Everyday Cryptography

Everyday Cryptography

Fundamental Principles
and Applications

KEITH M. MARTIN

Professor of Information Security
Information Security Group
Royal Holloway, University of London

OXFORD

UNIVERSITY PRESS

Great Clarendon Street, Oxford OX2 6DP

Oxford University Press is a department of the University of Oxford.
It furthers the University's objective of excellence in research, scholarship,
and education by publishing worldwide in

Oxford New York

Auckland Cape Town Dar es Salaam Hong Kong Karachi
Kuala Lumpur Madrid Melbourne Mexico City Nairobi
New Delhi Shanghai Taipei Toronto

With offices in

Argentina Austria Brazil Chile Czech Republic France Greece
Guatemala Hungary Italy Japan Poland Portugal Singapore
South Korea Switzerland Thailand Turkey Ukraine Vietnam

Oxford is a registered trade mark of Oxford University Press
in the UK and in certain other countries

Published in the United States
by Oxford University Press Inc., New York

© Keith M. Martin 2012

First published 2012
Reprinted with corrections 2012

British Library Cataloguing in Publication Data
Data available

Library of Congress Cataloging in Publication Data
Library of Congress Control Number: 2011944049

Typeset by Cenveo Publisher Services
Printed in Great Britain
on acid-free paper by
Clays Ltd, St Ives plc

ISBN 978-0-19-969559-1

Preface

Cryptography is a subject whose relevance to everyday life has undergone a dramatic transformation. Cryptography used to manifest itself in the public imagination through its historical use, primarily to protect military communications, and through recreational puzzles. However, largely due to the development of computer networks, particularly the Internet, most of us now use cryptography on a daily basis.

Cryptography is fundamental to the provision of a wider notion of information security. Electronic information can easily be transmitted and stored in relatively insecure environments. This has resulted in fundamental changes to the risks to which information is exposed. As the financial impact of information security incidents rises, so does the need for information security protection and control. Cryptography is a vital technology that underpins many of these controls. It provides a suite of basic mechanisms for implementing the security services that protect electronic information, such as confidentiality, data integrity and authentication. Cryptography does not secure information on its own, but many technical mechanisms for protecting information have cryptography at their core.

Cryptography is thus an important subject for anyone with an interest in information security. Other reasons for the wide interest in cryptography as a subject are:

- Cryptography plays an interesting political role. It is a key technology during times of conflict. Its modern use presents society with several intriguing moral and political dilemmas.
- Cryptography has a wide intrinsic appeal to the general public. Many people are fascinated by 'secrets' and 'codes'. This has been successfully exploited by the mainstream media.

Who should read this book?

There have been many books written about cryptography, but what distinguishes the approach taken in this book is the combination of the following:

Fundamental principles It is intended to be both relevant and relatively timeless. It is easy to write a cryptography book that is quickly out of date. This book is intended to be just as relevant in ten years time as it would have been relevant ten years ago. This is because it is primarily concerned with the fundamental principles rather than technical details of current technology.

Application-focussed It is primarily concerned with the cryptography that a user or practitioner of information security needs to know. While there is a great deal of contemporary theoretical research on cryptography, few of these ideas make it through to real-world applications, which tend to deploy only well-tested and understood techniques. This book focusses on cryptography for everyday applications.

Widely accessible It is intended to be suitable as a *first* read on cryptography. It focusses on core issues and provides an exposition of the fundamentals of cryptography. Note that it deliberately does not concentrate on the mathematical techniques underpinning cryptographic mechanisms. This book is intended to be introductory, self-contained and widely accessible.

We will explain why cryptography is important, how it can be used, and what the main issues are regarding its implementation. The main requirements that guided the writing of this book were that it should:

1. assume no prior knowledge of cryptography;
2. require almost no prior knowledge of mathematics;
3. focus on the principles behind cryptography, rather than the mathematical details of how it works;
4. stress the practical issues that accompany the use of cryptography;
5. present cryptography within the context of it being an underlying technology that supports information security, rather than as a topic in its own right.

It can either be read as a self-contained introduction to cryptography or can be used to support an educational course on cryptography. To this end, some supporting activities have been linked to the main chapters. The intended audiences are primarily:

Users and practitioners of information security Cryptography is a subject of relevance to anyone who needs to secure digital data. This book is intended to be of interest to:

- general users of information technology who seek an understanding of how to protect their data;
- information technology professionals who need to apply security techniques to data;
- information security professionals whose role is to protect information;
- managers of organisations who seek an understanding of issues concerning data security.

Students of cryptography It could form the basis for an undergraduate or postgraduate course that covers the principles of cryptography without delving into the mathematical detail of the underlying algorithms. Indeed this book has been developed from precisely such a course. It may also be of interest to students studying the mathematics of cryptography, since it complements more mathematical treatises by providing a 'bridge' between the theory of cryptography and the real-world problems that it attempts to solve. For students who already know the 'how', this book will explain the 'why'.

General interest audience It has been written in order to appeal to a general science or engineering audience who seek a greater understanding of what cryptography is and how it works.

Background to this book

This book has grown from a cryptography course offered by the Information Security Group at Royal Holloway, University of London. Royal Holloway has been a research centre for cryptography since the early 1980s and has a long association with industrial and governmental applications of cryptographic techniques.

In 1992, Royal Holloway launched an MSc in Information Security, which was one of the first qualifications of its kind in the world. This provides a broad introduction to the wide discipline of information security. The core of this programme consists of information security management, cryptography, network security and computer security. The module on cryptography is significant because the students who attend it do not necessarily have a mathematical background, and neither are they particularly interested in acquiring one. What they need to know is precisely what cryptography does (and does not do) and how it can be used. They do not need to know exactly how it works. Many students commence this module with a degree of trepidation, but almost all emerge with a great feeling of achievement (and perhaps relief!), which strongly suggests that the pitch is right for this intended audience.

The original cryptography module at Royal Holloway was designed by Professor Fred Piper, who co-authored one of the first academic books on cryptography [29] in 1982 and has played an enormously significant role in the development of academic and industrial information security activities in the UK. Along with Professor Sean Murphy, he published the popular *Cryptography: A Very Short Introduction* in 2002 [157], which presents a significant 'contraction' of the material covered by the Royal Holloway module to a general audience.

I took over the main teaching of the Royal Holloway module in 2004. I have spent much of the last decade teaching cryptography to non-mathematical students, including industrial courses and presentations to young audiences. I have also taught cryptography both 'face-to-face' and 'online', since the Royal Holloway MSc in Information Security is also offered to distance learning students. This book, which could to an extent be regarded as a much expanded and more 'academic' version of [157], has arisen from the joys and challenges of all of these experiences.

Structure

The book is divided into four parts:

Part I: Setting the Scene. Chapters 1 to 3 provide fundamental background. The need for cryptography is motivated in Chapter 1 and some of the core security services that can be provided by cryptography are identified. The basic model of a cryptosystem is introduced and the use of cryptography is discussed. We look back at a number of historical encryption algorithms in Chapter 2. Most of these are unsuitable for modern practical use, but they illustrate many of the core ideas, as well as some basic encryption algorithm design principles. The differences between security in theory and practice are discussed in Chapter 3. It is shown that unbreakable cryptosystems exist, but are not practical, and that most practical cryptosystems are breakable in theory. The real world is always about compromise. We argue that the study of cryptography is essentially the study of a 'toolkit' of cryptographic primitives that can be assembled in different ways in order to achieve different security goals.

Part II: The Cryptographic Toolkit. Chapters 4 to 9 explore the various components that make up the cryptographic toolkit. This includes cryptographic primitives and the cryptographic protocols that combine them. We begin with the provision of confidentiality. There are two types of cryptosystem, and we look at the first of these with respect to providing confidentiality in Chapter 4, which deals with symmetric encryption. Different types of symmetric encryption algorithms are discussed, as are the different ways in which they can be used. In Chapter 5 we look at public-key encryption. The motivation for public-key encryption is explained and two important public-key cryptosystems are studied in some detail. In Chapter 6 we look at the way in which (symmetric) cryptography can be used to provide data integrity and the stronger notion of data origin authentication. We then look in Chapter 7 at cryptographic techniques for providing non-repudiation, focussing on digital signature schemes. Chapter 8 explains how cryptography can be used to provide entity authentication. This chapter also considers random number generation, which is often required for entity authentication mechanisms. Finally, in Chapter 9 we look at how these cryptographic primitives can be combined to form cryptographic protocols.

Part III: Key Management. In Chapters 10 and 11 we explore what is arguably the most important, and often overlooked, area of cryptography from a practical perspective: key management. This underpins the security of any cryptographic system and is the aspect of cryptography where users and practitioners are most likely to become involved in decisions concerning cryptography. In Chapter 10 we discuss key management in general terms, focussing on the management of secret keys. The life cycle of a cryptographic key is studied and some of the most common techniques for conducting the various phases of this life cycle are discussed. In Chapter 11 we look at further issues of key management that particularly relate to public-key cryptography.

Part IV: Applications. In Chapter 12 we 'tie up' the previous material by examining some applications of cryptography. Since many of the issues that were raised in the previous chapters require decisions that are application-dependent, we demonstrate how several important applications actually address them. In particular, we discuss why particular cryptographic primitives are used and how key management is conducted. While the cryptographic applications that we discuss are of interest in their own right, the main purpose is to link up the previously discussed ideas. This chapter is, inevitably, slightly more detailed than the previous ones.

Additional features of the book are:

Further reading. Each chapter includes a brief summary of resources that could be used in order to further pursue the topics discussed. These are only intended to be starting points, and are by no means comprehensive. These resources are normally a mix of accessible reading, important research articles, relevant standards and useful web links. Carefully directed web searches should also prove an effective means of finding further information.

Activities. Each chapter also has a list of activities, which are designed to enhance the understanding of the chapter material. Some activities have definitive answers, while many are open-ended. While these activities may be skipped, they are all designed to structure further exploration of the chapter material. Later chapters do not rely on the activities of previous chapters having been completed.

Mathematics Appendix. A short appendix containing some elementary background mathematics is included. It is intended that the book can be comfortably read without consulting this appendix. However, in order to have a deeper appreciation of some of the issues concerning certain cryptographic primitives, particularly public-key cryptosystems, it will help to have digested this material.

How to use this book

The book has an ongoing narrative and, as a result, the material is most effectively read in the order in which it is presented. That said, it is certainly possible to dip into topics as required.

The chapters could well (and do) form the outline of a course on practical cryptography. To this end, 'learning outcomes' are identified at the start of each chapter. While it is very hard to imagine that such a course could be considered complete if any of the chapter topics were omitted, the book contains a bit more material than can be comfortably covered in a typical semester-based course. A balanced course on practical cryptography should pay attention to all the core security services and illustrate them by discussing a range of appropriate mechanisms, however, some of the chapter material could selectively be omitted if necessary. Key management is an essential topic to cover and should not be skipped. A run through two or three of the applications in Chapter 12 would probably suffice. At Royal Holloway we run separate tutorials for those students who lack confidence in the basic mathematics. The material in the Mathematics Appendix is comfortably covered in four or five one-hour example-based teaching sessions.

Alternative reading

There is a wealth of alternative literature on cryptography, thus presenting a healthy range of options for a reader wishing to pursue cryptography from a variety of different perspectives.

A substantial number of cryptography books focus on presenting the mathematical aspects of cryptography. Many of these are textbooks targeted at computer science or mathematics undergraduate students. For our purposes, most of these books go into too much mathematical detail of cryptographic algorithms and most provide insufficient detail on the practical aspects of cryptography. Arguably the best of these books is Stinson [185]. Other recommended titles include Buchmann [43], Katz and Lindell [105], Hoffstein, Pipher and Silverman [100], Mollin [125], Paar and Pelzl [149], Smart [178], Stallings [182], Trappe and Washington [191] and Vaudenay [194]. More specialist approaches include Koblitz [109], which presents cryptography for number theorists, and Talbot and Welsh [189], which presents cryptography from a complexity theory perspective.

For those seeking even more detail, there are numerous books that are primarily aimed at cryptographic researchers. While most of these are highly specialised, there are a few that have sufficiently wide coverage to merit mention. These include the biblical, but slightly dated Menezes, van Oorschot and Vanstone [123], the theoretical foundation texts of Goldreich [90, 91] and Mao [119].

Of more relevance are books concerned with applied cryptography. Schneier [168] is perhaps one of the best-known books on cryptography. While highly readable, it is not suitable for supporting a structured course on cryptography and is now dated. Ferguson, Schneier and Kohno [75] (which is an updated and expanded version of [74]) covers broadly similar topics to this book, but in a very different style. In particular, it tends more towards giving advice to practitioners, rather than presenting a wider discussion of the related issues. Dent and Mitchell [55] explain cryptography in terms of the existing international standards in this area. More focussed perspectives include Kenan [107], which discusses the use of cryptography to protect databases, and St Denis [181], which discusses cryptography for software developers. Other books cover wider aspects of information security and mention aspects of cryptography and its application in passing, rather than as a focus. Recommended titles of this type include Garfinkel and Spafford [88] and Anderson [23].

Finally there are several introductions to cryptography that claim to present the subject to more general audiences. The best of these is Piper and Murphy [157], as discussed earlier. The other books of this type tend to lack balance and depth, but for readers seeking a 'cheerful' introduction to cryptography we recommend Mel and Baker [122] and Cobb [47].

We include a section on further reading at the end of each chapter that provides some more focussed sources of alternative information. Amongst these are references to relevant standards. These are particularly important since, as we will continuously stress throughout the book, the cryptographic mechanisms that we will present are generally simplified. No cryptographic mechanisms discussed in this book should be implemented before consulting relevant standards. We will not mention all cryptographic standards (a comprehensive list is provided in Dent and Mitchell [55]) but will make reference to standards produced jointly by ISO, the *International Organization for Standardization*, and IEC, the *International Electrotechnical Commission*. We will also mention internet standards from the *Internet Engineering Task Force* (IETF), whose standards begin with the prefix RFC, and some standards produced by the *Institute of Electrical and Electronics Engineers* (IEEE). The US *National Institute of Standards and Technology* (NIST) is a particularly influential body that oversees *Federal Information Processing Standards* (FIPS), which are amongst the most important standards in cryptography. Of particular relevance to cryptography is NIST's *Computer Security Resource Center* (CSRC) [131], which is developing a cryptographic toolkit of recommended cryptographic algorithms and techniques. The CSRC regularly publishes *Special Publications*, which include recommendations about how to use cryptography, several of which we will make reference to. For those who wish to follow the 'cutting edge' of cryptographic research, one of the best places to find the latest research results is to seek proceedings from relevant conferences published in Springer's *Lecture Notes in Computer Science* (LNCS) series. As a source of general information on cryptography, the Wikipedia entries on cryptographic topics tend to be of fairly high quality and accuracy, and we highlight several in passing.

Acknowledgements

I am a great lover of books and always read the acknowledgements of any book with curiosity, many of which provide some insight into writing itself. My own writing experience appears to have been similar to many others: years of graft, endless revision and obsession. And like most authors, although I have put in hours of work, the final version would not have existed without a little bit of help from some friends.

While the words were crafted in a number of different geographical locations, including the UK, Malaysia, New Zealand and Poland, their ultimate origin is the many years of interaction with Royal Holloway MSc Information Security students from all over the world, only some of whom I have actually met. I thank them all for their many fascinating questions and perspectives, many of which continue to reshape my own. These are the joys of a teacher.

I would like to thank a number of colleagues and friends (I would like to think that all are both) who read and commented on parts of the manuscript: Carlos Cid, Jason Crampton, Mick Ganley, Qin Li, Miss Laiha Mat Kiah, Kenny Paterson, Maura Paterson and Geong Sen Poh. I reserve a special mention to Frederik Mennes, who not only provided detailed feedback throughout, but also succeeded in persuading me to restructure the book at a well-advanced stage. It is always painful to admit that someone else is right! For details on some of the cryptographic applications I had to seek expertise from knowledgeable sources, most of whom kindly commented on my interpretations of their information. I am extremely grateful to Peter Howard (Vodafone) for his many informative lectures at Royal Holloway on mobile telecommunications security. David Main and Mike Ward kindly provided comment on the material on EMV and made sure that I maintained impartiality. I am grateful to Allan Tomlinson for fielding my many questions on cryptography for video broadcasting and to Godot for giving me access to material about the eID card scheme, about which nobody else in the world knows more than he. And thanks to Cerulean, who helped to draft the original version of the Mathematics Appendix and who has held a hand of cryptographic numeracy out to many past MSc students during his lunchtime maths classes.

Turning ideas and learning materials into a book is not a straightforward exercise. I am extremely grateful to Doug Stinson and Bob Stern for giving me the confidence to take the plunge. I could not have asked for better support from Johnny Mackintosh (and his alter ego Keith Mansfield) at OUP. Thanks for being a believer in flexible deadlines. Writing a book is easy compared to finding a differentiating title in the congested cryptography book market. Nobody worked harder on this than Sandra Khan who offered me sixty-five possible titles, of which the current one was an adaptation due to Jason Crampton of number fifty.

My career route from timorous teenager into cryptographic researcher involved many people, some of whom I would like to single out for reasons that only I truly understand: Ian Anderson, Martin Anthony, Mick Ganley, Stuart Hoggar, Wen-Ai Jackson, Lars Knudsen, Chris Mitchell, Christine O'Keefe, Bart Preneel, Vincent Rijmen, Matt Robshaw, Rei Safavi-Naini, Jennifer Seberry and Peter Wild.

And of course there is Fred: legend and mentor. In certain aspects this is Fred Piper's book, even though he did not write it. Fred has persuaded hundreds of students whose knees trembled at the mere mention of cryptography that they could actually love this subject. I have done my best to incorporate his vision of cryptography, and hope that I have succeeded. Despite decades as a professional cryptographer, Fred retains the ability to see the subject through the eyes of a novice and his read of the manuscript was crucial and insightful.

Finally, some people are more important than the written word can capture. My parents are a source of great influence and support. I became a mathematician because of my father, Henry Martin, who has always been an 'oracle' (but not a random one) in my life. And, however fascinating cryptography might be, it is vital to be reminded every day that there are many other things of even greater value. Anita, Kyla and Finlay, I owe you much, much more than the many days and evenings that you lent to me to write this book. Boo, three times over.

Contents

List of Figures

List of Tables

Part I
Setting the Scene

Basic Principles

This chapter serves as an introduction to the environment in which cryptography finds common use today. We discuss the need for cryptography, as well as the basic language and concepts that are used to describe a cryptographic system.

> **At the end of this chapter you should be able to:**
> - Justify the need for information security.
> - Identify some of the essential security requirements of the modern world.
> - Appreciate the most significant risks to which information is exposed.
> - Identify a number of different security services that cryptography can provide.
> - Describe the basic model of a cryptosystem.
> - Recognise the differences between symmetric and public-key (asymmetric) cryptosystems.
> - Appreciate the importance of identifying the assumptions about what an attacker knows about a cryptosystem.
> - Discuss what it means to break a cryptosystem.

1.1 Why information security?

It is very likely that anyone reading this book already understands the need for information security, and hence cryptography. However, we need to consider this question, at least briefly, because it is extremely important that we understand the role of cryptography in securing information. We will use the term *information security* in a generic sense to describe the protection of information and information systems. This involves the use of many different types of security technologies, as well as management processes and controls. *Cryptography* provides the techniques that underpin most information security technologies. This chapter will explore this concept in more detail. More precise explanations of the core definitions relating to cryptography are provided in Section 1.4.1.

1.1.1 The rising profile of information security

Even as recently as the end of the last century, cryptography was a topic of which only specialists and interested users were aware. In fact, this probably also applies to the much broader discipline of information security. So, what has changed?

Information is not a new concept and has always been of value. Society has always dealt with information that has needed some level of protection and has always used processes to safeguard that information. There is nothing new about the need for information security.

Likewise, cryptography is not a new science, although some would say that it has only recently been formally treated as such. It has been used for centuries to protect sensitive information, especially during periods of conflict.

However, information security is now a subject with a relatively high profile. Most people use information security mechanisms on a daily basis. Information security incidents are widely reported in the media. Information security protection features on government agendas. The reason for this increased profile has been the development of computer networks, particularly the Internet. This development has not necessarily resulted in an increase in the amount of information in the world, but data is now easier to generate, access, exchange and store. The benefits of lower communication and storage costs, as well as increased connectivity and higher processing speeds, have encouraged automation of business processes. As a result, more and more applications and services are conducted electronically. Since all this electronic data has the potential to be transmitted and stored in environments that are relatively insecure, the need for information security has become paramount.

The rise in significance of information security has brought with it an increase in the importance and widespread use of cryptography. As we shall see, cryptography lies at the heart of most technical information security mechanisms. As a result, cryptography has become something that most people use in everyday applications. Once largely the domain of government and the military, cryptography is now deployed on devices that can be found in the pockets of almost every consumer of technology.

1.1.2 Two very different office environments

It is worth briefly considering precisely what types of physical security mechanisms we used to rely on prior to computer communication. Indeed, we still rely on many of these in physical situations. The fact that these security mechanisms cannot easily be applied to electronic environments provides the central motivation for defining cryptographic mechanisms.

AN OLD OFFICE

Imagine an office where there are no computers, no fax machines, no telephones and no Internet. The business conducted in this office relies on information coming from both external and internal sources. The employees in this office need to be able to make decisions about the accuracy and authenticity of information. In addition, they need mechanisms for controlling who has access to information. So, what basic security mechanisms allow people working in such an office to make decisions about the security of information that they receive and process?

We can fairly safely assume that most information dealt with in this office is either spoken or written down. Some basic security mechanisms for spoken information might be:

- facial or vocal recognition of people known to staff in the office;
- personal referrals or letters of introduction for people not known to staff in the office;
- the ability to hold a private conversation in a quiet corner of the room.

Some basic security mechanisms for written information might be:

- recognition of handwriting of people known to staff in the office;
- handwritten signatures on documents;
- sealing documents in an envelope;
- locking a document in a filing cabinet;
- posting a letter in an official post box.

Note that these security mechanisms are not particularly strong. For example, people who do not know each other well could misidentify a voice or face. An envelope could be steamed open and the contents altered. A handwritten signature could be forged. Nonetheless, these mechanisms tend to provide 'some' security, which is often 'good enough' security for many applications.

A MODERN OFFICE

Now consider a modern office, full of computers that are networked to the outside world via the Internet. Although some information will undoubtedly be processed using some of the previous mechanisms, for reasons of convenience and efficiency there will be a vast amount of information handled by electronic communication and storage systems. Imagine that in this office nobody has considered the new information security issues.

Here is a list of just some of the security issues that staff in this office should be considering:

- How can we tell whether an email from a potential client is a genuine inquiry from the person that it claims to have come from?
- How can we be sure that the contents of an electronic file have not been altered?

- How can we be sure that nobody else can read an email that we have just sent to a colleague?
- How can we accept an electronic contract received by email from a client on the other side of the world?

Without the adoption of some information security mechanisms, the answer to all of these questions is probably 'with great difficulty'. While even a non-expert may notice that a physical envelope has a damaged seal (and hence get suspicious), it is almost impossible to recognise whether an unprotected email has been accessed by an unauthorised party. It is certainly possible to communicate much more easily in this modern office, but there is a real case for claiming that we have much less inherent security in this environment than in the strictly physical world of the old office.

1.1.3 Differing perspectives

It should already be clear that there is a need for translation of the basic security mechanisms used in the physical world into mechanisms suitable for application in an electronic environment. In essence, this is what modern cryptography is all about. A central aim of this book is to demonstrate precisely what role cryptography plays in this translation process.

If this book was just about cryptography itself, then we could immediately proceed to a discussion of cryptographic mechanisms. However, this book is not just about the principles, but also the *application* of cryptography. We thus need to understand in a wider sense how cryptography fulfils a role in the provision of information security.

We now identify three different perspectives on the use of cryptography. The vested interests that these represent have helped to shape the modern use of cryptography.

INDIVIDUAL PERSPECTIVE

Cryptography is a technology just like any other. Thus the perspective of many individuals is that they have a right to use cryptography for any purpose that they deem fit. As we later discuss, using cryptography to encrypt data can serve a similar function to sealing a document in an envelope in the physical world. Thus, why should individuals be denied the right to use encryption? Further, many people regard cryptography as a technology that enables them to realise other rights. Foremost amongst these are rights to privacy and freedom of expression.

BUSINESS PERSPECTIVE

For businesses, computer networks, especially open networks such as the Internet, provide both great opportunities and significant risks. From a business perspective, cryptography is a technology that can be used in order to implement information security controls which, ultimately, result in the business making more money than if these controls were not adopted.

It is a common misconception that business automation is often driven by a desire for increased security. This is in fact very rarely the case. An important early business application of cryptography was the adoption of automatic teller machines in the banking industry. These were introduced not to increase security, but to increase availability, and hence to increase business. It is arguably easier to defraud an automatic teller machine than it is to extract money improperly from the counter of a bank.

Business automation usually leads to a significant change in the threats to which a business is exposed. Unless these are carefully addressed, business automation can lead to a decrease in the level of security. The main business security requirement is thus that increased automation and adoption of technologies such as cryptography should not lead to a decrease in the overall security of conducting business. For example, when the GSM system was developed for mobile telecommuniations (see Section 12.3), the designers intended that GSM should be 'as secure' as landlines.

GOVERNMENT PERSPECTIVE

Sometimes governments have conflicting requirements with respect to information security. On the one hand, they may wish to promote competitive business. They can do this by reducing costs and obstacles to business operation, such as reducing trade barriers and harmonising laws and regulations. On the other hand, governments may wish to control crime and manage issues of national security. They may try to do this by imposing certain barriers and introducing other laws and regulations.

In the case of cryptography, these different governmental roles have sometimes led to conflicts of interest. The fundamental problem they face is that the traditional model of a cryptosystem (which we discuss in Section 1.4.3) involves 'good' users deploying encryption to protect themselves from 'bad' attackers who attempt to access their information. However, from a government perspective it may be the case that they perceive 'bad' users are deploying encryption to hide their information from 'good' attackers (such as law enforcement officers) who could foil their activities if they had access to this information.

CONFLICTS OF INTEREST

These different perspectives clearly lead to potential conflicts of interest. For example:

- Some governments have a history of attempting to impose export controls on cryptographic algorithms, which clashes with individual freedom and business needs for the deployment of strong encryption in commercial products.
- Some governments have introduced regulations requiring access, in certain circumstances, to encrypted data. This has the potential to clash with individual

desires for privacy, as well as business needs for the protection of commercial secrets.

Indeed, cryptographic technology is sometimes labelled as a *dual use good*, which means that it is considered to be a technology with the potential to be both beneficial or harmful, depending on the perspective taken on a particular cryptographic application.

1.1.4 The importance of security infrastructure

The security commentator Bruce Schneier wrote a book called *Applied Cryptography* in the early 1990s. A few years later he wrote a book on computer security called *Secrets and Lies*. He claimed that during the writing of the second book he had an 'epiphany' in which he realised that all the cryptographic mechanisms in *Applied Cryptography* were almost immaterial compared to the 'real' security problems associated with the provision of a complete information security system. The biggest problem was not designing the cryptographic mechanisms themselves. The real problem was making the cryptography actually work in a practical system through the provision of an entire information security architecture, of which cryptography was only a small, but vital, component.

This is an important issue and one that needs to be kept in mind throughout this book. Cryptography, just like any security technology, cannot be made to work without having the infrastructure in place to support its implementation. By 'infrastructure' we mean the procedures, plans, policies, management, whatever it takes, to make sure that the cryptographic mechanisms actually do the job for which they were intended.

We will consider certain aspects of this infrastructure. However, there are many aspects of this infrastructure that are well beyond the scope of our discussions. Ideally, computer operating systems should be designed and used securely, networks should be implemented and configured securely, and entire information systems should be planned and managed securely. A perfectly good cryptographic mechanism can fail to deliver its intended security services if any one of these other areas of the security infrastructure fail.

This holistic attitude to information security is one that must always be kept in mind whenever a cryptographic application is designed or used. One of the aims of this book is to identify which elements of this wider security infrastructure are particularly relevant to the effectiveness of a cryptographic application.

1.2 Security risks

We now consider the types of risk to which information is typically exposed. We examine a very basic communication scenario and discuss some of the factors that determine the choice of security mechanisms deployed to address these risks.

1.2.1 Types of attack

Risks to information can be assessed by identifying different types of possible attack that can be applied. These attacks are often classified by the type of action that an attacker is able to perform.

PASSIVE ATTACKS

The main type of *passive attack* is unauthorised access to data. This is a passive process in the sense that the data and the processes being conducted on that data remain unaffected by the attack. Note that a passive attack is often likened to 'stealing' information. However, unlike stealing physical goods, in most cases theft of data still leaves the owner in possession of that data. As a result, information theft may go unnoticed by the owner. Indeed, it may even be undetectable.

ACTIVE ATTACKS

An *active attack* involves either data being changed in some way, or a process being conducted on the data. Examples of active attacks include:

- unauthorised alteration of data;
- unauthorised deletion of data;
- unauthorised transmission of data;
- unauthorised changing of the origin of data;
- unauthorised prevention of access to data (*denial of service*).

We will see that cryptography can be used as a tool to help prevent most passive and active attacks. A notable exception is denial of service. There is very little protection that cryptography can provide against this type of attack. Defence against denial of service normally requires security controls in other parts of the security infrastructure.

1.2.2 Security risks for a simple scenario

We now examine a very simple communication scenario and consider what security risks might exist. The simple scenario depicted in Figure 1.1 features a sender (who in the cryptographic world is often called *Alice*) and a receiver (who is usually called *Bob*). Alice wishes to transmit some information in an email to Bob. If Alice and Bob are to have any assurances about the security of the email that they have just exchanged then they should ask themselves some serious questions.

8

Figure 1.1. Simple communication scenario

For example, Alice might ask herself:

- Am I happy that anyone could read this email, or do I only want Bob to see it?
- How can I make sure that my email reaches Bob without being changed?
- Am I prepared (or allowed) to take any measures to protect my email before I send it?

Bob might ask himself:

- How can I have confidence that this email actually came from Alice?
- Can I be sure that this is the email that Alice intended to send me?
- Is it possible that Alice could deny in the future that she sent me this email?

This simple communication scenario (or variations thereof) is one that we will regularly return to when we consider different types of cryptographic mechanism. However, it is important to realise that not all applications of cryptography conform to this simple communication scenario. For example, we may need to secure:

- a broadcast environment, where one sender is streaming data to a large number of receivers;
- a data storage environment, which may not have an obvious recipient.

At this stage it suffices to appreciate that there are other basic scenarios that each come with their own players and security risks.

1.2.3 Choosing security mechanisms

Alice and Bob's concerns in Section 1.2.2 may seem rather paranoid. Some people regularly encrypt emails and so might regard these concerns as being important, while other people rarely encrypt emails and might regard the questions raised by Alice and Bob as being slightly absurd, or at least 'over the top' (for more discussion of this particular issue, see Section 12.7.2).

9

These contradictory perspectives are not surprising. Risk is subjective, and risks differ between applications. Indeed the assessment and management of risk is a major information security topic in its own right and one that many organisations devote entire departments to studying. It is prudent to think about questions such as those identified in Section 1.2.2, but whether we act on them and introduce security controls to address them is another issue altogether.

In fact there are at least three different issues to consider when contemplating the use of any security mechanism, including a cryptographic control:

Appropriateness. *Is it the right tool for the job?* It is important to understand the precise properties that a cryptographic mechanism will provide. One aim of this book is to explain how the various tools of cryptography can (and in some cases cannot) be used to provide different notions of security.

Strength. *Why put in an expensive burglar alarm in situations where a warning sign would suffice?* Different information security mechanisms provide different levels of protection for data, just as different security mechanisms in the physical world provide a range of strengths of physical protection.

Cost. *Do the security gains justify the costs?* The cost of a security mechanism is of fundamental importance. By 'cost' we do not necessarily mean monetary value. Cost can be measured in terms of ease of use and efficiency of operation, as well as directly in terms of financial worth. As we will see throughout Chapter 12, in many real applications it is cost considerations that determine the security mechanism adopted, rather than the strength of security that the mechanism provides. In the past, some military and government sectors may have opted for strong security, whatever the cost, but in most modern environments this is not appropriate. A sensible commercial question might be: *what strength of security is appropriate given the value of our assets?* A more commonly asked question of modern security managers however is: *what strength of security can we obtain within our budgetary constraints?* One of the challenges of managing security in such environments is to make a case for having information security controls. This case can often be built on the argument that good security may succeed in reducing other costs.

Returning to our email example, an *appropriate* tool for preventing emails from being read by unauthorised parties is encryption. The *strength* of the encryption used is dependent on the cryptographic algorithm and the number of decryption keys (which we will discuss later). The *cost* is that it is necessary to buy and install suitable software, manage the relevant keys, configure the email client appropriately and incur some small time and communication costs every time the software is used.

So, is it worth encrypting an email? There is of course no general answer, since this very much depends on the value of the information in the email and the perceived risks. However, an overall aim of this book is to advise how cryptography can help in this type of situation and what the related issues are. We will focus on explaining the appropriateness and strength of various cryptographic mechanisms, however, we will also indicate where issues of cost may arise. Hopefully you will then be able to make up your own mind.

1.3 Security services

A *security service* is a specific security goal that we may wish to achieve. We now introduce the main security services that we will be concerned with in this book. Note that while security services sometimes relate directly to human beings, more often they relate to computers or other devices (often operating on behalf of human beings). While this potential difference is an important issue that can have important security implications (see also Section 8.3), we will normally avoid concerning ourselves with it directly and use the generic terms *user* and *entity* in an interchangeable way to mean whoever, or whatever, is taking part in the processing of data in an information system.

1.3.1 Basic definitions

Confidentiality is the assurance that data cannot be viewed by an unauthorised user. It is sometimes referred to as *secrecy*. Confidentiality is the 'classical' security service that can be provided by cryptography and is the one implemented by most historical applications. While it remains an important security service, there are many modern applications of cryptography that do not require the provision of confidentiality. Even when confidentiality is wanted, it is rare for it to be the only security service that is required.

Data integrity is the assurance that data has not been altered in an unauthorised (which includes accidental) manner. This assurance applies from the time that the data was last created, transmitted or stored by an authorised user. Data integrity is not concerned with the *prevention* of alteration of data, but provides a means for *detecting* whether data has been manipulated in an unauthorised way.

Data origin authentication is the assurance that a given entity was the *original source* of received data. In other words, if a technique provides data origin authentication that some data came from Alice then this means that the receiver Bob can be sure that the data did originally come from Alice at some time in the past. Bob does not necessarily care exactly *when* she sent it, but he does care that Alice is the source of the data. Nor does he care from which immediate source he obtained the data, since Alice could have passed the data to an intermediary for forwarding (as is the case when data is passed over the Internet, where the immediate source of data may be a web server or router). For this reason, data origin authentication is sometimes referred to as *message authentication* since it is primarily concerned with the authentication of the data (message) and not who we are communicating with at the time the data is received.

11

Non-repudiation is the assurance that an entity cannot deny a previous commitment or action. Most commonly, non-repudiation is the assurance that the original source of some data cannot deny *to a third party* that this is the case. Note that this is a stronger requirement than data origin authentication, since data origin authentication only requires this assurance to be provided to the receiver of the data. Non-repudiation is a property that is most desirable in situations where there is the potential for a dispute to arise over the exchange of data.

Entity authentication is the assurance that a given entity is involved *and currently active* in a communication session. In other words, if a technique provides entity authentication of Alice then this means that by applying the technique we can be sure that Alice is really engaging with us *now*, in 'real time'. If we fail to establish this temporal aspect of entity authentication (which requires the adoption of a *freshness* mechanism, see Section 8.2) then we have failed to achieve entity authentication. In certain contexts, entity authentication is referred to as *identification* because it is concerned with determining *who am I communicating with now, in real time?*

1.3.2 Relationships between security services

It is important to recognise that these basic security services are all essentially *different*, even though on first encounter they may seem similar. The following statements further illustrate this.

DATA ORIGIN AUTHENTICATION IS A STRONGER NOTION THAN DATA INTEGRITY

In other words, if we have data origin authentication then we also have data integrity (but most certainly not the other way around).

To see that data origin authentication would be meaningless without data integrity, suppose that Alice has sent us some data. If we have no data integrity then we cannot be sure that the data received has not been changed by an attacker in transit. The actual data that we received might therefore have come from the attacker and not from Alice. How could we possibly claim to have data origin authentication from Alice in this case? We have thus tied ourselves in a logical knot. Therefore data origin authentication can only be provided if data integrity is also provided. It can be helpful to think of data origin authentication as a stronger version of data integrity. More precisely, data origin authentication is data integrity with the extra property of assurance of the identity of the original source of the data.

A commonly offered attempt at a counter-example to this relationship is recognition of the source of a broken voice message over a noisy channel (such as a telephone call). Since the voice message is audibly broken, we clearly do not have data integrity. However, because the voice is recognisable it could be argued that we do know the source of the voice data. This, though, is *not* an example of data origin authentication without data integrity. Even if the speaker's voice is recognisable, since an attacker could be inserting noise into the broken message signal we cannot be certain that *all* the data we receive has come from the speaker whose voice we recognise. Data origin authentication must apply to the entire received message, not just parts of it.

Note that in almost all environments where we wish to detect deliberate modification of data, we will require data origin authentication. The weaker notion of data integrity without data origin authentication is normally only required in situations where the sole integrity concern is accidental modification of data.

NON-REPUDIATION OF A SOURCE IS A STRONGER NOTION THAN DATA ORIGIN AUTHENTICATION

We have to be slightly careful when making statements about non-repudiation, since this security service can be applied in different situations. However, when applied to the source of some data (which is the context that we will focus on in this book) then it is clear that non-repudiation cannot be provided without data origin authentication (and hence data integrity) also being provided. We can only bind the source to the data, in a manner that cannot be later denied, if we have assurance that the data itself is from that source. As noted earlier, non-repudiation also typically requires this binding to be verifiable by a third party, which is a stronger requirement than that for data origin authentication.

DATA ORIGIN AUTHENTICATION AND ENTITY AUTHENTICATION ARE DIFFERENT

Data origin authentication and entity authentication are different security services. The best way to see this is to look at applications that require one, but not the other.

Data origin authentication is useful in situations where one entity is forwarding information on behalf of another, for example, in the transmission of an email message over a public network. Entity authentication is unlikely to be meaningful in this case since there may be significant delays between the time that the message is sent, the time that the message is received and the time that the message is actually read. However, whenever the message is read we would like assurance of the identity of the creator of the email. This is provided by data origin authentication.

On the other hand, entity authentication is the main security service required when accessing resources. A user logging on to a computer is required to provide real-time evidence of their identity. Normally, entity authentication is provided either by presenting a credential (such as a password) or performing a cryptographic computation. In both cases, entity authentication is provided by demonstrating an ability to conduct this process correctly and does not necessarily require the origin of any data to be checked.

DATA ORIGIN AUTHENTICATION PLUS A FRESHNESS CHECK CAN
PROVIDE ENTITY AUTHENTICATION

As we have just discussed, data origin authentication on its own is only concerned with the origin of data, and not whether the sender of data is currently active. However, if we carefully combine data origin authentication with some sort of freshness check then we can often achieve entity authentication, since we know where the data originated *and* we know that the originator is involved in the current communication session. We will see examples of this in Section 8.5 and Chapter 9.

CONFIDENTIALITY DOES NOT IMPLY DATA ORIGIN AUTHENTICATION

A common mistake is to believe that providing data confidentiality (primarily through encryption) also provides assurance of who sent the data and that it is correct. There are special situations where this is a reasonable deduction, but it is generally not true. Where both of these security services are required (which is the case for many cryptographic applications) then they should both be provided explicitly, either by using separate cryptographic mechanisms or one that is specially designed to provide both services. We will discuss this issue in further detail in Sections 6.3.1 and 6.3.6.

1.4 Fundamentals of cryptosystems

Having set the scene, it is now time to look at the concept of a cryptosystem. We examine the basic model of a cryptosystem and explain fundamental terminology that will be used throughout the rest of the book. We also explain the crucial difference between two important types of cryptosystem.

1.4.1 Different cryptographic concepts

Before proceeding further, it is important to explain some common cryptographic terminology.

Cryptography is a generic term used to describe the design and analysis of mechanisms based on mathematical techniques that provide fundamental security services. We will use *cryptography* in a generic sense, but a more formally accurate term is *cryptology*, which is the scientific study of *cryptography* (the design of such mechanisms) and *cryptanalysis* (the analysis of such mechanisms). It is appropriate to think of cryptography as the establishment of a large toolkit of different techniques, the contents of which can either be used on their own, or combined, in security applications.

A *cryptographic primitive* is a cryptographic process that provides a number of specified security services. If cryptography is a toolkit, then cryptographic primitives are the basic generic tools in that kit. Examples of cryptographic primitives that we will later discuss are block ciphers, stream ciphers, message authentication codes, hash functions and digital signature schemes.

A *cryptographic algorithm* is the particular specification of a cryptographic primitive. A cryptographic algorithm is essentially a 'recipe' of computational steps (rules such as 'add these two values together' or 'replace this value by an entry from this table'). An algorithm is a sufficiently detailed specification that a computer programmer could implement it. For example, AES is a cryptographic algorithm that specifies a block cipher. The term *cipher* is sometimes associated with a cryptographic algorithm, particularly historical algorithms such as those that we discuss in Chapter 2.

A *cryptographic protocol* is a sequence of message exchanges and operations between one or more parties, at the end of which a series of security goals should have been achieved. Examples of cryptographic protocols that we will discuss include the STS protocol (see Section 9.4.2) and SSL/TLS (see Section 12.1). Cryptographic protocols typically employ a number of different cryptographic primitives at various stages. If cryptographic primitives are tools in the cryptography toolkit, then a cryptographic protocol is a way of taking a number of these tools and using them in a specific way in order to achieve more complex security goals. We discuss cryptographic protocols in Chapter 9.

A *cryptosystem* (or *cryptographic scheme*) is often used rather generically to refer to the implementation of some cryptographic primitives and their accompanying infrastructure. Thus, while a cryptosystem that is being used to provide data confidentiality might use a block cipher, the 'cryptosystem' may also include the users, the keys, the key management, etc. This term is most often used in association with cryptographic primitives that provide data confidentiality. A cryptosystem is sometimes also referred to as a *cipher system*.

1.4.2 Cryptographic primitives for security services

Having introduced the notion of a cryptographic primitive, we now indicate which common cryptographic primitives can be used to implement the various security services defined in Section 1.3.1. Table 1.1 provides a mapping from our list of security services onto some of the cryptographic primitives that we will encounter in the remainder of the book. It shows the common use of cryptographic primitives *used on their own* to achieve security services. Note that we use the generic term 'encryption' in Table 1.1 to represent a range of cryptographic primitives, including block ciphers, stream ciphers and public-key encryption.

The immediately striking aspect of Table 1.1 is its sparseness with respect to 'Yes' entries. In particular, none of these primitives provides entity authentication when used on their own. However, if we relax the requirement *used on their own* and replace this with *can be used to help provide* then we obtain the much more 'positive' Table 1.2.

Table 1.1: Mapping of primitives used on their own to provide security services

	Confidentiality	Data integrity	Data origin auth.	Non-repudiation	Entity auth.
Encryption	Yes	No	No	No	No
Hash function	No	Sometimes	No	No	No
MAC	No	Yes	Yes	Sometimes	No
Digital signature	No	Yes	Yes	Yes	No

Table 1.2: Mapping of primitives that can be used to help provide security services

	Confidentiality	Data integrity	Data origin auth.	Non-repudiation	Entity auth.
Encryption	Yes	Yes	Yes	Yes	Yes
Hash function	Yes	Yes	Yes	Yes	Yes
MAC	No	Yes	Yes	Yes	Yes
Digital signature	No	Yes	Yes	Yes	Yes

The entries in Table 1.2 should not be agonised over at too great a length, especially as we have yet to discuss any of the primitives described there. The main point is to indicate how intricately related the various standard cryptographic primitives are and, in particular, to flag that they are often combined to achieve security services. For example:

- Encryption can be used to design a message authentication code (MAC), which provides data origin authentication (see Section 6.3.3).
- Hash functions can be used to store special types of confidential data (see Section 6.2.2).
- In certain circumstances, MACs can be used to provide non-repudiation (see Section 7.2).
- Digital signatures can be used in entity authentication protocols (see Section 9.4).

In the second part of this book we develop the cryptographic toolkit in terms of these different security services. Chapters 4 and 5 will focus on providing confidentiality. Chapter 6 looks at mechanisms for providing data integrity and data origin authentication. Chapter 7 is concerned with the provision of non-repudiation. Chapter 8 considers entity authentication.

For the remainder of this chapter, and indeed Chapters 2 and 3, we continue with our background to cryptography mainly from the perspective of providing confidentiality. This is for two reasons:

1. Confidentiality is the 'oldest' security service. The historical development of cryptography is thus easiest to illustrate in terms of the provision of confidentiality.
2. Confidentiality is the most 'natural' security service. By this we mean that when presented with the idea of cryptography, confidentiality is the first security service that occurs to the majority of people.

1.4.3 Basic model of a cryptosystem

We now examine a simple model for a cryptosystem that is providing confidentiality. This basic model is depicted in Figure 1.2. We make two restrictions in order to keep things as straightforward as possible. Please keep them in mind throughout the discussion.

1. The only security service required for this cryptosystem is confidentiality. Hence the cryptographic primitive that is used within this cryptosystem is one that provides data confidentiality, such as a block cipher, a stream cipher, or a public-key encryption scheme. Although the rest of this chapter will focus on *encryption* and *encryption algorithms*, most of the issues that we address are relevant to other types of cryptographic primitive.
2. The basic model that we describe is for a *communications* environment (in other words, Alice sending information to Bob across a communication channel of some sort). This basic model will look slightly different if we want data confidentiality in a different environment, such as for secure data storage.

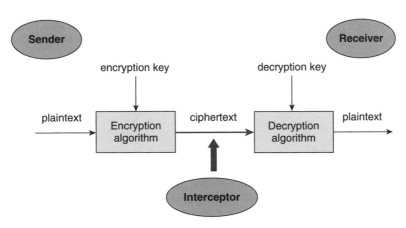

Figure 1.2. Basic model of a cryptosystem

Figure 1.2 depicts a sender who wishes to transfer some data to a receiver in such a way that any party intercepting the transmitted data cannot determine the content. The various components of the model are as follows:

The *plaintext* is the raw data to be protected during transmission from sender to receiver. Raw data of this type is sometimes referred to as being *in the clear*. This is also often (ambiguously) referred to as the *message*. The intention is that at the end of the process only the sender and the receiver will know the plaintext. In particular, an interceptor cannot determine the plaintext.

The *ciphertext* is the scrambled version of the plaintext that results from applying the encryption algorithm (and the encryption key) to the plaintext. It is sometimes referred to as the *cryptogram*. The ciphertext is not a secret and can be obtained by anyone who has access to the communication channel. In certain contexts this access is referred to as *eavesdropping*.

The *encryption algorithm* is the set of rules that determines, for any given plaintext and encryption key, a ciphertext. Using our terminology more appropriately, it is a cryptographic algorithm that takes as input a plaintext and an encryption key, and outputs a ciphertext. The choice of encryption algorithm must be agreed between sender and receiver. An interceptor may or may not know the encryption algorithm used (see Section 1.5.3).

The *decryption algorithm* is the set of rules that determines, for any given ciphertext and decryption key, a unique plaintext. In other words, it is a cryptographic algorithm that takes as input a ciphertext and a decryption key, and outputs a plaintext. The decryption algorithm essentially 'reverses' the encryption algorithm and is thus closely related to it. An interceptor may or may not know the decryption algorithm used (see Section 1.5.3).

The *encryption key* is a value that is known to the sender. The sender inputs the encryption key into the encryption algorithm along with the plaintext in order to compute the ciphertext. The receiver normally also knows the encryption key. It may or may not be known by an interceptor (see Section 1.4.8).

The *decryption key* is a value that is known to the receiver. The decryption key is related to the encryption key, but is not always identical to it. The receiver inputs the decryption key into the decryption algorithm along with the ciphertext in order to compute the plaintext. The interceptor must not know the decryption key. It may or may not be known by the sender (see Section 1.4.7). We call the collection of all possible decryption keys the *keyspace*.

An *interceptor* (in a more general setting we also refer to an *adversary* or an *attacker*) is an entity other than the sender or receiver who attempts to determine the plaintext. The interceptor will be able to see the ciphertext. The interceptor may know the decryption algorithm (see Section 1.5.3). The one piece of information that the interceptor must never know is the decryption key.

To encrypt the plaintext the sender needs access to the encryption key and the encryption algorithm. The plaintext must be encrypted at the sender's end within a secure environment. Cryptography cannot protect the plaintext before it has been converted into the ciphertext.

To decrypt the ciphertext the receiver needs access to the decryption key and the decryption algorithm. The receiver must keep the decryption key secret. The ciphertext must be decrypted at the receiver's end within a secure environment. Once the plaintext has been computed at the receiver's end then the receiver must take measures to protect (or destroy) it.

There are two common misconceptions about this basic model, which are worth clarifying straight away:

1. **Encryption does not prevent communication interception**. There are security techniques that can be employed to prevent interception of communicated data, but encryption is not one of them. What encryption does is to render intercepted data unintelligible to anyone who does not have access to the appropriate decryption key. As such, encryption is a suitable tool to use to protect data being exchanged over open networks.

2. **Encryption of the communication channel does not guarantee 'end-to-end' confidentiality**. It is true that (appropriate) encryption should guarantee that an interceptor who only has access to the ciphertext cannot decrypt it. However, the plaintext itself may be vulnerable at places within the system that are not protected by the encryption process. For example, the plaintext may exist in the clear on either the sender or receiver's computer. Other security mechanisms may be needed in order to protect plaintext data elsewhere in the system.

We note that since it does not make any sense to specify an encryption algorithm without specifying the decryption algorithm, we follow wider convention by using the term *encryption algorithm* to implicitly include the decryption algorithm. When dealing with the details we may refer to the *encryption process* or the *decryption process* but we assume that a specification of the *encryption algorithm* includes a specification of both processes.

This basic model of a cryptosystem may appear at this stage rather abstract. In Chapter 2 we will examine a number of simple cryptosystems of this type that will serve as illustrative examples.

1.4.4 Codes

The word 'code' is not one that we will be using within the context of cryptography, although it is a term that is often associated informally with cryptography. There are many different interpretations of the concept of a 'code'.

Most generally, the term 'code' is often used for any scheme where data is replaced by alternative data before being sent over a communication channel. This replacement is usually dictated by the contents of a *codebook*, which states precisely which replacement data to use. A good example is *Morse Code*, which replaces the letters of the alphabet with short sequences of dots and dashes. Note that Morse Code has nothing to do with secrecy, since the codebook in this case is well known. Morse Code was designed to efficiently transmit messages over telegraph wires. Another example of a code is ASCII, which provides a means of converting keyboard symbols into data suitable for processing on a computer (see the Mathematics Appendix).

If a codebook is kept secret, and is only known by the sender and the receiver of some data, then the resulting code can be regarded as a type of cryptosystem. In this case the encryption algorithm is simply to replace the plaintext with its matching ciphertext entry in the codebook. The decryption algorithm is the reverse process. The encryption (and decryption) key is the codebook specification itself. For example, Morse Code is not a cryptosystem because there is only one way of replacing letters by dots and dashes. However, if the rule for replacing letters by dots and dashes was kept secret from everyone except a chosen sender and receiver, then we could regard this as a cryptosystem.

In general, cryptosystems based on codebooks only tend to be referred to as 'codes' when the codebook describes ways of replacing dictionary words by other words. Thus the term 'code' is most likely to be encountered in reference to historical cryptosystems or recreational puzzles. The types of cryptosystem that we will be most interested in do not convert words into words, but rather convert sequences of ones and zeros into other sequences of ones and zeros. While we could produce 'codebooks' for these modern cryptosystems, the codebooks would have to be so large that they would be impractical to use.

The term 'code' is also often used as an abbreviated form of *error-correcting code*. This is a technique that can be deployed in order to enable the recovery of correct data from 'noisy' data containing accidental errors that are introduced in an unreliable channel. Error-correcting codes have nothing to do with preventing data from being seen by unauthorised users. While they are related to data integrity, error-correcting codes do not protect data from being *deliberately* manipulated by an attacker. Therefore, we cannot really regard them as cryptographic primitives.

1.4.5 Steganography

Another concept often confused with cryptography is *steganography*, which is also concerned with preventing unauthorised users from accessing plaintext data. However, the basic assumptions behind the use of steganography are rather different from those of cryptography. Steganography is essentially the study of *information hiding*. The main aim of steganography is for a sender to transfer a plaintext to a receiver in such a way that only the receiver can extract the plaintext because only the receiver knows that a hidden plaintext exists in the first place, and how to look for it (for example, by extracting information from a digital image). In steganography an 'interceptor' may well be unaware that observed data contains hidden information. This is quite unlike cryptography, where an interceptor is normally fully aware that data is being communicated because they can see the ciphertext. Their problem in this case is that they cannot determine what data the ciphertext represents.

Cryptography and steganography are used in quite different applications. They can also be used together. In this case, steganography can be used to hide a ciphertext. This creates two layers of security:

1. The first layer, steganography, tries to hide the fact that a ciphertext exists in the first place.
2. In the event that this use of steganography is detected and the ciphertext is found, the second layer, cryptography, prevents the plaintext from being known.

We will not discuss steganography any further in this book. While it does potentially have niche applications, and might in some cases be regarded as a potential threat to an information system, steganography is rarely employed to secure information systems.

1.4.6 Access control

It is worth observing that there are in fact three different approaches that can be taken to providing data confidentiality. The one that we are most interested in is encryption, since this provides protection independently of the location where the data resides. As we have just seen, steganography relies on 'hiding' the data. A third approach is to control access to the (unencrypted) data. *Access control* is a major topic in its own right. Indeed, much of our data is not protected through the use of encryption, but rather through access control mechanisms on computers that use a combination of software and hardware techniques to prevent unauthorised users from accessing data.

Encryption can be regarded as a means of implementing a type of access control, where only those with access to the appropriate decryption key can access protected data. However, they are normally separate mechanisms. Indeed, just as we saw for steganography, they can be used together to provide two separate layers of security. Access control can be used to restrict access to data, which is itself encrypted. Thus an attacker who manages to get around the access control mechanism only manages to retrieve encrypted data.

1.4.7 Two types of cryptosystem

There are two different types of cryptosystem and understanding the differences between them is crucial. The difference hinges on the relationship between the encryption and the decryption key. In any cryptosystem these two values must obviously be closely related since we cannot expect to be able to encrypt a plaintext with one key and then later decrypt the resulting ciphertext with a totally unrelated key. The precise relationship between these keys defines not only the type of cryptosystem, but also all of its resulting properties.

In *symmetric cryptosystems* the encryption key and the decryption key are essentially the same (in situations where they are not *exactly* the same, they are extremely closely related). All cryptosystems prior to the 1970s were symmetric cryptosystems. Indeed, symmetric cryptosystems are still widely used today and there is no sign that their popularity is fading. The study of symmetric cryptosystems is often referred to as *symmetric cryptography*. Symmetric cryptosystems are also sometimes referred to as *secret key cryptosystems*.

In *public-key cryptosystems* the encryption key and the decryption key are fundamentally different. For this reason, public-key cryptosystems are sometimes referred to as *asymmetric cryptosystems*. In such cryptosystems it is 'impossible' (we often use the phrase *computationally infeasible* to capture this impossibility) to determine the decryption key from the encryption key. The study of public-key cryptosystems is often referred to as *public-key cryptography*.

Symmetric cryptosystems are a 'natural' concept. In contrast, public-key cryptosystems are quite counterintuitive. How can the decryption key and the encryption key be 'related', and yet it be impossible to determine the decryption key from the encryption key?

The answer lies in the 'magic' of mathematics. It is possible to design a cryptosystem whose keys have this property, but it is not obvious how to do so. Within the context of cryptographic history, the concept of public-key cryptography is relatively new and there are far fewer public-key algorithms known than symmetric algorithms. They are, however, extremely important as their distinctive properties have useful applications, as we will see.

1.4.8 Secrecy of the encryption key

We already know that in any cryptosystem an interceptor must not know the decryption key. In a symmetric cryptosystem, the encryption key and the decryption key are the same. It follows that in a symmetric cryptosystem there is only one key, and that this key is used for both encryption and decryption, which is why it is often referred to as a *symmetric key*. The sender and the receiver must be the only people who know this key.

On the other hand, in a public-key cryptosystem the encryption key and the decryption key are different. Further, the decryption key cannot be determined from the encryption key. This means that as long as the receiver keeps the decryption key secure (which they must in any cryptosystem) there is no need for the corresponding encryption key to be kept secret. It follows that the encryption key could, at least in principle, be made publicly available (hence the term *public* key) so that anyone could look it up and use it to send a ciphertext to the receiver. In contrast, the associated decryption key is usually called the *private* key, since it is a 'private' value known only to that particular receiver.

In order to clarify this fundamentally different property, it can be helpful to consider a physical world analogy that usefully demonstrates the main difference between symmetric and public-key cryptosystems. This is the analogy of locking a piece of paper in a box in order to provide confidentiality of a message written on the paper. The piece of paper is the analogue of the plaintext. The locked box containing the paper is the analogue of the ciphertext. Encryption can be thought of as being analogous to the process of locking up the piece of paper, and decryption analogous to the process of unlocking it. This analogy is particularly appropriate since the physical locking process also involves the use of keys.

We consider two different types of lock that are widely available in the physical world, as illustrated in Figure 1.3:

1. *Conventional locks* are those normally found on filing cabinets, cars or windows. In this case the sender needs a key to lock the paper in the box. The receiver needs an identical copy of the key to later unlock it. Thus, when using a conventional lock the sender and the receiver need to share the same key. This is analogous to symmetric cryptosystems.

2. *Self-locking locks* are those found on padlocks and often on the front doors of houses. These locks do not require a key to conduct the locking operation (a padlock can simply be snapped shut and a front door can often just be closed). When using a self-locking lock, the sender does not need a key to lock the paper

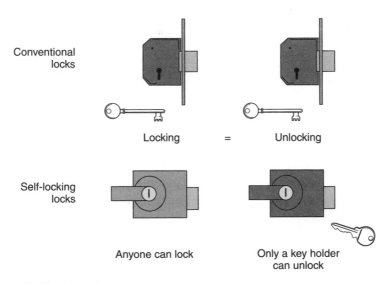

Figure 1.3. Physical lock analogy for the two types of cryptosystem

23

Table 1.3: Basic properties and terminology for keys in the two types of cryptosystem

	Relationship between keys	Encryption key	Decryption key
Symmetric cryptosystems	same key	symmetric	symmetric
Public-key cryptosystems	different keys	public	private

in the box. However, the receiver does need a key to open it. This is almost analogous to public-key cryptosystems. We say 'almost' analogous because, to make this analogy strictly accurate, we have to assume that the ability of anyone to lock the box without a key is 'equivalent' to having a key to lock the box that is made available to anyone who wants it.

We note that the term *secret key* is rather ambiguous, since it is often applied to both symmetric and private keys. We thus reserve the use of this term to situations where we we refer to either (or both) symmetric and private keys (mainly in Chapter 10). The relationship and terminology for encryption and decryption keys in the two types of cryptosystem is summarised in Table 1.3.

The ability to make encryption keys public makes the concept of public-key cryptography seem extremely attractive for a number of different applications. However, public-key cryptography comes with its own set of problems and one of the aims of this book is to explain the various advantages and disadvantages of using symmetric and public-key cryptosystems. As we will learn later, symmetric and public-key cryptosystems are often both implemented and used together in real information systems.

1.5 Cryptosystem security assumptions

We now consider what resources it is reasonable to assume that an attacker of a cryptosystem has access to. We begin by looking at standard assumptions and attack models. We then have a short discussion about the extent to which revealing the details of the encryption algorithm might affect the security of a cryptosystem.

1.5.1 Standard assumptions

In order to assess the security of a cryptosystem we must first establish exactly what assumptions we are making about potential attackers of the cryptosystem. Identifying assumptions about the capabilities of attackers is standard practice in all areas of information security and forms part of the larger process of *risk assessment*. If we underestimate an attacker's capabilities then the resulting security might be inadequate. It thus makes sense to be slightly conservative and take a 'worst-case' view.

In cryptography there are three standard assumptions that are normally made concerning an attacker's ability. These are that the attacker knows:

All ciphertexts sent using the cryptosystem. It is entirely reasonable to assume that an attacker has access to all the ciphertexts sent using the cryptosystem. These are not hidden from public view by the encryption process.

Some corresponding pairs of plaintexts and ciphertexts. At first glance, this might not seem such an obvious assumption to make, however, there are many circumstances where an attacker could have access to corresponding pairs of plaintexts and ciphertexts. Just some possible scenarios are:

- The receiver has been careless in failing to keep decrypted ciphertexts secret.
- The attacker has intelligently guessed some predictable plaintexts. A good example is predictable document headers.
- The attacker has been able to influence the choice of plaintexts encrypted by the sender.
- The attacker has (temporary) access to either the encryption or decryption device. Note that this does not imply that the attacker knows the encryption or decryption key. The keys might be embedded in secure hardware and the attacker only has access to the interface of the machine that conducts the encryption (decryption) process. Obviously, we assume that the attacker does not have permanent access to the decryption device, otherwise they are in a very strong position!
- We are using a public-key cryptosystem where the encryption key is known to any potential attacker. Thus an attacker can generate pairs of corresponding plaintexts and ciphertexts at their leisure.

The details of the encryption algorithm. This is the standard assumption that sometimes causes the most confusion. We consider this issue in Section 1.5.3.

1.5.2 Theoretical attack models

Simple attacks on cryptosystems have historically been classified using the following terminology:

ciphertext-only attacks require the attacker to know the encryption algorithm and some ciphertext;

known-plaintext attacks require the attacker to know the encryption algorithm and some plaintext/ciphertext pairs;

chosen-plaintext attacks require the attacker to know the encryption algorithm and some plaintext/ciphertext pairs that correspond to plaintexts chosen by the attacker.

These are increasingly powerful attacks, since an attacker who can *choose* which plaintext/ciphertext pairs to examine is clearly in a better position than an attacker who can only see arbitrary plaintext/ciphertext pairs.

Our 'standard assumptions' do not clearly differentiate between known and chosen-plaintext attacks, since this depends on whether the attacker can only see plaintexts chosen by the sender or was able to select plaintexts for encryption. It is safest to assume that an attacker has been able to choose the plaintexts for which they know plaintext/ciphertext pairs. Most modern cryptosystems (and all public-key cryptosystems) are thus designed to withstand chosen-plaintext attacks.

While it will suffice for us to remember the three standard assumptions about the knowledge of an attacker, it is worth recognising that cryptographic researchers often have even more stringent assumptions about the possible attack model. For example, in one strong theoretical model of security of a cryptosystem, an attacker should not be able to tell the difference between ciphertext that is produced using the cryptosystem and randomly generated data. While this is a good property that any cryptosystem should aspire to, for many practical applications it might be questionable whether it is strictly necessary to pass this 'test'.

1.5.3 Knowledge of the encryption algorithm

As promised, we now consider the validity of the standard assumption that an attacker knows the encryption algorithm. There tend to be two different approaches to designing encryption algorithms, which result in most encryption algorithms being classified as either:

publicly known algorithms: the full details of the algorithm are in the public domain and can be studied by anyone;
proprietary algorithms: the details of the algorithm are only known by the designers and perhaps a few selected parties.

In the case of publicly known encryption algorithms, an attacker knows the encryption algorithm. In the case of proprietary encryption algorithms, an attacker may well know the name of the encryption algorithm and certain basic properties, but it is not intended that they know any of the details of how it performs the encryption and decryption processes.

Note that the term 'proprietary' is often used in other contexts to describe something that has an 'owner' (an individual or organisation) and may have been patented, hence our use of this term is slightly unusual. It is possible for a publicly known algorithm to be patented by an 'owner', and indeed there are several high-profile examples. Further, it is not necessarily the case that a proprietary algorithm has any patent issues, although its use will necessarily be restricted.

THE IMPACT OF KERCKHOFFS' SECOND PRINCIPLE

At first glance, proprietary encryption algorithms would seem to be much more sensible, since they offer two distinct advantages:

1. Hiding the details of the algorithm will make life much harder for any attacker who tries to attack any cryptosystem using this algorithm. Hiding the encryption algorithm thus provides an extra 'layer' of security.
2. Proprietary encryption algorithms can be designed to meet the specific needs of a particular application.

However, there is a danger in relying on this first advantage. This is because there are many real examples of the details of proprietary encryption algorithms eventually becoming publicly known. This could happen if:

- a device on which the encryption algorithm is implemented is captured and expert attackers are able to investigate this device and somehow extract the algorithm (this process is often called *reverse engineering*);
- the details of the algorithm are accidentally or deliberately leaked to the public domain.

For this reason alone it is very unwise to *rely* on making an encryption algorithm proprietary. In fact, good cryptographic designers work on the principle that a proprietary encryption algorithm should still be secure in the event that the encryption algorithm becomes publicly known.

This principle is the most famous of six cryptosystem design principles that were identified by Auguste Kerckhoffs in the 19th century. More precisely, Kerckhoffs stated that the cryptographic algorithm *should not be required to be secret*. This principle is often misinterpreted as stating that the cryptographic algorithm should be publicly known, and hence rely only on the secrecy of the decryption key. However, Kerckhoffs did not say this. He simply pointed out that proprietary algorithms should not rely on their 'extra layer of security' and should be designed in such a way that public exposure of the algorithm does not compromise the security (more literally, he stated that the algorithm *must be able to fall into the hands of the enemy without inconvenience*).

THE CASE FOR PUBLICLY KNOWN ALGORITHMS

There are many reasons why it might be preferable to use a publicly known algorithm:

Scrutiny. A cryptographic algorithm that is in the public domain has the chance to be studied by a wide range of experts. If they all agree that the algorithm seems to be a good one then there are strong reasons to believe that the algorithm is secure. Such an algorithm could then be adopted by public standardisation bodies. In contrast, a proprietary algorithm may only have been assessed by a handful of experts.

Interoperability. It is much easier to adopt and implement publicly known algorithms in open networks. If an organisation wishes to regularly secure communications with external clients then use of a proprietary algorithm means that all the clients will either have to be given the algorithm specification, or the software or hardware necessary to run it.

Transparency. Businesses may find it easier to convince a trading partner that their systems are secure if the security techniques that they employ, which includes the cryptographic algorithms, are open to assessment by their partners. If an algorithm is proprietary then partners may want to perform independent evaluations of its strength.

WHAT HAPPENS IN PRACTICE?

The different advantages and disadvantages associated with proprietary and publicly known algorithms mean that their adoption is application dependent. In practice, both proprietary and publicly known algorithms are used in modern information systems.

Proprietary algorithms are normally only adopted by organisations (such as governments) that are large enough to be able to employ their own high-quality cryptographic design teams. They are also typically only used in closed environments where interoperability issues are less problematic.

The vast majority of applications of cryptography use publicly known algorithms. Indeed, in any commercial environment it is probably unwise to rely on the security of any cryptosystem that claims to use a proprietary algorithm unless the source of the cryptosystem design can be identified and is regarded as being highly reputable.

1.5.4 Use of publicly known algorithms

We have just observed that one possible advantage of publicly known algorithms is that a wide range of experts will have had the chance to evaluate such algorithms. However, designing cryptographic algorithms requires a great deal of knowledge, experience and skill. Many well-qualified (and less-qualified!) people have designed cryptographic algorithms, but very few ever gain sufficient public confidence to become recommended for use in real applications. It is thus very important to appreciate that:

- just because an algorithm is publicly known does not imply that it *has* been studied by a wide range of experts;
- even if a publicly known algorithm has been fairly well scrutinised, it may not be wise to deploy it in an application from a security perspective (for example, the level of scrutiny may not be sufficient);
- relatively few publicly known algorithms are actually deployed in applications;
- very few publicly known algorithms are widely supported across different applications.

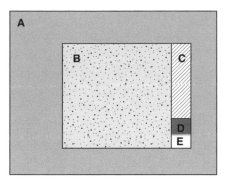

Figure 1.4. Taxonomy of publicly known encryption algorithms

To emphasise these points, Figure 1.4 presents a conceptual taxonomy of publicly known encryption algorithms. While this taxonomy is artificial, it is designed to emphasise the prudent 'conservatism' of adoption of publicly known encryption algorithms. The zones in the figure can be interpreted as follows:

Unstudied algorithms (Zone A). This consists of a substantial number of encryption algorithms that have been proposed by designers, but never subjected to any serious analysis. There may well be some very good algorithms in this zone, but they have not been scrutinised enough to be relied upon. Algorithms in this zone include those used by a number of commercial products that claim to have designed their own encryption algorithm. Great caution should be applied before relying on such products.

'Broken' algorithms (Zone B). This consists of the many publicly known encryption algorithms that have been analysed and subsequently found to be flawed.

Partially studied algorithms (Zone C). This consists of a reasonable number of publicly known encryption algorithms that have undergone some analysis without significant security weaknesses being found, but which have not subsequently attracted a great deal of attention. The most likely reason for this is that they do not appear to offer any significant benefits over algorithms in the next two zones. As a result, even though there may be very good algorithms in this zone, the extent to which they have been studied is probably not sufficient to justify deploying them in an application without good reason.

Respected algorithms (Zone D). This consists of a very small number of publicly known encryption algorithms that have been subject to a great deal of expert scrutiny without any flaws being found. These algorithms might reasonably be regarded as being secure enough to deploy in an application. Some of the algorithms in this zone may appear in standards. However, they are not 'default' encryption algorithms and so there is the potential for interoperability problems when they are used, since they are not as widely deployed as encryption algorithms in Zone E.

Default algorithms (Zone E). This consists of a handful of publicly known encryption algorithms that are widely recognised and deployed. These are regarded as safe choices and likely to be supported by many cryptographic applications.

Note that a publicly known encryption algorithm may well move between these zones over time. The only modern encryption algorithms that we will make specific references to in this book are (or used to be) either default or respected algorithms. It would normally be unwise to deploy a publicly known encryption algorithm that belongs to any other zone.

1.6 Breaking cryptosystems

We now discuss the much misunderstood concept of 'breaking' a cryptosystem. We will focus on:

- Cryptosystems providing confidentiality based on encryption algorithms. We note that the general principles apply to other cryptosystems supporting other cryptographic primitives.
- 'Breaks' that are directly related to the underlying cryptographic primitives. There are many ways in which a cryptosystem could be 'broken' which have nothing to do with the underlying cryptographic primitives. We discuss these further in Section 3.2.

1.6.1 Some useful preliminaries

An important objective of this book is to explain cryptography without the need for skills in mathematics. While we fully intend to honour this objective, there are some very basic pieces of notation and terminology that we will need. At the risk of insulting the intelligence of some readers, this is a good place to make them clear. Other (optional) mathematical ideas are relegated to the Mathematics Appendix.

BINARY NUMBERS

It is important to realise that although we will discuss some historical encryption algorithms in Chapter 2 which operate on letters of the alphabet, all the 'real' cryptographic algorithms that we will discuss in this book are designed to run on computers, and thus process information (including plaintexts, ciphertexts and cryptographic keys) as *binary* data consisting of zeros and ones. Individual zeros and ones are conventionally referred to as *bits* and groups of eight bits are referred to as *bytes*.

For much of our discussion we can probably 'get away' with just considering binary data as sequences of zeros and ones. However, it is important to realise that a sequence (we sometimes refer to this as a *string*) of zeros and ones such as 1101001 does actually represent a *binary number*. A full explanation of binary numbers and how they relate to the more familiar decimal numbers is provided in the Mathematics Appendix. This also includes an explanation of *hex*, which is most useful to us as a compact way of representing binary numbers.

XOR

Modern symmetric cryptographic algorithms process binary data by conducting various different operations on the data. One common operation is to compute the *exclusive or*, better known as XOR, of two binary strings (numbers). This is essentially the equivalent of 'addition' for binary numbers. Thus, every time that we refer to the binary operation XOR, it is reasonable to interpret this as 'adding' the two binary strings together. When we refer to this operation in text we use the term XOR, but when we write XOR in mathematical notation we commonly use the symbol $\oplus$ (which itself indicates that we are conducting a type of 'addition'). The XOR operation is described in more detail in the Mathematics Appendix.

EXPONENTIATION

A mathematical operation that we will often need to refer to is *exponentiation*. This means raising a number to a *power*, which means multiplying the original number by itself a certain number of times. Commonly we will need to raise the number 2 to various powers. We use the conventional notation 2^k to mean 'raising the number 2 to the power k', which means multiplying 2 by itself k times. In other words:

$$2^k = 2 \times 2 \times \cdots \times 2,$$

where there is a total of k occurrences of 2 on the right. As an example with $k = 4$:

$$2^4 = 2 \times 2 \times 2 \times 2 = 16.$$

More generally, we use the notation a^b to mean raising a to the power b, which just means multiplying the number a by itself b times. In other words:

$$a^b = a \times a \times a \times \cdots \times a,$$

where there is a total of b occurrences of a on the right. As an example with $a = 3$ and $b = 5$:

$$3^5 = 3 \times 3 \times 3 \times 3 \times 3 = 243.$$

Another simple fact that we will need later is that if we raise a to the power b, and then raise the result to the power c, then this is the same as raising a to the power $b \times c$. In other words:

$$(a^b)^c = a^{b \times c}.$$

As an example with $a = 2$, $b = 3$ and $c = 4$:

$$(2^3)^4 = 8^4 = 4096 = 2^{12} = 2^{3 \times 4}.$$

We will also use the fact that if we raise a to the power b, and then raise the result to the power c, then this is the same as raising a to the power c and then raising the result to the power b. In other words:

$$(a^b)^c = (a^c)^b.$$

Using our previous example:

$$(2^3)^4 = 4096 = (2^4)^3.$$

CONCATENATION

At various points in our coverage of cryptographic mechanisms we will need a mathematical notation to mean the very simple process of writing two pieces of data (or numbers) 'next to one another'. We say that the data (or number) x is *concatenated* to the data y, and write this as $x \mathbin{\|} y$. In other words, $x \mathbin{\|} y$ consists of x (written on the left) next to y (written on the right). For example, the concatenation of $x = 1101$ and $y = 11100011$ is:

$$x \mathbin{\|} y = 110111100011.$$

1.6.2 Key lengths and keyspaces

Before proceeding further, it is important to understand various concepts relating to the number of possible different decryption keys in a cryptosystem, which we refer to as the *size* of the keyspace. This is important because one strategy for an attacker of a cryptosystem is to try to determine the decryption key, hence the size of the keyspace is certainly something that the attacker will be interested in. The majority of cryptosystems have a fixed size of keyspace. However, it is worth noting that:

- Some cryptosystems can provide a choice of size of keyspace. For example, the encryption algorithm AES can be used in three different 'settings', each of which has a different size of keyspace (see Section 4.5). While a cryptosystem using AES may select just one of these 'settings', it is also possible that it could support more than one.
- For some cryptosystems the size of the keyspace is highly flexible. For example, both the Vigenère Cipher (see Section 2.2.4) and one-time pad (see Section 3.1.3) have keyspaces whose sizes can (at least in theory) be made arbitrarily large.

Since the size of the keyspace in modern cryptosystems can be enormous, we tend to focus attention on the *length* of a cryptographic key (often also referred to as the *size* or *strength* of the key), which is the number of bits that it takes to represent the key. For example, the cryptographic key 10011010 has length eight. The length of a cryptographic key is referred to more commonly than the size of the keyspace.

Regarding the relationship between key length and the size of the keyspace, there is an important difference between symmetric and public-key cryptosystems:

Symmetric cryptosytems. By and large, the length of the key can be used to determine the size of the keyspace. If the key length is k bits (which we sometimes refer to by saying that we have a k-*bit key*) then the size of the keyspace is 2^k, since there are two choices (0 or 1) for each of the bits of the key, and thus the number of possible keys is:

$$2 \times 2 \times \cdots \times 2 = 2^k.$$

We used the caveat 'by and large' because some symmetric cryptosystems specify that particular keys should not be used, thus the keyspace is sometimes slightly smaller than 2^k. Also, some symmetric cryptosystems use keys that contain redundant bits (for example, while DES keys are normally 64 bits long, 8 of these bits are redundant and hence the effective key length is only 56 bits).

Public-key cryptosystems. The length of the decryption key provides an *indication* of the size of the keyspace, although the precise relationship between the length of the decryption key and the size of the keyspace will depend on which public-key cryptosystem is being used. We discuss this in more detail in Section 5.4.3.

Note for symmetric cryptosystems that while the the length of a 256-bit key is indeed double the length of a 128-bit key, the size of the keyspace associated with a 256-bit key is vastly greater than that of a 128-bit key. To be precise, it is 2^{128} times as big!

The notions of the length of a key and the size of the keyspace are thus related and we often use these terms fairly interchangeably, keeping in mind the above discussion.

1.6.3 Breaking encryption algorithms

An encryption algorithm is often referred to as being *broken* if a method of determining the plaintext from the ciphertext is found that does not involve being legitimately given the decryption key. This is an extremely uncomfortable definition to work with since we will shortly see that under this definition *every* encryption algorithm can be broken. It might be better to suggest that an encryption algorithm is broken if a *practical* method to do this is found, but this too has problems, which we will come to in a moment.

The process of trying to determine a plaintext from a ciphertext is conducted under the standard assumptions of Section 1.5.1. In many cases, 'breaks' of encryption algorithms also involve large quantities of corresponding plaintext and ciphertext pairs being used during the cryptanalysis. There are generally two types of break:

1. A method of determining the decryption key directly is found. This is the most powerful type of break, since obtaining knowledge of the decryption key allows decryption of all other ciphertexts that were generated using the corresponding encryption key.
2. A weakness in the encryption algorithm is discovered that leads directly to a plaintext being deduced from the corresponding ciphertext without first determining the decryption key.

Determining the decryption key is the most common, and most natural, way of breaking an encryption algorithm, so we will focus on this type of break in the subsequent discussion.

It is very important to be aware of the fact that the term 'break' comes with a substantial health warning. Deciding when a method of determining the plaintext from a ciphertext is actually feasible (or relevant) is subjective and depends, to an extent, on what it is reasonable to expect an attacker to be able to do. It is thus highly plausible that an encryption algorithm that is regarded as 'broken' with respect to one application might still be suitable for another.

Another point, which we will make repeatedly, is that the most likely point of failure in any cryptosystem is in the management of the cryptographic keys. If a decryption key is inadequately protected then the cryptosystem becomes useless, regardless of the strength of the underlying encryption algorithm. It is surprisingly common for key management failures to be confused with breaks of encryption algorithms, especially in the media.

1.6.4 Exhaustive key searches

There is one important method that can be used to 'break' almost all known encryption algorithms (we will discuss the only exception in Section 3.1.3). This attack is so important that it provides a security 'benchmark' against which the effectiveness of other attacks can be measured.

CONDUCTING AN EXHAUSTIVE KEY SEARCH

An *exhaustive key search* can be conducted by an attacker who is in possession of a target ciphertext that has been encrypted using a known encryption algorithm. The attacker:

1. selects a decryption key from the keyspace of the cryptosystem;
2. decrypts the target ciphertext using that decryption key;
3. checks to see if the resulting plaintext 'makes sense' (we discuss this concept in a moment);

4. if the plaintext does make sense then the attacker labels the decryption key as a *candidate decryption key*;
5. if the attacker can confirm that this decryption key is the correct decryption key then the attacker stops the search, otherwise they select a new decryption key from the keyspace and repeat the process.

In other words, an exhaustive key search involves decrypting the ciphertext with different decryption keys until candidates for the correct decryption key are found. If the correct decryption key can be identified as soon as it is tested then the attacker stops the search as soon as it is found. If it cannot be identified then the attacker searches all possible decryption keys until the list of candidate decryption keys is complete. This type of attack is sometimes also referred to as a *brute-force attack*, since in its simplest form it involves no sophisticated knowledge of the cryptosystem other than the encryption algorithm used.

IDENTIFYING CANDIDATE DECRYPTION KEYS

In order to decrypt a target ciphertext 'correctly', an attacker conducting an exhaustive key search needs to be able to recognise when they have found candidates for the correct decryption key. The attacker thus needs some information that can be used to identify candidate decryption keys. This type of information could be:

Some known plaintext/ciphertext pairs: the attacker could then apply each decryption key to the known ciphertexts to see if that decryption key successfully decrypts the known ciphertexts into the corresponding known plaintexts.

Knowledge of the plaintext language: if the plaintext is in a known language, such as English, then the attacker will be able to use the statistical properties of the language to recognise candidate plaintexts, and hence candidate decryption keys.

Contextual information: the attacker may have other information concerning the plaintext that allows candidate decryption keys to be identified (for example, perhaps the plaintext has a specific format or begins with a particular known string of characters).

DETERMINING THE CORRECT DECRYPTION KEY

Suppose now that an attacker is not able to immediately identify the correct decryption key and thus generates a list of candidate decryption keys. If only one candidate decryption key is found then the attacker can of course reasonably deduce that this is the correct decryption key. If more than one candidate decryption key is found then the attacker will not necessarily be able to identify the correct decryption key from this list, unless they obtain some extra information (such as another valid plaintext/ciphertext pair).

However, it should be noted that the list of candidate decryption keys is likely to be very small. For example, suppose that a highly regarded encryption algorithm with a keyspace of size 2^{128} is being used. If an attacker already knows one plaintext/ciphertext pair then it can be shown that an exhaustive key search that uses this known plaintext/ciphertext pair to identify candidate decryption keys for a new target ciphertext will result in at most a handful of candidate decryption keys. This is because the chances that a different decryption key to the correct one also successfully decrypts the known ciphertext into the known plaintext is extremely small. Use of the knowledge of a second plaintext/ciphertext pair will almost always be sufficient to identify the correct decryption key.

However, even without determining precisely which of a short list of candidate decryption keys is the correct decryption key, an attacker may still have enough information to proceed. To see this, suppose that the plaintext is the launch date for a new product and the attacker is a commercial rival. If the attacker has just reduced 2^{128} possible decryption keys to just three (say) candidate decryption keys then this is a spectacularly significant achievement from a security perspective. Even if all three candidate plaintexts are plausible (in this case they would all have to be plausible launch dates), the attacker could:

- proceed to develop three separate courses of action, each based on a different candidate launch date of the rival's product;
- simply guess which one is correct, since they have a one third chance of being correct.

Thus in most cases it is normally assumed that an exhaustive key search results in the attacker 'knowing' the correct decryption key and hence the correct plaintext, even if in practice they are left with a small degree of doubt. Indeed, in some cases it is probably reasonable to assume that an attacker can identify the correct decryption key as soon as it is tested, hence they do not need to complete a search of the entire keyspace.

PROTECTING AGAINST EXHAUSTIVE KEY SEARCHES

An exhaustive key search is indeed exhausting to conduct manually, but this is precisely the type of process that computers can perform with ease. To withstand an exhaustive key search there must be so many different decryption keys to try out that the search becomes impossible to conduct in practice (it either takes too much time or costs too much money). This is why most practical cryptosystems must have a sufficiently large keyspace that an exhaustive key search is infeasible.

We now briefly consider how big 'sufficiently large' might be. We make the assumptions that:

- All possible keys in the keyspace are available and equally likely to be selected. If this is not the case then the keyspace is smaller than we think and the subsequent analysis may be invalid.
- The attacker can identify the correct decryption key as soon as it is tested.

Estimating exactly how much time is needed to conduct an exhaustive key search requires assumptions about the resources available to an attacker. A good place to start is to try to estimate the amount of time that it might take an attacker to test one decryption key. We can then use this estimate to assess how long an exhaustive key search might take. We first need one piece of statistical information. Namely, if the size of the keyspace of an encryption algorithm is 2^k then the laws of probability imply that, on average, an attacker can expect to find the correct decryption key in 2^{k-1} decryption attempts.

This is quite an intuitive statement. It says that an attacker can, on average, expect to find the correct decryption key about halfway through an exhaustive key search. It might be the first key that they try (lucky!) and it might be the last key that they try (unlucky!) but, on average, they will find it halfway through.

We can use this information to estimate how large a keyspace needs to be in order to reasonably withstand an exhaustive key search that takes one year. There are approximately 3×10^7 seconds in one year, which is approximately 2^{25} seconds (see the Mathematics Appendix for an explanation). For a number of assumed computational strengths of an attacker, Table 1.4 shows the approximate length of decryption key that is needed in order to protect against an exhaustive key search lasting one year.

To see where the figures in Table 1.4 come from, consider the third row. Note that one thousand is approximately 2^{10} and that one million is approximately 2^{20}. Thus in one year, one thousand processors testing one million keys per second will be able to test an approximate total of

$$2^{25} \times 2^{10} \times 2^{20} = 2^{55}$$

keys. This means that a keyspace of 2^{56} should suffice to make it likely that an exhaustive key search will, on average, take a full year. In other words, if we estimate that an attacker has one thousand processors that can each test one million keys per second then, if we want security for one year, the minimum key length that we should consider is 56 bits. In practice we would be wise to use keys longer than this, just to be on the safe side.

Note that, somewhat ironically, the threat of an exhaustive key search presents a case (at least in theory) for slowing down the speed of a decryption algorithm. While slowing down decryption makes the cryptosystem *slightly* more

Table 1.4: Key lengths needed to protect against an exhaustive key search that takes one year

Strength of attack	Key length
Human effort of one key per second	26 bits
One processor testing one million keys per second	46 bits
1000 processors testing one million keys per second	56 bits
One million processors testing one million keys per second	66 bits

cumbersome to use, it has the potential to make an exhaustive key search *much* more cumbersome to conduct. We give an example of a cryptographic primitive that has been deliberately slowed down for this reason in Section 8.4.2. Nonetheless, most applications tend to choose to maximise decryption speeds in order to make the cryptography as 'seamless' as possible. Hence making sure that the keys are sufficiently long is the only protection against an exhaustive key search.

1.6.5 Classes of attack

Although we do not plan to discuss the details of many cryptanalytic attacks, it is important to be aware of the types of attack that cryptosystems are commonly subjected to. A simple classification of the most common classes of cryptanalytic attack is as follows:

Generic attacks. These are attacks that apply to a wide range of cryptographic primitives and do not normally employ knowledge of the working of the primitive itself. We have already discussed the most important member of this class, the exhaustive key search. Other examples are:

- *Dictionary attacks.* This term is used in a number of different contexts, all of which relate to attacks that involve compiling a type of 'dictionary'. For example:
  - An attacker of a simple cryptosystem (for example, one using a block cipher in ECB mode, see Section 4.6.1) with a fixed key might be able to build a dictionary which consists of ciphertexts corresponding to plaintexts that the attacker has been able to learn by some means. For example, if the plaintexts correspond to dates that an event will occur on, the attacker will learn the plaintext when they later observe the event occurring. When a future ciphertext is seen, the attacker looks up the dictionary in the hope that the observed ciphertext is listed, in which case the attacker can read off the corresponding plaintext.
  - An attacker exploits a key derivation process (see Section 10.3.2) where keys are derived from passwords. In this case the attacker compiles a dictionary of likely passwords and then derives the resulting keys from them, which are then used in an 'intelligent' exhaustive key search.
- *Time memory tradeoff attacks.* These are related to both exhaustive key searches and dictionary attacks, and are based on balancing computational and memory resources in attempts to determine decryption keys. For example:
  - An attacker builds tables which consist of ciphertexts corresponding to specific (commonly sent) plaintexts encrypted using a large number of keys. When a ciphertext is seen that the attacker suspects may correspond to one of the commonly sent plaintexts, the attacker looks up the tables in the hope that the observed ciphertext is listed, in which case the attacker can then read off which key is likely to have been used. The size of the tables that the attacker needs to store in memory can be traded off against the time saved by table lookups.

Primitive-specific attacks. These are attacks that apply generically to a specific class of cryptographic primitives. Examples include:

- *Differential* and *linear cryptanalysis.* These two cryptanalysis techniques are primarily targeted against block ciphers, which are now explicitly designed to try to resist them.
- *Birthday attacks.* This simple attack can be conducted against any hash function and is the baseline attack that determines the output length for modern hash functions (see Section 6.2.3).
- *Statistical attacks.* There is a suite of simple statistical attacks that can be conducted against deterministic generators (see Section 8.1.4) and any modern deterministic generator should be resistant to them.

Algorithm-specific attacks. These are attacks that are designed for use against a specific cryptographic algorithm. Often such attacks are variants of more generic attacks that have been tailored to the working of the specific algorithm.

Side-channel attacks. This is an important class of attacks that are not against the theoretical design of a cryptographic primitive, but rather the way in which the primitive is *implemented.* An increasing number of side-channel attacks are being discovered and thus implementers of cryptography need to pay close attention to developments in this area. Examples include:

- *Timing attacks.* These exploit the fact that different processor computations take slightly different times to compute. Hence, by measuring such timings, it may be possible to learn information about the nature of a computation that a processor is trying to conduct. For example, it may be possible to determine a key by noting the timings of several different operations conducted using that key.
- *Power analysis.* These attacks are similar to timing attacks except that power consumption is used to obtain information about the nature of the underlying computations.
- *Fault analysis.* These attacks involve an attacker inducing errors in a cryptosystem and studying the resulting output for useful information.
- *Padding attacks.* These attacks exploit the fact that plaintext usually needs to be 'padded' before processing (see Section 4.3.2). By manipulating this process and monitoring resulting error messages it can be possible to learn important information about the nature of the underlying data.

1.6.6 Academic attacks

It is notable that the majority of attacks on modern cryptographic algorithms come from the academic community. However, these are often *academic attacks* in both their origin and applicability. Recall that the idea of 'breaking' a cryptographic algorithm is a subjective one and depends on what attack capabilities are considered to be reasonable. Security of modern encryption algorithms tends to be set very conservatively, so that even a very good attack that significantly improves on an exhaustive key search may still be well beyond a practical attacker's capabilities. Indeed, many academic attacks involve quite unrealistic assumptions and thus do not have practical impact (for example, they require an impractical number of deliberately chosen plaintext/ciphertext pairs). Others only have practical security implications for some types of application. Nonetheless, the fact that any attack was found at all might be a cause for concern, particularly if the attack technique has the potential to be improved.

Thus caution should be applied before reacting to claims that a particular cryptographic algorithm has been broken. It is important to recognise that without context and detail, such a claim on its own has very little meaning. More detailed information should always be sought and, if necessary, expert opinion should be obtained.

1.7 Summary

In this chapter we motivated the need for cryptography and discussed issues concerning its use. In particular, we introduced the basic model of a cryptosystem, as well as important terminology. There are a number of lessons that have emerged:

- The need to secure information is not a new concept, but the environment within which information needs to be secured has changed significantly.
- Cryptography provides the technical means to replicate some of the fundamental security requirements of the physical world in an electronic environment.
- Cryptography can offer strong protection, but only against certain specific threats. It is just as important to be aware of the security threats that cryptography does not protect against, as to be aware of those threats that it does address.
- There are two different types of cryptosystem, symmetric and public-key. These have significantly different properties and each type of cryptosystem has its own inherent advantages and disadvantages, which we will discuss in later chapters. Symmetric and public-key cryptosystems are often combined in real systems.
- In order to assess the security offered by a cryptosystem, it is important to establish clear assumptions about what an attacker can do, and what resources they might make available to attack the cryptosystem.

1.8 Further reading

Cryptography provides fundamental mechanisms for supporting information security. A reader wishing to explore information security in more detail has plenty of options. A good starting place is Schneier [170], which provides a very accessible overview of different computer security problems and, in particular, places the role of cryptography in context. A wider education in information security requires, at a minimum, a broad understanding of information security management, network security and computer security. While there are increasing numbers of texts on specialist aspects of these subjects, we recommend Dhillon [56] and Purser [159] for general introductions to the management of information security, Stallings [183] for network security, and Bishop [34] and Gollmann [92] for introductions to computer security. Anderson [23] provides an interesting read of relevance to all of those subjects, including cryptography. Although only of indirect relevance to cryptography, Stoll [187] is an entertaining story for anyone seeking further motivation for securing information systems.

Levy's highly recommended Crypto is a fascinating read, which covers the dramatic development of cryptography in the latter decades of the 20th century. The 'crypto politics' that surrounded these events provides a rich perspective on the different attitudes and perspectives that are held about cryptography. Levy brings this subject alive through interesting profiles of some of the main parties involved during this influential period. This book has been published under two different subtitles [117, 118] and, although sometimes hard to get hold of, is worth tracking down.

The different security services that we have introduced in this chapter are notoriously hard to formally define. Menezes, van Oorschot and Vanstone [123] contains a number of useful definitions, while Dent and Mitchell [55] cover the approach taken by ISO. For an introduction to coding theory, and how it relates to cryptography, approachable reads include Biggs [33] and Welsh [198]. More information about access control can be found in Gollman [92] and Anderson [23]. An accessible introduction to steganography and how it relates to cryptography is Wayner [197], while Fridrich [85] provides a more detailed discussion of steganographic principles and techniques. Walton [195] provides a thought-provoking perspective on the changes that have occurred in the application environment in which cryptography is deployed since the early 1970s, and the subsequent implications. A useful portal for laws and regulations relating to cryptography is maintained by Bert-Jaap Koops [110].

Auguste Kerckhoffs' original article [108] is available online, as are various translations of his six principles for cryptosystem design. We have only touched on very basic attack models for cryptosystems in this chapter. An indication of the stronger and more rigorous attack models used to design modern cryptosystems can be found in, for example, Katz and Lindell [105] and Stinson [185]. The study of side-channel attacks is a very active area of current research, with The Side Channel Cryptanalysis Lounge [64] being a recommended starting point.

Finally, we mention two interesting perspectives on cryptography. Matt Blaze [35] takes our analogy between encryption and physical locks much further. Blaze caused a real stir in the locksmith world when he first published this article, which is an interesting read and illustrates lessons that can be learnt by both the cryptographic and locksmith communities from studying one another's design methodologies. Young and Yung [206] discuss a number of ways in which cryptography can be exploited by attackers in order to attack computer systems, which is quite the opposite intention of most cryptographic applications.

1.9 Activities

1. Unauthorised access to information could also be reasonably described as 'stealing' information. What is one significant difference between 'stealing' information and 'stealing' physical goods?

2. Consider the two common (but analogous) scenarios of sending a letter in the post and sending an email message.

    (a) Write down a few lines that summarise the differences between these two processes with respect to:
        i. ease of creation of a message;
        ii. ease of sending a message;
        iii. ease of interception of a message;
        iv. ease of forgery of a message;
        v. ease of repudiation (denial of sending) of a message.
    (b) Having outlined the differences in process, now comment in each case on how the two scenarios differ with respect to the security mechanisms in place at each stage.
    (c) Is there an equivalent of *registered post* for sending an email?
    (d) Is there an equivalent of *secure email* for sending a letter by post?
    (e) In your opinion, which scenario is 'more secure' than the other?

3. For each of the physical world and the electronic world, provide two examples of the following:

    (a) Two weak security mechanisms that, when adopted together, represent a fairly strong security mechanism.
    (b) A strong security mechanism that, when used incorrectly, becomes a weak security mechanism.
    (c) A strong security mechanism that, when used without an appropriate security infrastructure, becomes a weak security mechanism.

4. Provide an example of at least one application (if there are *any* such applications) where:

    (a) data integrity is more important than data confidentiality;
    (b) entity authentication is more important than data origin authentication;
    (c) entity authentication and data origin authentication are both required;
    (d) data origin authentication is necessary but non-repudiation is not necessarily required;
    (e) data integrity is required but not data origin authentication;
    (f) data origin authentication is required but not data integrity;
    (g) entity authentication is provided using more than one mechanism.

5. Explain the differences between providing confidentiality through cryptography, steganography and access control mechanisms.

6. In the 19th century, Auguste Kerckhoffs defined six design principles for encryption algorithms.

    (a) State Kerckhoffs six design principles.
    (b) Do these six design principles still hold today?
    (c) Translate these six design principles into a more appropriate language for the cryptographic algorithms that are used today on modern computers.

7. A government department decides that it needs to use encryption to protect communication between itself and its international counterparts. At a meeting with its counterparts it is decided to develop a proprietary cryptographic algorithm for this purpose.

    (a) Is this decision justifiable?
    (b) What risks are being taken?

8. There are some encryption algorithms that are *almost publicly known* in the sense that most of the details are published, but some components of the encryption algorithm are kept secret (proprietary).

    (a) What are the advantages and disadvantages of this approach?
    (b) Do you think this captures the 'best of both worlds' or the 'worst of both worlds' with respect to knowledge of the encryption algorithm?

9. It is generally good practice in most situations to adopt publicly known and well-established encryption algorithms such as the AES. Some people might argue that this approach is akin to 'putting all of your eggs into one basket' and is inherently risky since, if a serious flaw is found in AES, then the implications could be disastrous.

    (a) Although diversity can be a good thing in many aspects of life, explain why it is not necessarily good when it comes to use of encryption algorithms.
    (b) How should we mitigate against the risk that a leading encryption algorithm, such as AES, does get unexpectedly broken in the near future?

10. Consider the zoned classification of publicly known encryption algorithms in Section 1.5.4:

    (a) For each of the classification zones, explain the potential disadvantages of using an encryption algorithm belonging to that zone.
    (b) To what extent do you think that such a zoning applies to publicly known cryptographic mechanisms for providing other security services, such as data origin authentication?

11. Suppose that an attacker has got hold of 128 bits of ciphertext that have been encrypted using an encryption algorithm whose keys are known to be 128 bits long. How effective is an exhaustive key search if:

(a) The attacker does not know the encryption algorithm that was used?

(b) The attacker knows the encryption algorithm, but does not know any previous plaintext/ciphertext pairs, and knows that the plaintext is randomly generated?

(c) The attacker knows the encryption algorithm, one previous plaintext/ciphertext pair, and knows that the plaintext is randomly generated?

12. Dan Brown's best seller *Digital Fortress* [42] features a machine which, it is claimed, can 'break' most cryptosystems. Comment on the practicality of building such a machine.

13. Explain why a cryptographic designer might reasonably claim that the main security goal for designing a symmetric encryption algorithm is to make sure that the best attack against it is an exhaustive key search.

14. We often lose perspective of very large numbers.

(a) Place the following values in order of increasing size:
   - number of possible 40-bit keys
   - number of possible 90-bit keys
   - number of possible 128-bit keys
   - number of web pages indexed by Google
   - number of stars in our galaxy
   - number of stars in the universe
   - number of species of bird on Earth
   - number of seconds since the beginning of the universe

(b) For each of the above, identify how many bits would be required to represent symmetric keys in a keyspace of that size.

15. Encryption algorithm ALEX has a 40-bit key and encryption algorithm CARLOS has a 48-bit key. Assume that you have sufficient computing power to use an exhaustive key search to find the key of ALEX in one day.

(a) Assuming that they have similar computational complexity, how long would you expect it to take to find the key of CARLOS by means of an exhaustive key search?

(b) Assume now that the (bad) design of CARLOS allows it to be run in two separate stages such that it is possible to conduct an exhaustive key search for the first 40 bits of a CARLOS key and then perform a separate exhaustive key search for the last 8 bits. How long do you now expect to take to recover a CARLOS key by means of an exhaustive key search?

16. The following table specifies a cryptosystem based around a very simple encryption algorithm with four different plaintexts A, B, C and D (one corresponding to each column) and four different ciphertexts **A**, **B**, **C** and **D**. The encryption algorithm has five different keys K_1, K_2, K_3, K_4, K_5 (one corresponding to each row). By writing $E_K(P)=$**C** to mean that the encryption

of plaintext P using encryption key K is C, the entire cryptosystem is defined as follows:

$$E_{K_1}(A)=\mathbf{B} \quad E_{K_1}(B)=\mathbf{C} \quad E_{K_1}(C)=\mathbf{D} \quad E_{K_1}(D)=\mathbf{A}$$
$$E_{K_2}(A)=\mathbf{B} \quad E_{K_2}(B)=\mathbf{C} \quad E_{K_2}(C)=\mathbf{A} \quad E_{K_2}(D)=\mathbf{D}$$
$$E_{K_3}(A)=\mathbf{D} \quad E_{K_3}(B)=\mathbf{B} \quad E_{K_3}(C)=\mathbf{A} \quad E_{K_3}(D)=\mathbf{C}$$
$$E_{K_4}(A)=\mathbf{A} \quad E_{K_4}(B)=\mathbf{B} \quad E_{K_4}(C)=\mathbf{D} \quad E_{K_4}(D)=\mathbf{C}$$
$$F_{K_5}(A)=\mathbf{C} \quad E_{K_5}(B)=\mathbf{D} \quad E_{K_5}(C)=\mathbf{A} \quad E_{K_5}(D)=\mathbf{B}$$

(a) What is the size of the keyspace?
(b) If an interceptor sees the ciphertext **B** then which plaintext can he rule out?
(c) What is the ciphertext that results from encrypting plaintext B with K_3, and is this a problem?
(d) Could we replace the bottom right-hand entry of the table with $E_{K_5}(D)=\mathbf{C}$?
(e) Suppose that we define a sixth key K_6 by the rule $E_{K_6}(P)=E_{K_5}(E_{K_1}(P))$ for each plaintext P. In other words, for example, $E_{K_6}(A)=E_{K_5}(E_{K_1}(A))=E_{K_5}(B)=\mathbf{D}$. What are the values for $E_{K_6}(B)$, $E_{K_6}(C)$ and $E_{K_6}(D)$?
(f) Could we use a table such as this to represent a real cryptosystem?

17. Explain whether the following scenarios are possible for a symmetric cryptosystem:

    (a) two different plaintexts encrypt to the same ciphertext under different keys (in other words, $E_{K_1}(P_1) = E_{K_2}(P_2) = C$);
    (b) two different plaintexts encrypt to the same ciphertext under the same key (in other words, $E_K(P_1) = E_K(P_2) = C$);
    (c) a plaintext encrypts to the same ciphertext under two different keys (in other words, $E_{K_1}(P) = E_{K_2}(P) = C$).

18. In most of this chapter we assumed that cryptography was being used to protect data in a communication scenario. However, cryptography can also be used to protect stored data. Which of the issues that we discussed in this chapter are exactly the same regardless of whether cryptography is being used to protect transmitted data or stored data, and which of these are subtly different? (You might like to consider who the likely players are in the basic model of a cryptosystem being used to protect stored data, which security questions they might ask, etc.)

19. Most people generally regard cryptography as a 'force for good', which can be used to help protect computer systems.

    (a) Explain why government organisations might not always regard cryptography as a 'force for good'.
    (b) Can you think of any ways in which cryptography could be used as a tool to *attack* computer systems?

20. In certain jurisdictions, cryptographic technology is subject to export controls.

    (a) Find an example of a country that currently has export controls on cryptographic technology and summarise the extent of these controls.
    (b) What potential problems do export controls present, given that cryptography is deployed in everyday applications?

21. In contrast to our usage, the term 'proprietary' is often used to describe something that is subject to a patent.

    (a) Find some examples of encryption algorithms that, using our terminology, are:
        i. publicly known and subject to patent issues;
        ii. proprietary but not subject to patent issues;
        iii. proprietary and subject to patent issues.
    (b) Do you think that it is more, or less, likely that a proprietary encryption algorithm is subject to patent issues than a publicly known encryption algorithm?

2 Historical Cryptosystems

We now discuss a number of simple historical cryptosystems. These cryptosystems are unsuitable for modern use, but they are simple to understand and help to illustrate many of the issues discussed in Chapter 1, including the basic model of a cryptosystem. These historical cryptosystems also provide us with simple examples that allow some fundamental cryptosystem design principles to be explored.

> **At the end of this chapter you should be able to:**
>
> - Describe a number of simple historical cryptosystems.
> - Relate a number of historical cryptosystems to the basic model of a cryptosystem.
> - Appreciate the direction of some historical advances in cryptosystem design.
> - Illustrate properties of these historical cryptosystems that make them unsuitable for modern use.
> - Formulate some fundamental design principles for a modern cryptosystem.

Before we proceed further, it is worth noting that all the cryptosystems that we will discuss in this chapter have four common features:

Symmetric. They are all symmetric cryptosystems. Indeed, they all predate the discovery of public-key cryptography.

Confidentiality. They are all designed to provide confidentiality only.

Alphabetic. They are all described as operating on alphabetic characters. This is in contrast to modern cryptosystems which generally operate on numbers, most commonly binary numbers. This has some implications: for example, we normally consider the size of the keyspace of these cryptosystems rather than discuss key length (see Section 1.6.2).

Unsuitable. Each, in their own different way, is completely unsuitable for use in modern cryptographic applications. In most cases this is because they are not secure enough.

47

2.1 Monoalphabetic ciphers

We begin with some very basic examples of historical cryptosystems.

2.1.1 Caesar Cipher

The *Caesar Cipher* tends to be the first example in any introduction to cryptography. Although it is a very straightforward cryptosystem, there are basic lessons to be learned from studying it. The cryptosystem that we describe is sometimes referred to as the *Shift Cipher*, with the name 'Caesar Cipher' occasionally used in a more restricted way to describe the Shift Cipher when the particular shift of three is used.

DESCRIPTION OF THE CAESAR CIPHER

The idea of the Caesar Cipher is to encrypt each letter of the alphabet by the letter obtained by 'shifting' the alphabet a secret number of positions. One way of visualising this is to:

1. Write out the plaintext letters of the alphabet A to Z, in order, twice (one after the other).
2. Imagine a 'sliding ruler' consisting of one copy of the ciphertext letters of the alphabet A to Z, in order. This 'sliding ruler' can be shifted to any position underneath the plaintext letters.
3. Sender Alice and receiver Bob both agree on a secret *shift*, which is represented by a number between 0 and 25.

In order to encrypt a plaintext letter, Alice positions the sliding ruler underneath the first set of plaintext letters and slides it to the right by the number of positions of the secret shift. The plaintext letter is then encrypted to the ciphertext letter underneath it on the sliding ruler.

The result of this process is depicted in Figure 2.1 for an agreed shift of three positions. In this case, plaintext HOBBY is encrypted to ciphertext KREEB.

On receiving the ciphertext, Bob, who also knows the secret shift, positions his sliding ruler in the same way as Alice. He then replaces the ciphertext letter on the sliding ruler with the plaintext letter above it. Hence ciphertext NHVWUHO is decrypted to KESTREL.

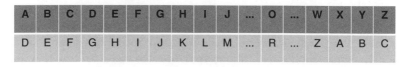

A	B	C	D	E	F	G	H	I	J	...	O	...	W	X	Y	Z
D	E	F	G	H	I	J	K	L	M	...	R	...	Z	A	B	C

Figure 2.1. Encryption using the Caesar Cipher with a shift of three

FITTING THE CAESAR CIPHER TO THE BASIC MODEL

The Caesar Cipher can be fitted to the basic model of a cryptosystem that we introduced in Section 1.4.3. The various components of this model are:

Plaintext/Ciphertext: these are both represented by strings of letters from the alphabet A to Z.

Encryption key: this is the number representing the secret shift.

Decryption key: this is also the number representing the secret shift, so this is a symmetric cryptosystem.

Keyspace: there are 26 possible different shifts, each of which corresponds to a possible key, so the keyspace has size 26.

Encryption algorithm: this can be represented by the algorithm –

1. slide the ruler to the right by the secret shift length;
2. replace the plaintext letter by the ciphertext letter beneath it.

Decryption algorithm: this can be represented by the algorithm –

1. slide the ruler to the right by the secret shift length;
2. replace the ciphertext letter by the plaintext letter above it.

MATHEMATICAL DESCRIPTION OF THE CAESAR CIPHER

Strictly as an aside (which can comfortably be skipped at this stage), the Caesar Cipher can more efficiently be described using simple mathematical notation. To do so, we represent the letters A to Z by the numbers 0 to 25 (in other words, we identify A with 0, B with 1, C with 2, and so on). The Caesar Cipher key is already a number between 0 and 25.

The advantage of doing this is that the process 'slide the ruler to the right' can now be more elegantly described as a simple modular addition (see Section 5.1.3 and the Mathematics Appendix for an explanation of modular arithmetic). If we want to encrypt the plaintext letter H using the key 3 then, since H is represented by the number 7, we can use modular arithmetic to describe the encryption process as:

$$7 + 3 = 10 \bmod 26.$$

Thus the ciphertext is K, which is the letter represented by 10. Similarly, the encryption of plaintext letter Y, which is represented by 24, can be written as:

$$24 + 3 = 1 \bmod 26,$$

and hence the ciphertext is B. More generally, let P denote the numerical representation of a plaintext letter (where P does not necessarily correspond to the letter P, but can represent any plaintext letter) and K be any key. Then encrypting plaintext P using key K produces the ciphertext letter C represented by the number:

$$C = P + K \bmod 26.$$

In other words, the ciphertext can be computed by adding the plaintext P and the key K and then reducing the sum modulo 26. In a similar way, decryption consists of subtracting the key K from the ciphertext C and then reducing modulo 26. In other words, the decryption algorithm can be described as:

$$P = C - K \bmod 26.$$

INSECURITY OF THE CAESAR CIPHER

Hopefully it should already be evident that a bank should not adopt the Caesar Cipher to protect its financial records! It is useful, however, to be able to articulate the problems with the Caesar Cipher precisely, using cryptographic terminology.

There are several reasons why the Caesar Cipher is not a secure cryptosystem, some of which we will discuss with respect to later cryptosystems. By far the most obvious, and serious, is the size of the keyspace. With only 26 possible keys to try out, an exhaustive key search is well within the means of an attacker armed with a pencil, a scrap of paper, and five minutes to spare! The attacker simply tries each of the 26 keys to obtain 26 candidate plaintexts. If the plaintext is recognisable (for example, it is in English) then the correct one should be obvious.

Note that if the plaintext does not contain identifiable redundancy (suppose it consists of randomly chosen letters) then an exhaustive key search is still highly effective as it reduces the number of candidate plaintexts to 26. Even if the original plaintext was just five letters long, without any knowledge of the ciphertext all we know is that the plaintext is one of

$$26^5 = 26 \times 26 \times 26 \times 26 \times 26 = 11881376$$

possible plaintexts consisting of five letters. Once we have seen the ciphertext, we can reduce this to just 26 candidates, which is dramatic progress.

In Section 3.1.3 we will discuss the only very special (and impractical) circumstance when the Caesar Cipher *is* a secure cryptosystem.

2.1.2 Simple Substitution Cipher

Our next example is the *Simple Substitution Cipher*, which is a considerable improvement on the Caesar Cipher. Like the Caesar Cipher, however, we will see that this cryptosystem is also fundamentally flawed. We start with a useful definition.

PERMUTATIONS

A *permutation* of a set of objects is an arrangement of the objects in some order. For example, (A, B, C), (B, C, A) and (C, A, B) are all permutations of the letters A, B and C. The total number of possible permutations of A, B and C is:

$$3 \times 2 \times 1 = 6.$$

A permutation of all the letters of the alphabet is the 26 letters of the alphabet arranged in some order. The most natural permutation is $(A, B, C, \ldots, Z)$, but $(Z, Y, X, \ldots, A)$ is also a permutation, and so is any arrangement such as $(G, Y, L, \ldots, X, B, N)$. The total number of such permutations is:

$$26 \times 25 \times 24 \times \cdots \times 3 \times 2 \times 1,$$

which is such a big number that we normally write it using the notation 26! (which is read as 26 *factorial*) In general, if we have n objects then the total number of possible permutations is:

$$n! = n \times (n - 1) \times (n - 2) \times \cdots \times 3 \times 2 \times 1.$$

DESCRIPTION OF THE SIMPLE SUBSTITUTION CIPHER

The Simple Substitution Cipher can be described as follows:

1. Write the letters $A, B, C, \ldots, Z$ in their natural order.
2. Alice and Bob agree on a randomly selected permutation of the letters of the alphabet.
3. Underneath the letters $A, B, C, \ldots, Z$, write out the chosen permutation of the letters of the alphabet.

Alice encrypts plaintext letters by replacing them (*substituting* them) with the permutation letter that is directly beneath them in the table.

This process is depicted in Figure 2.2. In the example shown, the chosen permutation is $D, I, Q, \ldots, G$. The plaintext *EAGLE* is encrypted to *TDZOT*.

On receiving the ciphertext, Bob, who also knows the randomly chosen permutation, just replaces each ciphertext letter on the bottom row with the

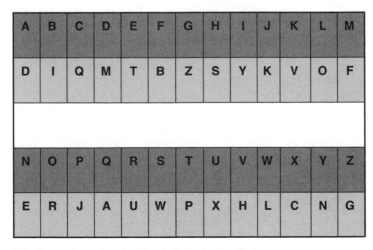

A	B	C	D	E	F	G	H	I	J	K	L	M
D	I	Q	M	T	B	Z	S	Y	K	V	O	F
N	O	P	Q	R	S	T	U	V	W	X	Y	Z
E	R	J	A	U	W	P	X	H	L	C	N	G

Figure 2.2. Encryption using the Simple Substitution Cipher

corresponding plaintext letter in the top row. Hence ciphertext *IXGGDUM* is decrypted to *BUZZARD*.

FITTING THE SIMPLE SUBSTITUTION CIPHER TO THE BASIC MODEL

The Simple Substitution Cipher can also be fitted to the basic model of a cryptosystem of Section 1.4.3. The various components of this model are:

Plaintext/Ciphertext: these are again both defined on the simple alphabet consisting of the single letters A to Z.
Encryption key: this is the chosen permutation of the letters of the alphabet.
Decryption key: this is the same as the encryption key, so this is a symmetric cryptosystem.
Keyspace: this is the number of possible permutations of letters of the alphabet (we discuss this shortly).
Encryption algorithm: this can be represented by the algorithm –

1. write the chosen permutation of letters underneath the naturally ordered letters of the alphabet;
2. replace the plaintext letter by the ciphertext letter beneath it.

Decryption algorithm: this can be represented by the algorithm –

1. write the chosen permutation of letters underneath the naturally ordered letters of the alphabet;
2. replace the ciphertext letter by the plaintext letter above it.

KEYSPACE OF THE SIMPLE SUBSTITUTION CIPHER

We have just seen that the key used in the Simple Substitution Cipher is a permutation of the letters of the alphabet. This means that the size of the keyspace of the Simple Substitution Cipher is the number of possible different permutations of the letters of the alphabet (since each choice of permutation is a possible key), which we know is 26! So, *how big* is 26!? Amazingly, 26! is approximately:

$$4 \times 10^{26} = 400\ 000\ 000\ 000\ 000\ 000\ 000\ 000\ 000.$$

To obtain an idea of just how big that is, there are an estimated 10 sextillion (that's 10^{22}) stars in our universe. That means that the Simple Substitution Cipher has about 40000 times more keys than there are stars in our universe.

In Section 4.4 we will discuss the symmetric encryption algorithm DES, which was the most important symmetric encryption algorithm of the late 20th century. DES uses keys that are 56 bits long, which means that the size of the keyspace of DES is 2^{56}. By using a useful conversion between powers of 2 and powers of 10 (see Mathematics Appendix) we can see that the size of the keyspace of DES is somewhere between 10^{16} and 10^{17}. This is much smaller than the keyspace of the Simple Substitution Cipher, being 'only' about $\frac{1}{100\ 000}$ of the number of stars in our universe.

The Simple Substitution Cipher therefore has a keyspace that is not just bigger than the keyspace of DES, it is *dramatically* bigger than the keyspace of DES. In fact, 4×10^{26} is approximately 2^{88}. As we will see in Section 10.2, this means that an exhaustive key search for a Simple Substitution Cipher key is close to the limit of what is currently practically feasible.

INSECURITY OF THE SIMPLE SUBSTITUTION CIPHER

There is no doubt that the Simple Substitution Cipher is a considerable improvement on the Caesar Cipher. Perhaps most significantly, the keyspace is so big that modern computer systems are not yet powerful enough to comfortably search through all the possible choices of key. The Caesar Cipher can be thought of as a highly restricted version of the Simple Substitution Cipher, where only 26 of the possible 4×10^{26} letter permutations can be selected as the key.

However, the Simple Substitution Cipher has a critical design flaw, which means that even with this enormous keyspace, this cryptosystem is easily broken under most circumstances.

2.1.3 Frequency analysis

A good cryptanalyst needs many skills, including the ability to think laterally. In order to 'break' a cryptosystem every available piece of information should be used. We are about to see that cryptosystems such as the Caesar Cipher and the Simple Substitution Cipher have a significant problem that can be exploited. Intriguingly, this exploit arises because of the typical nature of *plaintexts*.

THE NATURE OF PLAINTEXTS

The job of a cryptographer would arguably be much simpler if cryptosystems were only used to protect plaintexts consisting of randomly generated data. But, typically, they are not! In many situations, a plaintext is a meaningful string of letters that represents words, sentences, perhaps even an entire book, expressed in a language such as English. In any language there are certain letters, or combinations of letters, that occur far more often than others, hence languages are highly structured. Table 2.1 shows approximate letter frequencies for the English language.

The letter frequencies in Table 2.1 are expressed to three decimal places, indicating that, for example, in every 100 000 letters of typical English text we would expect about 8167 As, 12 702 Es, but only 74 Zs. Of course, this is just an approximation, but the inference is clear: given any plaintext string in English, there are likely to be far more occurrences of the letter E than the letter Z.

LETTER FREQUENCY ANALYSIS

The next observation we need to make is that both the Caesar Cipher and the Simple Substitution Cipher have the property that once we have chosen the

Table 2.1: Approximate letter frequencies for the English language [29]

Letter	Frequency	Letter	Frequency	Letter	Frequency
A	8.167	B	1.492	C	2.782
D	4.253	E	12.702	F	2.228
G	2.015	H	6.094	I	6.966
J	0.153	K	0.772	L	4.025
M	2.406	N	6.749	O	7.507
P	1.929	Q	0.095	R	5.987
S	6.327	T	9.056	U	2.758
V	0.978	W	2.360	X	0.150
Y	1.974	Z	0.074		

key *the same plaintext letter is always encrypted to the same ciphertext letter.* Cryptosystems where the encryption algorithm has this property are usually referred to as being *monoalphabetic ciphers.* Given a ciphertext, suppose that we:

- Know that it has been encrypted using a monoalphabetic cipher, in our case the Simple Substitution Cipher. This is reasonable, since we normally assume knowledge of the encryption algorithm used (see Section 1.5.1).
- Know the language in which the plaintext is expressed. This is reasonable, since in most contexts we either know this or could at least guess.

The following strategy then presents itself:

1. Count the frequency of occurrence of letters in the ciphertext, which can be represented as a histogram.
2. Compare the ciphertext letter frequencies with the letter frequencies of the underlying plaintext language.
3. Make an informed guess that the most commonly occurring ciphertext letter represents the most commonly occurring plaintext letter. Repeat with the second most commonly occurring ciphertext letter, etc.
4. Look for patterns and try to guess words. If no progress is made then refine the previous guesses and try again.

As an example, consider the ciphertext letter histogram generated in Figure 2.3 for an English plaintext using an unknown Simple Substitution Cipher key. It would be reasonable from this histogram to guess that:

- ciphertext H represents plaintext E;
- ciphertext W represents plaintext T;

Figure 2.3. Example of Simple Substitution Cipher ciphertext letter frequencies

- ciphertexts L, Q, R and U represent plaintexts A, O, I and N (in some order);
- ciphertexts C, M and T (none of which occur in our sample ciphertext) represent plaintexts J, X and Z (in some order).

While a degree of trial and error might be needed before we establish exactly what the correct matches are, we now have a reduced choice with respect to the remaining letters. The general strategy for proceeding should be clear. It should also be evident that we are unlikely to need to determine the whole key, since once enough letters are known we will probably be able to guess the rest of the plaintext.

The above process might sound a little bit ad hoc, but it reduces the challenge of decrypting the ciphertext to nothing more than a recreational puzzle, especially if useful information such as the positions of word breaks is also available. This process is easily automated by a computer. As a result, there are widely available letter frequency analysis tools that provide almost instant decryption of ciphertexts generated by the Simple Substitution Cipher.

LIMITATIONS OF LETTER FREQUENCY ANALYSIS

There are two circumstances under which letter frequency analysis is quite likely to fail:

1. if the plaintext letters do not conform to the 'normal' expected letter frequencies;
2. if the plaintext is too short for reliable frequencies to be computed.

In the first circumstance we will struggle to make correct guesses. The most extreme scenario is when the plaintext is randomly generated, in which case the plaintext letters all occur equally often and hence our ciphertext letter histogram is flat. In this case we will be stuck, although it should be noted that we will at least have learnt *something* about the plaintext since we will be able to determine which positions in the plaintext the same unknown plaintext letters occur, which may or may not be useful.

In the second circumstance, the ciphertext letter frequencies may not be reliable enough for us to make deductions about which plaintext letter corresponds to which ciphertext letter. We will discuss what 'too short' might mean for the Simple Substitution Cipher in a moment.

SUFFICIENCY OF KEYSPACE SIZE

We have just seen how the Simple Substitution Cipher can easily be broken despite its large keyspace. This is because it fails to 'destroy' the fundamental structure of the underlying plaintext, even though it disguises the actual letters themselves.

This leads us to the important design principle that *having a large keyspace is necessary to make an exhaustive key search impractical to conduct, but it is not sufficient to guarantee the security of a cryptosystem.* Putting this another way, in a quote attributed to Martin Hellman, one of the co-authors of the first published paper on public-key cryptography: *a large key is not a guarantee of security but a small key is a guarantee of insecurity.* Surprisingly, this design principle does not always seem to be understood by the sales teams of encryption products, who sometimes claim that the main security advantage offered by their products is that they have an incredibly large number of possible keys.

2.1.4 A study of theory versus practice

Before leaving the topic of monoalphabetic ciphers, it is worth using letter frequency analysis of the Simple Substitution Cipher to illustrate a point that we will keep returning to throughout our investigation of cryptography: the differences between theory and practice.

THEORY: UNIQUENESS OF THE PLAINTEXT

We have just observed that the Simple Substitution Cipher can provide reasonable protection for very short plaintexts. As an illustration, consider plaintexts consisting of just three letters. With only three ciphertext characters to work with, an attacker is faced with so many possible three-letter plaintexts that could encrypt into a given three-letter ciphertext, that it is probably fair to describe the Simple Substitution Cipher as being unbreakable.

To illustrate this, if we are given a three-letter ciphertext MFM then letter frequency analysis is useless, but we do know that the first and the third plaintext letter must be the same. The plaintext could be BOB, or POP, or MUM, or NUN, or …

However, given a 'reasonable' length of ciphertext, we know that letter frequency analysis becomes very effective. So how much ciphertext does it take for the apparently hard problem of decrypting a short ciphertext to transform into the easy problem of decrypting a longer ciphertext?

Although there is no simple answer to this question, an important observation is that as the number of ciphertext letters increases, the number of possible plaintexts that could have resulted in that ciphertext must decrease. At some point this number will decrease to the point where only one plaintext is possible. The obvious question is: *how many letters do we need before only one plaintext is possible?*

For the Simple Substitution Cipher applied to English plaintexts, this number is usually regarded as being around 28 ciphertext letters. This means that:

1. If we have significantly less than 28 ciphertext letters then there are probably many meaningful plaintexts that could have resulted in the ciphertext.
2. As we approach 28 ciphertext letters then the number of possible meaningful plaintexts that could have resulted in the ciphertext steadily decreases.
3. Once we have 28 ciphertext letters we can be fairly sure that there is only one meaningful plaintext that could have resulted in the ciphertext.
4. If we have hundreds of ciphertext letters then it is virtually a certainty that there is only one meaningful plaintext that results in the ciphertext.

PRACTICE: STATISTICAL INFORMATION

Our previous discussion is all about what is possible in theory. It does not necessarily tell us about what can happen in practice. If we have 28 ciphertext characters generated by a Simple Substitution Cipher with underlying plaintext language English, then there is probably only one possible plaintext that could have resulted in this ciphertext. But can it be found in practice?

The answer is, frustratingly, probably not. The effectiveness of letter frequency analysis increases with the amount of ciphertext available, but 28 letters is generally not enough statistical information. In practice, some people suggest that, for English plaintexts, at least 200 ciphertext letters are needed in order to be fairly confident that the letter frequency statistics will be reliable enough to conduct an effective letter frequency analysis, although it will often work with fewer letters than this.

THE GAP BETWEEN THEORY AND PRACTICE

There is thus a significant 'gap' between theory and practice. If we have between 28 and 200 ciphertext characters then there will almost certainly only be one meaningful plaintext that results in the target ciphertext, but it will probably be difficult to determine. The situation we have just discussed is summarised in Table 2.2.

This type of discussion will not prove particularly useful in our exploration of modern cryptosystems. Nor will we be discussing monoalphabetic ciphers in the remainder of this book, although it should be noted that *substitution* is widely used as a component of modern cryptographic algorithms. The point in having this discussion is to demonstrate that sometimes there is a significant gap between the theory of cryptanalysis and the practice of breaking cryptosystems. In this case,

Table 2.2: Letter frequency analysis: theory versus practice

Theory	Number of ciphertext letters	Practice
Many plaintexts	*Less than 5*	Many plaintexts
Reducing to 1	*Between 5 and 27*	Hard to find
1	*28*	Hard to find
1	*Between 29 and 200*	Getting easier to find
1	*More than 200*	Easy to find

theory suggests that the Simple Substitution Cipher is not fit for use if a plaintext is anywhere close to 28 letters long (which effectively makes it useless for most applications). However, practice suggests that if it was used to encrypt a 50-letter plaintext then we might well 'get away with it'. In this case, this gap arises from the fact that theory only tells us that something exists, not how to find it.

2.2 Historical advances

In Section 2.1 we observed that all monoalphabetic ciphers can be broken using letter frequency analysis. We now look at a number of more sophisticated historical cryptosystems. These cryptosystems use various different techniques to defeat single letter frequency analysis. It is these techniques that we are particularly interested in, since they illustrate good cryptosystem design principles. Despite this, none of the cryptosystems presented here are appropriate for use in modern applications for reasons that we will indicate.

2.2.1 Design improvements

Before proceeding, it is worth reflecting on design features that could be built into a cryptosystem in order to make single letter frequency analysis harder to conduct or, better still, ineffective. Three possible approaches are:

1. *Increase the size of the plaintext and ciphertext alphabets.* The cryptosystems that we have looked at thus far all operate on single letters. We can describe this by saying that the *plaintext* (and *ciphertext*) *alphabet* is the set of all single letters. When we conduct letter frequency analysis, we are only trying to match 26 possible ciphertext letters to 26 possible plaintext letters, which is generally not a particularly difficult task. If there were a larger number of choices for each unit of plaintext (ciphertext) then frequency analysis would certainly be harder.

58

2. *Allow the same plaintext letter to be encrypted to different ciphertext letters.* Letter frequency analysis is easy to perform on monoalphabetic ciphers. If we allow several ciphertext letters to represent the same plaintext letter then letter frequency analysis becomes more difficult.

3. *Make the choice of ciphertext letter that is used to encrypt a plaintext letter depend on the position that the plaintext letter occupies within the plaintext.* This is a particular example of the previous approach. By introducing a dependency on the position that a letter occupies within the plaintext (*positional dependency*) then a letter occurring in two different positions within the plaintext is likely to be encrypted into two different ciphertext letters, again helping to defeat letter frequency analysis.

We now look at three historical cryptosystems, each of which uses one or more of these techniques in order to defeat single letter frequency analysis.

2.2.2 Playfair Cipher

The *Playfair Cipher* is an unusual cryptosystem because it operates on pairs of letters (*bigrams*). The Playfair Cipher consists of a preprocessing stage and then an encryption stage.

PREPROCESSING FOR THE PLAYFAIR CIPHER

The plaintext requires a degree of preprocessing before it can be encrypted. We now describe this process and explain why each step is necessary.

1. *Replace J's with I's*: The Playfair Cipher is based on a 5 × 5 square grid (the *Playfair Square*) with 25 positions, each of which contains a different letter of the alphabet. Thus one letter of the alphabet cannot appear in this grid and must be discarded. It makes most sense for this to be a fairly uncommon letter. There is nothing special about the selection of the letter J, other than it does not occur often in English. The choice of replacement of the letter J by the letter I is because of the superficial resemblance between these two letters. A number of variants of the Playfair Cipher could be designed that remove a different unpopular letter and replace it by another of the remaining letters.

2. *Write out the plaintext in pairs of letters*: This is done because the Playfair Cipher operates on bigrams, and hence processes the plaintext in 'blocks' of two letters.

3. *Split identical pairs by inserting a Z between them*: The Playfair Cipher relies on the two letters in each plaintext bigram being different. If a plaintext bigram currently consists of two identical letters then the letter Z is inserted between them in the plaintext in order to separate them. There is nothing special about the selection of the letter Z. Any other unpopular letter could be chosen instead. Indeed, if two Z's occur together in a bigram of the plaintext then some other letter must be inserted between them.

4. *Rewrite the modified plaintext in pairs of letters*: Check to see whether there has been a 'knock on' effect that has resulted in a new plaintext bigram consisting of two identical letters. If this is the case then repeat the previous step until there are no such bigrams.

5. *If the final number of letters is odd then add Z to the end*: This is done in order to guarantee that the entire plaintext can be partitioned into bigrams. If there is an odd number of letters then the last letter needs a partner in order to be processed. Again, Z is used simply because it is an unpopular letter in English. If the last plaintext letter is itself a Z then a different final character will need to be used.

ENCRYPTION USING THE PLAYFAIR CIPHER

The Playfair Square, which forms the key of the Playfair Cipher, consists of a five-by-five grid, where each entry contains a unique letter of the alphabet other than J. Having preprocessed the plaintext according to the outlined procedure, the plaintext is encrypted as follows:

1. If two plaintext bigram letters lie *in the same row* of the Playfair Square then replace each letter by the letter on its right in the Playfair Square (if one of the letters lies in the fifth entry of the row then replace it by the letter in the first entry of the row).

2. If two plaintext bigram letters lie *in the same column* of the Playfair Square then replace each letter by the letter beneath it in the Playfair Square (if one of the letters lies in the fifth entry of the column then replace it by the letter in the first entry of the column).

3. Otherwise:

   a Replace the first plaintext bigram letter by the letter in the Playfair Square occurring in
      • the same row as the first bigram letter, and
      • the same column as the second bigram letter.

   b Replace the second plaintext bigram letter by the letter in the Playfair Square occurring in
      • the same column as the first bigram letter, and
      • the same row as the second bigram letter.

EXAMPLE OF A PLAYFAIR CIPHER

An example is very useful for mastering the subtleties of the Playfair Cipher.

Figure 2.4 shows an example of a Playfair Square. We use this as the key to encrypt the plaintext NATTERJACK TOAD. Ignoring the space between the two words, we preprocess the plaintext in preparation for encryption, as follows:

1. First, replace the single occurrence of J with an I, resulting in NATTERIACKTOAD.

S	T	A	N	D
E	R	C	H	B
K	F	G	I	L
M	O	P	Q	U
V	W	X	Y	Z

Figure 2.4. Example of a Playfair Square

2. We write out the plaintext as a sequence of pairs of letters:

NA TT ER IA CK TO AD.

3. We observe that the second bigram consists of TT, so we must insert a Z in between the two Ts, to get NATZTERIACKTOAD.

4. We rewrite the modified plaintext as a sequence of pairs of letters:

NA TZ TE RI AC KT OA D,

and note that there are now no bigrams with repeated letters.

5. Finally, we need to add a Z to the end in order to complete the last bigram:

NA TZ TE RI AC KT OA DZ.

We then proceed to encrypt these bigrams as follows:

1. The letters of the first bigram NA lie together in the same row of the Playfair Square in Figure 2.4, so NA is encrypted using this square to DN.

2. The letters in the next bigram TZ do not lie together in the same row or column. They thus define the corners of a rectangle in the Playfair Square. The encryption rule says that in this case they are encrypted to the two letters occurring at the other two corners of this rectangle. Thus TZ is encrypted to DW. Similarly, TE is encrypted to SR, and RI is encrypted to HF.

3. The letters AC lie in the same column, so they are encrypted to CG.

4. The letters KT do not lie in the same row or column, so KT is encrypted to FS. Similarly, OA is encrypted to PT.

5. Finally, DZ lie in the same column, so are encrypted to BD (note that since Z is in the last row, it is encrypted to the letter in the first row, D).

The final ciphertext is thus DNDWSRHFCGFSPTBD.

To decrypt this ciphertext, the receiver will reverse the encryption process using the Playfair Square in Figure 2.4 to obtain NATZTERIACKTOADZ. They will hopefully 'guess' that the two Zs are redundant and remove them to recover NATTERIACKTOAD. A knowledge of European amphibians should then allow the correct plaintext to be obtained!

CRYPTANALYSIS OF THE PLAYFAIR CIPHER

Is the Playfair Cipher a secure cryptosystem? The first thing to check is the size of the keyspace. The key is an arrangement of the letters A to Z (excluding J) in a square. Since every arrangement of these letters corresponds to a different key, the number of possible keys is the number of possible arrangements. This is the number of possible permutations of 25 letters, which is approximately 10^{25}. Thus the keyspace is very large, being slightly smaller than that of the Simple Substitution Cipher, but significantly more than that of DES (see Section 2.1.2). A determined attacker with a great deal of money, time and computing resources could search this keyspace, but it would be a mammoth task.

Neither is single letter frequency analysis an option for an attacker. Continuing our example, there are three occurrences of the letter A in the plaintext NATTERJACK TOAD, but these are encrypted to the ciphertext letters N, C and T, respectively. This means that frequency analysis of single letters will not be effective.

There is, however, an alternative frequency analysis that will succeed against the Playfair Cipher. A cryptanalyst could generalise the single letter technique to look at frequencies of bigrams. This works in a similar way to letter frequency analysis but is more complex to conduct, for three reasons:

1. There are $25 \times 24 = 600$ possible Playfair bigrams, hence frequency analysis will be more complex than for single letters, notwithstanding the need to compute accurate bigram statistics. However, bigram frequencies can be very revealing. For example, in English plaintext the bigram TH is by far the most common, so it should be relatively simple to detect this bigram if we have enough ciphertext.
2. A considerable amount of ciphertext will be needed before these bigram statistics can be used to conduct an effective bigram frequency analysis of a Playfair ciphertext. It is likely that thousands, rather than hundreds, of ciphertext letters will be needed.
3. The last two difficulties are enhanced by the fact that two letters next to one another in the original plaintext are not necessarily encrypted together, since they may occur in adjacent bigrams. For example, in the plaintext THE MOTH, the bigram TH occurs twice in the plaintext, but only the first occurrence is encrypted as a TH, since this plaintext gets split into bigrams TH EM OT HZ during preprocessing.

Breaking the Playfair Cipher is thus feasible, but is a rather tedious task that requires a considerable amount of data processing. This is why the Playfair Cipher was regarded as secure at the start of the 20th century. However, that same century saw the development of computers, which thrive on the routine processing of vast volumes of data. Thus the Playfair Cipher is now regarded as an insecure cipher, and 'easy' to break given sufficient ciphertext.

LESSONS FROM THE PLAYFAIR CIPHER

There are several important lessons to be learnt from the Playfair Cipher.

Avoiding the monoalphabetic property makes frequency analysis harder. Cryptanalysis is now much harder. Letter frequency analysis has been rendered ineffective by designing an encryption algorithm that does not encrypt plaintext letters by the same ciphertext letter each time they occur. The main technique for achieving this has been to encrypt the plaintext in pairs of letters, thus increasing the size of the plaintext (and ciphertext) alphabet from 26 single letters to 600 plaintext bigrams. The cost of this progress has been a more complex encryption and decryption process.

Avoiding the monoalphabetic property is not enough. We have seen that although single letter frequency analysis is defeated, cryptanalysis is only *slightly* harder. Assuming that a sufficiently long ciphertext is observed, it is still possible to conduct an analysis of the ciphertext based on this enlarged plaintext alphabet, by analysing frequencies of ciphertext bigrams.

Efficiency can be traded-off against security. The design of the Playfair Cipher represents an efficiency–security tradeoff, where we gain security at a slight cost to efficiency. It is possible to imagine that we could invent a generalisation of the Playfair Cipher that operates on *trigrams* (triples of plaintext letters). It would be even more complex to specify and encrypt than the Playfair Cipher, but if we designed it well then it might defeat bigram frequency analysis. However, it will itself be prone to trigram frequency analysis (harder to conduct, but possible using computers). For example, given enough ciphertext then it should be possible to identify the common English trigram THE.

We will see many more efficiency–security tradeoffs in the rest of our study of cryptography. We will also see that frequency analysis (of blocks of bits) is a relevant attack on modern cryptosystems, so our discussion of the Playfair Cipher is of much more than just historical interest.

2.2.3 Homophonic encoding

An alternative means of defeating single letter frequency analysis is to tackle the letter frequencies head on. The idea behind *homophonic encoding* is to encrypt plaintext letters by a number of different ciphertext characters in order to directly confuse the ciphertext symbol frequency statistics (we say *symbol* rather than *letter* here because, after homophonic encoding has been applied, there are many more ciphertext symbols than there are letters in the alphabet). This technique is best explained by means of an example.

EXAMPLE OF HOMOPHONIC ENCODING

The aim of homophonic encoding is to design a cryptosystem whose ciphertext alphabet histogram is close to being 'flat' (in other words, every ciphertext symbol occurs approximately equally often). We achieve this by increasing the ciphertext alphabet.

A possible homophonic code for use with English plaintexts can be devised from Table 2.1 of English letter frequencies, as follows. Suppose that we choose a ciphertext alphabet of 1000 symbols. This means that instead of 26 letters, each ciphertext character is one of these 1000 symbols. We then secretly divide the 1000 ciphertext symbols into 26 groups. Each group is then associated with one specific plaintext letter. From Table 2.1 we see that:

- Plaintext letter A occurs approximately 8.2% of the time, so we assign 82 ciphertext symbols for encrypting A.
- Plaintext letter B occurs approximately 1.5% of the time, so we assign 15 ciphertext symbols for encrypting B.
- Plaintext letter C occurs approximately 2.8% of the time, so we assign 28 ciphertext symbols for encrypting C.

We continue this process for the whole plaintext alphabet. Thus, for example, the letter E is assigned 127 ciphertext symbols, the letter T is assigned 90 ciphertext symbols, and the letters J, Q, Y and Z are all assigned only one ciphertext symbol.

To encrypt a plaintext letter, one of the ciphertext symbols in the group associated with that letter is chosen at random by the sender Alice. It does not matter which symbol is chosen, but it does matter that the process used to choose it is random. The receiver Bob, who also knows how the 1000 ciphertext symbols have been divided and assigned to plaintext letters, is able to decrypt this ciphertext letter since there is only one plaintext letter assigned to any given ciphertext symbol.

SINGLE LETTER FREQUENCY ANALYSIS OF HOMOPHONIC ENCODING

To see the advantage of homophonic encoding, think now about trying to conduct single letter frequency analysis. We assume once again that the plaintext is in English.

Suppose that we have a ciphertext consisting of 1000 symbols, which encrypts a plaintext that consists of 1000 English letters. We know from Table 2.1 that amongst these 1000 letters of the plaintext we can expect:

- One occurrence of the plaintext letter Z. Hence the ciphertext symbol associated with Z should occur just once amongst the 1000 ciphertext symbols.
- 127 occurrences of the plaintext letter E. However, every time that E is encrypted using our homophonic code, it is replaced by a randomly selected symbol from the group of 127 ciphertext symbols associated with E.

If we are *extremely lucky* then amongst these 1000 ciphertext symbols each ciphertext symbol could occur just once. In practice (with very high probability) this will not happen, since some of the ciphertext symbols will occur more than once and a few will not occur at all. However, it should be clear that for very long plaintexts, one million characters, say, the histogram of ciphertext symbols will be approximately flat, with each ciphertext symbol occurring approximately 1000 times.

As a result of this observation, frequency analysis of single ciphertext symbols will be a waste of time. Such analysis will tell us nothing about the frequency of the underlying plaintext letters.

PROBLEMS WITH HOMOPHONIC ENCODING

Homophonic encoding is designed precisely to counter single letter frequency analysis. It does not automatically prevent frequency analysis of bigrams, although our example of homophonic encoding will involve analysing one million bigrams, which will require a substantial amount of ciphertext to be obtained before being effective. However, there are two more significant problems with homophonic encoding that all but rule it out as a practical encryption technique:

Key size. The key for a homophonic code consists of the specification of assigned ciphertext symbols to plaintext letters. *Very crudely* (an accurate measurement is beyond our mathematical ambitions), this involves storing a table that contains a list of the ciphertext symbols assigned to each plaintext letter. Each ciphertext symbol appears once in this table. If we do this on a computer then we need to represent this table in binary. We note that each symbol from a set of size 1000 can be represented by 10 bits when represented in binary (this follows from the relationship between binary and decimal numbers, which is discussed further in the Mathematics Appendix). So our key is, very approximately, $1000 \times 10 = 10\,000$ bits long. By the standards of modern cryptosystems this is very large (for example, AES has a key size of between 128 and 256 bits, as discussed in Section 4.5).

Ciphertext expansion. We have extended our plaintext alphabet from 26 letters to a ciphertext alphabet of 1000 symbols. This means that it takes more information (think of *information* as the number of bits needed) to represent the ciphertext than it takes to represent the plaintext. In other words, the ciphertext is much bigger than the plaintext. Very roughly, we need:

- 5 bits to represent each of the 26 plaintext letters, but;
- 10 bits to represent each of the 1000 ciphertext symbols.

Hence each 5-bit plaintext letter will be encrypted to a 10-bit ciphertext symbol. This increase in the size of the ciphertext is often referred to as *message expansion* and is generally regarded as an undesirable property of a cryptosystem because the ciphertext becomes more 'expensive' to send across the communication channel.

Of course, we have based the above analysis on our example of a homophonic code that uses 1000 ciphertext symbols. It is possible to design simpler, less effective, homophonic codes that use fewer ciphertext symbols (another example of the efficiency–security tradeoff). However, most homophonic codes have extremely large keys and involve some degree of message expansion.

LESSON FROM HOMOPHONIC ENCODING

Homophonic encoding defeats single letter frequency analysis by increasing the size of the ciphertext (but not the plaintext) alphabet, thus enabling a given plaintext letter to be encrypted to different ciphertext letters. A good homophonic code arguably provides quite a secure cryptosystem. However, the biggest lesson from studying homophonic encoding is that the price to be paid for strong security is sometimes not worth paying. Good homophonic encoding comes at a significant cost in terms of key size and message expansion. It is unlikely that many modern security applications will be willing to bear these costs when they can get all the security they need from a much more efficient cryptosystem.

2.2.4 Vigenère Cipher

The last historical cryptosystem that we will look at is the famous *Vigenère Cipher*, which was for a significant period in history regarded as being such a secure cryptosystem that it was regularly used for protecting sensitive political and military information and referred to as the 'indecipherable cipher'. The Vigenère Cipher is of interest to us because it illustrates the use of positional dependency to defeat single letter frequency analysis.

ENCRYPTION USING THE VIGENÈRE CIPHER

The Vigenère Cipher is fairly straightforward to understand. The key of the Vigenère Cipher consists of a string of letters that form a *keyword*. Associating the letters A, B, . . . , Z with the numbers 0, 1, . . . , 25, respectively, the encryption process proceeds as follows:

1. write out the keyword repeatedly underneath the plaintext until every plaintext letter has a keyword letter beneath it;
2. encrypt each plaintext letter using a Caesar Cipher, whose key is the number associated with the keyword letter written beneath it.

Figure 2.5 provides an example of the Vigenère Cipher with keyword DIG, where the plaintext appears in the top row and the ciphertext appears in the bottom row. Thus, for example, the first plaintext letter A is shifted using a Caesar Cipher with shift 3 (corresponding to keyword letter D) to obtain the ciphertext letter D. The second plaintext letter, which is also A, is shifted using a Caesar Cipher with shift 8 (corresponding to keyword letter I) to obtain ciphertext letter I. The third plaintext letter, which is R, is shifted using a Caesar Cipher with shift 6 (corresponding to keyword letter G) to obtain ciphertext letter X. The rest of ciphertext is produced in a similar way. Decryption is just the reverse process.

The important point to note is that, for example, the plaintext letter A is encrypted to three different ciphertext letters (D, G and I). The critical fact that

A	A	R	D	V	A	R	K	S	E	A	T	A	N	T	S
D	I	G	D	I	G	D	I	G	D	I	G	D	I	G	D
D	I	X	G	D	G	U	S	Y	H	I	Z	D	V	Z	V

Figure 2.5. Example of encryption using the Vigenère Cipher

determines whether we use D, G or I to encrypt a particular occurrence of A in the plaintext is the *position* of A in the plaintext. When A occurs in positions 1 and 13 we use D, when A occurs at position 6 we use G, and when A occurs at positions 2 and 11 we use I. Note also that the ciphertext letter V occurs twice in our example ciphertext, but that each occurrence represents a different plaintext letter. This is because V is the encryption of plaintext letter N using key I, and is also the encryption of plaintext letter S using key D.

These properties both make basic single letter frequency analysis of the Vigenère Cipher apparently ineffective. Into the bargain, unlike for homophonic encoding, there is no message expansion. This all helped to establish the Vigenère Cipher's historical reputation of being practical and 'indecipherable'.

CRYPTANALYSIS OF THE VIGENÈRE CIPHER

The key in the Vigenère Cipher is the keyword. This means that the size of the keyspace can be adjusted by choosing different lengths of keyword. A short keyword does not offer much security since an exhaustive keyword search could then be used to break the Vigenère Cipher. However, a keyword of length 13 already offers 26^{13} keywords, which is approximately 2.5×10^{18} possible keys (a larger keyspace than that of DES), and a keyword of length 28 offers 26^{28}, which is approximately 4.2×10^{39} possible keys (a larger keyspace than that of 128-bit AES). Thus the size of the keyspace is not an issue for the Vigenère Cipher if a reasonably long keyword is used.

Unfortunately, despite its promise and rather illustrious history of application, the Vigenère Cipher is easily broken. The critical observation is that the Vigenère Cipher can be viewed as a sequence of Caesar Ciphers employed in strict rotation. To see this, consider the example in Figure 2.5. We can consider this example as a rotation of three Caesar Ciphers. The first Caesar Cipher has key D (a shift of 3). We use this Caesar Cipher to encrypt the first plaintext letter, and then use it again for the plaintext letters in positions 4, 7, 10, 13 and 16. The second Caesar Cipher has key I and we use it to encrypt the second plaintext letter, and then use it again for the plaintext letters in positions 5, 8, 11 and 14. Finally, the third Caesar Cipher has key G and we use it to encrypt the third plaintext letter, and then use it again for the plaintext letters in positions 6, 9, 12 and 15.

We know from Section 2.1.1 that the Caesar Cipher is easy to break. The problem facing the attacker is that they do not know which Caesar Ciphers are being used for which plaintext letter positions. This is because the attacker does not know the keyword. However, observe that if the attacker learns the *length* of the keyword then they will at least know which positions the *same* Caesar Cipher is being used, even if they do not know which key is being used for each position. In our example, if the attacker learns that the keyword has length three, then they will know that one Caesar Cipher is being used to encrypt the plaintext letters in positions 1, 4, 7, 10, 13 and 16, a second is being used for positions 2, 5, 8, 11 and 14, and a third for positions 3, 6, 9, 12 and 15. The attacker can then:

1. divide the Vigenère Cipher ciphertext into a sequence of component Caesar Cipher ciphertexts, one sequence corresponding to each letter of the keyword;
2. break each of the component Caesar Cipher ciphertexts individually, using single letter frequency analysis (assuming that there is sufficient length of ciphertext to render this effective);
3. put the component plaintexts obtained in the last step back together in sequence, to obtain the plaintext for the Vigenère Cipher.

This attack is depicted in Figure 2.6, where the ciphertext from the example in Figure 2.5 is split into three rows, based on the knowledge that the length of the keyword is three. The letters in each row can now be regarded as ciphertext corresponding to a component Caesar Cipher and each can be broken separately using single letter frequency analysis. Even though this example has too few ciphertext letters to be very effective, the double occurrence of ciphertext letters in each row (component Caesar Cipher) is already a useful clue. This is certainly a more difficult analysis to conduct than for the Simple Substitution Cipher, because recognising the correct plaintext corresponding to the component Caesar Ciphers is more difficult. However, it is definitely possible, and certainly a task that a computer can make fairly routine, given enough ciphertext.

Note that without knowledge of the keyword length the attacker cannot conduct this attack. However, there are some surprisingly simple statistical techniques that can be applied to the ciphertext to allow the attacker to make

D		D	G	U	H	D	V
I		I	D	S	I	V	
G		X	G	Y	Z	Z	

Figure 2.6. Cryptanalysis of the Vigenère Cipher

an intelligent (and normally very accurate) estimate of the length of the keyword. We will not describe the details here, but they work well and have led to the Vigenère Cipher being primarily regarded as something of historical interest only.

That said, there are two important observations that can be made about the Vigenère Cipher:

1. The security of the Vigenère Cipher improves with the length of the keyword since the component Caesar Ciphers become harder to break (and thus there are fewer plaintext characters encrypted with each component Caesar Cipher). In the extreme case where the length of the keyword is the *same* as the length of the plaintext, a separate Caesar Cipher is used to encrypt each plaintext letter, which makes it impossible to determine the correct plaintext without the key. In this case the Vigenère Cipher has indeed become 'indecipherable' . We will discuss this very special cryptosystem in Section 3.1.3.

2. The design principle of using a sequence of component encryption processes in rotation is an effective one and has been used by many well-known historical cryptosystems. One example is the encryption process of the Enigma machine, which can be regarded as a rotation of substitutions based on a long key.

LESSON FROM THE VIGENÈRE CIPHER

The Vigenère Cipher counters single letter frequency analysis, and indeed more sophisticated frequency analysis, through the introduction of positional dependency. The longer the keyword, the greater the diffusion of the frequency statistics. Despite this, however, it is insecure.

Probably the most important lesson that we can draw from the Vigenère Cipher is that security of a cryptosystem is only ever relative to our understanding of attacks. The Vigenère Cipher was believed to be secure for a long time. Only when it was noticed that statistical techniques could be used to determine the keyword length was its weakness exposed.

This is just as true for modern cryptosystems. We certainly have more knowledge and understanding of cryptographic design principles than back in the days when the Vigenère Cipher was regularly used. However, it is a virtual certainty that someone reflecting back on modern cryptography one hundred years into the future will be able to say the same thing about current techniques. Breakthroughs in cryptanalysis can happen suddenly and unexpectedly. They are not always sophisticated or require deep mathematical knowledge.

We will keep this lesson in mind as we study modern cryptographic techniques. Probably the only effective counter to this issue is to encourage the development of cryptographic primitives that work in different ways and rely on different security assumptions. We can choose to design cryptographic primitives conservatively, but we can never guarantee security against an unknown future.

2.3 Summary

In this chapter we have examined a number of historical cryptosystems. Although none of these cryptosystems are suitable for modern use, they provide several important design lessons for modern cryptosystems. These include:

- A large keyspace is necessary in a practical cryptosystem, but a large keyspace alone does not guarantee security.
- It is possible to break a cryptosystem without first determining the key. Designers of cryptosystems thus need to worry about much more than just protection of the key.
- The ciphertext produced by a cryptosystem should disguise the statistics of the underlying plaintext alphabet.
- Effective techniques for disguising plaintext statistics include increasing alphabet size, ensuring that plaintext letters encrypt to a variety of different ciphertext letters, and introducing positional dependency, but these properties alone do not guarantee security.
- Efficiency and security are often traded off against one another when designing a cryptosystem.
- It is unlikely that anyone will use a cryptosystem where the balance of efficiency versus security is inappropriate. In particular, secure cryptosystems that are inefficient to use in practice are not attractive for most applications.
- We can design cryptosystems to be secure against attacks that we know and understand, but unknown attacks could be discovered at any time in the future.

Most of the modern cryptosystems that we will later examine have been designed with these lessons in mind.

2.4 Further reading

There are many books that explain historical cryptosystems and an interested reader should have no trouble finding them. These include general texts such as Stinson [185] and books more dedicated to classical cryptography such as Spillman [180]. Many of these will provide more details on how to break the Vigenère Cipher (see also [176] for this).

One of the most compelling publicists of the links between historical and modern cryptography has been Simon Singh. His influential and very readable The Code Book [176] has some very interesting background information on historical cryptography (and much more), and was made into a five-part television series called The Science of Secrecy. He has produced a version of this book for younger audiences [177], as well as maintaining a website [175] from which a related CD-ROM can be downloaded.

If a more detailed history of cryptography is of interest then Kahn [104] provides the definitive chronicle of wartime cryptology. Several books such as Hodges [99], Paterson [155] and Smith [179] focus on the vital role that cryptography, and cryptographers, played during the Second World War. An impressive web resource on historical cryptosystems is provided by Dirk Rijmenants [162] and includes several simulators, including one for the Enigma machine.

Cryptography, both historical and contemporary, has proved an attractive subject for more mainstream media and entertainment. Foremost amongst these has been Dan Brown, whose books often contain references to cryptography. The most famous is The Da Vinci Code [41], which does not really contain any true cryptography but does feature a 'cryptographic heroine' Sophie Neveu who was notably (for our purposes) trained at Royal Holloway and thus would surely have benefitted enormously from this book! Dan Brown's Digital Fortress [42] features an impressive machine which is claimed to have the power to break all known cryptosystems (we discussed the practicality of this in Chapter 1). Other popular novels concerning cryptography include Enigma by Robert Harris [98] and Cryptonomicon by Neal Stephenson [184]. Cryptography has also been the focal subject of several films, including Enigma and Sneakers.

For those who want to 'play' further with historical cryptosystems of the type considered in this chapter then there are several books devoted to cryptographic puzzles, such as Gardner [87]. By far the best way of further pursuing these is, however, to use an online tool. We cannot recommend highly enough the free open source e-learning application CrypTool [52], which is easy to install and use. CrypTool has implementations of all the historical cryptosystems that we discussed in this chapter. It is possible not just to encrypt and decrypt using these cryptosystems, but also to conduct cryptanalysis through letter frequency analysis software, run Vigenère Cipher cryptanalysis tools, and much more. We will also recommend CrypTool activities in subsequent chapters, since it is just as valuable a tool for experimenting with contemporary cryptography.

2.5 Activities

1. The Caesar Cipher is our first historical cryptosystem and has numerous flaws.

   (a) Decrypt the Caesar Cipher ciphertext: IT STY ZXJ RJ YT JSHWDUY DTZW UFXXBTWI
   (b) The Caesar Cipher has an inadequate keyspace. What other problems does it have that make it insecure?
   (c) The Caesar Cipher is often described as having a fixed shift of three positions. Explain why in this case the Caesar Cipher is not really a cryptosystem at all.
   (d) Is ROT13 a cryptosystem?

2. The Caesar Cipher can be implemented by two 'wheels', where each wheel has the letters of the alphabet written on it and the inner wheel can be rotated within the outer wheel. Explain how to encrypt and decrypt with the Caesar Cipher using such an implementation.

3. The Simple Substitution Cipher is a major improvement on the Caesar Cipher.

   (a) In what different ways is it an improvement?
   (b) If a Simple Substitution Cipher is used (with an unknown key) and we intercept the ciphertext OXAO then which of the following four-letter words could be the plaintext: JOHN, SKID, SPAS, LOOT, PLOP, OSLO?
   (c) If a Simple Substitution Cipher is used (with an unknown key) and we intercept the ciphertext BRKKLK then what do we know about the plaintext?
   (d) Suppose that in the case of intercepting BRKKLK we also know that the plaintext is the name of a country. What is the plaintext?
   (e) What important lesson does the BRKKLK example illustrate?

4. The *Atbash Cipher* consists of replacing 'plaintext' letters A, B, C to Z by the 'ciphertext' letters Z, Y, X to A, respectively.

   (a) 'Decrypt' XZKVIXZROORV.
   (b) How would you describe the relationship between the Atbash Cipher and the Simple Substitution Cipher?

5. Explain how you might adjust the normal English letter frequencies depicted in Table 2.1 in order to conduct single letter frequency analysis, given that the context of a plaintext is:

   (a) a personal letter;
   (b) part of the technical manual for a SUN SOLARIS operating system;
   (c) a document written in Polish.

6. Decrypt the following ciphertext, which was obtained from English plaintext using a Simple Substitution Cipher (to make things slightly easier we have included the characters [space] and [.] in the ciphertext in the same positions that they appear in the plaintext):

   UGVPQFG OQ OLG PQCWNG. QDG EZF ZN SQW OLG NOCBGDON OQ VGEWD EHQCO ZDSQWFEOZQD NGPCWZOJ. OLZN FGEDN LEWB UQWY. LQUGRGW UG EVNQ UEDO OLGF OQ GDMQJ OLGFNGVRGN. OLG PQCWNG EDB OLG VGPOCWGN NLQCVB HG SCD XVGENG VGO CN YDQU ZS OLGWG EWG EDJ XWQHVGFN NQ OLEO UG PED EOOGFXO OQ PQWWGPO OLGF.

7. The ciphertext MBR OJFGA SWNTE CNK QJDIL NURW MBR XHMR was obtained by encrypting the plaintext THE QUICK BROWN FOX JUMPS OVER THE GATE using a Simple Substitution Cipher.

   (a) How much of the key is determined if this plaintext/ciphertext pair are known?

(b) How many different possible keys could have been used to encrypt the plaintext?

(c) Decrypt the ciphertext MBR TRHLRP WHE HTHV CWND PNEYNE ZNN, which is known to have been encrypted with the same key.

(d) What lesson can be learnt from conducting this exercise?

8. The Playfair Cipher represents one improvement over monoalphabetic ciphers.

(a) Decrypt the following ciphertext using the Playfair key depicted in Figure 2.4:

NR SH NA SR HF CG FL TN RW NS DN NF SK RW TN DS XN
DS BR NA BI ND SN CR NT WO TQ FR BR HT BM FW MC

(b) Explain what method could be used to attack the Playfair Cipher by attempting to decrypt ciphertext without knowledge of the decryption key.

(c) Some of the preprocessing rules for the Playfair Cipher are somewhat arbitrary. Suggest an alternative set of preprocessing rules for the Playfair Cipher.

9. Alice wishes to regularly send Bob a plaintext message P_1 or P_2. On each occasion she chooses to send either P_1 or P_2, but on average she chooses the plaintext P_1 twice as often as she chooses the plaintext P_2. Each time, Alice uses a (very simple) symmetric cryptosystem, with the same fixed key K, to encrypt the plaintext. When she chooses P_1, the ciphertext is $C_1 = E_K(P_1)$; when she chooses P_2, the ciphertext is $C_2 = E_K(P_2)$. Suppose that an attacker knows that the only possible plaintext messages are P_1 and P_2.

(a) Suppose that the attacker does not know that Alice chooses P_1 twice as often as P_2. What observation will the attacker, who can only see the ciphertexts sent from Alice to Bob, make?

(b) Suppose that the attacker learns that Alice chooses P_1 twice as often as she chooses P_2. What does the attacker now learn?

(c) Explain how homophonic encoding can be used in this case to make it more difficult for the attacker to learn anything useful from observing ciphertexts.

10. The example of homophonic encoding that we gave in Section 2.2.3 was designed to make it appear as if each plaintext letter occurs equally often. For each of the following specific requirements, and based on Table 2.1, design a homophonic code for use with English plaintexts that has significantly less message expansion than the example we gave (in each case also comment on the resulting message expansion):

(a) The plaintext letter E appears to occur equally often to the plaintext letter P.

(b) Plaintext vowels all appear to occur equally often.

(c) It is hard for an attacker to identify the eight most frequently occurring plaintext letters in English.

11. The Vigenère Cipher is of historical importance.

    (a) Encrypt MY HOME IS NEW ZEALAND using a Vigenère Cipher with keyword KEA.
    (b) The ciphertext JNHYSMCDJOP was obtained by encrypting an English word using a Vigenère Cipher:
        i. The first and ninth letters of the plaintext are identical. What does this tell you about the key?
        ii. Given that the keyword length is less than 7, the third and fourth letters of the plaintext are F and O, respectively, and that A is a letter in the keyword, find the keyword and the plaintext.
    (c) If the keyword of a Vigenère Cipher has repeated letters, does this make it any easier to break?

12. In this chapter we suggested a technique for cryptanalysing the Vigenère Cipher. Discuss at least two different situations where it will be hard to break the Vigenère Cipher using the technique that we described.

13. In this exercise we consider the Simple Substitution Cipher as a 5-bit block cipher. The letters $A = 1, B = 2, C = 3, \ldots, Z = 26$ are first represented as binary strings (5 bits per letter) as follows: $A = 00001, B = 00010, C = 00011, \ldots, Z = 11010$. Let the key of a Simple Substitution Cipher be given by (plaintext in top row above is replaced by bold ciphertext in bottom row):

A	B	C	D	E	F	G	H	I	J	K	L	M
G	**R**	**K**	**Z**	**L**	**A**	**B**	**X**	**T**	**N**	**M**	**E**	**Q**
N	O	P	Q	R	S	T	U	V	W	X	Y	Z
W	**F**	**V**	**Y**	**U**	**S**	**P**	**J**	**H**	**O**	**D**	**I**	**C**

    (a) Write the plaintext TODAY as a binary string.
    (b) Encrypt TODAY using the above cryptosystem and write the ciphertext as a binary string.
    (c) Change the second bit of the above ciphertext and then decrypt this altered ciphertext.
    (d) How many bits of the resulting plaintext are incorrect?

14. What are the implications of a known-plaintext attack on:

    (a) The Caesar Cipher?
    (b) The Simple Substitution Cipher?
    (c) The Vigenère Cipher?

15. Although the Simple Substitution Cipher and the Playfair Cipher are simple enough to conduct encryption and decryption by 'hand', their keys are not straightforward to memorise.

74

(a) Suggest a technique for producing keys for these cryptosystems that makes the resulting keys easier to remember.

(b) To what extent does use of such a technique make these cryptosystems easier to break?

16. A historical cryptosystem that we have not discussed is the *Affine Cipher*.

(a) Find out how to encrypt and decrypt using an Affine Cipher.

(b) What is the size of the keyspace of an Affine Cipher?

(c) Explain how to attack an Affine Cipher.

3 Theoretical versus Practical Security

In this chapter we consider the relationship between theoretical and practical security of a cryptosystem. This is a subject that we touched upon briefly in Chapter 2. The concept of perfect secrecy is introduced and a cryptosystem is exhibited that has this property. However, as always, nothing comes for free. The compromises that real systems adopt for reasons of practicality are investigated with the intention of working towards a notion of practical security of a cryptosystem.

Note that, once again, the focus of this chapter is on cryptosystems that are being used to provide confidentiality. However, the main lessons learnt from this chapter have wider implications for provision of other types of cryptographic service.

At the end of this chapter you should be able to:

- Explain the concept of perfect secrecy.
- Recognise that, in theory, there exist 'unbreakable' cryptosystems.
- Appreciate the limitations of theoretical security.
- Identify some of the issues involved in assessing practical security.
- Recognise that there are (at least) two significantly different levels of computational complexity.
- Appreciate that selection of a cryptographic primitive should be considered as part of a wider cryptographic process.
- Formulate a notion of practical security.

3.1 Theoretical security

In Section 1.6 we described a cryptosystem as being *broken* if a method of determining the plaintext from the ciphertext was found that did not involve being legitimately given the decryption key. We also discussed one method that can, at least in theory, be used to break any cryptosystem: an exhaustive key search.

In this section we will discuss a cryptosystem that can be *proven* to be unbreakable. We will even see that an exhaustive key search is of limited use against this cryptosystem.

3.1.1 Perfect secrecy

The notion of a cryptosystem being 'unbreakable' is modeled by the concept of *perfect secrecy*.

MOTIVATING PERFECT SECRECY

An exhaustive key search can always be launched against any cryptosystem. However, there is an even more basic attack that can also always be conducted against a cryptosystem that does not even involve trying to obtain the decryption key: an attacker can simply try to *guess* the plaintext.

Guessing the plaintext is an attack that can never be prevented. Of course, for long and complicated plaintexts it is very unlikely that an interceptor will be able to guess the plaintext correctly, but there will always be a *chance* (ideally a very small one) that they could. Note that guessing the plaintext becomes a much more plausible attack when the number of possible plaintexts is small, such as when the plaintext is a four-digit PIN or a short password.

DEFINING PERFECT SECRECY

It is thus useful to come up with a notion of security in which guessing the plaintext is essentially the best attack that the interceptor can deploy. We say that a cryptosystem has *perfect secrecy* if, after seeing the ciphertext, an interceptor *gets no extra information about the plaintext other than what was known before the ciphertext was observed.*

This can be a slightly confusing concept when met for the first time, so it is worth reading it again and then noting the following:

- We are not saying that in a cryptosystem with perfect secrecy the interceptor has *no information* about the plaintext. For example, the interceptor may already know that the next ciphertext sent will represent the encryption of a four digit PIN. What we are saying, however, is that the interceptor does not learn any *more* information about the plaintext from seeing the ciphertext. In other words, after seeing the ciphertext representing the four-digit PIN, the interceptor will still only know that it represents a four-digit PIN, and will have gained no other information about the value of the PIN. On the other hand, had a symmetric encryption algorithm with just 50 keys been used, then, on seeing the ciphertext, the interceptor would be able to deduce that the PIN was one of 50 different possible PINs simply by trying out the 50 possible decryption keys. In this case, by seeing the ciphertext, the interceptor would have learnt some useful information about the plaintext.

- If a cryptosystem has perfect secrecy then the interceptor might as well just try to guess the plaintext based on the knowledge that they already had about it *before* seeing the ciphertext. The interceptor could try to guess the key rather than the plaintext, but in a cryptosystem with perfect secrecy the most efficient strategy is to directly guess the plaintext for two reasons:
    1. The interceptor might have useful knowledge about the plaintext already (for example that one plaintext is sent more regularly than the others). Guessing the plaintext based on this information will be more likely to be successful than guessing the key.
    2. Even if the interceptor has no information about the plaintext, guessing the plaintext is still more efficient than guessing the key because the interceptor does not need to perform a decryption after having guessed the key.
- Perfect secrecy is a theoretical notion that is a consequence of the properties of the underlying encryption algorithm. Even if a cryptosystem has perfect secrecy, there is nothing to stop attacks on other components of the cryptosystem from occurring. For example, perfect secrecy provides no protection against a particularly aggressive attacker visiting the sender with a large crowbar and requesting the key! We return to this issue shortly.

3.1.2 A simple cryptosystem offering perfect secrecy

We now demonstrate a very simple cryptosystem that offers perfect secrecy.

DESCRIPTION OF THE CRYPTOSYSTEM

Consider the following situation. An investor has to make a major financial decision regarding whether to purchase additional stock in a shareholding, or whether to sell his existing shares. At 14.00 he intends to inform his broker which instruction to follow. The decision is highly sensitive, so the investor wants to encrypt it to prevent competitors from learning his intent.

Table 3.1 describes a suitable cryptosystem for use in this scenario. This cryptosystem has two keys K_1 and K_2, two plaintexts BUY and SELL, and two ciphertexts 0 and 1. The notation $E_K(\text{data})$ means the ciphertext created by encrypting the data using key K. The cryptosystem works as follows:

1. Investor and broker agree on a randomly chosen key in advance (either K_1 or K_2).
2. Once the investor makes his investment decision, he looks up Table 3.1 and reads the ciphertext in the row corresponding to the chosen key and the column corresponding to the chosen decision. For example, if the key is K_1 and the investor is selling then the ciphertext selected will be 1.
3. At 14.00 the investor sends the single ciphertext bit to the broker.
4. The broker looks up the row of Table 3.1 corresponding to the chosen key and establishes which column the ciphertext bit lies in. He then deduces that the

Table 3.1: Simple one-time pad for protecting two plaintexts

	BUY	SELL
Key K_1	$E_{K_1}(\text{BUY}) = 0$	$E_{K_1}(\text{SELL}) = 1$
Key K_2	$E_{K_2}(\text{BUY}) = 1$	$E_{K_2}(\text{SELL}) = 0$

decision corresponds to that column. In our above example, the broker checks the row corresponding to K_1 and sees that 1 lies in the column corresponding to SELL. So the broker deduces that the plaintext is SELL.

THE ATTACKER'S VIEW

Now we look at this cryptosystem from an attacker's viewpoint. It is important to appreciate that Table 3.1 completely specifies the cryptosystem being used. We can thus assume that the attacker has full knowledge of the details of Table 3.1. However, the attacker does not know which key (row) the investor and broker have chosen. The attacker is in the following situation:

Before seeing the ciphertext. We assume that the attacker has no idea whether the investor will buy or sell. If the attacker wants to base a financial decision on the likely outcome then the attacker might as well guess either BUY or SELL.

After seeing the ciphertext. The attacker knows that the combination of key and plaintext must correspond to one of the entries in Table 3.1 that consists of the observed ciphertext. The question remains, which one? From the attacker's perspective:

1. If the ciphertext bit was 0 then either:
   - the key was K_1 and the plaintext was BUY;
   - the key was K_2 and the plaintext was SELL.
2. If the ciphertext bit was 1 then either:
   - the key was K_1 and the plaintext was SELL;
   - the key was K_2 and the plaintext was BUY.

It is easy to see from the above analysis that, regardless of which ciphertext bit was sent, the attacker has not learnt anything useful about the plaintext since each plaintext remains equally likely. In other words, even after having seen the ciphertext, the attacker's best strategy is just to guess the plaintext. This cryptosystem therefore provides perfect secrecy.

COMMENTS ON THE SIMPLE CRYPTOSYSTEM

Note that not every cryptosystem provides perfect secrecy. Suppose that the investor had foolishly decided to use the Simple Substitution Cipher. In this case the ciphertext for BUY will be three characters long and the ciphertext for SELL will be four characters long. Knowing that the plaintext is either BUY or SELL, seeing the ciphertext will allow any attacker to deduce the plaintext immediately. In this case, seeing the ciphertext gives away *all* the information about the plaintext.

Table 3.1 depicts a simple cryptosystem that offers perfect secrecy when there are only two plaintexts. Of course it is not a *secure* cryptosystem since anyone can guess the correct plaintext with a 50% chance of being correct. However, the important point is that the ciphertext does not provide any information that is useful to an attacker. Thus an attacker might as well guess the plaintext without seeing the ciphertext. This is the best that can ever be achieved by any cryptosystem.

3.1.3 One-time pads

The simple cryptosystem offering perfect secrecy that we have just described is an example of a cryptosystem known as a *one-time pad*.

PROPERTIES OF A ONE-TIME PAD

Although there are many different versions and ways of describing a one-time pad, they all have the same three essential properties:

The number of possible keys is greater than or equal to the number of possible plaintexts. If the number of keys is less than the number of plaintexts then guessing the key is easier than guessing the plaintext, thus the cryptosystem does not provide perfect secrecy. In most one-time pads the number of possible keys is equal to the number of possible plaintexts.

The key is selected uniformly at random from the key space. By *uniformly* we mean that each key is equally likely to be chosen. Suppose that this is not the case. Recall our example in Section 3.1.1 of a cryptosystem that is being used to encrypt four-digit PINs. Suppose that the PINs themselves are chosen uniformly at random but that the interceptor knows that certain keys are more likely to be chosen than others. Then the best strategy for the interceptor is to guess one of these more likely keys. Since this strategy will have a greater probability of success than guessing the plaintext, although the cryptosystem may still be pretty good, it will not offer perfect secrecy.

A key should only be used 'once'. We will explain why this is the case in just a moment. This property is why a one-time pad is *one-time*. Note that this does not mean that after a key has been used then this key must never be used again. What it means is that each time a one-time pad is used, the current key should be discarded and a new key should be selected uniformly at random from the keyspace. If, *by chance*, the same key is selected on two different occasions then that is fine, since an attacker cannot predict when this might happen.

Note that these three properties do not *define* a one-time pad since there are cryptosystems that have these properties but do not have perfect secrecy. The property that defines a one-time pad is perfect secrecy. However, if a cryptosystem is a one-time pad then it must have these three properties.

In two seminal papers in the late 1940's, Claude Shannon demonstrated that one time pads are essentially the only cryptosystems with perfect secrecy. There are, however, various different ways of describing a one-time pad. We will look at three of them.

ONE-TIME PAD FROM THE VIGENÈRE CIPHER

Recall that at the end of Section 2.2.4 we commented that there is one special circumstance under which the Vigenère Cipher is a secure cryptosystem. Under this special circumstance it is a cryptosystem with perfect secrecy, in other words it is a one-time pad. This is when:

1. the length of the keyword is the same as the length of the plaintext;
2. the keyword is a randomly generated string of letters;
3. the keyword is used only once.

If these three conditions all hold then it should be clear that the three properties of a one-time pad are met by this special Vigenère Cipher. To see that the first one-time pad property holds, note that if the keyword consists of n randomly generated letters then there are 26^n possible keys. On the other hand there are at most 26^n possible plaintexts. If the plaintext is in a language such as English there will be considerably fewer than 26^n possible plaintexts, since many strings of n letters will not be meaningful.

Using this interpretation of a one-time pad we can demonstrate the power of this cryptosystem. Suppose that this one-time pad is used to send the plaintext LEOPARD using keyword CABBDFA. From our description of the Vigenère Cipher in Section 2.2.4, we can easily establish that the resulting ciphertext is NEPQDWD.

Now cast ourselves in the role of the adversary. We see ciphertext NEPQDWD and we know that a Vigenère one-time pad was used. Since the keyword has length seven and was chosen at random, we are in a very poor position because for *every* possible seven-letter plaintext there exists a keyword that could have been used. Even if we already know that the plaintext is the name of a species of wild cat whose name consists of seven letters, it could still be:

• CHEETAH (keyword LXLMKWW);
• PANTHER (keyword YECXWSN);
• CARACAL (keyword KEYQBWS).

81

An exhaustive key search is futile since every possible plaintext is a valid candidate. We might as well just try to guess the plaintext.

Note that it is tempting to claim that the adversary *does* learn something when they see the ciphertext because they see the *length* of the ciphertext. This might tell the adversary the length of the plaintext, which is certainly information about the plaintext, unless we are careful. There are two different perspectives from which this issue can be addressed:

Fixed length plaintext. The first perspective, which we adopted in the above example, is that the adversary *already knows* the length of the plaintext. In this case the adversary gains no further information from seeing the length of the ciphertext.

Maximum length plaintext. The second perspective, which is probably more realistic, is that the adversary already knows the *maximum possible* length of the plaintext. We thus assume that the maximum length of plaintext that the sender and receiver will ever send using this cryptosystem (in this case a maximum number of m plaintext letters) is a publicly known parameter, and hence is known by the adversary. The sender then:

1. agrees a keyword of length m letters with the receiver;
2. if the plaintext is less than m letters long then the sender adds some extra letters to make the plaintext m letters long (this example of adding 'redundant' information to a plaintext is often called *padding*, which we will discuss further in Section 4.3.2);
3. encrypts the extended plaintext using the keyword of m letters.

As a result of this approach, the adversary always sees a ciphertext of length m. The adversary thus does not learn anything new about the length of the plaintext from seeing the length of the ciphertext because:

- the maximum length m is public knowledge, hence the adversary learns nothing from seeing an m letter ciphertext other than what they already knew: that the plaintext cannot be more than m letters long;
- the true plaintext length is hidden.

This one-time pad also reveals a redeeming (but not very useful) property of the Caesar Cipher. Since it can be thought of as a Vigenère Cipher with keyword of length one, we see immediately that if we only send a single letter of ciphertext, choose the Caesar Cipher key randomly, and use that key only once, then the Caesar Cipher has perfect secrecy. Unfortunately there are not many applications for such a cryptosystem!

CONSEQUENCES OF KEY REUSE IN A ONE-TIME PAD

Recall that an important property of a one-time pad is that keys should only be used once. We now demonstrate why this is the case. To keep things really simple we will use the Caesar Cipher one-time pad to encrypt single letter plaintexts.

Suppose that two plaintext letters P_1 and P_2 have been encrypted using the *same* one-time pad key K (in other words key K has been used twice) to produce two ciphertext letters C_1 and C_2. This means that an attacker knows that both C_1 and C_2 have arisen by shifting P_1 and P_2 the same number of positions. Thus the attacker learns that the number of letters between C_1 and C_2 is the same as the number of letters between P_1 and P_2. This does not immediately tell the attacker what either P_1 or P_2 is, but it is certainly information that the attacker did not have before.

We can make this statement more precise by using the mathematical description of the Caesar Cipher from Section 2.1.1 (this requires a basic understanding of modular arithmetic, which we do not properly introduce until Section 5.1.3, so can be skipped if preferred). We have:

$$C_1 \;=\; P_1 + K \bmod 26$$
$$C_2 \;=\; P_2 + K \bmod 26.$$

Since an attacker can see C_1 and C_2, the attacker can subtract C_1 from C_2 to get:

$$C_2 - C_1 \;=\; (P_2 + K) - (P_1 + K) \bmod 26$$
$$=\; P_2 - P_1 \bmod 26,$$

since the keys K cancel each other out. Thus the attacker learns the value $P_2 - P_1$, which is the 'difference' between plaintext P_2 and plaintext P_1.

Could this relationship between P_1 and P_2 be of any real use to the attacker? An example to illustrate that it *could* be of use is as follows. Suppose that the single letter plaintexts represent two different days of the month within a 26-day period on which a major advertising campaign will be run. Alice encrypts these two days using the same key K and sends them to her colleague Bob. The attacker comes from a rival firm who wishes to know the campaign days. By learning the difference between P_2 and P_1 the attacker does not learn the dates of the campaign, but does learn the number of days between the two events. This in itself might be useful. The point here is that seeing two ciphertexts encrypted using the same key gives away *some* information about the plaintexts. Thus the property of perfect secrecy is lost if we reuse a one-time pad key.

Things get much more serious as soon as the first advertising campaign is actually run on date P_1. Since the attacker knows the difference between the launch days, they can now work out the date P_2 of the second run. Even worse, since the attacker now knows a corresponding plaintext/ciphertext pair, they can determine the key by working out the shift that was used. This can also be written mathematically as:

$$C_1 - P_1 = (P_1 + K) - P_1 = K \bmod 26.$$

Any further ciphertexts encrypted using key K can now be decrypted by the attacker.

The above attack is an example of a known-plaintext attack (see Section 1.5.2). Note that this is not indicative of a problem with the notion of perfect secrecy, since perfect secrecy is based on an interceptor who conducts ciphertext-only attacks. The attack does, however, reinforce the point that one-time pad keys should only be used once.

ONE-TIME PAD FROM A LATIN SQUARE

We can generalise the simple cryptosystem from Section 3.1.2 to obtain another one-time pad. This version is represented by a square table that has n rows, n columns and n different table entries (values appearing in the table). The cryptosystem in Table 3.1 is an example of this table for the case $n = 2$. Just as in the cryptosystem in Table 3.1, we associate:

- the n rows of the table with n different keys;
- the n columns of the table with n different plaintexts;
- the n different entries in the table with n different ciphertexts;
- the encryption of a plaintext (column) using a key (row) with the table entry in the row corresponding to the key and the column corresponding to the plaintext.

This table is public information and represents a full description of the cryptosystem. It is essentially a *look-up table*, where the ciphertext for any plaintext and key can be obtained by inspection. The only difference between the sender/receiver and the adversary is that the sender/receiver know which row of this look-up table to use. But this is a very significant difference.

Note that every possible plaintext is associated with a column of the table. Hence the plaintext LION might be the 17th column and the plaintext TIGER might be the 149th column. How this is done is not important, what is important is that the association is made. By doing so, in this one-time pad we do not have to worry about the issue of the length of the ciphertext giving away any information. This is because the plaintext length is no longer revealed by a ciphertext since the 'mapping' from plaintexts to columns has protected us from this issue.

Such a look-up table could be constructed for any cryptosystem, including modern cryptosystems using AES (see Section 4.5). However, the size of the table (the number of rows and columns) would be so large that there is no point in even beginning to consider trying to represent the likes of AES as such a table. For AES this table would have 2^{128} columns and at least 2^{128} rows!

For such a table to form the basis of a one-time pad and hence offer perfect secrecy, we need to have the following two properties:

Every row contains every table entry precisely once. A table without this property is not a cryptosystem. This is because some row (key) K must contain some table entry (ciphertext) C at least twice. If Alice and Bob choose key K and Alice sends ciphertext C, then Bob will not know which of the two occurrences of C in row K Alice meant to send, hence Bob will be uncertain which plaintext is being sent. In other words, Bob cannot decrypt this ciphertext.

Every column contains every table entry precisely once. A table without this property cannot provide perfect secrecy. If some column (plaintext) P contains a table entry (ciphertext) C twice, then because there are n rows and n possible ciphertexts, some table entry (ciphertext) C' must *not* occur in column P. If Alice sends ciphertext C' to Bob then the attacker will know that the corresponding plaintext cannot be P. In other words, from seeing the ciphertext C', the attacker learns *something* about the corresponding plaintext.

Squares with the above two properties are known to mathematicians as *Latin squares* and have been popularised by puzzle solvers as *Sudoku squares* (which are Latin squares that have additional properties). Table 3.2 provides an example for the case $n = 5$.

For the square in Table 3.2 to actually form a one-time pad we need to make sure that the key is chosen uniformly at random and is only used once.

VERNAM CIPHER

The most common one-time pad is the version that applies to binary plaintexts and keys (as opposed to the versions applied to letters of the alphabet and numbers from 1 to n that we have just described). This version is often called the *Vernam Cipher*.

The Vernam Cipher can be described as follows:

- Let the plaintext be a string of bits $P_1, P_2, \ldots, P_n$ (where P_i means the ith bit of the plaintext).
- Randomly generate a key that consists of n bits $K_1, K_2, \ldots, K_n$.
- Encrypt plaintext bit P_i by XORing it to key bit K_i to obtain ciphertext bit C_i (for an explanation of the XOR function, see Section 1.6.1 and the

Table 3.2: Latin square one-time pad for protecting five plaintexts

	P_1	P_2	P_3	P_4	P_5
K_1	1	2	3	4	5
K_2	2	3	4	5	1
K_3	3	4	5	1	2
K_4	4	5	1	2	3
K_5	5	1	2	3	4

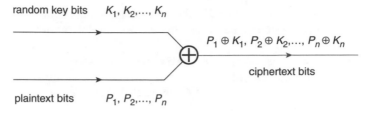

Figure 3.1. The Vernam Cipher

Mathematics Appendix). In other words:

$$C_1 = P_1 \oplus K_1$$
$$C_2 = P_2 \oplus K_2$$
$$\vdots$$
$$C_n = P_n \oplus K_n.$$

This process is depicted in Figure 3.1. Decryption is almost identical, since the receiver computes $P_i = C_i \oplus K_i$ to recover each plaintext bit from each ciphertext bit.

The Vernam Cipher is a one-time pad under the condition that every string of key bits is used just once. Of course we cannot *guarantee* that we will not generate the same string of bits some time in the future. So long as the bits are randomly generated then the next time we generate a string of bits it is very unlikely that it has been used before. We will discuss random generation in more detail in Section 8.1.

The Vernam Cipher is closely related to all the previous one-time pads:

1. Recalling that XOR is the same as 'adding' two binary numbers (which is actually addition modulo 2), we see that it is the same as our mathematical description of the Caesar Cipher one-time pad, where instead of working modulo 26 we are working modulo 2 (see Section 5.1.3 and the Mathematics Appendix for more explanation);
2. We could write out the Vernam Cipher as an enormous Latin square, but why bother when we already have such a simple and efficient description of it?

When we refer to the one-time pad at any later stage in our cryptographic discussion we could, in theory, be discussing any of these versions of this cryptosystem. However, all of our modern cryptosystems are designed to process strings of bits, so it is probably best to think of a one-time pad as the Vernam Cipher.

3.1.4 Theoretical security summary

We end this discussion of theoretical security by summarising the main points:

- Perfect secrecy captures the notion of an 'unbreakable' cryptosystem.
- A one-time pad provides perfect secrecy.
- There are many different ways of describing a one-time pad but the underlying cryptosystem is essentially the same.
- A one-time pad always has the three properties described in Section 3.1.3.
- A cryptosystem with the three properties described in Section 3.1.3 is not necessarily a one-time pad, since it must also have perfect secrecy. One of the activities for this chapter encourages the design of such a cryptosystem.

3.2 Practical security

In Section 3.1 we introduced the idea of perfect secrecy and noted that it provides an ideal notion of confidentiality in the sense that no cryptosystem can do better than perfect secrecy. We went on to exhibit various one-time pads, which are cryptosystems that provide perfect secrecy. Should our study of cryptography, at least for providing confidentiality, stop here?

It all sounds too good to be true, and it is. In this section we begin by explaining why a one-time pad is not the answer to all our problems. This section, as a whole, discusses the following conundrum: *a theoretically secure cryptosystem might not be secure in practice, while a theoretically breakable cryptosystem might be secure in practice.*

We start the justification of this statement by looking at the security of a one-time pad in practice.

3.2.1 One-time pad in practice

There are a number of practical problems with using a one-time pad to encrypt data. These are largely to do with key management. This makes them significant problems, since one of the biggest challenges in making cryptography work in real systems is providing the right key management support, as we will discuss in much greater detail in Chapters 10 and 11.

KEY MANAGEMENT ISSUES WITH A ONE-TIME PAD

There are three key management issues that make a one-time pad a very impractical cryptosystem to employ in real applications. These directly arise from each of the three fundamental properties of a one-time pad (see Section 3.1.3):

Length of the key. The requirement that a one-time pad key is as long as the plaintext is prohibitive for most applications. This has particular ramifications for two aspects of key management:

- Since these potentially enormous keys must be stored in an environment with maximum security, this has implications for *key storage* (see Section 10.5).
- Somehow these potentially enormous keys must be made available to anyone who requires access to them (this will be the sender and receiver in our basic communications model of Section 1.4.3). This process is known as *key establishment* (see Section 10.4). Since one-time pad key establishment must be conducted using a secure technique that does not leak any information about the key, common key establishment techniques such as encryption using another key cannot be used. (Unless of course the encryption of the key is done using a one-time pad, in which case we now face the problem of securely establishing the key that was used to encrypt our first key!)

Random generation of the key. A one-time pad key must be truly randomly generated and hence cannot be generated using a deterministic generator (see Section 8.1), which is the way most keys are generated in practice. Thus *key generation* for a one-time pad is an expensive key management process (see Section 10.3).

One-time use. Having gone through a costly key generation, establishment and storage process, the resulting key can then only be used on one occasion.

Note that if a key establishment mechanism exists for one-time pad keys that are as long as the plaintext then it is reasonable to wonder why that mechanism cannot then be used to securely transfer the plaintext itself. Why bother with a one-time pad? However, it may be easier to distribute the key in advance by a convenient and secure means, potentially before the plaintext is even known. Historically, one-time pad keys were distributed to agents using carefully engineered manual 'drops' (for example, meeting on a park bench in Vienna at a pre-arranged time). An agent was then ready to receive secret messages at whatever time in the future they were sent. We will discuss more modern versions of key establishment techniques in Section 10.4, however they tend to be similar to this historical example in the sense that they rely on relatively complex key establishment operations being conducted in advance, thus allowing on-the-fly encryption to subsequently take place.

ONE-TIME PADS IN PRACTICE

The key management overheads required to support a one-time pad are clearly too much for routine cryptographic application. However, there are two situations in which these might not be so unrealistic:

In high-security environments. If costly key management techniques can be justified due to the value of the data being protected, use of a one-time pad could be viable. Indeed, it is widely believed that the Washington–Moscow hotline used to be protected by a one-time pad. The term *pad* dates back to the physical media on which espionage agents in the field used to store one-time pad keys during high security missions. It is, however, unlikely that a one-time pad is still used in many such applications, largely because more conventional cryptosystems have become much more advanced and hence the key management costs and inconvenience are no longer justified. It is possible, although far from certain, that we may see more use of one-time pads in future environments supporting quantum key establishment (see Section 10.4.3 for further discussion).

For very short messages. The key management problems of a one-time pad are greatly reduced when the plaintext is short. If Alice wishes to send ten randomly generated bits to Bob then she can easily randomly generate a 10-bit key using a manual technique (coin tosses, for example). Secure key establishment and storage are still necessary, but are much more manageable for ten bits compared to, say, the number of bits required for encryption of a hard disk.

Although one-time pads are rarely used in modern applications, some of the properties of a one-time pad are highly attractive, not the least its simplicity of encryption. The most practical instantiation of a one-time pad, the Vernam Cipher, is very fast to use since encryption and decryption consist of XOR operations. We will see in Section 4.2 that there is an important class of symmetric encryption algorithms (namely, *stream ciphers*) that essentially 'emulate' a one-time pad in order to obtain this property.

3.2.2 Cover time

With the exception of those based on a one-time pad, all the cryptosystems that we will discuss, and that will be encountered in real-world systems, are theoretically breakable. This might, at first, sound rather alarming. However, keeping in mind the deficiencies of a one-time pad, this statement should be interpreted as pragmatic, rather than disturbing.

So what do we mean by 'theoretically breakable'? Or, looking at it from the other perspective, what might we mean by 'practical security'? This very complex question is one that we will attempt to answer throughout the remainder of this book. We will see that most modern cryptosystems are regarded as secure in practice because the known theoretical attacks take too much operational time to conduct. In other words, conducting these attacks in 'reasonable' operational time requires resources that are unrealistic for any imaginable attacker of the cryptosystem.

There is no universal notion of practical security that is meaningful for every possible application environment. However, there are some useful concepts that can help us work towards such a notion within a particular application context.

The first of these concerns the intended lifetime of a plaintext. The *cover time* is the length of time for which a plaintext must be kept secret. Clearly the cover time of different plaintext data varies considerably. For example:

- the cover time for a daily password might be twenty-four hours;
- some financial records need to be stored by law for seven years, hence this is likely to also be their cover time;
- the cover time for some stored government records could be one hundred years.

A very basic design principle for determining practical security could thus be to ensure that no known attack on the cryptosystem can be conducted in less than the cover time of the plaintext. We saw in Section 1.6.4 that exhaustive key search is one known attack that can be applied to any cryptosystem, hence this design principle certainly includes the requirement that an exhaustive key search takes longer than the cover time.

One drawback of defining practical security in such terms is that it is framed in terms of *known* attacks. If a new attack is developed after some data has been encrypted that results in it becoming possible to attack a ciphertext in less than the cover time of the underlying plaintext, then we have a problem. We can of course re-encrypt the plaintext data, but any attacker who has managed to get hold of the original ciphertext will now be in a strong position.

Nonetheless, cover time is one example of a useful concept that helps people who are protecting data to make decisions about how best to apply cryptography to it.

3.2.3 Computational complexity

The next aspect of practical security that is worth formalising concerns the time taken to conduct an attack. This requires an understanding of two separate pieces of information:

1. what computational processes are involved in known attacks on the cryptosystem;
2. how much time it takes to conduct these processes.

The first of these is the task of a cryptanalyst. However, for modern established cryptosystems that have already undergone a rigorous analysis, the computational processes involved should be fairly well understood. This is because, in order to demonstrate security, a well-designed cryptosystem is usually built around a computational problem that is widely perceived to be hard to solve. Such a cryptosystem will have, at its heart, at least one computational process that is understood and widely believed to be very slow to conduct.

Establishing the time required to conduct an attack against a cryptosystem thus requires a formal way of measuring how long the computational process required to break the cryptosystem takes to run. What we thus need is a way of measuring the time that it takes to run a process.

COMPLEXITY OF SIMPLE PROCESSES

We now look at the most common measure of processing time. All processes, not just cryptographic ones, are implemented by means of some algorithm, which specifies the machine operations required to conduct that process. The *complexity* of an algorithm gives, for each possible length of input to the algorithm, the time needed to run the algorithm for that length of input.

The length of input is measured in terms of the number of bits of input. The time is measured in terms of the number of basic machine operations (such as adding two bits, or comparing two values) that it takes to run the algorithm. This time is usually an approximation, rather than an attempt to measure the number of operations precisely.

This is best illustrated by examples. The complexity of some basic processes are shown in Table 3.3.

POLYNOMIAL AND EXPONENTIAL TIME

The study of the complexity of algorithms is an entire field of mathematical science in itself. It will suffice for us to observe that there are two very important general classes of process, determined by their complexity. A process can be conducted in:

Polynomial time if the time taken to execute the process for an input of size n is not greater than n^r, for some number r. Informally, polynomial-time

Table 3.3: Complexity of some basic processes

Operation	Complexity	Explanation
Addition of two n-bit numbers	n	Ignoring carrying, when a computer adds two numbers it performs one addition for every bit in the lengths of the input numbers.
Multiplication of two n-bit numbers	n^2	Computers multiply numbers in a similar way to the way we perform 'long multiplication'. Thus we have n different additions to perform, one for every bit of the length of the input numbers.
Raising a number to an n-bit power	n^3	This process consists of n operations, each of which is either a squaring or a multiplication, both of which take n^2 operations, hence n^3 in total (using the method known as *Repeated Squares*).
Exhaustive key search for an n-bit key	2^n	This involves trying out every possible n-bit key, of which there are 2^n.

processes are 'quick' on all inputs of 'reasonable' size. From Table 3.3 we see that multiplication of two n-bit numbers has complexity n^2 and thus can be conducted in polynomial time. Thus multiplication is an easy process to conduct. Likewise, we see that addition and raising a number to a power are easy processes to conduct.

Exponential time if the time taken to execute the process for an input of size n is approximately a^n, for some number a. Informally, exponential-time processes are 'slow' on all inputs of 'reasonable' size. As n increases, the length of time necessary to run the necessary algorithm increases dramatically, until it is impossible in practice to compute the result. If a bigger value of a is chosen then this trend is exacerbated. From Table 3.3 we see that an exhaustive key search has complexity 2^n and thus can be conducted in exponential time. Thus an exhaustive key search takes a long time to conduct, irrespective of the computer(s) on which it is performed.

Note that:

1. Just because a process is *easy* to conduct does not necessarily mean that it is *efficient* to conduct. For example:

   - multiplication can always be computed in a relatively short time with respect to the size of the input numbers but, as the size of the input numbers increases, the length of time it takes to process a multiplication might not always be acceptable;
   - raising a number to a power (*exponentiation*, which confusingly runs in *polynomial time*!) is also easy to conduct, but is generally regarded as being relatively computationally expensive.

   In fact, much work has been devoted to reducing the complexity of common polynomial-time processes such as multiplication and exponentiation in an attempt to make them faster to compute.

2. Just because a process is *generally* hard to conduct does not mean that it is *always* hard to conduct. For example, an exhaustive key search is quite feasible if n is small enough. The point is that if a process runs in exponential time then, as n grows larger, the time needed to conduct the process grows exponentially. Thus, after a certain point, the process takes too long to be realistically conducted using current computing capabilities.

In terms of the design of cryptosystems, it should be clear that encryption and decryption processes must run in polynomial time. Ideally an attacker who does not have access to the decryption key should be required to conduct an exponential-time process in order to obtain the plaintext or the decryption key from the ciphertext.

Note that Table 3.3 contains a slight oversimplification. A complete exhaustive key search for a modern symmetric algorithm with an n-bit key actually involves 2^n decryptions, each of which should consist of a polynomial-time operation. Hence the complexity is really $2^n \times n^r$, for some unspecified r. However, 2^n increases so much more rapidly than n^r that we can effectively 'forget' about the time taken to run decryption for each of the keys in the search. We thus describe the complexity in terms of the more significant computational requirement, which is the vast number of keys that must be searched.

These ideas about complexity are very powerful because they tell us about the general behaviour of algorithms. Note that as time goes by, computers get faster, following a much-quoted trend known as *Moore's Law*, so an exhaustive search for a particular input value of n that was once thought impractical might become feasible in the future. We will discuss how this has happened for DES in Section 4.4. However, knowing that an exhaustive key search runs in exponential time tells us that if computers continue to work in the way that they do today then there will always be a (relatively small) value of n beyond which it is impossible in practice to conduct the search.

COMPUTING REAL ATTACK TIMES

Complexity provides an abstract notion of time that is based on computer operations. To convert this into a real notion of time we need to know how much real time it takes to run these basic computer operations. This of course depends on the processor speed of the computer(s) used. To compute real attack times, we thus proceed as follows:

1. estimate the computer speed (in terms of number of operations performed per second);
2. calculate the real time to conduct the process for an input of n bits by the formula:

$$\frac{\text{complexity of process evaluated at } n}{\text{computer speed}} \text{ seconds.}$$

For example, an exhaustive key search has complexity 2^n. Thus, if we estimate that our computer is capable of processing one million operations per second then an exhaustive search for a 30-bit key will take:

$$\frac{2^{30}}{10^6} \text{ seconds.}$$

Since 2^{30} is approximately 10^9, the real-time search will take approximately:

$$\frac{10^9}{10^6} = 10^3 = 1000 \text{ seconds,}$$

which is just under 18 minutes.

The dramatic difference between polynomial time and exponential time is best seen by looking at the rate of increase of real computational time of some processes, expressed in Table 3.4 based on a computer speed of one million operations per second. All the calculations in Table 3.4 were computed using the technique just described.

93

Table 3.4: Real time of computation for sample complexities

Complexity	n = 10	n = 30	n = 50
n	0.00001 s	0.00003 s	0.00005 s
n^3	0.001 s	0.027 s	0.125 s
2^n	0.001 s	17.9 minutes	37.7 years
3^n	0.059 s	6.5 years	200 million centuries

LIMITATIONS OF COMPLEXITY

We have just seen that complexity theory is useful for giving some indication of the time that certain computations will take. It can thus be used to estimate the time that an attacker will take to successfully attack a cryptosystem using the best known technique. We have already seen precisely how to do this if the best known technique is exhaustive key search.

It is thus desirable to base the security of a cryptosystem on a computational problem whose complexity is beyond the realistic capabilities of computer systems that are likely to be employed by an attacker. Determining what an attacker's computational capability is likely to be, both now and at any time within the cover time of the data to be protected, is part of risk management and is an aspect of information security that is beyond the scope of our study.

Note that, as previously observed, decryption of a ciphertext without the key should involve an exponential-time process. However, returning to our attempts to define practical security, it must be noted that establishing the complexity of any known attacks is important and useful, but brings no guarantees of practical security. There are several reasons why this is the case:

There may be undiscovered theoretical attacks. As mentioned earlier, we can only be sure that known theoretical attacks have a complexity that is beyond the realistic computing power of any attacker. There may be other attacks out there waiting to be discovered that have lower complexity and are practical to conduct.

Complexity only deals with the general case. Complexity can be used to indicate that *on average* an attack takes a certain time to conduct. This does not, however, guarantee that a particular manifestation of that attack will not be successful in less time. For example, there is always a chance (albeit a very small one) that an exhaustive key search might result in the right key being found on the very first decryption attempt.

Implementation issues. Certain practices may compromise the notion of the complexity of an attack. For example, suppose that an ill-informed organisation decides to change key on a daily basis and employs the simple technique of requesting the encryption of the plaintext 00 . . . 0 every morning in order to confirm whether the receiver has the correct key for the day. Knowing that this practice is being used, an attacker could well invest the time and memory space in order to establish a massive database that contains the encryption of 00 . . . 0 under every possible key in the keyspace (this would be impractical to do for every possible plaintext, but potentially feasible to do for this one plaintext). The attacker could then wait for the morning confirmation message to be sent to the organisation from the receiver, and then consult this database in order to establish what key is being used. The point here is that an exhaustive search for the key is still hard, but a bad implementation practice has made it possible to search for the key using a different technique.

Key management. Most effective attacks on cryptosystems exploit bad key management practices. Complexity theory tells us nothing about the feasibility of exploiting bad key management to conduct an attack.

Any real notion of practical security needs to take these types of issue into account.

3.2.4 Design process of a cryptosystem

The following chapters will focus on describing cryptographic primitives and how they work. However, it is extremely important from a practical security perspective to recognise that the primitives themselves must always be considered as part of a process, rather than isolated mechanisms. The process that surrounds a cryptographic primitive includes the following:

SELECTION OR DESIGN OF A PRIMITIVE

The selection of a cryptographic primitive depends on the application requirements. For example, with respect to selection of an encryption algorithm, this part of the process may involve asking questions such as:

- should we use symmetric or public-key encryption?
- what requirements and/or restrictions on the key length exist?
- should we adopt a publicly known encryption algorithm or develop our own proprietary encryption algorithm?

Throughout our discussion of cryptographic primitives we will investigate some of the properties that influence this selection (design) process. Note that in many cases the financial or operational constraints may dictate the use of certain primitives. For example, an organisation might be forced to use a specific primitive in order to comply with a relevant application standard.

MODE OF USE

Cryptographic primitives can be used in different ways in order to achieve different security goals. For example, symmetric encryption algorithms can be:

- implemented in specific ways in order to achieve particular properties (we discuss these different *modes of operation* in Section 4.6);

- used as the basis for the design of other cryptographic primitives (for example, we will see in Chapter 6 that block ciphers can be used to design hash functions and message authentication codes);
- adopted within cryptographic protocols to provide different security services (we will see in Section 9.4 that encryption algorithms can be used as components of protocols that provide entity authentication).

IMPLEMENTATION

As anyone with practical security experience will know only too well, security technology is worthless without careful implementation. Developers do not always understand cryptography and how to use it. There have been many instances in the past of basic errors being made at the implementation stage, which later have disastrous consequences. Two potential problems with cryptographic implementations are:

Implementation tricks. All cryptographic primitives slow down an application, and some cryptographic primitives do so substantially (particularly public-key primitives). This has led to the development of various implementation 'tricks' to speed up certain cryptographic primitives. It is important that these are done in such a way that they do not inadvertently affect the security of the primitive itself.

Backwards compatibility measures. Developers sometimes make provision for *backwards compatibility*, which allows an application to be used with legacy systems that are not running the latest version software and/or hardware. Making such provisions can sometimes result in parts of a cryptographic mechanism being bypassed.

Also of great significance to the resulting security of a cryptosystem is whether its implementation is in software or hardware. Software-based cryptography is much more vulnerable to attack since the primitive and its keys will typically reside in memory and be vulnerable to attacks on the computing platform. For example, malicious code on a platform might seek to locate and export cryptographic keys. Hardware-based cryptography is generally more secure, with the best protection being provided when specialised hardware security modules are deployed. We examine this issue in more detail in Section 10.5.

We will not discuss implementation issues in any great detail in this book. Implementation security, including the development of secure software, is a topic of more general significance and is one that should be studied as part of any wider information security education.

KEY MANAGEMENT

The management of the cryptographic keys used by a cryptographic primitive is a vital part of the cryptographic process. We discuss this topic in detail in Chapter 10 and Chapter 11.

3.2.5 Evaluating security

One of the most difficult aspects of cryptography is making an accurate assessment of the security of a given cryptosystem. We separate this discussion into assessing the security of cryptographic primitives, protocols and cryptosystems.

ASSESSING THE SECURITY OF A CRYPTOGRAPHIC ALGORITHM

Historically, the security of cryptographic algorithms (and protocols) relied on a rather informal approach that considered known attacks on the algorithm, such as an exhaustive key search, and then designed the algorithm so that it was believed that these attacks would not work. Often the arguments put forward to justify the resulting 'security' were not particularly rigorous, and in many cases were experimental. This process resulted from the fact that cryptographic algorithm design is as much about engineering as mathematics.

The problem with such an informal approach is that it does not provide any real notion of 'proof' that a cryptographic algorithm is secure. With this in mind, cryptographic researchers have gradually been developing and adopting methodologies for attempting to provide stronger arguments for the security of cryptographic algorithms. This concept of *provable security* attempts to assess the security of a cryptographic algorithm by starting from some assumptions about the attack environment (captured by a *security model*), and then showing that the security of the cryptographic algorithm can be formally linked (*reduced*) to the difficulty of a computational problem that is better understood.

There are two potential problems with this type of approach:

The starting assumptions may not be the right ones. For example, there may be attacks that have not been considered in the security model.

The computational problem might not be as difficult as thought. Provable security arguments are essentially translations from one relatively poorly understood concept (the cryptographic algorithm) into a better understood concept (the computational problem). However, this does not guarantee any 'security' in the event that the computational problem is not as hard as originally believed.

Provable security is thus not really a 'proof' of cryptographic algorithm security. Nonetheless, it is a substantially better approach than the informal one of the past. A security proof within a sensible security model should thus be regarded as important evidence in favour of the overall security of a cryptographic algorithm.

Arguably the best assessment benchmark for a cryptographic algorithm remains exposure and breadth of adoption. As we observed in Section 1.5, the most highly regarded cryptographic algorithms tend to be those that have been widely scrutinised and implemented. To this end, several standardisation bodies, including ISO/IEC, NIST and IEEE, have standards that identify cryptographic algorithms that have been widely studied by experts and recommended for adoption. Some, but not all, of these cryptographic algorithms have proofs of security within specific security models.

ASSESSING THE SECURITY OF A CRYPTOGRAPHIC PROTOCOL

As we will discover in Chapter 9, cryptographic protocols are very complex objects to analyse. Their security is also assessed using both informal analysis and more rigorous formal methodologies. In addition to provable security techniques for cryptographic protocols, there have been attempts to define logical methods of arguing the security of a cryptographic protocol. These establish basic logical statements relating to security and attempt to build a cryptographic protocol for which certain security 'truths' hold.

One of the main problems with formal approaches to cryptographic protocol analysis is that the cryptographic protocols used in real applications are often quite complex and hard to capture in a formal model. However, even being able to formally analyse part of a cryptographic protocol is arguably a significant improvement on informal analysis techniques.

As well as general standards for specific types of cryptographic protocol, there are many cryptographic applications whose underlying cryptographic protocols are industry standards that have been approved by committees. We will discuss several of these in Chapter 12. Where the standards body concerned has sufficient cryptographic expertise, recommendations can be relied upon as a reasonable means of security assessment. However, in Section 12.2 we will discuss one case where development of an industry standard did not appear to involve the appropriate level of cryptographic expertise.

ASSESSING THE SECURITY OF A CRYPTOSYSTEM

Hardest of all to assess is the security of an entire cryptosystem. As this involves not just the cryptographic algorithms and protocols, but also the wider infrastructure, we have to be realistic about the extent to which this can be rigorously done. There are standards for many cryptosystem components, for example key management, which can be used to benchmark such an assessment. There are formal evaluation criteria for security products and there are organisations that are licensed to conduct evaluations against these benchmarks. Researchers are also looking into formal methods for evaluating the security of particular components of the overall infrastructure, for example, formal evaluation of the implementation of a particular cryptographic algorithm or protocol.

We cannot capture the assessment of security of a cryptosystem in just a few sentences. Rather, it is hoped that, by the end of this book, the breadth of what it might mean to assess the security of a cryptosystem should be clear.

3.2.6 Adequate security

One of the points that we will keep returning to when considering the security of real cryptosystems, especially in Chapter 12, is that in many application environments it is acceptable to adopt levels of security that are short of 'ideal'. This is because the potential benefits of *adequate security*, for example, in terms of efficiency, may outweigh the benefits of stronger security.

Clearly the decision to make such a tradeoff must be made from an informed viewpoint, which considers the realistic threat environment within which the cryptosystem will be used. As part of this analysis, it is worth considering exactly what process a potential attacker might have to go through in order to benefit from an attack on a cryptosystem:

Motivation. The attacker must want to attack the cryptosystem in the first place. There are many applications where, realistically, there are no motivated attackers. For example, the vast majority of email users do not encrypt their emails. Many of these users would probably use a secure email package if they believed in the existence of an attacker who routinely wanted to read their email (see Section 12.7.2).

Knowledge. An attacker with the motivation must also have the knowledge to conduct an attack. Even an attack that can largely be 'automated', for example, by downloading a software attack tool, often still requires an amount of expertise (albeit fairly small) to conduct. There may be many potential attackers with enough knowledge, but this is only a threat if one of them is likely to be motivated to conduct it.

Action. An attacker must actually proceed with an attack. Even with the motivation and the knowledge, there may be barriers that prevent an attacker from proceeding. These could be logistical, for example an attacker requires the right opportunity, perhaps access to a specific computer terminal, which might never arise. Or these could be conceptual. For example, an attacker may desire to access a colleague's files, and may have the knowledge of how to do so, but knows that this action would represent a breach of the organisation's computer use policy, which could result in the attacker losing their job.

Success. An attacker has to succeed with their attack. For many attacks on a cryptosystem, success is far from guaranteed. For example, an attacker with access to a user's ATM card can usually only make three attempts to guess the PIN before the card account is suspended.

Benefit. An attacker has to gain benefit from the attack. Even if the attacker successfully attacks the cryptosystem, the results may not be of great use to the attacker. For example, a plaintext with a short cover time could be encrypted using a fairly weak encryption algorithm. The attacker may well be able to conduct an exhaustive key search, but if this takes longer than the cover time then the plaintext should no longer be of value by the time the attacker finds it. As another example, which we will discuss in more detail in Section 6.2, an attacker might be successful in finding a collision for a hash function, but they will only benefit if that collision is meaningful.

In some application environments, the very idea that there *might* be a motivated attacker is enough to require that the application be 'locked down' using a high-grade cryptosystem. In others, it may suffice to rely on the benefits of a fairly easily conducted attack being quite small. What is vitally important is that this attack process is thought through when making a decision about what level of cryptosytem security is deemed to be adequate.

3.2.7 Towards a notion of practical security

Hopefully it should be evident that the term *practical security* describes an abstract idea rather than a concept for which we will ever be able to propose a clear definition. There are several fundamental problems with trying to define practical security:

Coverage. It involves too many separate factors to capture in one clear notion. For example, in order to evaluate practical security we need to conduct activities that include:

- evaluating the existence and abilities of potential attackers;
- assessing the likely computing power of an attacker;
- determining the complexity of known attacks;
- considering the security of cryptographic implementations;
- evaluating the effectiveness of key management processes;
- forming a notion of what levels of risk to accept.

Subjectivity. It is a subjective issue. What is regarded as practically secure from one perspective may not be from another. For example:

- Academics publishing research on cryptosystems set such demanding notions of security that it is not uncommon for academic breaks of cryptosystems to have relatively little impact on security in real environments (see Section 1.6.6).
- Different application sectors hold different views of risk. For example, in 1988 the National Security Agency in the USA removed its endorsement of DES, but in the same year the National Bureau of Standards reaffirmed the use of DES in the financial sector. This suggests that the two organisations may have had different notions of practical security.

Evolution. Hard as it is to formulate practical security at any given moment in time, an additional complication is that most of the inputs, such as attack capability and risk models, vary over time. Practical security thus needs to be continuously reassessed.

In order to assess practical security, it is thus necessary to fully understand the entire security and business requirements of a particular environment, which is well beyond the scope of this book. Indeed, the skills that this requires have wider application than just to cryptosystems and require a broad information security education to perform.

As a last observation, even after having formulated a notion of practical security, in a real environment it may not be possible to provide the determined degree of practical security. A more realistic security target might simply be 'inadequate security, but the best that we can afford'. However, the formulation of a notion of practical security at least allows such a decision to be placed in appropriate context.

3.3 Summary

In this chapter we have investigated the difference between providing security in theory and providing security in practice. We introduced the concept of perfect secrecy, which is in some sense the best security that a cryptosystem can ever provide. We described various versions of the only cryptosystem that has perfect secrecy and then explained why it cannot normally be used in real applications. We then explored the notion of practical security. We looked at ways of measuring the strength of a cryptosystem in terms of the difficulty of performing attacks against it. Finally, we commented on the difficulty of proposing a precise notion of practical security.

A number of important points arose during this discussion:

- It is impossible to guarantee the security of a cryptosystem. Even if it is theoretically secure, it may be insecure in practice.
- It is quite acceptable in practice (indeed, necessary) to use cryptosystems that are theoretically breakable.
- Every attempt should be made to formulate a notion of practical security for a given environment. This will inevitably involve tradeoffs, estimates and evaluations of what levels of risk to accept. Formulating this notion will be difficult.

3.4 Further reading

Alternative explanations of a one-time pad can be found in almost any book on cryptography. The foundations of information theory and perfect secrecy were first set out by Claude Shannon in two important papers [173, 174]. Shannon is regarded as a father figure in this area and much about his life and works (including copies of these papers) can be found on the web. Historical uses of one-time pads are discussed in Kahn [104]. The story of the Venona project [32] includes a fascinating example of the dangers involved in implementing a one-time pad in practice.

Concerning practical security, Harel [97] provides a readable introduction to the limitations of computational ability in modern computers, including reference to complexity theory and cryptography. Talbot and Welsh [189] provide an introduction to cryptography from a complexity theory perspective. Aspects of the wider cryptographic process that we will only pay passing reference to are covered well by other authors. Anderson [23] provides several examples of what can go wrong in real systems when the wider process is not carefully considered. Another good article by Anderson on this subject discusses why cryptosystems fail [22], as does the similar essay by Schneier on security pitfalls in cryptography [169]. There are many examples of the 'gap' that can arise between the theory and practice of cryptography, see for example Paterson and Yau [154]. With respect to implementation, McGraw [121] is an excellent introduction to secure software development and Ferguson, Schneier and Kohno [75] dedicate a chapter to implementation of cryptography.

The development of security models within which to evaluate the security of cryptographic algorithms is an active area of research. A good introduction to the most important formal provable security models for cryptographic algorithms can be found in Katz and Lindell [105]. Evaluation of security products, including those featuring cryptosystems, is a very difficult task. The most recognised framework for such evaluation is the Common Criteria [51].

3.5 Activities

1. The version of one-time pad that operates on alphabetic letters (associating A=0, B=1, etc.) is being used and the ciphertext DDGEXC is intercepted:

   (a) If the plaintext was BADGER then what was the key?
   (b) If the plaintext was WOMBAT then what was the key?
   (c) How many different plaintexts could have resulted in this ciphertext if the plaintext is not necessarily a word in English?
   (d) How many different plaintexts could have resulted in this ciphertext if the plaintext is a word in English?

2. Design a one-timed pad based on a Latin square that can be used to encrypt the seven plaintexts: BUY TODAY, BUY TOMORROW, BUY THE DAY AFTER TOMORROW, SELL TODAY, SELL TOMORROW, SELL THE DAY AFTER TOMORROW, DO NOTHING.

3. The following three squares have been suggested as potential one-time pads for protecting four plaintexts:

	P_1	P_2	P_3	P_4		P_1	P_2	P_3	P_4		P_1	P_2	P_3	P_4
K_1	2	1	4	3	K_1	2	1	4	3	K_1	2	1	4	3
K_2	4	3	1	4	K_2	4	3	1	2	K_2	4	3	1	2
K_3	1	2	3	1	K_3	1	2	3	4	K_3	3	2	4	1
K_4	3	4	2	2	K_4	3	4	2	1	K_4	1	4	2	3

(a) Which of these 'cryptosystems' is a one-time pad?

(b) For each of the 'cryptosystems' that is not a one-time pad, explain by means of at least one example why this is not the case.

4. Exhibit, by means of a table, a cryptosystem that satisfies the three properties of Section 3.1.3 but does not have perfect secrecy.

5. Explain why it is reasonable to claim that a one-time pad is 'immune' to an exhaustive key search.

6. The *unicity distance* of a cryptosystem is the approximate number of ciphertext letters that are required before, given a ciphertext of that length, there is likely to be only one meaningful plaintext and encryption key that could have been used to obtain that ciphertext. What is the unicity distance of a one-time pad?

7. Suppose that for convenience the users of a symmetric cryptosystem choose to remember each of their encryption keys as a trigram (three alphabetic characters, not necessarily carrying any meaning in English, for example ASF, ZZC, BED, etc.).

(a) What is the maximum size of the key space that they can use?

(b) How many bits long are the keys if they are represented in binary?

(c) Let your answer to part (b) be n. It would thus be tempting to describe this cryptosystem as using n-bit keys (because it does, if they are written in binary). Anyone hearing this would therefore be tempted to assume that the key space is of size 2^n. But what percentage of this number is the actual key space in this example?

(d) What important practical lesson have we just learnt?

8. What misuse of a one-time pad by the Soviets greatly assisted the NSA during the Venona project?

9. Determine how long (years, days, hours, seconds) it will take one million computers, each capable of processing one million operations per second, to:

(a) multiply two 1000-bit numbers together;

(b) perform a complete exhaustive search for a 128-bit key;

(c) find the correct key (on average) while performing an exhaustive search for a 128-bit key.

10. Suppose we want a cover time of 10 years for a particular plaintext. You see an advert for a encryption product from Cqure Systems that claims: *Our encryption product is so strong that even taking into account future improvements in computer power, a complete exhaustive search of the key space will take 40 years!* Do you think you should buy it?

11. Browsing the latest security products you see an advert for an encryption product from MassiveDataProtect that claims: *Our encryption product is based on one-time pad unbreakable encryption to provide 100% security for your data.* Do you think you should buy it?

12. Consider the following three possible strategies for designing modern encryption algorithms. These are to base the security of the algorithm on:

    (a) a well-studied computational problem that is not believed to be possible to solve based on computation that can be conducted in polynomial time;
    (b) a known, but poorly studied, computational problem that is not believed to be possible to solve based on computation that can be conducted in polynomial time;
    (c) making the description of the encryption algorithm so complex that it is not clear what problem it is necessary to solve in order to break it.

    Discuss the advantages and disadvantages of each of the above approaches, keeping in mind that most modern encryption algorithms are designed using the first strategy.

13. A much-quoted indicator of improvements in computer capability over time is Moore's Law.

    (a) After whom is this law named?
    (b) Precisely what did Moore originally 'predict'?
    (c) What other aspects of computer performance should be taken into account when attempting to predict future computer capability?
    (d) How do people regard Moore's Law as having stood the test of time and what is its own predicted future?

14. Suppose that you have been asked at work to recommend the strength of encryption needed to protect the contents of a database. Draw up a list of some of the questions that you think you will need to answer before you can meaningfully attempt to establish a notion of practical security for this application.

15. It is impossible to secure a cryptosystem against attacks that we do not know about. However, unforeseen attacks may well materialise, for example, through new improvements in cryptanalysis. What strategy might you adopt for trying to minimise your exposure to the risks of unforeseen attacks in terms of things you might do or procedures you might put in place?

Part II
The Cryptographic Toolkit

4 Symmetric Encryption

We have now completed our discussion of the fundamentals of cryptography. Recall from Chapter 1 that we interpreted cryptography as a toolkit and that cryptographic primitives were the basic tools in that toolkit. In this chapter we commence an investigation of the various primitives (tools) that cryptography provides for use as security mechanisms. We begin by studying symmetric encryption algorithms.

At the end of this chapter you should be able to:

- Recognise the basic differences between stream ciphers and block ciphers.
- Identify the types of application where stream ciphers and block ciphers are most appropriate.
- Appreciate the important role that DES has played in the history of modern cryptography.
- Identify the development history and basic design features of AES.
- Compare the properties of several different block cipher modes of operation.

4.1 Classification of symmetric encryption algorithms

In this introductory section we introduce an important classification of symmetric encryption algorithms. Note that:

- Encryption algorithms are the cryptographic primitives that most people associate with cryptography, since they are primarily designed for providing confidentiality. It is very important to recognise that encryption algorithms are just one of the many components of the cryptographic toolkit, albeit important ones.
- This chapter deals with one class of encryption algorithms, namely *symmetric* encryption algorithms. Public-key encryption is discussed in Chapter 5.
- While (symmetric) encryption algorithms are primarily designed as confidentiality mechanisms, they can be used, either directly or as building blocks, in

the provision of other security services. We will see examples of this in later chapters.

Since digital data consists of binary strings, we can think of a symmetric encryption algorithm as a process for converting one binary string into another binary string. A symmetric encryption algorithm must therefore:

1. take as input a sequence of plaintext bits;
2. perform a series of operations on these bits;
3. output a sequence of bits that forms the ciphertext.

We can rather crudely classify symmetric encryption algorithms as either being:

Stream ciphers, if the plaintext is processed one bit at a time. In other words, the algorithm selects one bit of plaintext, performs a series of operations on it, and then outputs one bit of ciphertext.

Block ciphers, if the plaintext is processed in *blocks* (groups) of bits at a time. In other words, the algorithm selects a block of plaintext bits, performs a series of operations on them, and then outputs a block of ciphertext bits. The number of bits that are processed each time is normally a fixed number that is referred to as the *block size* of the block cipher. For example, the symmetric encryption algorithms DES and AES have block sizes of 64 and 128, respectively.

This rather simplistic classification is illustrated in Figure 4.1, where the block cipher has an (artificially small) block size of 12. We say 'simplistic' because:

- Stream ciphers could be regarded as block ciphers with a block size of one.
- Some symmetric encryption algorithms that are generally referred to as stream ciphers actually process data in bytes, and hence could be regarded as block ciphers with a block size of eight.

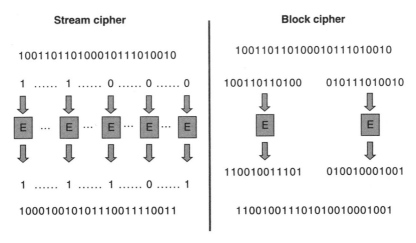

Figure 4.1. Stream ciphers versus block ciphers

107

- Block ciphers are often used in modes of operation that effectively convert them into stream ciphers. The block cipher is used to generate a keystream, which is then used to encrypt the data using a simple stream cipher. We will discuss this in more detail in Section 4.6.

Nonetheless, this classification is widely adopted because the properties of symmetric encryption algorithms with a 'small' block size vary significantly from those with a 'large' block size. It is fairly safe to assume that if a symmetric encryption algorithm is described as a block cipher then it is likely to have a block size of at least 64 bits.

Note that we could, at least in theory, also apply this classification to public-key encryption algorithms. The reason that we do not do this is because public-key encryption algorithms tend not to process binary data directly. Rather, they:

1. first convert the binary data into a different mathematical number representation, which typically requires several bits to be used for each plaintext 'number';
2. conduct the encryption processing on these 'numbers';
3. translate the resulting 'numbers' back into binary data.

We will see specific examples of this in Chapter 5. By operating in this manner, all public-key encryption algorithms are essentially block ciphers. For this reason, the terms *stream cipher* and *block cipher* are normally exclusively used with respect to symmetric encryption algorithms.

4.2 Stream ciphers

We have already come across one important stream cipher in Section 3.1.3, the Vernam Cipher. Recall that the Vernam Cipher is a one-time pad that operates on binary strings. We call it a stream cipher because it operates bitwise, encrypting each bit using the XOR operation.

We argued in Section 3.2.1 that the Vernam Cipher is not practical because it suffers from onerous key management issues. Stream ciphers can be thought of as attempts to 'simulate' the Vernam Cipher by using short keys to generate longer one-time keys. By doing so we can achieve some of the desirable properties of a one-time pad while mitigating some of the key management problems.

4.2.1 Model of a stream cipher

A model of a simple stream cipher is illustrated in Figure 4.2. Encryption and decryption in this simple stream cipher are both performed using the XOR operation, exactly as for the Vernam Cipher. The significant difference between

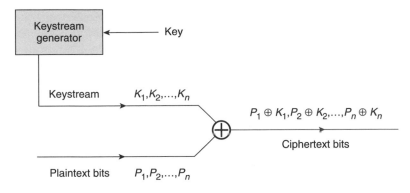

Figure 4.2. Model of a simple stream cipher

this simple stream cipher and the Vernam Cipher is that, rather than using a sequence of randomly generated key bits that is as long as the plaintext, a stream cipher:

1. Uses a key that is normally much shorter than the length of the plaintext (a typical key length would be 128 bits).
2. Converts this (short) key into a continuous stream of bits known as the *keystream* by means of a *keystream generator*. The keystream generator, which is the main 'engine' of the stream cipher, converts the short key into continuous keystream by means of a carefully designed mathematical process.

In order to decrypt the resulting ciphertext, the receiver needs to be in possession of:

- the same short key; and
- the same keystream generator.

The keystream generator is part of the stream cipher specification. If two parties agree on which stream cipher to use then they are, by default, agreeing on which keystream generator to use. In fact, technically, the encryption of the plaintext in this simple stream cipher is just the XOR of the plaintext with the keystream, and decryption is just the XOR of the ciphertext with the keystream. Thus the real work in designing a good stream cipher goes into designing the keystream generator. For this reason, when we refer to a particular *stream cipher* we tend to really be referring to the design of a particular keystream generator. Note that:

- Keystream generators are examples of *deterministic generators* (see Section 8.1.4). Keystream generators produce output that appears to be randomly generated, but is actually not randomly generated. We often term this *pseudorandom* (literally, 'fake random').
- The Vernam Cipher can be thought of as a stream cipher whose keystream is truly randomly generated (see Section 8.1.3).

- We referred to the stream cipher in Figure 4.2 as *simple* because many modern stream ciphers are slightly more complicated. For example, some stream ciphers use several different keystream generators and then combine their keystreams in a more complex way than just simple XOR. However they are never designed so differently from this simple model that the basic properties of our simple stream cipher are lost, so the simple model will suffice for our discussion.

4.2.2 Key management of stream ciphers

We have suggested that stream ciphers are 'practical' simulations of the Vernam Cipher. As evidence in support of this claim, recall the three key management problems that we identified in Section 3.2.1 concerning the use of a one-time pad in practice.

Length of the key. In a one-time pad the key has to be as long as the plaintext. Although the keystream for a stream cipher needs to be as long as the plaintext, the actual key that is used to generate it (and which must be distributed and stored) is much shorter.

Random generation of the key. In a one-time pad the key has to be truly randomly generated, which involves costly generation techniques. The keystream in a stream cipher is pseudorandom and thus is much cheaper to generate.

One-time use. We need to be careful here. A keystream generator is a deterministic process in the sense that every time the same key is input into the keystream generator, it will result in the same keystream being output. Thus if we reuse a stream cipher key to produce the same keystream and then encrypt two plaintexts using the same portion of keystream then, just as for a one-time pad, the 'difference' between the two ciphertexts will tell us the difference between the two corresponding plaintexts (see Section 3.1.3). This situation can be avoided either by:

- using the stream cipher keys only once;
- never reusing the same portion of keystream;
- instead of using the initial key, a unique key could be derived from the initial key each time the stream cipher is used; for example, we could incorporate some time-variant data (we will discuss key derivation in Section 10.3.2);
- making the keystream itself depend on some time-variant data (we will see several examples of this in Section 4.6).
- making the method of combining the plaintext with the keystream more complex.

Key management for stream ciphers, just as for any symmetric cryptographic primitives, is thus all about managing relatively short symmetric keys. This is not an easy task, but it is generally regarded as being an easier task than managing one-time pad keys.

4.2.3 The impact of errors

One of the aspects that differs between stream and block ciphers is the impact of errors. It is thus worth first discussing the different types of error that could occur in a communication system.

Transmission errors are errors that occur in the communication channel. A 1-bit transmission error occurs if a 0 becomes a 1, or a 1 becomes a 0, somewhere on the communication channel. This is sometimes referred to as a *bit-flip*.

Transmission losses occur when bits get lost in the communication channel. A 1-bit transmission loss occurs if one bit of data is lost in the communication channel, but both the previous and the subsequent bits are correctly received.

Computational errors are errors that occur somewhere during a (cryptographic) computation. A 1-bit computational error occurs if the output of a cryptographic computation results in an incorrect 1 instead of a correct 0, or an incorrect 0 instead of a correct 1.

Transmission errors and losses are probably the most commonly encountered of these errors. Indeed, in environments where data is sent over potentially noisy or unreliable channels, both of these errors may be expected.

All of these types of error are potentially bad news for a cryptosystem. However, cryptosystems differ in the extent to which these errors cause problems. We say that *error propagation* has occurred if a number of errors in the ciphertext (regardless of error type) result in a greater number of errors in the resulting plaintext. In the simplest case of a 1-bit error in the ciphertext, error propagation occurs if this has an impact of more than one erroneous bit in the resulting plaintext.

In general, error propagation is regarded as a bad thing since it represents an escalation of the number of errors when we convert the damaged ciphertext into plaintext. However, there are situations where this impact could have positive benefits. For example, suppose encryption is being used to protect some financial data but no additional data integrity mechanisms are being used. If there is no error propagation then a 1-bit error in the ciphertext will probably result in a 1-bit error in the plaintext. This might not be easily noticeable to the receiver but it could have massive impact on the meaning of the plaintext (for example, some crucial transaction figure might be altered on a balance sheet). If error propagation occurs then the plaintext errors are much more likely to be noticed (for example, the number on the balance sheet is significantly out of expected range). Note, however, that such reliance on error propagation in order to provide a very weak notion of data integrity is extremely unadvisable. It would be much safer to use a proper data integrity mechanism rather than rely on error propagation to provide this very weak notion of data integrity. We will discuss suitable mechanisms in Chapter 6.

Observe that error propagation has nothing to do with preventing errors occurring in the first place. Neither is error propagation anything to do with correcting errors when they do occur. This requires the use of special error-correcting codes, which are not regarded as cryptographic primitives (see Section 1.4.4).

4.2.4 Properties of stream ciphers

Stream ciphers have a number of attractive properties that make them the favoured encryption mechanism in a number of important applications:

No error propagation. Since stream ciphers encrypt the plaintext bit by bit, a 1-bit transmission error will only result in a 1-bit error in the plaintext. For this reason, stream ciphers are popular in communications applications, especially where the communication channel is of poor quality and errors are inevitable. For example, stream ciphers are often used in the protection of mobile communications (see Section 12.3). Stream ciphers are also used to protect private mobile radio systems, such as those used by emergency services and taxi operators.

Speed. The simple encryption process (based on XOR) results in stream ciphers being extremely fast to operate, which makes them very attractive for applications that require real-time encryption of data, which is again the case in mobile telecommunications. Their simplicity also makes stream ciphers relatively straightforward to implement.

On-the-fly encryption. Bitwise encryption means that large chunks of plaintext do not sit around in registers before being encrypted. This makes stream ciphers attractive to applications such as secure terminals, where individual keystrokes should be protected immediately on entry.

The main problem with stream ciphers is:

Need for synchronisation: Since stream ciphers process data bitwise, it is vital that the sender and receiver keep their keystream in perfect synchronisation. The consequences of a 1-bit transmission loss are potentially disastrous, since subsequent decryptions will be conducted using the wrong bits of the keystream. Procedures are thus required to allow periodic resynchronisation of the keystream. There are many different ways in which this could be done. One method is to regularly restart the keystream using a fresh key. This could either be done after a fixed period of time, or after the sending of a special resynchronisation sequence. Some modern stream ciphers are designed to have special resynchronisation properties, but we will not discuss these here.

As we will see in Section 4.6, block ciphers are often deployed in modes of operation that essentially convert them into stream ciphers in order to benefit from some of the above properties.

4.2.5 Examples of stream ciphers

Despite their attractive properties, individual stream ciphers have never achieved the 'fame' and ubiquitous implementation of block ciphers such as DES and AES. In some ways this is surprising, but there are two possible reasons why things have turned out this way:

Proprietary designs. There are many proprietary stream cipher algorithms. Indeed, the historical trend has been very loosely towards proprietary stream ciphers and publicly known block ciphers, although there are many exceptions to this. The reasons for this trend are due to many factors, including:

- adoption of stream ciphers in closed networking environments or commercial arenas where compatibility issues are easily addressed;
- adoption of stream ciphers in high-security applications where internal cryptographic design expertise is justifiable and available.

Lower versatility. Viewed as general components within the cryptographic toolkit, stream ciphers could be argued to be less useful and more specialised than block ciphers. Stream ciphers are normally only ever used for encryption. Block ciphers can be used in the design of other cryptographic primitives such as hash functions and MACs. Significantly, as we will see in Section 4.6, block ciphers can be used as keystream generators, essentially turning them into stream ciphers. This latter reason may well be the most powerful explanation, since many applications actually implement a stream cipher although the algorithm used to do so is a block cipher!

Having said that, there are a number of stream ciphers that have become very well known, either due to their widespread use or due to their adoption by a ubiquitous application. Examples include:

RC4: This is a simple, fast stream cipher with a relatively low level of security. It is probably the most widely implemented stream cipher in software and is widely supported by the likes of SSL/TLS (see Section 12.1), WEP (see Section 12.2) and Microsoft Office.
A5/1: One of the stream cipher algorithms used in GSM to secure the communication channel over the air from a mobile phone to the nearest base station.
E0: The stream cipher algorithm used to encrypt Bluetooth communications.

It is interesting to note that both RC4 (designed by Ron Rivest and a registered trademark of RSA Data Security) and A5/1 (designed by the SAGE group of the European Telecommunications Standards Institute) were both originally proprietary designs, both of which have become publicly known over time (see Section 1.5.3).

4.3 Block ciphers

We now discuss block ciphers, which operate on blocks of plaintext bits. Block ciphers are not better or worse than stream ciphers, they are just different. Block ciphers are arguably one of the most versatile of all cryptographic primitives. By the end of our study of the cryptographic toolkit, we will have seen them used for many more purposes than the provision of confidentiality.

4.3.1 Model of a block cipher

The basic model of a block cipher is depicted in Figure 4.3. A block cipher takes as input a plaintext block and a key, and outputs a ciphertext block. Normally the block size is fixed, and the block of ciphertext produced by the block cipher is usually the same length as the plaintext block.

The block size is not as critical to the security of a block cipher as the length of the key, but there are some security issues relating directly to the block size:

- If the block size is too short then the number of different plaintext blocks that can ever be encrypted may be uncomfortably small (if the block size is m then there is a maximum of 2^m such plaintext blocks). If an attacker is able to discover the plaintext blocks corresponding to some previously sent ciphertext blocks then, as we discussed in Section 1.6.5, it is possible that an attacker could launch a type of dictionary attack by building up a dictionary of plaintext/ciphertext pairs sent using that encryption key. A larger block size makes this attack harder because the dictionary needs to be larger.
- If the block size is too large then the block cipher becomes inefficient to operate, particularly for short plaintexts that are shorter than the block size. Such plaintexts will need to be padded before being encrypted (see Section 4.3.2).
- It is preferable that the block size is a multiple of 8 (or even better 16, 32 or 64) for implementation purposes, since these are the most common word lengths (the basic atomic units of information used by modern computer processors).

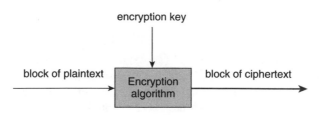

Figure 4.3. Model of a block cipher

114

Choosing a block size thus involves a compromise between security and efficiency. DES has a block size of 64. Modern block cipher algorithms such as AES tend to have a block size of 128.

4.3.2 Properties of block ciphers

Unlike stream ciphers, block ciphers tend not to be associated with generic properties. This is because block ciphers vary so much in their technical design. However, as a general rule, block ciphers are associated with:

Versatility. Block ciphers are not just used for encryption, but also as components of other cryptographic primitives such as MACs and hash functions.

Compatibility. Well-respected block ciphers such as AES are the most widely implemented and used encryption algorithms, resulting in them becoming default choices of encryption algorithm for many applications. This aids compatibility.

Adaptability. Block ciphers can be implemented in different modes of operation (see Section 4.6) in order to achieve different properties.

Two aspects of block ciphers that may not always be desirable are:

Error propagation. This is inevitable if a block cipher is used in the simple manner depicted in Figure 4.3. For example, a 1-bit transmission error only changes one bit of a ciphertext block, but the result of decrypting this erroneous ciphertext block will be a plaintext block with, on average, half of its bits incorrect. This is because:

1. A good block cipher should have the property that two ciphertext blocks that differ in just one bit (or, indeed, any number of bits) should have corresponding plaintext blocks that have no apparent relationship (they are *independent* of one another). To understand why, recall that our standard assumptions in Section 1.5.1 assume that an attacker knows plaintext/ciphertext pairs. If an attacker sees a new ciphertext block that differs from a ciphertext block that they already know the corresponding plaintext block for (even if this new ciphertext block differs only in one bit) then the attacker should not be able to predict any bits of the new plaintext block. If they could, then the block cipher would have to be regarded as insecure.

2. If two plaintext blocks P_1 and P_2 have no apparent relationship then this means that for every bit in P_1, the corresponding bit in P_2 should be 'unpredictable'. This means that there is a half chance that the corresponding bit in P_2 is different, and a half chance that it is the same. (If it was always different then it would be very predictable!) Thus, on average, P_1 and P_2 will have half of their bits in common, and these coinciding bits happen 'by chance'. Importantly, however, although an attacker can expect that, on average, half

of the bits coincide, they will not be able to predict exactly *which* bits will be the same.

Need for padding. Block ciphers operate on fixed block sizes (such as 128 bits) but the length of most plaintexts is not a multiple of the block size. For example, a 400-bit plaintext fills three 128-bit blocks but then has

$$400 - (3 \times 128) = 400 - 384 = 16$$

bits left over. The last group of bits needs to be 'filled out' with redundant information so that the length of the final plaintext is a multiple of the block size. In our example, the remaining 16 bits need to have 112 redundant bits added to them to make up a full block. The process of filling up the last block is referred to as *padding*. This might not seem to be a big deal, but there are a couple of issues that arise concerning padding:

1. Padding introduces a degree of inefficiency. For example, if we only want to send a plaintext of one ASCII character (8 bits) then using AES in the manner of Figure 4.3 would require a significant message expansion from 8 bits to 128 bits.
2. Padding can introduce insecurity into a cryptosystem. There have been examples in the past of padding schemes being exploited to break cryptosystems. For this reason padding should only be introduced by following a recognised *padding scheme*. These typically involve introducing fixed bit patterns or encoding information such as the length of the plaintext into the padded bits.

4.3.3 Block cipher algorithms

In contrast to stream ciphers, there are dozens of publicly known block ciphers that are available for use. The choice can seem daunting. However the ground rules for selecting a publicly known encryption algorithm that we outlined in Section 1.5.4 very much apply here. While there are many publicly known block cipher algorithms, there are relatively few that can be classified according to the terminology of Section 1.5.4 as either *respected* or *default*. Some examples of prominent block ciphers are:

AES: A default block cipher based on the encryption algorithm *Rijndael* that won the AES design competition. We discuss AES in greater detail in Section 4.5.
DES: The default block cipher of the 1980s and 1990s, but now a 'broken' block cipher, due primarily to its small key size. The two variants based on repeated DES applications commonly known as *Triple DES* are still respected block ciphers, although there are now faster block ciphers available. We discuss DES and Triple DES in greater detail in Section 4.4.
IDEA: A respected block cipher with a block size of 64 and a key size of 128, dating from 1991. IDEA has been supported by a number of applications, including

early versions of PGP, but its adoption has been restricted, partly due to patent issues.

Serpent: A respected block cipher with a block size of 128 bits and key lengths of 128, 192 or 256, which was an AES competition finalist. The designers of Serpent are generally regarded as having made slightly different tradeoffs between security and efficiency than AES, opting for a slower, but some suggest more secure, design.

Twofish: This respected block cipher with a block size of 128 and a variable key length was also one of the AES finalists. It is based on the earlier block cipher *Blowfish*, which has a block size of 64.

There are several different approaches to designing block ciphers. The next two sections will not just look at two of the most influential modern block ciphers, but will also provide a very high level illustration of two different block cipher design approaches.

4.4 The Data Encryption Standard

The most well-known, well-studied, and well-used block cipher proposed to date is the *Data Encryption Standard*, better known simply as DES. It is important to be familiar with DES because of its historical importance and influence on modern cryptography. It is also based on an interesting and influential design concept. Although DES is no longer a recommended block cipher, important variants on the original proposal are still in widespread use, as we will discuss in Section 4.4.4.

4.4.1 Feistel Cipher

DES is based on what is known as a *Feistel Cipher*. Rather than being a specific cipher, a Feistel Cipher is a design blueprint from which many different block ciphers could be derived. DES is just one example of a Feistel Cipher, but by far the most famous one.

ENCRYPTION USING A FEISTEL CIPHER

A pictorial representation of a Feistel Cipher is shown in Figure 4.4. We describe this algorithm in terms of a block size of 64 bits, although there is no need for a Feistel Cipher to have a 64-bit block size. Encryption using a Feistel Cipher consists of the following steps:

1. Split the 64 bits of plaintext into the left 32 bits L_0 and the right 32 bits R_0.
2. Apply a carefully designed mathematical function f that takes as input the key K and R_0, and computes the output $f(R_0, K)$.
3. XOR the output of the mathematical function with L_0, to compute a new 32-bit sequence $X = L_0 \oplus f(R_0, K)$.

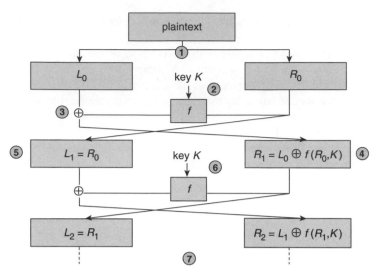

Figure 4.4. A Feistel Cipher

4. Let the new 'right 32 bits' R_1 be X.
5. Let the new 'left 32 bits' L_1 be the previous 'right 32 bits' R_0.
6. Repeat the process from step 2 to step 5, except using R_1 instead of R_0, and L_1 instead of L_0. This sequence of steps (step 2 to step 5) is known as a *round* of the block cipher. The function f used is often referred to as the *round function*.
7. Repeat step 6 for as many rounds as specified by the algorithm design. Once the last round (round number m) is completed then the last 'left 32 bits' L_m are joined with the last 'right 32 bits' R_m to form the 64 bits of the ciphertext, which is formed by concatenating R_m and L_m (in that order).

CHOOSING THE ROUND FUNCTION

Although it might look quite complicated at first, the algorithmic steps involved in encrypting a plaintext block using a Feistel Cipher are actually very straightforward and easy to implement (we have just specified the algorithm, which could easily now be converted into a computer programme). The difficult part of designing a Feistel Cipher is the choice of the round function f. This function needs to have several important properties that are beyond the scope of our discussion. Indeed, most of the design work of any Feistel Cipher, such as DES, concerns the choice of the round function.

DECRYPTION USING A FEISTEL CIPHER

The cleverness of the Feistel Cipher design concept only becomes clear when we consider decryption. It turns out that decryption is almost the same as encryption and that this holds regardless of the choice of the round function f. Instead of starting with 64 bits of plaintext, we input 64 bits of ciphertext into the start of the Feistel Cipher algorithm and then process it in exactly the same way as described in Figure 4.4. The end result will be the correct 64 bits of plaintext. This is more than just a convenience, since it greatly assists implementation of a Feistel Cipher because almost the same algorithm can be used for both encryption and decryption. In particular, the same piece of hardware can be used for both processes.

The reason that we say *almost* the same is that in real instances of the Feistel Cipher, such as DES, instead of using the whole encryption key during each round, a round-dependent key (often referred to as a *subkey*) is derived from the encryption key. This means that each round uses a different key, although all these subkeys are related to the original key. In the case of decryption, the only difference is that these subkeys must be used in the reverse order to encryption.

Note that the final swapping of L_m and R_m in step 7 of the Feistel Cipher is crucial. If we did not swap these around at the end of step 7 then the resulting ciphertext could not be decrypted using the same algorithm.

NUMBER OF ROUNDS

The number of rounds used in a Feistel Cipher is part of the design specification of a particular instance of the Feistel Cipher. DES, for example, uses 16 rounds. The design principle regarding the number of rounds is fairly straightforward. The more rounds there are, the more secure the resulting block cipher generally becomes. This is intuitive, since the plaintext becomes 'more scrambled' and an exhaustive key search takes slightly longer. However, the more rounds there are, the more inefficient the resulting encryption (and decryption) process becomes. This design decision once again concerns an efficiency–security tradeoff.

4.4.2 Specification of DES

DES is an example of a Feistel Cipher. It has a 64-bit block size, a 64-bit key length and uses 16 rounds. Note that DES has an effective key length of 56 bits, since 8 of the 64 bits of the key are not used by the encryption algorithm (they are check bits). Knowing that DES is based on the Feistel Cipher blueprint, all that is required to fully specify DES is:

- the round function, which is based on taking groups of input bits and replacing (*substituting*) them according to some rules based on tables known as *S-boxes*;
- the *key schedule*, which identifies which bits of the key are used to form the subkeys for any given round;
- any additional processing steps; for example, DES conducts an *initial permutation* of all the input bits before the first encryption round begins, and then performs the inverse of this permutation to all the output bits immediately after the last encryption round has been completed.

The details of the DES specification are technical and need not concern us here. DES is a publicly known block cipher, so the details are widely available.

4.4.3 Brief history of DES

DES is an extremely important block cipher, not just because variants of it are still heavily in use today, but also because it has an interesting and significant history, which we will only briefly cover here. This discussion is relevant because many of the issues concerned with the development of DES could arise again in the future.

MILESTONES IN THE HISTORY OF DES

In 1973, the National Bureau of Standards (NBS) in the United States published a call for proposals for an encryption algorithm standard. This was a historic moment, as prior to this call cryptography had been something of a 'black art' during the 20th century, practised mainly by military and national security organisations. The NBS recognised the need for a cryptographic algorithm to protect the increasingly commercial use of computer communications.

Initially there were no replies but, after issuing a second call in 1974, IBM was encouraged to submit an encryption algorithm that they had been developing. The submission of this algorithm and subsequent discussion with the National Security Agency (NSA) resulted in an encryption algorithm being published for public comment in 1975. After a due consultation process, this algorithm was adopted as a federal standard in 1976 and published as DES in 1977.

The use of DES became mandatory for Federal Agencies in 1977 and, after adoption in the banking standard ANSI X3.92, found widespread use throughout the international financial industry. Indeed, DES became the de facto international standard encryption algorithm, a status which it held until the establishment of AES. Although DES was predicted to have a 15-year lifespan, the NSA removed its endorsement of DES in 1988. However, the NBS reaffirmed the use of DES in the same year, largely to appease the financial industry, which by then relied heavily upon it.

The NBS, now known as the National Institute of Standards and Technology (NIST), finally acknowledged that DES no longer offered adequate cryptographic protection by issuing a call for a new algorithm in 1998. This process resulted in the AES, which we will discuss in Section 4.5.

EARLY DESIGN CRITICISMS

DES has proved to be a very well designed block cipher, since to date there have been no significant cryptanalytic attacks on DES other than exhaustive key search. There have been some academic breaks, involving techniques known as *differential* and *linear cryptanalysis*, but these attacks have not threatened DES in practice.

120

DES has, however, been subjected to several different design criticisms over the years:

Secret design criteria. Although the full description of DES, including the round function and key schedule, was published, their design criteria (in other words, *why* they were chosen to be that way) were not. This resulted in some people becoming suspicious that 'trapdoors' might exist, whereby the designers could easily subvert a DES encryption through knowledge of some secret technique. These fears appear to have been unfounded. In particular, the public discovery of differential cryptanalysis in the 1990s revealed that the design of DES seems to protect against this type of cryptanalytic attack. Thus, intriguingly, the designers of DES must have known about this technique long before its public discovery.

Potentially undesirable keys. It was pointed out that certain DES keys are not suitable for use. For example, some keys are described as 'weak' because encryption and decryption using these keys has the same effect. It is debatable whether this is actually a problem. In any case, there are only a few such keys and their use can easily be avoided.

Inadequate key length. The main criticism of DES, even in 1975, was that the effective key length of 56 bits was not adequate. Indeed, there were (never substantiated) accusations that the NSA had influenced the selection of a relatively small effective key length in order to keep exhaustive search for a DES key within their capabilities. Whether these claims were true may never be known. What is true is that 56 bits is inadequate protection today for most applications.

DES KEY SEARCHES

The security analysis of DES, right from the outset, has mainly focussed on the difficulty of exhaustively searching for a DES key. To place the subsequent discussion in some perspective, recall our computation of real attack times from Section 3.2.3. Suppose that we have a machine consisting of one million processors, each of which can test one million keys per second. How long is it likely to take before we find a DES key during an exhaustive key search?

DES effectively has a 56-bit key. A 56-bit key requires 2^{56} tests in order to search the key space completely. Since 2^{56} is approximately equal to 7.2×10^{16}, and since we are able to test $10^6 \times 10^6 = 10^{12}$ keys every second, a complete search will take:

$$\frac{7.2 \times 10^{16}}{10^{12}} = 7.2 \times 10^4 \text{ seconds,}$$

in other words about 20 hours. This means that we will probably find the correct key in about half that time, or about 10 hours (see Section 1.6.4).

These are straightforward mathematical facts. The real issue is how likely it is that an attacker has access to a machine this powerful in order to exhaustively search for a DES key. The historical debate about security of DES has essentially

Table 4.1: DES key search efforts

Year	Source	Implemented?	Cost in US$	Search time
1977	Diffie & Hellman	No	20 million	12 hours
1993	Wiener	No	10.5 million	21 minutes
1993	Wiener	No	1.5 million	3.5 hours
1993	Wiener	No	600,000	35 hours
1997	Internet	Yes	Unknown	140 days
1998	EFF	Yes	210,000	56 hours
2007	COPACOBANA	Yes	10,000	6.4 days

been a debate about the potential availability and cost of powerful computing devices. Some milestones in this debate, which are summarised in Table 4.1, are:

1977: Partly in response to their concerns over the key length of DES, Whit Diffie and Martin Hellman estimated that a search machine could be built for $20 million dollars, a sum that they did not rule out being within the capabilities of government security agencies such as the NSA. It is probably fair to say that in 1977 nobody really believed that anyone would invest this kind of money to build such a machine. It is also doubtful whether such a machine could practically have been built at that time.

1993: Mike Wiener proposed the figures in Table 4.1 for the development of a specified DES key search machine. The development of his machine cost a further $500,000. There was no evidence that anyone had actually built such a machine. These figures only worried a few people but it was acknowledged that such a machine was beginning, at least conceptually, to become feasible to build.

1997: In an extraordinary effort, a DES key was found using a massive group effort that harnessed parallel processing of the idle time of over 10 000 computers worldwide. At its peak, this effort processed 7000 million keys per second. (Note that this is significantly slower than our theoretical example at the start of this discussion!) As a cryptographic contribution this result was not surprising, since at these speeds of processing the search time was within expected bounds. What was extraordinary was the management feat of coordinating so many computers and successfully running them in this type of cooperative manner. What was also significant was that people had been motivated to conduct this search in the first place.

1998: The real breakthrough came when the Electronic Frontier Foundation (EFF), motivated by a desire to influence US government cryptography policy, built a piece of hardware called *Deep Crack* in order to search for a DES key. The machine cost $80,000 to design and $130,000 to manufacture. It processed just under 10^{11} keys per second, making it ten times slower than our theoretical machine. The design details were fully published, but the actual machine was not made available for public use. It did succeed, however, in convincing most people that DES was no longer secure enough for most applications.

2007: An indication of how insecure DES is for modern use comes from the ability to build powerful DES crackers at very little cost. The significance of dedicated hardware that became available was not so much the speed but the much reduced cost. For example, in 2007, the hardware device COPACOBANA was made available for a cost less than $10,000 and could search for a DES key in less than one week.

It is now well understood that anyone determined enough can exhaustively search for a DES key. Although DES is still used in a number of legacy applications, we can expect its use to decline steadily over time. Note that there is nothing wrong with using DES for applications with very short cover times, since the algorithm itself has not been attacked by anything other than theoretical (academic) attacks. In most modern applications, however, DES has largely been replaced by the likes of Triple DES and AES.

4.4.4 Triple DES

The progress on exhaustive key searches against DES in the 1990s began to cause disquiet amongst mainstream users of DES, such as those in the financial sector, especially as it takes an enormous amount of time and money to change encryption algorithms that are widely adopted and embedded in large security architectures.

The pragmatic response was not to abandon the use of DES completely, but to change the way in which DES is used. This resulted in Triple DES (sometimes known as 3DES). Confusingly, there are two variants of Triple DES known as *3-key Triple DES* (3TDES) and *2-key Triple DES* (2TDES). We will describe these separately.

3-KEY TRIPLE DES

The variant of Triple DES known as 3TDES is depicted in Figure 4.5.

Before using 3TDES we first generate and distribute a 3TDES key K, which consists of three different DES keys K_1, K_2 and K_3. This means that the actual 3TDES key has length $3 \times 56 = 168$ bits. To encrypt a 64-bit plaintext using 3TDES:

1. first encrypt the plaintext using single DES with key K_1;
2. now *decrypt* the result of step 1 using single DES with key K_2;
3. finally, encrypt the result of step 2 using single DES with key K_3; the result of this encryption is the ciphertext.

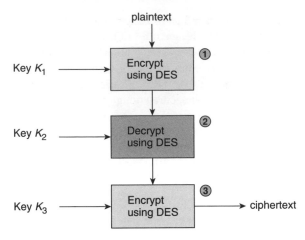

Figure 4.5. Encryption using 3TDES

Decryption of a 3TDES ciphertext consists of the reverse process. In other words, we first decrypt using K_3, then *encrypt* with K_2, and finally decrypt with K_1.

At first encounter 3TDES may seem rather confusing because the second encryption step is actually a single DES *decryption*. We could replace this with a single DES encryption, thus making 3TDES a triple encryption process using single DES, however, this is not preferred for implementation reasons. By structuring Triple DES as an encrypt–decrypt–encrypt process, it is possible to use a 3TDES (hardware) implementation for single DES by setting K_1, K_2 and K_3 to be the same value. This provides backwards compatibility, since an organisation can convert to 3TDES while continuing to be able to secure links to other organisations that are still using legacy systems based on single DES.

2-KEY TRIPLE DES

The variant of Triple DES known as 2TDES is identical to 3TDES except that K_3 is replaced by K_1. In other words we encrypt with K_1, then decrypt with K_2, and then encrypt with K_1 again. Hence 2TDES has a key length of 112 bits. Note that although both the first and third steps involve encrypting with K_1, the results in each case are different since the 'plaintexts' on which the encryption operation is conducted are different.

TRIPLE DES IN PRACTICE

Triple DES had a brief spell of being the 'default' global encryption algorithm, corresponding to the period between the practical evolution of DES key searches and the adoption of AES.

The lack of attacks on the underlying DES mechanism carry through to Triple DES so, as an encryption algorithm, Triple DES is highly regarded. Note, however, that the key lengths of the two versions of Triple DES are slightly deceiving. Since the encryption is conducted as three separate processes, there are several techniques for exploiting this. A *meet-in-the-middle attack* involves storing tables of single encryptions and decryptions and looking for appropriate matches that might indicate which single DES keys have been used as part of the Triple DES key. The existence of this type of attack against double encryption of DES (*Double DES*) explains why this technique for strengthening DES was not adopted.

The best meet-in-the-middle attack reduces the *effective security* of 3TDES to about 112 bits. By this we mean that, for example, the true security of 3TDES is roughly equivalent to an exhaustive key search for a 112-bit key. A different attack reduces the effective security of 2TDES to about 80 bits. Thus although both 3TDES and 2TDES are significantly more secure than single DES, their security is less than the key lengths suggest. The effective security also means that both variants of Triple DES are significantly less secure than AES. Nonetheless, 3TDES has sufficient effective security to be suitable for current applications.

Encryption using Triple DES is clearly a much slower process than encryption using single DES. One of the design specifications for AES, as we will discuss shortly, was that AES should be faster than Triple DES. In fact AES is reported to be about six times faster than Triple DES in software.

Thus, unless there are legacy reasons for using Triple DES (and legacy reasons can be very valid reasons), the case for using Triple DES ahead of AES is not strong, since AES provides better security and performance. However, there is no doubt that Triple DES will remain an important encryption technique for many years to come, since it underpins the security of many important applications such as the EMV standards for supporting electronic payments (see Section 12.4).

4.5 The Advanced Encryption Standard

The symmetric encryption algorithm that is now most likely to be encountered in a new application is the *Advanced Encryption Standard* or AES. In this section we provide a brief introduction to AES.

4.5.1 Development of AES

In 1998, NIST issued a call for proposals for a new block cipher standard to be referred to as the AES. The three main requirements for candidate algorithms proposed by NIST were:

1. the block size should be 128 bits;
2. the block cipher should be designed to offer variable key lengths of 128, 192 and 256 bits, in order to allow for future developments in exhaustive key

search efforts; these key lengths are all currently well beyond the capabilities of state-of-the-art exhaustive key search techniques;

3. the block cipher had to operate at a faster speed than Triple DES across a range of different computing platforms.

In contrast to the development of DES, it was specified that the selection process would be by an open public 'competition' and that the chosen algorithm and design details must be made freely available. There are probably two reasons why such a decision was made:

Confidence: to allay the suspicions that hung over the development process for DES and thus to maximise public confidence in, and international adoption of, the resulting encryption standard;

Expertise: to benefit from the dramatic increase in public expertise in cryptology that had taken place between the 1970s and the 1990s by:

- encouraging the best cryptographic designers to take part;
- obtaining the widest scrutiny of the candidate algorithms.

The result of this call was 15 candidate proposals, which were quickly reduced to 11. In 1999, after a public consultation process, this was reduced to five candidates. Finally in 2000, the winning algorithm *Rijndael* was selected. Rijndael was designed by two Belgian cryptographers, Joan Daemen and Vincent Rijmen, who at that time were working for a Belgian card payment organisation and a Belgian university, respectively. While Rijndael was selected on merit, and after significant scrutiny by international experts, it did no harm to the confidence in the process that the final selection was not from the US and was designed by a partnership between the commercial and academic sectors. The principal reasons for Rijndael's final selection were due to performance issues and not security issues. The four other finalists in the AES process, MARS, RC6, Serpent and Twofish, are also highly regarded.

Federal Information Processing Standard FIPS 197, the Advanced Encryption Standard, was published in 2001 and contained a slightly modified version of Rijndael. This standard specifies AES as a symmetric encryption algorithm that may be used by US Government organisations (and others) to protect sensitive information.

4.5.2 Design of AES

Unlike DES, AES is not designed to an explicit blueprint such as the Feistel Cipher. However, it is based on a design principle often referred to as a *substitution-permutation network*. This simply means that the design is based on a series of linked operations, some of which involve replacing inputs by specific outputs (*substitutions*) and others involve shuffling bits around (*permutations*). A detailed specification of AES is beyond our scope, however, we will provide at least a conceptual overview of the encryption process.

AES ENCRYPTION

It is worth noting that AES performs all its computations on bytes rather than bits. Hence AES first interprets the 128 bits of a plaintext block as 16 bytes. AES then computes a number of rounds. Similarly to DES, each of these rounds uses a different 128-bit round key, which is calculated from the original AES key and the details of which can be found in the AES key schedule (part of the AES algorithm that we will not discuss further). Unlike DES, the number of rounds is variable, depending on the length of the AES key. AES employs 10 rounds for 128-bit keys, 12 rounds for 192-bit keys and 14 rounds for 256-bit keys.

One round of AES is depicted in Figure 4.6. Each round takes 16 bytes of input and produces 16 bytes of output by applying the following four processes:

Byte substitution: The 16 input bytes are substituted by looking up a fixed table (S box) whose details form part of the algorithm. The 16 new bytes that result are arranged in a square consisting of four rows and four columns.

Shift rows: Each of the four rows of the square resulting from the byte substitution process is shifted to the left. Any entries that 'drop off' are then re-inserted on the right. More precisely, the first row is left alone, the second row is shifted one (byte) position to the left, the third row is shifted two positions to the left and the fourth row is shifted three positions to the left. The result is a new square consisting of the same 16 bytes, with the property that all the entries that used to be in one column have been moved so that they now lie in different columns.

Mix columns: Each column of four bytes is now transformed using a special mathematical function, the details of which form part of the algorithm. This function takes as input the four bytes of one column and outputs four completely new bytes, which replace the original column. The result is another new square consisting of 16 new bytes.

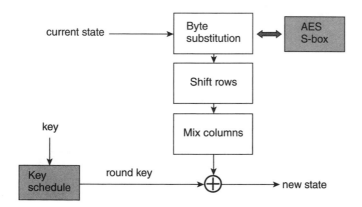

Figure 4.6. One AES encryption round

127

Add round key: The 16 bytes of the square resulting from the mix-columns process are now considered as 128 bits and are XORed to the 128 bits of the round key. If this is the last round then the output is the ciphertext. Otherwise, the resulting 128 bits are interpreted as 16 bytes and we begin another round, commencing with a new byte substitution process.

The most important issue to note is that the whole AES encryption process is based on a series of table lookups and XOR operations, which are very fast operations to perform on a computer. It is this speed of processing on a number of different computing platforms that gave the original Rijndael algorithm the edge during the AES selection process.

AES DECRYPTION

Decryption of an AES ciphertext simply consists of conducting the encryption process in the reverse order. In particular:

- each round consists of the four processes conducted in the order: *add round key, mix columns, shift rows, byte substitution*;
- each process 'reverses' the corresponding encryption process: for example, *add round key* involves XORing the ciphertext with the appropriate round key, while *mix columns* involves applying the inverse of the function used during encryption;
- the round keys are applied in the opposite order to encryption;

Hence, unlike for a Feistel Cipher, the encryption and decryption algorithms do have to be separately implemented, although they are very closely related.

4.5.3 AES today

AES is now widely adopted and supported in both hardware and software, including for low-cost environments such as RFID. While there has been a great deal of scrutiny and analysis of AES, there have thus far been no practical cryptanalytic attacks against AES. There have been some academic attacks against the 192- and 256-bit key versions of AES that are more effective than an exhaustive key search. Nonetheless, AES is widely believed to offer good security for the foreseeable future. As it was arguably designed using a more effective process than DES, pending any surprising cryptanalytic breakthroughs, these claims have reasonable grounding.

In contrast to DES, AES has built-in flexibility of key length, which allows a degree of 'future-proofing' against progress in the ability to perform exhaustive key searches.

However, just as for DES, the use of AES only guarantees security if it is correctly implemented and good key management is applied. In particular, there have been some very impressive side-channel attacks (see Section 1.6.5) against AES implementations, indicating the point that we want to keep emphasising during this discussion: the actual cryptographic design is a relatively 'easy' part of the cryptographic process. The hard part is securely implementing cryptography in a real system.

4.6 Modes of operation

Block ciphers are extremely versatile cryptographic primitives that can be used to provide a large number of different security properties. We mentioned in Section 3.2.4 that determining the way in which a cryptographic primitive is used affects the resulting properties that it provides.

One example of using a block cipher in an 'unconventional' way (by which we mean a way that does not strictly conform to the basic model of a cryptosystem proposed in Section 1.4.3) is Triple DES. In this case the block cipher was used in a different way in order to increase the level of security that it provides against exhaustive key search.

In this section we present several different *modes of operation* of a block cipher. These are operational rules for a generic block cipher that each result in different properties being achieved when they are applied to plaintexts consisting of more than one block. In theory, any block cipher could be used in any of these different modes of operation. The decision concerning which mode of operation to use will in practice be influenced by the application and the desired properties.

The modes of operation that we study are certainly not the only modes of operation proposed for block ciphers, but they are amongst the most established and commonly used modes of operation. They will suffice to illustrate the importance of selecting an appropriate mode of operation before applying a block cipher in practice.

4.6.1 Electronic Code Book mode

The first mode of operation is *Electronic Code Book* (ECB) mode. This mode of operation will not result in any surprises because ECB mode is just terminology for the intuitive way of using a block cipher that we depicted in Figure 4.3 and have thus far been assuming in our discussions. The main reason that we will discuss ECB mode at all is to identify its deficiencies.

HOW ECB MODE WORKS

In ECB mode we take the first block of plaintext and encrypt it with the key to produce the first block of ciphertext. We then take the second block of plaintext and encrypt it with the key to produce the second block of ciphertext, etc.

The derivation of the name for this mode of operation comes from the fact that, once the key is determined, encryption could (at least in theory) be conducted using an enormous codebook that is consulted to find out which ciphertext block replaces which plaintext block. Note that this code book would correspond to one row of the corresponding look-up table that can be constructed for any block cipher, as we discussed when considering the Latin square version of a one-time pad in Section 3.1.3.

PROBLEMS WITH ECB MODE

There are several good reasons why ECB mode is rarely used to encrypt long plaintexts consisting of many blocks:

Ciphertext manipulations. If a block cipher is used in ECB mode then some ciphertext manipulations are undetectable. By this we mean that an attacker could alter the ciphertext in such a way that the receiver might still get a meaningful plaintext after they decrypt the manipulated ciphertext. For example, an attacker could:

- replay (part of) an old ciphertext;
- delete certain blocks of ciphertext;
- rearrange the blocks of ciphertext in a different order;
- repeat certain ciphertext blocks.

Of course, to conduct most of these attacks without being detected, the attacker will have to rely on the resulting manipulated plaintext being meaningful, but there are many situations where this is a distinct possibility. For example, as depicted in Figure 4.7, an attacker with access to the contents of a database containing encrypted data fields P_1 and P_2 could swap the two corresponding encrypted entries C_1 and C_2. While the attacker may not know precisely what the result of this change will be, the attacker might have some idea of the likely implications. For example, if the entries are encrypted examination marks for students whose names were stored in plaintext on the database, the attacker may have prior knowledge of the students' abilities and thus deduce

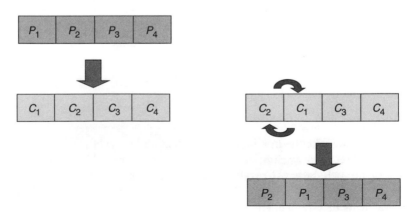

Figure 4.7. Ciphertext manipulation in ECB mode

that swapping the encrypted marks of good student A and bad student B will result in an increased grade for bad student B.

Statistical attacks. In Section 2.1 we saw that letter frequency analysis could easily be conducted against a monoalphabetic cipher. In some sense we can consider a block cipher being used in ECB mode to be a 'mono-block-ic' cipher, since the same plaintext block is always encrypted into the same ciphertext block. While undoubtedly much more difficult to perform than letter frequency analysis, it is still possible for ciphertext block statistics to be used to analyse a block cipher used in ECB mode. This will be particularly effective if the block cipher is regularly used to encrypt a small set of plaintexts. Again, the example of a partially encrypted examination database provides a good example, where there may only be one hundred possible plaintexts in the examination mark database field, and hence only one hundred different ciphertexts ever computed.

Dictionary attacks. In Section 4.3.1 we observed that relatively long block sizes are desirable to protect against dictionary attacks, where an attacker compiles a dictionary of known plaintext/ciphertext pairs that have been generated using a specific key. This is particularly dangerous in applications where certain fixed plaintexts are sent regularly. An extreme example of this is the situation that we described in Section 3.2.3, where a fixed plaintext was sent at the start of every day. While choosing a large block size makes this a more complex task (see Section 4.3.1), a dictionary attack of this sort is always theoretically possible if a block cipher is used in ECB mode.

All three of these problems arise because, when the same key is used in ECB mode, a plaintext block is always encrypted to the same ciphertext block. Note that none of these problems with ECB mode can be reduced by using a stronger (securer) block cipher since the issues described have nothing to do with the strength of the encryption algorithm. Rather, these issues arise only because of the way in which the block cipher is used.

Since the statistical attack that we just discussed is a generalisation of letter frequency analysis, it is worth recalling the three design principles that we identified in Section 2.2.1 for overcoming letter frequency analysis and consider how these might apply to modern block ciphers:

1. *Increase the size of the plaintext and ciphertext alphabets.* This corresponds to increasing the size of the block, since the 'alphabets' that the block cipher operates on consist of all possible blocks. This suggests that using larger block sizes is better from a security perspective, which is something that we already observed in Section 4.3.1.
2. *Allow the same plaintext letter to be encrypted to different ciphertext letters.* We saw the importance of this principle when we studied the likes of the Vigenère Cipher in Section 2.2.4. It would thus be a good idea for us to allow the same plaintext block to be encrypted to different ciphertext blocks, which is exactly what does *not* happen in ECB mode.

131

3. *Make the choice of ciphertext letter that is used to encrypt a plaintext letter depend on the position that the plaintext letter occupies within the plaintext.* This positional dependency is one way of achieving the previous design principle. One way of instantiating this, translated into our block cipher terminology, is to require a ciphertext block to depend not just on the current plaintext block, but also on previous plaintext or ciphertext blocks. An encryption mechanism with this property is sometimes referred to as being *message dependent*.

The first principle is dealt with in the design of a block cipher. It would thus be a good idea to have some alternative modes of operation that incorporate properties suggested by the latter two design principles. We will now look at three different modes of operation that do precisely this. The first two modes of operation use message dependency to achieve positional dependency, while the third mode of operation uses a different technique. These modes of operation are all preferred to ECB mode, which is rarely used in practice except for encrypting plaintexts consisting of just one block.

4.6.2 Cipher Feedback mode

The next mode of operation that we look at is *Cipher Feedback* (CFB) mode. This mode of operation is so called because each ciphertext block gets 'fed back' into the encryption process in order to encrypt the next plaintext block.

ENCRYPTION USING CFB MODE

There are several variants of CFB mode. The basic version of CFB mode encryption is illustrated in Figure 4.8, where E represents the encryption algorithm of the block cipher. We will assume in our discussion that E has a block size of 128 bits, however, it could be any value. The top and bottom boxes represent temporary *registers* of 128 bits, which will hold intermediate values that are needed in order to perform the encryption process. The contents of these registers will change throughout the encryption process. The CFB encryption process proceeds as follows:

1. We must first put something into the top register. This 'something' must be 128 bits long. This block of bits is often referred to as an *initialisation vector* (or IV), since its purpose is simply to initialise the process. The IV:

   - has to be known by the sender and receiver; they could agree on this over a public channel, or the sender could include it as the first 128 bits that are sent to the receiver;
   - does not strictly *have* to be secret and could be sent to the receiver in the clear, however, in practice it sometimes is secret;
   - is normally recommended to be 'unpredictable' rather than a block of 128 bits that could be predicted in advance by an attacker;
   - should only be used once with the same key.

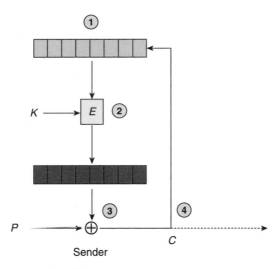

Figure 4.8. Encryption using CFB mode

2. Encrypt the contents of the top register with the key and place the result in the bottom register. Note, however, that even though we have just performed encryption using the block cipher:
   - the 'plaintext' block that we have just encrypted was not the current plaintext that we are trying to encrypt (we have not used this yet);
   - the 'ciphertext' block that we have just produced is not the final ciphertext (clearly it cannot be, since it was not computed using the current plaintext block).
3. Take the first plaintext block P_1 and XOR this to the contents of the bottom register. The result of this is C_1, our first block of ciphertext.
4. Send C_1 to the receiver, but also replace the contents of the top register with C_1. We have just *fed back* the ciphertext!
5. Now repeat from step 2. In other words, encrypt the contents of the top register (which now contains C_1) with the key; place the result in the bottom register; take the next plaintext block P_2 and add this to the contents of the bottom register to obtain the next block of ciphertext C_2; send C_2 to the receiver and replace the contents of the top register with C_2. Continue in this manner until the last plaintext block has been added to the contents of the bottom register and passed on to the receiver.

Essentially what is happening in the above encryption process is that the previous ciphertext block is encrypted with the key, and then the result is XORed to the current plaintext block. It should be clear that CFB mode differs significantly from ECB mode because the ciphertext corresponding to a given plaintext block depends not just on that plaintext block and the key, but also on the previous

133

ciphertext block (which in turn depends on the previous plaintext block, the key and the ciphertext block before that, etc.). In other words, the ciphertext block depends on the current plaintext block and all those that came before it. In this sense it really is message dependent. Unlike in ECB mode, when using the same key in CFB mode it should not be the case that the same plaintext block is always encrypted to the same ciphertext block because:

- each time a particular plaintext block needs to be encrypted, unless the whole plaintext message that precedes it is the same as on some previous occasion, the resulting ciphertext block should be different;
- even if the whole plaintext message that precedes a particular plaintext block is the same, by choosing a different IV on each occasion, we should get a different ciphertext block.

DECRYPTION USING CFB MODE

Decryption using CFB mode is very similar to encryption and is illustrated in Figure 4.9. The CFB decryption process is:

1. Start by placing the agreed IV in the top register.
2. Encrypt the contents of the top register with the key and place the result in the bottom register. The bottom register now contains exactly the same value as the sender had in their bottom register when they generated the first ciphertext block.

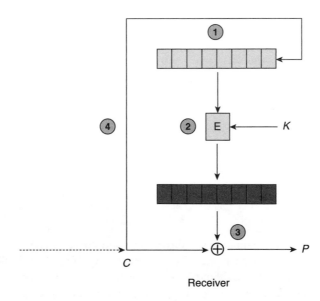

Figure 4.9. Decryption using CFB mode

134

3. Take the first ciphertext block C_1 and XOR this to the contents of the bottom register. Since the contents of the bottom register match that of the sender just before the sender encrypted P_1, the result of this is P_1, our first block of plaintext.

4. Now replace the contents of the top register with C_1. (We have just fed back that ciphertext again.)

5. Repeat again from step 2. In other words, encrypt the contents of the top register (which is now C_1) with the key; place the result in the bottom register; take the next ciphertext block C_2 and add this to the contents of the bottom register (because the contents of the bottom register now match that of the sender just before the sender encrypted P_2, the result of this is P_2); replace the contents of the top register with C_2. Continue in this manner until the last ciphertext block has been added to the contents of the bottom register to generate the last plaintext block.

A very strange feature of CFB mode is that we actually *decrypt* the ciphertext using only the *encryption* process of the block cipher. When using CFB mode we never use the decryption algorithm of the block cipher to 'decrypt' anything! This at first may seem paradoxical.

However, thinking about CFB mode in a slightly different way, it should be apparent that CFB mode is really converting a block cipher into a type of stream cipher. The encryption algorithm is never used directly to encrypt the plaintext, but is rather used as a keystream generator to produce keystream that is placed in the bottom register. This keystream is then XORed to the plaintext in the style of a stream cipher. Thus the receiver also uses the encryption algorithm to generate the same keystream that is needed to decrypt the ciphertext. This observation is crucial to understanding part of the motivation behind the design of modes of operation such as CFB mode. By converting a block cipher into a stream cipher through the use of CFB mode, we may gain some of the advantageous properties of a stream cipher that were discussed in Section 4.2.4, while preserving the advantageous properties of a block cipher that were discussed in Section 4.3.2.

REDUCED FEEDBACK CFB MODE

One of the advantages of a stream cipher that was identified in Section 4.2.4 was the ability to perform on-the-fly encryption. We now briefly indicate how CFB mode can be used to provide this.

At the beginning of our discussion we mentioned that there are several variants of CFB mode. Most practical implementations of CFB mode operate in a slightly different way to the processes described in Figures 4.8 and 4.9. The main difference is that these variants tend to process the plaintext in groups of bits that are smaller than the block size of the encryption algorithm.

For example, when using an encryption algorithm with a block size of 128 bits in *8-bit CFB mode*, the plaintext is processed in units of 8 bits at a time. Thus only 8 of the 128 bits in the bottom register are XORed to the plaintext, producing only 8 bits of ciphertext. These 8 bits of ciphertext are then fed back into the top register. Because they are not sufficient to replace the current contents of the top register, they are instead inserted into one end of the top register and the existing entries are shifted along, with the 8 furthest bits dropping out altogether.

This reduced feedback CFB mode has a significant advantage for certain types of application. For example, if we are processing 8-bit ASCII characters that are being input into a secure terminal then we can encrypt the characters immediately and do not have to wait until a full block (128 bits in our example) of data has been entered at the terminal. This reduces the time the input data spends sitting in unencrypted form in an input register.

IMPACT OF TRANSMISSION ERRORS IN CFB MODE

Recall that CFB mode deliberately incorporates message dependency in order to overcome the weakness of ECB mode. One possible disadvantage of making the encryption of one plaintext block dependent on the entire preceding encryption process is that transmission errors could propagate. For example, if one ciphertext bit gets changed from 1 to 0 during transmission then clearly the decryption of that ciphertext block will be incorrect. However, it might seem inevitable that (because of the feedback process) all subsequent ciphertext blocks will also be decrypted wrongly. We are about to see just how clever the design of CFB mode is.

Suppose that we are using CFB mode as depicted in Figure 4.9 using a block cipher with a block size of 128. Suppose also that a 1-bit transmission error occurs in ciphertext block C_i, but that all previous ciphertext blocks are received correctly. Clearly all the previous plaintext blocks P_1 up to P_{i-1} are unaffected, since they were recovered prior to C_i arriving. The situation when the erroneous block C_i is processed is depicted in Figure 4.10.

1. When C_i is received, the current content of the bottom register consists of the encryption of C_{i-1} and is therefore correct, since C_{i-1} was received correctly. However, when the correct contents of the bottom register are added to the incorrect ciphertext block C_i, the resulting plaintext block P_i is incorrect.
2. The incorrect C_i is now fed back into the top register. This incorrect value is encrypted and then placed in the bottom register. The bottom register thus now contains an incorrect value. When the next correct ciphertext block C_{i+1} is received, it is XORed to the incorrect contents of the bottom register. The result is another incorrect plaintext block P_{i+1}.
3. The correct C_{i+1} is now fed back into the top register. This correct value is encrypted and then placed in the bottom register. The bottom register thus now contains a correct value. When the next correct ciphertext block C_{i+2} is received, it is XORed to the correct contents of the bottom register. The result is a correct plaintext block P_{i+2}.
4. The error has now worked its way out of the system and, assuming that subsequent ciphertext blocks do not contain transmission errors, the remaining plaintext blocks will be recovered correctly. We thus see that a 1-bit error in the

136

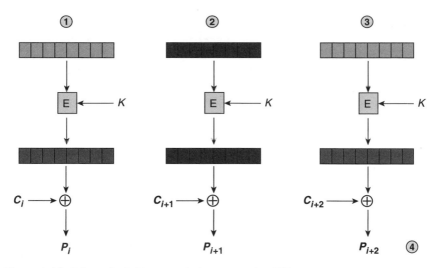

Figure 4.10. Effect of a 1-bit transmission error using CFB mode

ciphertext propagates to affect two blocks of plaintext. After this, CFB mode recovers and proceeds without further errors.

It is worth being a bit more precise about just *how wrong* these two affected plaintext blocks are:

- The value C_i contains just one incorrect bit and is XORed to a correct value. Thus the resulting incorrect P_i is in fact only incorrect in the same bit position of the error in C_i. (Whether a 1-bit plaintext error is serious will of course depend on the nature of the plaintext.)
- When C_i is encrypted as part of the decryption process for the incorrect P_{i+1}, the resulting 128 bits placed in the bottom register are 'very wrong'. This is because, as discussed in Section 4.3.2, even though the erroneous C_i is only wrong in one bit, the result of encrypting this value should be that about half of the 128 bits in the bottom register are wrong. These are then XORed to the correct C_{i+1}, resulting in P_{i+1} also having about half of its bits incorrect.

Assuming that all the later ciphertext blocks have no transmission errors, this really is a good outcome and shows that CFB mode cleverly contains transmission errors and has very limited error propagation.

PADDING IN CFB MODE

Another advantage of CFB mode concerns padding. Recall our earlier example from Section 4.3.2 of a 400-bit plaintext being encrypted using a block cipher with a 128-bit block length. If we use ECB mode then we need to split the plaintext into four separate blocks, the last of which only contains 16 bits of our plaintext. Thus we have to add 112 redundant padding bits to the fourth block.

137

However, if we use CFB mode then we do not have to do this. We process the first three 128-bit blocks as previously described. When the time comes to encrypt the fourth 'block', instead of padding we simply XOR the remaining 16 plaintext bits to the rightmost 16 bits of the contents of the bottom register and send the 16 resulting ciphertext bits. Likewise, the receiver only uses the rightmost 16 bits of the bottom register when decrypting these final 16 bits.

PROPERTIES OF CFB MODE

The main properties of CFB mode can thus be summarised as follows:

Message dependence. By incorporating message dependence, using a block cipher in CFB mode provides protection against ciphertext manipulation, frequency analysis and dictionary attacks.

Limited error propagation. Although error propagation does occur, it is strictly controlled and is not significantly worse than for ECB mode.

No synchronisation required. Even though CFB mode involves message dependence, it does not require synchronisation in the sense that the receiver could miss the beginning of the ciphertext and still succeed in decrypting from the point that the ciphertext is received. This is because the feedback (and hence the contents of the top and bottom registers) is determined only by the most recently received ciphertext block.

Efficiency. CFB mode is only slightly less efficient to implement than ECB mode when used with full feedback since the additional overhead consists of the extremely fast XOR operation. However, in this regard, the more common versions of CFB mode such as 8-bit CFB are less efficient since they involve repeated multiple encryptions for each block of plaintext. For example, 8-bit CFB mode using a 128-bit block cipher requires 16 encryption operations for each 128 bits of plaintext.

Implementation aspects. As discussed earlier, there is no need to pad the plaintext. In addition, there is no need to implement block cipher decryption when using CFB mode, which may save some implementation costs.

4.6.3 Cipher Block Chaining mode

An alternative way of providing message dependence is to use *Cipher Block Chaining* (CBC) mode. This has broadly similar properties to CFB mode, but is subtly different in the way it operates.

ENCRYPTION USING CBC MODE

CBC mode encryption is illustrated in Figure 4.11. The CBC encryption process proceeds as follows:

1. Put an initialisation vector (IV) into the top register. As for CFB mode, the IV has to be known by the sender and receiver (see Section 4.6.2 for discussion of how this could be facilitated).

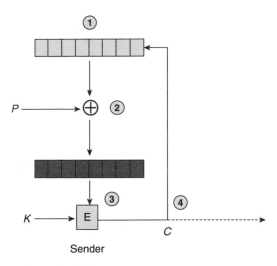

Figure 4.11. Encryption using CBC mode

2. Take the first plaintext block P_1 and XOR this to the contents of the top register. Put the result into the bottom register.
3. Encrypt the contents of the bottom register with the key. The result of this is C_1, our first block of ciphertext.
4. Send C_1 to the receiver, but also replace the contents of the top register with C_1.
5. Now repeat from step 2. In other words, add the contents of the top register (which is now C_1) to the next plaintext block P_2; place the result in the bottom register; encrypt the contents of the bottom register with the key to obtain the next block of ciphertext C_2; send C_2 to the receiver and replace the contents of the top register with C_2. Continue in this manner until the last plaintext block has been processed.

It should be clear that CBC mode also introduces message dependency since each ciphertext block depends on the current plaintext block and the previous ciphertext block (which itself depends on the previous plaintext block).

DECRYPTION USING CBC MODE

Decryption using CBC mode is illustrated in Figure 4.12, where in this case D represents the decryption algorithm of the block cipher. The CBC decryption process is as follows:

1. Put the agreed IV into the top register.
2. Take the first ciphertext block C_1 and decrypt it with the key, placing the result into the bottom register. The bottom register now contains exactly the same value as the sender had in their bottom register prior to the first encryption.
3. XOR the contents of the bottom register to the contents of the top register. The result of this is P_1, our first block of plaintext.

139

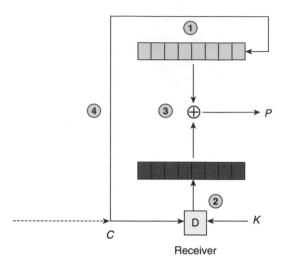

Figure 4.12. Decryption using CBC mode

4. Replace the contents of the top register with C_1.
5. Now repeat from step 2. In other words, decrypt the next block of ciphertext C_2 and place the result in the bottom register (the bottom register now contains exactly the same value as the sender had in their bottom register prior to the second encryption); add the contents of the bottom register to the contents of the top register, the result of which is the next plaintext block P_2; replace the contents of the top register with C_2. Continue in this manner until the last ciphertext block has been processed.

Put more concisely, in CBC mode the current plaintext block is added to the previous ciphertext block, and then the result is encrypted with the key. Decryption is thus the reverse process, which involves decrypting the current ciphertext and then adding the previous ciphertext block to the result.

IMPACT OF TRANSMISSION ERRORS IN CBC MODE

Just as we did for CFB mode, we now look at the effect of a 1-bit transmission error when CBC mode is used. Suppose that we are using CBC mode as depicted in Figures 4.11 and 4.12, using a block cipher with a block size of 128, and that a 1-bit transmission error occurs in ciphertext block C_i, but that all previous ciphertext blocks were received correctly. Clearly all the previous plaintext blocks P_1 up to P_{i-1} are unaffected since they were decrypted prior to C_i arriving. We now consider what happens when the erroneous block C_i is processed. This situation is depicted in Figure 4.13.

1. When C_i is received, it is decrypted, resulting in an incorrect value being placed in the bottom register. The current content of the top register consists of C_{i-1}

140

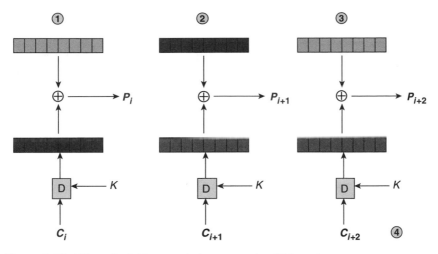

Figure 4.13. Effect of a 1-bit transmission error using CBC mode

and is therefore correct, since C_{i-1} was received correctly. However, when the incorrect contents of the bottom register are added to the correct contents of the top register, the resulting plaintext block P_i is incorrect.

2. The incorrect C_i is now put into the top register. When the next correct ciphertext block C_{i+1} is received, it is decrypted, resulting in a correct value being placed in the bottom register. However, the contents of the top register remain incorrect. When the correct contents of the bottom register are added to the incorrect contents of the top register, the resulting plaintext block P_{i+1} is incorrect.

3. The correct C_{i+1} is now put into the top register. When the next correct ciphertext block C_{i+2} is received, it is decrypted and the correct value is placed in the bottom register. The contents of the top register are now also correct and so the addition of the contents of the top and bottom registers results in a correct plaintext block P_{i+2}.

4. The error has now worked its way out of the system and assuming that subsequent ciphertext blocks do not contain transmission errors, the remaining plaintext blocks will be recovered correctly. We thus see that in a similar manner to CFB mode, although a 1-bit error in the ciphertext propagates to affect two blocks of plaintext, the process quickly recovers.

The extent to which these two plaintext blocks are incorrect can be established in a similar way to that of CFB mode. In fact the impact is the same as for CFB mode, except in the reverse order. In other words, the first incorrect plaintext block P_i is 'very wrong' (about half of its bits are incorrect) but the second incorrect plaintext block P_{i+1} is only incorrect in the same bit position that C_i is incorrect. Just as for CFB mode, CBC mode has recovered remarkably well from a 1-bit transmission error.

141

PROPERTIES OF CBC MODE

Although CBC mode is a different design to CFB mode (behaving much less like a stream cipher) the properties of CBC mode with respect to message dependency, error propagation and synchronicity are almost identical to those of CFB mode. However, it does not have the implementation benefits of CFB mode.

It is worth noting that CBC mode forms the basis for a well-known data origin authentication mechanism that we will discuss in Section 6.3.3. This brings implementation benefits for applications that require both symmetric encryption and data origin authentication and is perhaps why CBC mode has historically been the more popular of these two modes of operation.

4.6.4 Counter mode

The last of the modes of operation that we will describe in full is *Counter* (CTR) mode.

ENCRYPTION AND DECRYPTION USING CTR MODE

Counter mode can be thought of as a counter-based version of CFB mode without the feedback. The main difference is that we assume that both the sender and receiver have access to a reliable *counter*, which computes a new shared value each time a ciphertext block is exchanged. This shared counter is not necessarily a secret value, but both sides must keep the counter synchronised. Both encryption and decryption in CTR mode are depicted in Figure 4.14.

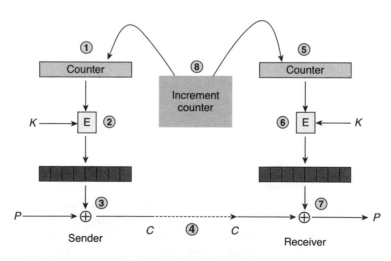

Figure 4.14. Encryption and decryption using CTR mode

Encryption proceeds as follows:

1. The initial value in the top register is the initial counter value. This value is the same for both the sender and the receiver and plays the same role as the IV in CFB (and CBC) mode.
2. As for CFB mode, encrypt the contents of the top register (the counter value) with the key and place the result in the bottom register.
3. As for CFB mode, take the first plaintext block P_1 and XOR this to the contents of the bottom register. The result of this is C_1, our first block of ciphertext.
4. Send C_1 to the receiver and update the counter, placing the new counter value into the top register (thus the counter update replaces the ciphertext feedback in CFB mode). Now repeat from step 2. Continue in this manner until the last plaintext block has been added to the contents of the bottom register and passed on to the receiver.

Thus CTR mode does not have message dependency (a ciphertext block does not depend on the previous plaintext blocks) but it does have positional dependency since a ciphertext block depends on the position of the current plaintext block within the message.

Decryption, which is similar to encryption, proceeds as follows:

5. Start by placing the initial counter value in the top register.
6. As for CFB mode, encrypt the contents of the top register (the counter value) with the key and place the result in the bottom register.
7. As for CFB mode, take the first ciphertext block C_1 and XOR this to the contents of the bottom register. The result of this is P_1, our first block of plaintext.
8. Update the counter, placing the new counter value in the top register.
9. Now repeat from step 6. Continue in this manner until the last ciphertext block has been added to the contents of the bottom register to generate the last plaintext block.

Thus, just like CFB mode, CTR mode does not involve the decryption process of the block cipher. This is because, just like CFB mode, CTR mode is really using the block cipher to generate a keystream, which is encrypted using the XOR function. In other words, CTR mode also converts a block cipher into a type of stream cipher.

PROPERTIES OF CTR MODE

The most obvious disadvantage of CTR mode is that it requires a synchronous counter. If this counter loses synchronisation then the subsequent plaintexts are all incorrectly recovered.

However, CTR mode preserves most of the other advantages of CFB mode. In addition it has some significant advantages over CFB mode and the other two modes of operation:

Error propagation. Like a dedicated stream cipher, CTR mode has the advantage that there is no error propagation. If a 1-bit error occurs in transmission then the corresponding plaintext is also only wrong in that one bit. This is because the incorrect ciphertext block is not fed back into any temporary registers that influence later decryptions.

Parallelisation. CTR mode lends itself very nicely to implementation environments that can exploit parallel computations, since the slow block cipher encryption computations can be computed independently (in advance) of the actual 'encryption' of the plaintext through the fast XOR operation. This is because there is no need to wait for any data to be 'fed back', as is the case for CFB and CBC modes. This property in particular has made CTR mode a popular mode of operation.

4.6.5 Other modes of operation

The four modes of operation that we have just discussed are all subtly different and have their own advantages and disadvantages. They are all used in real systems, particularly CBC and CTR modes. Table 4.2 attempts to summarise their key features. We assume full (not reduced feedback) CFB mode, although most of the properties are the same for reduced feedback CFB mode.

In addition to the four modes of operation that we have presented, many further modes of operation have been proposed. Some modes have been designed to have properties suitable for specific applications, such as XTS mode, which is designed to support full disk encryption (see Section 12.7.1). All the modes of operation we have described are only for use when the block cipher is being used to provide data confidentiality. If data origin authentication is also required then additional mechanisms such as a message authentication code should be used (see Section 6.3). Importantly, several other modes of operation, such as CCM mode, simultaneously offer both data origin authentication and confidentiality. We discuss these in a bit more detail in Section 6.3.6.

Table 4.2: Summary of properties of encryption-only modes of operation

Issue	ECB	CFB	CBC	CTR
Positional dependency	No	Yes	Yes	Yes
Error propagation for 1-bit transmission errors	One block	Two blocks	Two blocks	None
Synchronisation required	No	No	No	Yes
Requires encryption and decryption implementation	Yes	No	Yes	No
Requires plaintext padding	Yes	No	Yes	No
Easily parallelised	Yes	No	No	Yes

So, given an application that requires encryption using a block cipher, which mode of operation should be used? We have attempted to provide some basic information in this chapter but, as with all aspects of cryptography, it is advisable to consult best-practice guidelines and standards before selecting and implementing any mode of operation.

4.7 Summary

In this chapter we have concentrated on symmetric encryption algorithms. We looked at the two major classes of symmetric encryption algorithm, stream ciphers and block ciphers. Simple stream ciphers are fast and do not propagate errors, making them suitable for poor quality channels and for applications where errors are intolerable. Block ciphers do propagate errors (to a limited extent), but are quite flexible and can be used in different ways in order to provide different security properties, in some cases to achieve some of the benefits of stream ciphers. In particular we looked at two influential block ciphers, DES and its 'successor' AES. We then discussed different modes of operation of a block cipher and the different properties that they provide.

Perhaps the most important two messages to take away from this chapter are the following:

- Stream ciphers and block ciphers are different types of symmetric encryption algorithm. They have slightly different properties and are therefore suitable for different applications.
- The properties of cryptographic algorithms are not only affected by algorithm design, but also by the ways in which the algorithms are used. Different modes of operation can significantly change the properties of a block cipher.

4.8 Further reading

There is an abundance of cryptographic literature for those seeking more information about symmetric encryption algorithms. All the symmetric encryption algorithms that we discussed in this chapter are well known and details can be found in most recommended cryptography books. A good overview of symmetric encryption standards, including modes of operation, is Dent and Mitchell [55]. The ISO standard series relating to encryption mechanisms is ISO/IEC 18033 [12].

Until relatively recently there were few publicly known stream ciphers. Even well-used stream ciphers such as RC4 were originally proprietary designs, making the Wikipedia web portal [203] probably the best source of further information on it. A major development was the European eSTREAM project [164], which resulted in the development of a number of stream ciphers with a particular emphasis on those that would either run fast in software or be resource-efficient in hardware.

The most recent official formal specification of DES is FIPS 46-3 [77]. The fascinating history of the development of DES is covered well by Levy [117, 118]. The progress of exhaustive key search analysis against DES can be further explored by reading Diffie and Hellman's original analysis of DES [60], Wiener's blueprint for a DES exhaustive key search machine [199], Curtin and Dolske's account of publicly searching for DES keys using distributed techniques [53], the Electronic Frontier Foundation's breakthrough hardware design [84] (this book includes a discussion of the political motivation behind this work), and the dedicated hardware device COPACOBANA [50]. The latest official NIST specification of Triple DES is NIST 800-67 [140].

The AES is published as FIPS 197 [78]. A full technical explanation of the design methodology behind the AES can be found in Daeman and Rijmen [54]. Enrique Zabala's flash animations of Rijndael (essentially, the AES) [207] are excellent tools for visualising the AES encryption process. More details about the other block ciphers that we mentioned in this chapter can be found for IDEA [116], Twofish [171] and Serpent [24].

Of general relevance to all block ciphers, the modes of operation ECB, CFB, CBC, CTR and OFB (which we have not discussed) are all described in NIST Special Publication 800-38A [134] and ISO/IEC 10116 [1]. NIST also has special publications on CCM mode [135] and XTS mode [144], with more modes of operation likely to be standardised in the future. Meet-in-the-middle attacks and differential and linear cryptanalysis are all explained in detail in, for example, Vaudenay [194]. Several different padding techniques have been standardised, including in ISO/IEC 9797 [18], with the Wikipedia web portal [202] being a good place from which to explore current recommendations. The report by Blaze et al. [36] provided a benchmark for modern symmetric key lengths and the highly informative web portal by Giry [89] provides expert guidance that can be used to determine appropriate symmetric algorithm key lengths.

Most of the symmetric encryption algorithms that we mentioned in this chapter, as well as several of the modes of operation, have implementations in CrypTool [52]. We highly recommend simulating 1-bit transmission errors in CBC mode encryption using CrypTool in order to generate examples supporting the analysis in Section 4.6.3.

4.9 Activities

1. Explain the main benefits of using a stream cipher and illustrate your discussion by identifying application environments where:

   - stream ciphers are appropriate encryption mechanisms;
   - stream ciphers are inappropriate encryption mechanisms.

2. There are now a reasonable range of publicly known stream ciphers. Provide examples of (and ideally some information about) some publicly known stream

ciphers that are either published in international standards and/or adopted by commercial applications.

3. Find out what the difference is between *synchronous* and *self-synchronous* stream ciphers, using examples from this chapter to explain your answer.

4. The Feistel Cipher design is very clever.

   (a) Verify the claim that decryption using a Feistel Cipher is essentially the same as encryption. One way of explaining this is by using the simple equations that describe what happens at each round, although you can also explain this by describing the process in words.
   (b) From a practical (implementation) perspective, what are the significant advantages of the Feistel Cipher design structure?

5. Triple DES is a widely used block cipher whose design is motivated by practical considerations.

   (a) Explain what is meant by 'backwards compatibility'.
   (b) Describe three different ways in which keys could be chosen in order to make Triple DES backwards compatible with (single) DES.

6. Both Triple DES and the much weaker 'Double DES' are subject to attacks known as *meet-in-the-middle* attacks.

   (a) Find out, and then explain (roughly), how this type of attack works.
   (b) Explain why this type of attack is not so effective against AES.

7. Triple DES is just one idea for creating a stronger block cipher using DES. An alternative idea is DES-X, which is an encryption algorithm built from DES in the following way:

   - Let K_1 and K_2 be two 64-bit keys and let K be a DES key.
   - Let $DES_K(P)$ denote encryption of plaintext P using normal single DES with key K.
   - For a plaintext P we define the encryption of P using DES-X to be:

$$C = K_2 \oplus DES_K(P \oplus K_1).$$

   (a) What is the effective length of a DES-X key?
   (b) Explain how to decrypt a ciphertext using DES-X.
   (c) Is DES-X backwards compatible with single DES?

8. Suppose that we use AES with a 128-bit randomly generated key to encrypt a single block of 128 bits, and use the key only once. Is this an example of a one-time pad?

9. AES is a very popular symmetric encryption algorithm.

   (a) What applications of cryptography that you have used support the use of AES, and which key lengths do they recommend?

(b) AES is under great scrutiny from the cryptographic research community. Provide a 'layman's guide' to the latest cryptanalytic attacks that have been announced against AES and comment on their practical relevance.

(c) Suppose that one day an announcement is made that AES is too insecure for widespread use. What do you think the likely reaction will be from the various communities that this will affect?

10. If a block cipher is used in ECB mode then it is at least theoretically possible to conduct block frequency analysis.

(a) Suggest some circumstances, based on particular applications of encryption, which might result in it being possible for an attacker to conduct a practical block frequency analysis attack on a block cipher used in ECB mode.

(b) Can block frequency analysis still be conducted if the block cipher used is not known to an attacker?

11. At least in theory, the design of a block cipher is generally made more secure by:

- increasing the number of rounds used in a block cipher;
- using a block cipher with a larger block size.

    (a) For each of these techniques, explain why it might be more secure.

    (b) For each of these techniques, what are the associated practical disadvantages?

    (c) For each of these techniques, explain which of the three significant problems with ECB mode that we identified in Section 4.6.1 might be reduced.

    (d) Explain why it is inadvisable to apply either of these techniques to a published (standardised) block cipher such as AES.

12. More and more modes of operation of a block cipher are being proposed over time.

(a) What is the purpose of having different modes of operation of a block cipher?

(b) Why do you think there has been an increase in the number of modes of operation of a block cipher being proposed and standardised?

13. There is nothing, in theory at least, to prevent modes of operation from being applied to public-key encryption algorithms, which also process plaintexts in blocks of bits. Which of the modes of operation that we described in Section 4.6 could work if we use a public-key encryption algorithm instead of a symmetric encryption algorithm?

14. Many modes of operation of a block cipher essentially convert the block cipher into a stream cipher by using the encryption process of a block cipher as a keystream generator. This requires the output of the block cipher (ciphertext) to appear to be randomly generated. Explain why this is a reasonable (indeed desirable) property of a block cipher.

15. For each of the modes of operation discussed in Section 4.6, what is the effect of a 2-bit transmission error in the ciphertext if the two erroneous bits occur:

    (a) on the same ciphertext block?
    (b) on two consecutive ciphertext blocks?
    (c) on two ciphertext blocks that are separated by at least one error-free ciphertext block?

16. CFB mode is normally used in reduced feedback mode.

    (a) Sketch a diagram that illustrates how 8-bit CFB mode works when used with a block cipher operating on block sizes of 32 bits.
    (b) Explain what happens if there is a 1-bit transmission error in a ciphertext sent using this cryptosystem.

17. Modes of operation such as CFB and CBC require the use of an initial variable (IV), which must be known by both the sender and receiver. Discuss the pros and cons of the following suggestions for selection of IVs:

    (a) randomly generate each IV;
    (b) use a counter that is incremented after each message as the IV;
    (c) use the last ciphertext block of the previous message as the IV.

18. For each of the modes of operation that we discussed in Section 4.6:

    (a) What is the impact of the transmission loss of an entire block of ciphertext (in other words the ciphertext block is 'dropped')?
    (b) What is the impact of a 1-bit error as a result of a computational error during the encryption process itself (in other words, the error occurs at Alice's end when she computes ciphertext block C_i)?

19. There are several modes of operation proposed for block ciphers that we have not discussed in any detail. Choose an example of one such mode of operation.

    (a) What applications has your chosen mode of operation been designed for?
    (b) What properties does your mode of operation offer?
    (c) What is the impact of a 1-bit transmission error in your chosen mode of operation?

5 Public-Key Encryption

In this chapter we take our first detailed look at public-key cryptography. As for symmetric cryptography, our first chapter on this subject will primarily focus on using public-key cryptography for encryption. Throughout this discussion we will tend to refer to public-key 'cryptosystems'. This is because describing how to conduct public-key encryption involves a discussion of how to generate the necessary keys as well as how to conduct the encryption and decryption processes. In this chapter we will assume, by default, that a public-key cryptosystem is used to provide encryption. In later chapters we sometimes choose to make this more explicit by referring to *public-key encryption schemes*.

We first consider the motivation behind the concept of public-key cryptography and identify some of the problems that need to be solved before it can be used effectively. We will then turn our attention to two of the best-known public-key cryptosystems. Note that in contrast to our treatment of symmetric encryption, we will make an attempt to explain the mathematical details behind these two public-key cryptosystems. There are two main reasons for this:

1. Public-key encryption is less intuitive than symmetric key encryption, hence it merits several proofs of concept. Seeing, and hopefully understanding, is believing!
2. The algorithms used in public-key encryption are easier to describe than those used in symmetric encryption since they rely on simple mathematical ideas and not relatively complex engineering.

However, it is perfectly acceptable to skip over the mathematical details of these public-key cryptosystems without losing track of the main issues. For those who wish for more grounding in these basic mathematical ideas, we have included background material in the Mathematics Appendix.

At the end of this chapter you should be able to:

- Explain the basic principles behind public-key cryptography.
- Recognise the fundamental problems that need to be solved before public-key cryptography can be used effectively.
- Describe a simple version of the RSA cryptosystem.

- Describe a simple version of the ElGamal cryptosystem.
- Compare the basic properties of RSA, ElGamal and elliptic-curve-based approaches.
- Identify the main uses of public-key cryptography.

5.1 Public-key cryptography

We begin this chapter with an overview of the principles behind public-key cryptography.

5.1.1 Motivation for public-key cryptography

Public-key cryptography was initially invented in order to overcome some of the problems with symmetric cryptography. It is important that we begin our discussion by clearly understanding what these are.

PROBLEMS WITH SYMMETRIC CRYPTOGRAPHY

Recall that in a symmetric cryptosystem the same key is used to encrypt and decrypt. There is nothing conceptually problematic with this requirement but it has implications that may not always be desirable. The idea behind public-key cryptography arose from an attempt to overcome two of the most restrictive implications of symmetric cryptography:

Symmetric trust. Since the sender and receiver have to share the same symmetric key, there is an implication that, to an extent, the sender and receiver 'trust' one another. This 'trust' arises since anything cryptographic that the sender can do (by deploying the symmetric key), the receiver can also do (by deploying the same key). We will see in Chapter 7 how problematic this requirement is for at least one cryptographic service.

Key establishment. The sender and the receiver need to agree on a symmetric key in advance of use of a symmetric cryptosystem. Thus the sender and receiver need to have access to a secure key establishment mechanism (see Section 10.4).

Both of these implications are quite constraining. Consider, just as an example, an application such as an online store. A potential customer, browsing the store for the first time, has no reason to trust the store, nor has any pre-existing relationship with the store. Yet they may wish to make a purchase from this store and benefit from the use of cryptography to protect any data that is communicated to and from the store during the transaction. Symmetric cryptography, on its own, is unsuitable for use in this situation.

We will see shortly that public-key cryptography can be used in an attempt to overcome these problems. We apply the caveats because, as always, there are

151

issues that need to be resolved before we can comfortably claim that public-key cryptography *does* overcome these problems. We will see in Chapter 11 that public-key cryptography still requires an *indirect* trust relationship between entities employing it. We will see in Section 5.5 that one of the most compelling uses of public-key cryptography is actually to support the establishment of symmetric keys.

HISTORY OF PUBLIC-KEY CRYPTOGRAPHY

There was no public-key cryptography until the final quarter of the last century. Thus, in terms of cryptographic history, public-key cryptography is a relatively new idea. The timing of its invention is, however, more than coincidental. This is because the problematic issues that we have just associated with symmetric cryptography are relatively simple to overcome in the types of application environment in which cryptography was used prior to the 1970s. These were typically large, closed organisations such as governments, the military and big financial corporations. Symmetric cryptography was perfectly suitable for use in such organisations, and indeed still is, because:

- trust relationships exist between users of cryptography, since they are typically part of the same, or allied, organisations;
- symmetric key establishment can be facilitated and managed by an organisation's internal procedures and policies.

It was only with the spread of more open computer networks that a genuine need arose for deploying cryptography in environments where the problems with using symmetric cryptography present a significant challenge.

The invention of public-key cryptography is an interesting tale in itself. The intrigue lies in the fact that years after the 'public' mid-1970s invention of public-key cryptography in the US, it emerged that the idea had also been discovered several years earlier by UK government researchers. What is particularly poignant is that the UK government researchers had set aside the idea, primarily due to practical implementation concerns. Addressing some of these concerns is the subject of Chapter 11.

5.1.2 Properties of public-key cryptosystems

We now work towards a blueprint for a public-key cryptosystem that identifies the properties that we might want from such a system.

THE BRIEFCASE PROTOCOL

We have just observed that using symmetric encryption to protect a communication channel requires a trust relationship between the two communicating entities and prior establishment of a symmetric key. In fact this is not strictly true, as we will see in the following example, which we term the *briefcase protocol*. We begin with a physical analogy.

Suppose that Alice wishes to send a secure message to Bob, whom she has not met before and with whom she has no previous trust relationship. As this is a physical message, Alice will secure it by locking it in a briefcase. By 'secure', we mean that we want to make sure that nobody can see this message during its transportation (in other words, we want confidentiality over the communication channel). As Alice has not had any prior trust relationship with Bob, we assume that Bob does not already share a key with Alice. Figure 5.1 shows that, perhaps surprisingly, establishment of some sort of a secure channel is possible.

1. Alice begins by obtaining a padlock. Only Alice has the key to this padlock.
2. Alice places the message into the briefcase, locks the briefcase using the padlock and hands the locked briefcase to a courier, who transports it to Bob.
3. Bob obtains a padlock of his own. Once Bob receives the briefcase, he adds a second lock to the briefcase and returns the briefcase to the courier, who takes it back to Alice.
4. Alice removes her padlock and hands the briefcase to the courier, who once again transports it to Bob.
5. Bob removes his padlock and opens the briefcase to obtain the message.

The briefcase protocol achieves our stated goal because the message is kept confidential throughout its three journeys between Alice and Bob, since the briefcase is always locked by at least one padlock belonging to either Alice or Bob. Although this version secures a physical message, it is possible to produce a cryptographic equivalent of the protocol shown in Figure 5.1.

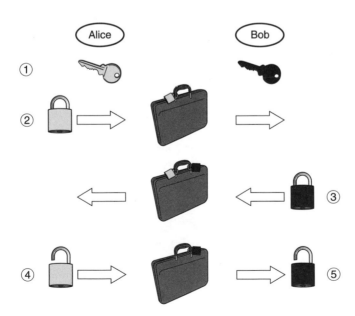

Figure 5.1. The briefcase protocol

However, nothing ever comes for free. There are two major problems with the briefcase protocol:

Authentication. The very freedom that we gain through being able to securely communicate with an entity that we had no prior trust relationship with, comes with a significant vulnerability. This is a lack of assurance that we have indeed securely communicated with the entity that we *think* we are communicating with. Alice has no guarantees (other than the word of the courier) that it is Bob who applies the second padlock. There is no authentication of any type in the briefcase protocol. While it is true that we did not specify authentication in our requirements, the briefcase protocol illustrates the dangers of omitting authentication as a requirement in such a scenario.

Efficiency. The briefcase protocol involves three journeys (or *passes*) between Alice and Bob. This is clearly inefficient since we normally require a message to be passed securely using just one communication. We must do better than this because in many applications communication bandwidth is expensive.

A BLUEPRINT FOR A PUBLIC-KEY CRYPTOSYSTEM

The briefcase protocol shows us that it is possible to exchange a secure message between two parties who have not previously established a shared key. We can thus use the briefcase protocol as a reference point from which to derive a blueprint (a 'wish list' if you like) for the properties that a public-key cryptosystem should have. This is formed by identifying some of the attractive properties of the briefcase protocol and some of the properties that were not provided:

1. *The keys used to encrypt and decrypt should be different.* The briefcase protocol achieves this in the sense that the final key used by Bob to 'decrypt' is different from the key used by Alice to 'encrypt' the message. This is a necessary property if we are to overcome the problems with symmetric cryptography discussed in Section 5.1.1.

2. *Anyone who wants to be a receiver needs a unique decryption key.* We will generally refer to this key as a *private key* (we prefer this to the ambiguous use of *secret key*, which is a term shared with symmetric cryptography). The briefcase protocol achieves this since everyone uses their own padlock, the key for which acts as a private key since only the key holder can unlock it.

3. *Anyone who wants to be a receiver needs to publish an encryption key.* We will generally refer to this key as a *public key*. One of the problems with the briefcase protocol is that this notion of a public key is not explicitly present. Since we have no 'public keys' we are unable to target a specific recipient for the message in the briefcase.

4. *Some guarantee of the authenticity of a public key needs to be provided.* It is necessary to be confident of the correct 'owner' of a public key otherwise we will still have the authenticity problem of the briefcase protocol. In the

154

early days of public-key cryptography it was envisaged that this guarantee could be provided by publishing the public keys in a 'directory', rather like a phone book. Currently a more popular way of doing this is to embed the public key in a *public-key certificate*. We will discuss this issue in more detail in Section 11.1.

5. *It should not be feasible to deduce the plaintext from knowledge of the ciphertext and the public key.* This is just one of the standard security assumptions that we introduced in Section 1.5.1. Public keys and ciphertexts are known values and so we must assume that an attacker has knowledge of them.

6. *It should not be feasible to deduce the private key from the public key.* While the public and private keys will need to be related in some way, we must make sure that the private key cannot be deduced from knowledge of the public key.

A BETTER BRIEFCASE ANALOGY?

Perhaps a more accurate analogy for a public-key cryptosystem is thus the following. Suppose that, once again, Alice wishes to send a secure message to Bob by placing it into a locked briefcase. Instead of the previous protocol, Bob now obtains a padlock and somehow gets the padlock to Alice. He could either send it to Alice, or he could distribute thousands of copies of the padlock around the world so that Alice can easily acquire one when she needs it. Alice locks the briefcase using Bob's padlock and sends the locked briefcase back to Bob, who then unlocks it using his key and obtains the message.

In this analogy, Alice faces two challenges. Firstly she has to acquire Bob's padlock. We suggested two options for doing this, but a real public key will be much easier to make available to Alice! Secondly, and more significantly, Alice has to be sure that it really is Bob's padlock that she is using. This is the issue of 'authenticity' of the public key. In this analogy it is not clear how to solve this (perhaps Bob will need to have his padlock engraved in a way that Alice can easily recognise). We devote much of Chapter 11 to discussing how to do this in practice for public-key cryptosystems.

5.1.3 Some mathematical preliminaries

In order to explain the public-key cryptosystems in this chapter we will need to introduce a little bit of basic mathematics. However, taking the time to absorb these fairly elementary ideas will greatly enrich the understanding of how public-key cryptosystems work. If these ideas cause some difficulty then there are a couple of approaches that could be taken:

1. Take a short break from reading this chapter in order to study the background material in the Mathematics Appendix. This will not take long and explains all that is needed. This is the approach that we recommend since we genuinely believe that it is not hard, even for those with a fear of mathematics, to fully understand these very elegant public-key cryptosystems.

2. Skip through the mathematics and just try to grasp the essence of what is going on. This is a perfectly valid option, although the details of these public-key cryptosystems will probably remain something of a 'fuzzy cloud'.

The main mathematical ideas that we will need are the following.

PRIMES

A *prime number*, which we will simply refer to as a *prime*, is a number for which there are no numbers other than itself and 1 that divide into the number 'neatly' (in other words, without a remainder). Such neatly dividing numbers are termed *factors*. For example, 17 is a prime since the only numbers that divide neatly into 17 are 1 and 17. On the other hand, 14 is *not* a prime since 2 and 7 both divide neatly into, and are thus factors of, 14. There are an infinite quantity of primes, with the smallest ten primes being 2, 3, 5, 7, 11, 13, 17, 19, 23 and 29. Primes play a very important role in mathematics, and a particularly important role in cryptography.

MODULAR ARITHMETIC

The public-key cryptoystems that we will describe do not operate directly on binary strings. Instead they operate on *modular numbers*. There are only finitely many different modular numbers, in contrast to the types of numbers that we are most familiar with using. *Modular arithmetic* provides rules for conducting familiar operations such as addition, subtraction and multiplication on these modular numbers. The good news is that modular numbers, and modular arithmetic, are concepts that most people are familiar with, even if they have never described them in such terms. An introduction to modular numbers and modular arithmetic is provided in the Mathematics Appendix.

SOME NOTATION

We will also introduce some simple notation. The important thing to remember about notation is that it is just shorthand for words. We could replace any mathematical equation with a sentence having the same meaning. However, the resulting sentences often become cumbersome and awkward. Notation helps to keep statements precise and clear.

Firstly, the symbol $\times$ is usually used to mean 'multiply'. Thus $a \times b$ is shorthand for 'a multiplied by b'. However, it will sometimes be convenient to write this statement even more concisely. Thus we will sometimes drop the $\times$ symbol and just write ab. Thus 'a multiplied by b', $a \times b$ and ab all mean exactly the same thing. If we write an equation $y = ab$ then this means that 'the number y is equal to the number a multiplied by the number b'.

Secondly, when we write two numbers in brackets, separated by a comma, then this is just a convenient way of saying that these two numbers are to be regarded as a 'package' and that we cannot have one without having the other. Thus if we say that a key is (a, b) then all that this means is that the key is made up of the numbers a and b together. The key is not just a, and neither is it just b, the key consists of both. Note, however, that we also use brackets in mathematics just to keep symbols 'together' (much as we do in sentences such as this one). Thus the following two pieces of notation have quite different meanings:

- $(p-1)(q-1)$ means the number $p-1$ multiplied by the number $q-1$ (without the brackets the statement would be confusing);
- $(p-1, q-1)$ means that the number $p-1$ and the number $q-1$ should be treated as a pair of numbers that occur together as a package (for example, they form a cryptographic key).

Note that brackets are sometimes used in other mathematical texts to mean different things.

5.1.4 One-way functions for public-key cryptography

Having stated the blueprint for a public-key cryptosystem, we now need to consider how such a public-key cryptosystem can be designed. The first step in this direction is to state more precisely the properties that we need public-key encryption to satisfy.

TRAPDOOR ONE-WAY FUNCTIONS

Public-key encryption can be thought of as a function that anyone should be able to compute, since the encryption key is public. This function has two obvious properties:

The function should be 'easy' to compute. In other words, it should be computable in polynomial time. If this is not the case then it will be impractical to encrypt anything.

The function should be 'hard' to reverse. In other words, any algorithm for finding an input from an output should run in exponential time. If this is not the case then an attacker might be able to efficiently determine a plaintext from knowledge of a ciphertext and the public encryption key.

A function that has the above properties is often referred to as a *one-way function* (see also Section 6.2.1).

However, public-key encryption should not always be a one-way function. Rather, it should *almost* always be a one-way function. We have omitted one important aspect. While the encryption operation should be one-way as far as most entities are concerned, there is one entity who should be able to determine the plaintext from a ciphertext, namely the intended recipient of the ciphertext! If the encryption function is completely one-way then it is certainly secure, but impractical for most applications (see Section 6.2.2 for a notable exception).

What we need is a special piece of technical 'magic' that will allow the genuine receiver to overcome the one-way property of the encryption function. One-way functions for which there exists a *trapdoor* of this type, knowledge of which allows the plaintext to be obtained from the ciphertext, are referred to as *trapdoor one-way functions*.

Thus, to design a public-key cryptosystem, we will need to find a trapdoor one-way function. The receiver will need to know the trapdoor, and be the only entity who knows the trapdoor. This trapdoor will form the receiver's private key.

MULTIPLICATION OF TWO LARGE PRIMES

We will temporarily set aside the need for trapdoors and look at two one-way functions on which we could potentially base a public-key cryptosystem. The first one-way function is multiplication of two large primes.

It is easy to take two primes and multiply them together (the result is normally called the *product*). If the numbers are fairly small then we can do this in our heads, on a piece of paper, or perhaps on a calculator. Once they get bigger (and bigger) it is still easy to write a computer program to compute the product. The reason is that, as we observed in Section 3.2.3, multiplication can be conducted in polynomial time. Multiplication of two primes is computationally easy.

However, given the product of two primes, the problem of working out what these two primes are (known as *factoring* because it involves determining the factors) is surprisingly hard. When we say 'hard', this of course applies to the general case. Table 5.1 indicates the level of difficulty of factorisation for a range of numbers that are the product of two primes. Note that factorisation is *unique*, meaning that there is only one possible pair of prime factors for each product. This observation explains the last two entries in Table 5.1. The last entry is implied from

Table 5.1: Examples of the difficulty of factoring the product of two primes

Challenge number	Difficulty of solution
15	Everyone can do this instantly
143	Doable with a little thought
6887	Should not take more than a few minutes
31897	A calculator is now useful
20-digit number	A computer is now required
600-digit number	This is impossible in practice
600-digit even number	One factor immediate, other easily computed
600-digit number with small factor	One factor easily found, other easily computed

a factorisation algorithm that works by dividing the target number by every prime, starting with the smallest ones. If the primes are very large then this algorithm fails to find a factor in polynomial time, but if one of the primes is small then it will find this factor very quickly.

Multiplication of two large primes is *believed* to be a one-way function. We say 'believed' because nobody has been able to prove that it is hard to factor. However, enough experts have devoted sufficiently many years to studying the problem without making significant progress that it seems a reasonable assumption

Maybe one day someone will find a method of factoring efficiently. Apart from becoming famous, and probably rich, a wider implication will be that any public-key cryptosystem whose security relies on multiplication of two primes being a one-way function will immediately be broken. One such public-key cryptosystem is RSA, which we study in Section 5.2.

MODULAR EXPONENTIATION WITH A LARGE MODULUS

The second one-way function that we will look at is *modular exponentiation*. In Section 1.6.1 we noted that exponentiation just means raising a number to a power. Hence *modular* exponentiation means raising a number to a power modulo some other number (this latter number is the *modulus*). A more detailed explanation of modular arithmetic is provided in the Mathematics Appendix.

Modular exponentiation thus involves raising a number a to the power b and then calculating the result modulo n, for some number n. We tend to write this as:

$$a^b \bmod n.$$

For example, raising 3 to the power 5 modulo 7 involves first calculating:

$$3^5 = 3 \times 3 \times 3 \times 3 \times 3 = 243$$

and then computing:

$$243 \bmod 7 = 5.$$

We have already noted in Section 3.2.3 that exponentiation can be conducted in polynomial time. Since this is also true for modular exponentiation, it is regarded as an easy operation.

However, given the result of a modular exponentiation, and only the numbers a and n (where n is a prime), calculating the number b that was used to compute the modular exponentiation is believed to be a hard problem, assuming that n is large. This difficult problem is often referred to as the *discrete logarithm problem*.

In other words, given numbers a and n (where n is prime), the function

$$f(b) = a^b \bmod n,$$

is believed to be a one-way function, since computing $f(b)$ is easy but, given $f(b)$, working out what b is appears to be hard.

NON-MODULAR EXPONENTIATION

The discrete logarithm problem might look hard enough without the added complication of modular arithmetic. However, there is a big difference between computing normal logarithms (given a and a^b, find b) and computing discrete logarithms (do the same thing, but working modulo n). Finding logarithms is in fact much easier without modular arithmetic. To get a feeling for this, consider a closely related problem: the taking of square roots.

We will try to find the square root of 1369. Here is a good strategy:

1. Start with a guess, say 40. The square of 40 (in other words 40 × 40) is easy to compute. It is 1600, which is too big.
2. Try something smaller, such as 30. The square of 30 is 900, which is too small.
3. Now try an intermediate value, such as 35. The square of 35 is 1225. This is still too small, but it is fairly close.
4. Now try something just a little bit bigger than 35, but smaller than 40, such as 37. The square of 37 is 1369, which is our target. Thus the square root of 1369 is 37.

It is clear that the above 'strategy' is actually a simple algorithm that we could use to find the square root of any number. This iterative algorithm essentially makes educated guesses at the answer, modifying the next guess based on the result of the previous one. It is efficient to run and thus computing square roots is clearly easy.

But what about computing square roots modulo a number? We will try to find the square root of 56 modulo 101. We might as well try the strategy that worked so well last time.

1. Start with a guess, say 40. The square of 40 is 1600. Reducing 1600 modulo 101 we get the answer 85. So the square of 40 modulo 101 is 85, which is too big.
2. Try something smaller, say 30. The square of 30 is 900, which is 92 modulo 101. This is even bigger, which is strange because 30 was smaller than our first guess.

We have just observed that the square of 30 modulo 101 is 'bigger' than the square of 40 modulo 101. Thus the algorithm that we designed for computing square roots, which was based on an intuitive notion of numerical order, no longer works. Generally, computing square roots modulo a number is regarded as being much harder than for normal integers. Thus squaring a number is an easy function to compute and to reverse for normal integers, but could be regarded as a one-way function when computed using modular arithmetic. Modular exponentiation can be regarded as a one-way function for similar reasons.

The moral of this short side discussion is that if we want to design one-way functions then modular arithmetic is a good concept on which to base our design, because it makes certain types of computation much harder than when it is not used.

5.2 RSA

The RSA cryptosystem was one of the first proposed, and remains one of the most-used, public-key cryptosystems today. It is named after the three researchers Ron Rivest, Adi Shamir and Len Adleman who first published the idea behind it. RSA is surprisingly straightforward to understand if the simple mathematics behind it can be grasped. It is important to have read Section 5.1.3 before continuing.

5.2.1 Setting up RSA

All the real work in RSA occurs during key generation. This should not be surprising since the 'clever' part of any public-key cryptosystem is in designing a relationship between two keys that allows one to reverse the effect of the other, while allowing one of them to be publicly known. Note that we do not have to be quite so mathematically clever when generating symmetric keys, which 'just' requires an ability to randomly generate numbers (see Section 8.1). The wider issues associated with key generation are discussed in more detail in Section 10.3.

GENERATING AN RSA KEY PAIR

We are now ready to generate an RSA key pair. The 'we' in this case is anyone who is setting up an RSA key pair. This could be someone generating a key pair for themselves, or a trusted key centre generating a key pair for a client. If we wish to set up a network of users who may want to communicate with one another using RSA then *every* user in the network will need to run this key pair generation process, or have the trusted key centre run it for them. We proceed as follows:

Generating the modulus. Let n be the product of two large primes p and q. In other words, let $n = pq$. By *large*, we typically mean a minimum of 512 bits long, preferably even longer. Thus p and q are very large primes, and n is an even larger number. Finding primes of this size is not straightforward, but there are known processes for generating them. The number n that is produced in this step is usually referred to as an *RSA modulus*.

Generating e. We select a 'special' number e. The number e cannot be just any number. For example, it must be greater than 1 and less than $(p - 1)(q - 1)$. The precise mathematical property that e must have is that there must be no numbers that divide neatly into e and into $(p - 1)(q - 1)$ except for 1. The mathematical term for this property is that e and $(p - 1)(q - 1)$ are *coprime*. Consider the following simple example:

- Let $p = 3$ and $q = 7$. In this case $(p - 1)(q - 1) = 2 \times 6 = 12$. Any suitable choice of e must have the property that there are no numbers that neatly divide into e and 12, except for 1.
- $e = 2$ is no good, since 2 is a factor of both 2 and 12. For a similar reason we can also rule out all multiples of 2, namely $e = 4$, $e = 6$, $e = 8$ and $e = 10$.

161

- $e = 3$ is no good, since 3 is a factor of both 3 and 12. For a similar reason we can also rule out all multiples of 3, namely $e = 6$ and $e = 9$.
- The remaining choices are $e = 5$, $e = 7$, and $e = 11$. Since in each case there is no number that divides into these choices of e and 12, other than 1, all these choices of e are valid.

Unlike in this 'toy' example, for the sizes of p and q that we tend to use in real RSA implementations we will find that many numbers less than $(p - 1)(q - 1)$ have the right property to be used as e.

Forming the public key. The pair of numbers (n, e) form the RSA public key and can be made available to anyone who wishes to send encrypted messages to the holder of the private key (which we have not yet generated). The primes p and q must not be revealed. Recall that although n is part of the public key, the fact that multiplication of two primes is a one-way function (see Section 5.1.4) should prevent them from being discovered by any entities not entitled to know them. Note that occasionally we may refer to the public key as simply being e. This is only done in situations where the value of the RSA modulus n is clear and assumed.

Generating the private key. We compute the private key d from p, q and e. The private key d is uniquely determined by the public key (n, e), meaning that given an n and an e there can only ever be one possible value d. This is essentially the clever part of RSA, since it is the mathematical relationship between e and d that makes RSA work. We thus have to be precise about how to find this value d.

In mathematical terminology, the private key d is the *inverse of e modulo* $(p - 1)(q - 1)$ (see the Mathematics Appendix for more details). What this means is that d is the unique number less than $(p - 1)(q - 1)$ that, when multiplied by e, is equal to 1 modulo $(p - 1)(q - 1)$. Written mathematically (which is much simpler) this relationship is expressed by:

$$ed = 1 \bmod (p - 1)(q - 1).$$

It is sufficient just to accept that, if we choose e correctly, such a d exists and is unique. Conveniently, there is a simple algorithm to compute d. This algorithm is known as the *Extended Euclidean Algorithm*, which takes as input p, q and e, and outputs d. The Extended Euclidean Algorithm can be computed in polynomial time by anyone who knows p and q. However, anyone who does not know p and q cannot run it to find d. This is why it is important that $n = pq$ is difficult to factor. If n was easy to factor then an attacker could compute p and q and then run the Extended Euclidean Algorithm to obtain d.

It is worth providing an example of RSA key generation, just to make sure that the process is clear. This example will, of course, use numbers that are *far too small* to be used in practice. Just keep in mind that the primes we use are just six bits long, rather than the thousands of bits long that is often recommended for RSA implementations.

Generating the modulus. Let $p = 47$ and $q = 59$. Thus:

$$n = pq = 47 \times 59 = 2773.$$

Generating e. Select $e = 17$, which is a valid choice since there is no number that divides into 17 and $(p - 1)(q - 1) = 46 \times 58 = 2668$, except for 1.

Forming the public key. The pair of numbers $(n, e) = (2773, 17)$ form the public key and can be made available to anyone whom we wish to be able to send us encrypted messages.

Generating the private key. Input $p = 47$, $q = 59$ and $e = 17$ to the Extended Euclidean Algorithm. The output will be $d = 157$. We can check that this result is correct by computing:

$$de = 17 \times 157 = 2669 = 1 \bmod 2668.$$

The private key is $d = 157$, which is a value that only we know.

5.2.2 Encryption and decryption using RSA

Once an RSA key pair has been set up, the hard work is done. Encryption and decryption are relatively simple processes to understand.

RSA ENCRYPTION

Suppose that we wish to send some plaintext to someone whose public key is (n, e).

The first point to note is that RSA does not directly operate on strings of bits, but rather on numbers modulo n. Thus our first task is to represent the plaintext as a series of numbers less than n. We will not discuss exactly how to do this here, but it is not any more difficult than the process of converting an English plaintext into a string of bits that can be processed by a block cipher such as AES. So long as everyone using RSA agrees to the same 'rules' for performing this conversion, everything will work.

We thus assume that every plaintext is a number less than n. Note that these numbers must be less than n. If we allow a plaintext to be greater than n then we will not be able to represent it uniquely since we will not be able to tell the difference between, for example, the plaintext 5 and the plaintext $n + 5$, since both of these would be considered by RSA to be equal to 5 (because $n + 5 = 5 \bmod n$).

Suppose that we now want to encrypt the first plaintext P, which is a number modulo n. The encryption process to obtain the ciphertext C is very simple:

$$C = P^e \bmod n.$$

In other words, the ciphertext C is equal to the plaintext P multiplied by itself e times and then reduced modulo n. This means that C is also a number less than n.

Returning to our numerical example, if the plaintext is $P = 31$ then encrypting using public key (2773, 17) results in:

$$C = 31^{17} = 587 \bmod 2773.$$

Recall from Table 3.3 that exponentiation (raising a number to a power) has polynomial complexity, which means that it is efficient to compute. Note also, however, that Table 3.3 illustrates that exponentiation is not *as efficient* as processes such as addition and multiplication. This means that encryption is fast, but not as fast as simpler operations, such as those that form the basis for most symmetric encryption algorithms. This observation has important implications, which we return to in Section 5.5.

RSA DECRYPTION

The decryption process for RSA is just as straightforward. Suppose that the holder of public-key pair (n, e) has just received a ciphertext C. All the receiver does is to raise C to the power of their private key d. The result will be the plaintext P. In other words:

$$P = C^d \bmod n.$$

Returning again to our numerical example, the ciphertext $C = 587$ can be decrypted using private key 157 to obtain:

$$P = 587^{157} = 31 \bmod 2773.$$

The million dollar question is, of course, *why does this work*? We suggest that you either choose just to accept that it works, or alternatively read the Mathematics Appendix for an explanation.

5.2.3 Security of RSA

There are two obvious ways of trying to break RSA. Indeed, these apply to any public-key cryptosystem. An attacker can either attempt to:

1. decrypt a ciphertext without knowledge of the private key;
2. determine the private key directly from the public key.

Clearly the second attack is more powerful than the first, since an attacker who can perform the second attack can then decrypt subsequent ciphertexts. We now consider these two attack strategies.

DECRYPTING A CIPHERTEXT WITHOUT KNOWLEDGE OF THE PRIVATE KEY

Consider trying to decrypt an RSA ciphertext without the private key. Recall that we specified in Section 5.1.4 that a public-key encryption function should be a trapdoor one-way function. By assuming that we do not know the private key, we are thus assuming that we do not know the trapdoor. Thus to assess the difficulty of determining the plaintext directly from the ciphertext, we need to assess the effectiveness of the one-way function that lies at the heart of RSA.

We need to take a closer look at the function that is being used for RSA encryption. The encryption process in RSA involves computing the function:

$$C = P^e \bmod n.$$

An attacker who observes C, and has knowledge of e and n (but not d), needs to work out what the value P is. Computing P from C, e and n is regarded as a hard problem (fortunately!) and thus the encryption function of RSA is believed to be a one-way function.

Although this hard problem might look familiar, it is in fact the first time that we have come across it. It is commonly referred to as the *RSA problem*. It superficially resembles the discrete logarithm problem that we discussed in Section 5.1.4, however, there are two subtle differences:

1. In the discrete logarithm problem we are given C, P and n and we try to find e. In the RSA problem we are given C, e and n and we try to find P.
2. In the discrete logarithm problem that we discussed in Section 5.1.4 we worked modulo a prime, whereas in the RSA problem our modulus is the product of two primes.

These are important differences. Hence the RSA encryption function and modular exponentiation are regarded as two different one-way functions. In fact the RSA encryption function is more closely related to the one-way function consisting of squaring a number modulo n that we mentioned in Section 5.1.4. In this case we are not squaring, but we are raising numbers to the power e. The difficult reversal in this case is not taking the square root, but taking the eth root modulo n.

Nobody knows *precisely* how difficult the RSA problem is to solve, but it is *widely believed* to be equivalent in difficulty to factoring. Thus the RSA encryption function is *widely believed* to be a trapdoor one-way function, where the trapdoor is knowledge of the private key d.

DETERMINING THE PRIVATE KEY DIRECTLY FROM THE PUBLIC KEY

There is one way in which an attacker could determine an RSA private key d from an RSA public key (n, e). This is by:

1. factoring n, in other words working out what p and q are;
2. running the Extended Euclidean Algorithm to determine d from p, q and e.

In fact it can be shown that the problem of factoring and the problem of determining an RSA private key directly from an RSA public key are *equivalent* in the sense that if we can solve one of these problems then we can solve the other problem.

Consequently, in order to obtain a private key using mathematical techniques (rather than doing something much easier such as stealing a hardware token that contains a private key) it is necessary to be able to factor an RSA modulus. So long as there remains no efficient method of factoring $n = pq$, obtaining an RSA private key directly from an RSA public key will be regarded as hard.

RSA SECURITY SUMMARY

The security of RSA thus depends on two separate functions being one-way:

The RSA encryption function. The RSA encryption function is a trapdoor one-way function, whose trapdoor is knowledge of the private key. The difficulty of reversing this function without the trapdoor knowledge is believed (but not known) to be as difficult as factoring.

Multiplication of two primes. The difficulty of determining an RSA private key from an RSA public key is known to be equivalent to factoring the modulus n. An attacker thus cannot use knowledge of an RSA public key to determine an RSA private key unless they can factor n. Because multiplication of two primes is believed to be a one-way function, determining an RSA private key from an RSA public key is believed to be very difficult.

If either of these two functions turns out *not* to be one-way then RSA will be broken. In particular, if someone develops a technique for factoring efficiently (breaking the second of the one-way functions) then RSA will no longer be safe for use. Such a situation will arise if a practical quantum computer can be built (see Section 5.4.4). It is for this reason that the latest results on progress in the design of factorisation algorithms are often quoted in the press next to articles predicting security disasters. Rather like the race between designers of machines that can perform exhaustive key searches and the recommended length of symmetric keys, there is a similar race between designers of factorisation algorithms and the recommended length of the modulus n for use in RSA. We discuss how large n should be in Section 5.4.3.

5.2.4 RSA in practice

As with most of the cryptographic primitives that we discuss, our explanation of RSA is simplified in order to emphasise the main design aspects. There are a number of attacks on specific instances of RSA that we will not outline in any detail here. For example, there are:

- attacks when d is very small;
- attacks when e is very small;
- attacks if the same message is sent to many receivers with the same low value of e;
- various side-channel attacks (see Section 1.6.5).

Just as with other cryptographic primitives that we have discussed, it is essential that RSA is not deployed in any real implementation in exactly the way that we have described . Rather, the latest best-practice guidelines outlined in the relevant standards should be consulted and followed. In particular, it should be noted that real implementations of RSA are advised to feature *probabilistic encryption*, which we explain in Section 5.3.4.

5.3 ElGamal and elliptic curve variants

Despite its relatively high profile, RSA is not the only public-key cryptosystem, just the most well-established one. RSA is definitely the best-known public-key cryptosystem whose security is assumed to be based on the difficulty of factoring. Of the other public-key cryptosystems proposed, several are based on different versions of the discrete logarithm problem. Some of the most important variants of these are based on the use of *elliptic curves* (see Section 5.3.5) and offer some significant practical benefits over RSA. Rather than describing approaches based on elliptic curves directly, we will discuss the *ElGamal* cryptosystem, for several important reasons:

1. ElGamal is the public-key cryptosystem on which elliptic curve variants are based;
2. ElGamal does not require further significant mathematical concepts;
3. ElGamal forms the basis for several other important cryptographic primitives, such as the Digital Signature Algorithm (see Section 7.3.6).

5.3.1 Setting up ElGamal

We now describe how to set up key pairs for use in ElGamal. Each user who wishes an ElGamal key pair conducts the following process:

Choose a large prime p. We will present a simplified version of ElGamal that works with numbers modulo p. In practice, ElGamal is often based on a slightly more general number system (and in the case of elliptic curve variants, is based on quite different number systems). By 'large' we mean a prime of similar size length to an RSA modulus. Thus a reasonable length would be in the order of 1024 to 2048 bits.

Choose a special number g. The special number g must be what is known as a *primitive element* modulo p. This number must be between 1 and $p - 1$, but cannot be *any* such number because not all numbers in this range are primitive. It suffices to accept g as being 'special', but if you wish to learn more about what *primitive* means then see the Mathematics Appendix.

Choose the private key. The private key x can be any number bigger than 1 and smaller than $p - 1$. We assume that the private key is generated using a suitably random process, which results in it being extremely unlikely that two users of the same system have the same private key.

Compute the last part of the public key. The value y is computed from the parameters p, g and the private key x as follows:

$$y = g^x \bmod p.$$

The ElGamal public key consists of the three parameters (p, g, y)

As an example, suppose that $p = 23$ and that $g = 11$ (we confirm that 11 is a primitive element modulo 23 in the Mathematics Appendix). The private key x can be any number bigger than 1 and smaller than 22, so we choose $x = 6$. The value y is then computed as follows:

$$y = 11^6 = 9 \bmod 23.$$

Thus the private key is 6 and the public key is $(23, 11, 9)$.

5.3.2 Encryption and decryption using ElGamal

While the generation of an ElGamal key pair is arguably simpler than the equivalent process for RSA, encryption and decryption are slightly more complex than RSA.

ELGAMAL ENCRYPTION

Suppose that we wish to send a plaintext to someone whose ElGamal public key is (p, g, y). ElGamal encryption operates on numbers modulo p. Thus the first task is to represent our plaintext as a series of numbers modulo p. Just as we did for RSA, we assume that there is some agreed method of doing this.

Suppose that we now want to encrypt the first plaintext P, which we have already represented as a number modulo p. The encryption process to obtain the ciphertext C is as follows:

1. randomly generate a number k;
2. compute two values C_1 and C_2, where:

$$\begin{aligned} C_1 &= g^k \bmod p, \\ C_2 &= Py^k \bmod p; \end{aligned}$$

3. send the ciphertext C, where C consists of the two separate values (C_1, C_2), sent together.

We now look more carefully at C_1 and C_2 in order to determine what role in the ciphertext each plays:

- The value k is randomly generated for this ciphertext, and *only* for this ciphertext. The next time a plaintext is encrypted, even if it is exactly the same plaintext as before, a new k should be randomly generated (we discuss why this is important in Section 5.3.4). Thus we can think of k as being a temporary (one-time) 'key'. The first component C_1 of the ciphertext is $g^k \bmod p$. Recall from Section 5.1.4

that modular exponentiation (of which this is an example) is believed to be a one-way function. This means that calculating C_1 is easy, but determining k from C_1 is believed to be hard. Thus C_1 is best thought of as a one-way representation of the temporary key k.

- The second ciphertext component C_2 is a function of the plaintext P, the public key component y and the temporary key k. More precisely, it is P multiplied by y^k, and then reduced modulo p. Thus C_2 can be thought of as the encryption of P using both the public-key component y and the temporary key k.

Using the above interpretation, we see that C_2 is in some sense the 'real' encryption of P using both y and a temporary key k. The receiver knows the matching private key x, so it would be reasonable to assume that they should be able to reverse any encryption process that uses the public-key component y. However, k is a one-time value that the receiver does not know, since the sender generated it on the fly during this particular encryption process. Thus the receiver must have some means of 'removing' the impact of the temporary key k.

The importance of C_1 should now be clear. It is the means of communicating information about the temporary key k to the receiver in a way that does not allow an attacker, who can observe C_1 since it is part of the ciphertext, to determine k from C_1. Of course, the receiver cannot determine k directly from C_1 either, but we will see shortly that this does not matter. ElGamal has been designed in a very clever way that allows the holder of the private key to reverse both the use of y and k in the encryption process.

Using the ElGamal key pair that we generated in the previous example, the plaintext $P = 10$ is encrypted as follows:

1. randomly generate a number, say $k = 3$;
2. compute the two values C_1 and C_2, where:

$$C_1 = 11^3 = 20 \bmod 23,$$

$$C_2 = 10 \times 9^3 = 10 \times 16 = 160 = 22 \bmod 23;$$

3. send the ciphertext $C = (C_1, C_2) = (20, 22)$.

ELGAMAL DECRYPTION

To decrypt the ciphertext (C_1, C_2) using private key x, the following two steps are required:

1. compute $(C_1)^x \bmod p$;
2. divide C_2 by the result of step 1:

$$P = \frac{C_2}{(C_1)^x} \bmod p.$$

Once again there are good reasons for these two steps. The first step allows the receiver to use their private key x to modify C_1 in a way that allows the effect of the temporary key k to be 'removed' in the second step. The receiver will never learn exactly what value of temporary key k the sender used, but they will learn enough to be able to remove its impact on the ciphertext. In the second step the plaintext is extracted from the ciphertext using the private key x.

Why does this work? Just as we did for RSA, we address this question in the Mathematics Appendix, allowing the option of just accepting that it does! However, it is worth noting that the explanation relies on nothing more than simple rearrangements of the above formula and does not require any significant results from mathematics.

Before looking at a simple example, we make one observation. The second decryption step involves dividing one number by another modulo p. Formally there is no such thing as 'division' in modular arithmetic. This process of 'dividing' a number a by a number b modulo p is instead carried out by multiplying a by the *modular inverse* of b (a number that is usually represented by b^{-1} and which is discussed in more detail in the Mathematics Appendix). Thus it would strictly be more accurate to describe the process of decrypting (C_1, C_2) using private key x as:

1. compute $(C_1)^x \bmod p$,
2. (a) calculate the modular inverse of $(C_1)^x$ modulo p, which we write as $((C_1)^x)^{-1}$;
   (b) $P = C_2 \times ((C_1)^x)^{-1} \bmod p$.

The only potentially awkward decryption computation is thus calculating the modular inverse. However, modular inverses can be calculated very easily using the same Extended Euclidean Algorithm that we used to set up an RSA key pair (see Section 5.2.1).

Continuing our example, to decrypt the ciphertext $C = (C_1, C_2) = (20, 22)$ using private key $x = 6$:

1. compute $20^6 = 16 \bmod 23$,
2. (a) calculate the modular inverse of 16 modulo 23, which we write as 16^{-1}; using the Extended Euclidean Algorithm, we find that $16^{-1} = 13 \bmod 23$;
   (b) $P = 22 \times 13 = 10 \bmod 23$.

Since $P = 10$ was indeed the plaintext that we started with, the decryption has been successful.

5.3.3 Security of ElGamal

Just as we did for RSA in Section 5.2.3, we will consider two different approaches that could be taken in order to break ElGamal.

DECRYPTING A CIPHERTEXT WITHOUT KNOWLEDGE OF THE PRIVATE KEY

The most obvious attack on an ElGamal ciphertext (C_1, C_2) is to determine the temporary key k. An attacker who can determine k can then compute y^k, and then 'divide' C_2 by this to obtain the plaintext P. To obtain k the attacker could either try to extract k from:

1. $C_1 = g^k \bmod p$;
2. $C_2 = Py^k \bmod p$, which is difficult because the attacker does not know P.

Thus C_1 looks the best bet, since both C_1 and g are known to the attacker. However, determining k from knowledge of $g^k \bmod p$ involves solving the discrete logarithm problem that we discussed in Section 5.1.4. It is thus widely *believed* (but not *proven*), that we need to solve the discrete logarithm problem in order to obtain an ElGamal plaintext directly from an ElGamal ciphertext.

DETERMINING THE PRIVATE KEY DIRECTLY FROM THE PUBLIC KEY

To conduct the more powerful attack of determining an ElGamal private key directly from an ElGamal public key, we need to work out x from knowledge of $y = g^x \bmod p$. Once again, this requires a process for solving the discrete logarithm problem. Thus directly determining the private key is also believed to be hard.

ELGAMAL SECURITY SUMMARY

We have just seen that both the 'obvious' attacks on ElGamal appear to only be viable if a means of efficiently solving the discrete logarithm problem can be found. Thus ElGamal is believed to be a strong public-key cryptosystem.

5.3.4 ElGamal in practice

There are several important aspects of ElGamal that deserve further discussion.

USE OF SYSTEM-WIDE PARAMETERS

One interesting aspect of ElGamal is that the values p and g can be treated as *system-wide parameters*, which are publicly known values that are shared by all the users of the system. In this case we can regard the public key of a particular user as simply being the value y. The main cost of this is that the users have to agree to use the same system-wide parameters, but the benefit is that key generation becomes slightly more straightforward.

PROBABILISTIC ENCRYPTION

ElGamal is an example of what is often termed *probabilistic encryption*. This is because each time the same plaintext is encrypted using the same public key, the resulting ciphertext should be *different* since the ciphertext relies on a randomly generated temporary key k as well as the public key y.

The obvious cost of probabilistic encryption is that it requires the random generation of a number. This could be regarded as disadvantageous in comparison to cryptosystems that do not appear to require this, such as the version of RSA that we described in Section 5.2.

However, a significant advantage of probabilistic encryption is that it prevents the following attack on a public-key cryptosystem. Suppose that a ciphertext to a known recipient has been observed by an attacker, who then proceeds to:

1. make an informed guess as to the value of the plaintext;
2. encrypt the guessed plaintext using the known recipient's public key;
3. if the result matches the observed ciphertext then the guess was correct; if not, try another guess of the plaintext.

This attack is particulary effective in situations where there are limited choices for the plaintext, for example, if the plaintext is a database entry from a limited range. In some sense, this attack could be regarded as an 'informed' *exhaustive plaintext search*.

Note that this attack does not apply to symmetric cryptosystems. This is because the encryption key is secret. Even if the attacker knows that the plaintext comes from a small set of potential values (perhaps even just two), the attacker cannot conduct this attack because *any* encryption key could have been used. This is why the attacker has to exhaustively search through all the potential symmetric keys instead.

Probabilistic encryption makes an exhaustive plaintext search attack impractical to conduct because the attacker now also has to guess the temporary key k that was used in order to encrypt any plaintext guess. If k is randomly generated using a secure process, such as those discussed in Section 8.1.4, then the attacker now has to exhaustively try *all* the possible values of k for *every* guess of the plaintext. This will almost certainly be infeasible.

In practice the security benefits of probabilistic encryption are sufficiently significant that even RSA tends to be implemented in a probabilistic manner, typically by introducing randomly generated values into the way that the plaintext is padded prior to encryption. One well-respected scheme for doing this is known as *RSA-OAEP*. The minor disadvantage of requiring random generation can be partially offset by conducting some of this work in advance and storing the results. For example, in ElGamal the calculation $C_1 = g^k$ does not involve the plaintext P and thus could have been computed earlier and just looked up from a table at the time of encryption.

MESSAGE EXPANSION

Most of the previous encryption algorithms that we have studied encrypt a plaintext into a ciphertext of identical length. ElGamal shares the property of homophonic encoding (see Section 2.2.3) that the ciphertext is *longer* than the plaintext. We previously referred to this property as *message expansion*. More precisely, an ElGamal ciphertext is twice as long as the corresponding plaintext, since each plaintext unit is a number modulo p, while its corresponding ciphertext consists of two numbers modulo p. This represents a potential cost in terms of bandwidth and storage.

For this reason ElGamal is rarely implemented in practice in the form that we have just described. However, as we will shortly discuss, elliptic-curve-based variants of ElGamal allow the size of the keys to become sufficiently small that, despite this message expansion, they are often preferred over RSA for efficiency reasons.

5.3.5 Elliptic Curve Cryptography

Elliptic Curve Cryptography (ECC) is a phrase used to describe a suite of cryptographic primitives and protocols whose security is based on special versions of the discrete logarithm problem. Instead of using the numbers modulo p, ECC is based on different sets of numbers. These numbers are associated with mathematical objects called *elliptic curves*. There are rules for adding and computing multiples of these numbers, just as there are for numbers modulo p. We will not concern ourselves here with any of the details of elliptic curves or how to combine the points on such a curve.

ECC includes a number of variants of cryptographic primitives that were first designed for modular numbers. As well as variants of ElGamal encryption, these include an elliptic-curve-based variant of the Diffie–Hellman key agreement protocol (see Section 9.4.2), and an elliptic-curve-based variant of the Digital Signature Algorithm (see Section 7.3.6).

The advantage of switching from numbers modulo p to points on an elliptic curve is that it is believed that the discrete logarithm problem is *much harder* when applied to points on an elliptic curve. The important implication of this is that an equivalent security level can be obtained for shorter keys if we use elliptic-curve-based variants. We will show the approximate extent of this reduction in Section 5.4.

The many advantages of shorter keys, both in terms of key management and efficient computation (see Section 10.2), make elliptic-curve-based variants highly attractive for many application environments. ECC primitives are being increasingly adopted, especially in resource-constrained environments.

5.4 Comparison of RSA, ElGamal and elliptic curve variants

Since RSA and elliptic-curve-based variants of ElGamal are the most commonly deployed public-key cryptosystems, in this section we present a brief comparison.

5.4.1 Popularity of RSA

Historically there is no doubt that RSA has been by far the most popular public-key cryptosystem. There are several possible reasons for this:

Maturity. RSA was one of the first public-key cryptosystems to be proposed and was the first to gain widespread recognition. Thus, in many senses, RSA is the 'brand-leader'.

Lack of message expansion. ElGamal involves message expansion by default, which made its use potentially undesirable. Note that while 'textbook' RSA does not, RSA-OAEP involves a degree of message expansion.

Marketing. The use of RSA was marketed from an early stage by a commercial company. Indeed, it was at one stage subject to patent in certain parts of the world. ElGamal has not had such successful commercial backing. However, ECC does, and there are a number of patents on ECC primitives.

5.4.2 Performance issues

In comparison with most symmetric encryption algorithms, neither RSA nor any variants of ElGamal are particularly efficient. The main problem is that in each case encryption involves exponentiation. We saw in Section 3.2.3 that exponentiation has complexity n^3. This means that it is easy to compute but is not as efficient as other more straightforward operations such as addition (complexity n) and multiplication (complexity n^2).

In this respect RSA is more efficient for encryption than ElGamal variants, since it only requires one exponentiation (and by choosing the exponent e to have a certain format this can be made to be a faster than average exponentiation computation), whereas ElGamal variants need two. However, we already noted in Section 5.3.4 that the computation of C_1 could be done in advance and so some people argue that there is very little difference in computational efficiency.

In contrast, decryption is slightly more efficient for ElGamal variants than for RSA. This is because running the Extended Euclidean Algorithm, which is necessary for ElGamal-based decryption, is a more efficient computation than an exponentiation, which is necessary for RSA decryption.

There has been a lot of work invested in trying to speed up the exponentiation process in order to make RSA and ElGamal variants more efficient. A combination of clever engineering and mathematical expertise has led to faster implementations, but they are all slower than symmetric computations. For this reason none of these public-key cryptosystems are normally used for bulk data encryption (see Section 5.5).

5.4.3 Security issues

In order to compare different public-key cryptosystems, we first need to establish a means of relating the security of one public-key cryptosystem to another.

KEY LENGTHS OF PUBLIC-KEY CRYPTOSYSTEMS

Just as for symmetric cryptosystems, the length of a private (decryption) key is an important parameter of a public-key cryptosystem and is one that can be used to compare different public-key cryptosystems. A complicating factor is that keys in public-key cryptosystems are:

- first specified in terms of 'numbers';
- then converted into binary strings for implementation.

As a result, unlike in symmetric cryptosystems, the actual length in bits of a private key will vary, since a smaller 'number' will involve fewer bits when it is converted into binary. Thus we tend to regard the 'length' of a private key as the maximum length that the private key could possibly be.

In order to determine the (maximum) length of a private key we have to consider the specifics of the public-key cryptosystem. For example, in RSA the decryption key d is a number modulo n. This means that the decryption key can be any number less than n. Hence the maximum number of bits that we need to represent an RSA private key is the smallest number k such that:

$$2^k \geq n.$$

This might sound a bit complicated since, given the modulus n, we would appear to have to perform some calculation before we can determine the length in bits of an RSA private key. However, the good news is that key length is of sufficient importance that we tend to approach this issue the other way around. In other words, public-key cryptosystems tend to be referred to directly in terms of their maximum private key lengths. When someone refers to *1024-bit RSA*, they mean that the modulus n is 1024 bits long when written in binary and thus that the maximum private key length is also 1024 bits. This means that the actual modulus n, when considered as a 'number', is much (much) bigger than 1024. More precisely, the modulus n will be a number in the range:

$$2^{1023} \leq n < 2^{1024},$$

since these are the numbers that have 1024 bits when written in binary.

COMPARING SECURITY OF PUBLIC-KEY CRYPTOSYSTEMS

Comparing the security of two different public-key cryptosystems, especially if they are based on different computationally hard problems, is a task best left to the experts. It is not usually easy to come up with direct comparisons of their relative security. As we further discuss in Section 10.2, this issue is further complicated by the fact that assessment tends to be subjective and the relative security may change over time, for example, if progress is made on solving one hard problem but not another.

Security comparisons tend to be expressed in terms of the key length. In other words, for a given perceived level of security, the required key length to achieve this security level for each public-key cryptosystem is determined. A common benchmark for the 'perceived level' of security is to use the difficulty of exhaustive key searches for given symmetric key lengths. For example, a perceived level of security defined by a symmetric key length of 128 bits means that solving the underlying hard problem for the given public-key cryptosystem is believed to be as hard as conducting an exhaustive key search for a 128-bit symmetric key.

EXHAUSTIVE KEY SEARCHES FOR PRIVATE KEYS

Note that we almost never consider the concept of an exhaustive search for the private key of a public-key cryptosystem. This is because:

1. An 'uninformed' exhaustive search of all possible private keys is normally impossible because the key lengths involved are so much larger than for symmetric cryptosystems. A complete exhaustive search for a 1024-bit RSA private key will involve trying 2^{1024} keys, which is clearly an impossible task, keeping in mind that searching for a 128-bit symmetric key is regarded as infeasible for the foreseeable future!
2. An 'informed' exhaustive key search would consist of only trying private keys that have the necessary mathematical properties. For example, not all 1024-bit numbers are possible values of d for RSA. To perform such a search we need a means of determining which keys are valid candidates for private keys. The catch is that finding that means of determining candidates tends to be related to solving the underlying hard problem. In the case of RSA, in order to determine whether a number is a candidate for d we first need to know the factorisation of n.
3. Most importantly, an exhaustive private key search is generally not the most efficient method of attacking a public-key cryptosystem. The equivalent 'benchmark' attack on a public-key cryptosystem is the best-known attack on the underlying hard problem (factoring, in the case of RSA).

As a result it tends to be more appropriate to focus on trying to solve the underlying hard problem rather than attempting an exhaustive search for the private key of a public-key cryptosystem.

RELATIVE KEY LENGTHS

Table 5.2 shows the estimated equivalence between key lengths for RSA (represented by the bit length of the modulus n), ElGamal (represented by the bit length of the group size p) and elliptic-curve-based ElGamal variants (represented by the bit length of the underlying elliptic curve group), based on one example of expert opinion. It also indicates the bit length of a symmetric key for which an exhaustive key search provides the perceived level of security.

Note that the values in Table 5.2 represent respected guidance at a particular moment in time. It would be prudent to check the latest opinions and information on such equivalences.

One interesting issue to note about the key lengths in Table 5.2 is that it is believed that we get equivalent security for the same key length in both RSA and basic ElGamal. For example, the equivalent security for an RSA modulus of 1776 bits requires an ElGamal modulus p of the same length. However, crucially,

Table 5.2: ECRYPT II key length equivalence recommendations (2010) [66]

RSA modulus	ElGamal group size	Elliptic curve	Symmetric equivalent
816	816	128	64
1008	1008	144	72
1248	1248	160	80
1776	1776	192	96
2432	2432	224	112
3248	3248	256	128
15424	15424	512	256

employing elliptic-curve-based ElGamal variants at the same perceived security level requires keys of only 192 bits, which is significantly shorter.

Currently 1024 bits is regarded as an acceptable general key length for RSA, with 2048 bits recommended for those who want an extra safety margin. For elliptic-curve-based ElGamal variants, 160 bits is acceptable and 224 bits provides a safety margin. However, these recommendations are subject to change over time. We will discuss key lengths again, from a key management perspective, in Section 10.2.

5.4.4 The future for public-key cryptosystems

As we have seen, the security of a (good) symmetric cryptosystem primarily relies on the difficulty of conducting an exhaustive key search. On the other hand, the security of a public-key cryptosystem is based on the difficulty of solving some underlying hard computational problem. As we discussed in Section 5.2.3, the security of RSA is believed to be based on the difficulty of factoring while, as we discussed in Section 5.3.3, the security of ElGamal is believed to be based on the difficulty of solving the discrete logarithm problem. As suggested by Table 5.2, both of these problems are regarded as hard, and neither one is regarded as easier than the other.

There are considerable advantages to be gained from ensuring that we retain efficient public-key cryptosystems that are based on different hard problems. If, one day, someone develops an efficient method for factoring large numbers then the discrete logarithm problem might, at least in theory, still be secure. That said, there are some experts who hold the opinion that if a breakthrough occurs that results in one of these problems no longer being regarded as hard, then there may be similar implications for the other one. Only time will tell.

Of more concern is that both of these problems are no longer regarded as hard if an attacker has access to a *quantum computer*, which is a computer that is based on the principles of quantum mechanics and is capable of conducting an exponential number of simultaneous computations. It is known that a quantum computer can both factor and compute discrete logarithms in polynomial time. Quantum computers are still just conceptual and it remains unclear on what timescale practical quantum computers could actually be built. Nonetheless there is considerable interest in developing public-key cryptosystems whose security is based on hard problems that cannot (apparently) be efficiently solved by a quantum computer.

5.5 Uses in practice of public-key cryptosystems

We began this chapter by looking at the motivation behind the introduction of public-key cryptosystems. We then examined two examples of public-key cryptosystems. But what are public-key cryptosystems used for in practice?

5.5.1 Restrictions on use of public-key cryptosystems

Despite their attractive properties, there are two significant factors that restrict the application of public-key cryptosystems:

Computational costs. As noted in Section 5.4.2, public-key encryption and decryption are relatively expensive computations to perform. This means that in applications where processing speed is important (in other words, almost every application!) it is often regarded as a good idea to restrict the number of public-key encryption and decryption operations that are performed. This is by far the most important restriction on use of these public-key cryptosystems.

Long-plaintext security issues. All our discussion of public-key encryption in this chapter has involved encryption of single plaintexts that can be represented by one 'unit' of public-key encryption. For example, we assumed that a plaintext to be encrypted using an RSA public key (n, e) could be represented as a number less than n. If we want to encrypt a longer plaintext then we first have to split the plaintext up into separate 'units' and then encrypt these separately. If we consider each of these plaintexts as 'blocks' (which is a reasonable analogy) then, by default, we would be encrypting these separate blocks using the public-key equivalent of ECB mode for a block cipher. This gives rise to several security issues that we discussed in Section 4.6.1, all of which were resolved by proposing different modes of operation for block ciphers. However, there are no alternative modes of operation proposed for public-key encryption. (This is, of course, primarily because of the lack of demand, due to the computational issue just discussed.) Thus, from a security perspective, it might also be wise to restrict the use of public-key encryption to single plaintexts, where by 'single' we mean that the entire plaintext can be encrypted in one computation.

Thus there is a strong case *from both an efficiency and a security perspective* for limiting the use of public-key encryption to 'occasional' short plaintexts.

5.5.2 Hybrid encryption

There are many applications where we want to use public-key encryption for the benefits discussed in Section 5.1.1, but where the plaintexts are long and thus we cannot use public-key encryption for the reasons just discussed in Section 5.5.1. The elegant and simple solution to this conundrum is known as *hybrid encryption*. If Alice wants to encrypt a (long) plaintext and send it to Bob, she:

1. generates a symmetric K and public-key encrypts the symmetric key K using the public key of Bob;
2. symmetrically encrypts the plaintext using K.

Alice then sends both of these ciphertexts to Bob. On receiving the two ciphertexts, Bob:

1. recovers the symmetric key K by decrypting the first ciphertext using his private key;
2. recovers the original plaintext by decrypting the second ciphertext using K.

This hybrid encryption process is depicted in Figure 5.2.

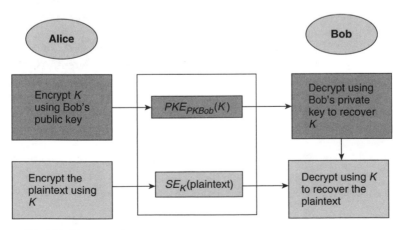

Figure 5.2. Hybrid encryption

Note from Table 5.2 that a symmetric key can always be represented as a short plaintext with respect to the recommended lengths of security parameters for public-key cryptosystems. Indeed, a 128-bit AES key is small enough to be encrypted as a single plaintext using any of the public-key cryptosystem parameters in Table 5.2, including those of an elliptic-curve-based cryptosystem offering just 64 bits of symmetric security (although it would be rather bizarre to do this since the effective security of the hybrid encryption would be reduced to just 64 bits).

In this way hybrid encryption gains the best of both cryptographic worlds by benefitting from:

Speed. The speed of symmetric key encryption is utilised for the encryption of the plaintext.

Convenience. The key management convenience of public-key cryptosystems enables two entities who do not have a direct trust relationship to securely communicate.

For encryption in open networks, hybrid encryption is essentially the default technique. We will see examples of this in Section 12.1 and Section 12.7.

5.5.3 Other uses of public-key cryptosystems

In addition to hybrid encryption, public-key encryption is often used in cryptographic protocols (see Chapter 9) where it is typically used to encrypt short messages. The only other application for which public-key cryptosystems are commonly employed is for the provision of a very different security service where the 'plaintext' to be 'encrypted' is short. This application is not for confidentiality purposes (hence our use of the quotation marks) and will be the subject of Chapter 7.

We note that this chapter has dealt exclusively with 'conventional' public-key encryption. There is, however, another family of public-key cryptosystems that tends to be referred to as *identity-based public-key cryptography*. The main difference between identity-based cryptosystems and cryptosystems such as RSA lies in the key management issues, which are significantly different. As a result, the potential applications for both types of cryptosystem are quite different. We will postpone discussion of identity-based public-key cryptography until Section 11.4.2.

5.6 Summary

In this chapter we have investigated public-key encryption. We looked at the general problem of designing a public-key cryptosystem and then studied two public-key cryptosystems in some detail. We have also looked at how the properties of public-key cryptosystems are most effectively harnessed in applications.

The main issues that we covered were:

- Public-key cryptosystems provide the potential for two entities who do not share a symmetric key to employ cryptography to secure data that they exchange.
- Public-key encryption requires the use of a trapdoor one-way function.
- RSA is a well-respected and widely-deployed public-key cryptosystem whose security is based on the belief that factoring large numbers is difficult.
- ElGamal is a public-key cryptosystem whose security is based on the belief that solving the discrete logarithm problem is difficult.
- Variants of ElGamal that are based on elliptic curves offer the significant benefit that keys are shorter than in either RSA or basic ElGamal.
- Public-key cryptosystems are less efficient to operate than most symmetric cryptosystems. As a result public-key encryption is usually employed in a process called hybrid encryption, which exchanges a symmetric key that is then used for bulk data encryption.

The significant advantages to applications opened up by public-key cryptosystems led to a revolution in cryptography in the mid-1970s, with a further boom in interest following the development of the Internet in the 1990s. Public-key cryptosystems are only likely to grow in importance in the coming years.

Public-key cryptography, to an extent, 'solves' the problem of symmetric key establishment. However, as we indicate in more detail in Section 10.1.3, it 'replaces' this problem with one of authenticating public keys. None of the advantages of public-key cryptosystems can be fully exploited unless we have some level of assurance that public keys are indeed associated with the entities to which we believe they belong. This is a subject that we will discuss in detail in Chapter 11.

5.7 Further reading

The history of the development of public-key cryptography is fascinating and, as well as providing further motivation for this chapter, is well worth learning more about. Good accounts can be found in Levy [117, 118] and Singh [176]. Also well worth a read is the account by Ellis of the earlier British discovery of public-key cryptography [69].

We have tried to be self-contained with respect to the minimum background mathematics required for understanding the public-key cryptosystems in this chapter. Most mathematical introductions to cryptography such as Menezes, van Oorschot and Vanstone [123] and Stinson [185] provide more technical details including, for example, details of the Extended Euclidean Algorithm. Several mathematical introductions to cryptography such as Pipher, Hoffstein and Silverman [100] and Smart [178] have a particular focus on public-key cryptography. All these books also provide information on how to generate large primes for use in practical public-key cryptosystems, which is a topic that we have not discussed.

The paper by Diffie and Hellman [59] that first introduced the world to the idea of public-key cryptography is quite accessible. Also fascinating from a historical perspective is Diffie's personal account of the first ten years of public-key cryptography [58]. The idea behind RSA was first published by Rivest, Shamir and Adleman [163] in 1978. A survey of attacks on RSA is provided by Boneh [39]. Further technical details on how to implement RSA are provided by the Public-Key Cryptography Standards (PKCS) [115]. The first of these standards PKCS#1 includes details of RSA-OAEP, which is one of the most popular methods of implementing RSA. ISO/IEC 18033 [12] includes public-key encryption and standards for hybrid encryption. Dent and Mitchell [55] include a good overview of these and other relevant standards.

The ElGamal cryptosystem was published by ElGamal [68]. The background mathematics behind elliptic curve cryptography can be found in many general texts such as Mollin [125] and Stinson [185], however, Koblitz [109] and Washington [196] have very detailed introductions. Those seeking information about implementing elliptic curve cryptography should consult Hankerson, Menezes and Vanstone [96]. An alternative source of information is the ECC Tutorial from Certicom [45]. Commercial standards for elliptic curve cryptography are developed by the Standards for Efficient Cryptography Group (SECG) [172] and are also defined in ISO/IEC 15946 [10].

A portal for comparing advice on key lengths for public-key cryptosystems is provided by Giry [89]. Moses [126] is a short position paper on the likely impact of quantum computing on the future of cryptography. A more technical survey of public-key cryptosystems that are resistant to quantum computers is Perlner and Cooper [156]. One such scheme called NTRU is described in the draft standard IEEE P1363.1 [147]. CrypTool [52] has an implementation of RSA and a good simulation of hybrid encryption.

5.8 Activities

1. The *briefcase protocol* depicted in Figure 5.1 shows that it is possible to exchange a confidential message between two entities who have not shared a key.

   (a) Design a cryptographic analogy of the briefcase protocol that uses symmetric encryption instead of locking the briefcase with a padlock.

(b) This cryptographic analogy of the briefcase protocol does not always work; what property does a symmetric cryptosystem need to have for it to work?

(c) Give an example of a symmetric cryptosystem that has this property.

2. Which of the following statements are true?

(a) The RSA cryptosystem will be broken if large primes can be factored.

(b) The ElGamal cryptosystem is not used in practice because of security concerns.

(c) RSA encryption is efficient to compute, whereas ElGamal encryption is not.

(d) RSA encryption does not involve significant message expansion.

(e) The security of the ElGamal cryptosystem is equivalent to solving the discrete logarithm problem.

3. RSA operates on plaintexts that are modular numbers, thus we must have some means of converting plaintext and ciphertext into modular numbers. This activity suggests different ways in which this conversion can be done.

(a) Use ASCII to write the plaintext CAT as a string of 21 bits.

(b) Divide this bit string into seven blocks of three bits and write each as an integer from 0 to 7.

(c) Encrypt each of these seven blocks using RSA, where $p = 3$, $q = 5$ and $e = 3$, writing the resulting ciphertext as a sequence of seven integers in the range 0 to 14.

(d) Using four bits per number, convert the ciphertext to a bit string.

(e) Write the ciphertext in hex.

4. Consider setting up RSA with $p = 7$ and $q = 11$.

(a) What are the suitable values for e?

(b) If $e = 13$, what is the value of d?

(c) What is the largest 'block size' in bits that we could use for RSA encryption using these parameters?

5. An ElGamal cryptosystem can be implemented in such a way that all users share the same system-wide parameters p and g. This raises the question as to whether it is possible for all users of an RSA cryptosystem to share a common modulus n.

(a) Suppose that Alice and Bob have each generated their own RSA public keys with the same modulus n but different public exponents e_A and e_B. Explain why Alice will be able to decrypt encrypted messages sent to Bob (and vice versa).

(b) Suppose that a trusted third party generates Alice and Bob's RSA key pairs for them. Find out, perhaps by consulting external resources, whether it is now acceptable for Alice and Bob to share a common modulus n.

6. Over the years there have been various factoring 'challenge' competitions set up.

   (a) What do you think the purpose of these factoring challenges is?

   (b) What is the largest RSA challenge number to have been factored?

7. Certain RSA encryption exponents e are regularly chosen because they have a special format. An example is $e = 2^{16} + 1$.

   (a) What are the advantages of RSA exponents that have this type of format?

   (b) Explain why it is not a problem if more than one user has the same encryption exponent e.

   (c) Why is it generally not advisable to choose RSA decryption keys d that have a similar format?

   (d) Under what special circumstances might there be a case for allowing decryption keys d to have special formats (similar, but not necessarily identical to the above example)?

8. RSA-OAEP is a standard for the practical implementation of RSA encryption. Explain how RSA-OAEP differs from the 'textbook' RSA described in this chapter.

9. Two of Alice's public-key components in a simple ElGamal cryptosystem are $p = 17$ and $g = 3$.

   (a) If Alice's private key is $x = 5$, what is her public key?

   (b) What is the ciphertext corresponding to the plaintext $P = 4$ if the randomly generated number $k = 2$ is used?

10. Elliptic Curve Cryptography provides approaches that are attractive for many applications.

   (a) Why are elliptic-curved-based variants more popular than the original ElGamal, on which they are based?

   (b) Provide some examples of applications supporting ECC primitives (either for encryption or other security services).

   (c) Do you think that there is much of a future for RSA, given the advantages of elliptic-curve-based approaches?

11. RSA and ElGamal both require the use of large primes. Find out how primes can be generated that are sufficiently large for use in practical public-key cryptosystems.

12. Compile a list of cryptographic applications that implement hybrid encryption.

13. Explain why, in general, public-key cryptosystems have longer key lengths than symmetric cryptosystems.

14. Why are modes of operation not relevant, and have thus not been proposed, for public-key encryption?

15. Public-key cryptography has been invented on at least one occasion prior to the public discovery by Diffie and Hellman in 1976.

(a) What is *non-secret encryption*?

(b) Who was Britain's equivalent of Rivest, Shamir and Adleman and when did he come up with his idea?

(c) Why were these ideas not published?

16. Quantum computers will have a significant impact on the practice of cryptography.

(a) What is the likely impact on public-key cryptography if a practical quantum computer can be built?

(b) How fast can an exhaustive key search be conducted on a quantum computer?

(c) What is the likely impact on symmetric cryptography if a practical quantum computer can be built?

17. There have been various side-channel attacks against public-key cryptosystems.

(a) Provide a short description of one such attack.

(b) Why do you think public-key cryptosystems are particularly vulnerable to certain types of side-channel attack?

18. Public-key cryptography normally works under the assumption that public keys are, as defined, public pieces of information. However, some people have suggested that, in certain circumstances, it might make sense to keep public keys secret. This means that only those who *need* to know a public key are given it by some secure means, and they are required to store the public key as a secret.

(a) What are the potential costs and benefits of using *secret* public keys?

(b) Can you think of any applications where this idea might have some value?

6 Data Integrity

Thus far we have concentrated on using cryptography to provide confidentiality. In this chapter we begin our investigation of cryptographic mechanisms that are designed to provide other security services. It is important to appreciate that much of our previous discussion, which was framed around encryption, also applies to the wider use of cryptography. In particular the discussions on security assumptions in Section 1.5 and the breaking of cryptosystems in Section 1.6 are directly applicable.

The focus of this chapter is on the provision of data integrity. We will look at mechanisms that provide only a 'light' notion of data integrity, as well as those that provide the stronger notion of data origin authentication. This chapter will only discuss data integrity mechanisms that are either symmetric or have no key. In Chapter 7 we will consider mechanisms based on asymmetric cryptography that also provide data integrity.

At the end of this chapter you should be able to:

- Appreciate that there are different levels of data integrity.
- Identify the different properties of a hash function.
- Comment on different applications of a hash function and which properties they require.
- Recognise the significance of the length of the output of a hash function.
- Explain how to use a MAC to provide data origin authentication.
- Describe two different approaches to constructing a MAC.
- Compare different ways of combining MACs with encryption to provide confidentiality and data origin authentication.

6.1 Different levels of data integrity

Data integrity is a slightly confusing security service because it is often referred to in different contexts. The best way of identifying the context is to consider the

186

strength of a potential 'attack' against the integrity of some data. For our purposes, we will consider four different levels of data integrity that can be provided by considering four increasing levels of attack:

Accidental errors. This first level of data integrity provides protection only against accidental errors. Such errors are most likely to occur through noise in a communication channel. Data integrity mechanisms that offer this level of data integrity include error-correcting codes (see Section 1.4.4) and simple checksums such as *cyclic redundancy checks* (CRCs). These techniques involve the computation of a digest that is appended to the original data. The digest is computed using a simple mathematical computation that is based on the data. Since the digest can be computed by anyone, these mechanisms offer no protection against an active attacker. We will not further discuss mechanisms in this category, since their integrity protection is weak.

Simple manipulations. The second level of data integrity protects against simple manipulations. Mechanisms providing protection only against accidental errors often have the property that if the data is changed in a particular way then the new integrity digest can be predicted without needing to formally recalculate it. For example, the integrity digest of the XOR of two messages might be the XOR of the two integrity digests. Hash functions are examples of mechanisms that can prevent simple manipulations, since they have inherent security properties that prevent this. However, an active attacker can still defeat integrity mechanisms in this category since the integrity digest can still be computed by anyone. This second category is only distinct from the first category in that an active attacker cannot 'shortcut' the computation of a new digest by manipulating old ones. We will discuss hash functions in Section 6.2.

Active attacks. The third level of data integrity protects against active attacks. Unlike the previous two categories, mechanisms in this category must be able to prevent an attacker from creating a 'valid' integrity digest on some data for which they have not previously seen an integrity digest. This strong notion of data integrity normally requires data origin authentication, since the most natural way of preventing active attacks of this type is to provide a binding between the underlying data and the source that created it. The main cryptographic mechanisms for providing this level of data integrity are MACs, which we discuss in Section 6.3.

Repudiation attacks. The fourth level of data integrity protects against a creator of an integrity digest who attempts to later deny that they created the digest. This level is necessary in applications where a 'proof' of data integrity that can be verified by a third party is required. This corresponds to non-repudiation of the source of data. We will postpone discussion of mechanisms in this category until Chapter 7, which focusses on digital signature schemes. Note, however, that under certain circumstances MACs can provide this level of data integrity (see Section 7.2).

6.2 Hash functions

Hash functions are probably the most versatile of all cryptographic primitives. They are extremely useful and appear in all sorts of surprising applications. As a standalone tool, they have few uses. However, no cryptographic designer should ever leave home without one! Such is their ubiquity that when an unexpected attack was announced in 2004 against several of the most widely deployed hash functions, there was considerable concern. Their many important and varied uses include:

As strong one-way functions. Hash functions are sometimes used to 'encrypt' highly confidential data that does not require 'decryption', such as passwords (see Section 6.2.2).

To provide a weak notion of data integrity. Hash functions can be used to provide checks against accidental changes to data and, in certain cases, deliberate manipulation of data (see Section 6.2.2). As such they are sometimes referred to as *modification detection codes* or *manipulation detection codes*.

As components to build other cryptographic primitives. Hash functions can be used to construct different cryptographic primitives such as MACs (see Section 6.3.4) and digital signature schemes with appendix (see Section 7.3.4).

As a means of binding data. Hash functions are often used within cryptographic protocols to bind data together in a single cryptographic commitment.

As sources of pseudorandomness. Hash functions are sometimes used to pseudorandomly generate numbers for use in cryptography, with an important example being the generation of cryptographic keys (see Section 10.3).

Note that the term 'hash function' has several other wider meanings in the field of computer science. While we will use the term 'hash function' because our context is clear, our hash functions are sometimes more specifically referred to as *cryptographic hash functions*.

6.2.1 Properties of a hash function

A *hash function* is a mathematical function (in other words, a process for converting a numerical input value into a numerical output value) that has two important practical properties and three security properties. Before we review these properties, it is important to appreciate the following:

Hash functions do not have a key. The security properties that a hash function delivers are all provided without the hash function using a key. In this respect they are unusual cryptographic primitives. Note that the term 'keyed hash function' is sometimes used for a *message authentication code*, which we will discuss in Section 6.3.

Hash functions are publicly computable. We always assume that an attacker knows the details of a hash function. Just as for encryption algorithms, this is the safest security assumption, for all the same reasons that we discussed in Section 1.5.3. Since hash functions do not involve a secret key, this means that anyone (in particular an attacker) can compute a valid hash for any input value.

PRACTICAL PROPERTY 1: COMPRESSES ARBITRARY LONG INPUTS INTO A FIXED LENGTH OUTPUT

What this means is that regardless of how much data is input, a hash function generates an output (or *hash*) that is always the same fixed length. This process of applying the hash function to the input data is often referred to as *hashing* the data. In general this hash is much smaller than the data that was input to the hash function. Thus a hash function performs the useful task of *compressing* data. Functions with this property are sometimes called *compression functions*. Because a hash is a small piece of data that represents a larger piece of data, it is sometimes referred to as a *digest*, and the hash function referred to as a *message digest function*.

Most of the hash functions that we are likely to come across in cryptography convert binary inputs into binary outputs. If the binary output of a particular hash function is n bits long then we refer to the hash function as an *n-bit hash function*. Popular practical values for n lie between 160 and 512 bits (we discuss this issue further in Section 6.2.3).

Note that an immediate consequence of the fact that the output of a hash function is (much) smaller than the input is that for any given hash there are likely to be many inputs that compress to the same hash value. To see that this is true, consider PINs for payment cards. The process of taking a client's personal information (name, address, bank details) and using a PIN derivation function to generate from this a four-digit PIN is a good example of a compression function. In practice, a PIN derivation function may or may not be a hash function (see, for example, Section 10.6) but it must be a compression function. If a country has 60 million bank users and PINs consist of only four digits (a maximum of 10 000 different PINs) then there will be many people who end up with the same PIN. If we do this process randomly then, on average, there will be 6000 people with the same PIN.

PRACTICAL PROPERTY 2: EASY TO COMPUTE

This means that it should be 'easy' (in terms of efficiency and speed) to compute a hash function. In other words, for a hash function h and input x it should be a fast operation to compute $h(x)$. The ubiquitous use of hash functions would not be appropriate if hash functions did not have this property.

Note that in Section 3.2.3 we provided a simple classification of ease of computation of operations. In terms of complexity theory, practical property 2 demands that a hash function can be computed in polynomial time. In fact any useful hash function is required to be a very fast function to compute (not just 'easy', but in fact 'very easy'). In general a practical hash function is expected to be much faster to compute than even a symmetric encryption operation.

SECURITY PROPERTY 1: PREIMAGE RESISTANCE

A hash function should be *preimage-resistant*, which means that it should be 'hard' (in terms of efficiency and speed) to reverse a hash function. In other words, for a hash function h, given an output (hash) value z it should be a difficult operation to find any input value x that hashes to z (in other words, $h(x) = z$). The term 'preimage-resistant' comes from the fact that the output $h(x)$ of a function h is often called the *image* of x, and hence x is referred to as a *preimage* of $h(x)$.

Note that preimage resistance is often 'lazily' defined as *given $h(x)$, it is hard to determine x*. This is 'lazy' because preimage resistance is actually a much stronger property than that. Recall that because the hash function is a compression function, there will be many inputs with the same hash. Preimage resistance means that if we obtain a hash value $h(x)$ that was obtained by hashing x (but we do not know what x was) then it is not just hard to find x, it is hard to find *any* input that hashes to $h(x)$.

In terms of complexity theory, security property 1 demands that reversing a hash function involves a process that runs in exponential time. Indeed, for all application purposes we require a hash function to be 'impossible' to reverse in any practical sense. Note that functions with practical property 2 and security property 1 are often referred to as *one-way functions*, as we mentioned in Section 5.1.4.

SECURITY PROPERTY 2: SECOND PREIMAGE RESISTANCE

The second security property is similar, but subtly different, to preimage resistance. A hash function should be *second-preimage-resistant*, which means that given an input and its hash it should be hard to find a *different* input with the *same* hash. In other words, for a hash function h, given an input x and its output (hash) value $h(x)$ it should be a difficult operation to find any other input value y such that $h(y) = h(x)$.

Essentially the difference between the first two security properties is the starting premise. Preimage resistance protects against an attacker who only has a hash value (no input value) and is trying to reverse the hash function. Second preimage resistance protects against an attacker who has an input value and its hash, and now wants to find a different input value that results in the same hash.

Another way of thinking about this is to return to our earlier example of payment card PINs. Recall that we observed that there will be many bank customers with the same PIN. Consider your own bank and your own PIN. All the other customers with the same PIN as you can be thought of as second preimages of your bank's PIN derivation function. It is desirable that the PIN derivation function is second-preimage-resistant since this makes it difficult for you to work out who they are! (Strictly speaking, this analogy assumes that the PIN derivation function is publicly known, which it may not be.)

SECURITY PROPERTY 3: COLLISION RESISTANCE

The third security property that a hash function should have is *collision resistance*, which means that it should be hard to find two different inputs (of any length) that, when fed into the hash function, result in the same hash being computed. This property is sometimes described as requiring a hash function to be *collision-free*. In other words, for a hash function h, it is hard to find two different inputs x and y such that $h(x) = h(y)$.

Note that, as we observed during our discussion of practical property 1, it is impossible for a hash function *not* to have collisions. The point is that these collisions should be hard to find. This makes it very difficult for an attacker to find two input values with the same hash.

Going back to our PIN analogy, security property 3 states that, even though many people share the same PIN, it should be very hard to find any two people who have the same PIN.

RELATIONSHIPS BETWEEN THE THREE SECURITY PROPERTIES

The three security properties of a hash function are summarised in Figure 6.1. While these three security properties are related, they are all *different*. The best way to see this is to look at some different hash function applications and identify the security properties that they require, which we do in Section 6.2.2.

There is only one clear relationship between the security properties: if a function is collision-resistant then it is second-preimage-resistant. If a function h is collision-resistant then it is hard to find any pair of values x and y for which $h(x) = h(y)$. Since this is true for *any* pair of values, it is true that given a *particular*

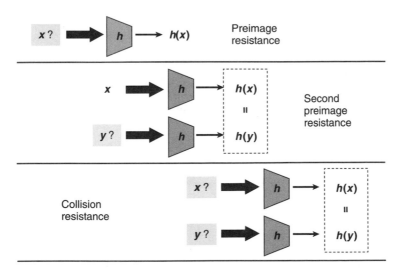

Figure 6.1. Three security properties of a hash function

191

x it is hard to find a different y such that $h(x) = h(y)$. In other words, the function h is also second-preimage-resistant. This makes intuitive sense. If finding *any* collision is hard, finding a *particular* collision will also be hard (indeed, it is *harder*).

A useful analogy is to consider a group of people, where each person is associated with an input value x. We can consider the first name of person x as a 'hash' $h(x)$ of that person's identity. It is much more likely that we will be able to find any two people x and y with the same first name $h(x) = h(y)$ than it is that we will be able to select one person whose name is (say) Bart, and then find another person in the group whose name is also Bart. The same is true for birthdays, as we will discuss more formally in Section 6.2.3.

The implication for hash functions, from an attacker's perspective, is that collisions are always easier to find than second preimages. Hence attackers of hash functions tend to focus on looking for collisions, and likewise designers of hash functions try to make collisions as hard as possible to find.

Lastly, it is worth noting that while these three security properties are all different and, as we will shortly see, they tend to be required by different types of application, cryptographers have historically designed hash functions to have all three of these security properties. There are three main reasons for this:

Potential for reuse. Although a hash function may be employed in an application that requires just one of the three security properties, it can be useful to already have it implemented in case it is later needed for use in a different application that requires a different security property. Hash functions are often regarded as the 'Swiss army knife' of the cryptographic toolkit because of this multifunctional capability.

Need for multiple properties. Some applications of hash functions require more than one of the security properties.

Similarity of the properties. It is rather difficult to design a dedicated function specifically for any of the three security properties and not the others. This is partly because it has thus far been impossible to mathematically *prove* that a function has any of these three security properties. It is only possible to design a function that is *believed* to have these three security properties. This has had serious implications in the past, as we will discuss in Section 6.2.4.

6.2.2 Applications of hash functions

We now look at three examples of applications of hash functions, each one requiring a different security property.

APPLICATION REQUIRING PREIMAGE RESISTANCE

Hash functions provide a simple, and widely adopted, way of implementing password storage protection. The idea is to store the passwords in a password file in 'disguised' form so that they can be checked, yet anyone who gains access to the password file (including perhaps the system administrator) cannot recover the passwords themselves. In this application a hash function is used to provide an unusual type of confidentiality for stored data. The unusual aspect is that the data itself (the password) never needs to be recovered. As a result, this type of confidentiality can be provided by a cryptographic primitive that does not use a key.

In advance of a logon attempt, a user's identity I is stored in the password file, next to the result of passing the user's password P through a hash function h. In other words, the password file consists of a table of pairs of the form $(I, h(P))$. Note that the passwords themselves are not stored in the password table.

The password-based logon process, which we discuss at greater length in Section 8.4, for a user attempting to access resources on a device is depicted in Figure 6.2 and operates as follows:

1. The user enters their identity I when prompted by the logon screen.
2. The user enters their password P when prompted by the logon screen.
3. The authentication application running on the device inputs the password P to the hash function and computes $h(P)$.
4. The authentication application running on the device looks up the table entry in the password file corresponding to identity I and compares the stored value of the hashed password with the value $h(P)$ that it has just calculated in step 3. If the entries match then the user is authenticated. Otherwise the user is rejected.

To appreciate the security property that this application requires of the hash function, we need to consider an attacker's perspective. The role of the hash

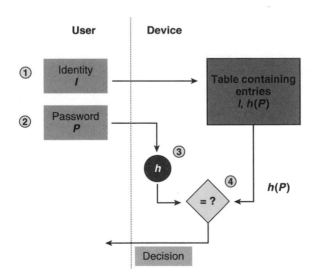

Figure 6.2. Use of a hash function to protect stored passwords

function is to protect data in the password file. We will temporarily ignore the real weakness in this type of system, which is the user's password management (that discussion can wait until Section 8.4). An attacker who has access to the password file is able to see hashes of passwords. We do not want this information to allow the attacker to determine passwords. Hence the important property that we require is *preimage resistance*. Note that the other two security properties do not concern us greatly:

Second preimage resistance. If the attacker does not know a valid password for the system then second preimage resistance is not an issue. If the attacker does know a valid password P for the system then second preimages of the hash of that password are still not particularly interesting:

- If all users are logging into a shared resource then there is no need for an attacker to seek another password with the same hash when the one he already knows will get him into the system!
- If users are logging on to private accounts and the attacker observes that another user has the same hashed password $h(P') = h(P)$ then the attacker knows that entering the known password P will also gain access to that user's account. Hence there is no apparent need for the attacker to determine the second preimage P'.

Collision resistance. Finding collisions for the hash function, in other words finding two passwords with the same hash, does not really benefit an attacker for similar reasons. The only possible beneficiary would be a malicious user who finds a collision, adopts one of the passwords and then persuades another user to adopt the other. The malicious user could now log on to both accounts with the same password. But a user with such powers of manipulation could easily subvert the system without going to the effort of seeking hash function collisions.

So it is primarily preimage resistance that we need for protecting password files. It is worth making two further observations before we leave this example:

1. Password file protection does not really require the compression property of hash functions since passwords tend to be short. All we technically need for this application is a one-way function. That said, hash functions tend to be the default one-way functions in most applications. In Section 8.4 we give an example of a one-way function that is not a compression function.
2. While the hash function provides a level of protection against an attacker who has access to the password file, in order to prevent attacks of the type that we discussed with respect to second preimage resistance, it is generally good practice to provide a further layer of security by 'hiding' the password file from attackers. Encrypting the password file would be one appropriate technique for doing so. This also prevents an attacker from conducting a dictionary attack on the password file where they compute hashes for common password choices and look for matches in the password file (see also Section 1.6.5).

Choose Download Location
mediaCam AV 2.7

You have chosen to download **mediaCam AV 2.7**. Check the file details to make sure this is the correct program and version, and that your operating system is supported.

Download Details
Operating Systems 98/2k/Me/XP
File Name mediaCamAV2.7.2.0_Installer.exe
MD5 Hash 8642009dfd6658e0399586fb271348866
File Size 4.27 MB (4,474,880 bytes)

Figure 6.3. Use of a hash function for file checksums

APPLICATION REQUIRING SECOND PREIMAGE RESISTANCE

One of the highest profile applications of hash functions is for generating checksums that offer a lightweight data integrity check. This check falls into the Section 6.1 data integrity category of protection against simple manipulations.

Hash functions are commonly used for providing a degree of assurance to a user that they have downloaded a file correctly. Figure 6.3 gives an example of this process, which works as follows:

1. A file download site displays information about a piece of software (in this case *mediaCam AV 2.7*) and a link to the executable code (in this case *Installer.exe*). It also displays an *MD5 Hash* value, which identifies the name of a hash function (MD5) and provides a hash of the executable code. MD5 is a 128-bit hash function and so the hash is commonly displayed as a 32-character hex value.

2. A user who downloads the executable code can then recompute the hash by putting the code through the MD5 hash function. The user then checks the resulting hash against the one displayed on the file download site. If they match then the user is assured that the code they have downloaded corresponds to the code that the download site intended them to have.

We describe this as a 'lightweight' data integrity check because a hash function can never be used on its own to provide integrity against an active attacker. Since a hash function has no secret key, an attacker can always modify a file and then recompute a new hash that matches the modified file. In our above example this would then require the attacker to persuade the file download site to display this modified code with its new hash value (alternatively the attacker would need to modify the information on the file download site). However, if we believe that the security of the file download site is fairly good then we can increase our 'faith' in the data integrity of the downloaded file. If the download site is fully trusted and its processes are believed to be secure then we gain strong data integrity through the knowledge that neither the file nor the hash can be altered on the site itself. In summary:

1. A hash function provides lightweight data integrity if used in isolation. It can only protect against accidental errors and simple manipulations (see Section 6.1).

195

2. A hash function can be used to provide stronger data integrity if combined with other security mechanisms. This can happen if, in particular, the hash itself is protected by another security mechanism. In our above example the security of the website might provide this assurance. Alternatively, the hash could be sent over a secure channel to anyone requiring stronger data integrity assurance.

To see what the most important security property is for this application, we need to consider what type of attack we are trying to prevent. Our main concern here is to prevent an attacker replacing the legitimate file with a corrupted file (perhaps malware). While this could be prevented by thorough security checks and processes on the file download site, it is reasonable to assume that these preventative measures might not be possible in some application environments. In order to successfully replace the file without being detected, an attacker must attempt to find another file whose hash matches the one on the download site and try to replace the link from *Installer.exe* to the corrupt code. One way of doing this would be if the attacker supplied the download site with some genuine code but then provided a link to the corrupt code for the site to point to. This would be a process failure by the download site, but it could certainly happen. In this case the attacker has some code and its hash, and tries to find a *different* piece of code with the *same* hash. Thus the security property we need in order to prevent this is *second preimage resistance*.

Neither of the other security properties are particularly relevant:

Preimage resistance. Since the executable code is not a secret, we are not concerned about preimage resistance. In fact we want the preimage of a hash to be known since the application requires this.

Collision resistance. Collisions are not meaningful in this application unless we can find two pieces of code with the same hash, one of which is potentially useful and one of which is malicious. This seems very unlikely. It is really collisions with respect to an already *known* piece of code that we are concerned with. Such collisions are second preimages.

APPLICATION REQUIRING COLLISION RESISTANCE

The third application that we describe relates to the use of hash functions to generate *cryptographic commitments*. These can be thought of as a type of 'binding promise'. The example scenario that we consider involves two suppliers, Alice and Bob, who wish to bid for a contract between their respective companies. Since they are both internal bidders, they decide to negotiate between themselves and not use a third party. In the physical world this situation could be resolved by sealing bids in an envelope and simultaneously exchanging them. However, we need to do this electronically and cannot assume that the messages are simultaneously exchanged.

Clearly if Alice states, 'We can do the job for 7000 euros', she then hands the initiative to Bob who could then undercut her and choose to bid 6999 euros.

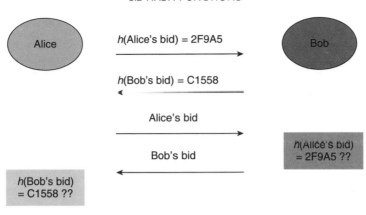

Figure 6.4. Use of a hash function for cryptographic commitments

A solution is for each party to determine their bid and then exchange a *commitment* ahead of time. They can then reveal their bids at leisure. The process, which is illustrated in Figure 6.4, runs as follows:

1. Alice determines her bid and then hashes it. This is her commitment. She sends the hash of her bid (but not the bid itself) to Bob. Bob stores the hash of Alice's bid.
2. Bob determines his bid and then hashes it. This is his commitment. He sends the hash of his bid (but not the bid itself) to Alice. Alice stores the hash of Bob's bid. The bidding stage is now closed.
3. Alice sends her bid to Bob. Bob computes the hash of Alice's bid and checks that it matches the hash that Alice sent in step 1. If it matches then he accepts Alice's bid as genuine.
4. Bob sends his bid to Alice. Alice computes the hash of Bob's bid and checks that it matches the hash that Alice sent in step 2. If it matches then she accepts Bob's bid as genuine.
5. Both parties are now aware of the two bids and accept them. The companies are now free, if they want, to accept the lower bid.

In any application involving the use of a hash function to provide commitments, the main security concern that arises is whether any of the parties could 'get out' of their commitment by some means. The way to get out of a commitment is to find an alternative input that hashes to the same commitment. In terms of the above application, this provides a cheating party with an option to select either of the inputs depending on the situation that unfolds during the bidding protocol. If Bob can find two bids with the same commitment then he can wait for Alice to reveal her bid and then strategically make a decision. He could choose a low-value input in order to win the contract (if it is lower than Alice's bid) or he could even wriggle out of the process by deliberately losing through submitting a higher bid (perhaps if Alice's bid is so high that Bob decides it is strategically advantageous to make her spend all her money).

The difference between this application and the file download application is that in this case there are many different collisions in the hash function that it could be useful for a cheating party to find. They are not just concerned with finding a collision for a *specific* input, but in fact collisions for a *range* of inputs. We thus need our hash function to offer *collision resistance*.

Note that this application requires *all three* security properties:

Preimage resistance. We need preimage resistance, otherwise each party might be able to determine the bid of the other party from the hash commitment.

Second preimage resistance. We need second preimage resistance for the same reasons that we need collision resistance (second preimages are just special types of collisions, as we observed in Section 6.2.1).

This example is of course a slightly artificial scenario, both in its simplicity and applicability. However, such commitments form genuine components of many more sophisticated cryptographic protocols, including complex applications such as electronic voting schemes.

Another important application of hash functions that relies on collision resistance is to digital signature schemes. We will examine this application in more detail in Section 7.3.4.

6.2.3 Attacking hash functions in theory

In Section 6.2.1 we noted that, from the attacker's perspective, finding collisions is normally the 'easiest' attack to conduct. In fact it is protection against collisions that primarily determines the output lengths of practical hash functions. Thus we will focus on finding collisions during our discussion of hash function attacks.

We will focus on the question: how many bits long should the hash of a message be in order for it to be regarded as secure? Since we are really worried about collision resistance, this question could be phrased as: how long does a hash have to be before finding collisions is hard?

Throughout this discussion we will keep in mind that, as we will see in Section 7.3.4, a popular application of hash functions is to apply them before creating a digital signature on a message. In other words, the digital signature is on the *hash* of the message and not the message itself. The consequences of finding a collision are serious for this type of application since if two messages can be found with the same hash then a badly behaving user could sign one message and then claim that the signature was on the other.

THE DANGERS OF A *VERY* SMALL HASH

Clearly a very small hash is a bad idea. For example, suppose that before digitally signing the message *Bruce owes Sheila $10* we hash it using a 2-bit hash function.

There are only four possible values for the resulting hash of this message: 00, 01, 10 or 11.

Sheila now receives this digitally signed message and, being the manipulative type, she decides to change the message to *Bruce owes Sheila $100*. Of course Sheila does not have the correct signature key, so she cannot digitally sign this message. However, because there are only four possible hashes, there is a 25% chance that the hash of the modified message is exactly the same as the hash of the original message. If it is, Sheila does not have to do anything further to conduct her attack. Since:

$$h(Bruce\ owes\ Sheila\ \$10) = h(Bruce\ owes\ Sheila\ \$100),$$

the signature on the message *Bruce owes Sheila $100* is exactly the same as the signature on the message *Bruce owes Sheila $10*. So now Sheila claims that she received the second message, and Bruce is in financial trouble. Consequently, the output length of a hash function must be sufficiently long that 'getting lucky' with the hash is not a reasonable attack strategy.

THE DANGERS OF A SMALL HASH

If we have a slightly longer hash, say a 10-bit hash, then we might reasonably regard 'getting lucky' as unlikely. In this case there are 2^{10} possible different hashes, which is about one thousand. So there is only a 0.1% chance of getting lucky by just guessing the hash value.

Suppose now, however, that a clerk approves payments by digitally signing them on behalf of an organisation that has approved the use of a 10-bit hash function. A certain Fred C. Piper intends to approach the clerk with a request for a payment of $200 to himself that he is confident will be authorised. Knowing that a 10-bit hash function is used, he can conduct the following attack:

1. First, he generates 1000 variants of a request for payment of $200 by adjusting the format of the request. For example:

    (a) *Pay Fred Piper $200*
    (b) *Pay F. Piper $200*
    (c) *Pay F.C. Piper two hundred dollars*
    (d) *Pay F.C. Piper two hundred dollars only*
    (e) *Pay two hundred dollars to Mr Fred Piper*
    (f) etc.

2. He now generates 1000 variants of a request for payment of $8000 in a similar way:

    (a) *Pay Fred Piper $8000*
    (b) *Pay F. Piper $8000*
    (c) *Pay F.C. Piper eight thousand dollars*
    (d) *Pay F.C. Piper eight thousand dollars only*

(e) *Pay eight thousand dollars to Mr Fred Piper*
(f) etc.

3. He calculates the hash of all 2000 of these different messages. Since there are only 1000 different possible values of the hash, there is a very good chance (although it is not 100%) that he will discover that the hash for one of the $200 messages is the same as the hash for one of the $8000 messages. We will assume that he is successful (and he almost certainly will be) and he discovers that:

$$h(Pay\ Fred\ Piper\ the\ sum\ of\ \$200) = h(We\ agree\ to\ pay\ F.\ C.\ Piper\ \$8000).$$

4. He presents the clerk with a request *Pay Fred Piper the sum of $200*. The clerk agrees to authorise the payment by digitally signing this request (which involves hashing the request message and then signing it).
5. Fred now sends his bank the digital signature on the hash of *Pay Fred Piper the sum of $200* but claims that it is on the message *We agree to pay F. C. Piper $8000*. Fred has a valid digital signature on this message.

There are two reasons why this attack was successful:

- In this example there are many potentially meaningful collisions. The nature of the example is more illustrative than realistic. A good way to reduce the number of meaningful collisions would be to insist, as many organisations do, that payment orders are formatted in a particular way and not left as open as this one was.
- The length of the hash is still too short. Even though 'getting lucky' with the hash is now a little bit more difficult than for our first example, it is still easy to find collisions by conducting a relatively small amount of work (in this case 2000 hash function computations).

So the lesson is that a hash must be sufficiently long that finding collisions is 'infeasible'. We now consider how many bits long a hash needs to be for this to be true.

BIRTHDAY ATTACKS

The output length of practical hash functions is formally determined by a well-known statistical result that is often referred to as the *birthday paradox*. It gets this name because it is often presented in terms of the number of people required in a room before it becomes more likely than not that two of them share the same birthday. The 'paradox' is that the number is smaller than most people expect (although this is really a 'surprise' rather than a paradox).

We will not worry ourselves with the mathematics behind the birthday paradox, but we do need to know what it tells us about finding collisions in hash functions. Thus, rather than people and birthdays, we will present the problem in a more general way.

m balls

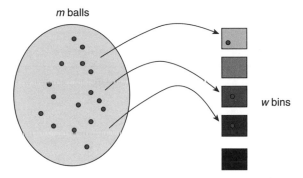

w bins

Figure 6.5. Experiment throwing *m* balls into *w* bins

Consider a (bizarre and pointless!) experiment where we take *m* balls and throw them randomly into a series of *w* bins, where *w* is a much smaller number than *m*. This situation is depicted in Figure 6.5.

What we are interested in learning is: *after how many throws is there a greater than half chance that one of the bins contains at least two balls?*

It would be reasonable to harbour some doubts as to whether we really are interested in learning the answer to this question! However, if we think of the balls as messages and the bins as hashes, then this question becomes: *after how many messages have been randomly selected is there a greater than half chance that one of the hashes matches at least two messages?* In more familiar cryptographic terminology, we are asking: *how many messages do we need to randomly select before there is a greater than half chance of a hash collision?*

This is a very useful number to learn because it represents the work effort that an attacker has to do if they conduct the following simple attack to find collisions:

1. pick a message at random, hash it and store the result in a database;
2. pick a new message at random, hash it and then check to see if that hash already exists in the database;
3. if it does then stop, since a collision has been found; if it does not then add the new hash to the database and repeat from step 2.

This is a simple, but powerful, attack that can be used against any hash function. Indeed, it can be thought of as the hash function 'equivalent' of exhaustive search for a symmetric key, since it forms the baseline attack that hash functions are measured against, just as exhaustive key search does for symmetric key encryption. Because its effectiveness is related to the birthday paradox, this attack is often called a *birthday attack*.

The answer to the question that we posed is that, on average, two balls are more likely than not to end up in the same bin (a collision is more likely than not to be found) after approximately *the square root of w* balls have been thrown (messages have been hashed). To interpret this properly, we note that an *n*-bit

Table 6.1: Hash lengths with respect to attacker work effort

Attacker's work effort	Hash length to stay secure against attacker
2^{64}	128
2^{80}	160
2^{112}	224
2^{256}	512

hash function has a total of 2^n possible hashes. This means that $w = 2^n$. So the above result states that a collision is more likely than not to be found after *the square root of 2^n* messages have been tried. The square root of 2^n is normally written in mathematical notation as $2^{\frac{n}{2}}$.

What this tells us is that, on average, an attacker who can conduct around $2^{\frac{n}{2}}$ hash computations can expect to find a collision. So the length of a practical hash function needs to be sufficiently long that this work effort is deemed unacceptable. Table 6.1 indicates what this means in terms of the length of the hash. For example, a well-designed 160-bit hash function (in other words, one that is believed to satisfy all the properties that we identified in Section 6.2.1) only requires an attacker to conduct an average of:

$$2^{\frac{160}{2}} = 2^{80}$$

hash function computations before they are more likely than not to have found a collision.

The issue of how many hash function computations are needed before a hash function is regarded as secure against a birthday attack is closely related to the similar question regarding how long a symmetric key should be in order to be secure against exhaustive key search. The similarity comes from the fact that both hash function and encryption operations are regarded as fast computations. We explore this issue further in Section 10.2. As we will discuss shortly, modern hash functions tend not to be designed with hashes of less than 160 bits, and in fact much longer hashes are widely recommended.

The original birthday paradox can also be solved using a similar argument. In this case the balls are people and the bins are birthdays. Since there are 365 possible birthdays, we can expect that around the square root of 365 (about 19) people will be required before two are more likely than not to share the same birthday. This is in fact a rather crude estimate, and a more accurate calculation reveals the answer to be closer to 23. Either way, it is not intuitive and seems surprisingly few. The surprise tends to arise because, rather than wondering how likely it is that *any* two people in the room share a birthday, we tend to focus on the chances that two of them have a *specific* birthday (such as our own one). What this tells us is that humans have a habit of confusing second preimages with collisions. Thus the birthday paradox itself has an important lesson for our understanding of hash functions.

6.2.4 Hash functions in practice

We have discussed at some length the various properties that a hash function should have and looked at several different applications of hash functions. We now discuss some of the hash functions that are used in practice.

HASH FUNCTION DESIGN

We will not discuss any particular hash function designs in detail, since hash functions are often relatively complex cryptographic primitives to describe, but the following notes present a brief indication of how hash functions have traditionally been designed.

- One popular design technique is to build *iterated hash functions*. Hash functions of this type are designed to operate in rounds, very much like a block cipher. Each round takes an input of a fixed size (typically a combination of the most recent message block and the output of the last round) and applies a *compression function* to produce an output of the required hash length. This process is repeated for as many rounds as are required to hash the entire message.
- The *Merkle–Damgard construction* is a particular type of iterated hash function that many modern hash functions are based on. This design has proved popular because it is possible to show that if the security properties that we want our hash function to have apply to the compression function used in each round, then these same security properties hold for the whole hash function.
- Hash functions can either be *dedicated designs* (meaning that they are designed explicitly as hash functions) or can be based on block ciphers. The latter constructions typically employ a block cipher in the design of a compression function, which is then iterated, as described above.

A BRIEF HISTORY OF MODERN HASH FUNCTIONS

Before we discuss some specific examples of hash functions, it is worth recalling that the birthday attack provides the benchmark attack on a hash function. The birthday attack tells us that, on average, collisions for an n-bit hash function are more likely than not to be found after around $2^{\frac{n}{2}}$ hash function computations. Thus any attack that can find collisions using fewer computations will be of interest. If the attack can find collisions using significantly fewer than $2^{\frac{n}{2}}$ computations then it may even be prudent to advise that the hash function should no longer be used.

We now briefly review some of the more well-known (families of) hash functions.

MD family: The hash function MD5 has been one of the most widely deployed hash functions, and was adopted as Internet Standard RFC 1321. It is a 128-bit hash function and is often used for file integrity checking (as we discussed in Section 6.2.2). MD5 was designed in 1991 to replace MD4, an earlier 128-bit hash function that was found to have flaws. In 2004, collisions were found in MD5. Subsequent refinements of the technique used to find collisions now mean that MD5 is no longer recommended for use.

SHA-1 family: The *Secure Hash Algorithm* SHA-0 was published by the National Institute of Standards and Technology (NIST) in 1993 as a 160-bit hash function. It was shortly replaced by an improved version known as SHA-1, which became the 'default' hash function of the late 1990s and the early years of the new century. SHA-1 is used in numerous security applications, including SSL/TLS (see Section 12.1) and S/MIME (see Section 12.7.2). In 2004, a technique for finding collisions was found for SHA-0 that takes approximately 2^{40} computations to conduct. This technique, which has subsequently been refined, involves considerably fewer computations than the birthday attack of 2^{80} and thus SHA-0 is considered as unfit for most uses. In 2005, a technique was proposed for finding collisions for SHA-1 after 2^{63} computations. This, again, is much faster than a birthday attack, casting significant doubts over the long-term future of SHA-1.

SHA-2 family: NIST published four further SHA variants, each of which is labelled by the number of bits of the hash output: SHA-224, SHA-256, SHA-384 and SHA-512 (collectively they are referred to as SHA-2). This family differ significantly in design from SHA-0 and SHA-1. The SHA-2 family is currently recommended for use by US Federal Agencies for all hash function applications.

RIPEMD family: This is a family of European hash functions designed by the open research community. They include RIPEMD-128 and RIPEMD-160. In 2004, a technique for finding collisions was found for the original version RIPEMD, which has been superseded by RIPEMD-128.

Whirlpool: This is a 512-bit hash function which is based on a modified version of AES (and shares one of the AES designers). Whirlpool has been adopted by several standards bodies and is available in open source cryptographic toolkits.

As there were relatively few respected hash function designs in widespread use prior to 2004, both MD5 and SHA-1 were widely deployed. Thus the discovery of techniques for finding collisions in MD5 and SHA-1 in 2004 provided a severe 'wake-up call' to designers and users of hash functions. Note that some of the collision-finding techniques can be regarded as 'academic attacks' (see Section 1.6.6) because they are of greater interest to cryptographic designers than users of hash functions. Nonetheless, cryptanalytic attacks improve over time and any hash function for which collisions can be generated in substantially fewer operations than a birthday attack is unlikely to have a long-term future.

Although the SHA-2 family of hash functions appear to be much stronger than previous hash functions and are significantly different from SHA-1, they are designed in a broadly similar way to SHA-1. As a result, new hash functions designs are being considered by the cryptographic community. This process was formally initiated by NIST who are leading an 'AES style' competition (see Section 4.5) for hash functions that can be relied on in the longer term. This SHA-3 process is expected to conclude in 2012.

6.3 Message authentication codes

In Section 6.2.2 we observed that hash functions can only provide a strong degree of data integrity if they are combined with other security mechanisms that protect the hash value from being manipulated. One such method is to introduce a key into the process of generating a 'hash'. Of course this means that we are no longer dealing with a 'hash function'.

In this section we discuss *message authentication codes*, more commonly simply referred to as MACs. These are symmetric cryptographic primitives designed to provide data origin authentication which, as we mentioned in Section 1.3.2, is a stronger notion than data integrity. This is one of the most commonly encountered mechanisms for providing data origin authentication (data integrity) and the most common symmetric technique. The other common mechanisms are digital signature schemes, which are public-key primitives that we will discuss in Chapter 7.

6.3.1 Does symmetric encryption provide data origin authentication?

Consider the following active attacks on a message:

1. unauthorised changing of part of a message;
2. unauthorised deletion of part of a message;
3. unauthorised sending of a false message;
4. trying to persuade the receiver that the message came from someone other than it did.

In most secure environments these are attacks that we would clearly like to prevent (or more realistically to *detect* in the event that they have occurred). It is often believed that if Alice and Bob share a symmetric key K and Alice encrypts a message and sends it to Bob then these attacks are prevented. After all, from Bob's perspective, *Alice is the only other person who knows the key K*, so surely nobody else could have tampered with the message in any way since it is encrypted. But is this argument valid?

Probably the most accurate answer to this question is that *it might be, but it is certainly not always valid*. Here are three situations that illustrate this:

ECB mode. Suppose that Alice and Bob use ECB mode (see Section 4.6.1) to encrypt their message (which is perhaps not the wisest choice). An attacker who intercepts the ciphertext on its way to Bob cannot determine the plaintext because he does not know key K. However, the attacker could rearrange the ciphertext blocks into a different order, or delete one or more of the ciphertext blocks. If the message is a sentence in English then there is a good chance that Bob might notice something odd when he decrypts the modified ciphertext block sequence, although there is certainly a chance that he might not. However, if the ciphertext consists of a sequence of database entries, one for each block, it may not be so easy to detect.

Stream cipher. Suppose that Alice uses a stream cipher to encrypt her message to Bob. An attacker knows that changing one bit of the ciphertext, which is often referred to as *bit flipping*, will change the corresponding bit of the plaintext. Although the attacker will not normally know the exact impact of making this change to the plaintext, there are many applications where the attacker may have a reasonable idea of what the impact is likely to be. For example, if the attacker knows that the first part of the message is a date then flipping the ciphertext bit has a reasonable chance of changing this to an alternative date.

Randomly generated plaintext. Suppose that Alice wishes to send a plaintext to Bob that appears to him to be 'randomly' generated in the sense that it is not in any natural language and does not contain any obvious structure. This is not such a strange proposition since, as we will learn in Section 10.4, a common technique for distributing symmetric keys is to encrypt them using another (higher level) symmetric key. The attacker is now in a very strong position because they can modify Alice's ciphertext block in any way they like and probably succeed in fooling Bob. This is because the plaintext looks 'randomly' generated and so Bob cannot tell the difference between a valid plaintext and a modified one. Even worse, if the attacker knows that Bob is expecting such a message, the attacker can send a false block to Bob (before Alice sends any data to Bob). When Bob decrypts this block he may think that it was the message from Alice and will decrypt it. Of course the attacker does not gain significantly because even the attacker does not know what the plaintext is that corresponds to the modified (or false) ciphertext block. However, in both of these cases data origin authentication has not been provided since Bob has been fooled into believing that some data came from Alice, when it actually came from the attacker.

It should thus be clear that, as a rule, *encryption does not provide data origin authentication*. It is thus good practice to use separate cryptographic mechanisms if both confidentiality and data origin authentication are required (see Section 6.3.6).

6.3.2 MAC properties

In essence, a MAC is a cryptographic checksum that is sent along with a message in order to provide an assurance of data origin authentication. The basic model of a MAC is shown in Figure 6.6. In this model the sender and receiver share a symmetric key K. The MAC takes as input the message and the key K. The sender transmits the message accompanied by the MAC. Note that we will assume that this message is sent in the clear, since we are only trying to provide data origin authentication, not confidentiality. If confidentiality is also required then the message will need to be encrypted. This raises some additional issues that we will not consider until Section 6.3.6.

Upon receipt of the message and the MAC, the receiver inputs the received message and the key into the MAC algorithm and recomputes the MAC. The receiver then checks whether this freshly recomputed MAC matches the MAC sent by the sender. If they do match then the receiver accepts the message and regards data origin authentication as having been provided. We will discuss precisely why this is appropriate in Section 6.3.3. Note that, just as in the basic model of a cryptosystem discussed in Section 1.4.3, we will always assume that an attacker knows the MAC algorithm but is unaware of the MAC key.

Note that if the MAC computed by the receiver does not match the MAC sent by the sender, the receiver cannot determine whether it is the message that has been altered or whether it is the origin that has been falsified. Nor do they know whether the message has been altered accidentally or deliberately. The receiver just knows that for some reason one of these events must have occurred.

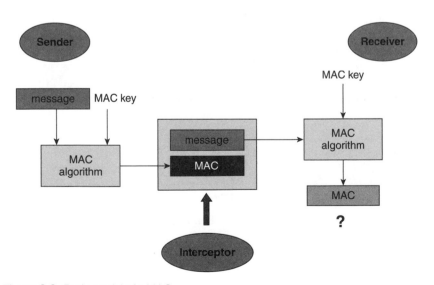

Figure 6.6. Basic model of a MAC

207

A MAC is superficially similar to a hash function with regard to the properties that it should have. However, there are several crucial differences that arise because of the involvement of a symmetric key. This is why MACs are able to provide data origin authentication and hash functions are not. As a comparison, we now review the properties we require of a hash function and discuss to what extent these are provided by a MAC:

Compression. A MAC does condense arbitrary long inputs into a fixed length output since it produces a fixed length digest of a message, regardless of how long the input message is.

Easy to compute. In hash functions this applies to *anyone*, however, this property is highly restricted for MACs. A MAC must be easy to compute for *anyone who knows the symmetric MAC key*, which is normally only the legitimate sender and receiver of a MAC. However, it must be hard to compute the correct MAC on a message for anyone who does *not* know the MAC key.

Preimage/second preimage/collision resistance. These properties are important for the security of hash functions since, without them, it might be possible for an attacker to manipulate the 'commitment' properties of a hash function. But MACs are not used for the wide range of applications that hash functions are used for. MACs are only used to provide data origin authentication of messages. We now consider separately the case of attackers, who do not know the MAC key, and legitimate MAC key holders:

1. A MAC is normally sent alongside a message, so an attacker is not really interested in the equivalent of preimage resistance (trying to work out the message from the MAC). Thus the only real goal of an attacker who does not know the MAC key is to try to come up with a MAC that is valid for a message that has not been legitimately sent. This attack is often referred to as a *MAC forgery*. Hence the security property that we really want for MACs is *MAC forgery resistance*, namely, that it is hard to find a valid message/MAC pair without knowledge of the MAC key.

   Note that in the context of providing data origin authentication, MAC forgery resistance is a general security property that covers all the types of attack that the hash function security properties were designed to stop. For example, suppose that an attacker views a legitimate message M and its MAC computed using key K, which we denote $MAC_K(M)$. The attacker could use this information (somehow) to try to find an alternative (fraudulent) message M' that has the same MAC when computed with key K. Since

$$MAC_K(M) = MAC_K(M')$$

the attacker can now present the message M' along with the observed MAC and will deceive the receiver into accepting it. This type of attack is precisely what second preimage resistance is designed to prevent in a hash function.

MAC forgery resistance also prevents this attack since conducting it involves finding a message/MAC pair without knowledge of K.

2. Legitimate MAC key holders (the sender and receiver) are in a position similar to that of everyone in the case of hash functions. Namely, they have the ability to produce a valid MAC on any message of their choosing. Since legitimate MAC key holders all have this same capability, we have to assume that they 'trust' each other, which is the case for any symmetric cryptographic primitive. We thus do not care whether they can find collisions or second preimages for MAC values. This is because we will never be able to use the cryptography alone to resolve any disputes between legitimate senders and receivers. We return to this point in Section 6.3.5.

Note that it would have been simpler to have an equivalently general security property as MAC forgery resistance for hash functions. Unfortunately this is impossible because the equivalent property would have to involve preventing attackers from computing the hash of a message. Since hash functions have no key, we can never stop attackers doing this.

Another subtle difference between hash functions and MACs is that the strong data integrity assurance provided by a MAC is only provided to the legitimate receiver of the MAC, who is the only other entity with the capability of verifying the correctness of the MAC. In contrast, the weak data integrity assurance provided by a hash function is provided to everyone.

Hopefully this rather involved discussion has illustrated how useful it is to introduce a key into a function that otherwise resembles a hash function. We now show precisely how this key can be used to provide data origin authentication.

6.3.3 CBC-MAC

The most well known examples of MAC algorithms are based on either using a block cipher or a hash function as a 'building block'. We will look at one example of each technique, beginning with block ciphers.

The first MAC design that we describe will hopefully look familiar. This MAC is commonly referred to as CBC-MAC and is based on a block cipher. An early banking standard defined CBC-MAC using DES, so the MAC operated on blocks of 64 bits. We present the CBC-MAC construction in a more general form. Any block cipher, such as AES, could be used.

COMPUTING CBC-MAC

We assume that the sender and receiver have both agreed in advance upon a symmetric key K. We also assume that the message M has been split into blocks of the same length as the block length of the block cipher (64 bits for DES or 128 bits for AES) in order to process it. In Figure 6.7 these blocks are labelled

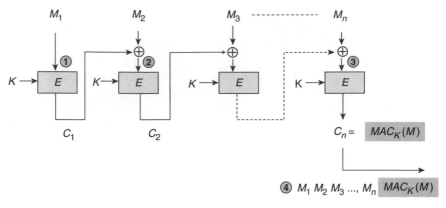

Figure 6.7. CBC-MAC

$M_1, M_2, \ldots, M_n$. If the message does not fit neatly into blocks then we pad the last block (see Section 4.3.2).

As illustrated in Figure 6.7, the sender computes the MAC as follows:

1. Take the first message block M_1 and encrypt it (using the block cipher) with the key K to obtain C_1.
2. XOR C_1 to the second message block M_2 and encrypt the result with the key K to obtain C_2.
3. Repeat this process until the second-last ciphertext block C_{n-1} has been XORed to the last message block M_n, and the result encrypted with key K to obtain C_n.
4. Send the message $M_1, M_2, \ldots, M_n$ to the receiver, accompanied by the last ciphertext block C_n. This last ciphertext block C_n is the MAC, which we denote $MAC_K(M)$.

The reason that this process is familiar (and the name CBC-MAC should have provided a significant clue) is because the MAC in CBC-MAC is the last ciphertext block of a computation that is very similar to encryption of the message using the CBC mode of operation that we discussed in Section 4.6.3.

The main difference between CBC encryption and CBC-MAC is the start of the process. For CBC encryption we need to artificially generate an initial block, hence both parties agree on an IV to use as this initial block. For CBC-MAC we are in the advantageous position of knowing the 'plaintext' (the message). Thus we can start the process using the first message block instead of creating an IV. After that, both CBC encryption and CBC-MAC conduct the same process of 'XOR then encrypt'.

Note also that in the case of CBC-MAC we discard all the intermediate 'ciphertext' blocks $C_1, C_2, \ldots, C_{n-1}$, since these are only temporary values that are generated on the way to obtaining the final MAC value.

CHECKING CBC-MAC

The computation of $MAC_K(M)$ can be performed by anyone who knows the MAC key K. The receiver obtains the message $M_1, M_2, \ldots, M_n$ and the MAC value $MAC_K(M)$, then simply:

1. Repeats the computation in Figure 6.7.
2. Checks that the output of this computation is the same value $MAC_K(M)$ that was received. If it is then the message is authenticated, otherwise it is rejected.

SECURITY OF CBC-MAC

The security of CBC-MAC relies on the security of the symmetric key K that is shared by the sender and receiver. Since we assume that the CBC-MAC process can be conducted by anyone, and that the message itself is not secret, the only information that an attacker does not have is the key K.

We can check the effectiveness of the MAC by reviewing the four attacks on data origin authentication that we mentioned in Section 6.3.1:

Unauthorised changing of part of a message. Any alteration of the message (including swapping message blocks around) will result in a different sequence of message blocks. Since the MAC is computed using all of these message blocks in a specific order, the MAC on the modified message will be different from that of the original message. To compute the new MAC, the key K will be needed. Only the sender and receiver know K, so unauthorised changing of a message is detectable.

Unauthorised deletion of part of a message. This is just the same argument as above.

Unauthorised insertion of a false message. The attacker can easily send a false message, but without knowledge of the key K they cannot compute the correct MAC on this message. Thus CBC-MAC allows us to detect this type of attack.

Trying to persuade the receiver that the message came from someone other than it did. Suppose that an attacker Archie (who shares a MAC key K' with receiver Bob) claims that the message came from him rather than the genuine sender Alice (who shares MAC key K with Bob). Since the message M has been sent along with $MAC_K(M)$, if Bob believes it came from Archie and computes $MAC_{K'}(M)$ then he will reject the MAC, since it is very unlikely that $MAC_K(M) = MAC_{K'}(M)$ just by chance.

Note that in this last scenario, the attacker Archie could intercept the message:

$$M, \ MAC_K(M)$$

from Alice, and replace it with:

$$M, \ MAC_{K'}(M),$$

211

and then claim that the message comes from himself (Archie). However, this is not an attack on data origin authentication since indeed this new message *does* come from Archie!

Thus CBC-MAC provides data origin authentication. Note in particular that the two examples that we gave in Section 6.3.1 of encryption failing to provide data origin authentication are now both detectable using CBC-MAC or, more generally, any reputable MAC algorithm:

- If an attacker swaps message blocks around then we can detect this using a MAC.
- If the message consists of randomly generated data then modification of it is detectable using a MAC.

Without knowledge of the key K, the attacker's best strategy is simply to attempt to guess the MAC. If the MAC is just one bit long then the attacker has a half chance of guessing the MAC correctly. However, in general, if the MAC is n bits long then there are 2^n possible MAC values to choose from, hence the attacker only has a $1/2^n$ chance of guessing. In the case of CBC-MAC as depicted in Figure 6.7 based on AES, $n = 128$, and hence the attacker will have to be very lucky indeed to guess the MAC correctly.

CBC-MAC IN PRACTICE

Our description of CBC-MAC presents the general idea. Practical reality is, as always, a little bit more complicated. The following notes are very important:

- Our description of CBC-MAC is oversimplified. In practice the final block C_n does not form $MAC_K(M)$, as depicted in Figure 6.7. Instead, C_n is subjected to some further processing before being turned into $MAC_K(M)$, in order to prevent some special forgery attacks. It is best to consult relevant standards before implementing a MAC of this type.
- It is possible to use just a portion of the output of CBC-MAC as the MAC, rather than the whole output. It does not matter exactly how much of this last block is sent as the MAC, so long as the sender and receiver agree on how much to use and that it is not so small that guessing the MAC becomes realistic. This is another efficiency–security tradeoff. In the original version of CBC-MAC (based on DES) just half of the 64 output bits were used as the MAC, the remainder being called the *MAC residue*. Note that MAC residues can be useful, as we will see in Section 10.4.2.

6.3.4 HMAC

We will now briefly look at another well-known and widely deployed MAC, this time based on a hash function. Our discussion in Section 6.3.2 should hopefully have made it clear that a very natural way to design a MAC might be to start with a hash function and then somehow build in the use of a key. This is precisely the idea behind the *Hash-based Message Authentication Code (HMAC)*. This type of MAC can, at least in theory, be constructed from any cryptographic hash function. Thus it is common to see HMAC more precisely being referred to as, for example, HMAC-MD5, where the suffix identifies the name of the underlying hash function.

The design of HMAC is very simple. Let h be a hash function and let K_1 and K_2 be two symmetric keys. Then the MAC on message M is computed as follows:

1. compute the hash of K_2 concatenated (see Section 1.6.1) with the message; in other words compute $h(K_2||M)$;
2. compute the hash of K_1 concatenated with the output of step 1; in other words compute:

$$h(K_1 \ || \ h(K_2||M) \ ).$$

Thus computing the MAC involves two applications of the underlying hash function, first to K_2 and the message, and then to K_1 and the first hash output. HMAC is simple and fast to implement. So what is the catch?

In some sense there is no catch, however, it is important to recognise that the security of HMAC depends on three separate things:

The security of the keys. HMAC employs two symmetric keys. Thus the length of an HMAC key can be regarded as the sum of the lengths of these two keys.

The security of the hash function. HMAC's security depends on the security of the underlying hash function. Thus it should be deployed using hash functions that have been approved for use in HMAC by recognised experts.

The length of the MAC output. Just as we discussed in Section 6.3.3, it is possible to use just part of the HMAC output as the actual MAC, but reducing its length will reduce security.

Perhaps the most 'delicate' of these three dependencies is the second one. As we discussed in Section 6.2.4, the security of hash functions is arguably a less 'mature' subject than the security of block ciphers. If a flaw is found in a hash function then it is possible (probable) that this flaw will have implications for the use of HMAC with that hash function. However, it is of course also true that HMAC could still then be used with an alternative underlying hash function.

It is important to note that:

- Once again we have presented a 'textbook' version of a cryptographic primitive rather than one ready for immediate implementation. In practice, it is normal in HMAC to introduce some padding after the keys in order to format the input for processing by the hash function.
- It is tempting to consider HMAC as 'over-engineered' and to just treat $h(K_2||M)$, the output from step 1, as a suitable MAC for message M. The problem with this approach is that, for many choices of hash function, it becomes possible for an

attacker to produce a valid MAC on a message *M'* that consists of *M* with some additional data appended to it. This is an example of MAC forgery, since the attacker has been able to compute a valid MAC on *M'* without knowing the key. Step 2 is thus necessary if we are to make a secure MAC from a hash function.

6.3.5 MACs and non-repudiation

Recall from Section 1.3.1 that non-repudiation is the assurance that an entity cannot deny any previous commitments or actions. The most important limitation of MACs is that they do *not* provide a non-repudiation service. To see this, consider what happens if the sender and receiver get involved in a dispute over whether a particular MAC was attached to a particular message. Do MACs provide a proof that a message was sent by the sender to the receiver?

The answer, at least in most cases, is no. Nobody can compute a MAC other than the sender and the receiver. This means that a MAC on a message is evidence that *either the sender or the receiver* computed it. This provides protection from any third-party claims to have computed it, but it does not protect the sender and receiver from one another. The sender could deny having sent the MAC and claim that the receiver forged it, or vice versa. Since it is impossible to determine which of the two parties computed the MAC, it is thus impossible to provide non-repudiation.

This 'limitation' of MACs arises because they are based on symmetric cryptography and thus require trust between the sender and receiver for their use. If non-repudiation is required then we normally need to look at techniques based on public-key cryptography. That said, there are situations where a MAC can be used to provide a non-repudiation service. We will discuss these situations in Section 7.2.

6.3.6 Using MACs with encryption

In our analysis of MACs we have assumed that we only wish to provide data origin authentication for a message. Thus our assumption was that the message was sent in the clear to the receiver. However, there are many applications where this is not a reasonable assumption.

The majority of cryptographic applications that require confidentiality also tend to require data origin authentication. Indeed, some people argue that true confidentiality can never be provided by the use of encryption on its own and hence confidentiality always needs to be accompanied by data origin authentication.

A practical issue that often arises in applications that require both of these security services is that there may be some message data that must not be encrypted, but should be authenticated. Examples of this might be a packet header that contains routing information, or a header that contains a key identifier that informs the recipient which key(s) to use in order to authenticate and decrypt. In the following discussion we will use the term *message* to refer to the data requiring confidentiality *and* data origin authentication, *associated data* to refer to the additional data requiring only data origin authentication, and *full message* to the combination of the message and the associated data.

There are two possible approaches to providing both confidentiality and data origin authentication. The first is to provide these using separate cryptographic primitives. The alternative approach is to use a cryptographic primitive that is explicitly designed to provide both security services.

USING SEPARATE PRIMITIVES

We observed in Section 6.3.1 that, in general, encryption does not provide data origin authentication. Hence, when both security services are required, the most obvious solution is to use two separate cryptographic primitives. In a symmetric setting the most natural way of realising this is to use symmetric encryption and a MAC. But in which order should these cryptographic primitives be applied?

MAC-then-encrypt. In this case:

1. the MAC is computed on the full message;
2. the message and the MAC are encrypted (but not the associated data);
3. the ciphertext, the associated data and the MAC are sent to the receiver.

The receiver first decrypts the ciphertext to recover the message and the MAC. The receiver then assembles the full message and checks the MAC. This order, which computes the MAC first, is perhaps the most aesthetic solution from a 'purist's' perspective, because it is the message itself that we want data origin authentication for, not its encrypted form. However, this does not necessarily mean that it is the most secure solution. Indeed, there are some security concerns about this approach.

Encrypt-then-MAC. In this case:

1. the message is encrypted;
2. the MAC is computed on the combination of the ciphertext and the associated data;
3. the ciphertext, the associated data and the MAC are sent to the receiver.

This might not seem the intuitive order in which to conduct the two cryptographic operations, but it has a distinct advantage. The receiver will first have to check the MAC on the ciphertext. If this check fails then the receiver will reject the received data without any need for decryption, thus saving some computation. In contrast, in the case of MAC-then-encrypt, the receiver must perform both operations. Encrypt-then-MAC also benefits from the existence of a theoretical security proof that suggests that it is a good way of combining the two operations.

Note that, regardless of which order is used, the encryption operation and the MAC operation should be computed using *different* cryptographic keys. This is because they are different cryptographic operations, providing different security services. Using different keys follows the best-practice principle of key separation, which we discuss in more detail in Section 10.6.1.

One cost of using separate operations is therefore that two different keys are needed in order to provide confidentiality and data origin authentication. It would thus be attractive if a cryptographic primitive that provides both services using just one key could be found. Another cost is that the two separate operations require the message data to be cryptographically processed twice, once for each of the operations. It would thus be better from an efficiency perspective if a cryptographic primitive could be designed that requires the message to be processed just once.

USING AN AUTHENTICATED-ENCRYPTION PRIMITIVE

An *authenticated-encryption primitive* is a symmetric cryptographic primitive that uses a single key to simultaneously provide both confidentiality and data origin authentication. We have already seen that block ciphers can be used to provide both confidentiality (in Section 4.3) and data origin authentication (in Section 6.3.3). Further, in Section 4.6 we saw that block cipher modes of operation can be used to achieve different properties. It should thus not be surprising that authenticated-encryption primitives are special modes of operation of a block cipher.

There are several different authenticated-encryption primitives proposed. All of these support the presence of associated data that does not require encryption. The differences between these primitives are mostly fairly subtle and largely to do with implementation and intellectual property issues. Examples include:

Counter with CBC-MAC (CCM) Mode. This mode is, almost literally, a combination of CTR mode (see Section 4.6.4) for encryption and a type of CBC-MAC (see Section 6.3.3) for data origin authentication. It essentially follows the MAC-then-encrypt construction, with the MAC itself separately encrypted using CTR mode. CCM mode has been standardised by NIST and is the subject of an Internet Standard, as well as being adopted by a number of significant applications, for example WPA2 (see Section 12.2.5). It requires two block cipher encryption operations for each message block (one for the CTR mode encryption and one for the CBC-MAC).

EAX mode. This mode of operation is heavily influenced by CCM mode, also being based on CTR mode and a special type of CBC-MAC called OMAC. EAX makes a number of improvements in comparison to CCM mode, amongst the most notable of which is that EAX does not require the length of the message to be known in advance (CCM employs the length of the message during its computation), thus allowing on-the-fly processing.

Offset Codebook (OCB) mode. In contrast to CCM mode, OCB mode uses techniques that are different from those that we have previously come across. OCB encryption consists of XORing each message block with a sort of counter both before and after it is encrypted with the block cipher. Like CTR mode, the computation of the resulting ciphertext is thus easily parallelised. Data origin authentication is provided by conducting a similar operation to encryption on a checksum based on the message blocks and then XORing a separate MAC computed on the associated data. Once again, the techniques used are easily parallelised. Significantly, OCB mode thus requires just one block cipher encryption operation for each message block. Like CCM mode it also requires one block cipher encryption for each block of associated data but, by decoupling this from the message block encryption, OCB mode is even more efficient if associated data only needs to be sent once at the start of a session. However, unlike CCM mode, OCB mode has patent issues that are likely to restrict its wide-scale adoption.

Authenticated-encryption primitives are relatively new in comparison to the modes of operation discussed in Section 4.6. One advantage of this is that their design has benefitted from the more rigorous modern requirements for formal security proofs (see Section 3.2.5). Because they tend to combine efficiency of processing with simpler key management, they are already being adopted by a range of applications, as we will see in Chapter 12. Since confidentiality and data origin authentication are almost always required together in an application, it is likely that the use of authenticated-encryption primitives will increase.

6.4 Summary

In this chapter we discussed cryptographic mechanisms for providing different levels of data integrity. Hash functions are multipurpose cryptographic primitives and our discussion included an examination of their many different properties and applications, not just those relating to data integrity. Hash functions, on their own, are fairly weak data integrity mechanisms, but they can be used as part of stronger mechanisms. We saw this in Section 6.3.4, where they were used in the construction of a MAC. We will see this again in Section 7.3.4 when they are used as components of digital signature schemes. MACs provide the stronger notion of data origin authentication and we reviewed two general techniques for constructing them.

Data integrity, in particular data origin authentication, is arguably a more important requirement than confidentiality in many modern applications. Very few applications that require confidentiality do not also require data origin authentication. Indeed, we have not yet finished our discussion of data origin authentication, since Chapter 7 is also dedicated to mechanisms that provide this important service.

6.5 Further reading

General introductions to hash functions can be found in most books on cryptography, ranging from the relaxed approach of Ferguson, Schneier and Kohno [75] through to the more formal treatment in Katz and Lindell [105]. More details about the theory behind birthday attacks can be found in most books, including a detailed explanation in Vaudenay [194].

While the properties and applications of hash functions are fairly stable, the actual hash functions that are used in applications will change significantly over the coming years. This is because the NIST SHA-3 competition will define the hash functions of the future and is not due to complete until 2012. The latest news, and ultimately the final results, of the NIST SHA-3 competition are best obtained from the official website [132]. Until then, the most commonly deployed hash functions are probably SHA-1 and the SHA-2 family, which are all described in FIPS 180-2 [80]. Other hash functions that we mentioned include RIPEMD-160 [62] and Whirlpool [28]. All these hash functions are included in ISO/IEC 10118 [2]. A good example of the relationship between academic attacks and real-world impact is the aftermath of the cryptanalysis of SHA-1 in 2005. The comments made by Bruce Schneier [166] indicate both the significance, and to an extent the lack of significance, of the immediate impact. A fun explanation of hash functions, their security properties and some of their applications can be found at Friedl [86].

More information about the MAC algorithms that we discussed in this chapter are provided by the full specifications of CBC-MAC in ISO/IEC 9797 [18] and HMAC in FIPS 198 [81] and RFC 2104 [113]. A good list of practical issues that need to be taken care of when implementing MACs is provided in Handschuh and Preneel [95]. A discussion of the order in which to conduct encryption and MAC can be found in Ferguson, Schneier and Kohno [75]. Further details of the authenticated encryption modes that we discussed can be found for CCM [135], EAX [30] and OCB [165] mode. Authenticated encryption modes are also standardised in ISO/IEC 19772 [13].

Playing with many of the hash functions mentioned in this chapter is made easy through the use of CrypTool [52]. Recommended is the hash demonstration, which allows minor changes to be made to an input file and then the similarity of the resulting hash outputs to be measured.

6.6 Activities

1. One class of weak data integrity mechanisms (which we did not discuss in any detail) can only detect accidental modification of data.

   (a) A single *parity check bit* consists of the XOR of all the bits in the data. What types of accidental errors will this simple integrity mechanism detect?
   (b) In what ways are cyclic redundancy checks (CRCs) better data integrity mechanisms than parity check bits?

    (c) Explain why a CRC is not a strong data integrity mechanism.

    (d) Identify two different applications that use CRCs to provide data integrity and explain why they do not need a stronger data integrity mechanism.

2. By considering the analogy of a birthday being a 'hash' of a person's identity, explain the following terms:

    (a) preimage resistance;

    (b) second preimage resistance;

    (c) collision resistance;

    (d) the birthday paradox.

3. The term *hash function* has a more general interpretation in computer science, where the hash functions that we have discussed are often called *cryptographic hash functions*.

    (a) Which properties are shared by *cryptographic hash functions* and the more general computer science *hash functions*?

    (b) What applications are there for such general hash functions?

4. Explain which of the practical and security properties of a hash function are most useful for the following applications:

    (a) storing a passphrase;

    (b) generating a short-lived key by hashing a long-term key;

    (c) HMAC;

    (d) digital signature schemes with appendix;

    (e) computer virus detection.

5. Which of the practical and security properties of a hash function do the following mathematical functions have:

    (a) Reducing a number modulo n?

    (b) Multiplying two primes together?

6. Explain in detail the extent to which a hash function can be used to provide data integrity.

7. PINs are a commonly used security mechanisms.

    (a) In a class of 120 students who have been assigned 4-digit PINs by their banks (and have not changed them) is it more, or less, likely that two students have the same PIN to protect their payment card?

    (b) Approximately how many students would you need to have in the class before a similar likelihood was expected if banks used 5-digit PINs instead?

8. An *exhaustive hash search* is an attack which repeatedly computes the output of a hash function for a large number of inputs.

    (a) What threats are posed by an exhaustive hash search?

    (b) What countermeasures can be used to protect against an exhaustive hash search?

9. Hash functions are sometimes used as a practical means of pseudorandomly generating numbers.

    (a) Why is it reasonable to expect a hash function to generate 'random' ouput?
    (b) What are the possible advantages of using a hash function as a pseudorandom number generator?

10. The SHA-3 'competition' is an AES-style process designed to standardise hash functions.

    (a) What were the SHA-3 hash function competition design criteria?
    (b) Based on the most current information that you can find, write a short report on this competition.

11. A block cipher with an unknown key is used in ECB mode to encrypt the plaintext: *The order is Karl, Andy, Fred and Ian. Ian and Andy have left.* All that is known about the block cipher is that:

    - it encrypts plaintext blocks consisting of two letters into ciphertext blocks consisting of two letters;
    - punctuation and spaces are ignored.

    Suppose that the original ciphertext is $C_1, C_2, C_3 \ldots, C_{23}$.

    (a) Find two numbers i and j such that $C_i = C_j$;
    (b) Decrypt the ciphertext:

    $$C_1, \quad C_2, \quad C_3, \quad C_4, \quad C_5, \quad C_{10}, \quad C_{11}, \quad C_6, \quad C_7, \quad C_8, \quad C_9, \quad C_{12},$$
    $$C_{13}, \quad C_{14}, \quad C_{15}, \quad C_{16}, \quad C_{17}, \quad C_6, \quad C_7, \quad C_{20}, \quad C_{21}, \quad C_{22}, \quad C_{23}$$

    (c) Decrypt the ciphertext:

    $$C_1, \quad C_2, \quad C_3, \quad C_4, \quad C_5, \quad C_{10}, \quad C_{11}, \quad C_{12}, \quad C_{13}, \quad C_{14}$$

    (d) Decrypt the ciphertext:

    $$C_{10}, \quad C_8, \quad C_6, \quad C_{17}, \quad C_6, \quad C_7, \quad C_{20}, \quad C_{21}, \quad C_{22}, \quad C_{23}$$

    (e) Find another sequence of ciphertext blocks that decrypt to a plausible plaintext.
    (f) What lesson about the delivery of security services does this example demonstrate?

12. Explain the extent to which a MAC prevents the following attacks:

    (a) unauthorised changing of part of a message;
    (b) unauthorised deletion of part of a message;
    (c) unauthorised sending of a false message;
    (d) unauthorised replaying of a previously sent message.

13. Alice and Charlie are flavour technicians at a food processing company. Alice shares key K_A with Boss Bob and Charlie shares key K_C with Bob. Suppose that:

- Alice sends an email message *My big idea for the next flavour of crisps is chicken korma* to Bob. She attaches $MAC_{K_A}(\text{message})$ to this message.
- Charlie intercepts the email message and thinks the idea is a very good one. Charlie has a dishonest streak and so he removes the MAC from Alice's message and replaces it by his own $MAC_{K_C}(\text{message})$. In other words, Charlie 'steals' Alice's message and passes it on to Bob with his own MAC, hence claiming the idea.

Thus Bob receives a message, with a correct MAC, that appears to come from Charlie. Unknown to Bob, however, the original message originated with Alice.

(a) Is this an example of a MAC being used without data origin authentication being provided?

(b) How could Alice have easily avoided this problem?

14. A simple proposal for a MAC algorithm consists of letting the MAC of message M (which consists of message blocks $M_1, M_2, \ldots, M_n$) be the AES encryption with key K of the XOR of all the message blocks. In other words:

$$MAC_K(M) = E_K(M_1 \oplus M_2 \oplus \cdots \oplus M_n).$$

Explain why this is a bad idea.

15. The description of CBC-MAC that we gave in Section 6.3.3 is oversimplified.

(a) Find out what additional operations are conducted in a version of CBC-MAC that is approved by a relevant standards body (for example, CMAC).

(b) Why is our simplified version of CBC-MAC regarded as insecure in practice?

16. HMAC describes a means of creating a MAC from a hash function.

(a) Provide an informal explanation of why the construction $h(K||M)$ of a MAC from a hash function is not regarded as secure, where:

- h is the underlying hash function;
- K is a symmetric key;
- M is a message.

(b) Explain one 'obvious' way of trying to create a hash function from a MAC.

(c) Why might the above technique not give you a secure hash function?

(d) How does the standardised version of HMAC differ from the simplified one in this chapter?

17. Suppose that Alice wishes to send a confidential message to Bob that starts with a delivery address. Alice decides to use a block cipher in CBC mode and sends the IV to Bob followed by the ciphertext.

(a) Explain why an attacker who modifies the IV has a good chance of changing the delivery address.

(b) What general fact about encryption does this attack illustrate?

(c) Suggest several different ways in which Alice could prevent the above attack from occurring.

18. Confidentiality and data origin authentication can be provided using separate operations by either the encrypt-then-MAC or MAC-then-encrypt constructions (see Section 6.3.6). However, a third possibility is to use the following *encrypt-and-MAC* construction:

   - the message is encrypted;
   - the MAC is computed on the full message;
   - the ciphertext, the associated data and the MAC are sent to the receiver.

   (a) Explain the process that the receiver follows to decrypt and check data received using this construction.
   (b) Compare this approach to the encrypt-then-MAC and MAC-then-encrypt constructions.

19. Some modes of operation have been proposed that provide both data origin and confidentiality.

   (a) What are the advantages of combining the provision of these two security services in one cryptographic process?
   (b) Identify some applications that use such a mode of operation.
   (c) What are the possible disadvantages of using a combined mode of operation, as opposed to implementing two separate security mechanisms?

20. In this chapter we have seen several examples of cryptographic 'recycling' (building cryptographic mechanisms from other cryptographic mechanisms). This might make sense from an efficiency perspective, but to what extent do you think it makes sense from a security perspective? (Present both a case 'for' and a case 'against'.)

7 Digital Signature Schemes

In this chapter we consider digital signature schemes, which are the main cryptographic mechanisms for providing non-repudiation. We start by looking at general requirements for a digital signature scheme. We then examine several ways in which a digital signature scheme could be realised. We also discuss important issues concerning the adoption and use of digital signatures.

At the end of this chapter you should be able to:

- Explain general requirements for a digital signature scheme.
- Recognise that not all digital signature schemes rely on public-key cryptography.
- Appreciate the important role that hash functions play in creating some types of digital signature scheme.
- Explain two different methods of creating a digital signature scheme based on RSA.
- Compare the various properties of digital and handwritten signatures.
- Identify some points of vulnerability in any practical digital signature scheme.

7.1 Digital signatures

The term *digital signature* is somewhat provocative in the sense that it infers a digital analogue of handwritten signatures. We will later discuss the precise extent to which this is true. For now, we will use this loose connection to motivate a cryptographic perspective on what it means to provide non-repudiation.

7.1.1 The basic idea

In Section 1.3.1 we defined non-repudiation to be the assurance that an entity cannot deny a previous commitment or action. Non-repudiation is a vital service for any application which requires evidence that a particular entity has generated

223

some data, often at a specific moment in time. In a communication scenario this normally means that the receiver of data wants evidence of the fact that the data was created by the sender. This requirement is especially relevant in business applications where there is potential for dispute over exchanged data.

Note that this requirement is for evidence that could, at least in theory, be presented to a third party for independent assessment. This is a stronger requirement than *assurance* that a particular entity has generated some data, which is how we defined data origin authentication. In particular, data origin authentication may provide assurance to the *receiver* but does not, in general, provide evidence that could be presented to a *third party*. This is precisely what normally happens when a MAC is used. A basic application of a MAC convinces the receiver, but not a third party, who cannot tell whether the sender genuinely created the MAC or whether the receiver forged it using the shared key, as discussed in Section 6.3.5. We will qualify 'normally' in Section 7.2, when we consider situations where a MAC may suffice to provide a degree of non-repudiation.

The primary purpose of a digital signature is to bind an entity to some data in a way that can be independently checked by a third party. Note that the entity being bound to the data could be, for example:

- the creator of the data;
- the owner of the data;
- an entity who is formally 'approving' the data.

We will use the term *signer* for the entity who creates a digital signature (regardless of their precise relationship to the data) and the term *verifier* for any entity who receives digitally signed data and attempts to check whether the digital signature is 'correct' or not. We say that the verifier attempts to *verify* the digital signature by checking whether it is *valid* for the given data and claimed signer.

7.1.2 Electronic signatures

It is quite natural to associate the term 'signature' with non-repudiation mechanisms because handwritten signatures are the most important non-repudiation mechanisms used in the physical world. However, it is also important to apply caution when using this analogy because handwritten signatures have complex properties that do not all necessarily translate into the electronic world. Some of these properties are desirable ones, that are hard to emulate. Others are rather undesirable, and can be 'improved upon' by using digital techniques. We will discuss these issues in more detail in Section 7.4.3.

That said, there is clearly a case for electronic techniques that can be applied in similar situations to those where handwritten signatures are utilised in the physical world. Recognising this, an important European Community Directive defines an *electronic signature* to be *data in electronic form attached to, or logically connected with, other electronic data and which serves as a method of authentication*.

This definition is deliberately vague and does not even suggest that the goal of such a mechanism is non-repudiation. An electronic signature under this loose definition could thus be, for example:

- typing a name into a web form;
- an electronic representation of a handwritten signature;
- a biometric template;
- network information that identifies a particular computer;
- a digital signature in the cryptographic sense (the main subject of this chapter).

Typing a name into a web form is clearly a very weak electronic signature. It does imply some intent on the part of the signer but is also very easy to forge. Nonetheless, there are applications where this type of electric signature probably suffices. However, the Directive also recognises the need for stronger notions of electronic signature in order to provide non-repudiation services. It proposes an *advanced electronic signature*, which is defined to be an electronic signature that, in addition, is:

1. uniquely linked to the signatory;
2. capable of identifying the signatory;
3. created using means under the sole control of the signatory;
4. linked to data to which it relates in such a way that subsequent changes in the data are detectable.

This notion is much closer to what we expect from a cryptographic non-repudiation mechanism and is likely to have been formulated with cryptographic digital signatures very much in mind. We will look at some of the practical issues associated with the notion of an advanced electronic signature in Section 7.4.

7.1.3 Digital signature scheme fundamentals

While we noted in the last section that electronic signatures could be provided using a variety of different types of mechanism, we will now focus on electronic signatures that can be provided by cryptographic mechanisms. We thus restrict the term *digital signature* to mean an electronic signature that was generated using a cryptographic primitive.

REQUIREMENTS FOR A DIGITAL SIGNATURE SCHEME

We will define a *digital signature scheme* to be a cryptographic primitive that provides:

Data origin authentication of the signer. A digital signature validates the underlying data in the sense that assurance is provided about the integrity of the data and the identity of the signer.

Non-repudiation. A digital signature can be stored by anyone who receives it as evidence. This evidence could later be presented to a third party who could use the evidence to resolve any dispute that relates to the contents and/or origin of the underlying data.

Note that digital signature schemes are often deployed simply for their ability to provide data origin authentication. They are the main public-key cryptographic primitive for providing data origin authentication and the obvious choice for applications that require data origin authentication but cannot, normally for key management reasons, use a MAC.

In order to provide these two security services, a digital signature on some data will need to be computed from:

The data. Since a digital signature provides data origin authentication (and non-repudiation) it is clear that the digital signature itself must depend on the data and cannot be a completely unrelated piece of information. Note that although its computation must involve the data, it could be transmitted and stored separately from the data. This is in contrast to handwritten signatures, as we discuss in Section 7.4.3.

A secret parameter known only by the signer. Since a digital signature provides non-repudiation, its calculation must involve a secret parameter that is known only by the signer. If any other entity knows this secret parameter then it will be impossible to tell whether it was the signer or the other entity who computed the digital signature. The only possible situation where this might be acceptable is if the other entity is totally trusted by all parties involved in the signing and verifying of digital signatures, which is a scenario that we discuss in Section 7.2.

BASIC PROPERTIES OF A DIGITAL SIGNATURE SCHEME

There are three basic properties that any practical digital signature scheme should normally have:

Easy for the signer to sign data. From a practical perspective, there is no point in having a digital signature scheme that requires the signer to compute complex operations in order to generate a digital signature. The signing process should be as efficient as possible.

Easy for anyone to verify a message. Similarly, the verification of a digital signature should be as efficient as possible.

Hard for anyone to forge a digital signature. In other words, it should be practically impossible for anyone who is not the legitimate signer to compute a digital signature on some data that appears to be valid. By 'appears to be valid' we mean that anyone who attempts to verify the digital signature is led to believe that they have just successfully verified a valid digital signature on some data.

7.2 Non-repudiation using symmetric techniques

Non-repudiation is, by definition, rather an 'asymmetric' requirement in that it demands a capability that is linked to a specific entity, not one that is shared with any other entity (unlike confidentiality, for example). It should thus not be a surprise that digital signature schemes are normally provided using techniques associated with public-key cryptography. That said, there are several special circumstances where symmetric techniques based on MACs can be used to provide non-repudiation.

7.2.1 Arbitrated digital signature schemes

The first case arises when there exists a trusted third party, the *arbitrator*, who participates in the transfer of data and generates evidence that can be used to settle any disputes. Both the signer and verifier trust the arbitrator. Disputes are settled based on the premise that a statement is true if the arbitrator says that it is true.

An example of an *arbitrated digital signature scheme* is illustrated in Figure 7.1. Prior to using the scheme in Figure 7.1, it is assumed that all the parties involved have agreed upon a method for computing MACs. Further, the signer and the arbitrator share a symmetric MAC key *KS*, and the verifier and the arbitrator share a symmetric MAC key *KV*. To generate a digital signature on some data:

1. The signer computes a MAC on the message using key *KS*. The sender then sends the message and the MAC to the arbitrator. (This message includes an indication of the identities of the signer and the intended verifier.)

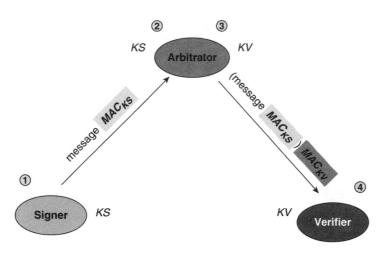

Figure 7.1. An arbitrated digital signature scheme

2. The arbitrator uses key *KS* to verify the correctness of the MAC received from the signer. If it is correct then the arbitrator continues, otherwise the process is aborted.

3. The arbitrator computes a new MAC on all the data that was received from the signer. In other words, the MAC is computed using key *KV* on both the message *and* the MAC that was computed by the signer using *KS*. The arbitrator then forwards everything sent by the signer, plus this new MAC, to the verifier.

4. The verifier uses key *KV* to verify the correctness of the MAC received from the arbitrator. If it is correct then the verifier accepts this as a 'digital signature' on the message, otherwise the verifier rejects the signature. Although the verifier cannot check the first MAC, there is no need for the verifier to do so since the arbitrator has already verified this MAC for them.

We now check that this scheme does indeed have the required security services of a digital signature scheme:

Data origin authentication. The second MAC (computed using *KV*) provides the verifier with data origin authentication of the message that was passed on by the arbitrator. The first MAC (computed using *KS*) provides the arbitrator with data origin authentication of the message from the signer. The verifier trusts the arbitrator to behave honestly. Therefore the verifier has assurance through the second MAC that the arbitrator, who is trusted, had assurance through the first MAC that the message came from the signer. Under the trust assumptions of this model, the verifier does indeed have data origin authentication of the signer.

Non-repudiation. Suppose that a dispute arises at a later date and that the signer falsely denies digitally signing the message. The verifier can present the full data that was received from the arbitrator as evidence of the data exchange. The presence of the valid MACs essentially states that the verifier received the message from the arbitrator, who vouched that it came from the signer. While the verifier could have forged the second MAC (computed using *KV*), the verifier could certainly not have forged the first MAC (computed using *KS*) because the verifier does not know key *KS*. The arbitrator (or indeed any judicator who is given access to the appropriate MAC keys) will rule in favour of the verifier in this case.

The scheme in Figure 7.1 thus provides the two security services that we need. With respect to the properties, digital signature generation is a fairly efficient process since it involves the creation of two MACs, and these are efficient to compute. Verification is also efficient since it involves checking one MAC. Note, however, that only a verifier who has a trust relationship (shared key) with the arbitrator can verify a MAC. Assuming that a reputable MAC algorithm is used, the only entity who can forge a digital signature of this type is the arbitrator, which is of course why all users of this scheme have to trust the arbitrator.

Thus the arbitrated digital signature scheme as depicted in Figure 7.1 does satisfy our notion of a digital signature scheme. However, this is not a scheme seen that often in practice. The main practical difficulty with implementing arbitrated signatures is the potential 'bottleneck' of having to pass every single signature generation process through the arbitrator. It is worth noting that in the physical world there are many processes that have a similar message flow to arbitrated digital signature schemes, for example, many legal processes.

7.2.2 Asymmetric trust relationships

A simpler example of MACs being used to provide non-repudiation arises in situations where the signer and the verifier are in very different positions regarding their perceived level of trust. For example, suppose that the signer is the client of a major bank, who is the verifier. The client 'signs' data using a MAC that was based on a MAC key, which in turn was generated by the bank and issued to the client on a smart card. We assume that the bank in control of the underlying key management of this system has a strong reputation for honesty and integrity with respect to its underlying infrastructure.

Now suppose that the client tries to deny 'signing' (generating a MAC on) some data on which there appears to be a valid MAC. If the MAC algorithm is strong and the underlying security architecture is properly implemented then the client's only defence can be that the bank must have created this MAC and is trying to 'frame' the client. However, how likely is it that a judge will rule in favour of the client in this case? Even though both entities could, in theory, have generated the MAC, the bank is a more powerful entity in this scenario and one in which there is normally a much greater degree of perceived trust. This *could* therefore be regarded as a relationship between a relatively untrusted entity (the client) and a trusted entity (the bank). In such cases it might be arguable that a MAC suffices to provide non-repudiation, because one party will never 'cheat'.

Of course, the above scenario allows plenty of room for debate! In fact, such a debate has played itself out in courtrooms over the years when clients have accused banks of 'phantom withdrawals' from Automatic Teller Machines, which utilise symmetric cryptography to protect transactions. It should be clear by now that the cryptography is unlikely to be at fault in such a scenario. Thus the challenge for the client is to persuade the court that the banking accounting infrastructure is flawed in some way. The bank, on the other hand, will be trying to persuade the court that either the client is lying or, more likely, a genuine transaction took place without the client being aware (the card was 'borrowed' by a family member, for example). It is not common in such court cases for anyone to suggest that the MACs on the ATM transaction are not true non-repudiation mechanisms and could have been forged by the bank.

7.2.3 Enforced trust

A third scenario where MACs could provide non-repudiation is where all cryptographic computations take place in hardware security modules (HSMs). These are special trusted hardware devices that have protection against tampering and are discussed in more detail in Section 10.5.3. We can then use MACs generated using keys that are only valid for MAC creation by one signer and MAC verification by one verifier (but not the other way around). For example:

- the MAC key K_{AB} is only allowed to be used by Alice's HSM to create MACs that can be verified by Bob's HSM;
- a separate MAC key K_{BA} is only allowed to be used by Bob's HSM to create MACs that can be verified by Alice's HSM.

So long as these usage rules are enforced by the HSMs, a judge will be able to decide if some data and an accompanying MAC was generated by the alleged signer. If Alice tries to deny generating some data on which a valid MAC using K_{AB} has been found, the judge will rule against her since the HSMs are trusted to enforce the usage rule that only Alice's HSM creates MACs using K_{AB}. This judgement also relies on the belief that although Bob's HSM contains K_{AB}, it only uses it to verify MACs sent to it by Alice, never to create MACs. In this way we have turned a symmetric key into the type of secret parameter only known by the signer that is necessary for non-repudiation.

7.3 Digital signature schemes based on RSA

We now discuss what most people would regard as 'true' digital signature schemes, which are those based on public-key cryptography. Indeed, Whit Diffie, one of the authors of the seminal research paper proposing public-key cryptography, has indicated that his motivation for the idea was substantially driven by a desire to find a means of creating 'digital signatures' and not public-key encryption. We will present a basic model of a digital signature scheme and describe two digital signature schemes based on RSA.

7.3.1 Complementary requirements

Keeping in mind our concerns about arbitrated digital signature schemes in Section 7.2.2, it is preferable to avoid the direct involvement of a third party in the generation of digital signatures. This leads us to some very simple requirements for a digital signature scheme, which we indicate in Table 7.1. As can be seen, these requirements have more than a passing resemblance to

Table 7.1: Comparison of requirements between digital signature and public-key encryption schemes

Digital signature scheme requirements	Public-key encryption scheme requirements
Only the holder of a secret can digitally sign some data	'Anyone' can encrypt some data
'Anyone' can verify that a digital signature is valid	Only the holder of a secret can decrypt some encrypted data

the basic requirements for a public-key encryption scheme that we discussed in Section 5.1.2.

The respective requirements are so similar that it seems natural to attempt to use a public-key cryptosystem in some way to produce a digital signature scheme. The most naive method of trying to produce a digital signature scheme would be to start with a public-key cryptosystem and for each user to:

- somehow use the private decryption key of the public-key cryptosystem to create digital signatures;
- somehow use the public encryption key of the public-key cryptosystem to verify digital signatures.

This compelling approach, in some cases, almost works. However, there are several reasons why this approach is indeed 'naive':

Technical constraints. We have to check that the technical details (the underlying mathematics) make sense if the roles of these two keys are reversed. In particular, if encryption and decryption are very different operations then it may not be possible just to swap the keys around in this manner.

Processing constraints. In the event that the technical details do still work, the roles may only easily reverse for 'textbook' versions of the cryptographic primitives. Real versions, based on accepted standards, often involve additional processing stages (adding padding, for example) that will not enable the operations to be swapped around so easily.

Key management constraints. It is not wise to use the same keys for two different applications. We will discuss this issue in more detail in Section 10.6.1, although it can easily be addressed by having two pairs of keys, one for decryption/encryption and one for signing/verifying.

Nonetheless, this naive approach certainly looks promising. We will see shortly that for the 'textbook' RSA cryptosystem, the underlying mathematics does in fact allow this role reversal of the keys. Hence this approach does form the basis for RSA digital signature schemes.

7.3.2 Basic model of a digital signature scheme

We assume that anyone who wishes to be able to digitally sign data is in possession of a public-key pair. Only the signer knows their 'private' key and the corresponding 'public' key is made available to anyone by whom the signer wishes their digital signatures to be verified. This could be by making it publicly-available. It is very important, however, that we do not use this key pair for decryption/encryption and signing/verifying (see Section 10.6.1). Thus we will refer to the 'private' key in this case as the *signature key* and the 'public' key as the *verification key*. The basic model of a digital signature scheme is shown in Figure 7.2.

The *signature algorithm* takes as input the data that is being signed and the signature key. The output is the *digital signature*, which is then sent to the verifier. The verifier inputs the digital signature and the verification key into the *verification algorithm*. The verification algorithm outputs some data, which should be the same data that was digitally signed. Using this output the verifier makes a decision on whether the digital signature is valid.

7.3.3 Two different approaches

There are two different approaches to designing digital signature schemes. Recall that a digital signature is essentially a cryptographic value that is calculated from the data and a secret parameter known only by the signer. A verifier who wishes to verify the correctness of this digital signature will need to run the verification

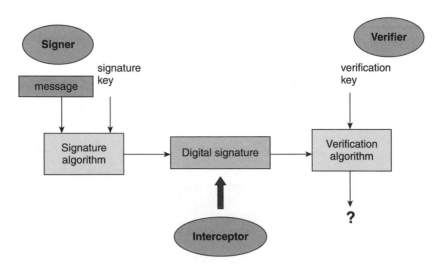

Figure 7.2. Basic model of a digital signature scheme

algorithm and, from the results of this process, will need to be able to determine whether the digital signature is valid. An important question to ask is: how will the verifier know which data this digital signature matches?

This question is particularly relevant if the data being digitally signed has no apparent recognisable structure (it could, for example, be an encrypted cryptographic key). After all, the digital signature itself will hopefully not have any apparent structure since it is the output of a cryptographic algorithm. This digital signature could well have been modified by an attacker. When the verifier runs the verification algorithm, the result that is output (assuming that this resembles the underlying data) will also have no apparent structure. So how will the verifier be able to determine whether the data that has been output is the correct data?

There are two different methods that are used to provide the verifier with this assurance.

Send the verifier the data that is being digitally signed. Data that is digitally signed is not, by default, confidential. In many situations it is acceptable to send the data along with the digital signature. The verifier now verifies the digital signature and is also able to see the data that was supposed to be digitally signed. Digital signature schemes that use this technique are called *digital signature schemes with appendix* because the data is sent with the digital signature as an 'appendix'.

Add redundancy to the data that is being signed. A more subtle technique is to make the data that is being digitally signed 'recognisable' by adding redundancy before computing the digital signature. In this case it now suffices to just send the digital signature itself. On verification, the verifier will recover some data from the digital signature. If this recovered data has the correct redundancy format then the verifier will accept that data as being correct, otherwise they will reject it. Digital signature schemes that use this technique are called *digital signature schemes with message recovery* because the data can be 'recovered' from the digital signature itself.

We will now look at examples of each of these two techniques. Both digital signature schemes are based on RSA and, to an extent, on the naive digital signature scheme that we proposed in Section 7.3.1. However, it is important to recognise that RSA is rather special in this regard since the naive approach does not generally work for arbitrary public-key cryptosystems.

7.3.4 RSA digital signature scheme with appendix

We require all signers and verifiers to agree on the use of a particular hash function as part of this scheme. In the following we will deliberately use the terms 'encryption' and 'decryption' in quotes because, while they refer to applying the RSA encryption and decryption algorithms, they do not refer to encryption and decryption of data for confidentiality purposes.

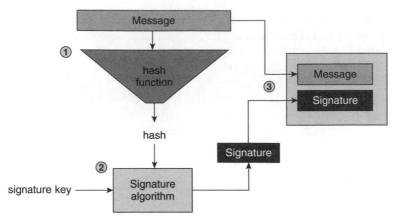

Figure 7.3. Creation of an RSA digital signature with appendix

THE SIGNING PROCESS

Figure 7.3 illustrates the process of creating an RSA digital signature with appendix.

1. The signer starts by hashing the data that is to be signed. We will shortly explain why.
2. The signer now signs the hashed data. This process simply involves 'encrypting' the hashed data using RSA as the encryption algorithm and the signer's signature key as the 'encryption' key. Note that signing involves 'encrypting' with the 'private' key of the signer, in contrast to the use of RSA for providing confidentiality when we encrypt using the public key of the receiver (see Section 5.2.2). This signed hash is the digital signature.
3. The signer sends to the verifier two pieces of information:

   (a) the data itself;
   (b) the digital signature.

   These do not have to be sent together, but the verifier will need both pieces of information before they can verify the digital signature.

THE VERIFICATION PROCESS

Figure 7.4 illustrates the process of verifying an RSA digital signature with appendix.

1. The verifier's task is to compare two separate pieces of information. To compute the first of them, the verifier takes the received data and applies the hash function to it in order to obtain the hash of the received data.
2. The verifier now 'decrypts' the digital signature using RSA as the decryption algorithm and the verification key of the signer as the 'decryption' key.

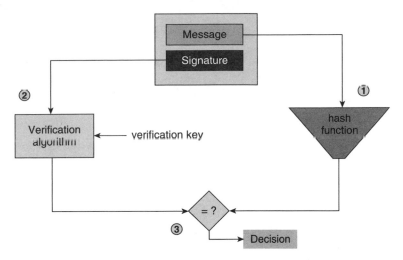

Figure 7.4. Verification of an RSA digital signature with appendix

Note again that this use of the signer's 'public' key for 'decryption' contrasts with the use of RSA for providing confidentiality. The result of this should be the hashed data, since the verification key should 'undo' the 'encryption' using the signature key.

3. The verifier now compares the two results. If the hash of the received data from step 1 matches the hashed data recovered in step 2 then the verifier accepts the digital signature as valid, otherwise the verifier rejects the digital signature.

REASONS FOR HASHING

The only 'surprising' part of the RSA digital signature scheme with appendix is the involvement of a hash function. The use of the hash function is essential for a number of reasons, which we now outline:

Efficiency. Recall that RSA operates on 'blocks' of bits, where each block is of approximately the same size as the RSA modulus. If the data to be signed is longer than one block then, without first hashing the data, we will need to split the data into separate blocks, each of which will need to be signed separately. As discussed in Section 5.4.2, RSA signature creation and verification processes are relatively computationally expensive since they rely on modular exponentiation. It is thus inefficient to sign (and verify) a large amount of data using RSA. However, when using a digital signature scheme with appendix the verifier is sent the data anyway, so it is sufficient to sign a 'representative' of the data. The hash of the data is a relatively small digest of the data that depends on the whole data. Assuming that the hash function has all the security properties that we discussed in Section 6.2.1, digitally signing a hash of the data is as good as digitally signing the data itself.

235

Preventing modification attacks. Suppose that data consists of more than one block and, rather than first using a hash function, each block is separately signed as discussed above. Then since these signature blocks are not linked together in any way, an attacker could perform a variety of active attacks on the digital signature. For example, if the data $m_1 \mid\mid m_2$ (meaning the concatenation of m_1 and m_2) has been split into blocks m_1 and m_2 then the digital signature is of the form:

$$m_1 \mid\mid m_2 \mid\mid sig(m_1) \mid\mid sig(m_2).$$

An attacker could swap component blocks and their component signatures around to forge a signature on the data $m_2 \mid\mid m_1$ (the original data with the two blocks presented in the reverse order):

$$m_2 \mid\mid m_1 \mid\mid sig(m_2) \mid\mid sig(m_1).$$

This attack is prevented by using the hash function h. In this case the digital signature is:

$$m_1 \mid\mid m_2 \mid\mid sig(\,h(m_1 \mid\mid m_2)\,).$$

An attacker could still swap around the data blocks m_1 and m_2, but in order to forge the signature on $m_2 \mid\mid m_1$ they would need to compute $sig(\,h(m_2 \mid\mid m_1)\,)$, which is impossible without knowledge of the signer's signature key.

Preventing existential forgeries. An attacker is said to be able to create an *existential forgery* if it is possible for the attacker to create a valid digital signature on some data that has not previously been signed. The above modification attack is an example of this. However, it would be even more concerning if an attacker could create an existential forgery from scratch. If we do not use the hash function then an attacker can create such a forgery, as follows:

1. randomly generate a value r (this will be the digital signature);
2. apply the signer's verification key to r to compute a value m (this will be the data).

It should be clear that r will appear to be a valid digital signature for data m. Of course the attacker has no control over what m is, thus it could be argued that this is not a serious attack. However, if the data to be signed has no apparent structure (for example, it is an encrypted cryptographic key) then this is a potentially serious attack. Anyway, the very fact that an attacker can generate existential forgeries so easily is highly disconcerting. Once again, use of the hash function prevents this type of forgery. This is because the value m in our forgery process is now the hash of some data, thus the attacker will need to reverse (find a preimage for) the hash function in order to find out what data the attacker has just forged a digital signature on.

RSA IS SPECIAL

We have mentioned several times that RSA is 'special' in that it allows the naive digital signature scheme to be realised by essentially swapping the roles of private and public keys in an RSA cryptosystem. In general, we cannot obtain a digital signature scheme from an arbitrary public-key cryptosystem in this way. Similarly, we cannot obtain a public-key cryptosystem by swapping the roles of the signature and verification keys of any digital signature scheme.

RSA has a special property that facilitates this. Let the verification key of the signer be (n, e) and the signature key be d. To sign data m, the signer first computes $h(m)$ and then digitally signs $h(m)$ by raising it to the power d modulo n:

$$sig(m) = h(m)^d \bmod n.$$

The signer then sends m and $sig(m)$ to the verifier. To verify this digital signature, the verifier computes $h(m)$ and then verifies $sig(m)$ by raising it to the power e modulo n. The verifier now checks to see if:

$$h(m) = sig(m)^e \bmod n.$$

If it does then the verifier accepts the digital signature.

We need to determine why this works. Firstly, observe that by one of the basic rules of exponentiation (see Section 1.6.1):

$$sig(m)^e = (h(m)^d)^e = h(m)^{de} \bmod n.$$

When we multiply two numbers together it does not matter which number we write first (for example, $2 \times 3 = 3 \times 2 = 6$), thus:

$$h(m)^{de} = h(m)^{ed} = (h(m)^e)^d \bmod n.$$

However, we know from our study of RSA as a public-key encryption scheme in Section 5.2.2 that raising something to the power e and then to the power d is equivalent to 'encrypting' it with a 'public' key and then 'decrypting' it with a 'private' key. We saw that for RSA this gets us back to where we started, since decryption of an encrypted plaintext recovers the original plaintext. Thus:

$$(h(m)^e)^d = h(m) \bmod n,$$

which is what we hoped would happen.

So what is special about RSA? In fact there are two special features:

Similarity of processes. The first special property is that the encryption and decryption processes are essentially the same. Encryption and decryption both use simple modular exponentiation.

Symmetry of exponentiation. The second special property is that raising a number to a power d and then to a power e has the same effect as raising a number to a power e and then to a power d. This makes it possible to 'swap' the roles of the encryption and decryption keys and thus convert an encryption scheme into a digital signature scheme. Most other public-key cryptosystems and digital signature schemes do not have sufficient symmetry of this type to allow such a swap to be conducted.

However, once again, it is worth repeating our caveat of Section 7.3.1. The above argument applies only to the 'textbook' versions of RSA. Real RSA encryption schemes and RSA digital signature schemes with appendix, do not work quite as simply as we have just described, where by 'real' we mean those that follow established standards such as PKCS and employ schemes such as RSA-OAEP for encryption and RSA-PSS for digital signatures. Instead, they involve additional processing stages that result in this straightforward key pair swap not being possible. That said, it is this symmetry of the simple 'textbook' versions that permits the very existence of both RSA encryption and RSA digital signature schemes, hence the observations in this section are relevant.

7.3.5 RSA digital signature scheme with message recovery

We now describe an RSA digital signature scheme based on the second approach that was identified in Section 7.3.3. Before we describe this scheme, it is worth identifying what advantages this second approach might offer.

ADVANTAGES OF DIGITAL SIGNATURE SCHEMES WITH MESSAGE RECOVERY

There are a couple of disadvantages with the digital signature schemes with appendix approach:

1. It requires the use of a hash function, so it might be advantageous to design schemes where no hash function is required.
2. Both the data and the digital signature need to be sent to the verifier. This involves a degree of message expansion, since the message that is sent is necessarily longer than the underlying data that is digitally signed.

The reasons we discussed for hashing, rather than signing the data directly, primarily applied to 'long' data that needs to be split into more than one block for direct processing using RSA. However, if the data to be signed is less than one RSA block in length (in other words, less than the length of the RSA modulus) then the case for hashing before signing is not so strong. Digital signature schemes with message recovery are typically proposed for precisely this situation. This is why they are sometimes also referred to as *digital signature schemes for short messages*.

Recall from Section 7.3.3 that if the data does not accompany the digital signature then the verifier faces the problem of recognising the correct data that is associated with the digital signature. Digital signature schemes with message recovery address this problem by adding redundancy to the data before it is signed, in order to later make it recognisable to a verifier. The data to be digitally signed must therefore be sufficiently short that it remains less than one RSA block in length *after* this redundancy has been added.

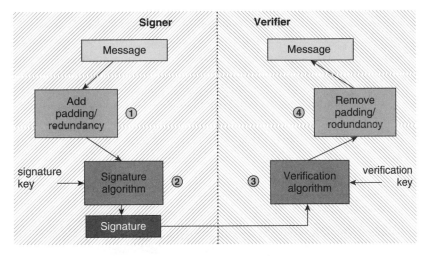

Figure 7.5. Signing and verifying using an RSA digital signature scheme with message recovery

SIGNING AND VERIFYING USING A DIGITAL SIGNATURE SCHEME WITH MESSAGE RECOVERY

We assume that each potential user of the scheme is equipped with an RSA signature/verification key pair. Figure 7.5 illustrates the process of creating and verifying an RSA digital signature with message recovery.

1. Some predefined redundancy is added to the data prior to signing. This has no content value and will primarily be used as a means for the verifier to identify that the recovered data is correct.
2. The formatted data (data plus redundancy) is signed using RSA. In other words, the formatted data is 'encrypted' using the signature key of the signer. The result of this 'encryption' is the digital signature. The digital signature is sent on its own to the verifier (there is no need to send the data this time).
3. The verifier checks the digital signature by 'decrypting' it with the signer's verification key. If all is well, the result is the correct formatted data.
4. The verifier removes the redundancy to extract the data from the formatted data. If the redundancy has the expected format then the verifier accepts the digital signature on the data as valid, otherwise the verifier rejects it.

To see why this works, suppose that an attacker intercepts the digital signature on its way to the verifier and modifies it before sending it on to the verifier. When the verifier 'decrypts' this modified digital signature with the signer's verification key, for the same error propagation reasons that we discussed in Section 4.3.2 for block ciphers, the result should have no apparent relationship to the original formatted data. Thus, in particular, the redundancy should not have the expected format and hence the verifier will reject the digital signature. A similar argument applies if an attacker attempts to directly forge a digital signature with message recovery.

REDUNDANCY TECHNIQUES

Exactly what should the predefined redundancy that we add during the digital signature creation process look like? Simple examples of redundancy, which serve only as illustrations, include:

- repeating the data twice, with the second copy concatenated to the first;
- adding a fixed data string;
- adding a counter that specifies the length of the data;
- adding a hash of the data.

Any of these techniques could be used in theory, so long as the technique is agreed by all potential users of the digital signature scheme. However, just like in other areas of cryptography, it is vital that appropriate standards are consulted before adopting a technique for adding redundancy. There have been sophisticated attacks against cryptosystems that exploit poor redundancy processes and so advice should be sought on what the current recommendations are for suitable methods of adding redundancy.

DIGITAL SIGNATURE SCHEMES WITH MESSAGE RECOVERY AND CONFIDENTIALITY

It is worth observing that digital signature schemes with message recovery do not provide confidentiality. It is tempting to believe that, because we do not send the data along with the digital signature, we are also 'hiding' the underlying data from an attacker. This belief can be fuelled by the fact that a digital signature should have no apparent structure, since it is essentially a piece of 'ciphertext' generated using RSA. There are two fallacies at play here:

1. Attempting to determine the underlying data from the digital signature is not an 'attack' at all. Digital signature schemes are not designed to provide confidentiality. In Section 7.4.2 we will consider what to do if confidentiality is also needed.
2. *Anyone* who has access to the signer's verification key can work out the data from the digital signature by following the legitimate verification process. Thus the data is only superficially 'hidden' inside the digital signature.

7.3.6 Other digital signature schemes

Although there have been many different proposals for digital signature schemes, only two substantially different types of digital signature scheme have thus far been widely adopted.

The first type consists of digital signature schemes based on RSA. We have discussed two examples of such schemes. The second type consists of schemes loosely based on ElGamal. Unlike RSA, the encryption and decryption operations in ElGamal are not easily swapped around. Thus, while such schemes are motivated by ElGamal encryption, they need to be designed in a fundamentally different way. The most well known of these is the *Digital Signature Algorithm* (DSA), which was standardised by the US Government as the *Digital Signature Standard*. The DSA is a digital signature scheme with appendix that is strongly motivated by ElGamal, but works in a different way. There is also an important variant based on elliptic curves known as ECDSA, which offers similar advantages over the DSA to those gained by using elliptic-curve-based variants of ElGamal encryption (see Section 5.3.5).

It is also quite common for digital signature schemes with appendix to be identified by combining the names of the digital signature scheme and the underlying hash function that is used. Hence the use of RSA-MD5 indicates the RSA digital signature scheme with MD5 as the underlying hash function. Similarly, ECDSA-SHA2 indicates the ECDSA signature scheme with SHA2 as the underlying hash function. Since digital signature schemes with appendix can, at least in theory, be combined with *any* underlying hash function, this nomenclature is primarily informative, since RSA-MD5 and RSA-SHA2 are essentially the same RSA digital signature scheme.

7.4 Digital signature schemes in practice

In this section we will consider practical issues that concern digital signature schemes in general, rather than being specific to any particular scheme.

7.4.1 Security of digital signature schemes

We will assume that we are using a respected digital signature scheme and that the platform on which the digital signature scheme is being used is 'trustworthy'. There are three cryptographic components of a digital signature scheme that could be exploited by an attacker.

SECURITY OF THE SIGNATURE KEY

We noted in Section 7.1.3 that in order for a user to generate a digital signature on some data, it is necessary for the user to have knowledge of a secret, which takes the form of the user's signature key. The signature key is thus, in some sense, an implied 'identity' of the signer. To compute a digital signature the signer combines this 'identity' with the data to be signed using the digital signature algorithm.

The two security services that are provided by a digital signature scheme both rely on the assumption that only the signer knows the signature key. If evidence is found that a particular signature key was used to create a digital signature (successful verification of the digital signature is sufficient evidence) then it is assumed that the owner of that signature key must have created the digital signature. More precisely, this provides:

Data origin authentication of the signer, since the ability to create a valid digital signature demonstrates that the originator of the data that was signed must have known the signature key;

Non-repudiation, since it is assumed that the *only* user with knowledge of the signature key is the signer, thus allowing the digital signature to be presented to a third party as evidence that the data was signed by the signer.

This has a very serious implication. It is important to observe that anyone who knows the signature key can use this to sign data. For the purposes of a digital signature scheme the signer *is* their signature key. If an attacker succeeds in obtaining someone else's signature key then the attacker is effectively able to 'become' the victim whenever the attacker uses the signature key to create digital signatures. This is an example of *identity theft*.

By using a respected digital signature scheme, we can fairly safely assume that an attacker will not be able to determine a signature key by exploiting the underlying cryptography. The real danger comes from attacks that either exploit poor key management procedures or break physical protection mechanisms (for example, circumnavigating the protection of a smart card on which the signature key is stored). In some cases it may not be necessary to learn the signature key since it may be sufficient to obtain the device on which it is stored and then instruct the device to use the key.

The implication of these observations is that whenever a digital signature scheme is deployed, it is vital that users protect their signature keys using appropriate methods. While protection of keys is always important in cryptography, signature keys are particulary sensitive for the reasons just discussed. We will examine appropriate methods for protection of (signature) keys in Section 10.5.

SECURITY OF THE VERIFICATION KEY

Verification keys are not as sensitive as signature keys, since they are 'public' keys that are disseminated to anyone who needs to be able to verify a digital signature. Nonetheless, suppose that an attacker can persuade Charlie that Alice's verification key is actually the verification key of Bob. Now, when Alice digitally signs some data, Charlie will verify it and believe that the data was digitally signed by Bob. Note that the attacker does not need to obtain Alice's signature key. Of course the attacker cannot forge any digital signatures using this attack, so it is a less serious (but potentially easier) attack than obtaining a signature key.

An interesting related attack for handwritten signatures occurs when a new payment card that is being mailed out to a user is intercepted by an attacker in the postal system. The attacker can then sign the user's name in the attacker's handwriting on the back of the card and masquerade as the user (hopefully only until the first monthly bill is received). The attacker is able to conduct this attack without any knowledge of the victim's handwritten signature.

In order to prevent attacks of this type on verification keys, it is necessary to put into place sound processes for authenticating verification keys. This same problem arises for public keys that are being used for public-key encryption. We will discuss this topic in Chapter 11.

SECURITY OF THE HASH FUNCTION

Digital signature schemes with appendix could also be attacked, at least in theory, by finding collisions in the underlying hash function. We discussed an attack of this type in Section 6.2.3. It is thus very important that any hash function that is used to support a digital signature scheme with appendix provides collision resistance (see Section 6.2.1). If this is in any doubt then all digital signatures created using that hash function could become contestable.

7.4.2 Using digital signature schemes with encryption

Recall from Section 6.3.6 that many applications require both confidentiality and data origin authentication, which is a topic that we discussed within the context of symmetric cryptography. The case for requiring both of these security services is even stronger in environments using public-key cryptography. This is because the potentially wide availability of a public encryption key makes it easy for anyone to send an encrypted message to the public key owner, without it necessarily being clear who the originator of the message was.

In many applications it may thus be desirable to both encrypt and digitally sign some data. The main problem with trying to combine encryption and digital signatures in an application is that the two 'obvious' methods based on using two separate primitives have fundamental security problems. These problems are independent of the digital signature scheme that is used. We will assume in the following discussion that we are using a digital signature scheme with appendix.

Sign-then-encrypt. This essentially involves Alice digitally signing the data and then encrypting the data and the digital signature using Bob's public encryption key. However, in this case a bad recipient Bob can:

1. decrypt and recover the data and the digital signature;
2. encrypt the data and the digital signature using Charlie's public encryption key;
3. send this ciphertext to Charlie, who decrypts it and verifies Alice's digital signature.

The problem here is that Charlie has received a message that is both encrypted and digitally signed (by Alice). Charlie will want to reasonably conclude that this is evidence that Alice was the origin of the data (which she was), and that nobody else has been able to view the data en route from Alice to Charlie. But this, as we have just seen, is certainly not the case.

Encrypt-then-sign. This involves Alice encrypting the data using Bob's public encryption key and then digitally signing the ciphertext. The ciphertext and the digital signature are then sent to Bob. However, in this case an attacker who intercepts the resulting message can:

1. create their own digital signature on the ciphertext;
2. forward the ciphertext and the attacker's digital signature to Bob, who verifies the attacker's digital signature and then decrypts the ciphertext.

In this case Bob will want to conclude that the recovered data has been sent to him by the attacker. However, this is certainly not the case since the attacker does not even know what the data is.

The above problems did not arise in Section 6.3.6 due to the fact that the use of symmetric keys involves an implicit indication of the originator and intended recipient of a message. By their very nature, this is not the case for use of public keys. The simplest way of providing this assurance when using public-key cryptography is to make sure that:

- the data that is encrypted always includes the sender's identity;
- the data that is digitally signed always includes the receiver's identity.

If this is done then the 'attacks' on sign-then-encrypt and encrypt-then-sign are not possible.

An alternative solution is to use a dedicated cryptographic primitive that simultaneously encrypts and digitally signs data in a secure way. Such primitives are often referred to as *signcryption schemes* and can be regarded as the public-key cryptography equivalent of authenticated-encryption primitives (see Section 6.3.6). Signcryption schemes have not yet seen wide adoption, but they are beginning to be standardised, so this situation may change in the future.

7.4.3 Relationship with handwritten signatures

Earlier in Section 7.1.2 we commented on the importance of resisting any temptation to consider digital signatures as a direct electronic 'equivalent' of handwritten signatures. Now that we have discussed digital signatures at some length, it is time to look more closely at the relationship between these two concepts.

We proceed by considering a list of relevant issues and identifying the differences. The number of differences is striking. Hopefully this extensive comparison makes it clear that handwritten signatures and digital signatures are in many ways quite different in their properties. While some electronic applications for digital signatures are indeed analogous to physical applications of handwritten signatures, digital signatures provide more precise security properties at the cost of being more complex to implement.

ENVIRONMENTAL DIFFERENCES:

Form. A handwritten signature is a physical object, while a digital signature is electronic data. This difference is obvious but it has great significance, for example, with regard to the law (see later).

Signer. A handwritten signature must be generated by a human signer. On the other hand, signature keys for digital signatures do not have to be associated with a human signer. They could be held by groups of humans (for example, an organisation) or could belong to devices or software processes.

Signature creation. The ability to create a handwritten signature requires the presence of a human. Digital signatures require the existence of equipment in order to create a signature, such as a secure device on which to store the signature key and a computer to perform the signature creation.

Availability. Barring serious illness or accident, handwritten signatures are always available for use. Digital signatures depend on the availability of the various components of the infrastructure of the digital signature scheme, including computer systems and signature key storage devices.

SECURITY DIFFERENCES:

Consistency over messages. In theory, a handwritten signature is approximately the same every time that it is used, even to sign different messages. A crucial difference between handwritten and digital signatures is that digital signatures on different items of data are not the same. A digital signature depends on the underlying data. In cryptographic terminology, a digital signature is *message dependent*.

Consistency over time. While handwritten signatures have a reasonable degree of consistency, they tend to vary with the physical state (health, mood and concentration) of the signer. They also tend to gradually change over time. In contrast, a digital signature generated using a particular set of values is the result of a cryptographic computation and will be the same each time the same set of values are input.

Uniqueness to individuals. Handwritten signatures are biometrically controlled and thus it is reasonable to regard then as being unique to a particular signer. Many people have handwritten signatures that appear to be similar but there are experts who can fairly accurately distinguish handwritten signatures. On the other hand, digital signatures depend on a signature key and the underlying data. The issue of 'uniqueness' is thus only relevant if we consider digitally signing a fixed message. In this case the uniqueness of the digital signature to an individual depends on how unique a signature key is to an individual. Signature keys should be unique if they are generated properly. For example, recommended parameters for RSA should provide at least the equivalent security of a 128-bit symmetric key, which means that there should be at least 10^{40} possibilities for a signature key. Since this number dwarfs the number of people in the world, it is *extremely unlikely* that any two individuals will generate the same signature key.

Capability for precise verification. Handwritten signatures need an expert to verify precisely (from prior samples) and are normally rather imprecisely verified. On the other hand, digital signatures can be precisely verified by application of the correct verification key.

Ease of forgery. Handwritten signatures are easy to forge superficially, at least in a way that would fool most of the people for most of the time, but hard to forge in the presence of an expert. Digital signatures are very hard to forge if a sound security infrastructure is in place. However, if the infrastructure fails then they may be very easy to forge (for example, if an attacker obtains someone else's signature key). This feature of digital signature schemes has the potential to be quite concerning.

Security services. It is questionable whether a handwritten signature *formally* provides any of our cryptographic security services. A handwritten signature is normally a statement that the underlying data was seen and approved at some moment in time by the signer. It can be simple to change the data after a handwritten signature has been applied. The lack of message dependency also potentially makes it easy to transfer a handwritten signature from one document to another (see *ease of forgery*). Digital signatures do not have these problems since their underlying message dependency provides data origin authentication and non-repudiation, assuming that a supporting public-key management system is in place.

Levels of security. The security of a digital signature scheme can potentially be set to different levels through the use of different lengths of signature key and applying different levels of process checking within the underlying public-key management system (see Chapter 11). Handwritten signatures do not have such flexibility, although they too can be subjected to different levels of checking (for example, witnessed or notarised signatures).

The human-computer gap. A handwritten signature carries with it an implication that the signer has seen the entire document that was signed, even if they only sign a cover or the last page. However, a digital signature carries no such implication. It is quite possible for a human to digitally sign data that they have never seen, since the signing function is normally carried out by a computer. The human thus needs to 'trust' that all the components of the computer functioned correctly. This 'human–computer gap' may allow a signer to claim that he did not create, or was not aware of creating, a digital signature.

PRACTICAL DIFFERENCES:

Cost. Handwritten signatures are cheap to deploy. Digital signature schemes require a supporting infrastructure that provides technology, key management, etc. This makes digital signature schemes more expensive to implement.

Longevity. Handwritten signatures can be created for the lifetime of the signer, and are often valid beyond the signer's lifetime. Restrictions on the longevity of an agreement signed using a handwritten signature can be put in place by stating such limitations in the underlying data. Digital signatures can be created and verified until the time that the relevant key pair expires (see Section 10.2.1) or the verification key is revoked (see Section 11.2.3). Digital signatures may also be regarded as being valid beyond this time, depending on the application. To extend the lifetime of a digital signature, digital data can be resigned to create a new digital signature on the data, or be archived by a trusted third party (see Section 12.6.5).

Acceptability. Handwritten signatures are well accepted and their limitations understood. Despite their failure to provide strong security services, they are deployed in applications throughout the world for reasons of cost and availability. Digital signatures have not earned this level of use and their inherent complexity provides several possibilities for challenging the security services that they provide.

Legal recognition. Handwritten signatures are well respected and recognised in law throughout the world. Digital signatures are increasingly being recognised and appropriate laws being developed, but many jurisdictions do not yet recognise them, while others only recognise them for specific purposes.

FLEXIBILITY DIFFERENCES:

Binding to the underlying data. Handwritten signatures are, to an extent, physically bound to the object that they relate to, typically a piece of paper. Note however that this binding can be 'loose', for example, when a handwritten signature is only applied to the cover or last page of a document. In contrast, digital signatures can be sent and stored separately from the underlying data.

Support for multiple signatures. Some people have different handwritten signatures that they reserve for different purposes. However, any one individual is only likely to be able to reliably generate a small number of different handwritten signatures. On the other hand, there is no limit to the number of signature keys that any one individual can hold (they could have different signature keys for different applications) and hence no limit to the number of different digital signatures that one individual could generate for a fixed message.

Special signatures. Handwritten signatures have several important specialised forms, such as notarised and witnessed signatures, which have different status within law. It is possible to design digital equivalents of these. In fact it is possible to create many more specialised digital signatures. As noted above, the signer of a digital signature does not have to be a single human being. For example, various types of *group signature* are possible where a signature can be produced and proven to be from a group of entities without revealing who the actual signer was. Also, *blind signatures* can be generated, where signers sign data that they cannot see. An impressive variety of specialised digital signature schemes have been proposed by cryptographers, although relatively few of these have yet been implemented in applications.

7.4.4 Relationship with advanced electronic signatures

Before closing our discussion of digital signature schemes, it is worth returning to the definition of advanced electronic signature from Section 7.1.2 and noting the extent to which digital signatures comply with this notion. The four particular properties of an advanced electronic signature were:

Uniquely linked to the signatory. We discussed this issue under *uniqueness to individuals* in Section 7.4.3. A well-designed digital signature scheme should have signature keys that are uniquely linked to signatories.

Capable of identifying the signatory. A signatory can be 'identified' by verifying a digital signature that they created. This capability is primarily realised by providing a secure infrastructure that provides verifiers with confidence in the correct ownership of verification keys. This infrastructure is provided by a public-key management system and is the subject of Chapter 11.

Created using means under the sole control of the signatory. This is probably the most difficult of these properties to establish. Confidence that a digital signature could only be produced by the designated signatory is provided through many different factors in combination. It requires confidence in the supporting public-key management system, in particular the processes that surround the generation of signature keys. It also requires confidence in the ongoing management of the signature key, as well as confidence in the secure operation of the computing device that was used to compute the digital signature. Weaknesses in any of these could lead to the formulation of a case for arguing that a digital signature might have been created without the signatory being aware of what was happening. Most of these are key management issues, which we discuss in Chapters 10 and 11.

Linked to data to which it relates in such a way that subsequent changes in the data is detectable. Digital signatures provide this property by definition, since they provide data origin authentication.

248

7.5 Summary

In this chapter we have discussed digital signatures, the main cryptographic mechanism for providing non-repudiation of data. While it is possible under special circumstances to produce a 'digital signature' using symmetric techniques, digital signature schemes are normally regarded as being public-key primitives.

The main issues that we covered were:

- Digital signature schemes are in some senses complementary to public-key encryption schemes, providing data origin authentication and non-repudiation of data based on the belief that only a designated signatory is in possession of a signature key.
- There are two general techniques for designing a digital signature scheme: digital signature schemes with appendix and digital signature schemes with message recovery.
- The most popular digital signature schemes are based on RSA or DSA (ECDSA).
- Digital signatures have different properties and offer different guarantees to handwritten signatures.

We have also seen that, as for all cryptographic primitives, the security of digital signature schemes is intrinsically bound to the effectiveness of the management of the cryptographic keys on which they rely. We will address these challenges in much greater detail in Chapters 10 and 11.

7.6 Further reading

Digital signatures are one of the areas where cryptography interacts closely with the law. A good portal for links to different national approaches to accepting digital signatures is the Wikipedia entry on digital signatures and the law [200]. One of the most influential documents in this area, and one that we made explicit reference to, is the European Parliament Directive on electronic signatures [151].

The idea of a digital signature scheme was first proposed by Diffie and Hellman [59]. RSA digital signature schemes, including RSA-PSS, are fully specified in PKCS#1 [115]. The Digital Signature Standard is described in FIPS 186-3 [82]. This also includes a specification of ECDSA, although a useful alternative description can be found in Johnson, Menezes and Vanstone [102]. Digital signature schemes with appendix are the subject of ISO/IEC 14888 [7], while digital signature schemes with message recovery are treated in ISO/IEC 9796 [17]. Digital signature schemes based on elliptic curves are defined in ISO/IEC 15946 [10]. An interesting standard which deals with non-repudiation based on symmetric techniques, as well as considering a number of non-repudiation mechanisms using trusted third parties, is ISO/IEC 13888 [6]. This standard also covers non-repudiation in a much more general sense than we have, including other types of non-repudiation, such as non-repudiation of delivery of a message. As always, an excellent overview of the relevant digital signature standards is provided in Dent and Mitchell [55].

We have hopefully made it very clear that although digital signatures have a passing resemblance to handwritten signatures, they are fundamentally different. Another version of this message appeared in Bruce Schneier's Crypto-Gram Newsletter [167]. A good overview of the issues surrounding digital signature schemes is also provided in Ford and Baum [83]. It is possible to compute and verify digital signatures, as well as run a simulation of RSA digital signature schemes with appendix, using CrypTool [52].

7.7 Activities

1. The definition of 'electronic signature' proposed in Section 7.1.2 is very open.

   (a) What processes or technologies can you think of that might satisfy this definition?
   (b) To what extent do your proposals satisfy the definition of an advanced electronic signature?

2. MACs do not by default provide non-repudiation.

   (a) Explain why this is the case.
   (b) Under what conditions might a MAC be used to provide non-repudiation?

3. RSA is unusual in that the encryption algorithm can be used as part of the process of generating a digital signature.

   (a) Write down the mathematical operations involved in RSA encryption and verification of an RSA digital signature with appendix.
   (b) Identify the 'special' property of RSA that allows it to be used both for encryption and digital signatures.
   (c) Explain why this apparent 'symmetry' between RSA encryption and digital signatures is not so relevant in practice.

4. RSA digital signatures rely on the security of the supporting hash function.

   (a) Explain why it is important that the hash function has collision resistance.
   (b) Discuss whether it is important that the hash function has preimage resistance.

5. For an application environment of your choice using an RSA digital signature scheme with appendix, order the following risks with respect to both likelihood of occurrence and security implications:

   - an attacker factorises the RSA modulus;
   - a smart card containing the signature key is stolen;
   - a collision is found in the underlying hash function;

- an attacker persuades a verifier to use an incorrect verification key;
- a second preimage is found for the underlying hash function;
- an attacker extracts the signature key from a smart card on which it is stored;
- an attacker persuades the signer to digitally sign some fraudulent data;
- a flaw in the RSA algorithm is found that compromises the digital signature scheme security.

6. There are several reasons why it is good practice to separate RSA digital signature key pairs and RSA encryption key pairs.

   (a) If Alice is using the same RSA key pair for both digital signatures and encryption, explain how Bob could forge Alice's signature on a message of his choice if Alice is 'foolish' enough to help him.
   (b) Why is this a more powerful attack than the existential forgery that we described in Section 7.3.4?
   (c) What other reasons are there for keeping these key pairs separate?

7. The Digital Signature Algorithm (DSA) is related to ElGamal.

   (a) Is the DSA a digital signature scheme with appendix or with message recovery?
   (b) Explain how to generate a DSA signature/verification key pair.
   (c) Describe the process of creating a DSA signature.
   (d) Describe the process of verifying a DSA signature.
   (e) What is the basis for the security of DSA?
   (f) Provide a short comparison of the DSA and RSA digital signature schemes.

8. What key lengths and lengths of hash function outputs would you currently recommend for use with digital signatures based on:

   (a) RSA?
   (b) DSA?
   (c) ECDSA?

9. Digital signature schemes with message recovery rely on the data being signed having some structured redundancy added to the data prior to being input into the signing algorithm.

   (a) Explain why this redundancy is necessary.
   (b) Find out how this redundancy is added for a particular digital signature scheme with message recovery that has been standardised by a recognised standards body.

10. It is possible that an application using public-key cryptography might require both confidentiality and data origin authentication of a message to be provided. One possible solution is to use a signcryption scheme. Prepare a short report on signcryption schemes, which includes information about how they work, the extent to which they are being standardised, and potential applications.

11. It is possible that an application using symmetric encryption might also require non-repudiation based on a digital signature scheme. Compare different ways of combining these two cryptographic primitives.

12. In Section 7.4.3 we discussed a range of issues in which digital signatures and handwritten signatures differ. Prepare a two-minute summary of this discussion for your line manager which outlines the differences that you regard as the most fundamental.

13. Determine the extent to which digital (electronic) signatures are currently supported by the laws that apply to the country in which you currently reside.

14. Bob has successfully verified a digital signature that appears to come from Alice. However, Alice is convinced that she did not create this digital signature. What 'defence' arguments could Alice use in her denial of the digital signature?

15. There have been many digital signatures proposed with additional properties. One of these is *blind signatures*.
    (a) What is a blind signature?
    (b) Provide a physical world analogy for a blind signature.
    (c) What potential applications are there for blind signatures?
    (d) Describe one method of producing blind signatures that is based on RSA.

8 Entity Authentication

The last security service that we will discuss in detail is entity authentication. This is probably the security service that is provided by the most diverse range of mechanisms, including several that are not inherently cryptographic. Naturally our focus will be on the use of cryptography to provide entity authentication. Since many cryptographic entity authentication mechanisms rely on randomly generated numbers, we will choose this chapter to have a discussion about random number generation. We will also discuss the wider notion of providing freshness in cryptography.

> ## At the end of this chapter you should be able to:
>
> - Discuss a number of different mechanisms for randomly generating values that are suitable for use in cryptography.
> - Compare different techniques for providing freshness.
> - Recognise a number of different approaches to providing entity authentication.
> - Appreciate the limitations of password-based approaches to providing entity authentication.
> - Explain the principle behind dynamic password schemes.

8.1 Random number generation

The relationship between cryptography and randomness is extremely important. Many cryptographic primitives cannot function securely without randomness. Indeed, there are many examples of cryptosystems failing not because of problems with the underlying cryptographic primitives, but because of problems with their sources of randomness. It is thus vital that we understand what randomness is and how to produce it.

8.1.1 The need for randomness

Most cryptographic primitives take structured input and turn it into something that has no structure. For example:

- The ciphertext produced by a block or stream cipher should have no apparent structure. If this is not the case then useful information may be provided (leaked) to an attacker who observes the ciphertext. Indeed, there are many applications where ciphertext is used as a source of randomness. We have already seen this in Section 4.6.2 when we observed that ciphertext can be used to generate keystream for a 'stream cipher'.
- The output of a hash function should have no apparent structure. Although we did not state this explicitly as one of our hash function properties, we noted in Section 6.2.2 that hash functions are often used to generate cryptographic keys.

Just as importantly, many cryptographic primitives *require* sources of randomness in order to function. For example:

- Any cryptographic primitive that is based on symmetric keys requires a source of randomness in order to generate these keys. The security of symmetric cryptography relies on the fact that these keys cannot be predicted in any way.
- Many cryptographic primitives require the input of other types of randomly generated numbers such as salts (see Section 8.4.2) and initial variables (see Section 4.6.2). We have also seen in Section 5.3.4 that public-key cryptosystems are normally probabilistic, in the sense that they require fresh randomness each time that they are used.
- We will see in Chapter 9 that sources of randomness are very important for providing freshness in cryptographic protocols.

Given this intricate relationship, we could probably have had a general discussion about random number generation almost anywhere in our review of mechanisms for implementing security services. However, we choose to have it now because a significant number of the cryptographic mechanisms for providing entity authentication require randomly generated numbers as a means of providing freshness. We will discuss freshness mechanisms in Section 8.2. We will discuss randomness in the specific context of cryptographic key generation in Section 10.3.

8.1.2 What is randomness?

People have been trying for hundreds of years to define precisely what is meant by the word 'random'. In fact 'randomness', by its very nature, defies classification rules. Nonetheless, we all have an intuitive feel for what 'random' should mean.

These notions are all to do with ideas such as 'unpredictability' and 'uncertainty'. We would like randomly generated numbers in general to be hard to predict and appear to have no relationship with previous randomly generated numbers. By the same measure, we would like randomly generated bits to be apparently unpredictable sequences of bits.

Ironically, however, although randomness is hard to define, there are many ways that we would like randomness to behave that are easily identifiable. A random number generation process is often assessed by applying a series of statistical tests. Many of these tests are fairly intuitive and include checks such as, on average, over the generation of many random outputs:

- does 1 appear in the output of the process approximately as often as 0 does?
- does a 0 follow a 1 in the output of the process approximately as often as a 1 follows a 1?
- does the string 000 occur in the output of the process approximately as often as the string 111?

Human intuition often confuses randomness with evenly spaced distributions. For example, many people believe that the binary string 10101010 is more likely to have been produced by a truly uniform random source than the binary string 11111111. In fact, the probability that a uniform random source produces these two outputs is exactly the same, and is equal to the probability that it produces a string with no apparent pattern such as 11010001. By the same token, some bank customers get concerned when the bank issues them with the PIN 3333, when in fact this should be just as unlikely to occur as the PIN 7295. (Of course, a bank customer is perhaps more likely to change a PIN to something like 3333, so there is a genuine case for considering 3333 to be a less secure PIN in practice, but it is not a failure of the bank's random PIN generation process!) Statistical tests provide rigorous methods for assessing a random generation process that are much more reliable than human intuition.

8.1.3 Non-deterministic generators

There are two general approaches to generating randomness. First we will look at *non-deterministic* generation, which relies on unpredictable sources in the physical world. This is a compelling, but often expensive, approach to producing randomness. On the other hand, there are many situations where we are willing to compromise and use a 'cheaper' source of randomness. In this case, *deterministic* generation techniques, which we examine in Section 8.1.4, can be adopted.

A *non-deterministic generator* is based on the randomness produced by physical phenomena and therefore provides a source of 'true randomness' in the sense that the source is very hard to control and replicate. Non-deterministic generators can be based on hardware or software.

HARDWARE-BASED NON-DETERMINISTIC GENERATORS

Hardware-based non-deterministic generators rely on the randomness of physical phenomena. Generators of this type require specialist hardware. Generally speaking, these are the best sources of 'true' randomness. Examples include:

- measurement of the time intervals involved in radioactive decay of a nuclear atom;
- semiconductor thermal (Johnson) noise, which is generated by the thermal motion of electrons;
- instability measurements of free running oscillators;
- white noise emitted by electrical appliances;
- quantum measurements of single photons reflected into a mirror.

Hardware-based generators provide a continuous supply of randomly generated output for as long as the power required to run the generator lasts, or until the process ceases to produce output. However, because specialist hardware is required, these types of generator are relatively expensive. In some cases the randomly generated output is produced too slowly to be of much practical use.

SOFTWARE-BASED NON-DETERMINISTIC GENERATORS

Software-based non-deterministic generators rely on the randomness of physical phenomena detectable by the hardware contained in a computing device. Examples include:

- capture of keystroke timing;
- outputs from a system clock;
- hard-drive seek times;
- capturing times between interrupts (such as mouse clicks);
- mouse movements;
- computations based on network statistics.

These sources of randomness are cheaper, faster and easier to implement than hardware-based techniques. But they are also of lower quality and easier for an attacker to access or compromise. When using software-based techniques it may be advisable to combine a number of different software-based non-deterministic generators.

NON-DETERMINISTIC GENERATORS IN PRACTICE

Non-deterministic generators work by measuring the physical phenomena and then converting the measurements into a string of bits. In some cases the initial binary string that is generated may need some further processing. For example, if the source was based on mouse clicks then periods of user inactivity may have to be discarded.

Regardless of the underlying technique used, there are two problems with non-deterministic generators:

1. They tend to be expensive to implement.
2. It is, essentially, impossible to produce two identical strings of true randomness in two different places (indeed, this is the very point of using physical phenomena as a randomness source).

For these reasons, in most cryptographic applications deterministic sources of randomness tend to be preferred.

8.1.4 Deterministic generators

The idea of a *deterministic* random generator may sound like an oxymoron, since anything that can be determined cannot be truly random. The term *pseudorandom* (which we introduced in Section 4.2.1) is often used to describe both a deterministic generator and its output.

BASIC MODEL OF A DETERMINISTIC GENERATOR

A *deterministic generator* is an algorithm that outputs a pseudorandom bit string, in other words a bit string that has no apparent structure. However, as we just hinted, the output of a deterministic generator is certainly not randomly generated. In fact, anyone who knows the information that is input to the deterministic generator can completely predict the output. Each time the algorithm is run using the same input, the same output will be produced. Such predictability is, in at least one sense, the opposite of randomness.

However, if we use a *secret* input into the deterministic generator then, with careful design of the generation process, we might be able to generate output that will have no apparent structure. It will thus *appear* to have been randomly generated to anyone who does not know the secret input. This is precisely the idea behind a deterministic generator. The basic model of a deterministic generator is shown in Figure 8.1.

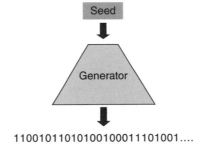

Figure 8.1. Basic model of a deterministic generator

The two components of this model are:

A seed. The secret information that is input into the deterministic generator is often referred to as a *seed*. This is essentially a cryptographic key. The seed is the only piece of information that is definitely not known to an attacker. Thus, to preserve the unpredictability of the pseudorandom output sequence it is important both to protect this seed and to change it frequently.

The generator. This is the cryptographic algorithm that produces the pseudorandom output from the seed. Following our standard assumptions of Section 1.5.1, we normally assume that the details of the generator are publicly known, even if they are not.

DETERMINISTIC GENERATORS IN PRACTICE

A deterministic generator overcomes the two problems that we identified for non-deterministic generators:

1. They are cheap to implement and fast to run. It is no coincidence that deterministic generators share these advantages with stream ciphers (see Section 4.2.4), since the keystream generator for a stream cipher is a deterministic generator whose output is used to encrypt plaintext (see Section 4.2.1).
2. Two identical pseudorandom outputs can be produced in two different locations. All that is needed is the same deterministic generator and the same seed.

Of course, deterministic generators are, in some sense, a bit of a cheat. They generate pseudorandom output but they require random input in the form of the seed to operate. So we still require a source of randomness for the seed. If necessary, we also require a means of securely distributing the seed.

However, the seed is relatively short. It is normally a symmetric key of a standard recommended length, such as 128 bits. We are still faced with the problem of generating this seed, but once we address this we can use it to produce long streams of pseudorandom output. The use of relatively expensive non-deterministic generators might be appropriate for short seed generation. Alternatively, a more secure deterministic generator could be used for this purpose such as one installed in secure hardware (see Section 10.3).

The case for using deterministic generators is similar to the case we made for using stream ciphers in Section 4.2.2. Deterministic generators thus provide an attractive means of converting relatively costly random seed generation into a more 'sustainable' source of pseudorandom output. As remarked earlier, however, deterministic generators are often points of weakness in real cryptosystems. It is important to identify potential points of weakness:

Cryptanalysis of the generator. Deterministic generators are cryptographic algorithms and, as such, are always vulnerable to potential weaknesses in their design. Use of a well-respected deterministic generator is probably the best way of reducing associated risks. However, it is not uncommon for cryptographic applications to use well-respected encryption algorithms but employ 'home-made' deterministic generators to produce keys. This may arise because some system designers are wise enough not to attempt to build their own encryption algorithms, but fail to appreciate that designing secure deterministic generators is just as complex.

Seed management. If the same seed is used twice with the same input data then the same pseudorandom output will be generated. Thus seeds need to be regularly updated and managed. The management of seeds brings with it most of the same challenges as managing keys, and presents a likely target for an attacker of a deterministic generator. Thus most of the issues concerning key management discussed in Chapter 10 are also relevant to the management of seeds.

We end this brief discussion of generating randomness by summarising the different properties of non-deterministic and deterministic generators in Table 8.1.

8.2 Providing freshness

Before we discuss entity authentication mechanisms, there is one important set of mechanisms that we need to add to our cryptographic toolkit. These are not really cryptographic 'primitives' because, on their own, they do not achieve any security goals. *Freshness mechanisms* are techniques that can be used to provide assurance that a given message is 'new', in the sense that it is not a *replay* of a message sent at a previous time. The main threat that such mechanisms are deployed against is the capture of a message by an adversary, who then later replays it at some advantageous time. Freshness mechanisms are particularly important in the provision of security services that are time-relevant, of which one of the most important is entity authentication.

Table 8.1: Properties of non-deterministic and deterministic generators

Non-deterministic generators	Deterministic generators
Close to truly randomly generated output	Pseudorandom output
Randomness from physical source	Randomness from a (short) random seed
Random source hard to replicate	Random source easy to replicate
Security depends on protection of source	Security depends on protection of seed
Relatively expensive	Relatively cheap

Note that what entity authentication primarily requires is a notion of *liveness*, which is an indication that an entity is currently active. A freshness mechanism does not provide this by default, since just because a message is 'new' does not imply that the sender is 'alive'. For example, an attacker could intercept a 'fresh' message and then delay relaying it to the intended receiver until some point in the future. When the receiver eventually receives the message they may well be able to identify that it is fresh (not a replay) but they will not necessarily have any assurance that the sender is still 'alive'. However, all freshness mechanisms can be used to provide liveness if they are managed appropriately, particularly by controlling the window of time within which a notion of 'freshness' is deemed acceptable.

There are three common types of freshness mechanism, which we now review.

8.2.1 Clock-based mechanisms

A *clock-based* freshness mechanism is a process that relies on the generation of some data that identifies the time that the data was created. This is sometimes referred to as a *timestamp*. This requires the existence of a clock upon which both the creator of the data and anyone checking the data can rely. For example, suppose that Alice and Bob both have such a clock and that Alice includes the time on the clock when she sends a message to Bob. When Bob receives the message, he checks the time on his clock and if it 'matches' Alice's timestamp then he accepts the message as fresh. The granularity of time involved might vary considerably between applications. For some applications the date might suffice, however, more commonly an accurate time (perhaps to the nearest second) is more likely to be required.

Clock-based freshness mechanisms seem a natural solution, however, they come with four potential implementation problems:

Existence of clocks. Alice and Bob must have clocks. For many devices, such as personal computers and mobile phones, this is quite reasonable. It may not be so reasonable for other devices, such as certain types of smart token.

Synchronisation. Alice's and Bob's clocks need to be reading the same time, or sufficiently close to the same time. The clocks on two devices are unlikely to be perfectly synchronised since clocks typically suffer from *clock drift*. Even if they drift by a fraction of one second each day, this drift steadily accumulates. How much drift is acceptable before Bob rejects the time associated with a message? One solution might be to only use a highly reliable clock, for example one based on a widely accepted time source such as universal time. Another solution might be to regularly run a resynchronisation protocol. The most obvious solution is to define a window of time within which a timestamp will be accepted. Deciding on the size of this *window of acceptability* is application dependent and represents a tradeoff parameter between usability and security.

Communication delays. It is inevitable that there will be some degree of communication delay between Alice sending, and Bob receiving, a message. This tends to be negligible compared to clock drift and can also be managed using windows of acceptability.

Integrity of clock-based data. Bob will normally require some kind of assurance that the timestamp received from Alice is correct. This can be provided by conventional cryptographic means, for example using a MAC or a digital signature. However, such an assurance can only be provided when Bob has access to the cryptographic key required to verify the timestamp.

8.2.2 Sequence numbers

In applications where clock-based mechanisms are not appropriate, an alternative mechanism is to use *logical* time. Logical time maintains a notion of the order in which messages or sessions occur and is normally instantiated by a *counter* or *sequence number*.

The idea is best illustrated by means of an example. Suppose Alice and Bob regularly communicate with one another and wish to ensure that messages that they exchange are fresh. Alice can do this by maintaining two sequence numbers for communicating with Bob, which are counters denoted by N_{AB} and N_{BA}. Alice uses sequence number N_{AB} as a counter for messages that she sends to Bob, and sequence number N_{BA} as a counter for messages that she receives from Bob. Both sequence numbers work in the same way. We illustrate the case of N_{AB}.

When Alice sends a message to Bob:

1. Alice looks up her database to find the latest value of the sequence number N_{AB}. Suppose that at this moment in time $N_{AB} = T_{new}$.
2. Alice sends her message to Bob along with the latest sequence number value, which is T_{new}.
3. Alice increments the sequence number N_{AB} by one (in other words, she sets $N_{AB} = T_{new} + 1$) and stores the updated value on her database. This updated value will be the sequence number that she uses next time that she sends a message to Bob.

When Bob receives the message from Alice:

4. Bob compares the sequence number T_{new} sent by Alice with the most recent value of the sequence number N_{AB} on his database. Suppose this is $N_{AB} = T_{old}$.
5. If $T_{new} > T_{old}$ then Bob accepts the latest message as fresh and he updates his stored value of N_{AB} from T_{old} to T_{new}.
6. If $T_{new} \le T_{old}$ then Bob rejects the latest message from Alice as not being fresh.

This is just one example of the way in which sequence numbers can work. The basic principle is that messages are only accepted as fresh if the latest sequence number has not been used before. The simplest way of doing this is to make sure that, each time a new message is sent, the sequence number is increased.

Note that an alternative technique would be to associate each new message with a unique identification number, but not necessarily one that is bigger than the last one sent. In this case Bob would have to maintain a database that consisted of all previous identification numbers sent (not just the most recent one). He would then have to search this database every time that a new message was received in order to check that the identification number had not been used before. Clearly this would be inefficient in terms of time and storage space.

In the above example, note that Alice increments her sequence number N_{AB} by one each time that she sends a message, but Bob only checks whether $T_{new} > T_{old}$, not that $T_{new} = T_{old} + 1$, which is what we might expect. If $T_{new} > T_{old} + 1$ then this suggests that, between the last message Bob received and the current message, some messages from Alice to Bob have got lost. This might itself be a problem, so Bob will need to decide whether the fact that there are missing messages is important. However, the sequence number is primarily there to provide *freshness*. The fact that $T_{new} > T_{old}$ is enough to gain this assurance. It also allows Bob to resynchronise by updating his version of N_{AB} to the latest sequence number T_{new}.

It is worth briefly considering the extent to which sequence numbers address the four concerns that we raised with clock-based mechanisms:

Existence of clocks. The communicating parties no longer require clocks.

Synchronisation. In order to stay synchronised, communicating parties need to maintain a database of the latest sequence numbers. Our simple example included a mechanism for making sure that this database is kept up to date.

Communication delays. These only apply if messages are sent so frequently that there is a chance that two messages arrive at the destination in the reverse order to which they were sent. If this is a possibility then there remains a need to maintain the equivalent of a window of acceptability, except that this will be measured in terms of acceptable sequence number differences, rather than time. For example, Bob might choose to accept the message as fresh not just if $T_{new} > T_{old}$, but *also* if $T_{new} = T_{old}$, since there is a chance that the previous message from Alice to Bob has not yet arrived. Note that this issue is not relevant if either:

- delays of this type are not likely (or are impossible);
- Bob is more concerned about the possibility of replays than the implications of rejecting genuine messages.

Integrity of sequence numbers. Just as for clock-based time, an attacker who can freely manipulate sequence numbers can cause various problems in any protocol that relies on them. Thus sequence numbers should have some level of cryptographic integrity protection when they are sent.

The obvious *cost* of using sequence numbers is the need to maintain databases of their latest values. Another possible problem arises if sequence numbers have a limited size and eventually cycle around again. Nonetheless, this type of mechanism is popular in applications where maintaining synchronised clocks is unrealistic. The most compelling such example is probably mobile phone networks, where it is impractical to rely on millions of handsets throughout a network keeping an accurately synchronised notion of clock-based time (see Section 12.3.4).

8.2.3 Nonce-based mechanisms

One problem that is shared by both clock-based mechanisms and sequence numbers is the need for some integrated infrastructure. In the former this was a shared clocking mechanism, in the latter it was a synchronised database of sequence numbers. *Nonce-based* mechanisms do not have this need. Their only requirement is the ability to generate *nonces* (literally, 'numbers used only once'), which are randomly generated numbers for one-off use. Note that the term 'nonce' is sometimes used, more literally, to mean numbers that are *guaranteed* to be used only once. We will use it in a slightly more relaxed way to mean numbers that *with high probability* are used only once.

The general principle is that Alice generates a nonce at some stage in a communication session (protocol). If Alice receives a subsequent message that contains this nonce then Alice has assurance that the new message is fresh, where by 'fresh' we mean that the received message must have been created *after* the nonce was generated.

To see why freshness is provided here, recall that the nonce was generated randomly for one-off use. As we know from Section 8.1, a good random number generator should not produce predictable output. Thus it should be impossible for an adversary to be able to anticipate a nonce in advance. If the same nonce reappears in a later message then it must be the case that this later message was created by someone *after* the generation of the nonce. In other words, the later message is fresh.

We re-emphasise this important point by considering the simplest possible example. Suppose that Alice generates a nonce and then sends it in the clear to Bob. Suppose then that Bob sends it straight back. Consider the following three claims about this simple scenario:

Alice cannot deduce anything from such a simple scenario. This is not true, although it is true that she cannot deduce very much. She has just received a message consisting of a nonce from someone. It could be from anyone. However, it consists of a nonce that she has just generated. This surely is no coincidence! What this means is that it is virtually certain that whoever sent the nonce back to her (and it might not have been Bob) must have seen the nonce that Alice sent to Bob. In other words, this message that Alice has just received was almost certainly sent by someone *after* Alice sent the nonce to Bob. In other words, the message that Alice has just received is not authenticated, but it is fresh.

There is a chance that the nonce could have been generated before. This is certainly true, there is a 'chance', but if we assume that the nonce has been generated using a secure mechanism and that the nonce is allowed to be sufficiently large then it is a very small chance. This is the same issue that arises for any cryptographic primitive. If Alice and Bob share a symmetric key that was randomly generated then there is a 'chance' that an adversary could generate the same key and be able to decrypt ciphertexts that they exchange. What we can guarantee is that by generating the nonce using a secure mechanism, the chance of the nonce having been used before is so small that we might as well forget about it.

Since a nonce was used, Bob is sure that the message from Alice is fresh. This is not true, he certainly cannot. As far as Bob is concerned, this nonce is just a number. It could be a copy of a message that was sent a few days before. Since Bob was not looking over Alice's shoulder when she generated the nonce, he gains no freshness assurance by seeing it. If Bob has freshness requirements of his own then he should also generate a nonce and request that Alice include it in a later message to him.

Nonce-based mechanisms do not suffer from any of the problems that we identified for the previous freshness mechanisms, except for the familiar need to set a window of acceptance beyond which a nonce will no longer be regarded as fresh. After all, in our simple example we stated that Bob sent the nonce 'straight back'. How much delay between sending and receiving the nonce should Alice regard as being 'straight back'? Nonce-based mechanisms do, however, come with two costs:

1. Any entity that requires freshness needs to have access to a suitable generator, which is not the case for every application.
2. Freshness requires a minimum of two message exchanges, since it is only obtained when one entity receives a message back from another entity to whom they earlier sent a nonce. In contrast, clock-based mechanisms and sequence numbers can be used to provide freshness directly in one message exchange.

8.2.4 Comparison of freshness mechanisms

Choosing an appropriate freshness mechanism is application dependent. The appropriate mechanism depends on which of the various problems can best be overcome in the environment in which they will be deployed. Table 8.2 contains a simplified summary of the main differences between the three types of freshness mechanism that we have discussed.

Note that there are other differences that might be influential in selecting a suitable freshness mechanism for an application. For example, sequence numbers and nonces are not, by definition, bound to a notion of clock-based time. Hence, if using these mechanisms in an application that requires a notion of 'timeliness' (for

Table 8.2: Summary of properties of freshness mechanisms

	Clock-based	Sequence numbers	Nonce-based
Synchronisation needed?	Yes	Yes	No
Communication delays	Window needed	Window needed	Window needed
Integrity required?	Yes	Yes	No
Minimum passes needed	1	1	2
Special requirements	Clock	Sequence database	Random generator

example, for entity authentication) then they require a degree of management. For sequence numbers this management involves monitoring the time periods between received sequence numbers. For nonces, it involves monitoring the delay between sending and receiving the nonce.

8.3 Fundamentals of entity authentication

Recall from Section 1.3.1 that entity authentication is the assurance that a given entity is involved and currently active in a communication session. This means that entity authentication really involves assurance of both:

Identity. the identity of the entity who is making a claim to be authenticated;
Freshness. that the claimed entity is 'alive' and involved in the current session.

If we fail to assure ourselves of identity then we cannot be certain whom we are trying to authenticate. If we fail to assure ourselves of freshness then we could be exposed to *replay attacks*, where an attacker captures information used during an entity authentication session and replays it at a later date in order to falsely pass themselves off as the entity whose information they 'stole'.

The word *entity* is itself problematic. We will avoid philosophical questions and not propose any formal definition, other than to comment that an 'entity' in the subsequent discussion could be a human user, a device or even some data. To appreciate the problems of defining a rigorous notion of an 'entity', consider the following question: when someone types their password into a computer then is the entity that is being authenticated the person, or their password? This essentially relates to the same 'human–computer gap' that we commented on when discussing digital signatures in Section 7.4.3.

If entity authentication is only used to provide assurance of the identity of one entity to another (and not vice versa) then we refer to it as *unilateral* entity authentication. If both communicating entities provide each other with assurance of their identity then we call this *mutual* entity authentication. For example, when someone presents their card and PIN at an ATM then they are engaging in unilateral entity authentication to the bank. The bank does not authenticate itself to the customer. Indeed this 'weakness' of ATM authentication has been regularly exploited by attackers who present fake ATMs to bank customers in order to harvest their card details and PINs. If the entity authentication process had been mutual then the customer would have been able to reject the bank. In fact, ATMs attempt to weakly authenticate themselves simply by 'looking like' genuine ATMs, but a determined attacker can easily make something that defeats this by also 'looking like' a real ATM.

8.3.1 A problem with entity authentication

It is important to recognise that entity authentication is a security service that is only provided for an 'instant in time'. It establishes the identity of a communicating entity at a specific moment, but just seconds later that entity could be replaced by another entity, and we would be none the wiser.

To see this, consider the following very simple attack scenario. Alice walks up to an ATM, inserts her payment card and is asked for her PIN. Alice enters her PIN. This is an example of entity authentication since the card/PIN combination is precisely the information that her bank is using to 'identify' Alice. As soon as the PIN is entered, Alice is pushed aside by an attacker who takes over the communication session and proceeds to withdraw some cash. The communication session has thus been 'hijacked'. Note that there was no failure of the entity authentication mechanism in this example. The only 'failure' is that it is assumed (fairly reasonably in this case) that the communication that takes place just a few seconds after the entity authentication check is still with the entity who successfully presented their identity information to the bank via the ATM.

This instantaneous aspect of entity authentication might suggest that for important applications we are going to have to conduct almost continuous entity authentication in order to have assurance of the identity of an entity over a longer period of time. In the case of the ATM, we would thus have to request Alice to enter her PIN every time she selects an option on the ATM. This will really annoy Alice and does not even protect against the above attack, since the attacker can still push Alice aside at the end of the transaction and steal her money (we can at least prevent the attacker controlling the amount that is withdrawn).

Fortunately, cryptography can provide a means of prolonging an entity authentication check in many situations. The solution is to combine entity authentication with the establishment of a cryptographic key. Through the entity authentication we gain assurance that the key was established with the claimed entity. Every time the key is correctly used in the future then it should be the case that the entity who was authenticated is involved in that session, since nobody else should know the key. While this does not help us much in our scenario where the attacker is standing next to Alice at the ATM, it does help us defend against attackers who are attacking the ATM network and attempting to modify or send spoof messages over it. We will look at cryptographic protocols for implementing this process in Section 9.4.

8.3.2 Applications of entity authentication

Entity authentication tends to be employed in two types of situation:

Access control. Entity authentication is often used to directly control access to either physical or virtual resources. An entity, sometimes in this case a human user, must provide assurance of their identity in real time in order to have access. The user can then be provided with access to the resources immediately following the instant in time that they are authenticated.

As part of a more complex cryptographic process. Entity authentication is also a common component of more complex cryptographic processes, typically instantiated by a cryptographic protocol (see Chapter 9). In this case, entity authentication is normally established at the start of a connection. An entity must provide assurance of their identity in real time in order for the extended protocol to complete satisfactorily. For example, the process of establishing a symmetric key commonly involves mutual entity authentication in order to provide the two communicating entities with assurance that they have agreed a key with the intended partner. We discuss this scenario in more detail in Section 9.4.

8.3.3 General categories of identification information

One of the prerequisites for achieving entity authentication is that there is some means of providing information about the identity of a *claimant* (the entity that we are attempting to identify). There are several different general techniques for doing this. Note that:

- As we observed earlier, providing identity information is not normally enough to achieve entity authentication. Entity authentication also requires a notion of freshness, as discussed in Section 1.3.1.
- Different techniques for providing identity information can be, and often are, combined in real security systems.
- Cryptography has a dual role in helping to provide entity authentication:
  1. Some of these approaches involve identity information that may have little to do with cryptography (such as possession of a token or a password). Cryptography can still be used to support these approaches. For example, as we discussed in Section 6.2.2, cryptography can play a role in the secure storage of passwords.

2. Almost all of these approaches require a cryptographic protocol (the subject of Chapter 9) as part of their implementation.

We now review the main categories of identity information that are used when providing entity authentication.

SOMETHING THE CLAIMANT HAS

For human users, identity information can be based on something physically held by the user. This is a familiar technique for providing access control in the physical world, where the most common identity information of this type is a physical key. This technique can also be used for providing identity information in the electronic world. Examples of mechanisms of this type include:

Dumb tokens. By 'dumb' we mean a physical device with limited memory that can be used to store identity information. Dumb tokens normally require a reader that extracts the identity information from the token and then indicates whether the information authenticates the claimant or not.

One example of a dumb token is a plastic card with a magnetic stripe. The security of the card is based entirely on the difficulty of extracting the identity information from the magnetic stripe. It is quite easy for anyone determined enough to either build, or purchase, a reader that can extract or copy this information. Hence this type of dumb token is quite insecure.

In order to enhance security, it is common to combine the use of a dumb token with another method of providing identification, such as one based on something the user knows. For example, in the banking community plastic cards with magnetic stripes are usually combined with a PIN, which is a piece of identity information that is required for entity authentication but that is not stored on the magnetic stripe.

Smart cards. A smart card is a plastic card that contains a chip, which gives the card a limited amount of memory and processing power. The advantage of this over a dumb token is that the smart card can store secret data more securely and can also conduct cryptographic computations. However, like dumb tokens, the interface with a smart card is normally through an external reader.

Smart cards are widely supported by the banking industry, where most payment cards now include a chip as well as the conventional magnetic stripe (see, for example, Section 12.4). Smart cards are also widely used for other applications, such as electronic ticketing, physical access control, identity cards (see Section 12.6.3), etc.

Smart tokens. Smart cards are special examples of a wider range of technologies that we will refer to as *smart tokens*. Some smart tokens have their own user interface. This can be used, for example, to enter data such as a challenge number, for which the smart token can calculate a cryptographic response. We will discuss an application of this type in Section 8.5.

All types of smart token (including smart cards) require an interface to a computer system of some sort. This interface could be a human being or a processor connected to a reader. As with dumb tokens, smart tokens are often implemented alongside another identification method, typically based on something that the user knows.

SOMETHING THE CLAIMANT IS

One of the highest profile, and most controversial, methods of providing identity information is to base it on physical characteristics of the claimant, which in this case is normally a human user. The field of *biometrics* is devoted to developing techniques for user identification that are based on physical characteristics of the human body.

A biometric mechanism typically converts a physical characteristic into a digital code that is stored on a database. When the user is physically presented for identification, the physical characteristic is measured by a reader, digitally encoded, and then compared with the template code on the database. Biometric measurements are often classified as either being:

Static, because they measure unchanging features such as fingerprints, hand geometry, face structure, retina and iris patterns.

Dynamic, because they measure features that (slightly) change each time that they are measured, such as voice, writing and keyboard response times.

Identification based on biometrics is a compelling approach for human users because many biometric characteristics appear to be fairly effective at separating individuals. However, there are many implementation issues, both technical, practical and sociological. Hence biometric techniques need to be adopted with care.

We will not discuss biometrics any further here since they are of peripheral relevance to cryptography. We recognise biometrics primarily as a potentially useful source of identity information.

SOMETHING THE CLAIMANT KNOWS

Basing identity information, at least partially, on something that is known to the claimant is a very familiar technique. Common examples of this type of identity information include PINs, passwords and passphrases. This is the technique most immediately relevant to cryptography since identity information of this type, as soon as it is stored anywhere on a device, shares many of the security issues of a cryptographic key.

Indeed, in many applications, identity information of this type often *is* a cryptographic key. However, strong cryptographic keys are usually far too long for a human user to remember and hence 'know'. There is some good news and some potentially bad news concerning the use of cryptographic keys as identity information:

1. Most information systems consist of networks of devices and computers. These machines are much better at 'remembering' cryptographic keys than humans!

Thus, if the claimant is a machine then it is possible that a cryptographic key can be something that is 'known'.

2. Where humans are required to 'know' a cryptographic key, they normally activate the key by presenting identity information that is easier to remember such as a PIN, password or passphrase. Of course, this reduces the effective security of that cryptographic key from that of the key itself to that of the shorter information used to activate it. We revisit this issue in Section 10.6.3.

We will now proceed to look more closely at ways in which cryptography can be employed to assist in the provision of identity information based on something that the claimant knows.

8.4 Passwords

Passwords are still one of the most popular techniques for providing identity information, although they have many obvious flaws. We will briefly look at some of these flaws as motivation for enhanced techniques. We will also reexamine the use of cryptography for password protection. Note that in this section we use the term 'password' very loosely, since much of our discussion equally applies to the likes of PINs and passphrases.

8.4.1 Problems with passwords

The attractive properties of passwords are that they are simple and familiar. These are the reasons that they are ubiquitously used as identity information. However, they have several flaws that severely limit the security of any application that employs them:

Length. Since passwords are designed to be memorised by humans, there is a natural limit to the length that they can be. This means that the *password space* (all possible passwords) is limited in size, thus restricting the amount of work required for an exhaustive search of all passwords.

Complexity. The full password space is rarely used in applications because humans find randomly generated passwords hard to remember. As a result we often work from highly restricted password spaces, which greatly reduces the security. This makes dictionary attacks possible, where an attacker simply exhaustively tries all the 'likely' passwords and hopes to eventually find the correct one (see Section 1.6.5). Clever pneumonic techniques can slightly increase the size of a usable password space. Where users are requested to adopt complex passwords a usability–security tradeoff is soon reached, since it is more likely that a complex password will be transferred into 'something the claimant has' in the form of a written note, which in many cases defeats the purpose of using passwords in the first place. Moving from passwords to passphrases can improve this situation by significantly increasing the password space, however, many of the other problems with passwords remain.

Repeatability. For the lifetime of a password, each time that it is used it is exactly the same. This means that if an attacker can obtain the password then there is an (often significant) period of time within which the password can be used to fraudulently claim the identity of the original owner. One measure that can be taken to restrict this threat is to regularly force password change. However, this again raises a usability issue since regular password change is confusing for humans and can lead to insecure password storage practices.

Vulnerability. We have just noted that the consequences of 'stealing' a password can be serious. However, passwords are relatively easy for an attacker to obtain:

- they are most vulnerable at point of entry, when they can be viewed by an attacker watching the password holder (a technique often referred to as *shoulder surfing*);
- they can be extracted by attackers during social engineering activities, where a password holder is fooled into revealing a password to an attacker who makes claims, for example, to be a system administrator (an attack that is sometimes known as *phishing*);
- they can be obtained by an attacker observing network traffic or by an attacker who compromises a password database.

For the latter reason, passwords should be cryptographically protected at all times, as we will discuss in just a moment.

It is best to regard passwords as a rather fragile means of providing identity information. In particular, the problem of repeatability means that passwords on their own do not really provide entity authentication as we defined it, since there is no strong notion of freshness. In applications where strong entity authentication is required then passwords are best employed in conjunction with other entity authentication techniques, if at all. However, the advantages of passwords mean that they will probably always find use in applications where security is a relatively low priority.

8.4.2 Cryptographic password protection

Consider a large organisation that wishes to authenticate many users onto its internal system using passwords. One obvious way of implementing this is to use a system that compares offered passwords with those stored on a centralised password database. This presents the password database as a highly attractive target for attackers, since this database potentially contains a complete list of account names and passwords. Even if this database is managed carefully, the administrators of the system potentially have access to this list, which may not be desirable.

One area where cryptography can be used to help to implement an identification system based on passwords is in securing the password database. This is because, in order to authenticate a user, the system does not actually need to know a user's password. Rather, the device simply needs to know whether a supplied password is the correct one. The point is that while a user does need to enter the correct password, the system does not need to store a copy of this password in order to verify that it is correct.

In Section 6.2.2 we described an application of hash functions that implemented password database protection. The idea is to store hashes of the passwords, rather than the actual passwords in the password database. This allows them to be checked, while preventing anyone who gains access to the password database from recovering the passwords themselves. We observed that any function that is regarded as being one-way (which includes hash functions) could be used to provide this service.

As an example of a cryptographic primitive being used in a different way to create a one-way function, Figure 8.2 illustrates the basic idea behind the function that was used in many early UNIX operating systems for password database protection.

In the password database in the UNIX system, often identified by */etc/passwd*, every user has an entry that consists of two pieces of information:

Salt. This is a 12-bit number randomly generated using the system clock (see Section 8.1.3). The salt is used to uniquely modify the DES encryption algorithm (see Section 4.4) in a subtle way. We denote the result of this unique modification by DES+.

Password image. This is the result that is output after doing the following:

1. Convert the 8 ASCII character password into a 56-bit DES key. This is straightforward, since each ASCII character consists of 7 bits.

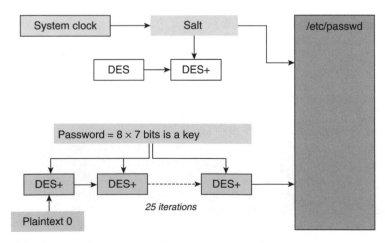

Figure 8.2. One-way function for UNIX password protection

2. Encrypt the plaintext consisting of all zeros (64 zero bits) using the uniquely modified DES+ with the 56-bit key derived from the password.
3. Repeat the last encryption step 25 times (in other words, we encrypt the all-zero string 25 times). This last step is designed to slow the operation down in such a way that it is not inconvenient for a user, but much more difficult for an attacker conducting a dictionary attack.

When a user enters their password, the system looks up the salt, generates the modified DES+ encryption algorithm, forms the encryption key from the password, and then conducts the multiple encryption to produce the password image. The password image is then checked against the version stored in /etc/passwd. If they match then the password is accepted.

8.5 Dynamic password schemes

As just observed, two of the main problems with passwords are vulnerability (they are quite easy to steal) and repeatability (once stolen they can be reused). A *dynamic password scheme*, also often refered to as a *one-time password scheme*, preserves the concept of a password but greatly improve its security by:

1. limiting the exposure of the password, thus reducing vulnerability;
2. using the password to generate dynamic data that changes on each authentication attempt, thus preventing repeatability.

Dynamic password schemes are important entity authentication mechanisms and are widely deployed in token-based technologies for accessing services such as internet or telephone banking.

8.5.1 Idea behind dynamic password schemes

At its heart, a dynamic password scheme uses a 'password function' rather than a password. If a claimant, which we will assume is a human user, wants to authenticate to a device, such as an authentication server, then the user inputs some data into the function to compute a value that is sent to the device. There are thus two components that we need to specify:

The password function. Since this function is a cryptographic algorithm, it is usually implemented on a smart token. In the example that we will shortly discuss, we will assume that this is a smart token with an input interface that resembles a small calculator.

The input. We want the user and the device to agree on an input to the password function, the result of which will be used to authenticate the user. Since the input must be fresh, any of the freshness mechanisms that we discussed in

Section 8.2 could be used. All of these techniques are deployed in different commercial devices, namely:

Clock-based. The user and the device have synchronised clocks and thus the current time can be used to generate an input that both the user and the device will 'understand'.

Sequence numbers. The user and the device both maintain synchronised sequence numbers.

Nonce-based. The device randomly generates a number, known as a *challenge*, and sends it to the user, who computes a cryptographic *response*. Such mechanisms are often referred to as *challenge–response* mechanisms.

8.5.2 Example dynamic password scheme

We now give an example of a dynamic password scheme.

DYNAMIC PASSWORD SCHEME DESCRIPTION

Before any authentication attempts are made, the user is given a token on which the password function has already been implemented in the form of a symmetric cryptographic algorithm A (this could be an encryption algorithm) with symmetric key K. While the algorithm A could be standard across the entire system, the key K is shared only by the server and the token held by the user. Note that a different user, with a different token, will share a different key with the server. Thus, as far as the server is concerned, correct use of key K will be associated with a specific user.

A further feature of this example scheme is that the user has some means of identifying themselves to the token, otherwise anyone who steals the token could pass themselves off as the user. In our example, this process will be implemented using a PIN. The token will only activate if the user enters the correct PIN.

Figure 8.3 shows an authentication attempt using this dynamic password scheme:

1. The server randomly generates a challenge and sends it to the user. It is possible that the user first sends a message to the server requesting that the server send them a challenge.
2. The user authenticates themselves to the token using the PIN.
3. If the PIN is correct then the token is activated. The user then uses the token interface by means of a keypad to enter the challenge into the token.
4. The token uses the password function to compute a response to the challenge. If algorithm A is an encryption algorithm then the challenge can be regarded as a plaintext and the response is the ciphertext that results from applying encryption algorithm A using key K. The token displays the result to the user on its screen.

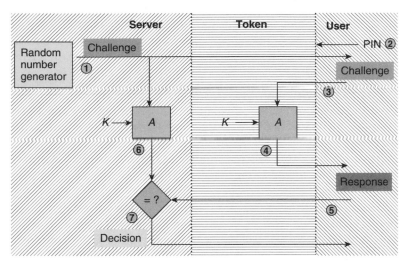

Figure 8.3. Example of a dynamic password scheme based on challenge–response

5. The user sends this response back to the server. This step might involve the user reading the response off the screen of the token and then typing it into a computer that is being used to access the authentication server.
6. The server checks that the challenge is still valid (recall our discussion in Section 8.2.3 regarding windows of acceptance for nonce-based freshness mechanisms). If it is still valid, the server inputs the challenge into the password function and computes the response, based on the same algorithm A and key K.
7. The server compares the response that it computed itself with the response that was sent by the user. If these are identical then the server authenticates the user, otherwise the server rejects the user.

ANALYSIS OF DYNAMIC PASSWORD SCHEME

The dynamic password scheme in Figure 8.3 merits a closer look, just to make sure that we appreciate both what has been gained in comparison to conventional passwords and the limitations of this idea.

Firstly, we establish the basis for assurance that the user is who they claim to be (the security 'bottom line'). From the perspective of the server, the only entity apart from itself that can compute the correct response is the only other entity in possession of both the algorithm A and the key K. The only other entity to know K is the token. The only way of accessing the token is to type in the correct PIN. Knowledge of the PIN is therefore the basis for assurance of authentication. So long as only the correct user knows the correct PIN, this dynamic password scheme will successfully provide entity authentication of the user.

275

This does not sound like a big improvement on password-based entity authentication, since we are essentially using a conventional password scheme to authenticate the user to the token. However, there are several significant improvements:

Local use of PIN. With regard to security at the user end, the main difference is that the user uses the PIN to authenticate themselves to a small portable device that they have control over. The chances of the PIN being viewed by an attacker while it is being entered are lower than for applications where a user has to enter a PIN into a device not under their control, such as an ATM. Also, the PIN is only transferred from the user's fingertips to the token and does not then get transferred to any remote server.

Two factors. Without access to the token, the PIN is useless. Thus another improvement is that we have moved from *one-factor* authentication (something the claimant knows, namely the password) to *two-factor* authentication (something the claimant knows, namely the PIN, *and* something the claimant has, namely the token).

Dynamic responses. The biggest security improvement is that every time an authentication attempt is made, a different challenge is issued and therefore a different response is needed. Of course, because the challenge is randomly generated there is a *very small* chance that the same challenge is issued on two separate occasions. But assuming that a good source of randomness is used (see Section 8.1) then this chance is so low that we can dismiss it. Hence anyone who succeeds in observing a challenge and its corresponding response cannot use this to masquerade as the user at a later date.

DYNAMIC PASSWORD SCHEMES IN PRACTICE

The relative ease of use and low cost of dynamic password schemes has seen their use increase significantly in recent years. They are now fairly popular entity authentication mechanisms for applications such as online banking (for example, EMV-CAP, discussed in Section 12.4.5). There is a great deal of variation in the ways in which these schemes operate. As well as varying in the underlying freshness mechanism, they also vary in the extent to which the user authenticates to the token. Techniques include:

- the user authenticates directly to the token (as in our example);
- the user presents some authentication data, such as a PIN, to the server; this could happen:
  - directly, for example the user presents the PIN to the server using a separate communication channel such as a telephone line;
  - indirectly, for example, the PIN is also an input into the cryptographic computation on the token, thus allowing it to be checked by the server when it conducts the verification step;

- there is no authentication between the user and the token (in which case we have one-factor authentication that relies on the correct user being in possession of the token).

8.6 Zero-knowledge mechanisms

We now briefly discuss an even stronger cryptographic primitive that can be used to support entity authentication. *Zero-knowledge mechanisms* bring security benefits but have practical costs. Nonetheless, it is worth at least discussing the idea behind them, just to indicate that it is feasible, even though they are not as commonly implemented in real systems as the previously discussed techniques.

8.6.1 Motivation for zero-knowledge

The entity authentication techniques that we have looked at thus far have two properties that we might deem undesirable.

Requirement for mutual trust. Firstly, they are all based on some degree of trust between the entities involved. For example, passwords often require the user to agree with the server on use of a password, even if the server only stores a hashed version of the password. As another example, the dynamic password scheme based on challenge–response requires the smart token and the server to share a key. However, there are situations where entity authentication might be required between two entities who are potential adversaries and do not trust one another enough to share *any* information.

Leaking of information. Secondly, they all give away some potentially useful information on each occasion that they are used. Conventional passwords are catastrophic in this regard since the password is fully exposed when it is entered, and in some cases may even remain exposed when transmitted across a network. Our example dynamic password scheme is much better, but does reveal valid challenge–response pairs each time that it is run (see the remark about *key exposure* in Section 10.2.1).

It would seem unlikely that entity authentication could be provided in such a way that no shared trust is necessary and *no knowledge at all* is given away during an authentication attempt, but amazingly zero-knowledge mechanisms can do precisely this.

The requirement for a zero-knowledge mechanism is that one entity (the *prover*) must be able to provide assurance of their identity to another entity (the *verifier*) in such a way that it is impossible for the verifier to later impersonate the prover, even after the verifier has observed and verified many different successful authentication attempts.

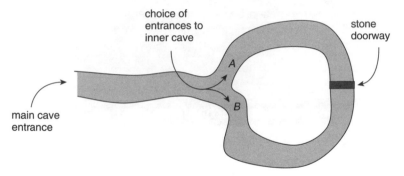

Figure 8.4. Popular analogy of a zero-knowledge mechanism

8.6.2 Zero-knowledge analogy

We will avoid discussion of the details of any zero-knowledge mechanism, but instead present a popular analogy in which we will play the role of verifier. The setting is a cave shaped in a loop with a split entrance, as depicted in Figure 8.4. The back of the cave is blocked by a stone doorway that can only be opened by using a secret key phrase. We wish to hire a guide to make a circular tour of the entire cave system but need to make sure in advance that our guide knows the key phrase, otherwise we will not be able to pass through the doorway. The guide, who will be our prover (the entity authentication claimant), is not willing to tell us the key phrase, otherwise there is a risk that we might go on our own tour without hiring him. Thus we need to devise a test of the guide's knowledge before we agree to hire him.

The guide has a further concern. For all he knows, we are from a rival guiding company and are trying to learn the key phrase. He wants to make sure that no matter how rigorous a test is run, we will not learn *anything* that could help us to try to work out what the key phrase is. Putting it another way, he wants to make sure that the test is a zero-knowledge mechanism that verifies his claim to know the key phrase.

So here is what we do:

1. We wait at the main cave entrance and send the guide down the cave to the place where it splits into two tunnels, labelled A and B. We cannot see this tunnel split from the main entrance, so we send a trusted observer down with him, just to make sure he does not cheat during the test.
2. The guide randomly picks a tunnel entrance and proceeds to the stone door.
3. We toss a coin. If it is heads then we shout down the cave that we want the guide to come out through tunnel A. If it is tails then we shout down the cave that we want the guide to come out through tunnel B.
4. The observer watches to see which tunnel the guide emerges from.

Suppose we call heads (tunnel *A*). If the guide comes out of tunnel *B* (the wrong entrance) then we decide not to hire him since he does not appear to know the key phrase. However, if he comes out of tunnel *A* (the correct entrance) then one of two things have happened:

- The guide got lucky and chose tunnel *A* in the first place. In that case he just turned back, whether he knows the key phrase or not. In this case we learn nothing.
- The guide chose tunnel *B*. When we called out that he needed to come out of tunnel *A*, he used the key phrase to open the door and crossed into tunnel *A*. In this case the guide has demonstrated knowledge of the key phrase.

So if the guide emerges from tunnel *A* then there is a 50% chance that he has just demonstrated knowledge of the key phrase. The problem is that there is also a chance that he got lucky.

So we run the test again. If he passes a second test then the chances that he got lucky twice are now down to 25%, since he needs to get lucky in both independent tests. Then we run the test again, and again. If we run n such independent tests and the guide passes them all, then the probability that the guide does not know the key phrase is:

$$\frac{1}{2} \times \frac{1}{2} \times \cdots \times \frac{1}{2} = \left(\frac{1}{2}\right)^n = \frac{1}{2^n}.$$

Thus we need to insist on n tests being run, where $\frac{1}{2^n}$ is sufficiently small that we will be willing to accept that the guide almost certainly has the secret knowledge. Meanwhile, the guide will have done a great deal of walking around the cave system and using the key phrase, without telling us any information about the key phrase. So the guide will also be satisfied with the outcome of this process.

8.6.3 Zero-knowledge in practice

An obvious question to ask about the zero-knowledge analogy is why we did not just stand at the cave split, send the guide down one tunnel, and then request that he came out of the other tunnel. This would demonstrate knowledge of the key phrase without revealing it. The reason is that this was indeed just an 'analogy' for the way in which cryptographic zero-knowledge mechanisms work.

Cryptographic zero-knowledge mechanisms require a number of 'runs' (or *rounds*) of a test of knowledge of a cryptographic secret, with each round passed bringing greater assurance to the verifier that the prover knows a cryptographic secret. However, each round also involves more computation and adds to the time taken to make the entity authentication decision. Zero-knowledge mechanisms normally use techniques similar to those of public-key cryptography which, as we discussed in Section 5.4.2, are typically more computationally expensive than those of symmetric cryptography. Thus zero-knowledge primitives are more expensive mechanisms to use than the previous entity authentication mechanisms that we have discussed.

8.7 Summary

In this chapter we discussed mechanisms for providing entity authentication. Since strong entity authentication mechanisms require an assurance of freshness, we first reviewed freshness mechanisms. Since an important means of providing freshness mechanisms is challenge–response, which relies on random number generation, we began with a discussion of random number generation. Thus, some of this chapter dealt with issues of wider significance than entity authentication.

However, our treatment of entity authentication was also incomplete. One of the most important classes of cryptographic mechanism for providing entity authentication are authentication and key establishment (AKE) protocols. We have chosen to defer our discussion of AKE protocols until Section 9.4. The reason that we delay is because consideration of AKE protocols really requires a better understanding of what a cryptographic protocol is.

Lastly, we note that entity authentication is a service that is often provided in combination with other services. While there are applications where one entity is simply required to identify itself to another, in many applications the real reason for requiring entity authentication is to provide a platform on which other security services can be built. Hence entity authentication mechanisms are often components of more complex cryptographic protocols. Again, AKE protocols will provide an example of this.

8.8 Further reading

Generating good randomness is one of the most essential requirements for many cryptosystems. A good overview of appropriate techniques can be found in RFC 4086 [63]. Another source of reliable information is ISO/IEC 18031 [11]. NIST 800-22 [145] provides a suite of statistical tests of randomness, which can be used to measure the effectiveness of any random generator. Ferguson, Schneier and Kohno [75] has an interesting chapter on practical random generation. An informative and fun site about randomness and its applications beyond cryptography, which also provides output from a non-deterministic generator, is maintained by Mads Haahr [94]. CrypTool [52] has implementations of various statistical randomness tests.

Ferguson, Schneier and Kohno [75] also have an informative chapter on using clocks as freshness mechanisms. There are also discussions of different freshness mechanisms in Menezes, van Oorschot and Vanstone [123], and Dent and Mitchell [55]. The Network Time Protocol provides a means of synchronising clocks in packet-switched networks such as the Internet and is specified in RFC 1305 [124].

Entity authentication is a security service that can be implemented in a variety of different ways, many of which involve cryptography being used alongside other technologies. A comprehensive overview of smart cards, smart tokens and their applications is provided by Mayes and Markantonakis [120]. A detailed investigation of different biometric techniques can be found in Jain, Flynn and Ross [101], while Gregory and Simon [93] is a more accessible introduction to biometrics.

An interesting set of experiments were conducted by Yan et al. [205] concerning memorability and security of passwords as entity authentication mechanisms. There is a good chapter on password security in Anderson [23]. FIPS 181, the Automated Password Generator [76], creates pronounceable passwords from DES, illustrating the use of cryptographic primitives as a source of pseudorandomness. A survey of alternatives to conventional passwords based on graphical techniques was conducted by Suo, Zhu and Owen [188]. Of more significant cryptographic interest are dynamic password schemes. RSA Laboratories are one of the main commercial providers of products implementing dynamic password schemes and they maintain several interesting simulations of their products, as well as providing a home for the One-Time Password Specifications (OTPS) [114]. Wikipedia provides a good portal page on dynamic password schemes [201] that includes comparisons of different approaches to generating dynamic passwords and mentions various other commercial vendors of products implementing dynamic password schemes.

The main ISO standard relating to entity authentication is ISO/IEC 9798 [19], which includes a part relating to zero-knowledge mechanisms. Examples of zero-knowledge mechanisms can be found in, for example, Stinson [185] and Vaudenay [194]. The original inspiration for the zero-knowledge protocol analogy that we described is Quisquater et al. [72].

8.9 Activities

1. Cryptography and randomness are connected in many different ways:
    (a) Provide some examples of why randomness is needed in cryptography.
    (b) Provide some examples of how cryptography can be used to provide randomness.

2. Suggest appropriate mechanisms for generating randomness for the following applications:
    (a) generating a cryptographic key on a laptop for use in an email security application;
    (b) generating a master key for a hardware security module;
    (c) generating keystream for a stream cipher on a mobile phone;

(d) generating a one-time pad key for a high-security application;

(e) generating a nonce on a server for use in a dynamic password scheme.

3. In Section 8.1.3 we provided some examples of software-based non-deterministic random number generation techniques. Find out which (combinations of) these techniques are currently recommended from:

   (a) a security perspective;
   (b) a practical perspective.

4. One technique for proving freshness is to use a clock-based mechanism.

   (a) What standard means are there of providing an internationally recognised notion of clock-based time?
   (b) Explain why it is important to protect the integrity of a timestamp.
   (c) Describe in detail how to provide integrity protection for a timestamp.

5. In practice we often have to be more pragmatic about implementing security controls than the theory suggests:

   (a) Under what circumstances might it make sense for an application that employs sequence numbers to accept a sequence number as 'fresh' even if the most recently received sequence number is not greater in value than the previously received sequence number?
   (b) Suggest a simple 'policy' for managing this type of situation.

6. A nonce, as we defined it in Section 8.2.3, is in most cases a pseudorandom number.

   (a) Explain why this means that we cannot guarantee that a particular nonce has not been used before.
   (b) What should we do if we require a *guarantee* that each nonce is used at most once?
   (c) The terms *nonce* and *salt* are used in different areas of cryptography (and not always consistently). Conduct some research on the use of these terms and suggest, in general, what the difference is between them.

7. For each of the following, explain what problems might arise if we base a freshness mechanism on the suggested component:

   (a) an inaccurate clock;
   (b) a sequence number that regularly cycles around;
   (c) a nonce that is randomly generated from a small space.

8. Freshness and liveness are closely related concepts.

   (a) Explain the difference between freshness and liveness by providing examples of applications that require these slightly different notions.
   (b) For each of the freshness mechanisms discussed in this chapter, explain how to use the freshness mechanism to provide a check of liveness.

9. What is the size of the password space if we permit passwords to consist only of:

    (a) eight alphabetic characters (not case sensitive);
    (b) eight alphabetic characters (case sensitive);
    (c) six alphanumeric characters (case sensitive);
    (d) eight alphanumeric characters (case sensitive);
    (e) ten alphanumeric characters (case sensitive);
    (f) eight alphanumeric characters and keypad symbols (case sensitive);

10. FIPS 181 describes a standard for an automated password generator.

    (a) What desirable password properties do passwords generated using FIPS 181 have?
    (b) How does FIPS 181 generate the required randomness?

11. Let E be a symmetric encryption algorithm (such as AES), K be a publicly known symmetric key, and P be a password. The following function F has been suggested as a one-way function suitable for storing passwords:

$$F(P) = E_K(P) \oplus P.$$

    (a) Explain in words how to compute $F(P)$ from P.
    (b) Since the key K is publicly known, explain why an attacker cannot reverse $F(P)$ to obtain P.
    (c) What advantages and disadvantages does this one-way function have over the UNIX password function described in Section 8.4.2?

12. An alternative function for storing passwords is *LAN Manager hash*.

    (a) Which applications use LAN Manager hash?
    (b) Explain how LAN Manager hash uses symmetric encryption to protect a password.
    (c) What criticisms have been made about the security of LAN Manager hash?

13. Passwords stored on a computer in encrypted form are a potential attack target. Explain how encrypted passwords can be attacked by using:

    (a) an exhaustive search;
    (b) a dictionary attack;
    (c) rainbow tables.

14. Biometric technologies provide a source of identity information that could be used as part of an entity authentication mechanism based on use of an electronic identity card.

    (a) What biometric technology might be suitable for such an application?
    (b) What issues (technical, practical and sociological) might arise through the use of your chosen biometric technology?

(c) Where might you also deploy cryptographic mechanisms in the overall implementation of such a scheme?

15. There are several commercial technologies for implementing dynamic passwords based on security tokens that employ a clock-based mechanism. Find a commercial product based on such a mechanism.

   (a) What 'factors' does your chosen product rely on to provide authentication?
   (b) In what ways is your chosen technology stronger than basic (static) passwords?
   (c) Explain how the underlying mechanism in your chosen technology differs from the challenge–response mechanism that we looked at in Section 8.5.
   (d) Find out how your chosen technology manages the issues that were raised in Section 8.2.1 concerning clock-based mechanisms.

16. Explain how to implement a dynamic password scheme based on the use of sequence numbers.

17. A telephone banking service uses a dynamic password scheme that employs a clock-based mechanism but does not use any authentication between the user and the token.

   (a) What is the potential impact if the token is stolen?
   (b) How might the bank address this risk through token management controls and authentication procedures?

18. Explain why a stream cipher would be a poor choice for the encryption mechanism used to compute responses to challenges in a dynamic password scheme based on challenge–response.

19. Some online banks implement the following dynamic password scheme:

   • When a user wishes to log on they send a request for a 'one-time' password in order to access the banking service.
   • The bank generates a one-time password and sends this by SMS to the user's mobile phone.
   • The user reads the SMS and enters the one-time password in order to access the service.
   • If the presented one-time password is correct, the user is given access to the service.

   Compare this approach with the dynamic password schemes that we discussed in this chapter, from a:

   (a) security perspective;
   (b) efficiency perspective;
   (c) business perspective (costs, processes, business relationships).

20. Our list of general categories of identification information in Section 8.3.3 is by no means exhaustive.

    (a) Another possible category of identification information is *somewhere the claimant is*. Provide an example of entity authentication based on location information.

    (b) Can you think of any other categories of identification information?

21. In Table 1.2 we provided a mapping of cryptographic primitives that can be used to help provide different cryptographic services (rather than largely providing these services on their own). Now that we have completed our review of cryptographic primitives, attempt to explain all the 'yes' entries in this table by providing examples of each primitive being used as part of the provision of the relevant service.

9 Cryptographic Protocols

We have now completed our review of the most fundamental cryptographic primitives that make up the cryptographic toolkit. We have seen that each primitive provides very specific security services that can be applied to data. However, most security applications require different security services to be applied to a variety of items of data, often integrated in a complex way. What we must now do is examine how cryptographic primitives can be combined together to match the security requirements of real applications. This is done by designing cryptographic protocols.

We begin this chapter with a brief introduction to the idea of a cryptographic protocol. We then examine and analyse some very simple cryptographic protocols. Finally, we discuss the important class of cryptographic protocols that provide entity authentication and key establishment.

At the end of this chapter you should be able to:

- Explain the concept of a cryptographic protocol.
- Analyse a simple cryptographic protocol.
- Appreciate the difficulty of designing a secure cryptographic protocol.
- Justify the typical properties of an authentication and key establishment protocol.
- Appreciate the significance of the Diffie–Hellman protocol and variants of it.
- Compare the features of two authentication and key establishment protocols.

9.1 Protocol basics

We begin by providing two different, but related, motivations for the need for cryptographic protocols.

9.1.1 Operational motivation for protocols

It is rare to deploy a cryptographic primitive in isolation to provide a single security service for a single piece of data. There are several reasons for this. Many applications:

Have complex security requirements. For example, if we wish to transmit some sensitive information across an insecure network then it is likely that we will want confidentiality *and* data origin authentication guarantees (see Section 6.3.6 and Section 7.4.2).

Involve different data items with different security requirements. Most applications involve different pieces of data, each of which may have different security requirements. For example, an application processing an online transaction may require the purchase details (product, cost) to be authenticated, but not encrypted, so that this information is widely available. However, the payment details (card number, expiry date) are likely to be required to be kept confidential. It is also possible that different requirements of this type arise for efficiency reasons, since all cryptographic computations (particularly public-key computations) have an associated efficiency cost. It can thus be desirable to apply cryptographic primitives only to those data items that strictly require a particular type of protection.

Involve information flowing between more than one entity. It is rare for a cryptographic application to involve just one entity, such as when a user encrypts a file for storage on their local machine. Most applications involve at least two entities exchanging data. For example, a card payment scheme may involve a client, a merchant, the client's bank and the merchant's bank (and possibly other entities).

Consist of a sequence of logical (conditional) events. Real applications normally involve multiple operations that need to be conducted in a specific order, each of which may have its own security requirements. For example, it does not make any sense to provide confidentiality protection for the deduction of a sum from a client's account and issue some money from a cash machine until entity authentication of the client has been conducted.

We thus require a process for specifying precisely how to apply cryptographic primitives during the exchange of data between entities in such a way that the necessary security goals are met.

9.1.2 Environmental motivation for protocols

An alternative motivation for cryptographic protocols comes from the environments in which they are likely to be deployed.

The idea of a *protocol* should be quite familiar. We engage in protocols in many aspects of daily life. For example, most cultures have established protocols that run when two people who have not met before are introduced to one another (such as smile, shake hands, then exchange business cards). Diplomatic protocols are an example of a more formally documented class of protocols. These are procedures designed to achieve diplomatic goals, independent of the culture and language of the participating countries and diplomats. Indeed, it is for the very reason that countries, languages and diplomats are all *different* that diplomatic protocols are necessary. A potentially more familiar example of a protocol is the sequence of procedural and legal processes involved in sale or purchase of a property within a particular legal jurisdiction.

For similar reasons, protocols are important for electronic communications. Different computing devices run on different hardware platforms, using different software, and communicate in different languages. When considering environments such as the Internet, it at first seems incredible that this diversity of devices can communicate with one another at all. The secret is protocols, in this case communication protocols. The communication protocol TCP/IP enables any device connected to the Internet to talk to any other device connected to the Internet. TCP/IP provides a common process for breaking data into small packets, addressing them, routing them through a network, reassembling them, and finally checking that they have arrived correctly. They can then be interpreted and processed by the receiving device.

In a similar way, a cryptographic protocol provides a common process that allows security goals to be achieved between a number of devices, regardless of the nature of the devices involved.

9.1.3 Components of a cryptographic protocol

A *cryptographic protocol* is a specification of all the events that need to take place in order to achieve some required security goals. In particular, a cryptographic protocol needs to specify:

The protocol assumptions – any prerequisite assumptions concerning the environment in which the protocol will be run. While this in practice involves assumptions about the entire environment (including, for example, security of devices used in the protocol), we will generally restrict our attention to clarifying the cryptographic assumptions, such as the strength of cryptographic primitives used and the possession of cryptographic keys by the participating entities. *What needs to have happened before the protocol is run?*

The protocol flow – the sequence of communications that need to take place between the entities involved in the protocol. Each message is often referred to as being a *step* or *pass* of the protocol. *Who sends a message to whom, and in which order?*

The protocol messages – the content of each message that is exchanged between two entities in the protocol. *What information is exchanged at each step?*

The protocol actions – the details of any actions (operations) that an entity needs to perform after receiving, or before sending, a protocol message. *What needs to be done between steps?*

If a cryptographic protocol is followed correctly, in other words all protocol messages are well formed and occur in the correct order, and all actions complete successfully, then hopefully the security goals will be met. If at some stage a protocol message is not received correctly, or an action fails, then the protocol itself is said to *fail* and none of the security goals can be safely considered to have been met. It is wise to have pre-specified rules for deciding how to proceed following a protocol failure. In the simplest case this might involve a rerun of the protocol.

Even in simple applications, such as sending an integrity protected message from one entity to another, we still need to spell out the precise steps that need to be taken in order to achieve the required security goal. Cryptography is thus always used within a cryptographic protocol of some sort, albeit sometimes a rather simple one.

However, most cryptographic protocols are complicated to design and analyse. It is failures in the design and implementation of cryptographic protocols that lead to many security weaknesses in real cryptographic applications. In this chapter we will explain some of the subtleties involved in protocol design and demonstrate some of the basic skills required to 'make sense' of a cryptographic protocol.

9.2 From objectives to a protocol

The design of a cryptographic protocol is a process that commences with a real security problem that needs to be solved and ends with the specification of a cryptographic protocol.

9.2.1 Stages of protocol design

There are three main stages to the process of designing a cryptographic protocol:

Defining the objectives. This is the problem statement, which identifies what the problem is that the protocol is intended to solve. While we will focus on security objectives, it is important to realise that there may be other objectives that are also important, particularly performance-related objectives.

Determining the protocol goals. This stage translates the objectives into a set of clear cryptographic requirements. The protocol goals are typically statements of the form *at the end of the protocol, entity X will be assured of security service Y*. We will see some examples shortly.

Figure 9.1. A simple cryptographic protocol providing non-repudiation

Specifying the protocol. This takes the protocol goals as input and involves determining some cryptographic primitives, message flow and actions that achieve these goals.

A very simple example of these stages would be the following:

Defining the objectives. Merchant Bob wants to make sure that a contract that he will receive from Alice cannot later be denied.

Determining the protocol goals. At the end of the protocol Bob requires non-repudiation of the contract received from Alice.

Specifying the protocol. A protocol to achieve this simple goal is given in Figure 9.1. In this protocol there is only one message, which is sent from Alice to Bob. This message consists of the contract, digitally signed by Alice. The notation Sig_{Alice} represents a generic digital signature algorithm. We do not specify *which* algorithm is to be used. Nor do we specify whether the digital signature scheme is with appendix or message recovery (see Section 7.3.3). We assume that if a digital signature scheme with appendix is used then part of Sig_{Alice}(contract) is a plaintext version of the contract.

9.2.2 Challenges of the stages of protocol design

The very simple example that we have just discussed is so elementary that it hides the complexity that is normally involved with each design stage of a cryptographic protocol. While we will shortly examine a slightly more complex protocol, it is important to note that most applications have much more sophisticated security requirements. This introduces complexity throughout the design process.

DEFINING THE OBJECTIVES

It can be very difficult to determine in advance exactly what security requirements a particular application has. Failure to get this correct from the outset is likely to have serious consequences. Thus great care needs to be taken to conduct a sufficiently rigorous risk analysis exercise in advance, so that the security objectives that are defined are complete.

DETERMINING THE PROTOCOL GOALS

The translation of the security goals into cryptographic requirements is, in theory, the most straightforward of the design stages. However, just like any translation exercise, this needs to be done by someone sufficiently expert that the conversion process is accurately conducted.

SPECIFYING THE PROTOCOL

Designing a cryptographic protocol that meets the specified goals can be a very difficult task. This difficulty often comes as a surprise to system designers without cryptographic expertise, who may be tempted to design their own cryptographic protocols. Even if strong cryptographic primitives are used, an insecure protocol will not meet the intended security objectives.

This is true even for the most basic security goals. In Section 9.4 we will discuss cryptographic protocols that are designed to meet the relatively straightforward security goals of mutual entity authentication and key establishment. Hundreds of cryptographic protocols have been proposed to meet these security goals, but many contain design flaws.

The simple message here is that, just as for the design of cryptographic primitives, all three of the design stages (but most importantly the last one) are best left to experts. Indeed, even among such experts, the process of designing cryptographic protocols that can be *proven* to implement specified cryptographic goals remains a challenging one (see Section 3.2.5).

STANDARDS FOR CRYPTOGRAPHIC PROTOCOLS

In the light of the difficulties just discussed about designing cryptographic protocols, one sensible strategy would be to only use cryptographic protocols that have been adopted in relevant standards. For example:

- the PKCS standards include some cryptographic protocols for implementing public-key cryptography;
- ISO/IEC 11770 specifies a suite of cryptographic protocols for mutual entity authentication and key establishment;
- SSL/TLS specifies a protocol for setting up a secure communication channel (see Section 12.1).

The adoption of standardised cryptographic protocols is highly recommended, however, there are two potential issues:

Application complexity. Many applications have sufficiently complex security goals that there may not be an already approved cryptographic protocol that meets the precise application security goals. For major applications it may be necessary to design an entirely new dedicated standard. For example, the *Trusted Computing Group* have had to design and standardise their own set of cryptographic protocols for the implementation of trusted computing. Indeed, unusually, this process required the design of a new cryptographic primitive as well as cryptographic protocols.

Precision of fit. If a standardised protocol is considered for use then it must be the case that the application security goals are precisely those of the standard protocol. If a standard protocol needs to be even slightly changed then it may be the case that the protocol no longer meets its original security goals. This issue also applies to cryptographic primitives themselves, since if we even slightly amend the key schedule of AES then the resulting algorithm is no longer AES.

9.2.3 Assumptions and actions

We now reconsider the simple cryptographic protocol shown in Figure 9.1. Recall the four components of a cryptographic protocol that we identified in Section 9.1.3, namely assumptions, flow, messages and actions. In fact, Figure 9.1 only describes the flow (one message from Alice to Bob) and the message (a contract digitally signed by Alice).

There are several problems that could arise with the protocol in Figure 9.1:

1. If Alice and Bob have not agreed on the digital signature scheme that they are going to use then Bob will not know which verification algorithm to use.
2. If Alice does not already possess a signature key then she will not be able to digitally sign the contract.
3. If Bob does not have access to a valid verification key that corresponds to Alice's signature key then he will not be able to verify the digital signature.
4. If Bob does not verify the digital signature received from Alice then he cannot have any assurance that Alice has provided him with correctly formed data that can later be used to settle a potential dispute.

ASSUMPTIONS

The simple protocol in Figure 9.1 only makes sense if we make the following *assumptions* regarding the environment in which the protocol is run. Before the protocol is run:

- Alice and Bob agree on the use of a strong digital signature scheme. *This addresses the first problem.*
- Alice has been issued with a signature key. *This addresses the second problem.*
- Bob has access to a verification key corresponding to Alice's signature key. *This addresses the third problem.*

Indeed, it may be appropriate to generalise these assumptions to one that states that before the protocol is run there exists a supporting public-key management system for overseeing the management of all required cryptographic keys (see Chapter 11).

ACTIONS

The description of the simple protocol in Figure 9.1 is only complete if we specify the following *action* that needs to take place as part of the protocol. After receiving the message from Alice:

- Bob verifies the digital signature received from Alice. *This addresses the fourth problem.*

This action should really be specified as part of the protocol itself. It is common practice to leave certain actions as implicit in the description of a cryptographic protocol. This, however, is slightly dangerous. For example, SSL/TLS is commonly adopted to secure the communication channel between a client and a web server (see Section 12.1). During this protocol the web server provides a digitally signed public-key certificate (see Section 11.1.2) to the client in order to facilitate entity authentication of the web server. The implicit action of *verifying the public-key certificate received from the web server* is often ignored, thus exposing this protocol to a range of attacks.

9.2.4 The wider protocol design process

While the focus of this chapter is on the *design* of cryptographic protocols, it is important to recognise that the design is only one stage in a wider process. Just as we discussed for cryptographic primitives in Section 3.2.4, it is more likely that security problems arise from failures to implement a cryptographic protocol properly. This can manifest itself in numerous ways, including:

- weakness in the implementation of a specific cryptographic primitive used by the protocol;
- instantiation of a cryptographic primitive used in the protocol by a weak cryptographic algorithm;
- failure to implement the entire protocol correctly (for example, omitting an important action);
- weakness in the supporting key management processes.

Coupled with the difficulties in designing secure cryptographic protocols that we discussed in Section 9.2.2, it should be clear that the entire deployment process of a cryptographic protocol requires great care.

9.3 Analysing a simple protocol

In this section we will look at another simple cryptographic protocol, but one that has more security goals than the example in Section 9.2. We argued throughout Section 9.2 that cryptographic protocol design was best left to experts, thus the reason for studying this simple application is to provide insight into the complexities of cryptographic protocol design, rather than to develop proficiency in it. There are two other reasons for studying such an example in some depth:

1. We will see that there are many different ways, each with its own subtle advantages and disadvantages, of designing a cryptographic protocol that meets some specific security goals.
2. While designing proprietary cryptographic protocols is not generally recommended, it is useful to be able to analyse, at least at a high level, whether a given cryptographic protocol achieves its goals.

9.3.1 A simple application

We now describe a simple security scenario. This is probably too simple a scenario to have any real application, however, even this scenario has sufficient complexity to provide us with an example that we can analyse.

THE OBJECTIVES

In this scenario we suppose that Alice and Bob have access to a common network. Periodically, at any time of his choosing, Bob wants to check that Alice is still 'alive' and connected to the network. This is our main security objective, which we will refer to as a check of liveness (see Section 8.2).

In order to make the example slightly more interesting, we assume that Alice and Bob are just two entities in a network consisting of many such entities, all of whom regularly check the liveness of one another, perhaps every few seconds. We thus set a secondary security objective that whenever Bob receives any confirmation of liveness from Alice, he should be able to determine precisely which liveness query she is responding to.

THE PROTOCOL GOALS

We now translate these objectives into concrete protocol goals. Whenever Bob wants to check that Alice is alive he will need to send a *request* to Alice, which she will need to respond to with a *reply*. When designing protocol goals to meet these objectives it can be helpful to consider what could go wrong, hence we will motivate each protocol goal by a potential failure of the protocol if this goal is not met.

At the end of any run of a suitable cryptographic protocol, the following three goals should have been met:

Data origin authentication of Alice's reply. If this is not provided then Alice may not be alive since the reply message might have been created by an attacker.

Freshness of Alice's reply. If this is not provided then, even if there is data origin authentication of the reply, this could be a replay of a previous reply. In other words, an attacker could observe a reply that Alice makes when she *is* alive and then send a copy of it to Bob at some stage after Alice has expired. This would be a genuine reply created by Alice. But she would not be alive and hence the protocol will have failed to meet its objectives.

Assurance that Alice's reply corresponds to Bob's request. If this is not provided then it is possible that Bob receives a reply that corresponds to a different request (either one of his own, or of another entity in the network).

Note that it is the combination of the first two goals that provides the basic guarantee that Alice is alive. However, we will see that the third goal not only provides more precision, but in some circumstances is essential.

Table 9.1: Notation used during protocol descriptions

r_B	A nonce generated by Bob
‖	Concatenation
Bob	An *identifier* for Bob (perhaps his name)
$MAC_K(data)$	A MAC computed on *data* using key K
$E_K(data)$	Symmetric encryption of *data* using key K
$Sig_A(data)$	A digital signature on *data* computed by Alice
T_A	A timestamp generated by Alice
T_B	A timestamp generated by Bob
ID_S	A session identifier

CANDIDATE PROTOCOLS

We will now examine seven candidate cryptographic protocols and discuss the extent to which they meet the three security goals. Most importantly, we will see that:

- there is more than one cryptographic protocol that meets these goals;
- some protocols only meet the goals if we make some additional assumptions;
- some protocols that appear at first to meet the goals, in fact, do not.

Table 9.1 indicates the notation used to describe the seven candidate protocols.

9.3.2 Protocol 1

Figure 9.2 shows the protocol flow and messages of our first candidate protocol. We describe this protocol in detail in order to clarify the notation.

PROTOCOL ASSUMPTIONS

There are three assumptions that we make before running this protocol:

Bob has access to a source of randomness. This is necessary because the protocol requires Bob to be able to generate a nonce. We naturally also assume that this generator is 'secure' in order to guarantee unpredictability of the output.

Alice and Bob already share a symmetric key K that is known only to them. This is necessary because the protocol requires Alice to be able to generate a MAC that Bob can verify.

Alice and Bob agree on the use of a strong MAC algorithm. This is necessary because if the MAC algorithm is flawed then data origin authentication is not necessarily provided by it.

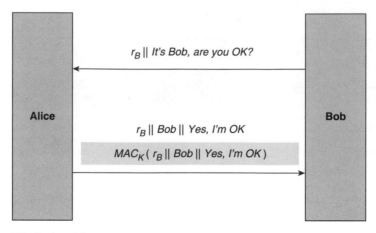

Alice

$r_B \|$ *It's Bob, are you OK?*

$r_B \|$ *Bob* $\|$ *Yes, I'm OK*

$MAC_K(\, r_B \| Bob \| Yes, I'm OK\,)$

Bob

Figure 9.2. Protocol 1

If Alice and Bob do not already share a symmetric key then they will need to first run a different protocol in order to establish a common symmetric key K. We will discuss suitable protocols in Section 9.4. Technically, if Alice and Bob have not already agreed on the use of a strong MAC algorithm to compute the MAC then Alice could indicate the choice of MAC algorithm that she is using in her *reply*.

PROTOCOL DESCRIPTION

Protocol 1 consists of the following steps:

1. Bob conducts the following steps to form the request:

   (a) Bob generates a nonce r_B (this is an implicit action that is not described in Figure 9.2, as is the fact that he stores it for later checking purposes).
   (b) Bob concatenates r_B to the text *It's Bob, are you OK?*. This combined data string is the request.
   (c) Bob sends the request to Alice.

2. Assuming that she is alive and able to respond, Alice conducts the following steps to form the reply:

   (a) Alice concatenates the nonce r_B to identifier *Bob* and the text *Yes, I'm OK.* We will refer to this combined data string as the *reply text*.
   (b) Alice computes a MAC on the reply text using key K (this is an implicit action). The reply text is then concatenated to the MAC to form the reply.
   (c) Alice sends the reply to Bob.

3. On receipt of the reply, Bob makes the following checks (all of which are implicit actions that are not shown in Figure 9.2):

   (a) Bob checks that the received reply text consists of a valid r_B (which he can recognise because he generated it and has stored it on a local database) concatenated to his identifier *Bob* and a meaningful response to his query (in this case, *Yes, I'm OK*).

(b) Bob computes a MAC on the received reply text with key K (which he shares with Alice) and checks to see if it matches the received MAC.

(c) If both of these checks are satisfactory then Bob accepts the reply and ends the protocol. We say that the protocol successfully *completes* if this is the case.

PROTOCOL ANALYSIS

We now check whether, if it successfully completes, Protocol 1 meets the required goals:

Data origin authentication of Alice's reply. Under our second assumption, the only entity other than Bob who can compute the correct MAC on the reply text is Alice. Thus, given that the received MAC is correct, the received MAC must have been computed by Alice. Thus Bob indeed has assurance that the reply (and by implication the reply text) was generated by Alice.

Freshness of Alice's reply. The reply text includes the nonce r_B, which Bob generated at the start of the protocol. Thus, by the principles discussed in Section 8.2.3, the reply is fresh.

Assurance that Alice's reply corresponds to Bob's request. There are two pieces of evidence in the reply that provide this:

1. Firstly, and most importantly, the reply contains the nonce r_B, which Bob generated for this run of the protocol. By our first protocol assumption, this nonce is very unlikely to ever be used for another protocol run, thus the appearance of r_B in the reply makes it almost certain that the reply corresponds to his request.

2. The reply contains the identifier *Bob*.

It will not be immediately obvious why both of these pieces of data are needed (the first might seem enough). However, in Protocol 3 we will discuss what might happen if the identifier *Bob* is removed from this protocol.

Thus we deduce that Protocol 1 does indeed meet the three security goals for our simple application. Note that all four of the components of a cryptographic protocol that we identified in Section 9.1.3 play a critical role in Protocol 1:

The protocol assumptions. If the protocol assumptions do not hold then, even when the protocol successfully completes, the security goals are not met. For example, if a third entity Charlie also knows the MAC key K then Bob cannot be sure that the reply comes from Alice, since it could have come from Charlie.

The protocol flow. Clearly the two messages in this protocol must occur in the specified order, since the reply cannot be formed until the request is received.

The protocol messages. The protocol goals are not necessarily met if the content of the two messages is changed in any way. For example, we will see in Protocol 3 what happens if the identifier Bob is omitted from the reply text.

The protocol actions. The protocol goals are not met if any of the actions are not undertaken. For example, if Bob fails to check that the MAC on the reply text matches the received MAC then he has no guarantee of the origin of the reply.

Informal assurance that Alice is indeed alive comes from the fact that a valid MAC is produced on a message that includes a newly generated nonce. Only Alice could have generated the MAC and, because she includes the nonce, she must have done this after Bob made his request. However, such informal arguments have no place in cryptographic analysis because it is the details that are important. We will later examine several protocols that appear to satisfy a similar informal analysis, but which fail to meet the security goals.

REMARKS

We have seen that Protocol 1 meets the security goals and hence is a suitable protocol to use in our simple application. We will use Protocol 1 as a 'benchmark' protocol against which later protocols will be compared. We have described Protocol 1 in greater detail than we intend to treat later protocols. By doing so, we have hopefully clarified notation and how to interpret the figures indicating protocol messages and flow.

9.3.3 Protocol 2

Figure 9.3 shows the protocol flow and messages of our second candidate protocol.

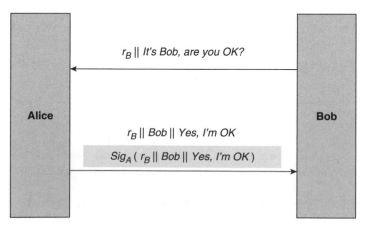

Figure 9.3. Protocol 2

PROTOCOL ASSUMPTIONS

As can be seen from Figure 9.3, Protocol 2 is very similar to Protocol 1. In fact, it is in the protocol assumptions that the main differences lie:

Bob has access to a source of randomness. As for Protocol 1.

Alice has been issued with a signature key and Bob has access to a verification key corresponding to Alice's signature key. This is the digital signature scheme equivalent of the second assumption for Protocol 1.

Alice and Bob agree on the use of a strong digital signature scheme.

PROTOCOL DESCRIPTION

The description of Protocol 2 is exactly as for Protocol 1, except that:

- Instead of computing a MAC on the reply text, Alice digitally signs the reply text using her signature key.
- Instead of computing and comparing the received MAC on the reply text, Bob verifies Alice's digital signature on the reply text using her verification key.

PROTOCOL ANALYSIS

The analysis of Protocol 2 is exactly as for Protocol 1, except for:

Data origin authentication of Alice's reply. Under our second assumption, the only entity who can compute the correct digital signature on the reply text is Alice. Thus, given that her digital signature is verified, the received digital signature must have been computed by Alice. Thus Bob indeed has assurance that the reply (and by implication the reply text) was generated by Alice.

We therefore deduce that Protocol 2 also meets the three security goals.

REMARKS

Protocol 2 can be thought of as a public-key analogue of Protocol 1. So which one is better?

- It could be argued that, especially in resource-constrained environments, Protocol 1 has an advantage in that it is more computationally efficient, since computing MACs generally involves less computation than signing and verifying digital signatures.
- However, it could also be argued that Protocol 2 has the advantage that it could be run between an Alice and Bob who have not pre-shared a key, so long as Bob has access to Alice's verification key.

The real differences between these two protocols are primarily in the key management issues that arise from the different assumptions. We will discuss these in much greater detail in Chapters 10 and 11. It suffices to note that this is such an application-dependent issue that many cryptographic protocols come in two different 'flavours', along the lines of Protocol 1 and Protocol 2.

A good example is the suite of authentication and key establishment protocols standardised in ISO 11770. Many of the protocols proposed in part 2 of ISO 11770, which is concerned with symmetric techniques, have public-key analogues in part 3 of the standard.

9.3.4 Protocol 3

From Figure 9.4 it should be clear that the protocol flow and messages of our third candidate protocol are almost identical to Protocol 1.

PROTOCOL ASSUMPTIONS

These are identical to Protocol 1.

PROTOCOL DESCRIPTION

This is identical to Protocol 1, except that in Protocol 3 the identifier *Bob* is omitted from the reply text.

PROTOCOL ANALYSIS

This is identical to Protocol 1, except for:

Assurance that Alice's reply corresponds to Bob's request. As argued for Protocol 1, the inclusion of the nonce r_B in the reply appears, superficially, to provide this assurance since r_B is in some sense a unique identifier of Bob's request. However, there is an attack that can be launched against Protocol 3 in certain environments which shows that this is not always true. Since the attacker plays the role of a 'mirror', we call this a *reflection attack* against Protocol 3. The attack is depicted in Figure 9.5.

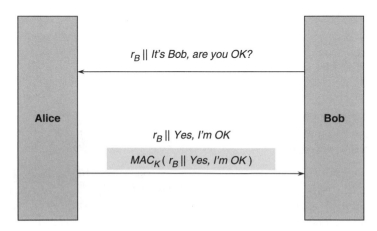

Figure 9.4. Protocol 3

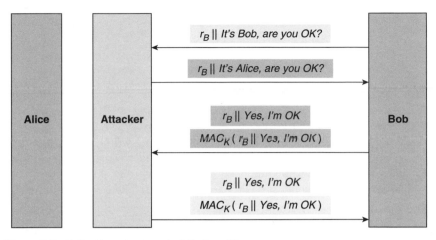

Figure 9.5. Reflection attack against Protocol 3

To see how the reflection attack works, we assume that an attacker is able to intercept and block all communication between Alice and Bob. We also assume that Bob normally recognises that incoming traffic may be from Alice through the use of the channel, rather than an explicit identifier. This is perhaps an unreasonable assumption, but we are trying to keep it simple. Thus, even if Alice is no longer alive, the attacker can pretend to be Alice by sending messages on this channel. The reflection attack works as follows:

1. Bob initiates a run of Protocol 3 by issuing a request message.
2. The attacker intercepts the request message and sends it straight back to Bob, except that the text *It's Bob* is replaced by the text *It's Alice*.
3. At this point it is tempting to suggest that Bob will regard the receipt of a message containing his nonce r_B as rather strange and will surely reject it. However, we must resist the temptation to anthropomorphise the analysis of a cryptographic protocol and recall that in most applications of this type of protocol both Alice and Bob will be computing devices following programmed instructions. In this case Bob will simply see a request message that appears to come from Alice and, since he is alive, will compute a corresponding reply message. He then sends this reply to Alice.
4. The attacker intercepts this reply message and sends it back to Bob.
5. Bob, who is expecting a reply from Alice, checks that it contains the expected fields and that the MAC is correct. Of course it is, because he computed it himself!

We can regard the reflection attack described in Figure 9.5 as two nested runs of Protocol 3:

- The first run is initiated by Bob, who asks if Alice is alive. He thinks that he is running it with Alice, but instead he is running it with the attacker.

301

- The second run is initiated by the attacker, who asks if Bob is alive. Bob thinks that this request is from Alice, but it is from the attacker. Note that this run of Protocol 3 begins *after* the first run of the protocol has begun, but completes *before* the first run ends. This is why we describe the two runs as 'nested'.

Thus, if this reflection attack is feasible, then Protocol 3 does not meet the third security goal. It is tempting to respond to this by pointing out that if this reflection attack is *not* feasible then Protocol 3 is secure. However, by this stage in our cryptographic studies it should be clear that this is not the attitude of a wise cryptographic designer. If there are circumstances under which a cryptographic protocol might fail then we should really consider the protocol as insecure.

A better response would be to repair Protocol 3. There are two 'obvious' options:

Include an action to check for this attack. This would involve Bob keeping a note of all Protocol 3 sessions that he currently has open. He should then check whether any request messages that he receives match any of his own open requests. This is a cumbersome solution that makes Protocol 3 less efficient. Further, the additional actions that Bob needs to perform during the protocol are not 'obvious' and, although they could be clearly specified in the protocol description, some implementations might fail to include them.

Include an identifier. A far better solution would be to include some sort of identifier in the reply that prevents the reflection attack from working. There is no point in doing so in the request since it is unprotected and an attacker could change it without detection. There are many different identifiers that could be used, but one of the simplest is to include the name of the intended recipient in the reply, in other words add an identifier *Bob* into the reply text. If we do this then we convert Protocol 3 into Protocol 1.

REMARKS

Protocol 3 has raised an important issue. Even when considering such a simple set of protocol goals, we have come up against a subtle attack. It is generally regarded as good practice in the design of cryptographic protocols to include the identifiers of recipients in protocol messages to prevent reflection attacks of this type.

There are several other general classes of attack that can be launched against cryptographic protocols. These include *interleaving attacks*, which exploit several parallel protocol sessions and switch messages from one protocol run into another. Hopefully our earlier remark in Section 9.2.2 about the dangers of inexperienced designers inventing their own cryptographic protocols is now better justified.

9.3.5 Protocol 4

Figure 9.6 shows the protocol flow and messages of our fourth candidate protocol.

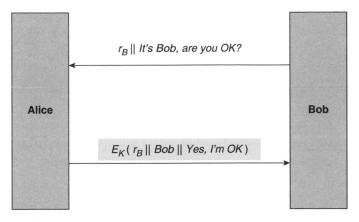

Figure 9.6. Protocol 4

PROTOCOL ASSUMPTIONS

These are identical to Protocol 1, except that we assume that Alice and Bob have agreed on the use of a strong symmetric encryption algorithm E (rather than a MAC). Note that, just as for the previous protocols, this assumption does not specify precisely how this encryption algorithm should be substantiated. Thus it could, for example, be either a stream cipher or a block cipher. If it is a block cipher then it could be using any mode of operation. We will see shortly that this ambiguity might lead to problems.

PROTOCOL DESCRIPTION

The description of Protocol 4 is exactly as for Protocol 1, except that:

- Instead of computing a MAC on the reply text, Alice uses E to encrypt the reply text using key K.
- Alice does not send the reply text to Bob.
- Instead of computing and comparing the received MAC on the reply text, Bob simply decrypts the received encrypted reply text.

PROTOCOL ANALYSIS

The analysis of Protocol 4 is exactly as for Protocol 1, except for the issue of data origin authentication of Alice's reply. We need to consider whether encryption can be used in this context to provide data origin authentication. There are two arguments:

The case against. This is perhaps the purist's viewpoint. Protocol 4 does not provide data origin authentication because encryption does not, in general, provide data origin authentication. We presented this argument in Section 6.3.1. A key management purist might also choose to point out there is inherent danger in using encryption to provide data origin authentication because the same key K might later be used for encryption, thus abusing the principle of key separation (see Section 10.6.1).

The case for. In Section 6.3.1 we outlined a number of problems that may arise if encryption is used to provide data origin authentication. These mainly arose when the plaintext was long and unformatted. However, in this case the reply text is short and has a specific format. Thus, if a block cipher such as AES is used then it is possible that the reply text is less than one block long, hence no 'block manipulation' will be possible. Even if the reply text is two blocks long and ECB mode is used to encrypt these two blocks, the format of the reply text is specific and any manipulation is likely to be noticed by Bob (assuming of course that he checks for it).

It is safest to argue that Protocol 4 does not meet the three security goals, since the 'case for' requires some caveats concerning the type of encryption mechanism used. For example, it is not likely to meet the goals if we implement E using a stream cipher.

There are cryptographic protocols in standards that do use encryption to deduce data origin authentication in the style of Protocol 4. Such standards normally include advice on what type of encryption mechanism it is 'safe' to use. Good advice in this case would be to use a block cipher in an authenticated-encryption mode of operation, as discussed in Section 6.3.6. We will see such an example in Section 9.4.3. However, encryption tends only to be used in this way if confidentiality of the message data is also required. In Protocol 4 this is not the case, so it would be much better to use Protocol 1.

9.3.6 Protocol 5

Protocol 5, depicted in Figure 9.7, is very similar to Protocol 1, except that the nonce generated by Bob is replaced by a timestamp generated by Bob.

PROTOCOL ASSUMPTIONS

These are the same as the assumptions for Protocol 1, except that the need for Bob to have a source of randomness is replaced by:

Bob can generate and verify integrity-protected timestamps. This requires Bob to have a system clock. Requiring T_B to be integrity-protected means that it cannot be manipulated by an attacker without subsequent detection of this by Bob. We discussed mechanisms for doing this in Section 8.2.1.

PROTOCOL DESCRIPTION

The description of Protocol 5 is exactly as for Protocol 1, except that:

- Instead of generating a nonce r_B, Bob generates an integrity-protected timestamp T_B. This is then included in both the request (by Bob) and the reply (by Alice).
- As part of his checks on the reply, Bob checks that the reply text includes T_B.

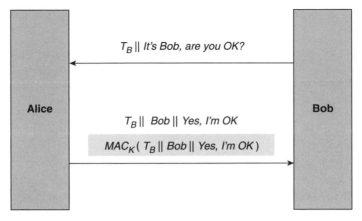

Figure 9.7. Protocol 5

PROTOCOL ANALYSIS

The analysis of Protocol 5 is similar to Protocol 1.

Data origin authentication of Alice's reply. As for Protocol 1.

Freshness of Alice's reply. The reply text includes the timestamp T_B, which Bob generated at the start of the protocol. Thus, by the principles discussed in Section 8.2.1, the reply is fresh.

Assurance that Alice's reply corresponds to Bob's request. There are two pieces of evidence in the reply that provide this:

1. The reply contains the timestamp T_B, which Bob generated for this run of the protocol. Assuming that the timestamp is of sufficient granularity that it is not possible for Bob to have issued the same timestamp for different protocol runs (or that it includes a unique session identifier), the presence of T_B indicates that the reply matches the request.
2. The reply contains the identifier *Bob*, preventing reflection attacks.

Thus Protocol 5 meets the three security goals.

REMARKS

Protocol 5 can be thought of as the 'clock-based' analogue of Protocol 1. Many cryptographic protocols come in two different 'flavours' such as Protocol 1 and Protocol 5, depending on the type of freshness mechanism preferred.

Note that there is no need for Alice to share a synchronised clock with Bob for Protocol 5 to work. This is because only Bob requires freshness, hence it suffices that Alice includes Bob's timestamp without Alice necessarily being able to 'make sense' of, let alone verify, it.

One consequence of this is that it is important that T_B is integrity-protected. To see this, suppose that T_B just consists of the time on Bob's clock, represented as an unprotected timestamp (perhaps just a text stating the time). In this case the following attack is possible:

1. At 15.00, the attacker sends Alice a request that appears to come from Bob but has T_B set to the time 17.00, which is a time in the future that the attacker anticipates that Bob will contact Alice.
2. Alice forms a valid reply based on T_B being 17.00 and sends it to Bob.
3. The attacker intercepts and blocks the reply from reaching Bob, then stores it.
4. The attacker hits Alice over the head with a blunt instrument. (Less violent versions of this attack are possible!)
5. At 17.00, Bob sends a genuine request to Alice (recently deceased).
6. The attacker intercepts the request and sends back the previously intercepted reply from Alice.
7. Bob accepts the reply as genuine (which it is) and assumes that Alice is OK (which she most definitely is not).

This attack is only possible because, in this example, we allowed the attacker to 'manipulate' T_B. By assuming that T_B is a timestamp that cannot be manipulated in such a way, this attack is impossible.

9.3.7 Protocol 6

Protocol 6 is shown in Figure 9.8.

PROTOCOL ASSUMPTIONS

These are the same as the assumptions for Protocol 1, except that the need for Bob to have a random generator is replaced by:

Alice can generate timestamps that Bob can verify. As part of this assumption we further require that Alice and Bob have synchronised clocks.

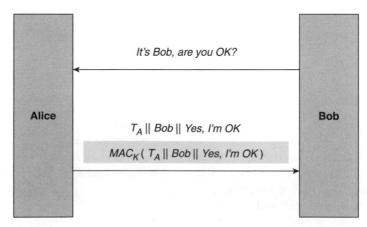

Figure 9.8. Protocol 6

PROTOCOL DESCRIPTION

The description of Protocol 6 is slightly different from Protocol 1, so we will explain it in more detail than the last few protocols.

1. Bob conducts the following steps to form the request:

   (a) Bob forms a simplified request message that just consists of the text *It's Bob, are you OK?*.
   (b) Bob sends the request to Alice.

2. Assuming that she is alive and able to respond, Alice conducts the following steps to form the reply:

   (a) Alice generates a timestamp T_A and concatenates it to identifier *Bob* and the text *Yes, I'm OK*, to form the reply text.
   (b) Alice computes a MAC on the reply text using key K. The reply text is then concatenated to the MAC to form the reply.
   (c) Alice sends the reply to Bob.

3. On receipt of the reply, Bob makes the following checks:

   (a) Bob checks that the received reply text consists of a timestamp T_A concatenated to his identifier *Bob* and a meaningful response to his query (in this case, *Yes, I'm OK*).
   (b) Bob verifies T_A and uses his clock to check that it consists of a fresh time.
   (c) Bob computes a MAC on the received reply text with key K and checks to see if it matches the received MAC.
   (d) If both these checks are satisfactory then Bob accepts the reply and ends the protocol.

PROTOCOL ANALYSIS

The analysis of Protocol 6 is similar to Protocol 1.

Data origin authentication of Alice's reply. As for Protocol 1.
Freshness of Alice's reply. The reply text includes the timestamp T_A. Thus, by the principles discussed in Section 8.2.1, the reply is fresh.
Assurance that Alice's reply corresponds to Bob's request. Unfortunately this is not provided, since the request does not contain any information that can be used to uniquely identify it.

Thus Protocol 6 does not meet all three security goals.

REMARKS

Protocol 6 has only failed on a technicality. It could easily be 'repaired' by including a unique session identifier in the request message, which could then be included in the reply text. Nonetheless, it requires rather more complicated assumptions than Protocol 1, which seem unnecessary for this simple application.

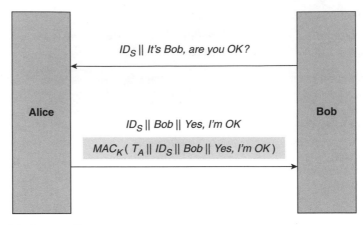

Figure 9.9. Protocol 7

9.3.8 Protocol 7

Our seventh protocol variant is closely related to Protocol 6, and is depicted in Figure 9.9.

PROTOCOL ASSUMPTIONS

These are the same as the assumptions for Protocol 6.

PROTOCOL DESCRIPTION

The description of Protocol 7 is almost the same as Protocol 6. The only differences are:

- Bob includes a unique session identifier ID_S in the request, which Alice includes in the reply text. This identifier is not necessarily randomly generated (unlike the nonces that were used in some of the previous variants).
- The reply text that is sent in the clear by Alice differs from the reply text on which Alice computes the MAC. The difference is that T_A is included in the latter, but not the former.

PROTOCOL ANALYSIS

The analysis of Protocol 7 is similar to Protocol 6. The inclusion of the session identifier ID_S is intended to remove the concerns about linking the reply to the request. The omission of T_A from the reply text that is sent in the clear at first just looks like a saving in bandwidth, since:

- Alice and Bob have synchronised clocks, by our assumptions,
- it is not strictly necessary that the data on which the MAC is computed matches the reply text, so long as Bob receives all the critical data that he needs to check the MAC.

However, there is a problem. Bob does not know T_A. Even if they have perfectly synchronised clocks, the time that Alice issues T_A will not be the same time that Bob receives the message due to communication delays. Thus Bob does not know all the reply text on which the MAC is computed, and hence cannot verify the MAC to obtain data origin authentication. The only option is for Bob to check all the possible timestamps T_A within a reasonable window and hope that he finds one that matches. While this is inefficient, it is worth noting that this technique is sometimes used in real applications to cope with time delays and clock drift (see Section 8.2.1).

REMARKS

Protocol 7 is easily fixed by including T_A in both versions of the reply text, as is done in Protocol 6. Nonetheless, this protocol flaw demonstrates how sensitive cryptographic protocols are to even the slightest 'error' in their formulation.

9.3.9 Simple protocol summary

That is enough protocol variants for now! Hopefully the important points have been highlighted as a result of this analysis:

There is no one correct way to design a cryptographic protocol. Of the seven variants that we studied, three provide all three security goals, despite being different protocols. The choice of the most suitable protocol design thus depends on what assumptions are most suitable for a given application environment.

Designing cryptographic protocols is hard. The deficiencies of several of these protocol variants are very subtle. Given that this application is artificially simple, the complexity of designing protocols for more intricate applications should be clear.

9.4 Authentication and key establishment protocols

The security goals of our simple protocol were rather basic, making it hard to justify the need for such a protocol in a real application. However, the dissection of the simple protocol variants has demonstrated the type of analytical skills required to examine more complex cryptographic protocols with more realistic collections of security goals.

We now reconsider *AKE protocols* (authentication and key establishment), which were introduced at the end of Chapter 8. There are literally hundreds of proposed AKE protocols, since an AKE protocol often has to be tailored to the precise needs of the application for which it is designed. However, the two main security objectives of an AKE protocol are always:

Mutual entity authentication, occasionally just unilateral entity authentication.

Establishment of a common symmetric key, regardless of whether symmetric or public-key techniques are used to do this.

It should not come as a surprise that these two objectives are required together in one protocol.

Need to authenticate key holders. Key establishment makes little sense without entity authentication. It is hard to imagine any applications where we would want to establish a common symmetric key between two parties without at least one party being sure of the other's identity. Indeed, in many applications mutual entity authentication is required. The only argument for not featuring entity authentication in a key establishment protocol is for applications where the authentication has already been conducted prior to running the key establishment protocol.

Prolonging authentication. The result of entity authentication can be prolonged by simultaneously establishing a symmetric key. Recall from Section 8.3.1 that a problem with entity authentication is that it is achieved only for an instant in time. In practice, we often desire this achievement to be extended over a longer period of time (a *session*). One way of doing this is to bind the establishment of a symmetric key to the entity authentication process. In this way, later use of the key during a session continues to provide confidence that the communication is being conducted between the parties who were authenticated at the instant in time that the key was established. Thus we can maintain, at least for a while, the security context achieved during entity authentication. Of course, exactly *how long* this can be maintained is a subjective and application-dependent issue.

9.4.1 Typical AKE protocol goals

We now break down the general security objectives of an AKE protocol being run between Alice and Bob into more precise security goals. These will not be universal for all AKE protocols, hence we will refer to these as 'typical' security goals that are to be achieved on completion of an AKE protocol:

Mutual entity authentication. Alice and Bob are able to verify each other's identity to make sure that they know with whom they are establishing a key.

Mutual data origin authentication. Alice and Bob are able to be sure that information being exchanged originates with the other party and not an attacker.

Mutual key establishment. Alice and Bob establish a common symmetric key.

Key confidentiality. The established key should at no time be accessible to any party other than Alice and Bob.

Key freshness. Alice and Bob should be happy that (with high probability) the established key is not one that has been used before.

Mutual key confirmation. Alice and Bob should have some evidence that they both end up with the same key.

Unbiased key control. Alice and Bob should be satisfied that neither party can unduly influence the generation of the established key

The motivation for the first five of these security goals should be self-evident. The last two goals are more subtle and not always required.

The goal of mutual key establishment is that Alice and Bob do end up with the same key. In many AKE protocols it suffices that key confirmation is *implicit*, with Alice and Bob assuming that they have established the same key because they believe that the protocol completed successfully. Mutual key confirmation goes one step further by requiring *evidence* that the same key has been established. This evidence is usually a cryptographic computation made using the established key.

Mutual key establishment does not impose any requirements on how the established key is generated. Hence, in many cases it may be acceptable that Alice (say) generates a symmetric key and transfers it to Bob during the AKE protocol, in which case Alice has full control of the choice of key. Unbiased key control is required in applications where Alice and Bob do not trust each other to generate a key. Alice may, for example, believe that Bob might, accidentally or deliberately, choose a key that was used on some prior occasion. Unbiased key control is normally achieved either by:

- Generating the key using a component of 'randomness' from each of Alice and Bob, so that the resulting key is not predictable by either of them. This is often termed *joint key control*.
- Using a trusted third party to generate the key.

We choose to distinguish between two families of AKE protocols. We will say that an AKE protocol is based on:

Key agreement, if the key is established from information that is contributed by each of Alice and Bob; we will discuss an AKE protocol based on key agreement in Section 9.4.2;

Key distribution, if the key is generated by one entity (which could be a trusted third party) and then distributed to Alice and Bob; we will discuss an AKE protocol based on key distribution in Section 9.4.3.

9.4.2 Diffie–Hellman key agreement protocol

The *Diffie–Hellman key agreement protocol*, which we will henceforth refer to simply as the *Diffie–Hellman protocol*, is one of the most influential cryptographic protocols. Not only does it predate the public discovery of RSA, but it remains the basis for the vast majority of modern AKE protocols based on key agreement. We will explain the idea behind the Diffie–Hellman protocol and then examine an example of an AKE protocol that is based on it.

IDEA BEHIND THE DIFFIE–HELLMAN PROTOCOL

The Diffie–Hellman protocol requires the existence of:

- A public-key cryptosystem with a special property, which we discuss shortly. We denote the public and private keys of Alice and Bob in this cryptosystem by (P_A, S_A) and (P_B, S_B), respectively. These may be temporary key pairs that have been generated specifically for this protocol run, or could be long-term key pairs that are used for more than one protocol run.
- A *combination function* F with a special property, which we discuss shortly. By a 'combination' function, we mean a mathematical process that takes two numbers x and y as input, and outputs a third number which we denote $F(x, y)$. Addition is an example of a combination function, with $F(x, y) = x + y$.

The Diffie–Hellman protocol is designed for environments where secure channels do not yet exist. Indeed, it is often used to establish a symmetric key, which can then be used to secure such a channel. It is important to remember that, unless otherwise stated, we assume that all the exchanged messages take place over an unprotected (public) channel that an attacker can observe and, potentially, modify. The basic idea behind the Diffie–Hellman protocol is that:

1. Alice sends her public key P_A to Bob.
2. Bob sends his public key P_B to Alice.
3. Alice computes $F(S_A, P_B)$. Note that only Alice can conduct this computation, since it involves her private key S_A.
4. Bob computes $F(S_B, P_A)$. Note that only Bob can conduct this computation, since it involves his private key S_B.

The special property for the public-key cryptosystem and the combination function F is that

$$F(S_A, P_B) = F(S_B, P_A).$$

At the end of the protocol Alice and Bob will thus share this value, which we denote Z_{AB}. As we will discuss in a moment, this shared value Z_{AB} can then easily be converted into a key of the required length. Since the private keys of Alice and Bob are both required to compute Z_{AB}, it should only be computable by Alice and Bob, and not anyone else (an attacker) who observed the protocol messages. Note that this is true despite the fact that the attacker will have seen P_A and P_B.

The somewhat surprising aspect of the Diffie–Hellman protocol is that *without sharing any secret information*, Alice and Bob are able to jointly generate a secret value by communicating only over a public channel. This was a revolutionary idea when it was first proposed in 1976, and remains a slightly counterintuitive one. This property makes the Diffie–Hellman protocol extremely useful.

INSTANTIATION OF THE DIFFIE–HELLMAN PROTOCOL

In order to fully specify the Diffie–Hellman protocol, we need to find a suitable public-key cryptosystem and a suitable function F. Fortunately, we will not need

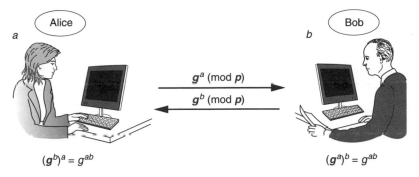

Figure 9.10. Diffie–Hellman protocol

any new public-key cryptosystems to describe the most common instantiation of the Diffie–Hellman protocol. This is because the ElGamal cryptosystem (see Section 5.3) has precisely the property that we need. Equally fortunately, the required function F is very simple.

Just as explained in Section 5.3.4 for ElGamal, we can choose two public system-wide parameters:

- a large prime p, typically 1024 bits in length;
- a special number g (a primitive element).

The Diffie–Hellman protocol is shown in Figure 9.10 and proceeds as follows. Note that all calculations are performed modulo p and thus we omit mod p in each computation for convenience. For a reminder of the basic rules of exponentiation, see Section 1.6.1.

1. Alice randomly generates a positive integer a and calculates g^a. This is, effectively, a temporary ElGamal key pair. Alice sends her public key g^a to Bob.
2. Bob randomly generates a positive integer b and calculates g^b. Bob sends his public key g^b to Alice.
3. Alice uses g^b and her private key a to compute $(g^b)^a$.
4. Bob uses g^a and his private key b to compute $(g^a)^b$.
5. The special combination function property that we need is that raising a number to the power a and then raising the result to the power b is the same as raising the number to the power b and then raising the result to the power a, which means that:

$$(g^a)^b = (g^b)^a = g^{ab}.$$

So Alice and Bob have ended up with the same value at the end of this protocol.

There are several important issues to note:

1. It is widely believed that the shared value $Z_{AB} = g^{ab}$ cannot be computed by anyone who does not know either a or b. An attacker who is monitoring the communication channel only sees g^a and g^b. Recall from Section 5.3.3 that

313

from this information the attacker is unable to calculate either a or b because of the difficulty of the discrete logarithm problem.

2. The main purpose of the Diffie–Hellman protocol is to establish a common cryptographic key K_{AB}. There are two reasons why the shared value $Z_{AB} = g^{ab}$ is unlikely to itself form the key in a real application:

   - Z_{AB} is not likely to be the correct length for a cryptographic key. If we conduct the Diffie–Hellman protocol with p having 1024 bits, then the shared value will also be a value of 1024 bits, which is much longer than a typical symmetric key.
   - Having gone through the effort of conducting a run of the Diffie–Hellman protocol to compute Z_{AB}, Alice and Bob may want to use it to establish several different keys. Hence they may not want to use Z_{AB} as a key, but rather as a seed from which to derive several different keys (see Section 10.3.2). The rationale behind this is that Z_{AB} is relatively expensive to generate, both in terms of computation and communication, whereas derived keys K_{AB} are relatively cheap to generate from Z_{AB}.

3. The protocol we have described is just one instantiation of the Diffie–Hellman protocol. In theory, any public-key cryptosystem that has the right special property and for which a suitable combination function F can be found, could be used to produce a version of the Diffie–Hellman protocol. In this case:

   - very informally, the special property of ElGamal is that public keys of different users can be numbers over the same modulus p, which means that they can be combined in different ways;
   - the combination function F, which is $F(x, g^y) = (g^y)^x$, has the special property that it does not matter in which order the two exponentiations are conducted, since:

$$F(x, g^y) = (g^y)^x = (g^x)^y = F(y, g^x).$$

It is not possible to use keys pairs from *any* public-key cryptosystem to instantiate the Diffie–Hellman protocol. In particular, RSA key pairs cannot be used because in RSA each user has their own modulus n, making RSA key pairs difficult to combine in the above manner. Hence, in contrast to Section 7.3.4, this time ElGamal is 'special'. Note that an important alternative manifestation of the Diffie–Hellman protocol is when an elliptic-curve-based variant of ElGamal is used (see Section 5.3.5), resulting in a protocol with shorter keys and reduced communication bandwidth.

ANALYSIS OF THE DIFFIE–HELLMAN PROTOCOL

We will now test the Diffie–Hellman protocol against the typical AKE protocol security goals that we identified in Section 9.4.1:

Mutual entity authentication. There is nothing in the Diffie–Hellman protocol that gives either party any assurance of who they are communicating with. The values a and b (and hence g^a and g^b) have been generated for this protocol run and cannot be linked with either Alice or Bob. Neither is there any assurance that these values are fresh.

Mutual data origin authentication. This is not provided, by the same argument as above.

Mutual key establishment. Alice and Bob do establish a common symmetric key at the end of the Diffie–Hellman protocol, so this goal is achieved.

Key confidentiality. The shared value $Z_{AB} = g^{ab}$ is not computable by anyone other than Alice or Bob. Neither is any key K_{AB} derived from Z_{AB}. Thus this goal is achieved.

Key freshness. Assuming that Alice and Bob choose fresh private keys a and b then Z_{AB} should also be fresh. Indeed, it suffices that just one of Alice and Bob choose a fresh private key.

Mutual key confirmation. This is not provided, since neither party obtains any explicit evidence that the other has constructed the same shared value Z_{AB}.

Unbiased key control. Both Alice and Bob certainly contribute to the generation of Z_{AB}. Technically, if Alice sends g^a to Bob before Bob generates b, then Bob could 'play around' with a few candidate choices for b until he finds a b that results in a $Z_{AB} = g^{ab}$ that he particularly 'likes'. This type of 'attack' is somewhat theoretical since, in practice, the values involved are so large that it would be very hard to conduct (Bob would probably have to try out too many choices of b). Hence it would seem reasonable to argue that joint (and hence unbiased) key control is achieved since any 'manipulation' that Bob can conduct is in most cases rather contrived.

Thus, from the above analysis, the Diffie–Hellman protocol achieves the goals relating to key establishment, but not the goals relating to authentication. We will now show that this is sufficiently problematic that this basic version of the Diffie–Hellman protocol is not normally implemented without further modification.

MAN-IN-THE-MIDDLE ATTACK ON THE DIFFIE–HELLMAN PROTOCOL

The *man-in-the-middle attack* is applicable to any situation where an attacker (Fred, in Figure 9.11) can intercept and alter messages sent on the communication channel between Alice and Bob. This is arguably the most well known attack against a cryptographic protocol and is one that the designers of any cryptographic protocol need to take measures to prevent.

The man-in-the middle attack works as follows (where all calculations are modulo p):

1. Alice begins a normal run of the Diffie–Hellman protocol depicted in Figure 9.10. She randomly generates a positive integer a and calculates g^a. Alice sends g^a to Bob.

2. Fred intercepts this message before it reaches Bob, generates his own positive integer f, and calculates g^f. Fred then claims to be Alice and sends g^f to Bob instead of g^a.

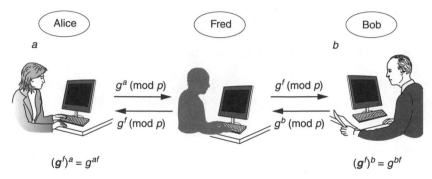

Figure 9.11. Man-in-the-middle attack against the Diffie–Hellman protocol

3. Bob continues the Diffie–Hellman protocol as if nothing untoward has happened. Bob randomly generates a positive integer b and calculates g^b. Bob sends g^b to Alice.

4. Fred intercepts this message before it reaches Alice. Fred then claims to be Bob and sends g^f to Alice instead of g^b.

5. Alice now believes that the Diffie–Hellman protocol has successfully completed. She uses g^f and her private integer a to compute $g^{af} = (g^f)^a$.

6. Bob also believes that it has successfully completed. He uses g^f and b to compute $g^{bf} = (g^f)^b$.

7. Fred computes $g^{af} = (g^a)^f$ and $g^{bf} = (g^b)^f$. He now has two different shared values, g^{af}, which he shares with Alice, and g^{bf}, which he shares with Bob.

At the end of this man-in-the-middle attack, all three entities hold different beliefs:

- Alice believes that she has established a shared value with Bob. But she is wrong, because she has established a shared value with Fred.
- Bob believes that he has established a shared value with Alice. But he is wrong, because he has established a shared value with Fred.
- Fred correctly believes that he has established two different shared values, one with Alice and the other with Bob.

Note that at the end of this man-in-the-middle attack, Fred cannot determine the shared value g^{ab} that Alice and Bob would have established had he not interfered, since both a and b remain secret to him, protected by the difficulty of the discrete logarithm problem. Nonetheless, Fred is now in a powerful position:

- If Fred's objective was simply to disrupt the key establishment process between Alice and Bob then he has already succeeded. If Alice derives a key K_{AF} from g^{af} and then encrypts a message to Bob using this key, Bob will not be able to decrypt it successfully because the key K_{BF} that he derives from his shared value g^{bf} will be different from K_{AF}.
- Much more serious is the situation that arises if Fred remains on the communication channel. In this case, if Alice encrypts a plaintext to Bob using

key K_{AF}, Fred (who is the only person who can derive both K_{AF} and K_{BF}) can decrypt the ciphertext using K_{AF} to learn the plaintext. He can then re-encrypt the plaintext using K_{BF} and send this to Bob. In this way, Fred can 'monitor' the *encrypted* communication between Alice and Bob without them being aware that this is even happening

This man-in-the middle attack was only able to succeed because neither Alice nor Bob could determine from whom they were receiving messages during the Diffie–Hellman protocol run. To solve this problem, we need to strengthen the Diffie–Hellman protocol so that it meets the authentication goals of Section 9.4.1 as well as the key establishment goals.

AKE PROTOCOLS BASED ON DIFFIE–HELLMAN

Although the basic Diffie–Hellman protocol that we described in Section 9.4.2 does not provide authentication, there are many different ways in which it can be adapted to do so.

We now describe one way of building in authentication. The *station-to-station* (STS) protocol makes an additional assumption that Alice and Bob have each established a long-term signature/verification key pair and have had their verification keys certified (see Section 11.1.2). The STS protocol is shown in Figure 9.12 and proceeds as follows (where all calculations are modulo p):

1. Alice randomly generates a positive integer a and calculates g^a. Alice sends g^a to Bob, along with the certificate *CertA* for her verification key.
2. Bob verifies *CertA*. If he is satisfied with the result then Bob randomly generates a positive integer b and calculates g^b. Next, Bob signs a message that consists of Alice's name, g^a and g^b. Bob then sends g^b to Alice, along with the certificate *CertB* for his verification key and the signed message.
3. Alice verifies *CertB*. If she is satisfied with the result then she uses Bob's verification key to verify the signed message. If she is satisfied with this, she signs a message that consists of Bob's name, g^a and g^b, which she then sends back to Bob. Finally, Alice uses g^b and her private key a to compute $(g^b)^a$.

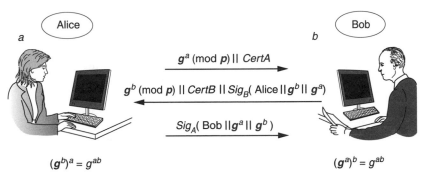

Figure 9.12. Station-to-station protocol

4. Bob uses Alice's verification key to verify the signed message that he has just received. If he is satisfied with the result then Bob uses g^a and his private key b to compute $(g^a)^b$.

With the exception of the first two, the extent to which the goals of Section 9.4.1 are met for the STS protocol are just as for the basic Diffie–Hellman protocol (in other words, they are all met except for key confirmation). It remains to check whether the first two authentication goals are now met:

Mutual entity authentication. Since a and b are randomly chosen private keys, g^a and g^b are thus also effectively randomly generated values. Hence we can consider g^a and g^b as being nonces (see Section 8.2.3). At the end of the second STS protocol message, Alice receives a digital signature from Bob on a message that includes her 'nonce' g^a. Similarly, at the end of the third STS protocol message, Bob receives a digital signature from Alice on a message that includes his 'nonce' g^b. Hence, by the principles that we discussed in Section 8.2.3, mutual entity authentication is provided, since both Alice and Bob each perform a cryptographic computation using a key only known to them on a nonce generated by the other party.

Mutual data origin authentication. This is provided, since the important data that is exchanged in the main messages is digitally signed.

Thus, unlike the basic Diffie–Hellman protocol, the STS protocol meets the first five typical AKE protocol goals of Section 9.3.1.

9.4.3 An AKE protocol based on key distribution

The STS protocol is an AKE protocol based on key agreement and the use of public-key cryptography. We will now look at an AKE protocol based on key distribution and the use of symmetric cryptography. This protocol is a simplified version of one from ISO 9798-2. This protocol involves the use of a trusted third party (denoted TTP).

PROTOCOL DESCRIPTION

The idea behind this AKE protocol is that Alice and Bob both trust the TTP. When Alice and Bob wish to establish a shared key K_{AB}, they will ask the TTP to generate one for them, which will then be securely distributed to them. The protocol involves the following assumptions:

- Alice has already established a long-term shared symmetric key K_{AT} with the TTP.
- Bob has already established a long-term shared symmetric key K_{BT} with the TTP.
- Alice and Bob are both capable of randomly generating nonces.

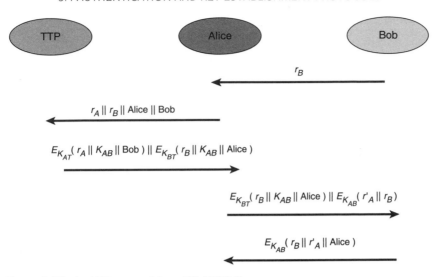

Figure 9.13. An AKE protocol from ISO 9798-2

There is a further assumption made on the type of encryption mechanism used, but we will discuss that when we consider data origin authentication. The protocol is shown in Figure 9.13 and proceeds as follows:

1. Bob starts the protocol by randomly generating a nonce r_B and sending it to Alice.
2. Alice randomly generates a nonce r_A and then sends a request for a symmetric key to the TTP. This request includes both Alice's and Bob's names, as well as the two nonces r_A and r_B.
3. The TTP generates a symmetric key K_{AB} and then encrypts it twice. The first ciphertext is intended for Alice and encrypted using K_{AT}. The plaintext consists of r_A, K_{AB} and Bob's name. The second ciphertext is intended for Bob and encrypted using K_{BT}. The plaintext consists of r_B, K_{AB} and Alice's name. The two ciphertexts are sent to Alice.
4. Alice decrypts the first ciphertext using K_{AT} and checks that it contains r_A and Bob's name. She extracts K_{AB}. She then generates a new nonce r'_A. Next, she generates a new ciphertext by encrypting r'_A and r_B using K_{AB}. Finally, she forwards the second ciphertext that she received from the TTP, and the new ciphertext that she has just created, to Bob.
5. Bob decrypts the first ciphertext that he receives (which is the second ciphertext that Alice received from the TTP) using K_{BT} and checks that it contains r_B and Alice's name. He extracts K_{AB}. He then decrypts the second ciphertext using K_{AB} and checks to see if it contains r_B. He extracts r'_A. Finally, he encrypts r_B, r'_A and Alice's name using K_{AB} and sends this ciphertext to Alice.
6. Alice decrypts the ciphertext using K_{AB} and checks that the plaintext consists of r_B, r'_A and Alice's name. If it does then the protocol concludes successfully.

319

PROTOCOL ANALYSIS

We now analyse this protocol to see if it meets the typical goals of an AKE protocol specified in Section 9.3.1.

Mutual entity authentication: We will divide this into two separate cases.

1. First we look at Bob's perspective. At the end of the fourth protocol message, the second ciphertext that Bob receives is an encrypted version of his nonce r_B. Thus this ciphertext is fresh. But who encrypted it? Whoever encrypted it must have known the key K_{AB}. Bob received this key by successfully using K_{BT} to decrypt a ciphertext, which resulted in a correctly formatted plaintext message consisting of r_B, K_{AB} and Alice's name. Thus Bob can be sure that this ciphertext originated with the TTP, since the TTP is the only entity other than Bob who knows K_{BT}. The format of this plaintext is essentially an 'assertion' by the TTP that the key K_{AB} has been freshly issued (because r_B is included) for use in communication between Bob (because it is encrypted using K_{BT}) and Alice (because her name is included). Thus the entity that encrypted the second ciphertext in the fourth protocol message must have been Alice because the TTP has asserted that only Alice and Bob have access to K_{AB}. Hence Bob can be sure that he has just been talking to Alice.

2. Alice's perspective is similar. At the end of the last protocol message, Alice receives an encrypted version of her nonce r_A'. This ciphertext, which was encrypted using K_{AB}, is thus fresh. In the third protocol message Alice receives an assertion from the TTP that K_{AB} has been freshly (because r_A is included) issued for use for communication between Alice (because it is encrypted using K_{AT}) and Bob (because his name is included). Thus the entity that encrypted the last protocol message must have been Bob, again because the TTP has asserted that only Alice and Bob have access to K_{AB}. Thus Alice can be sure that she has just been talking to Bob.

Note that our assertions that only Alice and Bob have access to K_{AB} of course assume that the TTP is not 'cheating', since the TTP also knows K_{AB}. However, the whole point of this protocol is that the TTP is *trusted* not to misbehave in this type of way.

Mutual data origin authentication: This is interesting, because we use symmetric encryption throughout this protocol and do not apparently employ any mechanism to explicitly provide data origin authentication, such as a MAC. While symmetric encryption does not normally provide data origin authentication, recall the 'case for' in our analysis of Protocol 4 in Section 9.3.5. Throughout our current protocol, the plaintexts are strictly formatted and fairly short, hence it might be reasonable to claim that encryption alone is providing data origin authentication, so long as a strong block cipher such as AES is used. However, the standard ISO 9798-2 goes further, by specifying that the 'encryption' used in this protocol must be such that data origin authentication is also essentially provided. One method would be to use an authenticated-encryption primitive, such as those discussed in Section 6.3.6. This goal is thus also met.

Mutual key establishment: At the end of the protocol Alice and Bob have established K_{AB}, so this goal is met.

Key confidentiality: The key K_{AB} can only be accessed by an entity who has knowledge of either K_{AT}, K_{BT} or K_{AB}. This means either the TTP (who is trusted), Alice or Bob. So this goal is met.

Key freshness: This goal is met so long as the TTP generates a fresh key K_{AB}. Again, we are *trusting* that the TTP will do this.

Mutual key confirmation: Both Alice and Bob demonstrate that they know K_{AB} by using it to encrypt plaintexts (Alice in the fourth protocol message; Bob in the last protocol message). Thus both confirm knowledge of the shared key.

Unbiased key control: This is provided because K_{AB} is generated by the TTP.

Thus we conclude that all the goals of Section 9.4.1 are provided. A similar AKE protocol is used by the widely deployed *Kerberos* protocol.

9.5 Summary

In this chapter we discussed cryptographic protocols, which provide a means for cryptographic primitives to be combined in ways that allow complex sets of security goals to be tailored to particular application environments. We focussed on a simple, but artificial, application in order to demonstrate that there are many different ways in which a cryptographic protocol can be designed, and also how sensitive the security of cryptographic protocols can be. We then looked at the important family of AKE protocols.

Perhaps the most important objective of this chapter was to provide an introduction into the art of designing and analysing cryptographic protocols. Two important caveats apply:

1. We do not recommend that anyone other than an expert attempts to design their own cryptographic protocols. Unless there are no alternatives, standard cryptographic protocols should be used. It is notoriously hard to design a secure cryptographic protocol since even minor changes to a secure protocol can result in an insecure protocol, as we have seen.

2. All our protocol analysis has been informal. There are a number of available techniques for attempting to formally prove the security of cryptographic protocols. While these need to be associated with some caveats of their own (see Section 3.2.5), their use is nonetheless preferable to the rather informal type of analysis that we have conducted in this chapter. Of course, as we have seen, informal analysis is often sufficient for establishing the insecurity of a cryptographic protocol.

9.6 Further reading

All books on cryptography feature cryptographic protocols, but relatively few provide introductions to protocols or discuss practical aspects of protocols. A relevant introduction to practical cryptographic protocols can be found in Ferguson, Schneier and Kohno [75].

The majority of important cryptographic protocols are essentially AKE protocols. A comprehensive overview of the many different approaches to designing an AKE protocol is Boyd and Mathuria [40]. Menezes, van Oorschot and Vanstone [123] have a useful chapter on AKE protocols. Dent and Mitchell [55] provide a summary of most significant standards for AKE protocols, including those appearing in ISO/IEC 9798 on entity authentication [19] and ISO/IEC 11770 on key establishment [4]. The popular Kerberos protocol is standardised in RFC 4120 [129]. SSL/TLS is one of the most widely used AKE protocols, with the latest version of TLS being specified by RFC 5246 [57] (see Section 12.1). The highly influential Diffie–Hellman protocol was first proposed in Diffie and Hellman [59] and is covered by RFC 2631 [160] and PKCS#3 [115]. CrypTool [52] includes a simulation of Diffie–Hellman. The STS protocol is due to Diffie, van Oorschot and Wiener [61]. A popular AKE protocol based on Diffie–Hellman is the Internet Key Exchange protocol (IKE), which is specified in RFC 4306 [106].

Every application of cryptography involves cryptographic protocols of some sort. One interesting set of cryptographic protocols that we made passing reference to were those for trusted computing, see for example Mitchell [65]. O'Mahony, Peirce and Tewari [146] describe a family of cryptographic protocols that have been proposed for electronic payment schemes. The interesting class of manual authentication protocols involve actions by human users. These feature in ISO/IEC 9798 [19] and are used in Bluetooth security [37]. We will look at several more cryptographic protocols during our discussion of cryptographic applications in Chapter 12.

9.7 Activities

1. There are many protocols that we have to conduct during our day-to-day lives. One example is the purchase of a property. Explain this protocol (you may choose to discuss the slightly less complex protocol for renting a property if you are unfamiliar with the purchase protocol), making sure you mention:

    - the entities involved;
    - the protocol assumptions;
    - the protocol flow;
    - the protocol messages;
    - the protocol actions.

2. A common security objective is to send a message from Alice to Bob in such a way that nobody else can read the message and that Bob can be sure that the message that he received did indeed come from Alice.

   (a) Identify the goals of a simple cryptographic protocol to meet this security objective.
   (b) Specify a simple cryptographic protocol based only on symmetric cryptography designed to meet these goals, including the assumptions, flow, messages and actions involved in the protocol.

3. Provide some simple examples of a cryptographic protocol failing to provide the intended security services that results from a problem with:

   (a) the protocol assumptions;
   (b) the protocol messages;
   (c) the protocol actions.

4. Design a protocol based on Protocol 1 in Section 9.3.2 that, in addition to the existing protocol goals, also allows Alice to confirm that Bob is alive.

5. The security objectives of a cryptographic protocol are for Alice to be able to send a highly confidential email message to Bob in such a way that:

   • Bob can prove to Charlie that the email came from Alice;
   • Alice receives confirmation that Bob received the email message.

   (a) Determine the protocol goals.
   (b) Propose a simple cryptographic protocol (including assumptions, flow, messages and actions) for achieving these goals.

6. Let $p = 23$ and $g = 11$ be system-wide parameters for the Diffie–Hellman protocol.

   (a) Show that if Alice chooses $a = 2$ and Bob chooses $b = 4$ then, by following the Diffie–Hellman protocol, both of them establish the same secret value.
   (b) What is the largest symmetric key length that Alice and Bob could safely derive directly from this shared secret?
   (c) Explain how attacker Fred can conduct a man-in-the-middle attack using the value $f = 3$.

7. Man-in-the-middle attacks do not just apply against the Diffie–Hellman protocol.

   (a) Explain how a man-in-the-middle attack against a generic cryptographic protocol works.
   (b) Is it possible to conduct a meaningful man-in-the-middle attack against the dynamic password scheme based on challenge–response that we described in Section 8.5?

8. For each of the typical AKE protocol goals defined in Section 9.4.1, explain what might go wrong if an AKE protocol fails to provide that goal.

9. Find out information about the Kerberos protocol. There are different versions of this protocol, but they all work in broadly similar ways.

    (a) What is the Kerberos protocol used for?
    (b) What entities are involved in the Kerberos protocol?
    (c) What assumptions need to be in place before use of the Kerberos protocol?
    (d) Informally describe the protocol flow and messages of the Kerberos protocol.
    (e) Explain the extent to which the Kerberos protocol meets the typical AKE protocol goals of Section 9.4.1.

10. By basing your ideas heavily on the protocol in Section 9.4.3, design a similar AKE protocol that uses clock-based freshness mechanisms instead of nonces.

11. Suppose that two different cryptographic protocols both achieve the same protocol goals and can thus be argued to be equivalent from a security perspective. What criteria do you suggest we use to compare these two protocols from an *efficiency* perspective?

12. A cryptographic protocol is normally considered to have to failed if some protocol message is not received correctly, or a protocol action fails. One option for proceeding is simply to rerun the protocol. Explain, by means of some illustrative examples, why straightforward rerunning of the protocol is not always the best way of proceeding.

13. Cryptographic protocols are notoriously difficult to design. Provide an informal explanation of the different approaches that are being taken towards trying to establish the formal security of cryptographic protocols.

14. Most of the cryptographic protocols that we discussed in this chapter were AKE protocols, whose primary goals are entity authentication and key establishment. Find at least two examples of cryptographic protocols that are not AKE protocols. For each of these protocols:

    (a) Identify the main protocol goals.
    (b) Briefly explain which cryptographic mechanisms are used to achieve these goals.

15. In Section 9.3.4 we mentioned *interleaving attacks* on cryptographic protocols, which can be launched against parallel executions of a protocol.

    (a) Find an example of a simple interleaving attack against a cryptographic protocol.
    (b) Explain what types of defence mechanism can be put in place against this type of attack.

Part III
Key Management

10 Key Management

K̲ey management is crucial to the security of any cryptosystem. Without secure procedures for the handling of cryptographic keys throughout their lifecycle, the benefits of the use of strong cryptographic primitives are potentially lost. Indeed, it could be argued that if key management is not performed correctly then there is no point in using cryptography at all.

Cryptographic primitives are rarely compromised through weaknesses in their design. However they are often compromised through poor key management. Thus, from a practical perspective, there is a strong case for arguing that this is the most important chapter in this book.

This chapter is intended to provide an understanding of the fundamental principles of key management. However, key management is a complex and difficult aspect of any cryptosystem. Since it is essentially the interface between cryptographic mechanisms and the security of a real system, key management must be closely tailored to the needs of a particular application or organisation. For example, different solutions will be needed for managing the keys of a bank, a military organisation, a mobile telephone network, and a home personal computer. *There is no one correct way of managing keys.* As such, the discussion in this chapter cannot be prescriptive. Nonetheless, the following treatment of key management will hopefully explain the main issues and provide useful guidelines.

At the end of this chapter you should be able to:

- Identify some fundamental principles of key management.
- Explain the main phases in the lifecycle of a cryptographic key.
- Discuss a number of different techniques for implementing the different phases in the lifecycle of a cryptographic key.
- Identify appropriate key management techniques for specific application environments.
- Appreciate the need for secure key management policies, practices and procedures.

10.1 Key management fundamentals

In this section we provide an introduction to key management. Most importantly, we identify the scope of key management and introduce the key lifecycle, which we will use to structure the discussion in the remainder of the chapter.

10.1.1 What is key management?

The scope of key management is perhaps best described as the *secure administration of cryptographic keys*. This is a deliberately broad definition, because key management involves a wide range of quite disparate processes, all of which must come together coherently if cryptographic keys are to be securely managed.

The important thing to remember is that cryptographic keys are just special pieces of *data*. Key management thus involves most of the diverse processes associated with information security. These include:

Technical controls. These can be used in various aspects of key management. For example, special hardware devices may be required for storing cryptographic keys, and special cryptographic protocols are necessary in order to establish keys.

Process controls. Policies, practices and procedures play a crucial role in key management. For example, business continuity processes may be required in order to cope with the potential loss of important cryptographic keys.

Environmental controls. Key management must be tailored to the environment in which it will be practiced. For example, the physical location of cryptographic keys plays a big role in determining the key management techniques that are used to administer them.

Human factors. Key management often involves people doing things. Every security practitioner knows that whenever this is the case, the potential for problems occurring is high. Many key management systems rely, at their very highest level, on manual processes.

Thus, while cryptographic keys represent an extremely small percentage of the data that an organisation needs to manage, much of the wider information security issues that the organisation has to deal with (such as physical security, access control, network security, security policy, risk management and disaster recovery) interface with key management. Paradoxically, we will also see that while key management exists to support the use of cryptography, we will also need to use cryptography in order to provide key management.

The good news is that much of key management is about applying 'common sense'. The bad news, of course, is that applying 'common sense' is often much more complex than we first imagine. This is certainly true for key management.

327

Recall from Section 3.2.1 that if key management was easy then we would all probably be using a one-time pad for encryption!

Note that while all cryptographic keys need to be managed, the discussion in this chapter is primarily aimed at *keys that need to be kept secret*. In other words, we focus on symmetric keys and the private keys of a public-key pair (that is, private decryption or signature keys). Public keys have such special key management issues that we devote Chapter 11 to considering them. That said, many of the broader issues discussed in this chapter also apply to public keys.

10.1.2 The key lifecycle

Another way of defining the scope of key management is to consider the *key lifecycle*, which identifies the various processes concerning cryptographic keys throughout their lifetime. The main phases of the key lifecycle are depicted in Figure 10.1.

Key generation concerns the creation of keys. We discuss key generation in Section 10.3.

Key establishment is the process of making sure that keys reach the end points where they will be used. This is arguably the most difficult phase of the key lifecycle to implement. We discuss key establishment in Section 10.4.

Key storage deals with the safekeeping of keys. It may also be important to conduct *key backup* so that keys can be recovered in the event of loss of a key and, ultimately, *key archival*. These are all discussed in Section 10.5.

Key usage is about how keys are used. As part of this discussion we will consider *key change*. We will also look at how a key's life ends in *key destruction*. These are all discussed in Section 10.6.

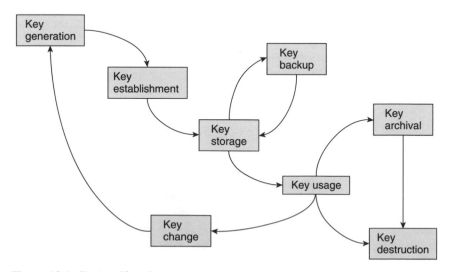

Figure 10.1. The key lifecycle

Note that the various phases in the key lifecycle are not always cleanly separated. For example, we saw in Section 9.4.2 how key agreement protocols such as the Diffie–Hellman protocol simultaneously generate and establish a symmetric key. Also, some phases are not always relevant. For example, key backup and key archival may not be necessary in some applications.

10.1.3 Fundamental key management requirements

There are two fundamental key management requirements that apply throughout the various phases of the key lifecycle:

Secrecy of keys. Throughout the key lifecycle, secret keys (in other words, symmetric keys and private keys) must remain secret from all parties except those that are authorised to know them. This clearly impacts all phases of the key lifecycle since, for example:

- if a weak key generation mechanism is used then it might be possible to determine information about a secret key more easily than intended;
- secret keys are vulnerable when they are 'moved around', thus secure key distribution mechanisms must be used;
- secret keys are perhaps most vulnerable when they are 'sitting around', thus key storage mechanisms must be strong enough to resist an attacker who has access to a device on which they reside;
- if secret keys are not destroyed properly then they can potentially be recovered after the supposed time of destruction.

Assurance of purpose of keys. Throughout the key lifecycle, those parties relying on a key must have *assurance of purpose* of the key. In other words, someone in possession of a key should be confident that they can use that key for the purpose that they believe it to be for. This 'purpose', may include some, or all, of the following:

- information concerning which entities are associated with the key (in symmetric cryptography this is likely to be more than one entity, whereas for public-key cryptography each key is normally only associated with one entity);
- the cryptographic algorithm that the key is intended to be used for;
- key usage restrictions, for example, that a symmetric key can only be used for creating and verifying a MAC, or that a signature key can only be used for digitally signing transactions of less than a certain value.

The 'assurance' necessarily includes some degree of data integrity that links (ideally binds) the above information to the key itself, otherwise it cannot be relied upon. Sometimes, perhaps rather casually, assurance of purpose is referred to as *authentication* of the key. However, assurance of purpose is often much more than identification of the entity associated with the key. Assurance of purpose impacts all phases of the key lifecycle since, for example:

- if a key is established without providing assurance of purpose then it might later be used for a purpose other than that for which it was originally intended (we will show how this could happen in Section 10.6.1);
- if a key is used for the wrong purpose then there could be very serious consequences (we will see an example of this in Section 10.6.1).

In some applications we require an even stronger requirement that assurance of purpose is *provable to a third party*, which might be the case for verification keys for digital signature schemes.

The need for secrecy of keys is self-evident and much of our subsequent discussion about the key lifecycle will be targeted towards providing it. Assurance of purpose of keys is more subtle and is often provided *implicitly*. For example, in the AKE protocol from ISO 9798-2 that we discussed in Section 9.4.3, Alice and Bob establish a shared AES encryption (say) key using a TTP, in each case receiving the key encrypted using a key known only to Alice or Bob and the TTP. In this case the assurance of purpose is implicitly provided through a combination of the facts that:

1. the key arrives shortly after a specific request for a shared AES encryption key;
2. the key has clearly come from the TTP (this case was argued in the protocol analysis in Section 9.4.3);
3. the name of the other communicating party is included in the associated ciphertext.

Assurance of purpose in the above example is largely facilitated by the fact that the parties relying on the key, Alice and Bob, are both part of a 'closed' system where they both share long-term symmetric keys with a TTP. In most environments where symmetric key cryptography is used, assurance of purpose is provided through similar implicit arguments. In contrast, public-key cryptography facilitates the use of cryptography in 'open' environments where there are no sources of implicit assurance of purpose of keys. Public keys can, literally, be public items of data. By default there are no assurances of whether a public key is correct, with whom it can be associated, or what it can be used for. Thus key management of public keys needs to focus much more explicitly on assurance of purpose of public keys. This is the main subject of Chapter 11.

Finally, the purpose of a key is not always intuitive. For example, we saw in Section 7.2.3 that a user who has a MAC key might not be allowed to use it both for MAC creation and verification. Similarly, a user might not be allowed to use a symmetric key for both encryption and decryption. We will also see in

Section 10.6.1 an example of a symmetric key that can only ever be used by anyone for encryption, never decryption.

10.1.4 Key management systems

We will use the term *key management system* to describe any system for managing the various phases of the key lifecycle introduced in Section 10.1.2. While throughout our discussion of cryptographic primitives we have cautioned against using anything other than a few respected, and standardised, cryptographic primitives, we have to take a more pragmatic view when it comes to key management systems. This is because a key management system needs to be aligned with the functionality and priorities of the organisation that implements it (we use the term 'organisation' in such a loose sense that this could be an individual). For example, a key management system may depend on:

Network topology. Key management is much simpler if it is only needed to support two parties who wish to communicate securely, rather than a multinational organisation that wishes to establish the capability for secure communication between any two employees.

Cryptographic mechanisms. As we will see in this chapter and Chapter 11, some of the key management system requirements of symmetric and public-key cryptography differ.

Compliance restrictions. For example, depending on the application, there may be legal requirements for key recovery mechanisms or key archival (see Section 10.5.5).

Legacy issues. Large organisations whose security partly depends on that of other related organisations may find that their choice of key management system is restricted by requirements to be compatible with business partners, some of whom might be using older technology.

Thus an organisation will, almost inevitably, have to think carefully about how to design and implement a key management system that meets its own needs. That said, there are a number of important standards relating to key management that provide useful guidance. There are inevitably many proprietary key management systems around, some closely related to these standards and others completely non-standard. It is also worth noting that most international standards for key management are lengthy documents, covering a multitude of key management areas, so that full compliance with such standards is extremely hard to achieve. Many organisations will comply with the 'spirit' of a standard rather than the 'letter' of the standard.

Key management is hard, and there are many different ways of approaching it. This raises a major concern: how can we get some level of assurance that a key management system is doing its job effectively? We will briefly revisit this issue in Section 10.7.

10.2 Key lengths and lifetimes

Before we discuss the lifecycle of cryptographic keys, we need to consider a couple of properties of the keys themselves, most significantly the key length.

We already know that, in general (but certainly not by default), longer keys are better from a security perspective. Longer symmetric keys take more time to exhaustively search for and longer public-key pairs tend to make the underlying computational problem on which a public-key cryptosystem is based harder to solve. So there is certainly a case for making keys as long as possible.

However, a cryptographic computation normally takes more time if the key is longer. In addition, longer keys involve greater storage and distribution overheads. Hence longer keys are less efficient in several important respects. Thus key length tends to be based on an efficiency–security tradeoff. We normally want keys to be 'long enough', but not more than that.

10.2.1 Key lifetimes

The issue of key length is closely linked to the intended *lifetime* (also often referred to as the *cryptoperiod*) of a cryptographic key. By this we mean that the key can only be used for a specified period of time, during which it is regarded as being *live*. Once that lifetime has been exceeded, the key is regarded as *expired* and should no longer be used. At this point it may need to be *archived* or perhaps *destroyed* (we discuss this in more detail in Section 10.6.4).

There are many reasons why cryptographic keys have finite lifetimes. These include:

Mitigation against key compromise. Having a finite lifetime prevents keys being used beyond a time within which they might reasonably be expected to be compromised, for example by an exhaustive key search or compromise of the storage medium.

Mitigation against key management failures. Finite key lifetimes help to mitigate against failures in key management. For example, forcing an annual key change will guarantee that personnel who leave an organisation during the year, but for some reason retain keys, do not have access to valid keys the following year.

Mitigation against future attacks. Finite key lifetimes help to mitigate against future advances in the attack environment. For this reason, keys are normally set to expire well before current knowledge suggests that they need to.

Enforcement of management cycles. Finite lifetimes enforce a key change process, which might be convenient for management cycles. For example, if keys provide access to electronic resources that are paid for on an annual subscription basis, then having a one-year key lifetime allows access to keys to be directly linked to subscriptions to the service.

Flexibility. Finite key lifetimes introduce an additional 'variable' which can be adjusted to suit application requirements. For example, a relatively short key (which is relatively inexpensive to generate, distribute and store) could be adopted under the pretext that the key lifetime is also suitably short. We will discuss an example of this in Section 10.4.1, where *data keys* are relatively short but expire quickly in comparison to *master keys*.

Limitation of key exposure. At least in theory, some information relating to a key is 'leaked' to an attacker every time the attacker sees a cryptographic value computed using that key. This is because the result of every cryptographic computation provides the attacker with information that they did not have before they saw the ciphertext. We refer to this as *key exposure*. However, this information is normally of little (often no) use to an attacker if the cryptographic algorithm is strong, hence in many applications key exposure is not a significant issue. Nonetheless, finite key lifetimes limit key exposure, should this be regarded as a concern.

10.2.2 Choosing a key length

The length of a cryptographic key is commensurate with the key lifetime, which in turn is related to the length of time for which cryptographic protection is required. We discussed one aspect of this issue in Section 3.2.2 when we considered the notion of cover time. Note, however, that there is an element of 'the chicken and the egg' in the relationship between key length and key lifetime:

- in an ideal world the key lifetime would be chosen and then a suitable key length selected;
- in the real world the key length may be dictated (for example, the key management system is based on the use of 128-bit AES keys) and thus the key lifetime is set to an appropriate time period.

Fortunately, the decision on key length is made much simpler by the limited number of standard cryptographic algorithms, which in turn present limited options for key lengths. Nonetheless, decisions will need to be made, particularly since some of the most popular cryptographic algorithms such as AES (see Section 4.5) and RSA (see Section 5.2) have variable key lengths.

The most important advice on selecting key length is to listen to the experts. From time to time, influential bodies will issue guidance on advised key lengths, and these should be carefully adhered to. Note that:

- Key length recommendations for symmetric cryptography tend to be algorithm-independent, since the security of respected symmetric encryption algorithms should be benchmarked against the difficulty of an exhaustive key search.

- Key length recommendations for public-key cryptography tend to be algorithm-specific, since the security of a public-key cryptosystem depends upon the perceived difficulty of the hard computational problem on which the algorithm is based (for example, factoring in the case of RSA).

Key length recommendations are usually presented in terms of a combination of potential attack environments and cover times. Table 10.1 provides an example, showing protection profiles and recommended symmetric key lengths.

There are several issues worth noting from Table 10.1:

1. Some of the key length recommendations are specifically linked to maximum recommended key lifetimes.
2. Although these recommendations are largely algorithm-independent, some further specific advice is given by ECRYPT II on the use of Triple DES, since Triple DES has a much weaker security than that suggested by its key length (see Section 4.4.4).

It should also be noted that:

Advice on key length is not unanimous. Ultimately these are subjective opinions, albeit hopefully informed ones. Before choosing a key length it is advisable to seek recommendations from more than one source.

Table 10.1: ECRYPT II protection profiles and symmetric key lengths (2011)

	Protection	Notes	Key length
1	Vulnerable to real-time attacks by individuals	Limited use	32
2	Very short term protection against small organisations	Not for new applications	64
3	Short-term protection against medium organisations; medium-term protection against small organisations		72
4	Very short term protection against agencies; long-term protection against small organisations	Protection to 2012	80
5	Legacy standard level	Protection to 2020	96
6	Medium-term protection	Protection to 2030	112
7	Long-term protection	Protection to 2040	128
8	'Foreseeable future'	Good protection against quantum computers	256

Advice on key length changes over time. It is wise to seek the latest and most accurate information before deciding on key lengths. It is possible, for example, that the advice in Table 10.1, and the key length comparisons in Table 5.2, may no longer be accurate.

10.3 Key generation

We now begin our discussion of the various phases in the key lifecycle. This begins with key generation, which is the creation of cryptographic keys. This is a critical phase of the key lifecycle. As we indicated at the start of Section 8.1, many cryptosystems have been found to have weaknesses because they do not generate their keys in a sufficiently secure manner.

Key generation processes for symmetric and public-key cryptography are fundamentally different. We will first look at ways of generating a symmetric key.

10.3.1 Direct key generation

Symmetric keys are just randomly generated numbers (normally bit strings). The most obvious method for generating a cryptographic key is thus to randomly generate a number, or more commonly a pseudorandom number. We have already discussed random number generation in Section 8.1 and any of the techniques discussed there are potentially appropriate for key generation. The choice of technique will depend on the application. Obviously, the strength of the technique used should take into consideration the importance of the cryptographic key that is being generated. For example, use of a hardware-based non-deterministic generator might be appropriate for a master key, whereas a software-based non-deterministic generator based on mouse movements might suffice for generating a local key to be used to store personal files on a home PC (see Section 8.1.3).

The only further issue to note is that for certain cryptographic algorithms there are sporadic choices of key that some people argue should not be used. For example, as mentioned in Section 4.4.3, DES has some keys that are defined to be *weak*. In the rare event that such keys are generated by a key generation process, some guidance suggests that they should be rejected. Issues such as this are algorithm-specific and the relevant standards should be consulted for advice.

10.3.2 Key derivation

The term *key derivation* is sometimes used to describe the generation of cryptographic keys from other cryptographic keys or secret values. Such 'key

335

laundering' might at first seem a strange thing to do, but there are several significant advantages of deriving keys from other keys:

Efficiency. Key generation and establishment can be relatively expensive processes. Generating and establishing one key (sometimes called a *base key*), and then using it to derive many keys, can be an effective technique for saving on these costs. For example, many applications require both confidentiality and data origin authentication. If separate cryptographic mechanisms are to be used to provide these two security services then they require an encryption key and a MAC key (see Section 6.3.6 for a wider discussion of this, and other options). As we will see in Section 10.6.1, it is good practice to make sure that the keys used for each of these mechanisms are different. Rather than generating and establishing two symmetric keys for this purpose, a cost-efficient solution is to generate and establish one key K and then derive two keys K_1 and K_2 from it. For example, a very simple key derivation process might involve computing:

$$K_1 = h(K||0) \quad \text{and} \quad K_2 = h(K||1),$$

where h is a hash function.

Longevity. In some applications, long-term symmetric keys are preloaded onto devices before deployment. Using these long-term keys directly to encrypt data exposes them to cryptanalysis (as indicated in Section 10.2.1). However, randomly generating a new key requires a key establishment mechanism to be used, which may not always be possible or practical. A good solution is to derive keys for use from the long-term key. In this way, so long as the key derivation process is understood by all parties requiring access to a key, no further key establishment mechanism is required and the long-term key is not exposed through direct use.

Key derivation must be based on a derivation function that is one-way (see Section 6.2.1). This protects the base key in the event that keys derived from it are later compromised. This is important because often many different keys are derived using a single base key, hence the impact of subsequently compromising the base key could be substantial.

There are standards for key derivation. For example, PKCS#5 defines how a key can be derived from a password or a PIN, which can be regarded as a relatively insecure type of cryptographic key, but one which is often long term (such as the PIN associated with a payment card). Key derivation in this case is defined as a function $f(P, S, C, L)$, where:

- f is a key derivation function that explains how to combine the various inputs in order to derive a key;
- P is the password or PIN;
- S is a string of (not necessarily all secret) pseudorandom bits, used to enable P to be used to derive many different keys;

- C is an iteration counter that specifies the number of 'rounds' to compute (just as discussed for a block cipher in Section 4.4.1, this can be used to tradeoff security against efficiency of the key derivation);
- L is the length of the derived key.

Obviously, the benefits of key derivation come at the cost of an increased impact in the event that a base key becomes compromised. This is just the latest of the many efficiency–security tradeoffs that we have encountered.

In Section 10.4.2 we will see another variation of this idea, where keys are derived from old keys and additional data.

10.3.3 Key generation from components

Direct key generation and key derivation are both processes that can be performed if one entity can be trusted to have full control of a particular key generation process. In many situations this is an entirely reasonable assumption.

However, for extremely important secret keys it may not be desirable to trust one entity with key generation. In such cases we need to distribute the key generation process amongst a group of entities in such a way that no members of the group individually have control over the process, but collectively they do. One technique for facilitating this is to generate a key in *component form*. We illustrate this by considering a simple scenario involving three entities: Alice, Bob and Charlie. Assume that we wish to generate a 128-bit key:

1. Alice, Bob and Charlie each randomly generates a *component* of 128 bits. This component is itself a sort of key, so any direct key generation mechanism could be used to generate it. However, given that key generation based on component form is only likely to be used for sensitive keys, the generation of components should be performed as securely as possible. We denote the resulting components by K_A, K_B and K_C, respectively.
2. Alice, Bob and Charlie securely transfer their components to a secure *combiner*. In most applications this combiner will be represented by a hardware security module (see Section 10.5.3). In many cases the 'secure transfer' of these components will be by manual delivery. For some large international organisations, this might even involve several of the components being physically flown across the world. The input of the components to the secure combiner is normally conducted according to a strict protocol that takes the form of a *key ceremony* (see Section 10.7.2).
3. The secure combiner derives a key K from the separate components. In this example, the best derivation function is XOR. In other words:

$$K = K_A \oplus K_B \oplus K_C.$$

Note that the key K is only reconstructed within the secure combiner and not output to the entities involved in the key derivation process. XOR is the 'best' type of key derivation function since knowledge of even two of the components does not leak any information about the derived key K. To see this, consider the case where Alice and Bob are conspiring to try to learn something about key K. Suppose that Alice and Bob XOR their components together to compute $R = K_A \oplus K_B$. Observe that $K = R \oplus K_C$, which means that $R = K \oplus K_C$. Thus R can be considered as the 'encryption' of K using a one-time pad with key K_C. We know from Section 3.1.3 that the one-time pad offers perfect secrecy, which means that knowing R (the 'ciphertext') does not leak any information about K (the 'plaintext').

Thus Alice, Bob and Charlie are able to jointly generate a key in such a way that all three of their components are necessary for the process to complete. If only two of the components are present then no information about the key can be derived, even if the components are combined. This process easily generalises to any number of entities, all of whom must present their components in order to derive the key. Even more ingenious techniques can be used to implement more complex key generation policies. For example, the *Shamir secret-sharing protocol* allows a key to be generated in component form in such a way that the key can be derived from any k of n components, where k can be any number less than n (in our previous example $k = n = 3$).

Component form can also be used in other phases of the key lifecycle, as we will see in Section 10.4 and Section 10.5.

10.3.4 Public-key pair generation

Since key generation for public-key cryptography is algorithm-specific, we will not treat it in detail here. As for symmetric key generation:

- Public-key pair generation often requires the random generation of numbers.
- Relevant standards should be consulted before generating public-key pairs.

However, in contrast to symmetric key generation:

- Not every number in the 'range' of the keyspace of a public-key cryptosystem is a valid key. For example, for RSA the keys d and e are required to have specific mathematical properties (see Section 5.2.1). If we choose an RSA modulus of 1024 bits then there are, in theory, 2^{1024} candidates for e or d. However, only some of these 2^{1024} numbers *can* be an e or a d, the other choices are ruled out.
- Some keys in public-key cryptosystems are chosen to have a specific format. For example, RSA public keys are sometimes chosen to have a specific format that results in them being 'faster than the average case' when they are used to compute exponentiations, thus speeding up RSA encryptions (or RSA signature

verifications if the public key is a verification key). There is no harm in such a deliberate choice of key since the public key is not a secret value. Clearly, if similar restrictions were placed on a private key then an attacker might benefit from having many fewer candidate private keys to choose from.

- The generation of a key pair can be slow and complex. Some devices, such as smart cards, may not have the computational resources to generate key pairs. In such cases it may be necessary to generate key pairs off the card and import them.

Thus, while key generation is always a delicate part of the cryptographic lifecycle, particular care and attention needs to be paid to the generation of public-key pairs. We will also discuss this issue in Section 11.2.2.

10.4 Key establishment

Key establishment is the process of getting cryptographic keys to the locations where they will be used. This part of the key lifecycle tends either to be relatively straightforward, or very hard, to manage. Key establishment is generally hard when keys need to be shared by more than one party, as is the case for most symmetric keys. It is relatively straightforward when:

The key does not need to be shared. This applies to any keys that can be locally generated and do not need to be transferred anywhere, such as symmetric keys for encrypting data on a local machine. Of course, if such keys are not locally generated then key establishment becomes hard again! We will consider this issue for private keys in Section 11.2.2.

The key does not need to be secret. This applies mainly to public keys. In this case key establishment is more of a logistical problem than a security issue. We also discuss this in Section 11.2.2.

The key can be established in a controlled environment. In some cryptographic applications it is possible to establish all the required keys within a controlled environment before the devices containing the keys are deployed. This is often termed *key predistribution*. While this makes key establishment fairly easy, there are still issues:

- Some key establishment problems are transferred into 'device establishment' problems. However, these may be less sensitive. For example, key predistribution can be used to preload keys onto mobile phones (see Section 12.3.5) or set-top boxes for digital television services (see Section 12.5.4). In this case the provider still needs to keep track of which customer receives which device, but this is likely to be a simpler problem than trying to load cryptographic keys onto a device that is already in the hands of a customer.
- In environments suited to key predistribution, it can be challenging to conduct post-deployment key management operations, such as key change (see Section 10.6.2). In such cases it may be necessary to establish entirely new devices.

We have already discussed some important techniques for key establishment:

- In Section 9.4 we discussed AKE (Authentication and Key Establishment) protocols. Many symmetric keys are established by means of an AKE protocol of some sort. We noted that AKE protocols can be classified into key distribution and key agreement protocols.
- In Section 9.4.2 we discussed the Diffie–Hellman protocol, which forms the basis for the majority of AKE protocols based on key agreement.
- In Section 5.5.2 we discussed hybrid encryption, which is a very common method of key establishment in environments where public-key cryptography is supported.

The rest of this section will focus on some special techniques for conducting symmetric key establishment, all of which could be regarded as being particular types of AKE protocol.

10.4.1 Key hierarchies

One of the most widely used techniques for managing symmetric keys is to use a *key hierarchy*. This consists of a ranking of keys, with high-level keys being more 'important' than low-level keys. Keys at one level are used to encrypt keys at the level beneath. We will see shortly how this concept can be used to facilitate symmetric key establishment.

PHILOSOPHY BEHIND KEY HIERARCHIES

There are two clear advantages of deploying keys in a hierarchy:

Secure distribution and storage. By using keys at one level to encrypt keys at the level beneath, most keys in the system can be protected by the keys above them. This allows keys to be securely distributed and stored in encrypted form.

Facilitating scalable key change. As we will discuss further in Section 10.6.2, there are many reasons why keys may need to be changed. Some of these reasons are concerned with the risk of a key being compromised, which is arguably more likely to happen to 'front-line facing' keys that are directly used to perform cryptographic computations, such as encryption of transmitted data. Use of a key hierarchy makes it relatively easy to change these low-level keys without the need to replace the high-level keys, which are expensive to establish.

However, one significant problem remains: how to distribute and store the keys at the top level of the hierarchy? The use of a key hierarchy focusses the key management problems onto these top-level keys. Effort can thus be concentrated on key management solutions for the top-level keys. The payoff is that if we get

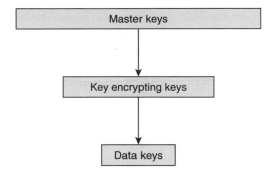

Figure 10.2. A three-level key hierarchy

the management of the top-level keys 'right', the management of the rest of the keys can be taken care of using the key hierarchy.

A SIMPLE KEY HIERARCHY

The idea of a key hierarchy is best illustrated by looking at a simple example. The 'simple' example shown in Figure 10.2 provides a key hierarchy that is probably good enough (and maybe even more complex than necessary) for the majority of applications. The three levels of this hierarchy consist of:

Master keys. These are the top-level keys that require careful management. They are only used to encrypt key encrypting keys. Since the key management of master keys is expensive, they will have relatively long lifetimes (perhaps several years).

Key encrypting keys. These are distributed and stored in encrypted form using master keys. They are only used to encrypt data keys. Key encrypting keys will have shorter lifetimes than master keys, since they have greater exposure and are easier to change.

Data keys. These are distributed and stored in encrypted form using key encrypting keys. These are the working keys that will be used to perform cryptographic computations. They have high exposure and short lifetimes. This may simply correspond to the lifetime a single session, hence data keys are often referred to as *session keys*.

Since the longevity of the keys in the hierarchy increases as we rise up the hierarchy, it is often the case that so does the length of the respective keys. Certainly keys at one level should be *at least as long* as keys at the level beneath. Note that the 'middle layer' of key encrypting keys may well be unnecessary for many applications, where it suffices to have master keys and data keys.

MANAGING THE TOP-LEVEL KEYS

Top-level (master) keys need to be securely managed, or the whole key hierarchy is compromised. Most key management systems using key hierarchies will employ

341

hardware security modules (HSMs) to store master keys. These top-level keys will never leave the HSMs in unprotected form. HSMs will be discussed in more detail in Section 10.5.3.

The generation of master keys is an extremely critical operation. Master keys are commonly generated, established and backed up in component form. We discussed component form in Section 10.3.3 and will discuss the establishment process for a master key from components in Section 10.7.2. If a master key needs to be shared between two different HSMs then one option is to generate the same master key from components separately on each HSM. An alternative is to run a key agreement protocol (see Section 9.4.2) between the two HSMs in order to establish a shared master key.

SCALABLE KEY HIERARCHIES

The notion of a key hierarchy works fine for a relatively simple network, but quickly becomes unmanageable for large networks. Consider a simple two-level hierarchy consisting of only master and data keys. If we have a network of n users, then the number of possible pairs of users is $\frac{1}{2}n(n-1)$. This means that, for example, if there are 100 users then there are $\frac{1}{2} \times 100 \times 99 = 4950$ possible pairs of users. Hence, in the worst case, we might have to establish 4950 separate master keys amongst the 100 HSMs in the network, which is not practical.

Alternatively, we could install the same master key in all HSMs. Data keys for communication between Alice and Bob could then be derived from the common master key and Alice and Bob's identities. However, compromise of Alice's HSM would now not only compromise data keys for use between Alice and Bob, but data keys between *any* pair of users in the network. This is not normally acceptable.

In such cases it is common to deploy the services of a trusted third party, whom all the users trust, which we will refer to as a *key centre* (KC). The idea is that each user in the network shares a key with the KC, which acts as a 'go between' any time any pairs of users require a shared key. In this way we reduce the need for 4950 master keys in a network of 100 users to just 100 master keys, each one shared between a specific user and the KC.

There are two key distribution appoaches to acquiring shared keys from a KC. We illustrate these using a very simple scenario. In each case we assume that Alice wishes to establish a shared data key K with Bob. We will also assume that both Alice and Bob have respectively established master keys K_{AC} and K_{BC} with the KC, and that a simple two-level key hierarchy is being employed. The two approaches are:

Key translation. In this approach the KC simply translates an encrypted key from encryption using one key to encryption using another. In this case the KC is acting as a type of *switch*. This process is depicted in Figure 10.3 and runs as follows:

1. Alice generates a data key K, encrypts it using K_{AC} and sends this to KC.

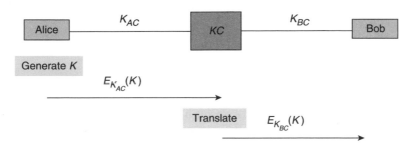

Figure 10.3. Key translation

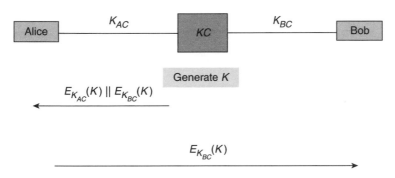

Figure 10.4. Key despatch

2. KC decrypts the encrypted K using K_{AC}, re-encrypts it using K_{BC} and then sends this to Bob.
3. Bob decrypts the encrypted K using K_{BC}.

Key despatch. In this approach the KC generates the data key and produces two encrypted copies of it, one for each user. This process, which we have already encountered in Section 9.4.3, is depicted in Figure 10.4 and runs as follows:

1. KC generates a data key K, encrypts one copy of it using K_{AC} and another copy of it using K_{BC}, and then sends both encrypted copies to Alice.
2. Alice decrypts the first copy using K_{AC} and sends the other copy to Bob.
3. Bob decrypts the second copy using K_{BC}.

The only real difference between these two key distribution approaches is who generates the data key. Both approaches are used in practice.

An alternative way of deploying key hierarchies for networks of many users is to use public-key cryptography and have a master public-key pair. We can think of hybrid encryption (as discussed in Section 5.5.2) as a two-level key hierarchy where the public key plays the role of a master key, which is then used to encrypt data keys. However, it is important to recognise that this approach comes with its own issues and does not do away with the need for a trusted third party of some sort. This now takes the form of a certificate authority, which we discuss in Section 11.1.2.

10.4.2 Unique key per transaction schemes

We now look at a different way of establishing a cryptographic key. *Unique key per transaction* (UKPT) schemes are so called because they establish a new key each time that they are used.

MOTIVATION FOR UKPT SCHEMES

Most of the previous key establishment mechanisms that we have discussed involve one, or both, of the following:

- Use of long-term (top-level) secret keys, for example, the use of master keys or key encrypting keys in key hierarchies.
- A special transfer of data explicitly for the purposes of key establishment. This applies to every technique that we have discussed thus far, except key predistribution.

While these are acceptable features in many environments, they may not be desirable in others. The first requires devices that can securely store and use long-term keys, and the second introduces a communication overhead.

One of the reasons that most of the previous schemes require these features is that the new key that is being established has been generated *independently*, in the sense that it has no relationship with any existing data (including existing keys). An alternative methodology is to generate new keys by deriving them from information already shared by Alice and Bob. We discussed derivation in Section 10.3.2, where the shared information was an existing key known to Alice and Bob. However, importantly, this shared information does not need to be a long-term secret key. Rather it can be a short-term key, other data, or a combination of the two.

If key derivation is used to generate new keys then the processes of key generation and key establishment essentially 'merge'. This brings several advantages:

1. Alice and Bob do not need to store a long-term key;
2. Alice and Bob are not required to engage in any special communication solely for the purpose of key establishment;
3. Key generation and establishment can be 'automated'.

APPLICATION OF UKPT SCHEMES

UKPT schemes adopt the methodology we have just described by updating keys using a key derivation process after each use. A good example of an application of UKPT schemes is retail point-of-sale terminals, which are used by merchants to verify PINs and approve payment card transactions. The advantages of a UKPT scheme all apply to this scenario:

1. Terminals have limited security controls, since they must be cheap enough to deploy widely. In addition, they are typically located in insecure public environments such as stores and restaurants. They are also portable, so that they can easily be moved around, hence easily stolen. (This is what we will refer to as a Zone 1 key storage environment in Section 10.5.3.) It is thus undesirable that they contain important top-level keys.
2. Transactions should be processed speedily to avoid delays, hence efficiency is important.
3. Terminals may be managed and operated by unskilled staff, hence full automation of the key establishment process is a necessity.

EXAMPLE UKPT SCHEMES

Consider a UKPT scheme operating between a merchant *terminal* and a *host* (a bank or card payment server). The terminal maintains a *key register*, which is essentially the running 'key' that will be updated after every transaction. We will describe a generic UKPT scheme in terms of the protocol that is run between the terminal and the host during a transaction. Note:

- We assume at the start of the protocol that the terminal and the host share an initial value that is stored in the terminal key register. This may or may not be a secret value (it might just be a seed designed to initiate the process).
- We will describe a simple protocol that uses a single *transaction key* to compute MACs on the exchanged messages. In reality, such protocols may be slightly more complex since, for example, an encryption key might also be needed to encrypt the PIN of the card.

Figure 10.5 illustrates our generic UKPT scheme:

1. The terminal derives the transaction key using the contents of the key register and shared information that will be available to the host.
2. The terminal sends a *request* message to the host. The transaction key is used to compute a MAC on the request message.
3. The host derives the transaction key (the technique for doing this varies between schemes, as we will shortly illustrate).
4. The host validates the MAC on the request message.
5. The host sends a *response* message to the terminal. The transaction key is used to compute a MAC on the response message.
6. The terminal validates the MAC on the response message.
7. The terminal updates the contents of the key register.

In order to produce a real UKPT scheme from the generic UKPT scheme of Figure 10.5, we need to answer three questions:

1. What is the initial value in the terminal key register?

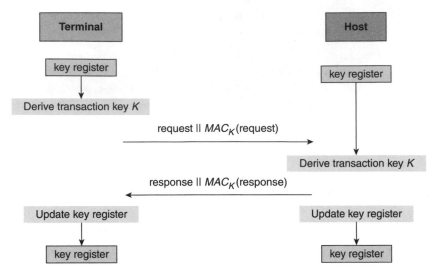

Figure 10.5. Generic UKPT scheme

2. How should the transaction key be derived so that the terminal and host derive the same key?
3. How should the terminal key register be updated so that the terminal and host update to the same value?

There are various ways in which these operations could be conducted in such a way that the terminal and host stay synchronised. Two examples of real UKPT schemes are:

Racal UKPT scheme. This scheme answers the three questions as follows:

1. The initial value is a secret seed, which is agreed between the terminal and the host.
2. The host maintains an identical key register to the terminal. The transaction key is derived from the key register and the card data (more precisely, the primary account number on the card), both of which are known by the terminal and the host.
3. At the end of the protocol, the new key register value is computed as a function of the old key register value, the card data (primary account number) and the transaction data (more precisely, the two *MAC residues* of the MACs on the request and response messages, both of which can be computed by the host and the terminal but neither of which are transmitted during the protocol, see Section 6.3.3). Both the terminal and the host conduct the same computation to update their key registers.

Derived UKPT scheme. This scheme is supported by Visa, amongst others, and answers the three questions as follows:

1. The initial value is a unique initial key that is installed in the terminal.
2. The transaction key is derived by the terminal from the contents of the terminal key register, a transaction counter, and the terminal's unique identifier. The host has a special base (master) key. The host does not need to maintain a key register, but can calculate this same transaction key from the base key, the transaction counter and the terminal identifier.
3. At the end of the protocol the new terminal key register value is derived from the old key register value and the transaction counter. The host does not need to store this value because it can compute transaction keys directly, as just described.

One of the most attractive features of the Racal UKPT scheme is that it has an in-built audit trail. If a transaction is successful then, since it relies on all previous transactions, this also confirms that the previous transactions were successful. A potential problem with the Racal UKPT scheme is synchronisation in the event that a transaction does not complete successfully.

The Derived UKPT scheme has the significant advantage that the host does not need to maintain key registers and can derive transaction keys directly. However, it suffers from the problem that an attacker who compromises a terminal (and thus obtains the value in the key register) will be able to compute future transaction keys for that terminal. In the Racal UKPT scheme such an attacker would also need to capture all the future card data. The Derived UKPT scheme also requires a careful initialisation process, since compromise of the terminal initial key leads to the compromise of all future transactions keys.

The problems with these UKPT schemes can all be addressed through careful management. UKPT schemes are very effective key management systems for addressing the difficulties associated with key establishment in the types of environment for which they are designed.

10.4.3 Quantum key establishment

We close our discussion of key establishment with a few words about a technique that has captured the public attention, but whose applicability remains to be determined.

MOTIVATION FOR QUANTUM KEY ESTABLISHMENT

In Section 3.1.3 we discussed one-time pads and argued that they represented 'ideal' cryptosystems that offered perfect secrecy. However, in Section 3.2.1 we pointed out substantial practical problems with implementing a one-time pad. These were all essentially key management problems, perhaps the most serious being the potential need to establish long, randomly generated symmetric keys at two different locations.

Tantalisingly, if a way could be found of making key establishment 'easy' then perhaps a one-time pad could be used in practice. This is one motivation for *quantum key establishment*, which is an attempt to make the establishment of long, shared, randomly generated symmetric keys 'easy'.

Note that quantum key establishment is often inappropriately described as 'quantum cryptography'. The latter name suggests that it is something to do with new cryptographic algorithms that are suitable for use to protect against quantum computers (see Section 5.4.4). Quantum key establishment is in fact a technique for establishing a conventional symmetric key, which can then be used in any symmetric cryptosystem, including a one-time pad. Of course, it does have some relevance to quantum computers, since a one-time pad still offers perfect secrecy if an attacker is in the fortunate position of having a quantum computer, whereas many modern encryption algorithms would no longer be secure (see Section 5.4.4). Nonetheless, quantum key establishment is only what it claims to be, a technique for key establishment.

THE BASIC IDEA

Quantum key establishment takes place over a *quantum channel*. This is typically instantiated by an optical fibre network or free space. Alice and Bob must have devices capable of sending and receiving information that is encoded as quantum states, often termed *qubits*, which are the quantum equivalent of bits on a conventional communication channel. These qubits are represented by *photons*. In a conventional communication channel, one simple way of establishing a symmetric key is for Alice to generate a key and then send it to Bob. The problem with this approach is that an attacker could be listening in on the communication and thus learn the key. Even worse, neither Alice nor Bob would be aware that this has happened.

The basic idea behind quantum key establishment is to take advantage of the fact that in a quantum channel such an attacker cannot 'listen in' without changing the information in the channel. This is a very useful property, which Alice and Bob can exploit to test whether an attacker has been listening to their communication.

The most well known quantum key establishment protocol is the *BB84 protocol*. While the following conceptual overview of this protocol is simplified and omits important background information, it should provide a flavour of the basic idea. The BB84 protocol involves the following steps:

1. Alice randomly generates a stream of qubits, and sends these as a stream of polarised photons to Bob.
2. Bob measures them using a *polarisation detector*, which will return either a 0 or a 1 for each photon.
3. Bob contacts Alice over a conventional authenticated channel (perhaps a secure email, a telephone call, or a cryptographically authenticated channel), and Alice then provides him with information that probably results in Bob discarding

approximately 50% of the measurements that he has just taken. This is because there are two different types of polarisation detector that Bob can use to measure each photon, and if he chooses the wrong one then the resulting measurement has only a 50% chance of being correct. Alice advises him over the authenticated channel which polarisation detector she used to encode each qubit, and Bob throws away the returns of all the wrongly measured photons.

4. Alice and Bob now conduct a check over the authenticated channel on the stream of bits that they think they have just agreed upon. They do this by randomly choosing some positions and then check to see if they both agree on the bits in these positions. If they find no discrepancies then they throw away the bits that were used to conduct the check, and form a key from the bits that they have not yet checked.

To understand why this protocol works, consider the position of an attacker. This attacker can take measurements of photons on the quantum channel and can listen in to all the discussion on the authenticated channel. However, if the attacker chooses to measure a photon on the quantum channel, and if the attacker uses the wrong detector (which will happen in approximately 50% of the measurements) then this process changes the polarisation, which in turn leads to Bob obtaining an incorrect output bit. Thus such activity will be detected with high probability by Alice and Bob when they do the 'spot check' of agreed bits. Alice and Bob can set this probability to be as high as they like, simply by increasing the number of bits that they check.

QUANTUM KEY ESTABLISHMENT IN PRACTICE

The theory behind quantum key establishment is certainly intriguing. However, the motivation for quantum key establishment is all about overcoming practical problems. Is quantum key establishment, itself, practical?

There are a number of substantial limitations of quantum key establishment. These include:

Distance limitations. Implementations of quantum key establishment are improving all the time. Nonetheless, it has still only been demonstrated to work over limited distances. For example, in 1988 it was shown to work over a 30 cm distance. This had improved by 2010 to around 150 km in an optical fibre network, and several demonstration networks had been built that used quantum key establishment. It is believed that a significant extension of the underlying mechanisms will be required if distances over 400 km are ever to be achieved in optical fibre networks. In contrast, there are no technical limits on the distance over which most conventional key establishment techniques can be used.

Data rates. There are limits to the rate at which key material can be exchanged over the quantum channel. This is also related to the distance over which the key establishment is being conducted.

Cost. Use of quantum key establishment requires expensive hardware devices and suitable quantum channels. Although the associated costs will doubtless reduce over time, most conventional key establishment techniques do not require such special technology.

The need for conventional authentication. Quantum key establishment requires a conventional means of authentication to be used. For example, in the BB84 protocol it is important that Alice and Bob establish an authenticated channel. How will they do this? One way is, of course, to use symmetric cryptography. So how do they establish the key used for authentication? If a conventional key establishment technique is used then the security of the quantum key establishment relies on the security of conventional key establishment. It could be argued that very little has been gained.

However, the biggest issue with quantum key establishment is really *whether it is needed at all*. Most of the other key establishment mechanisms that we have discussed are all very effective when used with strong cryptographic algorithms such as AES to support them. Are the costs of quantum key establishment really justifiable?

It is worth noting, however, that quantum key establishment does permit the continuous establishment of randomly generated keys. Quantum key establishment is probably best considered as a technique that has potential for high-security applications where it is felt that use of a one-time pad is merited. While it does rely on conventional authentication, it could be argued that this is not a big problem since the authenticated channel is only required for a relatively short period of time. In comparison, data protected using the resulting key may be kept secure for a long time. Nonetheless, it would seem unlikely that we will see widespread adoption of quantum key establishment.

10.5 Key storage

Secret keys need to be protected from exposure to parties other than the intended 'owners'. It is thus very important that they are stored securely. In this section we consider how to store keys. We will also discuss how to manage the potential loss or unavailability of keys.

10.5.1 Avoiding key storage

The best solution of all would be not to store cryptographic keys anywhere and just generate them on the fly whenever they are required. This is possible in some applications. Since the same key must be generated on the fly every time we need to use it, we require a deterministic key generator (see Section 8.1.4) to generate the key. Recall from Section 8.1.4 that deterministic generators require a seed, so we will require this seed to be consistently used each time we generate the key. But the seed also needs to be kept secure, so where do we store the seed?

For most applications that use this technique, the seed is stored inside the human brain in the form of a passphrase or strong password. This is precisely the technique adopted by some cryptographic software to protect private keys, which are encrypted using a key encrypting key (see Section 12.7.1) and then stored. The user generates a passphrase, which they are required to remember. The passphrase is then used as a seed for a deterministic generator that generates the key encrypting key on the fly. The key encrypting key is then used to decrypt the encrypted private key. The obvious drawback of this process is that the security of the stored key is now dependent on the security of the seed (passphrase) that is used to generate the key encrypting key. However, this is a pragmatic solution that represents a balance between security and usability that is appropriate for many types of application.

But it is not always possible to avoid storing a key. For example:

- Suppose that a symmetric key is being used to secure communication between Alice and Bob, who are in different locations. In some applications Alice and Bob may be able to locally generate the key precisely when they require it. However, in many other applications the key will need be stored somewhere, at least for a short while (for example, if Alice and Bob are both issued with the key in advance by a mutually trusted third party).
- Many uses of cryptography require long-term access to certain keys. For example, keys used for secure data storage may themselves need to be stored for a long time in order to facilitate future access to the protected data.
- Public-key pairs are expensive to generate. Generating them precisely when they are needed is inefficient. In many cases this is impossible, since the devices on which the private keys reside (for example, a smartcard) may have no user interface. Thus private keys almost always need to be securely stored.

10.5.2 Key storage in software

One option for storing a cryptographic key is to embed the key into software. As mentioned in Section 3.2.4, conducting any part of the cryptographic process in software comes with inherent risks. However, storing keys in software is much cheaper than storing keys in hardware so, as is often the case, the security risks have to be traded off against the cost benefits.

STORING KEYS IN THE CLEAR

By far the cheapest, and the riskiest, approach is to store keys in the clear in software. In other words, regard keys as pieces of data that are stored on a hard drive as unprotected data. Crazy though this sounds, this is often done. One common approach is to try to 'hide' the keys somewhere in the software. This is 'security by obscurity', which is always dangerous since it relies on the hider of the keys being 'smarter' than any attacker. In addition, there are two fundamental problems with hiding cryptographic keys in software:

1. The developer who designs the software will know where the keys are, so there is at least one potential attacker out there who knows where to look for the keys.
2. Assuming that the hidden keys are specific to different versions (users) of the software, an attacker who obtains two versions of the software could compare them. Any locations where differences are noted are potential locations of material relating to a key.

Even if these fundamental problems do not apply to a specific application, the underlying concerns about unprotected keys being stored in software are sufficiently serious that this approach is normally best avoided. Indeed, software storage of keys in the clear is explicitly forbidden by many key management systems and standards.

STORING KEYS USING CRYPTOGRAPHY

Fortunately, we are already very familiar with a technique that can be employed to protect data that resides in software on a computer system. We can encrypt it! While this might seem the obvious thing to do, it has only moved the goalposts, not removed them. In order to encrypt a key, we require a key encrypting key. So where do we store the key encrypting key? If it is a public key, where do we store the corresponding private key?

There are really only four options:

Encrypt it with yet another key. So where do we store that key?

Generate it on the fly. This is a fairly common approach that we discussed in Section 10.5.1 and is often taken for applications where a hardware-based solution is not viable.

Store it in hardware. This is probably the most common approach but, obviously, requires access to a suitable hardware device. The key encrypting key remains on the hardware device, which is also where all encryption and decryption using this key is performed. We discuss hardware storage of keys in Section 10.5.3.

Store it in component form. We introduced the idea of component form in Section 10.3.3. It can also be used for key storage. By using components we make the task of obtaining a key harder since, in order to recover the key, all of the necessary components need to be obtained. However, we have only partially solved the storage problem, since we still have to store the components somewhere. As components are essentially keys themselves, hence not easily memorised, the most common way to store components is on hardware (such as a smart card). Thus component form is really a strengthening of a hardware-based solution, not an alternative.

10.5.3 Key storage in hardware

The safest medium in which to store a cryptographic key is hardware. There are, of course, different types of hardware device, with varying levels of security.

HARDWARE SECURITY MODULES

The securest hardware storage media for cryptographic keys are *hardware security modules* (HSMs). These dedicated hardware devices that provide key management functionality are sometimes known as *tamper-resistant devices*. Many HSMs can also perform bulk cryptographic operations, often at high speed. An HSM can either be peripheral or can be incorporated into a more general purpose device such as a point-of-sale terminal.

While we have chosen to introduce HSMs as mechanisms for the secure storage of cryptographic keys, it is important to appreciate that HSMs are often used to enforce other phases of the key lifecycle.

Keys stored on HSMs are physically protected by the hardware. If anyone attempts to penetrate an HSM, for example, to extract a key from the device, tamper-resistant circuitry is triggered and the key is normally deleted from the HSM's memory. There are various techniques that can be used to provide tamper resistance. These include:

Micro-switches. A simple mechanism that releases a switch if an HSM is opened. This is not particularly effective, since a clever attacker can always drill a hole and use glue to force the switch off.

Electronic mesh. A fine-gauge electronic mesh that can be attached to the inside of an HSM case. This mesh surrounds the sensitive components. If broken, it activates the tamper-detection circuitry. This mechanism is designed to protect against penetrative attacks, such as drilling.

Resin. A hard substance, such as epoxy resin, that can be used to encase sensitive components. Sometimes electronic mesh is also embedded in resin. Any attempt to drill through the resin, or dissolve the resin using chemicals, will generally damage the components and trigger the tamper-detection circuitry.

Temperature detectors. Sensors that are designed to detect variations in temperature outside the normal operating range. Abnormal temperatures may be an indication of an attack. For example, one type of attack involves, literally, freezing the device memory.

Light-sensitive diodes. Sensors that can be used to detect penetration or opening of an HSM casing.

Movement or tilt detectors. Sensors that can detect if somebody is trying to physically remove an HSM. One approach is to use mercury tilt switches, which interrupt the flow of electrical current if the physical alignment of an HSM changes.

Voltage or current detectors. Sensors that can detect variations in voltage or current outside the normal operating range. Such anomalies may be indication of an attack.

Security chips. Special secure microprocessors that can be used for cryptographic processing within an HSM. Even if an attacker has penetrated all the other defences of an HSM, the keys may still remain protected inside the security chip.

Different HSMs may use different combinations of these techniques to build up a layered defence against attacks. An HSM is also typically backed up by a battery, so that it cannot be attacked simply by switching off the power supply.

KEY STORAGE ON AN HSM

There is at least one key, often referred to as a *local master key* (LMK), that resides inside the HSM at all times. Some HSMs may store many LMKs, each having its own specific use. Any other keys that need to be stored can either be:

1. stored inside the HSM;
2. stored outside the HSM, encrypted using an LMK.

In the latter case, when a key stored outside the HSM needs to be used, it is first submitted to the HSM, where it is recovered using the LMK and then used.

This approach places a great deal of reliance on the LMK. It is thus extremely important to back up the LMK (see Section 10.5.5) in order to mitigate against loss of the LMK. Such loss can occur if the HSM fails, or if it is attacked, since the tamper-resistance controls are likely to delete the HSM memory. Indeed this applies to any keys that are only stored inside the HSM. Thus we can see that the issue of whether to store a key inside or outside the HSM involves a tradeoff between:

Efficiency – storing keys inside the HSM is more efficient in terms of processing speed since they do not need to be imported and then recovered before use.

Need for backups – since every key only stored inside the HSM needs to be securely backed up, perhaps in component form.

OTHER TYPES OF HARDWARE

While HSMs are the securest hardware devices on which to store keys, there are numerous other hardware devices offering less security. Some of these devices might include some of the tamper-resistance measures that we outlined for HSMs, while others may just rely on the hardware itself to provide some resistance to attack.

One class of hardware devices are smart tokens, including smart cards, which we first discussed in Section 8.3.3. Smart tokens are designed to be portable and cheap, so the security measures deployed to protect them are limited. Thus while smart tokens are normally appropriate media for storing keys specific to a user, for example, the type of token used in Section 8.5 for generating dynamic passwords, they are typically not secure enough to store cryptographic keys that are critical for an entire system, such as a system master key.

COMMUNICATING WITH HARDWARE

The use of hardware is a good means of protecting stored keys, however, it relies on a secure interface between the processes outside the hardware and the processes inside the hardware. For example, without a secure interface it might be possible for an unauthorised party to take an encrypted key from a database outside the hardware and 'persuade' the hardware to decrypt and then use this key on their behalf to reveal the result of a cryptographic computation. The problem is that the hardware responds to external calls, which can come from any number of different applications. Most hardware requires an *Application Programming Interface* (API) that contains a large number of different commands such as generate key, verify PIN, validate MAC, etc. It is therefore possible that an attacker could utilise these commands.

The security of this interface relies on access control to applications and devices, which in turn is related to the security of the hardware computing platform and the physical security surrounding it. Thus HSMs for important applications such as banking systems are always located in tightly controlled environments, both logically and physically.

In order to exploit weaknesses in an API, an attacker needs to write an application and have communication access to the hardware. Such an attacker would probably need to be a 'privileged' insider. Nonetheless, some proof-of-concept attacks have been publicised against the APIs of commercial HSMs. We will give an example of an API attack in Section 10.6.1.

EVALUATING HARDWARE

Since hardware is often used for critical components of a key management system, it is essential to have high confidence that it is sufficiently secure to fulfill its role. Obviously, it is not in a security hardware vendor's interests to produce insecure products, so they normally maintain high levels of vigilance regarding the security of their products. They also spend a lot of time reviewing and analysing the associated APIs. There are several organisations that carry out independent evaluations of the physical protection offered by hardware, particularly HSMs. There are also standards for HSM security, the most important of which is FIPS 140, against which most HSMs are evaluated.

10.5.4 Key storage risk factors

The risks to key storage media depend not only on the devices on which keys are stored, but also on the environments within which the devices reside. This relationship is indicated in Figure 10.6, which identifies four zones based on different environmental and device controls.

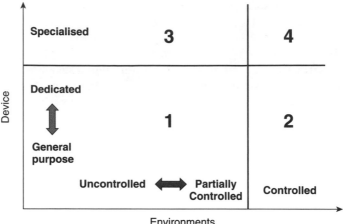

Figure 10.6. Key storage risk zones

The two dimensions depicted in Figure 10.6 represent:

Environments, which range from

Uncontrolled: public environments such as shops and restaurants, where it is not possible to implement strict access control mechanisms;

Partially controlled: environments such as general offices and homes, where it is possible to implement basic access control mechanisms (for example, a physical door key);

Controlled: environments such as high-security offices and military installations, where it is possible to implement strong access control mechanisms (for example, biometric swipe cards).

Devices, which range from

General purpose: general devices running conventional operating systems with their default in-built security controls (for example, a laptop);

Dedicated: dedicated devices that offer some specialist security controls, such as limited tamper resistance (for example, a point-of-sale terminal or a mobile phone);

Specialised: specialised devices whose main functionality is to provide security (for example, an HSM).

The four zones identified in Figure 10.6 are mainly conceptual, but illustrate the importance of both dimensions.

Zone 1. This is the lowest security zone and thus offers the highest risk. However, for many applications this may provide sufficient security. For example, a key stored in encrypted form on the hard disk of a home PC may well be good enough for protection of the user's personal files. Likewise, any keys stored under the limited protection of a portable point-of-sale terminal are probably still secure from anything other than attacks from experts.

Zone 2. The security offered by Zone 1 devices is increased substantially when they are moved into a controlled environment. In the extreme, a key stored in the clear in software on a general PC provides excellent security if the PC is not networked and is kept in a physically secure room with an armed guard at the door! More realistically, encrypted keys stored on PCs that are located in an office with strong physical security (such as smart card access control to the rooms) and good network security controls should have better protection than those on a PC located in a public library or an internet cafe.

Zone 3. Specialised devices sometimes have to be located in insecure environments because of the nature of their application. A good example is provided by Automated Teller Machines (ATMs), which need to be 'customer facing'. Such devices are thus exposed to a range of potentially serious attacks that are made possible by their environment, such as an attacker attempting to physically remove them with the intention of extracting keys back in a laboratory.

Zone 4. The highest-security zone is provided when a specialist device is kept in a controlled environment. This is not just the most secure, but the most expensive zone within which to provide solutions. This level of security is nonetheless appropriate for important keys relating to high-security applications such as data processing centres, financial institutions, and certification authorities.

Note that this conceptual 'model' could easily be extended. For example, we have not considered the different ways in which keys stored on the devices are activated (see Section 10.6.3).

10.5.5 Key backup, archival and recovery

We have spent most of our discussion about cryptography assuming that the use of cryptography brings security benefits. However, there are situations where use of cryptography can potentially have damaging consequences. One such situation arises if a cryptographic key becomes 'lost'. For example:

1. data stored in encrypted form will itself be lost if the corresponding decryption key is lost, since nobody can recover the data from the ciphertext;
2. a digital signature on a message becomes ineffective if the corresponding verification key is lost, since nobody has the ability to verify it.

The first scenario illustrates the potential need for *key backup* of critical secret keys. The second scenario more broadly illustrates the potential need for *key archival*, which is the long-term storage of keys beyond the time of their expiry.

Note that because key archival tends to apply to keys after they have expired, it appears in the key lifecycle of Figure 10.1 as a process occurring after key usage. However, we have included it in this section as it is closely related to key backup.

KEY BACKUP

It can be surprisingly easy to 'lose' critical cryptographic keys. As we discussed in Section 10.5.3, important keys are often stored on HSMs. An obvious attack against a Zone 3 (see Figure 10.6) HSM would be to physically attack the HSM to the point that one of its tamper-resistant triggers is activated and the device wipes its memory. The attacker does not learn the keys stored on the device but, without a backup, the potential impact on the organisation relying on the HSM is high. Even Zone 4 HSMs are subject to risks such as a careless cleaner bumping into a device and accidentally wiping its memory.

As noted at the start of this chapter, cryptographic keys are just pieces of data, so the backup of keys is not technically any more difficult than the backup of more general data. An obvious, but important, point is that the security of a key backup process must be as strong as the security of the key itself. For example, it would be unwise to back up an AES key by encrypting it using a DES key. The backed-up key will need to be stored on media that is subject to at least the same level of device and environmental security controls as the key itself. Indeed for the highest levels of key, the use of component form might be the only appropriate method for key backup.

KEY ARCHIVAL

Key archival is essentially a special type of backup, which is necessary in situations where cryptographic keys may still be required in the period between their expiry and their destruction. Such keys will no longer be 'live' and so cannot be used for any new cryptographic computations, but they may still be required. For example:

- There may be a legal requirement to keep data for a certain period of time. If that data is stored in encrypted form then there will be a legal requirement to keep the keys so that the data can be recovered. As an illustration, the London Stock Exchange requires keys to be archived for seven years.
- A document that has been digitally signed, such as a contract, may require the capability for that digital signature to be verified well beyond the period of expiry of the key that was used to sign it. Hence it may be necessary to archive the corresponding verification key to accommodate future requests. For example, Belgian legislation requires verification keys used for electronic signatures in online banking applications to be archived for five years (see also Section 12.6.5).

Managing the storage of archived keys is just as critical as for key backups. Once a key no longer needs to be archived, it should be destroyed.

KEY RECOVERY

Key recovery is the key management process where a key is recovered from a backup or an archive. Technically this is no harder than retrieving a key from any other type of storage, so the challenges all relate to the management processes that surround key recovery. Clearly it should not be possible to recover a key unless the recovery is suitably authorised.

Note that the term 'key recovery' is also associated with initiatives to force a 'mandatory' backup, also referred to as *key escrow*. The idea behind key escrow is that if any data is encrypted then a copy of the decryption key is stored (escrowed) by a trusted third party in such a way that, should it be necessary and the appropriate legal authority obtained, the decryption key can be obtained and used to recover the data. Such a situation might arise if the encrypted data is uncovered in the course of a criminal investigation. Many suggested key escrow mechanisms employed component form storage of escrowed keys in an attempt to reassure potential users of their security.

The idea of key escrow is fraught with problems, not the least being how to 'force' all users to use a cryptosystem that has an in-built key escrow facility. When routine key escrow was proposed in the early 1990s by the governments of a number of countries, including the UK and the US, business community concerns were sufficiently high that it was not pursued. Nonetheless, the ensuing debate about key escrow did help to raise the profile of the genuine need for key backup and key recovery in many cryptographic applications.

10.6 Key usage

Having considered the generation, establishment and storage of cryptographic keys, we now continue our study of the key lifecycle by looking at issues relating to key usage. The most important of these is key separation. We will also discuss the mechanics of key change, key activation and key destruction.

10.6.1 Key separation

The *principle of key separation* is that *cryptographic keys must only be used for their intended purpose*. In this section we consider why key separation is a good idea and discuss options for enforcing it.

THE NEED FOR KEY SEPARATION

The problems that can arise if key separation is not enforced can be serious. In many applications the need for key separation may be quite obvious. For example, it may be the case that encryption and entity authentication are conducted by distinct processes, each with their own particular requirements regarding key lengths. We will see an example of this in Section 12.2 when we look at WLAN security, where the process for encryption is 'locked down' across all applications, but the entity authentication process can be tailored to a specific application environment.

However, in other applications it may be tempting to use a key that has already been established for one purpose and then, for convenience, use it for some other purpose. We illustrate the potential dangers of doing this with two examples.

Example 1. Like passwords, PINs should not be stored anywhere in the clear. Hence PINs are often stored in encrypted form using a symmetric *PIN encrypting key*. This key should only ever be used to encrypt PINs. It should never be used to decrypt an encrypted PIN. In contrast, a normal symmetric data key is used both for encryption and decryption. If these two keys are somehow interchanged within an HSM then we have two serious problems. Firstly, it may become possible to decrypt and reveal a PIN. Secondly, it may not be possible to recover any normal data encrypted with the PIN encrypting key.

Example 2. Suppose we have an HSM with the following two security functions:

Function 1. This generates a four-digit PIN for a payment card by:

1. encrypting the card's 16-digit account number using a *PIN generation key*, and outputting the resulting ciphertext in hex form;
2. scanning the hex output for the first four digits in the range 0 to 9, but ignoring any in the range A to F, which are then used to form the PIN (additional measures need to be taken in the unlikely event that there are insufficient digits generated using this process to form a PIN);
3. outputting the resulting PIN in encrypted form.

Function 2. This generates a MAC on some input data by:

1. computing a simple CBC-MAC (using the version of CBC-MAC depicted in Figure 6.7, which is not recommended in practice) on the input data using a MAC key;
2. outputting the MAC in hex form.

Now suppose that an attacker is able to persuade the HSM to use the key from Function 1 to compute Function 2. In other words, the attacker is able to generate a MAC on the card's account number using the PIN generation key. The result will be that a MAC is output in hex form. Assuming that the same block cipher is used by both functions (in Function 1 to encrypt and in Function 2 to compute CBC-MAC) and since the account number is likely to be a short piece of data less than one block long, the MAC that is output will be the same as the encrypted account number that is produced in the first stage of Function 1. The attacker can then scan the MAC for the first four digits in the range 0 to 9, and hence determine the PIN.

These two examples both illustrate the potential dangers of not enforcing key separation. It might be argued that they are rather artificial examples for several reasons, one of which is that it should not be possible to force keys within an HSM to be used for purposes other than they were intended, especially as the keys

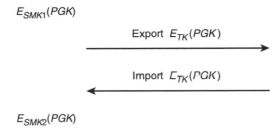

Figure 10.7. Key masquerade attack

involved will never appear in the clear outside the HSM. We now show how this could, at least in theory, happen.

As we will discuss shortly, one method of enforcing key separation in an HSM is to store keys in the HSM encrypted under a master key that is specific to one usage purpose. In this way, access to the key is directly linked to the use of a master key that identifies the key usage purpose. However, many HSMs have *export* and *import* functions that allow keys to be transferred between different HSMs. Keys are encrypted using a *transport key* during export and import. Figure 10.7 shows how this facility could, potentially, be used to change the apparent usage purpose of a key.

1. A PIN generation key *PGK* is stored on the HSM, encrypted by a *storage master key SMK*1, which is the local key on the HSM that is used to store PIN generation keys.
2. The HSM is instructed to export *PGK*. It thus decrypts the encrypted *PGK* using *SMK*1, then re-encrypts *PGK* using the transport key *TK*. This is then exported.
3. The HSM is then instructed by the attacker to import a new MAC key. The attacker submits *PGK*, encrypted under *TK*.
4. The HSM decrypts the encrypted *PGK* using *TK*, then re-encrypts it using storage master key *SMK*2, which is the HSM key used to store MAC keys. The HSM thus now regards *PGK* as a MAC key.

This attack will not be possible if different variants of transport key are used for separate export and import functions. However, due to interoperability issues between different vendors' solutions, transport key variants might not be permitted.

The above difficulties all arise through security weaknesses in the interface between the device on which the keys are stored and the outside world, which we already observed in Section 10.5.3 was an aspect of key management that can be problematic.

ENFORCING KEY SEPARATION

In order to avoid some of the problems that we have just illustrated, mechanisms are required to enforce key separation. This can be regarded as part of the wider provision of assurance of purpose of keys, which we discussed in Section 10.1.3. Keys are often unstructured bit strings, so there is no obvious way of distinguishing the purpose of a key from its basic form. There are two main techniques that can be used to enable the purpose of a key to be distinguished:

Encrypting a key using a specified variant key. This is a hardware-enforced method that we previously mentioned, which involves using specific higher-level keys to encrypt keys for particular purposes. For example, in Figure 10.7 the HSM used the key *SMK*1 to encrypt PIN generation keys, and key *SMK*2 to encrypt MAC keys. The HSM can interpret the usage based on the key encrypting key variant used. This technique can be applied to keys being distributed, as well as keys being stored. This method can be used to enforce any type of key separation (for example, the separation of the different MAC keys required to support the example in Section 7.2.3).

Embedding the key in a larger data block. This involves embedding the key into a larger data object that also includes a statement on the key usage. Three examples of this are:

Employing redundancy. As discussed in Section 4.4, a DES key has an effective length of 56 bits, but is usually a 64-bit value. Thus, there are 8 'spare' bits that can be used for other purposes. The original DES standard recommends that the spare bits be used to provide error detection in the event that a DES key becomes corrupted. Since the standard did not mandate this approach, the idea of *key tagging* was introduced. This allows the eight spare bits to define the key usage. When a key is presented in a command to an HSM, the tagging bits are checked by the HSM to ensure that the key is a valid key for the command that it is being used for.

Key blocks. This is a formatted data string that allows a key to be represented along with other data relating to the key. One example is the *ANSI TR-31* key block, which is depicted in Figure 10.8 and has the following fields:

- the *header* includes information that clarifies the purpose of the key;
- the *optional header* includes optional data such as the expiry date of the key;
- the *key* is encrypted using a suitable key encrypting key;
- the *authenticator* is a MAC on the rest of the key block, which provides data origin authentication (data integrity) of the key block data.

Public-key certificates. These are types of key block used to provide assurance of purpose for public keys. A public-key certificate often includes a field that

header (clear)	optional header (clear)	key (encrypted)	authenticator (MAC)

Figure 10.8. ANSI TR-31 key block

defines the key usage. We will discuss public-key certificates in more detail in Section 11.1.2.

It is important to realise that while distinguishing the purpose of a cryptographic key is helpful, it does not *enforce* key separation. Enforcement of key separation also requires procedural controls, which we discuss in Section 10.7.

KEY SEPARATION IN PRACTICE

At an intuitive level, the principle of key separation makes sense. Clearly, in an ideal world, having separate keys for separate purposes keeps things simple. However, the principle of key separation is precisely what it claims to be, namely, a 'principle'. Enforcing it does not come without potential costs. For example, enforcing it may mean that a key management system has more keys to manage than it would have if the principle is not enforced. It thus may be tempting to use keys for more than one purpose, just to reduce the number of keys that have to be managed. Of course, if we decide to use a particular symmetric key for both encryption and computing MACs then we could argue that the principle of key separation is still enforced since the 'purpose' of the key is both encryption and computing MACs! At least *thinking* about the principle of key separation has made us recognise these different uses of the key.

One example of a pragmatic compromise between the principle of key separation and practical issues is key derivation, which we discussed in Section 10.3.2. In this case a single *derivation key* might be stored and then used to derive separate encryption and MAC keys. Technically the same key is being used twice, since derivation is by means of a publicly known process, so the encryption and MAC keys are not as 'different' as we would like in the ideal world. Pragmatically, we are enforcing the principle of key separation by having two keys for the two different cryptographic operations.

The examples in this section have illustrated the dangers of not following the principle. The degree to which the principle of key separation is adhered to in a real application naturally depends on the specific priorities of the application environment. We will comment on key separation issues when we examine applications in Chapter 12.

10.6.2 Key change

Most key management systems require the ability to change keys.

THE NEED FOR KEY CHANGE

The need for a change of key tends to arise in two different types of circumstance:

Planned key changes. These will most likely occur at regular intervals. One reason for a planned key change might be the end of the key lifetime (see Section 10.2.1). Another reason might simply be to regularly practice key change procedures in preparation for an unplanned key change (the equivalent of a 'fire drill'). In some organisations this is the most common planned change, since their key lifetimes are very long.

Unplanned key changes. These may occur for a variety of reasons. Indeed, many of the reasons that we gave in Section 10.2.1 for having finite key lifetimes were to mitigate against unplanned events. An unplanned key change may thus be required if these unplanned events actually occur. For example:

- a key is compromised;
- a security vulnerability becomes apparent with the potential to lead to key compromise (such as an operating system vulnerability, a breakthrough in cryptanalysis, or a failure of a tamper-resistance mechanism in an HSM);
- an employee unexpectedly leaves an organisation.

Note that in some of these cases it may simply be enough to *withdraw* a key (remove it from active use), rather than change it. However, care must be taken before making this type of decision. For example, when an employee unexpectedly leaves an organisation on good terms then it may suffice to withdraw any personal keys that they held, such as any symmetric keys shared only by the employee and a central system, or any public-key pairs relating only to the employee. However, the employee might also have held *group keys* that are shared by several members of staff. It would be advisable to change these keys, since they are likely to remain in use after the employee's departure.

IMPACT OF KEY CHANGE

Key change can be a very expensive process, depending on the importance of the key being changed. An unplanned key change is particularly problematic, especially in the event of a key compromise, since it raises questions about any cryptographic operations that were conducted using the affected key, such as the confidentiality of any encrypted data. One likely consequence is that it will probably be necessary to also change any other keys encrypted using the affected key, which in turn raises questions about any cryptographic operations conducted using them.

The minimum impact of a key change is that a new key needs to be generated and established. However, the impact can be severe, especially in the case of high-level key compromise. For example, if a master key is compromised in a financial system then the resulting costs might include costs of investigation into the compromise, costs related to any 'rogue' transactions conducted using compromised keys, damage to reputation and loss of customer confidence. Recovery from unplanned key changes should be part of an organisation's wider disaster recovery and business continuity processes.

One situation where the damage caused by a key compromise might be limited is when the time of a cryptographic operation is logged and the time of key compromise is known. For example, in the case of a signature key being compromised, it might only be necessary to deem all signatures generated using the key after the time of compromise to be invalid.

MECHANISMS FOR CHANGING KEYS

As mentioned above, key change requires:

- generation and establishment of a new key;
- withdrawing the old key (and potentially destroying or archiving it).

Any of the mechanisms for these operations discussed elsewhere in this chapter could, in theory, be used to conduct these processes. Ideally, planned key changes should happen automatically and require very little intervention. For example, we saw in Section 10.4.2 that UKPT schemes automate planned key changes after every transaction. More intervention may be required in the case of unplanned key changes.

Obviously, high-level key changes are more complex to manage. For example, if a storage master key in an HSM goes through a planned change then all keys encrypted under the old storage master key will need to be decrypted, and then re encrypted using the new storage master key. In this case, since the storage master key has not been compromised, there is no need to change all the keys that were encrypted using it.

Note that key changes are not always easy to facilitate. Indeed, the *migration* process from one key to another can be particularly challenging and, where possible, needs to be carefully planned for in order to make the transition as smooth as possible.

CHANGING PUBLIC-KEY PAIRS

It is perhaps slightly surprising that key change is, in general, simpler to perform for symmetric keys. This is 'surprising' because key change forces a new key establishment operation, which is usually a more difficult process for symmetric keys. There are two reasons why changing public-key pairs is normally more challenging:

Knowledge of public keys. Since symmetric keys need to be carefully 'positioned' in a network so that entities relying on them have the right keys, a key management system tends to be fully 'in control' of where its symmetric keys are located. This, at least in theory, makes withdrawing a symmetric key straightforward. In contrast, the 'public' nature of a public key means that a key management system may have little control over which entities have knowledge of a public key. Indeed, in open environments such as the Internet, a public key could be known by anyone.

Open application environments. Symmetric cryptography tends to be employed in closed environments. Thus any key management system handling symmetric keys should have mechanisms and controls in place for key establishment that can be reused for key change. In contrast, public-key cryptography tends to be used in open environments where this may be more challenging.

Since private and public keys are interdependent, any requirement to change one of them requires the other also to be changed. Changing a private key is arguably simpler than changing a symmetric key. However, changing public keys requires special mechanisms, which we will discuss in Section 11.2.3.

10.6.3 Key activation

When assessing the security of any key management system, it is important to pay attention to the processes by which keys are *activated*, by which we mean that their use is 'authorised'. We observed in Section 8.3.3 that one problem with using identity information based on a cryptographic key for entity authentication can be that the effective security is not as strong as expected. This problem arose because in the scenario under discussion the key was activated by a less-secure mechanism, such as a password.

This potential problem applies more widely than just to entity authentication. Indeed, in any use of cryptography we have to instruct the device performing the cryptographic computation to select a particular key for use. If this all takes place within the confines of an HSM then we may have little to be concerned about. However, in many applications key activation requires human interaction.

As an example, consider a signature key stored on a computer for digitally signing emails. If RSA is being used then this signature key might, reasonably, be up to 2048 bits long, which is clearly a value that the human owner of the key will not be capable of memorising. When the user decides to digitally sign an email, the user needs to instruct the email client to activate their signature key. Several scenarios may now apply, depending on how the key is stored (if at all) on the computer. These include:

Key stored on the computer in the clear. In this case the user might activate the key simply by entering an instruction, perhaps selecting the key from a list of potential keys stored on the computer. Key activation is thus possible for anyone with access to the computer. In this case the effective security of the keys is simply linked to the security required to access the computer itself, which perhaps just requires a valid username and password.

Key stored on the computer in encrypted form. The user might activate the key in this case by being prompted to provide some secret identity information, such as a passphrase. This passphrase would then be used to generate the key that can be used to recover the signature key. In this case the effective security is linked to the security of the passphrase.

Key generated on the fly. In this case the key is not stored on the computer, but is generated on the fly. The activation of the key is thus linked to the generation of the key. Again, one way of implementing this is to request some identity information such as a passphrase from the user. Thus the effective security of the key is again determined by the security of this passphrase.

Key stored off the computer. Another option is that the key is stored on a peripheral device. The key activation takes place when the user connects the device to the computer. In this case the effective security is linked to the security of the peripheral device. This process may also require a passphrase to be used.

The above scenarios are just examples, but what they all illustrate is that, even though a 2048-bit key is being used to secure the application, the key activation process plays a vital role in determining the effective security that is in place. In particular, the 2048-bit key might be activated by an attacker through:

- compromise of a security mechanism used to activate the key (such as a passphrase);
- access to a device on which the key is stored.

10.6.4 Key destruction

When a key is no longer required for any purpose then it must be destroyed in a secure manner. The point at which key destruction is required may either be:

1. when the key expires (the natural end of the key's lifetime);
2. when the key is withdrawn (before its expiry, in the event of unplanned events such as those discussed in Section 10.6.2);
3. at the end of a required period of key archival.

Since keys are a special type of data, the mechanisms available for destroying keys are precisely those for destroying general data. Since keys are sensitive data, secure mechanisms must be used. Suitable techniques are sometimes referred to as *data erasure* or *data sanitisation* mechanisms.

It goes without saying that simply deleting a key from a device is not sufficient if the key is to be truly destroyed. Not only does this not destroy the key, but operating systems may well have other (temporary) copies of the key in different locations. Even if the key was stored on the device in encrypted form, this may be useful to a determined attacker. Many secure data destruction mechanisms involve repeatedly overwriting the memory containing the key with randomly generated data. The number of overwrites is normally configurable. It should also be noted that any other media storing information about keys, such as paper, should also be destroyed. Relevant standards provide guidance on how to do this.

10.7 Governing key management

We have repeatedly stressed in this chapter that key management is the main interface between the technology of cryptography and the users and systems that rely on it. To this extent, key management is a small, but important, part of the wider management of the security of an information system.

For a private user managing keys on their own machine, key management may simply involve the selection of appropriate techniques for conducting each of the relevant phases of the key lifecycle. However, key management is a much more complex process for an organisation, due to the diversity of processes that affect key management, which we outlined in Section 10.1.1.

Key management within an organisation thus needs to be governed by rules and processes. In this section we will briefly discuss some of the issues involved in governing key management effectively within an organisation.

10.7.1 Key management policies, practices and procedures

Within an organisation, the most common way to govern key management is through the specification of:

Key management policies. These define the overall requirements and strategy for providing key management. For example, a policy might be that all cryptographic keys are stored only in hardware.

Key management practices. These define the tactics that will be used in order to achieve the key management policy goals. For example, that all devices using cryptography will have an in-built HSM.

Key management procedures. These document the step-by-step tasks necessary in order to implement the key management practices. For example, the specification of a key establishment protocol that will be used between two devices.

Clearly, different organisations will have different approaches to the formulation of key management policies, practices and procedures, but the important outcome of this process should be that key management governance is:

By design: in other words, that the entire key management lifecycle has been planned from the outset, and not made up in response to events as they occur.

Coherent: the various phases of the key lifecycle are considered as linked component parts of a larger unified process and designed with this 'big picture' in mind.

Integrated: the phases of the key management lifecycle are integrated with the wider requirements and priorities of the organisation.

For commercial organisations, it may also make sense to publicise key management policies and practices, since this can be used as a mechanism for increasing confidence in their security practices. This is particularly relevant for organisations providing cryptographic services, such as Certificate Authorities (see Section 11.2.3).

The formulation of key management policies, practices and procedures also facilitates the auditing of key management, which is part of the wider process of auditing security. This is because not only can the policies, practices and procedures themselves be scrutinised, but the effectiveness of their implementation can then be tested.

10.7.2 Example procedure: key generation ceremony

We illustrate the potential complexities of key management governance by giving an example of an important type of key management procedure that might be required by a large organisation. This is that of a *key ceremony*, which can be used to implement key generation from components (as discussed in Section 10.3.3). Note that the key in question could be a top-level (master) symmetric key or top-level (root) private key, which needs to be installed into an HSM. The key might be:

- a new key being freshly generated;
- an existing key being re-established (from backed-up stored components).

The participants are:

Operation manager: responsible for the physical aspects, including the venue, hardware, software and any media on which components are stored or transported;

Key manager: responsible for making sure that the key ceremony is performed in accordance with the relevant key management policies, practices and procedures;

Key custodians: the parties physically in possession of the key components, responsible for handling them appropriately and following the key ceremony as instructed;

Witnesses: responsible for observing the key ceremony and providing independent assurance that all other parties perform their roles in line with the appropriate policies, practices and procedures (this might involve recording the key ceremony).

The key ceremony itself involves several phases:

Initialisation. The operation manager installs and configures the required hardware and software, including the HSM, within a controlled environment. This process might need to be recorded by witnesses.

Component retrieval. The components required for the key ceremony, held by the relevant key custodians, are transported to the key ceremony location. These key custodians may be from different organisations (departments) and may not be aware of each others' identities.

Key generation/establishment. The key is installed onto the HSM under the guidance of the key manager. This process will involve the various key custodians taking part in the key ceremony, but not necessarily simultaneously (for example, it may be required that the key custodians never meet). Throughout the key ceremony, the witnesses record the events and any deviations from the defined procedure are noted. At the end, an official record is presented to the key manager.

Validation. If necessary, following the completion of the key ceremony, the official record can be scrutinised to validate that the correct procedure was followed (perhaps as part of an audit).

This proposed key ceremony is meant only as an illustration, and precise details of key ceremonies will depend on local requirements. The point, however, is to demonstrate the importance of key management policies, practices and procedures. Regardless of the underlying cryptographic technology and hardware, the security of the key ceremony itself is down to an orchestrated sequence of actions by human beings, which can only be controlled by procedures of this type.

10.8 Summary

In this chapter we have discussed key management, the aspect of cryptography that is of greatest relevance to users of cryptography, since it is the part most likely to require decision making and process design in individual application environments. We have observed that key management is always necessary, but never easy. In particular, we have:

- Stressed the importance of keeping in mind the entire cryptographic key lifecycle, from key generation through to key destruction.
- Examined the various phases of the cryptographic key lifecycle in detail.
- Noted that key management must ultimately be governed by policies, practices and procedures.

This chapter dealt with management of keys that need to be kept secret. In the next chapter we examine further issues that arise when managing key pairs for use in public-key cryptography.

10.9 Further reading

Despite the importance of key management, it is often a topic that is overlooked in introductions to cryptography and there are few dedicated and comprehensive overviews of the topic. Probably the best overall treatment is NIST's recommendations for key management, published as NIST 800-57 [139]. The first part of this special publication provides a thorough grounding in key management and the second part includes advice on key management governance. NIST 800-130 [142] deals with the design of key management systems. The first part of ISO/IEC 11770 [4] presents a general overview and basic model for key management. Another relevant standard is ISO 11568 [3], which covers key management in the important application area of retail banking, as does the influential standard ANSI X9.24 [26]. Dent and Mitchell [55] provide a good overview of the contents of most of these key management standards.

The best place for advice on key lengths is the web portal managed by Giry [89]. We used the 2010 key length recommendations from the European project ECRYPT II [66] in Table 10.1, which is one of the resources linked to by [89]. NIST provide guidance on key derivation in NIST 800-108 [141] and on key derivation from passwords in NIST 800-132 [143], as does PKCS#5 [115]. Key generation by components is conducted using simple secret sharing schemes, a good introduction to which can be found in Stinson [185]. Unique key per transaction schemes are popular in the retail world and are described in banking standards. The Racal UKPT scheme has been standardised in UKPA Standard 70 [193] and the Derived UKPT scheme can be found in ANSI X9.24 [26].

We provided several references to key establishment mechanisms in Chapter 9, including Boyd and Mathuria [40] and ISO/IEC 11770 [4]. The BB84 protocol was first proposed by Bennett and Brassard [31], with an accessible description of it provided in Singh [176]. Scientific American ran a story on quantum key establishment by Stix [186]. There is quite a lot of misinformation around on the usefulness and likely impact of quantum key establishment. We recommend the practical analysis of Moses [126] and Paterson, Piper and Schack [152] as providing interesting perspectives.

Hardware security modules are fundamental components of many key management systems. One of the most influential standards in this area is FIPS 140-2 [79]. HSMs are also treated in the banking standards ISO 11568 [3] and ISO 13491 [5]. Attridge [27] provides a brief introduction to HSMs and their role in cryptographic key management. The zones of risk for key storage depicted in Figure 10.6 are based on ISO 13491 [5]. Ferguson, Schneier and Kohno [75] include a chapter on key storage, and Kenan [107] discusses key storage in the context of cryptographically protected databases. Bond [38] describes fascinating attacks on HSMs that had achieved a high level of FIPS 140 compliance. Dent and Mitchell [55] include a chapter on cryptography APIs.

The key block that we described in Figure 10.8 is from ANSI X9 TR-31 [25]. NIST has a special publication NIST 800-88 [137] relating to data deletion (sanitisation). Finally, the key generation ceremony that we described is loosely based on the ceremony described in [112].

10.10 Activities

1. Provide some examples of attacks that can be conducted if assurance of purpose of cryptographic keys is not provided as part of:

   (a) a fully symmetric hierarchical key management system deployed in a government department;

   (b) an open key management system supporting public–key (hybrid) cryptog-raphy to provide email security.

2. Guidance on key lengths changes over time.

   (a) Name two reputable sources for key length recommendations (other than the ECRYPT recommendations of Table 10.1) and explain why they are credible sources.

   (b) To what extent do their recommendations for symmetric key lengths 'match' the recommendations shown in Table 10.1?

   (c) Given a public–key cryptosystem, explain how experts might determine which key length for this algorithm is 'equivalent' to a symmetric key length of 128 bits.

3. Which of the following keys do you think should be the longest:

- a key protecting the PIN of a credit card in a point-of-sale terminal;
- a transaction (session) key protecting a large money transfer between two banks?

4. For each of the following, give an example (with justification) of an application of cryptography where it might make sense to deploy:

   (a) a flat key hierarchy with just one level;

   (b) a two-level key hierarchy;

   (c) a three-level key hierarchy.

5. UKPT schemes offer support for key management in special application environments.

   (a) Which of the phases of the key management lifecycle shown in Figure 10.1 is a UKPT scheme designed to make more straightforward?

   (b) Compare the impacts on the Racal and Derived UKPT schemes in the event that an attacker compromises a point-of-sale terminal and is able to access any keys stored in the terminal.

   (c) Compare the impacts on the Racal and Derived UKPT schemes if there is a communication error in the middle of a transaction.

   (d) Suggest some key management controls that are designed to overcome the 'weaknesses' of these two UKPT schemes.

6. Quantum key establishment technology is at a relatively early stage of maturity. Explore the 'state of the art' in quantum key establishment by finding out:

   (a) What is the longest distance over which a symmetric key has been established using quantum key establishment?

   (b) What are the best current data rates?

   (c) Which commercial organisations are selling quantum key establishment technology?

   (d) Which applications are deploying quantum key establishment technology?

7. Hardware security modules (HSMs) are commonly used to store cryptographic keys.

    (a) What benchmarks are used for evaluating the security of an HSM?
    (b) Which organisations carry out such evaluations?
    (c) Provide an example of a currently available commercial HSM technology and provide any details that you can about the security features that it uses.

8. Key backup is an important part of the cryptographic key lifecycle.

    (a) Why is it important to back up cryptographic keys?
    (b) In what ways might backup of cryptographic keys differ from backup of more general data on a computer system?
    (c) As system administrator of a small organisation deploying symmetric cryptography for protection of all traffic on the local intranet, suggest what techniques and procedures you will use for the backup (and subsequent management of backed-up) cryptographic keys.

9. In the past, the idea of mandatory key escrow in order to facilitate access to decryption keys during an authorised government investigation has been proposed.

    (a) Explain what is meant by mandatory key escrow.
    (b) What are the main problems with attempting to support mandatory key escrow within a key management system?
    (c) An alternative approach is to provide a legal framework within which targets of an authorised investigation are 'forced' by law to reveal relevant decryption keys. What are the potential advantages and disadvantages of this approach?
    (d) For the jurisdiction in which you currently reside, find out what (if any) mechanisms exist for supporting an authorised government investigation in the event that the investigators require access to data that has been encrypted.

10. Give an example of a real cryptographic application that:

    (a) 'enforces' the principle of key separation (explain why);
    (b) 'abuses' the principle of key separation (justify why, if possible).

11. Cryptographic keys need to be destroyed at the end of their lifetime. Find out what the latest recommended techniques are for destroying:

    (a) a data key that is stored on a laptop;
    (b) a master key that is stored on a server in a bank.

12. Key management must be governed by appropriate policies, practices and procedures.

    (a) Provide one example (each) of an appropriate policy statement, practice and procedure relating to passwords used to access a personal computer in an office.

(b) Give three different examples of things that might go wrong if an organisation fails to govern key management properly.

(c) For each of your chosen examples, indicate how appropriate key management governance might help to prevent the stated problem arising in the first place.

13. Suppose three users, Alice, Bob and Charlie, wish to use symmetric cryptography to protect files that are transferred between their personal computers. They decide:

   - not to use any standard secure file transfer package;
   - to encrypt files directly using an encryption algorithm implemented on their local machines;
   - send the encrypted files over any appropriate insecure channel (there is no need to consider what type of channel is used).

   Design a suitable key management system (including all phases of the key lifecycle) for supporting this application.

14. Cryptographic Application Programming Interfaces (APIs) provide services that allow developers to build secure applications based on cryptography.

   (a) What are the most popular cryptographic APIs in use today?

   (b) For a cryptographic API of your choice, write a short summary of the main services provided by the API, including the range of cryptographic primitives and algorithms that it supports.

   (c) What vulnerabilities might arise from potential misuse of a cryptographic API? (You might choose to illustrate this answer by providing examples of potential attacks, of which there are several that have been reported in the media.)

15. A payment card organisation has a key management system in place to manage the PINs that their customers use. It has the following features:

   - All PINs are generated using a PIN generation key PGK, which is a single length DES key.
   - PGK is generated from three components PGK_A, PGK_B and PGK_C, all of which are stored on smart cards held in a single safe.
   - The components PGK_A and PGK_B are backed up, but PGK_C is not.
   - When PGK is established from its components, the key generation ceremony specifies that the holders of each of the components must pass the smart card with their component to the internal auditor after they have installed it.
   - Some of the retail systems supporting the card payment system store PGK is software.
   - Customers are permitted to change their PIN using a telephone-based interactive voice recognition service.

   (a) What problems can you identify with this key management system?

   (b) Propose some changes to the key management system in order to overcome these problems.

16. It is sometimes suggested that a cryptographic key should not be used unnecessarily, since each use of a key 'exposes' its use to an attacker. Suppose that a cryptosystem is being used for encryption purposes.

    (a) What does an attacker potentially learn each time an encryption key is used?
    (b) Our standard assumptions about a cryptosystem suggest that an attacker knows corresponding pairs of plaintexts and ciphertexts, so do our standard assumptions contradict in any way this 'principle' of minimising key exposure?
    (c) To what extent do you think that key exposure is a real risk if the cryptosystem is using AES?
    (d) Provide some examples of key management techniques that reduce key exposure.

17. There are many different reasons why cryptographic keys need to be changed from time to time. This can be particularly problematic for long-term keys such as master keys. Suggest different ways in which an organisation could manage the process of changing (migrating) from the use of one master key to another.

18. It will be increasingly important in the future to use resources, including computing resources, as efficiently as possible. Explain what role key management can play in the 'greening' of information technology.

19. A 128-bit block cipher can be thought of as a family of 2^{128} different 'codebooks' (see Section 1.4.4), each of which defines how to convert any block of plaintext into a block of ciphertext under one specific key. One way to appear to avoid having to deal with some 'key management' issues for a particular hardware device might be to directly implement the 'codebook' corresponding to a particular key onto the device. Thus the hardware cannot be used with *any* block cipher key, but instead has an implementation of the unique version of the 'block cipher' that arises from one specific key.

    (a) In what types of application environment might this be an attractive idea?
    (b) What are the disadvantages of such an approach?
    (c) Does this approach make 'key management' any easier?

11 Public-Key Management

This chapter continues our investigation of key management by looking at particular issues that relate to public-key management. These issues primarily arise due to the need to provide assurance of purpose of public keys. It is important to state from the outset that this chapter should be regarded as an *extension* of Chapter 10 for public-key cryptography, not a *replacement*. Most of the key management issues discussed in Chapter 10 are also relevant to the management of key pairs in public-key cryptography.

The term *public-key infrastructure* (PKI) is often associated with key management systems for supporting public-key cryptography. We avoid it for several reasons:

1. The term 'PKI' is often used in confusing ways. In particular, it is often incorrectly used to refer to public-key cryptography itself, rather than the supporting key management system.
2. The notion of a PKI is strongly associated with a key management system that supports public-key certificates. While this is the most common approach to designing a public-key management system, it is not the only option. We will consider alternative approaches in Section 11.4.
3. The attention paid to the concept of a PKI rather deflects from the fact that all cryptosystems require key management systems to support them. We do not often hear the term *symmetric key infrastructure* (SKI), yet key management support for symmetric cryptography is just as essential as it is for public-key cryptography.

> **At the end of this chapter you should be able to:**
> - Explain the purpose of a public-key certificate.
> - Describe the main phases in the lifecycle of a public-key certificate.
> - Discuss a number of different techniques for implementing the different phases in the public-key certificate lifecycle.
> - Compare several different certificate-based public-key management models.
> - Be aware of alternative approaches to certificate-based public-key management.

11.1 Certification of public keys

Recall from our discussion in Section 10.1.3 that the main challenge for the management of public keys is providing assurance of purpose of public keys. In this section we introduce the most popular mechanism for providing this assurance of purpose, the *public-key certificate*.

11.1.1 Motivation for public-key certificates

We begin by recalling why we need assurance of purpose of public keys, since this is of crucial importance in public-key management.

A SCENARIO

Suppose that Bob receives a digitally signed message that claims to have been signed by Alice and that Bob wants to verify the digital signature. As we know from Chapter 7, this requires Bob to have access to Alice's verification key. Suppose that Bob is presented with a key (we do not concern ourselves with how this is done) that is alleged to be Alice's verification key. Bob uses this key to 'verify' the digital signature and it appears to be correct. What guarantees does Bob have that this is a valid digital signature by Alice on the message?

As is often the case in security analysis, the best way of approaching this question is to consider what might have gone wrong. Here are some questions that Bob would be strongly advised to consider, especially if the digital signature is on an important message:

Does the verification key actually belong to Alice? This is the big question. If an attacker is able to persuade Bob (incorrectly) that their verification key belongs to Alice, then the fact that the signature verification is successful will suggest to Bob that Alice signed the contract, when in fact it might have been signed by the attacker.

Could Alice deny that this is her verification key? Even if Bob does have Alice's correct verification key, Alice could deny that it belonged to her. If Alice denies signing the message and denies that the verification key belongs to her, then the fact that the signature verifies correctly is of little use to Bob, since he cannot prove who the signer was.

Is the verification key valid? Recall from Section 10.2 that cryptographic keys have finite lifetimes. It is possible that, even if Alice did use this verification key once, it is no longer a valid verification key for Alice since it has expired. Alice might have (naughtily!) signed the message with an expired key, knowing that the digital signature would not be legally accepted because she did not sign it with a signature key that was valid at the time of signing.

Is the verification key being used appropriately? It is generally regarded as good practice that cryptographic keys should have specifically designated uses. For example, in order to enforce the principle of key separation that we discussed in Section 10.6.1 it might be wise to have different RSA key pairs for encryption and digital signatures. Even more fine-grained usage policies are possible. For example, a particular digital signature key pair might only be authorised for use on messages that relate to transactions worth less than a particular limit (beyond which a different key pair needs to be used, perhaps consisting of longer keys). If Alice has used the signature key inappropriately (in our first example this might be by using an RSA private key designated for decryption use only, in the second case by using a signature key to sign a transaction above the limit) then even if the verification key confirms the result to be 'cryptographically' verified, the signature may not be valid in any legal sense.

PROVIDING ASSURANCE OF PURPOSE

The above scenario is pessimistic in its outlook, but it is important to observe that if we can provide assurance of purpose of verification keys then all of Bob's concerns should be put to rest. In particular we need to:

1. provide a 'strong association' between a public key and the *owner* of that key (the entity whose identity is linked to the public key);
2. provide a 'strong association' between a public key and any other relevant data (such as expiry dates and usage restrictions).

Once again, we emphasise that these issues are not unique to public keys but, as discussed in Section 10.1.3, are often provided implicitly for secret keys. Because public keys are usually publicly available, assurance of purpose must be provided explicitly.

PROVIDING A POINT OF TRUST

The concept of the provision of 'trust' will be a central theme in this chapter. This is because public-key cryptography lends itself to use in relatively open environments where common points of trust are not always present by default. This is in contrast to symmetric key cryptography, which we saw in Chapter 10 typically requires explicit points of trust to be deployed within a key management system, such as a trusted key centre.

The problem in designing any public-key management system is that we need to find a source for the provision of the 'strong association' between a public-key value and its related data. In public-key management systems this is often provided by introducing points of trust in the form of trusted third parties who 'vouch' for this association.

USING A TRUSTED DIRECTORY

Perhaps the crudest approach to providing assurance of purpose for public keys is to use a trusted 'directory', which lists all public keys next to their related data (including the name of the owner). Anyone requiring assurance of purpose of a public key, simply looks it up in the trusted directory. This is analogous to the idea of a telephone directory for telephone numbers.

While this approach may suffice for some applications of public-key cryptography, there are several significant problems:

Universality. The directory has to be trusted by all users of the public-key management system.

Availability. The directory has to be online and available at all times to users of the public-key management system.

Accuracy. The directory needs to be maintained accurately and protected from unauthorised modification.

In truly open application environments, such a trusted directory might potentially need to account for public keys associated with public-key owners throughout the world. Establishing a trusted directory that everyone trusts, is always online, and is always accurate, is likely to be impossible.

However, this basic idea does provide the required assurance of purpose. A more practical solution would be to provide assurance of purpose by distributing the functionality of the trusted directory in some manner. This motivates the notion of a public-key certificate, which we now discuss.

11.1.2 Public-key certificates

A *public-key certificate* is data that binds a public key to data relating to the assurance of purpose of that public key. It can be thought of as a trusted directory entry in a sort of distributed database.

CONTENTS OF A PUBLIC-KEY CERTIFICATE

A public-key certificate contains four essential pieces of information:

Name of owner. The name of the owner of the public key. This owner could be a person, a device, or even a role within an organisation. The format of this name will depend upon the application, but it should be a unique identity that identifies the owner within the environment in which the public key will be employed.

Public-key value. The public key itself. This is often accompanied by an identifier of the cryptographic algorithm with which the public key is intended for use.

Validity time period. This identifies the date and time from which the public key is valid and, more importantly, the date and time of its expiry.

Signature. The creator of the public-key certificate digitally signs all the data that forms the public-key certificate, including the name of owner, public-key value and validity time period. This digital signature not only binds all this data together, but is also the guarantee that the creator of the certificate believes that all the data is correct. This provides the 'strong association' that we referred to in Section 11.1.1.

Most public-key certificates contain much more information than this, with the precise contents being dictated by the certificate format that is chosen for use in

Table 11.1: Fields of an X.509 Version 3 public-key certificate

Field	Description
Version	Specifies the X.509 version being used (in this case V3)
Serial Number	Unique identifier for the certificate
Signature	Digital signature algorithm used to sign the certificate
Issuer	Name of the creator of the certificate
Validity	Dates and times between which the certificate is valid
Subject	Name of the owner of the certificate
Public-Key Info.	Public-key value; Identifier of public-key algorithm
Issuer ID	Optional identifier for certificate creator
Subject ID	Optional identifier for certificate owner
Extensions	A range of optional fields that include:
	Key identifier (in case owner owns several public keys);
	Key usage (specifies usage restrictions);
	Location of revocation information;
	Identifier of policy relating to certificate;
	Alternative names for owner.

the public-key management system. The most well known public-key certificate format is probably X.509 Version 3. The entries (or *fields*) of an X.509 Version 3 public-key certificate are shown in Table 11.1. The public-key certificate itself consists of all the information in Table 11.1 plus a digital signature on the contents, signed by the certificate creator.

INTERPRETING A PUBLIC-KEY CERTIFICATE

It is important to recognise that a public-key certificate binds the assurance-of-purpose data relating to a public key to the public-key value, but does *nothing more than this*. In particular:

A *public-key certificate cannot be used to encrypt messages or verify digital signatures*. A public-key certificate is simply a statement that the public key contained in it belongs to the named owner and has the properties specified in the certificate. Of course, once the certificate has been checked, the public key can be extracted from the certificate and then used for its specified purpose.

A public-key certificate is not a proof of identity. A public-key certificate can be made available to anyone who needs to use the public key contained in it, so presenting a public-key certificate is not a proof of identity. In order to identify someone using their public-key certificate it is necessary to obtain evidence that they know the private key that corresponds to the public key in the public-key certificate. This technique is commonly used in entity authentication protocols based on public-key cryptography. We saw an example in Section 9.4.2 when we studied the STS protocol.

PUBLIC-KEY CERTIFICATE CREATORS

It should be clear that the creator of a public-key certificate plays an extremely important role since this creator, by signing the certificate, is providing the guarantee that all the data relating to the public key (including the name of the owner) is correct.

A creator of a public-key certificate is referred to as a *certificate authority* (CA). The certificate authority normally plays three important roles:

Certificate creation. The CA takes responsibility for ensuring that the information in a public-key certificate is correct before creating and signing the public-key certificate, and then issuing it to the owner.

Certificate revocation. The CA is responsible for revoking the certificate in the event that it becomes invalid (see Section 11.2.3).

Certificate trust anchor. The CA acts as the point of trust for any party relying on the correctness of the information contained in the public-key certificate. To fulfil this role, the CA will need to actively maintain its profile as a trusted organisation. It may also need to enter into relationships with other organisations in order to facilitate wider recognition of this trust (see Section 11.3.3).

We will shortly discuss all of these roles in more detail.

RELYING ON A PUBLIC-KEY CERTIFICATE

Recall from Section 11.1.1 that the motivation for public-key certificates is to provide assurance of purpose of public keys. We thus need to establish exactly how the use of a public-key certificate provides this assurance.

There are three things that someone who wishes to rely on a public-key certificate (whom we will call a *relying party*) needs to be able to do in order to obtain assurance of purpose of the public key:

Trust the CA. The relying party needs to be able to trust (directly or indirectly) the CA to have performed its job correctly when creating the certificate. We will discuss exactly why a relying party might come to trust a CA in Section 11.3.

Verify the signature on the certificate. The relying party needs to have access to the verification key of the CA in order to verify the CA's digital signature on the public-key certificate. If the relying party does not verify this signature then they have no guarantee that the contents of the public-key certificate are correct. Of course, this transfers the problem to one of providing assurance of purpose of the CA's verification key. However, just as we saw for symmetric keys in Section 10.4.1, transferring a key management problem 'higher up a chain' allows for a more scalable solution. We will discuss this issue in more detail in Section 11.3.

Check the fields. The relying party needs to check all the fields in the public-key certificate. In particular, they must check the name of the owner and that the public-key certificate is valid. If the relying party does not check these fields then they have no guarantee that the public key in the certificate is valid for the application for which they intend to use it.

DIGITAL CERTIFICATES

It is worth noting that the principle of having some specific data digitally signed by a trusted third party can have other applications. Public-key certificates represent a special class of *digital certificates*. An example of another type of digital certificate is an *attribute certificate*, which can be used to provide a strong association between a specific attribute and an identity, such as:

- the identity specified is a member of the access control group *administrators*;
- the identity specified is over the age of 18.

Attribute certificates might contain several fields that are similar to a public-key certificate (for example, owner name, creator name, validity period) but would not contain a public-key value. Like a public-key certificate, the data that they contain is digitally signed by the creator in order to vouch for its accuracy.

11.2 The certificate lifecycle

Many of the details of the phases of the key lifecycle (Figure 10.1) that we discussed in Chapter 10 are just as valid for private keys as they are for symmetric keys. However, there are several important differences with respect to the lifecycle of public keys. In this section we will consider these lifecycle differences for a public-key certificate, which is essentially the embodiment of a public key.

11.2.1 Differences in the certificate lifecycle

We now recall the main phases of the key lifecycle from Figure 10.1 and comment on where differences lie:

Key generation. This is one of the phases which differs significantly. We have already observed in Section 10.3.4 that the generation of a public-key pair is an algorithm-specific, and often technically complex, operation. Having done this, creation of a public-key certificate is even harder from a process perspective, since it involves determining the validity of information relating to the public key. We will discuss this in more detail in Section 11.2.2.

Key establishment. Private key establishment is potentially easier than symmetric key establishment since the private key only needs to be established by one entity. Indeed, this entity could even generate the private key themselves (we discuss the pros and cons of this approach in Section 11.2.2). If another entity generates the private key then private key establishment may involve the private key being distributed to the owner using a secure channel of some sort, such as physical distribution of a smart card on which the private key is installed.

Public-key certificate establishment is not a sensitive operation, since the public-key certificate does not need to be kept secret. Most techniques can either be described as:

Pushing a public-key certificate, meaning that the owner of the public-key certificate provides the certificate whenever it is required by a relying party (for example, in the STS Protocol of Figure 9.12, both Alice and Bob pushed their public-key certificates to one another).

Pulling a public-key certificate, meaning that relying parties must retrieve public-key certificates from some sort of repository when they first need them. One potential advantage of pulling public-key certificates is that they could be pulled from a trusted database that only contains valid public-key certificates.

Key storage, backup, archival. We have discussed these processes from the perspective of private keys in Section 10.5. They are all less-sensitive operations when applied to public-key certificates.

Key usage. The principle of key separation, discussed in Section 10.6.1, applies equally to public-key pairs. Many public-key certificate formats, such as the X.509 Version 3 certificate format depicted in Table 11.1, include fields for specifying key usage.

Key change. This is the other phase of the key lifecycle that differs significantly for public-key pairs. We identified why this is the case in Section 10.6.2 and we will discuss potential techniques for facilitating key change in Section 11.2.3.

Key destruction. Destruction of private keys is covered by Section 10.6.4. Destruction of public-key certificates is less sensitive, and may not even be required.

The remainder of this section discusses key pair generation and key pair change, the two phases in the key lifecycle for which specific issues arise for the management of key pairs.

11.2.2 Certificate creation

We now discuss the creation of public-key certificates.

LOCATION OF KEY PAIR AND CERTIFICATE CREATION

It is important to be aware of the fact that we are dealing with two separate processes here:

- generation of the public-key pair itself;
- creation of the public-key certificate.

Key pair generation can be performed either by the owner of the public-key pair or a trusted third party (who may or may not be the CA). The choice of location for this operation results in different certificate creation scenarios:

Trusted third party generation. In this scenario, a trusted third party (which could be the CA) generates the public-key pair. If this trusted third party is not the CA then they must contact the CA to arrange for certificate creation. The advantages of this approach are that:

- the trusted third party may be better placed than the owner to conduct the relatively complex operations involved in generation of the public-key pair (see Section 10.3.4);
- the key pair generation process does not require the owner to do anything.

The possible disadvantages are that:

- the owner needs to trust the third party to securely distribute the private key to the owner; the only exception to this is if the private key is managed on behalf of the owner by the trusted third party, in which case processes must exist for securely managing 'access' to the private key when the owner needs to use it.
- the owner needs to trust the third party to destroy the private key after it has been distributed to the owner; an exception to this would be if the third party provides a backup and recovery service for the owner (see Section 10.5.5).

This scenario lends itself most naturally to closed environments where a trusted third party with the extra responsibilities outlined above can be established.

Combined generation. In this scenario, the owner of the key pair generates the public-key pair. The owner then submits the public key to a CA for generation of the public-key certificate. The main advantages of this approach are that:

- the owner is in full control of the key pair generation process;
- the private key can be locally generated and stored, without any need for it to be distributed.

The possible disadvantages of this approach are that:

- the owner is required to have the ability to generate key pairs;
- the owner may need to demonstrate to the CA that the owner knows the private key that corresponds to the public key submitted to the CA for certification (we discuss this shortly).

This scenario is most suitable for open environments where owners wish to control the key pair generation process themselves.

Self-certification. In this scenario, the owner of the key pair generates the key pair and certifies the public key themselves. This approach is certainly simple. However, it might seem a strange option, since a public-key certificate generated by a CA provides 'independent' assurance of purpose of a public key, whereas self-certification requires relying parties to trust in the assurance of purpose provided by the owner of the public key. However, if relying parties trust the owner then this scenario may be justifiable. Examples of situations where this might be the case are:

- the owner is a CA; it is not uncommon for CAs to self-certify their own public-keys, which is an issue that we will discuss in a moment;
- all relying parties have an established relationship with the owner and hence trust the owner's certification; for example, a small organisation using a self-certified public key to encrypt content on an internal website.

REGISTRATION OF PUBLIC KEYS

If either trusted third-party generation or combined generation of a public-key pair is undertaken then the owner of the public-key pair must engage in a *registration* process with the CA before a public-key certificate can be issued. This is when the owner presents their credentials to the CA for checking. These credentials not only provide a means of authenticating the owner, but also provide information that will be included in some of the fields of the public-key certificate. Registration is arguably the most vital stage in the process of generating a public-key certificate. It is also a process that varies greatly between different applications.

It is worth re-emphasising that the requirements for a registration process are not unique to public keys. It is also extremely important that a symmetric key is issued to the correct entities and that associated information (such as intended purpose of the key, expiry date and usage restrictions) is linked by some means to the key value. However, as we argued in Section 5.1.1 and Section 10.1.3, 'registration' of symmetric keys tends to be implicitly provided by the supporting key management system. It is important that registration is explicit for public keys, particularly in the case of combined generation.

In many application environments a separate entity known as a *Registration Authority* (RA) performs this operation. The roles of RA and CA can be separated for several reasons:

- Registration involves a distinct set of procedures that generally require an amount of human intervention, whereas certificate creation and issuance can be automated.
- Checking the credentials of a public-key certificate applicant is often the most complex part of the certificate creation process. Centralised checking of credentials represents a likely major bottleneck in the process, particularly for large organisations. There is thus a strong argument for distributing the registration activities across a number of local RAs, which perform the checking and then

report the results centrally. On the other hand, the security-critical processes associated with a CA, such as public-key pair generation and certificate signing, are probably best done within one well-defined business unit.

Whether the CA and RA roles are incorporated as one, or kept entirely separate, there remains an important problem to address: what credentials should be presented to the RA during registration?

The answer to this is, of course, application dependent. It is worth noting that many CAs issue different types of public-key certificate (sometimes referred to as *levels* of public-key certificate) depending upon the thoroughness of the registration process. Public-key certificates of different levels may then be used in different types of application. These certificates might have quite different properties. For example, the liability that the CA accepts responsibility for (with respect to any relying parties) might vary for different levels of public-key certificate. We now give some examples of credentials:

- A very low level of public-key certificate might simply require a valid email address to be presented at registration. The registration process might include checking that the applicant can receive email at that address. This level of credential is often enough for public-key certificates that can be obtained online at no cost.
- Registration for public-key certificates for use in a closed environment, such as an organisation's internal business environment, might involve presentation of an employee number and a valid internal email address.
- Commercial public-key certificates for businesses trading over the Internet might require a check of the validity of a domain name and the confirmation that the applicant business is legally registered as a limited company.
- Public-key certificates for incorporation into a national identity card scheme require a registration process that unambiguously identifies a citizen. This can be surprisingly complex to implement. Credentials might include birth certificates, passports, domestic utility statements, etc.

PROOF OF POSSESSION

If a public key and its certificate are created using combined generation then, strictly speaking, it is possible for an attacker to attempt to register a public key for which they do not know the corresponding private key. Such an 'attack' on a verification key for a digital signature scheme might work as follows:

1. The attacker obtains a copy of Alice's verification key. This is a public piece of information, so the attacker can easily obtain this.
2. The attacker presents Alice's verification key to an RA, along with the attacker's legitimate credentials.
3. The RA verifies the credentials and instructs the associated CA to issue a public-key certificate in the name of the attacker for the presented verification key.
4. The CA issues the public-key certificate for the verification key to the attacker.

The attacker now has a public-key certificate issued in their name for a verification key for which they do not know the corresponding signature key. At first glance this might not seem a very useful outcome for the attacker. However, a problem arises if Alice now digitally signs a message with her signature key, since the attacker will be able to persuade relying parties that this is actually the attacker's digital signature on the message. This is because the attacker's name is on a public-key certificate containing a verification key that successfully verifies the digital signature on the message.

This attack can be prevented if the CA conducts a simple check that the public-key certificate applicant knows the corresponding private key. This type of check is often referred to as *proof of possession* (of the corresponding private key). If the public key is an encryption key then one possible proof of possession is as follows:

1. The RA encrypts a test message using the public key and sends it to the certificate applicant, along with a request for the applicant to decrypt the resulting ciphertext.
2. If the applicant is genuine, they decrypt the ciphertext using the private key and return the plaintext test message to the RA. An applicant who does not know the corresponding private key will not be able to perform the decryption to obtain the test message.

It should be noted that proof of possession checks are only required in applications where the outlined 'attack' is deemed to be meaningful. Proof of possession does require a small overhead, so once again we encounter a potential tradeoff between the extra security gained by conducting the check versus the efficiency gained by omitting to do so.

GENERATING CA PUBLIC-KEY PAIRS

Public-key certificates involve a CA digitally signing the owner's public key together with related data. This in turn requires the CA to possess a public-key pair. This raises the interesting question of how assurance of purpose of the CA's verification key will be provided.

The most natural solution is to create a public-key certificate for the CA's public key. But who will sign the public-key certificate of the CA? This is an absolutely crucial question, since any compromise or inaccuracy of this public-key certificate may compromise all public-key certificates signed by the CA. The two most common methods of certifying the CA's verification key are:

Use a higher-level CA. If the CA is part of a *chain* of CAs (we discuss this in Section 11.3.3) then the CA may choose to have their public key certified by another CA. Of course, this does not address the question of who certifies the public key of the higher-level CA.

Self-certification. A top-level CA probably has no choice other than self-certification. It may suffice that this process involves making the public key available in high-profile media, such as daily newspapers. There is a strong case for arguing that a top-level CA's business model involves them being in such a position of trust that they have no motivation for providing incorrect information about their public keys. Hence publication of the information on their own website may suffice.

Note that wide distribution of the public key (certificate) of a CA is also extremely important, since all relying parties of the public-key certificates signed by the CA require this information. As an example, CAs who certify public keys that are used in web-based commercial applications need to have their public-key certificates incorporated into leading web browsers, or have them certified by a higher-level CA who has done this.

11.2.3 Key pair change

The second phase of the key lifecycle that is significantly different for public keys is key change.

REVOCATION OF PUBLIC-KEY CERTIFICATES

We explained in Section 10.6.2 that the main reason why key change is challenging for public keys is because it is almost impossible (and in many cases undesirable) to control who has access to a public key. This makes withdrawing an existing public key very difficult. This process is normally referred to as *revoking* the public key, since it involves 'calling back' information that has been released into the public domain and is now no longer valid. In contrast, establishing a new public key is relatively easy. Thus our discussion of key change for public keys will focus on public-key revocation.

We observe that it does not suffice just to establish a new public key, since we cannot always determine who has access to the old public key and hence we cannot guarantee that all holders of the old public key will realise that a new public key has been issued.

Revoking a public key essentially means revoking the public-key certificate. With this in mind, it is worth observing that there may be situations where a public-key certificate needs to be revoked and then a new public-key certificate created for the *same* public-key value. We will assume that revocation of a public-key certificate only takes place prior to its expiry date. A public-key certificate should not be relied on by any relying parties if its expiry date has been exceeded.

REVOCATION TECHNIQUES

Revocation of public-key certificates can only realistically be approached in one of three ways:

Blacklisting. This involves maintaining a database that contains serial numbers of public-key certificates that have been revoked. This type of database is often referred to as a *certificate revocation list* (or CRL). These CRLs need to be maintained carefully, normally by the CA who is responsible for issuing the certificates, with clear indications of how often they are updated. The CRLs need to be digitally signed by the CA and made available to relying parties.

Whitelisting. This involves maintaining a database that contains serial numbers of public-key certificates that are valid. This database can then be queried by a relying party to find out if a public-key certificate is valid. An example is the *Online Certificate Status Protocol* (OCSP), which has been standardised as RFC 2560. This is particularly useful for applications that require real-time information about the revocation status of a public-key certificate.

Rapid expiration. This removes the need for revocation by allocating very short lifetimes to public-key certificates. This, of course, comes at the cost of requiring certificates to be reissued on a regular basis.

Blacklisting is a common technique when real-time revocation information is not required. There are many different ways of implementing the blacklisting concept, often involving networks of distributed CRLs rather than one central CRL. The main problem with blacklisting is one of synchronisation. In particular, there are likely to be:

- reporting delays between the time that a public-key certificate should be revoked (for example, the time of a private key compromise) and the CA being informed;
- CRL issuing delays between the time that the CA is informed of the revocation of a public-key certificate and the time that the next version of the CRL is signed and made publicly available.

Thus, in theory, a relying party could rely on a public-key certificate in the gap period between the time the public-key certificate should have been revoked and the publication time of the updated CRL. This is an issue that must be 'managed' through suitable processes and procedures. For example:

- The CA should inform all relying parties of the update frequency of CRLs.
- The CA should clarify who is responsible for any damage incurred from misuse of a public key in such a gap period. It might be reasonable to address this by:
  - the CA accepting limited liability during gap periods;
  - relying parties accepting full liability if they fail to check the latest CRL before relying on a public-key certificate.

The means of conveying this information to relying parties is through publication of the key management policies and practices of a CA (see Section 10.7.1). The relevant documents for a CA are often referred to as *certificate policy statements* and *certificate practice statements*. They not only clarify the issues just discussed, but also the wider key management issues relating to public keys that the CA certifies.

11.3 Public-key management models

In this section we consider different public-key management models. We begin by discussing the issue of trusting CAs, particularly techniques for joining CA domains. We then examine the relationship between a relying party and a CA, and use this to define several different management models.

11.3.1 Choosing a CA

In a closed environment, the choice of who will play the role of a CA may be straightforward, since central administrative functions within an organisation are well placed to serve such a role. Choosing an organisation to play the role of a CA in an open environment is less straightforward. Currently, most CAs serving open environments are commercial organisations who have made it their business to be 'trusted' to play the role of a CA.

While CAs serving open environments can be regulated to an extent by commercial pressure (if they fail to offer attractive services or experience reputational damage then they are likely to suffer financially), the importance of their role may demand tighter regulation of their practices. Options for this include:

Licensing. This approach requires CAs to obtain a government license before they can operate. Government, thus, ultimately provides the assurance that a CA conforms to minimum standards.

Self-regulation. This approach requires CAs to form an industry group and set their own minimum operational standards through the establishment of best practices.

In the UK, licensing was considered in the 1990s but was met with considerable objections from industry. Currently the self-regulation approach is being adopted.

11.3.2 Public-key certificate management models

The owner of a public-key certificate has, by necessity, placed some trust in the CA who issued the certificate. This may be because the owner belongs to the same organisation as the CA (typically in closed environments) or because the owner and the CA have a direct business relationship (typically in open environments).

However, the same cannot necessarily be said for a relying party. Indeed, the relationship between a relying party and the public-key certificate owner's CA defines a number of distinct public-key certificate management models, which we now review.

CA-FREE CERTIFICATION MODEL

The *CA-free certification model* is depicted in Figure 11.1 and applies when there is no CA involved. In the CA-free certification model, the owner generates a key pair

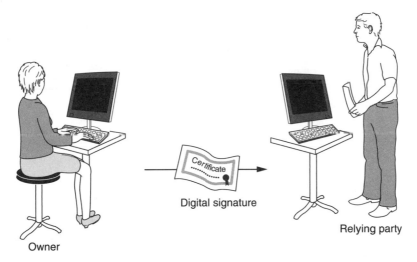

Figure 11.1. CA-free certification model

and then either self-certifies the public key or does not use a public-key certificate. Any relying party obtains the (self-certified) public key directly from the owner. For example, the owner could include their public key in an email signature or write it on a business card. The relying party then has to make an independent decision as to whether they trust the owner or not. The relying party thus carries all the risk in this model. A variation of this idea is the *web of trust* model, which we discuss in Section 11.4.1.

REPUTATION-BASED CERTIFICATION MODEL

The *reputation-based certification model* is depicted in Figure 11.2 and applies when the owner has obtained a public-key certificate from a CA, but the relying party has no relationship with this CA. Even if the relying party obtains the verification key of the CA, which enables them to verify the public-key certificate, because they do not have any relationship with the CA itself they do not by default gain assurance of purpose from verification of the certificate. They are left to *choose* whether to trust that the CA has done its job correctly and hence that the information in the public-key certificate is correct. In the worst case, they may not trust the CA at all, in which case they have no reason to trust any information affirmed by the CA.

The only assurance that they might gain is through the *reputation* of the CA that signed the public-key certificate. If the relying party has some trust in the reputation of the CA, for example, it is a well-known organisation or trust service provider, then the relying party might be willing to accept the information in the public-key certificate.

391

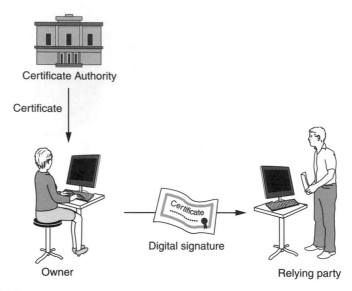

Figure 11.2. Reputation-based certification model

CLOSED CERTIFICATION MODEL

The *closed certification model* is depicted in Figure 11.3 and applies when the relying party has a relationship with the owner's CA. The closed certification model is the most 'natural' certification model, but is only really applicable to closed environments where a single CA oversees the management of all public-key

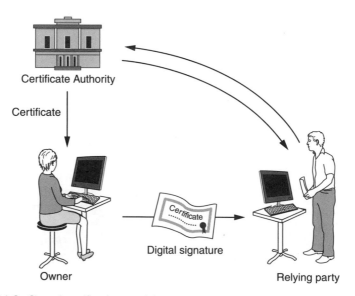

Figure 11.3. Closed certification model

certificates. In the closed certification model, the more onerous issues concerning public-key management, such as those relating to liability and revocation, are more straightforward to solve than for the other models. This is because public-key certificate owners and relying parties are all governed by the same certificate management policies and practices.

CONNECTED CERTIFICATION MODEL

The *connected certification model* is depicted in Figure 11.4 and applies when the relying party has a relationship with a trusted third party, which in turn has a relationship with the owner's CA. The trusted third party that the relying party has a relationship with could be another CA. In Figure 11.4 we describe it as a *validation authority* because its role is to assist the relying party to validate the information in the owner's public-key certificate. Strictly speaking, this validation authority may not necessarily be a CA.

We do not further specify the nature of the relationship between the owner's CA and the relying party's validation authority, since there are many different ways in which this could manifest itself. For example, the CA and validation authority could both be members of a federation of organisations who have agreed to cooperate in the validation of public-key certificates and have signed up to common certificate management policies and practices. The important issue is that, because the relying party has a relationship with the validation authority, the relying party essentially delegates the task of verifying the public-key certificate

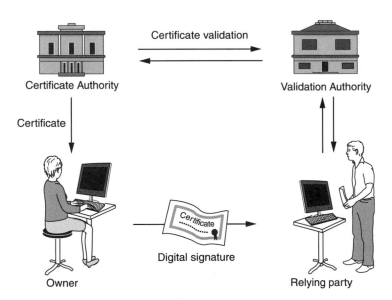

Figure 11.4. Connected certification model

393

to the validation authority. The validation authority can then do this through its relationship with the owner's CA.

The connected certification model is a pragmatic 'stretching' of the closed certification model, in order to allow public-key certificates to be managed in environments that are either:

open, in the sense that owners and relying parties are not governed by any single management entity;

distributed, in the case of a closed environment that is distributed, for example, a large organisation with different branches or regional offices.

11.3.3 Joining CA domains

The connected certification model is of particular interest since it allows public-key certificates to be used in environments where the owner and relying party do not have trust relationships with the same CA. We will now assume that both the owner Alice and relying party Bob have relationships with their own CAs, which we label CA1 and CA2, respectively (hence for simplicity we now assume that the validation authority in Figure 11.4 is a CA). We now consider the nature of the relationship between CA1 and CA2. In particular, we will look at techniques for 'joining' their respective *CA domains* and allowing certificates issued by CA1 to be 'trusted' by relying parties who have trust relationships with CA2.

CROSS-CERTIFICATION

The first technique for joining two CA domains is to use *cross-certification*, whereby each CA certifies the other CA's public key. This idea is depicted in Figure 11.5. Cross-certification implements a *transitive* trust relationship. By cross-certifying, relying party Bob of CA2, who wishes to trust a public-key certificate issued to Alice by CA1, can do so by means of the following argument:

1. I (Bob) trust CA2 (because I have a business relationship with CA2);
2. CA2 trusts CA1 (because they have agreed to cross-certify one another);

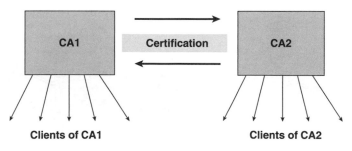

Figure 11.5. Cross-certification

3. CA1 has vouched for the information in Alice's public-key certificate (because CA1 generated and signed it);
4. Therefore, I (Bob) trust the information in Alice's public-key certificate.

CERTIFICATION HIERARCHIES

The second technique, which we also encountered in Section 11.2.2, is to use a *certification hierarchy* consisting of different levels of CA. A higher-level CA, which both CA1 and CA2 trust, can then be used to 'transfer' trust from one CA domain to the other. The simple certification hierarchy in Figure 11.6 uses a higher-level CA (termed the *root CA*) to issue public-key certificates for both CA1 and CA2. Relying party Bob of CA2, who wishes to trust a public-key certificate issued to Alice by CA1, can do so by means of the following argument:

1. I (Bob) trust CA2 (because I have a business relationship with CA2);
2. CA2 trusts root CA (because CA2 has a business relationship with root CA);
3. Root CA has vouched for the information in CA1's public-key certificate (because root CA generated and signed it);
4. CA1 has vouched for the information in Alice's public-key certificate (because CA1 generated and signed it).
5. Therefore, I (Bob) trust the information in Alice's public-key certificate.

CERTIFICATE CHAINS

The joining of CA domains makes verification of public certificates a potentially complex process. In particular, it results in the creation of *certificate chains*, which consist of a series of public-key certificates that must all be verified in order to have trust in the end public-key certificate. Just as an example to illustrate this complexity, consider the apparently simple CA topology in Figure 11.7. In this

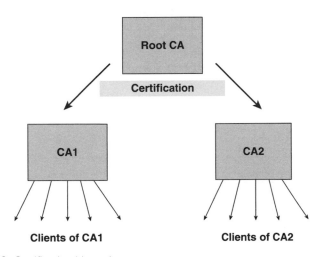

Figure 11.6. Certification hierarchy

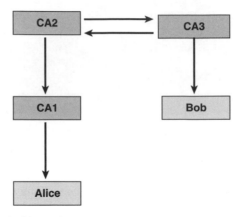

Figure 11.7. A simple CA topology

topology Alice has a relationship with CA1, which is a low-level CA whose root CA is CA2. Bob has a relationship with CA3, which has cross-certified with CA2. Now suppose that Bob wishes to verify Alice's public-key certificate. To do so, he will need to verify a certificate chain that consists of the three public-key certificates shown in Table 11.2.

In other words, Bob first verifies Alice's public-key certificate, which is signed by CA1. Then Bob needs to verify CA1's public-key certificate, which is signed by CA2. Finally, Bob verifies CA2's public-key certificate, which is signed by CA3. The certificate chain ends at CA3, since this is the CA that Bob has a relationship with and thus we assume that he trusts signatures by CA3.

Indeed, to properly verify the above certificate chain, for *each* of these public-key certificates Bob should:

1. verify the signature on the public-key certificate;
2. check all the fields in the public-key certificate;
3. check whether the public-key certificate has been revoked.

Table 11.2: Example of a certificate chain

Certificate	Containing public key of	Certified by
1	Alice	CA1
2	CA1	CA2
3	CA2	CA3

JOINING CA DOMAINS IN PRACTICE

While these techniques for joining CA domains appear to work in theory, it is less clear how well they work in practice. Issues such as liability start to become extremely complex when CA domains are joined in such ways. Our discussion of certificate chains has shown that even verification of a public-key certificate chain can be a complex process.

One of the highest profile examples of the connected certification model in practice is the *web based certification model* implemented by major web browser manufacturers. This can be thought of as a fairly 'flat' certification hierarchy, where commercial CAs have their root certificates embedded into a web browser. Rather than 'cross-certifying' amongst these root CAs, the browser manufacturer should ensure that CAs whose root certificates they accept have met certain business practice standards. This allows relying parties to gain some assurance of purpose of public-key certificates issued by CAs that they do not have direct business relationships with. It also implements the reputation-based model, since even relying parties who have no relationship with any CA can still gain some degree of trust in a public-key certificate, so long as they trust the web browser manufacturer to have vetted CAs to an appropriate level.

One of the problems with the web-based certification model is that the trust linkage between the root CAs is not particularly 'tight'. Arguably, a more serious problem is that relying parties are left to conduct a significant portion of the certificate chain verification process, since a web browser cannot automatically check that all the fields of each certificate are what the relying party is expecting. Relying parties cannot always be trusted to understand the importance of conducting these checks. Indeed, even informed relying parties may choose, for convenience, to omit these checks.

The connected certification model is probably most effective when the CAs involved have strong relationships, such as when they operate in what we referred to in Section 11.3.2 as a distributed environment. Some examples of this type of environment arise in the financial and government sectors.

11.4 Alternative approaches

As we have seen from the discussion in this chapter, there are many complicated issues to resolve when trying to implement a certificate-based approach to public-key management. There are a number of alternative approaches that attempt to resolve these by avoiding the use of public-key certificates. We now discuss two such approaches.

Note that the use of public-key certificates is more common than either of these alternative approaches. However, consideration of these approaches not only indicates that certificates are not the only option for public-key management, but also helps to place the challenges of public-key certificate management in context.

11.4.1 Webs of trust

In the CA-free certification model of Section 11.3.2, we noted that public keys could be made available directly by owners to relying parties without the use of a CA. The problem with this approach is that the relying party is left with no trust anchor other than the owner themselves.

A stronger assurance can be provided if a *web of trust* is implemented. Suppose that Alice wishes to directly provide relying parties with her public key. The idea of a web of trust involves other public-key certificate owner's acting as 'lightweight CAs' by digitally signing Alice's public key. Alice gradually develops a *key ring*, which consists of her public key plus a series of digital signatures by other owners attesting to the fact that the public-key value is indeed Alice's.

These other owners are, of course, not acting as formal CAs, and the relying party may have no more of a relationship with any of these other owners than with Alice herself. Nonetheless, as Alice builds up her key ring there are two potentially positive impacts for relying parties:

1. A relying party sees that a number of other owner's have been willing to sign Alice's public key. This is at least *some* evidence that the public key may indeed belong to Alice.
2. There is an increasing chance (as the key ring size increases) that one of the other owners is someone that the relying party knows and trusts. If this is the case then the relying party might use a transitive trust argument to gain some assurance about Alice's public key.

Webs of trust clearly have limitations. However, they represent a lightweight and scalable means of providing some assurance of purpose of public keys in open environments, where other solutions are not possible.

However, the extent to which webs of trust make a real impact is unclear since, for the types of open applications in which they make most sense, relying parties are often likely to choose to simply trust the owner (in many cases they may already have an established trust relationship).

11.4.2 Identity-based public-key cryptography

Recall that the main purpose of a public-key certificate is to bind an identity to a public-key value. Thus one way of eliminating the need for public-key certificates is to build this binding directly into the public keys themselves.

THE IDEA BEHIND IDPKC

One way in which this binding could be built in is if the public-key value can be uniquely derived from the identity. And one way in which *this* can be done is to make the public-key value and the identity *the same value*. This is the motivation behind *identity-based public-key cryptography* (IDPKC).

A significant difference between IDPKC and certificate-based approaches to management of conventional public-key cryptography is that IDPKC requires a trusted third party to be involved in private key generation. We will refer to this trusted third party as a *trusted key centre* (TKC), since its main role is the generation and distribution of private keys. The basic idea behind IDPKC is:

- A public-key owner's 'identity' *is* their public key. There is a publicly known rule that converts the owner's 'identity' into a string of bits, and then some publicly known rule that converts that string of bits into a public key.
- The public-key owner's private key can be calculated from their public key only by the TKC, who has some additional secret information.

In this way public-key certificates are not required, since the linkage between the owner's identity and the public key is by means of the publicly known rules. Despite the fact that public keys are easily determined by anyone, private keys are only computable by the TKC.

A MODEL FOR IDPKC ENCRYPTION

Figure 11.8 shows the process behind using IDPKC to encrypt a message from Alice to Bob. The model consists of the following stages:

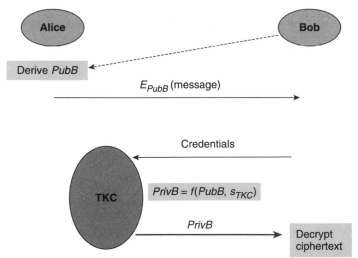

Figure 11.8. The IDPKC process

Encryption. Alice derives Bob's public key *PubB* from Bob's identity using the publicly known rules. Alice then encrypts her message using *PubB* and sends the resulting ciphertext to Bob.

Identification. Bob identifies himself to the TKC by presenting appropriate credentials and requests the private key *PrivB* that corresponds to *PubB*.

Private key derivation. If the TKC accepts Bob's credentials then the TKC derives *PrivB* from *PubB* and a system secret value s_{TKC}, known only by the TKC.

Private-key distribution. The TKC sends *PrivB* to Bob using a secure channel.

Decryption. Bob decrypts the ciphertext using *PrivB*.

One of the most interesting aspects of this IDPKC encryption model is that encryption can occur *before* private-key derivation and distribution. In other words, it is possible to send an encrypted message to someone who has not yet established a private decryption key. Indeed, they may not even be aware of the possibility of receiving encrypted messages! This is quite an unexpected property and one that certainly does not hold for conventional public-key cryptography.

It should also be noted that once a user has obtained their private key, there is no need for them to repeat the middle three stages until either *PubB* or the system secret s_{TKC} change. We return to this issue shortly.

IDPKC ENCRYPTION ALGORITHMS

The most important issue regarding algorithms for IDPKC is that *conventional public-key cryptosystems cannot be used for IDPKC*. There are two principal reasons for this:

1. In conventional public-key algorithms, such as RSA, it is not possible for *any* value to be a public key. Rather, a public key is a value that satisfies certain specific mathematical properties. Given an arbitrary numerical identity of a public-key owner, it is unlikely that this corresponds to a valid public key (it *might*, but this would be lucky, rather than expected).
2. Conventional public-key algorithms do not feature a system secret s_{TKC} that can be used to 'unlock' each private key from the corresponding public key.

For these reasons, IDPKC requires the design of different encryption algorithms that are explicitly designed for the IDPKC setting. Several such algorithms exist, but we will not discuss them in any further detail.

PRACTICAL ISSUES WITH IDPKC

While IDPKC directly solves some of the problems associated with certificate-based public-key cryptography, it results in some new issues. These include:

The need for an online, centrally trusted TKC. There is no getting around this requirement, which immediately restricts IDPKC to applications where the existence of such a trusted entity is acceptable and practical. Note in particular that:

- the TKC should be *online*, since it could be called upon at any time to establish private keys;
- only the TKC can derive the private keys in the system, hence it provides a source of key escrow, which can either be seen as desirable or undesirable (see Section 10.5.5);
- the TKC requires secure channels with all private key owners, with the similar advantages and disadvantages as discussed for trusted third-party generation of key pairs in Section 11.2.2, except that the TKC cannot 'destroy' the private keys as it always has the ability to generate them.

Nonetheless, there are many potential applications where the existence of such a TKC is reasonable, especially in closed environments.

Revocation issues. One of the problems with tying a public-key value to an identity is the impact of revocation of a public key, should this be required. If the public key has to change, we are essentially requiring the owner's 'identity' to change, which clearly might not be practical. An obvious solution to this is to introduce a temporal element into the owner's 'identity', perhaps featuring a time period for which the public key is valid. For example, Bob's public key might become *PubB3rdApril* for any encrypted messages intended for Bob on 3rd April, but change to *PubB4thApril* the next day. The cost of this is a requirement for Bob to obtain a new private key for each new day.

Multiple applications. Another issue is that it is no longer immediately obvious how to separate different applications. In conventional public-key cryptography, one owner can possess different public keys for different applications. By tying an identity to a public-key value, this is not immediately possible. One solution is again to introduce variety into the encryption key using, say, *PubBBank* as Bob's public key for his online banking application. However, it should be pointed out that IDPKC offers a potential advantage in this area since it is possible for the *same* public key *PubB* to be used across multiple applications, so long as different system secrets s_{TKC} are used to generate different private keys.

It is important to recognise that these issues are *different* issues to those of certificate-based public-key cryptography. This means that IDPKC presents an interesting alternative to conventional public-key cryptography, which may suit certain application environments better, but may not be suitable for others. For example, IDPKC may be attractive for low-bandwidth applications because there is no need to transfer public-key certificates, but will be unattractive for any application that has no central point of trust that can play the role of the TKC.

It is also important to realise that some of the challenges of certificate-based public-key cryptography remain. One example is that the need to register for public-key certificates is now simply translated into a need to register in order to obtain private keys.

MORE GENERAL NOTIONS OF IDPKC

The idea behind IDPKC is both compelling and intriguing, since it represents a quite different approach to implementing public-key cryptography. In fact, it is even more interesting than it first appears, since there is no need to restrict public keys to being associated with identities. They could take the form of almost any string of data.

One of the most promising extensions of the IDPKC idea is to associate public keys in an IDPKC system with *decryption policies*. The idea involves only a slight modification of the process described in Figure 11.8:

Encryption. Alice derives a public key *PubPolicy* based on a specific decryption policy using publicly known rules. For example, this policy could be *Qualified radiographer working in a UK hospital*. Alice then encrypts her message (say, a health record) using *PubPolicy* and (continuing our example) stores it on a medical database, along with an explanation of the decryption policy.

Identification. Qualified UK radiographer Bob, who wishes to access the health record, identifies himself to the TKC by presenting appropriate medical credentials and requests the private key *PrivPolicy* that corresponds to *PubPolicy*.

Private-key derivation. If the TKC accepts Bob's credentials then the TKC derives *PrivPolicy* from *PubPolicy* and a system secret value s_{TKC}, known only by the TKC.

Private-key distribution. The TKC sends *PrivPolicy* to Bob using a secure channel.

Decryption. Bob decrypts the ciphertext using *PrivPolicy*.

This example illustrates the power of being able to encrypt before the recipient obtains the private key since, in this example, Alice does not necessarily even know the recipient. This idea is being instantiated by *attribute-based* encryption schemes, which model decryption policies in terms of a set of *attributes* that a recipient must possess before the TKC will release the corresponding private key to them.

IDPKC IN PRACTICE

While IDPKC presents an interesting alternative framework for managing public-key cryptography, it is still early in its development. Cryptographic algorithms for implementing IDPKC are relatively new, although several are now well respected. Some commercial applications, including email security products (see Section 12.7.2), have already implemented IDPKC. While we have primarily discussed IDPKC in order to illustrate that there are public-key management alternatives to public-key certificates, it also represents a cryptographic primitive that is likely to be used more often in future applications.

11.5 Summary

In this chapter we have looked at particular key management issues that relate to the management of key pairs for use in public-key cryptography. We have focussed on the most common technique of using public-key certificates to provide assurance of purpose of public keys, and have discussed management of the various phases of the public-key certificate lifecycle.

The development of the Internet and World Wide Web triggered a significant interest in deploying public-key cryptography in the 1990s, since many applications (such as web-based commerce) require security technologies that work in open environments. However, every deployment of public-key cryptography requires the associated key pairs to be properly managed. Many security architects and developers discovered that the related key management issues that we have discussed in this chapter are more difficult to address than they first appear. In particular, while it is relatively easy to design management solutions on paper (for example, CRLs for the problem of key revocation), these solutions become very difficult to implement in the form of working procedures.

Public-key cryptography subsequently suffered a rather 'mixed press', perhaps due to over-hyped expectations and subsequent frustrations at the implementation challenges and costs. It is important to recognise that:

- the main difficulties associated with implementing public-key cryptography all arise due to key management issues and not the cryptographic technology itself;
- the key management challenges associated with implementing public-key cryptography are largely down to the nature of the environments in which it is implemented.

This latter remark is important. We have argued in this chapter that it is fairly straightforward to manage public keys in closed environments. However, these are precisely the environments in which fully symmetric key management systems can be implemented, and are hence normally preferred. Thus it could be argued that the only reason that public-key management is perceived to be difficult is because public-key cryptography tends to be implemented in challenging (open) environments where it is not possible to use symmetric cryptography to provide the necessary security services.

403

Finally in this chapter, we looked at some alternatives to using public-key certificates to manage public keys. We observed that each of these solves some problems, but introduces new ones. It is thus likely that alternatives such as IDPKC may find niche applications, but will never fully 'replace' the use of certificate-based approaches to public-key management.

11.6 Further reading

A good guide to certificate-based public-key management is Adams and Lloyd [21]. There are also informative chapters on public-key management in Garfinkel and Spafford [88], Ford and Baum [83], and Ferguson, Schneier and Kohno [75]. In terms of standards, the most well known public-key management standard is X.509, which is specified as part 8 of ISO 9594 [16]. This standard includes a public-key certificate format and a certificate revocation list format. The most-used public-key certificate format is X.509 v3, which is also specified in RFC 5280 [49] and often referred to as a PKIX certificate. Formats for attribute certificates are provided in RFC 3281 [73]. Other general standards relating to public-key management include ISO/IEC 15945 [9] and the banking standard ISO 15782 [8]. NIST 800-32 [133] provides an introduction to public-key management and outlines the approach taken by the US government. More specific standards include RFC 2511 [127] which deals with certificate requests and includes a proof of possession mechanism (there is also one in ISO 15945 [9]) and RFC 2560 [128], which describes OCSP. ISO 21188 [14] discusses governance of public-key management systems, including root key pair generation ceremonies.

Some organisations initially adopted public-key cryptography without necessarily being aware of all of the complexities of public-key management. Ellison and Schneier [70] produced a well-publicised note of caution that outlines ten 'risks' of public-key management. An interesting review of the public-key management issues experienced by a number of organisations is provided by Price [158]. For many people, the most familiar public-key management application is the use of public-key certificates to support SSL/TLS in web applications. A report by KPMG [111] outlines the fragility of this public-key management model by indicating a number of points of weakness, as well as indicating how these vulnerabilities can be addressed.

One alternative to using a certificate-based public-key management system is to use a web of trust, with the Wikipedia portal [204] being a good place to start for details and criticisms of this approach. Explanations of some identity-based encryption algorithms can be found in Stinson [185]. A more detailed investigation of IDPKC, including attribute-based encryption schemes, is Joye and Neven [103]. IEEE P1363.3 [148] is a draft standard that specifies a number of different IDPKC primitives. An interesting comparison of the different issues involved with implementing certificate-based and identity-based public-key cryptography is Paterson and Price [153].

11.7 Activities

1. Provide an argument for supporting the following three statements (which do not contradict one another):

    (a) The core issues that motivate the need to manage keys for symmetric cryptography and public-key cryptography are essentially the same.
    (b) Many phases of the key lifecycle for symmetric cryptography and public-key cryptography arc almost idcntical.
    (c) Many phases of the key lifecycle for symmetric cryptography and public-key cryptography are fundamentally different.

2. The term *public-key infrastructure* (PKI) is much more commonly discussed than the term *symmetric key infrastructure* (SKI). Why do you think this is the case?

3. The lifecycle of a cryptographic key depicted in Figure 10.1 does not just apply to symmetric keys. Sketch two copies of this lifecycle for the following types of 'key', indicating on each copy whether the various phases of the key lifecycle are, in general, easier or harder to manage than for symmetric keys:

    (a) private keys;
    (b) public-key certificates.

4. X.509 is just one example of a public-key certificate format. Find an example of a different public-key certificate format and compare it to the X.509 version 3 format depicted in Table 11.1:

    (a) Which fields are the same?
    (b) Explain any differences.

5. There are several different types of digital certificate.

    (a) What is a *code-signing certificate*?
    (b) What are the important fields of a code-signing certificate?
    (c) Discuss the potential impact of management failures in the different phases of the lifecycle of a code-signing certificate.

6. Registration is a very important phase of the public-key certificate lifecycle.

    (a) What general issues should be considered before selecting appropriate credentials for checking during a public-key certificate registration process?
    (b) Suggest candidate credentials that public-key certificate applicants should provide when applying for a student smart card for access to campus services.

7. The trusted third–party generation technique described in Section 11.2.2 is quite commonly adopted by large-scale applications where private keys are stored on smart cards.

    (a) Why is this technique attractive for such applications?
    (b) Why might the key pair generation be conducted by a third party that is different from the CA in such applications?

(c) What problems might arise if private signature keys that are required to have legal standing are generated using this technique?

8. Visit the website of a well-known commercial CA to establish:

   (a) what levels of public-key certificate they issue;
   (b) what credentials they require for registration for these different levels of public-key certificate;
   (c) what liability they accept for these different levels of public-key certificate;
   (d) how often they publish certificate revocation lists (CRLs);
   (e) how clients access CRLs;
   (f) what advice they provide clients concerning the importance of checking CRLs.

9. Suppose that Alice's public RSA encryption key *PKA* is certified by a root CA, which also has its own public RSA encryption key *PKC*. A cryptographic protocol requires the following computation:

$$E_{PKA}(E_{PKC}(\text{data})).$$

   In other words, Alice is required to encrypt a message using RSA that consists of data already encrypted using RSA by the CA.

   (a) Why might this be a problem?
   (b) Would the same problem arise if a symmetric key hierarchy was in place and a similar computation was made using symmetric keys at different levels in the hierarchy?

10. The article 'Ten risks of PKI' by Carl Ellison and Bruce Schneier [70] was written in 2000 and is widely available.

    (a) Briefly summarise the ten risks described in the article.
    (b) To what extent do you think these concerns remain valid today?

11. Provide an example of a real security incident that has arisen due to a failure in some phase of the public-key certificate lifecycle. For your chosen incident:

    (a) Explain what went wrong.
    (b) Explain why this was allowed to happen.
    (c) Explain how such an incident could have been prevented.

12. Some organisations choose to use a central CA to generate key pairs on behalf of their users and never release the private keys to the users, who can only activate services that require use of their private key through the CA itself.

    (a) How might a user go about 'activating' their private key on the CA's server?
    (b) What are the advantages of this approach to public-key management?
    (c) What problems might arise from this approach?
    (d) What application environments do you think that this approach might work best in?

13. One way of providing conformance between different CAs is to develop common standards that allow a CA to be measured against current best practices. Find an example of such a scheme (either national or industry-wide) and provide information about what it does.

14. Alice wishes to securely send an important message to Bob, who has a public encryption key that he generated himself. Neither Alice or Bob are part of any formal public-key certificate management system and Bob does not intend to acquire a public-key certificate for his public key. Suggest how Alice might obtain Bob's public key and acquire sufficient assurance of purpose of this key if:

    (a) Alice and Bob are friends;
    (b) Alice and Bob are remote business acquaintances;
    (c) Alice and Bob are strangers.

15. Continuing the theme of the previous activity, even for a large organisation there are certain situations where it is possible to provide assurance of purpose of a public key without creating a public-key certificate. Consider how this might be done for:

    (a) the public key of a CA;
    (b) an application where all public keys are embedded in hardware (such as an ATM).

16. Provide an example of an application where you think identity-based public-key cryptography (IDPKC) is more suitable for implementation than traditional public-key cryptography supported by public-key certificates. In particular, for your chosen application, explain:

    (a) the problems of a certificate-based approach;
    (b) the advantages of using IDPKC;
    (c) how you might overcome some of the practical issues associated with implementation of IDPKC.

17. We have only discussed IDPKC encryption in this chapter. It is possible to design identity-based digital signature schemes.

    (a) Describe a model similar to the one in Section 11.4.2 for IDPKC encryption that explains a potential process by which identity-based digital signatures might be created and verified.
    (b) To what extent do you think identity-based digital signature schemes offer any benefits compared to conventional digital signature schemes?

18. Consider the following medium-sized online travel business:

    • 160 staff are employed, 40 in the main national office and 15 in each of eight international offices;
    • the company sells package holidays, air tickets, travel insurance and travel accessories over the Internet;

- each office has its own intranet, as well as access to a common company-wide intranet connecting all the regional offices;
- the company provides many of its services through external suppliers;
- the company provides its own information security functionality (rather than outsourcing).

You are the member of the IT support team with responsibility for security.

(a) By considering the overall activities of the company, which security services are likely to be required on the various network links?

(b) Where would you choose to deploy symmetric and public-key cryptography (if at all)?

(c) Design a simple key management system to support this business, identifying the different keys required and how their lifecycle will be supported.

19. As well as electronic and advanced electronic signatures, the European Union Directive on Electronic Signatures defines a third class of electronic signatures known as *qualified electronic signatures*.

(a) Under what conditions does an advanced electronic signature become a qualified electronic signature?

(b) Explain what is meant by a *qualified certificate*.

(c) Explain how a suitable public-key management system can provide these necessary conditions.

(d) To what extent are advanced electronic signatures and qualified electronic signatures legally 'equivalent' to handwritten signatures?

Part IV

Applications

12 Cryptographic Applications

W e have now completed our discussion of the cryptographic toolkit and the management of cryptographic keys. We have spent much of this discussion highlighting issues that need to be addressed when making decisions about what type of cryptography to implement and how to support it. It is notable that many of these issues were dependent on the application environment. We thus avoided making any 'decisions' about such issues during our discussion. Rather, we focussed on presenting the pros and cons of relevant choices.

We will now examine a number of applications of cryptography. While these may well be of independent interest, the real reason that we are studying these applications is to indicate the types of decisions that have been taken in specific application environments with respect to issues that we left 'open' in the previous chapters.

While these applications are all important, and hopefully interesting, their selection has primarily been to provide different application environments where different decisions have been taken. We will see during this discussion that the 'right' decisions are not always taken, first time around at least. We will also see that many decisions are taken based on tradeoffs. The chosen applications are:

Cryptography on the Internet. SSL/TLS is one of the most ubiquitous cryptographic protocols and provides an excellent example of the use of hybrid encryption to support open application environments.

Cryptography for wireless local area networks. The development of the cryptography used in wireless local area network standards provides a number of important lessons in practical cryptographic design.

Cryptography for mobile telecommunications. GSM and UMTS provide good examples of cryptographic design in relatively closed application environments.

Cryptography for secure payment card transactions. The banking industry has been one of the longest commercial users of cryptography and a wide variety of different techniques are used to support different types of payment transaction.

Cryptography for video broadcasting. Pay-TV provides a fascinating application with relatively straightforward cryptography requiring the support of fairly sophisticated key management.

410

Cryptography for identity cards. The Belgian eID card provides a good example of a technology that makes public-key cryptography widely available for use by other applications.

Cryptography for home users. Our last application concerns the potential use of cryptography for securing everyday home user applications such as file encryption, disk encryption and email security.

It is important to note that we will not attempt to provide a comprehensive introduction to these applications, since we are only interested in the role that cryptography plays in supporting them. In particular, for each application, we will be exploring:

What are the security requirements?
What are the application constraints that influence decision-making?
Which cryptographic primitives are deployed?
Which cryptographic algorithms and key lengths are supported?
How is key management conducted?

Once again we stress that the main reason that these particular applications have been chosen is illustrative. It is likely that some of the cryptographic decisions taken for these, and similar, applications will change over time.

At the end of this chapter you should be able to:

- Appreciate the influence of application constraints on making decisions about how to deploy cryptography.
- Compare a number of different application environments and their cryptographic requirements.
- Recognise the role that cryptography plays in supporting a range of applications.
- Justify the decisions taken regarding deployment of cryptography in different application environments.
- Identify appropriate key management techniques for a range of application environments.

12.1 Cryptography on the Internet

Perhaps one of the highest-profile uses of cryptography, at least to users of the Internet, is the *Secure Sockets Layer* (SSL) protocol. SSL is one of the three most important cryptographic protocols for establishing a secure network channel. The Internet is often modelled as a four-layer *Internet Protocol Suite*. While SSL operates at the Transport Layer of the Internet Protocol Suite, secure channels can also be established at the higher Application Layer using the *Secure Shell* (SSH) protocol and at the lower Internet Layer using the *Internet Protocol Security* (IPsec) suite.

12.1.1 SSL background

SSL is a general communication security protocol for protecting data while it is being transferred between different locations. Although it has many applications, most users encounter SSL when securing a web connection between a client machine and a web server, for example, when making a purchase from an online store. SSL requires a reliable underlying transport protocol, hence its suitability for applications on the Internet running over the *Transmission Control Protocol* (TCP). Unlike many other applications of cryptography, the deployment of SSL is often made apparent to a user. When securing web sessions, an SSL connection may be indicated by:

- a dialogue box inviting the user to engage in a 'secure connection';
- the appearance of an icon, such as a padlock, on the web browser;
- the replacement of `http` by `https` in the web address displayed by the browser.

These indications provide a degree of assurance to the user that information exchanged during the session is 'secure', in contrast to traffic that is exchanged outside of an SSL-protected session.

SSL was developed by Netscape in the mid-1990s for use with their *Navigator* browser. It subsequently became the responsibility of the *Internet Engineering Task Force* (IETF), who develop standards for the Internet. In 1996, the IETF published a version known as *Transport Layer Security* (TLS). Subsequent versions of TLS have since been released. For simplicity, unless otherwise specified, we will choose to treat SSL and TLS as the same protocol and refer to this protocol as SSL.

12.1.2 SSL security requirements

SSL is designed to establish a 'secure channel' between two entities. To this end, the main security requirements are fairly standard, although SSL is designed to be highly configurable and all these 'requirements' are in fact optional:

Confidentiality. Data transferred over the secure channel should only be accessible to the entities at either end of the channel, and not by any attacker who monitors the channel.

Data origin authentication. Data transferred over the secure channel should be integrity-protected against an attacker who can conduct active attacks on the channel, including falsification of the origin of the data.

Entity authentication. In order to set up the secure channel, it should be possible to establish the identity of each communicating entity.

It is important to recognise that the secure channel enabled by SSL only operates between two specific applications, such as a client web browser and a web server. If the 'real' destination of data sent by the client web browser is a back-end database beyond the web server, then the transfer between the web server and the back-end database may require separate protection.

12.1.3 Cryptography used in SSL

SSL is designed for use in open environments, where it is unreasonable to expect communicating entities to have agreed or exchanged security-related information such as cryptographic keys. Such security-related information is often referred to as a *security association*. For example, in the case of a user wishing to make a purchase from an online store, there is no reason to suppose that the user has ever purchased anything from this store before. Indeed, the user may have only discovered the store just minutes before deciding to make a transaction. Thus an SSL session must have the capability of being established between 'strangers'.

As we know from Section 5.1.1, this is exactly the type of situation where public-key cryptography is most effective. However, given that the amount of data that we may want to exchange over the secure channel is unspecified, and thus may be large, it follows from our discussion in Section 5.5.2 that this situation lends itself naturally to hybrid encryption. Indeed, this is precisely how SSL works. In fact SSL uses a wide range of cryptographic primitives. For example:

1. public-key cryptography is used to enable symmetric key establishment;
2. digital signatures are used to sign certificates and facilitate entity authentication;
3. symmetric encryption is used to provide confidentiality;
4. MACs are used to provide data origin authentication and facilitate entity authentication.
5. hash functions are used as components of MACs and digital signatures, and for key derivation.

SSL also accommodates the fact that different entities involved in an SSL session may have different preferences for specific cryptographic algorithms and key lengths. Thus SSL supports a range of different algorithms, which include:

- many well-known block ciphers, such as AES, normally in CBC mode;
- HMAC, implemented using a choice of well-known hash functions such as SHA-256;
- digital signature algorithms such as RSA and DSA.

One of the first tasks to be performed at the start of an SSL session is for the two communicating entities to agree on which collection of these algorithms they will use to secure the session. The collection of different algorithms that they agree upon is often referred to as a *cipher suite*.

413

12.1.4 SSL protocols

SSL essentially consists of two cryptographic protocols:

Handshake Protocol. This protocol performs all the tasks that require agreement between the two entities before they set up the secure SSL channel. In particular, this protocol can be used to:

- agree on the cryptographic algorithms to be used to establish the secure channel;
- establish entity authentication;
- establish the keys that will be needed to secure the channel.

Record Protocol. This protocol implements the secure channel. This includes:

- formatting the data (for example, breaking it up into blocks);
- computing MACs on the data;
- encrypting the data.

SIMPLE SSL HANDSHAKE PROTOCOL DESCRIPTION

We will now describe the SSL Handshake Protocol. We will describe a 'simple' version of this protocol, which is only designed to provide unilateral entity authentication of the server to the client. This is the most common mode of use of the protocol, although we later indicate how mutual entity authentication can be added. Our description is simplified, since we primarily want to indicate the use of cryptography in this protocol. Note that the names that we use for the protocol messages are not strictly the same as the 'official' SSL message names. The message flow of the simplified SSL Handshake Protocol is indicated in Figure 12.1.

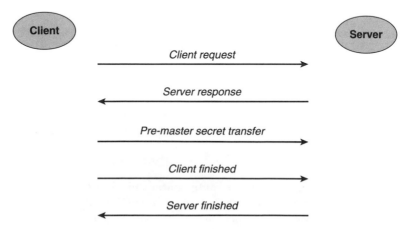

Figure 12.1. Simple SSL Handshake Protocol message flow

Client Request: This message from the client initiates the communication session and requests the establishment of an SSL-protected channel. As part of this request message, the client sends some data, including:

- a *session ID*, which acts as a unique identifier for the session;
- a pseudorandom number r_C, which will be used for the provision of freshness;
- a list of cipher suites that the client supports.

Server Response: The server responds by sending some initialisation data, including:

- the session ID;
- a pseudorandom number r_S, which is the server's freshness contribution to the protocol;
- the particular cipher suite that the server has decided to use (chosen from the list offered by the client).
- a copy of the server's public-key certificate, including details of any certificate chain required to verify this certificate.

At this point the client should check that the server's public-key certificate is valid. This will involve checking the validity of all the public-key certificates in the chain, as well as checking any relevant CRLs, as discussed in Section 11.3.3.

Pre-master Secret Transfer: The client now generates another pseudorandom number K_P, which it encrypts using the server's public key and sends to the server. Note that r_C and r_S are nonces used to provide freshness, hence they are not encrypted when they are exchanged. In contrast, K_P will be used to derive the keys that are used to secure the session, and hence must be protected when it is sent over the communication channel. This value K_P is referred to as the *pre-master secret* and is a value known only by the client and the server. (Note that it is also possible in SSL to choose to use the Diffie–Hellman protocol to establish K_P.)

The client and server are both now in a position to derive the keys that will be required to secure the SSL session. The first step in this process is to use a key derivation function to compute the *master secret* K_M. The key derivation function uses K_P as a key and takes as input, amongst other data, r_C and r_S. The client and server both then derive MAC and encryption keys from K_M (see our description of the SSL Record Protocol for details). From this point on, all messages that are exchanged are cryptographically 'protected'.

Client Finished. The client computes a MAC (the precise details of this process vary between versions, but most are based on HMAC) on the hash of all the messages sent thus far. This MAC is then encrypted and sent to the server.

Server Finished. The server checks the MAC received from the client. The server then computes a MAC on the hash of all the messages that have been sent thus far. This MAC is then encrypted and sent to the client.

415

Finally, the client checks the MAC received from the server.

ANALYSIS OF THE SIMPLE SSL HANDSHAKE PROTOCOL

We now confirm exactly how the simple SSL Handshake Protocol achieves its three main goals:

Agreement of cryptographic algorithms. This is achieved at the end of the second protocol message, when the server informs the client which cipher suite has been selected from the list provided by the client.

Entity authentication of the server. This relies on the following argument, assuming that the protocol run has been successful and that all checks (including certificate validity checks) have been correctly made:

1. The entity who sent the *Server Finished* message must know the master secret K_M, since the final check was correct and relied on knowledge of K_M.
2. Any entity other than the client who knows K_M must also know the pre-master secret K_P, since K_M is derived from K_P.
3. Any entity other than the client who knows K_P must know the private decryption key corresponding to the public-key certificate sent in the message *Server Response*, since this public key was used to encrypt K_P in the message *Pre-master Secret Transfer*.
4. The only entity with the ability to use the private decryption key is the genuine server, since the public-key certificate provided by the server in the message *Server Response* was checked and found to be valid.
5. The server is currently 'alive' because K_M is derived from fresh pseudorandom values (K_P and r_C) generated by the client and thus cannot be an old value.

Key establishment. SSL establishes several keys, as we will shortly discuss. These are all derived from the master secret K_M, which is a value that is established during the SSL Handshake Protocol. The master secret is derived from the pre-master secret K_P, which is a value that only the client and the server know.

Note that the *Client Finished* and *Server Finished* messages also provide retrospective data origin authentication of the entire message flow. This provides assurance that none of the messages exchanged during the SSL Handshake Protocol have been tampered with, which is particularly important since the opening messages of the protocol have no cryptographic protection.

SSL HANDSHAKE PROTOCOL WITH CLIENT AUTHENTICATION

The simple SSL Handshake Protocol does not provide mutual entity authentication, only entity authentication of the server. This is reasonable because many applications do not require client authentication at the layer of the network in which SSL is deployed. For example, when a user purchases goods from an online store, the merchant may not care about who they are communicating with, so long as they get paid at the end of the transaction. In this scenario, client authentication is more likely to be performed at the application layer, perhaps by using a password-based mechanism (see, for example, Section 12.4.4).

However, there are some applications of SSL, particularly in closed environments, where it may be useful to provide mutual entity authentication. In this case the simple SSL Handshake Protocol can be modified by adding an extra message from the client to the server after the message *Pre-master Secret Transfer*, as follows:

Client Authentication Data: The client sends a copy of its public-key certificate to the server. The public key in this certificate is used as a verification key. The certificate includes any details of the certificate chain required for verification. In addition, the client hashes all the protocol messages so far and digitally signs the hash using the client's signature key.

The server should now check that the client's public-key certificate (chain) is valid. The server should also verify the client's digital signature. If these checks are successful then the server has entity authentication assurance of the client by the following argument:

1. The entity who sent the *Client Authentication Data* message must know the signature key corresponding to the public key in the client's certificate, since the digital signature verified correctly.
2. The only entity who knows the signature key is the genuine client, since the public-key certificate provided by the client was checked and found to be valid.
3. The client is currently 'alive' because the digital signature was computed on a hash of some data that included the fresh pseudorandom value r_S generated by the server, and thus cannot be a replay.

SSL RECORD PROTOCOL

The SSL Record Protocol is the protocol used to instantiate the secure channel after the SSL Handshake Protocol has successfully completed. Before running the SSL Record Protocol, both the client and the server derive the cryptographic data that they will need to secure the session. This includes symmetric session keys for encryption, symmetric MAC keys and any required IVs. These are all generated using a key derivation function to compute a *key block*. This key derivation function uses K_M as a key and takes as input, amongst other data, r_C and r_S. The key block is then 'chopped up' to provide the necessary cryptographic data. In particular, the following four symmetric keys are extracted from the key block:

- K_{ECS} for symmetric encryption from the client to the server;
- K_{ESC} for symmetric encryption from the server to the client;
- K_{MCS} for MACs from the client to the server;
- K_{MSC} for MACs from the server to the client.

The SSL Record Protocol specifies the process for using these keys to protect traffic exchanged between the client and the server. For example, for data sent from the client to the server, the process is:

1. compute a MAC on the data (and various other inputs) using key K_{MCS};
2. append the MAC to the data and then pad, if necessary, to a multiple of the block length;
3. encrypt the resulting message using key K_{ECS}.

Upon receipt of the protected message, the server decrypts it using K_{ECS} and then verifies the recovered MAC using K_{MCS}. It is interesting to note that SSL uses a variant of the MAC-then-encrypt construction that we referred to in Section 6.3.6.

12.1.5 SSL key management

We now consider SSL key management issues by examining some of the phases of the key management lifecycle.

KEY MANAGEMENT SYSTEM

SSL essentially relies on two 'separate' key management systems:

Public-key management system. Since SSL is designed for use in open environments, it relies on an external key management system that governs the public-key pairs that are required by SSL users (which is *all users* if mutual entity authentication is required, or just users who are *servers* if only unilateral entity authentication is required). This key management system is beyond the scope of an SSL specification and is relied on to establish and maintain public-key certificates and information concerning their validity. If this system fails then the security provided by SSL is undermined.

Symmetric key management system. Within SSL is a self-contained symmetric key management system. SSL is used to generate symmetric sessions keys, which are designed to have limited lifetimes.

Of course these are not really independent key management systems, since there are aspects of the key management lifecycle where these two systems overlap. However, we separate them to indicate that there are certain aspects of key management that are beyond the scope of SSL itself.

KEY GENERATION

There are two types of keys deployed in SSL:

Asymmetric keys. These are generated using the public-key management system, which is not governed by the specification of SSL.
Symmetric keys. These are all generated within SSL. As described in Section 12.1.4, the session keys are all derived from the master secret that is established

following the SSL Handshake Protocol. Key derivation is a suitable technique for key generation because:

- it is a lightweight key generation technique, which does not impose significant overheads;
- it allows several different session keys to be established from just one shared secret;
- as the SSL Handshake Protocol is relatively expensive to run (it requires the use of public key cryptography), the shared master secret can be used to establish several batches of session keys, should this be desirable.

However, the generation of the master secret does rely on the client being able to randomly generate a pre-master secret. Should the client fail to do this securely using a suitable technique (see Section 8.1) then the subsequent generation of all the SSL session keys could be compromised.

The key lengths used in SSL are all negotiable and part of the cryptographic algorithm agreement process defined in the SSL Handshake Protocol.

KEY ESTABLISHMENT

The most important key establishment process in SSL is the establishment of the pre-master secret during the SSL Handshake Protocol. Probably the most common technique for conducting this is to use RSA public-key encryption during the protocol message *Pre-master Secret Transfer*. However, a variant based on Diffie–Hellman is also supported by SSL.

KEY STORAGE

Key storage is beyond the scope of SSL, but it relies on both the client and the server securely storing relevant secret keys. The most sensitive keys to store are the private keys, since they are relied upon across multiple SSL sessions. In contrast, the symmetric keys negotiated during the SSL Handshake Protocol are only used for a relatively short period of time. Nonetheless, if they are compromised then so are any sessions that they are used to protect.

KEY USAGE

One of the interesting design aspects of SSL is how it embraces the principle of key separation, discussed in Section 10.6.1. Separate encryption and MAC keys are derived from the master secret, which are then used to establish the secure channel. However, SSL takes this principle a step further by deploying separate keys for each communication direction, which provides security against reflection attacks (see Section 9.3.4). The cost of this is low because these separate keys are derived from the common master secret.

However, largely for convenience, SSL also abuses the principle of key separation. The master secret K_M is used not only as a key derivation key, but also as a MAC key. This is a good example of pragmatism in adoption of the principle of key separation. It is enforced for the vulnerable session keys that will be used for protecting data. It is relaxed for the less-exposed master secret, which is only publicly used to create MACs during the SSL Handshake Protocol.

12.1.6 SSL security issues

SSL is a popular communication protocol and is generally regarded as cryptographically 'strong' if used with respected cryptographic algorithms. Most security problems experienced using recent versions of SSL have arisen from aspects that are beyond the scope of the protocol specification. These include:

Process failures. The most common 'failure' of SSL arises when a client does not perform the necessary checks to validate the server's public-key certificate. A web user who is presented with a dialogue box warning them of their browser's inability to verify a public-key certificate is quite likely to disregard it and proceed with establishing an SSL session. Indeed, it is rather hard to place too much blame on them for doing so.

A particularly common manifestation of this problem on the Internet is when a rogue web server, holding a legitimate public-key certificate in its own name, tries to pass itself off as another web server. Even if the client web browser successfully verifies the rogue web server's certificate chain, if the client does not notice that the public-key certificate is not in the name of the expected web server then the rogue web server will succeed in establishing an SSL protected channel with the client. This is an entity authentication failure because the client has succeeded in setting up an SSL session, but it is not with the server that they think it is with. This failure is often exploited during phishing attacks.

Note that the above phishing attack is not a failure of the SSL Handshake Protocol. It is a failure in the surrounding processes that support the protocol. In this case the client has failed to conduct a protocol action (validating the server's certificate chain) with a sufficient degree of rigour.

Implementation failures. Because it is an open protocol that can be adopted for many different applications, on different platforms, by anyone, SSL is particularly vulnerable to implementation failures. Even if the protocol specification is followed correctly, it could fail if a supporting component is weak. For example, if the client uses a weak deterministic generator to generate the pre-master secret K_p then the protocol can be compromised because the session keys become too predictable.

Key management failures. As discussed in Section 12.1.5, if either the client or the server mismanages their cryptographic keys then the protocol can be compromised. For example, if an attacker obtains the server's private key then the attacker can recover the pre-master secret. The attacker can then compute all the resulting session keys and hence undermine any secure channel that these session keys are used to establish.

Usage failures. SSL has such a high profile that it runs the risk of being used inappropriately. Alternatively it may be appropriately deployed, but its security properties overestimated under the misapprehension that use of SSL 'guarantees' security. Perhaps the classic example of the latter is our default SSL application of securing the connection between a client web browser and the web server of an online store. Such stores often claim to offer a 'completely secure' service because they are deploying SSL. This of course tells the client nothing about the security of their payment card details after the web server has acquired them. After all, largely due to the use of SSL, criminals seeking payment card details are more likely to hack into a back-end database, rather than engage in large-scale monitoring of network traffic.

12.1.7 SSL design issues

Having discussed the use of cryptography in SSL at some length, we close by remarking on a few of the design issues that appear to have influenced the cryptographic choices made by the designers of SSL.

Support for a range of publicly known cryptographic algorithms. Since SSL (in this case we really mean TLS) is an open standard targeted at wide-scale public use, it is fundamental that it supports not just publicly known algorithms, but a *range of* publicly known algorithms. This supports cross-platform use and has helped to foster confidence in SSL as a protocol.

Flexibility. SSL is not only flexible in terms of the components that can be used to implement it, but it is also flexible in the ways in which it can be used (for example, to provide unilateral or mutual entity authentication). This, again, is because SSL has been targeted at a wide range of application environments.

Minimal use of public-key operations. The use of hybrid encryption restricts the number of public-key operations to the minimum necessary to establish a secure channel. Although we have not discussed this in any detail, SSL is also designed so that the relatively expensive SSL Handshake Protocol may not need to be rerun if a client requires another session with the same server within a specified time period.

Unbalanced computational requirements. Recall that in the SSL Handshake Protocol it is the client who is required to generate the pre-master secret and send it encrypted to the server. This means that the client performs one public-key *encryption* operation and the server performs one public-key *decryption* operation. One reason for this is that some public-key cryptosystems, and RSA is a good example, have certain public keys that are considerably more computationally efficient to use than others (see Section 10.3.4). Thus it is reasonable to assume that encryption is a faster operation than decryption. The design of SSL thus places a slight computational 'burden' on the server, which is the entity expected to have the greater computational ability.

12.2 Cryptography for wireless local area networks

It is extremely important to provide security for wireless networks, since these networks are particularly vulnerable to some types of external attack. However, one of the most interesting aspects of wireless network security is the cryptographic design errors that were made when developing certain wireless network security standards. In this section we look at the example of wireless local area networks and discuss the problems that have arisen in their underlying cryptographic design.

12.2.1 WLAN background

Many users of computers are accustomed to the inherent network 'security' provided by the use of physical wires to communicate between different devices. Although a determined attacker can 'tap' a wired communication, this requires physical access to the wires themselves. Hence many attacks on wired networks tend to focus on the machines at the ends of the wires; for example, by installing malicious software on a machine that monitors traffic being sent and received on the network by that machine.

The advent of wireless communication has brought numerous benefits, perhaps the most significant being convenience. An office or home can easily establish a network without messy wiring being installed. Also, networks can be established in places where they were once awkward to install, such as railway stations, restaurants and conference venues.

However, without the security provided by physical wires, wireless networks are much more vulnerable to attack. Without built-in security, the information exchanged over them can be monitored (and potentially modified) by anyone geographically close enough to access them. For example, access to a wired home network is, by and large, restricted to someone who can enter the building and physically access either the machines or the wires. In contrast, a wireless network is potentially accessible to someone located outside the building.

The type of wireless network that is typically deployed between devices in an office or home environment is known as a *wireless local area network* (WLAN). The international standards for WLAN communications are governed by the *Institute of Electrical and Electronics Engineers* (IEEE) and are collectively referred to as IEEE 802.11. The original version of the IEEE 802.11 standard was released in 1997, but there have been many amendments since then. Some devices that are certified to be compliant with IEEE 802.11 are labelled by the trademark *Wi-Fi*, which is an indicator of interoperability.

A simple WLAN architecture is shown in Figure 12.2. A *wireless access point* is a piece of hardware that acts as a bridge between the wireless network and a wired network (for example, the wired network that delivers a connection to the Internet from a home). The access point consists of a radio, an interface with the wired network and bridging software. A *device* is any computer (for example, a desktop

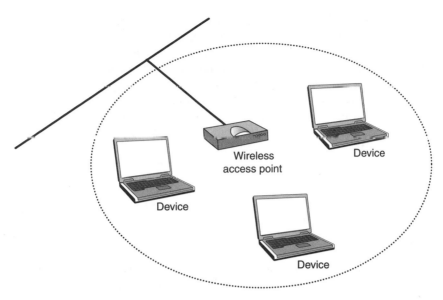

Figure 12.2. Simple WLAN architecture

PC, laptop or PDA) which has a wireless network interface card that allows it to communicate over a wireless network. A WLAN may consist of many devices all communicating with the one access point, or indeed may involve several different access points.

The original 802.11 standard defined the *Wired Equivalent Privacy* (WEP) mechanism to protect WLAN communication. WEP was designed to provide security at the data link layer, which means that it operates at a virtual networking layer that is close to being the equivalent of physical wires in a wired network. However, as we will shortly discuss, there were many serious problems with the deployment of cryptography in WEP. In 2002, an improved security mechanism known as *Wi-Fi Protected Access* (WPA) was proposed. This was intended to be a temporary solution, designed to improve security whilst being capable of running on legacy hardware. In the meantime a complete redesign of the underlying cryptographic components was underway, which was published as WPA2 in 2004 as part of the IEEE 802.11i standard. We will discuss all of these mechanisms for securing WLANs, because they not only represent an interesting and important application of cryptography, but the development process also provides several valuable cryptographic design lessons.

12.2.2 WLAN security requirements

The scope of the security requirements for a WLAN are defined by the notion that a WLAN should be *as secure as a wired network*. This idea is rather vague, since the two types of network are very different and such security equivalence cannot be precisely established or measured. However, the notion is useful because it provides a security 'target' that helps to influence certain design decisions. As an example, WLAN security mechanisms are not intended to prevent denial-of-service attacks, since a wired network is not inherently protected against these; returning to our scenario of a home network, an external attacker who is located outside a building with a wired home network could potentially cut a wire that supplied communications or power to the building. In Section 12.3 we will see that a similar notion of security has been used to define the scope of security requirements for mobile telecommunications.

With this scope in mind, the security requirements for a WLAN are:

Confidentiality. Data transferred over the WLAN should be kept confidential. As we remarked earlier, tapping a wired network takes a bit of effort, so a wireless network should also offer suitable protection.

Mutual entity authentication. Communicating entities can identify one another when setting up a WLAN connection. This is motivated by the fact that a degree of inherent (very weak) 'entity authentication' is provided by physical wires, but there are no such guarantees once we are in a wireless environment.

Data origin authentication. The source of all data transferred over the WLAN should be assured. This is because an attacker could easily modify data transmitted during a WLAN session after the initial entity authentication has been conducted. The original WLAN security standard WEP only provides a weak level of data integrity, which is not good enough.

12.2.3 WEP

There are three cryptographic design decisions that are common to all of the WLAN security mechanisms that we discuss:

- Since WLANs may be comprised of many different types of device, from different manufacturers, it is important that the cryptography used in a WLAN is widely available. Hence it would not be wise to deploy proprietary cryptographic algorithms.
- Since these mechanisms are dedicated to WLAN security and do not require the full flexibility of the likes of SSL, it makes sense to decide which cryptographic algorithms to use in advance and then deploy them universally, rather than require an expensive equivalent of the SSL Handshake Protocol to negotiate them.
- Since speed and efficiency are important, and WLANs are usually linked to some sort of fixed infrastructure, symmetric cryptography is a natural choice.

However, the cryptographic details of each of the proposed mechanisms vary considerably. We start by looking at the original proposal of WEP, which uses:

1. The stream cipher RC4 for encryption. A stream cipher is a reasonable choice, since a wireless communication channel is prone to errors (see Section 4.2.4).

The choice of RC4 was also reasonable at the time, since it was well respected and widely deployed in other applications, including SSL (although RC4 was originally a proprietary stream cipher, the details were publicly known by the time of the design of WEP). It would not be regarded as a good choice today, since the security of RC4 is no longer regarded as sufficient for modern applications.

2. A simple *CRC checksum* for data integrity. The problem with this type of checksum is that, in a similar way to using a hash function on its own to provide data integrity (see Section 6.2.2), an attacker can modify the data and then recompute the correct CRC checksum for the modified data. Hence this checksum can only be relied upon to detect accidental changes to the data.

3. A simple challenge–response protocol to provide entity authentication.

CONFIDENTIALITY AND INTEGRITY MECHANISMS IN WEP

In many ways, the cryptographic design of WEP was very naive. We now look at the mechanisms for providing confidentiality and data integrity in more detail, in order to illustrate some of the design errors.

The first WEP design decision was to use a *shared, fixed symmetric key* in each WLAN. This same key is used by all devices, for several different purposes, when communicating using a WEP-secured WLAN. This almost eliminates any issues regarding key establishment, however, it introduces considerable risks. In particular, if one of the devices is compromised then this key may become known to an attacker, and hence the entire network will be compromised. The original version of WEP only used a 40-bit key, but later adaptations allow much longer keys.

As discussed in Section 4.2.4, one problem with deploying a stream cipher such as RC4 is the need for synchronisation, especially in a potentially noisy channel such as a wireless one. Thus WEP requires each packet of data to be encrypted separately, so that loss of a packet does not affect the rest of the data being sent. This introduces a new problem. In Section 4.2.2 we discussed the negative consequences of re-using keystream for more than one plaintext. It follows that WEP requires a mechanism for making sure that the same keystream is not reused for subsequent packets.

The solution to this problem in WEP was to introduce an initialisation vector (IV), which just like the IVs used in several of the modes of operation of a block cipher (see Section 4.6), varies each time the WEP key is used to encrypt a packet. However, RC4 does not easily allow an IV to be incorporated into the encryption process, hence the WEP IV is directly appended to the key. In this way WEP defines a 'per-packet' key, which consists of a 24-bit IV appended to the WEP key.

If Alice wants to set up a secure WLAN connection with Bob, based on the shared, fixed WEP key K, the encryption process for each packet of data to be sent is depicted in Figure 12.3 and is as follows.

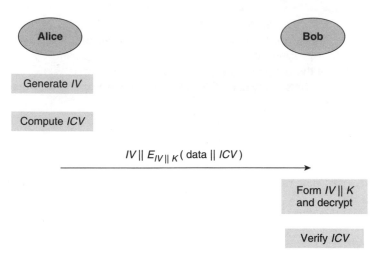

Figure 12.3. WEP encryption process

Alice:

1. generates a 24-bit pseudorandom initialisation vector *IV* and appends the WEP key *K* to *IV* to form the key:

$$K' = IV \| K;$$

2. computes a 32-bit CRC checksum *ICV* of the data, and appends this to the data;
3. encrypts the data plus *ICV* using key *K'*;
4. sends *IV* (in the clear) and the resulting ciphertext to Bob.

Bob then:

1. appends the WEP key *K* to the received *IV* to form the key *K'*;
2. decrypts the ciphertext using *K'* and extracts the checksum *ICV*;
3. verifies that the checksum *ICV* is correct.

If the verification of *ICV* is successful then Bob accepts the data packet.

ENTITY AUTHENTICATION IN WEP

The WEP entity authentication technique is very simple. It is based on the same challenge–response principle that we first discussed for dynamic passwords in Section 8.5 and that was used in several of the protocols analysed in Section 9.4. If Alice (a device) wants to identify herself to Bob (a wireless access point):

1. Alice sends a request to authenticate to Bob;
2. Bob sends a nonce r_B to Alice;

3. Alice uses WEP encryption to encrypt r_B (importantly for later, note from our above explanation of the WEP encryption process that this also involves Alice generating an IV that is used to 'extend' the WEP key).
4. Alice sends the IV and the resulting ciphertext to Bob;
5. Bob decrypts the ciphertext and checks that it decrypts to r_B; if it does, he authenticates Alice.

This simple protocol is based on Bob's assumption that only an authorised user such as Alice should know the WEP key K.

12.2.4 Attacks on WEP

WEP is perhaps the most criticised security standard ever proposed and there is very little right about it! We will briefly review some of the many concerns.

WEP KEY MANAGEMENT WEAKNESSES

We will start with key management. There are several serious problems with WEP key management:

Use of a shared fixed key. The WEP key K acts as an overall 'master key' for the WLAN and, as such, is a single point of failure. If the WEP key can be compromised (and it suffices that this compromise arises on just one of the entities forming the WLAN) and an attacker learns the WEP key then the entire WLAN security is compromised.

Exposure of the WEP key. In its role as a master key, the WEP key is unnecessarily 'exposed' through direct use as a component of an encryption key (see Section 10.4.1). It is also exposed in this way each time an authentication attempt is made.

No key separation. WEP abuses the principle of key separation (see Section 10.6.1) by using the WEP key for multiple purposes.

Key length. While WEP does allow the WEP key length to vary, the smallest RC4 key length is 40 bits, which is far too short to be secure against contemporary exhaustive key searches. Perhaps more problematically, many WEP implementations allow WEP keys to be generated from passwords which, if not long enough, reduce the effective keyspace that an attacker needs to search.

WEP ENTITY AUTHENTICATION WEAKNESSES

We now look at attacks concerning the entity authentication mechanism.

Rogue wireless access point. WEP only provides *unilateral* entity authentication from a device (Alice) to a wireless access point (Bob). This means that an attacker could set up a rogue access point and allow Alice to authenticate to it, without Alice realising that she was not dealing with the genuine access point.

Lack of session key. WEP does not establish a session key during entity authentication that is later used to protect the communication session. As a result, WEP entity authentication is only valid for the 'instant in time' at which it is conducted. WEP thus suffers from the potential for a 'hijack' of the communication session, as discussed in Section 8.3.1.

Keystream replay attack. Another serious problem is that there is no protection against replays of the WEP authentication process. An attacker who observes Alice authenticating to Bob is able to capture a plaintext (the challenge r_B and its CRC checksum) and the resulting ciphertext (the encrypted response). Since WEP uses the stream cipher RC4, the keystream can be recovered by XORing the plaintext to the ciphertext (see Section 4.2.1). We will denote this keystream by $KS(IV \| K)$, since it is the keystream produced by RC4 using the encryption key $IV \| K$. Note that this is not yet an 'attack', because our standard assumptions of Section 1.5.1 dictate that good stream ciphers are designed to offer protection against an attacker who knows corresponding plaintext/ciphertext pairs, and hence can recover keystream from this knowledge. However, this relies on the same keystream not being reused in a predictable manner (see Section 4.2.2). This is where WEP fails, since the attacker can now falsely authenticate to Bob as follows (and depicted in Figure 12.4):

1. The attacker requests to authenticate to Bob;
2. Bob sends a nonce r'_B to the attacker (assuming that Bob is properly generating his nonces, it is very unlikely that $r'_B = r_B$);
3. The attacker computes the CRC checksum ICV on r'_B. The attacker then encrypts $r'_B \| ICV$ by XORing it with the keystream $KS(IV \| K)$; note:
   - the attacker does not know the WEP key K, but does know this portion of keystream;
   - in line with WEP encryption, the attacker also first sends the IV that was observed during Alice's authentication session to Bob;
4. Bob decrypts the ciphertext, which should result in recovery of r'_B, in which case Bob accepts the attacker.

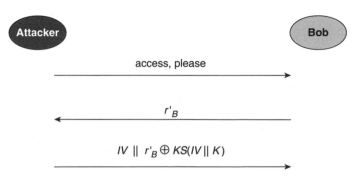

Figure 12.4. Keystream replay attack on WEP authentication

This attack works because WEP allows the attacker to 'force' Bob to use the same IV that Alice used in the genuine authentication session, and hence use the same encryption key $IV \parallel K$, which in turn validates the use of the previous keystream. Of course, having authenticated to the access point, the attacker cannot do much more since the attacker still does not know the WEP key K and hence cannot perform valid encryptions and decryptions. Nonetheless, the authentication process has been successfully attacked. Indeed, more generally, the use of a stream cipher in a challenge–response protocol is ill-advised (see the related activity at the end of Chapter 8).

WEP CONFIDENTIALITY AND INTEGRITY WEAKNESSES

We now identify some attacks on the confidentiality and integrity mechanisms in WEP. These include attacks that can reveal the WEP key to an attacker.

CRC manipulation attack. This attack exploits the fact that the CRC checksum used to provide data integrity is not a cryptographic primitive, but is a highly 'linear' function. This means that certain changes to the checksum output (ICV) can be used to deduce changes to the underlying data packet. Because of this, the encrypted ICV can be manipulated and then the receiver's behaviour (either to accept or reject a data packet) monitored in order to deduce information about an underlying data packet. In this way it might be possible to recover an unknown data packet without knowing the WEP key.

Birthday attack on IVs. The length of the IV in WEP is only 24 bits. This means that there are 2^{24} possible different IVs. From our discussions of birthday attacks in Section 6.2.3, we know that we can expect that if around 2^{12} (which is only about 4000) data packets are sent, then two of these data packets will probably have the same IV. Even if the IV is an ascending counter then, for example, if the access point transmits data at a rate of 11 megabits per second then all the IVs are exhausted after about five hours, after which the IV will necessarily repeat. If two data packets have the same IV then they will have been encrypted using the same RC4 key. As the WEP key is fixed, an attacker can expect, over time, to find large numbers of data packets that have been encrypted using the same encryption key. This is something that we observed in Section 4.2.2 is not desirable for stream ciphers. Note that this attack is independent of the length of the WEP key. In practice this is quite a hard attack to conduct but, unfortunately for WEP, there are even more serious attacks against the encryption mechanism.

Key recovery attack. Most seriously of all, the way that RC4 keys are formed from IVs can be exploited in order to define a clever statistical attack, which by 2010 had been refined to the point where it was possible to recover WEP keys with high probability after less than ten thousand data packets had been observed. Since the WEP key is fixed, this is a fatal flaw. While this attack is not obvious, it is easy to deploy using widely available tools.

WEP DESIGN FLAWS

The designers of WEP set out with an admiral goal to provide *enough* security, but not *excessive* security, in order to keep WLANs secure but efficient. In doing so they were attempting to establish a particular efficiency–security tradeoff. It is clear that they did not succeed and that they sacrificed too much security in the name of efficiency.

However, some of the problems with the WEP cryptographic design appear to arise not from knowledgeable tradeoffs, but from fundamental misunderstandings. These include:

Poor key management. The decision to use one shared, fixed, key in a WEP-protected WLAN to provide all the WEP security services is extremely risky. We have just seen that WEP encryption keys can be recovered given enough data packets. Such an attack would be regarded as very serious for any cryptosystem, even if it changed its keys regularly. For WEP, with its fixed key, this attack is disastrous.

Failure to appreciate the effective key length. The way that the RC4 encryption keys are formed in WEP provides a false sense of security with respect to key length. Even if the WEP key is a respectable length, the RC4 encryption key only varies in 24 bits each time that an encryption operation is performed. This leads to problems, such as our *birthday attack on IVs*.

Lack of a proper cryptographic data origin authentication mechanism. The poor choice of data integrity mechanism leads to attacks that can exploit the fact that CRC checksums can be manipulated. Data origin authentication should have been provided using a suitable cryptographic primitive. Given that WEP relies on symmetric encryption, the 'correct' tool for this job is a MAC.

Non-standard use of a cryptographic algorithm. WEP provides an excellent example of why it is important to use cryptographic algorithms in the intended way, and not to 'tinker' with them. The *key recovery attack* that we mentioned is not an attack on RC4. It is an attack on the fact that RC4 was not used in a standard way in WEP. Instead, the RC4 encryption keys were formed using a technique that was invented for WEP, but not one that had been sufficiently analysed by cryptographic experts. Since it was this technique that was exploited in the powerful key recovery attack on WEP, this shows that even a small change in the way that a cryptographic algorithm is used can result in an insecure cryptographic mechanism.

Weak entity authentication mechanism. The WEP entity authentication mechanism can be exploited in several different ways, as we discussed. Use of a stream cipher in this mechanism is highly inappropriate.

Thus WEP has provided us with a wide range of valuable cryptographic design lessons, many of which have wider implications.

12.2.5 WPA and WPA2

We now look at how WPA and WPA2 overcome the many problems with WEP.

MUTUAL ENTITY AUTHENTICATION AND KEY ESTABLISHMENT

In order to avoid all the problems relating to use of a shared, fixed WEP key, a key hierarchy (see Section 10.4.1) is employed. The top key in this key hierarchy is known as the *pairwise master key PMK*, which is a key that is shared between a device and a wireless access point. There are two ways in which this key *PMK* can be established:

1. *During an AKE protocol that is run between a device and a central authentication server.* Both WPA and WPA2 support the use of a central authentication server to provide authentication in a way that is scalable and can be tailored to fit the needs of the specific application environment. A wide range of authentication techniques are supported by the *Extensible Authentication Protocol* (EAP), which is a suite of entity authentication mechanisms that includes methods that deploy SSL (see Section 12.1) to secure a connection to an authentication server.

2. *As a pre-shared key that is programmed directly into the device and the wireless access point.* This is most suitable for small networks. The most common method for generating *PMK* is by deriving it from a password. Any users requiring access to the WLAN must be made aware of this password. A home user who purchases a wireless router may be provided with a (weak) default password from the manufacturer or service provider. It is important that this is changed on first installation to something less predictable.

Note that even if a device has successfully authenticated itself to a central authentication server and this server has passed *PMK* to the wireless access point, it is still necessary for the device to authenticate itself to the access point. Regardless of how *PMK* has been established, it forms the basis for this entity authentication process between the device and the access point. The master key *PMK* is also used to derive session keys using the following AKE protocol that runs between Alice (a device) and Bob (a wireless access point) and is shown in Figure 12.5:

1. Alice generates a nonce r_A and sends r_A to Bob.
2. Bob generates a nonce r_B. Bob then uses r_A, r_B and *PMK* to derive the following four 128-bit session keys:
   - an encryption key *EK*;
   - a MAC key *MK*;
   - a data encryption key *DEK*;
   - a data MAC key *DMK*.

431

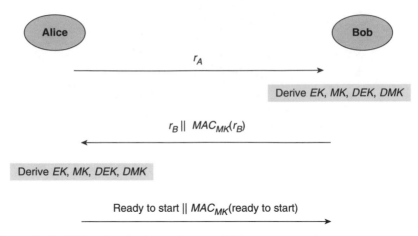

Figure 12.5. WPA authentication and key establishment protocol

3. Bob then sends r_B to Alice, along with a MAC computed on r_B using MAC key MK.
4. Alice uses r_A, r_B and PMK to derive the four session keys. She then checks the MAC that she has just received from Bob.
5. Alice sends a message to Bob stating that she is ready to start using encryption. She computes a MAC on this message using MAC key MK.
6. Bob verifies the MAC and sends an acknowledgement to Alice.

At the end of this protocol both Alice and Bob have achieved mutual entity authentication, since each has demonstrated knowledge of PMK by successfully computing MACs using MK, which is derived from PMK. (Strictly speaking, Bob has only achieved assurance that Alice is *one of* the authorised users of the WLAN, since there may be more than one user sharing PMK with Bob.) In addition, Alice and Bob have agreed on four session keys. Two of these, DEK and DMK, will be used to secure the data exchanged between Alice and Bob in the coming session (the fourth key EK plays a role in group key management, which we will not discuss).

CONFIDENTIALITY AND DATA ORIGIN AUTHENTICATION IN WPA

WPA and WPA2 differ in the way that they provide protection for the data exchanged during a communication session between a device and a wireless access point. Recall that WPA was designed as a temporary 'fix' of WEP, while WPA2 is a complete redesign.

While WPA still uses RC4, it features several design improvements:

- The RC4 encryption key is created by *mixing DEK* and an IV, rather than concatenating, as in WEP. Further, a separate encryption key is derived by such

432

a mixing for each packet sent. These simple changes are enough to prevent several of the attacks on WEP.

• Data origin authentication is provided using a MAC, rather than the easily manipulated CRC checksum used in WEP. The recommended MAC is a special lightweight mechanism tailored for WPA known as *Michael*.

While these are both definite improvements over WEP, they are both still unconventional cryptographic primitives, albeit ones that have been carefully designed by cryptographic experts.

CONFIDENTIALITY AND DATA ORIGIN AUTHENTICATION IN WPA2

WPA2 represents a complete redesign and uses standard cryptographic mechanisms. In particular, WPA2 adopts AES instead of RC4 as the underlying encryption algorithm.

WPA2 provides confidentiality and data origin authentication together in one mechanism by deploying AES in a protocol referred to as the *Counter Mode with CBC-MAC Protocol* (CCMP). CCMP is based on the CCM mode of operation of a block cipher that we discussed in Section 6.3.6. As indicated in Section 6.3.6, this avoids the need to provide these services using separate mechanisms. CCMP includes mechanisms for deriving fresh keys for each separate CCM 'encryption'. Note that if CCMP is used then it is only necessary to derive one data key during the WPA2 AKE protocol, instead of separate keys *DEK* and *DMK*.

12.2.6 WLAN security issues

Perhaps the most interesting aspect of WLAN security is that some of the problems have arisen from errors in cryptographic mechanism design, which is relatively unusual. As we have repeatedly observed, it is far more common for vulnerabilities to arise elsewhere, such as during implementation and key management (see Section 3.2.4). However, it would seem that WPA2 addresses all of the previous problems and provides good cryptographic protection. To date there have been no serious attacks on the cryptography used in WPA or WPA2.

The most vulnerable aspect of WPA2 security remains the potential for the *PMK* derivation in small (home) networks to rely on a weak password or passphrase. This is a very important issue because all the subsequent session keys are derived from this pre-shared key, and the mutual entity authentication process relies on *PMK* only being known by authorised devices and the wireless access point. If this type of key derivation is being used then all the potential problems with passwords and passphrases, such as those discussed in Section 8.4.1, apply to WPA2 security. There is also the potential risk that home users use default keys that are supplied with their equipment, rather than establish their own.

433

12.2.7 WLAN design issues

The main cryptographic design issues concerning WLAN security are as follows:

Use of symmetric cryptography. This is a sensible decision because WLANs transfer bulk traffic between networked devices, hence speed of encryption is important. For small networks, such as a home network, key establishment is straightforward. Larger enterprise WLANs may optionally choose to use public-key mechanisms as part of the initial authentication between a device and a central authentication server, but the core WPA2 security protocol CCMP uses only symmetric cryptography.

Use of recognised cryptographic mechanisms. This was not adhered to in WEP, where the cryptographic design was rather ad hoc. WEP thus provides a useful lesson regarding the potential folly of adopting unconventional mechanisms. In contrast, WPA2 adopts more widely accepted cryptographic mechanisms.

Flexibility, but only when appropriate. While WLANs may be deployed in quite different environments, they do not require the same cryptographic flexibility as open applications such as SSL. Thus it makes sense to 'lock down' the cryptographic mechanisms, where appropriate. WPA2 does this for the confidentiality and data origin authentication services. However, WPA2 allows for flexibility in choosing the initial entity authentication mechanism (between the device and a centralised authentication server), recognising that different environments may well have different approaches to identifying network users.

The potential need to cater for migration. When the flaws in WEP became apparent, it was clear that due to the difficulty of upgrading a widely deployed technology, any complete redesign of the WLAN security mechanisms could not be rolled out quickly. It was thus necessary to design a 'fix' that was based on the existing cryptographic mechanisms, which would provide 'good enough' security. The 'fix' is WPA, which is based on RC4. The 'complete redesign' is WPA2, which is based on AES.

12.3 Cryptography for mobile telecommunications

We now look at a very different application of cryptography, but one that most of us use almost every day. The aspect that makes it so different from the previous two applications that we have studied is the nature of the operating environment. Mobile telecommunication services are provided by companies who have agreed on certain operational standards in order to make their services compatible. Collectively they thus represent a sort of 'closed' environment, albeit one distributed across a substantial number of different organisations. We will see that this has influenced some of the cryptographic design decisions that have been taken.

12.3.1 GSM and UMTS background

In Section 12.2.1 we observed that there is an inherent level of physical security provided by a wired computer network. The same can be said for a wired telecommunications network. Thus, in a very similar way to the development of WLANs, the advent of mobile telecommunications brought with it a range of new threats that did not exist for traditional wired telecommunications networks.

These problems were not recognised by the designers of the first mobile phone systems. These used analogue signals and did not have suitable protection. Mobile handsets sent their serial numbers in the clear, leaving them highly susceptible to cloning. A cloned phone could then be used by an attacker at the expense of the genuine user. Eavesdropping on calls was also straightforward.

This situation was clearly unacceptable for everyone involved. It raised privacy concerns for mobile phone customers, as well as the considerable inconvenience of dealing with the aftermath of a phone cloning incident. More significantly, mobile telecommunications operators faced loss of revenue and reputation through incidents of fraud.

The shift from analogue to digital communications brought with it the opportunity to use cryptographic techniques to provide security. In doing so, the development of the *Global System for Mobile Communication* (GSM) standard by the *European Telecommunications Standards Institute* (ETSI) brought security to mobile telecommunications. We will look in some detail at the cryptographic aspects of GSM security. Third generation, or 3G, mobile phones are characterised by higher data transmission rates and a much richer range of services. We will briefly discuss the enhanced security of GSM's successor for 3G phones, the *Universal Mobile Telecommunications System* (UMTS).

The basic architecture of a mobile telecommunications network is shown in Figure 12.6. The network is divided into a large number of geographic *cells*, each of which is controlled by a *base station*. A mobile phone first connects with its nearest base station, which directs communications either to the home network of the mobile phone user or to other networks in order to transfer call data.

12.3.2 GSM security requirements

One of the main drivers behind GSM's security mechanisms was revenue protection. Mobile telecommunications is big business and mobile operators pay substantial sums for the frequency ranges that they use. It is very important to mobile operators that they charge the right customers for the services that these customers have genuinely used. However, because mobile telecommunications is a business, the security provided by GSM must be cost-effective and limited to that which is strictly necessary.

The overarching design guideline for GSM was that the resulting system should be *as secure as the Public Switched Telephone Network* (PSTN). This is very

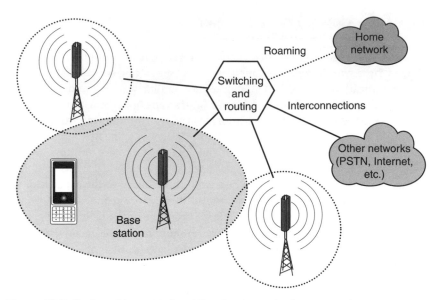

Figure 12.6. Basic architecture of mobile telecommunications network

much in the same spirit as the guidelines for developing WLAN security that we discussed in Section 12.2.2. It is widely rumoured that GSM was not designed to go further and provide *end-to-end security* (meaning security throughout the entire path from source to destination) because governments were keen to maintain the degree of intercept access that they have to the PSTN. This led to the following specific security requirements:

Entity authentication of the user. Mobile operators need to have strong assurance of the identity of users connecting with their services in order to reduce fraud. This issue is much simpler to deal with in traditional telephone networks, since a user needs to have physical access to the end of a telephone wire in order to use the services.

Confidentiality on the radio path. In simple terms, a mobile connection passes 'over the air' (the *radio path*) between the handset and a base station, after which it is passed through a switching centre and enters the traditional PSTN (see Figure 12.6). Thus in order to provide 'PSTN-equivalent security', the main link for which GSM needs to provide additional security is the radio path. Since this path is easily intercepted by anyone with a suitable receiver it is necessary to provide confidentiality on this radio path.

Anonymity on the radio path. GSM provides a degree of anonymity (confidentiality of the identity of users) on the radio path in order to prevent an attacker from linking the source of several intercepted calls. This is handled by using temporary user identities for each call, rather than permanent ones. We will not discuss this requirement further.

Notably, GSM did not specify the need for entity authentication of the mobile operator to the mobile phone, since at the time of development of GSM this was not regarded as a serious threat. This was because it was perceived to be extremely expensive for an attacker to masquerade as a mobile operator.

The meeting of these security requirements was subject to certain constraints:

- The security mechanisms should not be excessively strong, in order to avoid export control issues (which were more relevant in the period of GSM development, the 1990s, than they are today).
- The security mechanisms should not add significant overheads to the operation of the system, including call setup.

12.3.3 Cryptography used in GSM

The main cryptographic design decisions for GSM were:

A fully symmetric cryptographic architecture. While it is obvious that the need for fast real-time encryption of the radio link requires the use of symmetric cryptography, it might still be beneficial to deploy public-key cryptography to enable key establishment. However, GSM is an entirely closed system. All key material can be loaded onto the necessary equipment prior to it being issued to users, so there is no need to use public-key cryptography for this purpose.

Stream ciphers for data encryption. The requirement for fast real-time encryption over a potentially noisy communication channel means that, as we discussed in Section 4.2.4, a stream cipher is the most appropriate primitive.

Fixing the encryption algorithms. It is necessary that the mobile operators agree on which encryption algorithms to use, so that the devices on which they operate can be made compatible with one another. However, other cryptographic algorithms, such as those used in GSM authentication, do not have to be fixed. In the case of authentication, an individual mobile operator is free to choose the cryptographic algorithm that it deploys to authenticate its own users (since users of another mobile operator are not directly impacted by this decision).

Proprietary cryptographic algorithms. The designers of GSM chose to develop some proprietary cryptographic algorithms, rather than use open standards. We have discussed the pros and cons of this choice in Section 1.5.3. While the use of proprietary algorithms is not wise in many application environments, in the case of GSM there were three factors that favoured at least considering this option:

- GSM is a closed system, hence deploying proprietary algorithms is feasible.
- ETSI have a degree of cryptographic expertise, and maintain links with the open research community.

- The need for fast real-time encryption means that an algorithm designed explicitly to run on the hardware of a mobile phone will probably perform better than an 'off-the-shelf' algorithm.

The fundamental component involved in GSM security is the *Subscriber Identification Module* (SIM) *card*, which is a smart card (see Section 8.3.3) that is inserted into the mobile phone of the user. This SIM card contains all the information that distinguishes one user account from another. As a result, a user can potentially change phone equipment simply by removing the SIM and inserting it into a new phone. The SIM contains two particularly important pieces of information:

1. the *International Mobile Subscriber Identity* (IMSI), which is a unique number that maps a user to a particular phone number;
2. a unique 128-bit cryptographic key K_i, which is randomly generated by the mobile operator.

These two pieces of data are inserted onto the SIM card by the mobile operator before the SIM card is issued to the user. The key K_i forms the basis for all the cryptographic services relating to the user. The SIM card also contains implementations of some of the cryptographic algorithms required to deliver these services.

GSM AUTHENTICATION

Entity authentication of the user in GSM is provided using a challenge–response protocol, in a similar way to the dynamic password schemes that we discussed in Section 8.5. This is implemented as part of an AKE protocol, which also generates a key K_c for subsequent data encryption. GSM does not dictate which cryptographic algorithms should be used as part of this AKE protocol, but it does suggest one candidate algorithm and defines the way in which algorithms should be used.

As indicated in Figure 12.7, an algorithm A3 is used in the challenge–response protocol and an algorithm A8 is used to generate the encryption key K_c. Both of these algorithms can be individually selected by the mobile operator and are implemented on the SIM and in the operator's network. Both A3 and A8 can be loosely considered as types of key derivation function, since their main purpose is to use K_i to generate pseudorandom values.

In the following we use the notation $A3_K(data)$ to denote the result of computing algorithm A3 on the input *data* using key K (the notation $A8_K(data)$ should be similarly interpreted). If Alice (a mobile) is able to directly authenticate to Bob (the authentication centre of a mobile operator) then the GSM AKE protocol is as follows:

1. Alice sends an authentication request to Bob.
2. Bob generates a 128-bit randomly generated challenge number *RAND* and sends it to Alice.

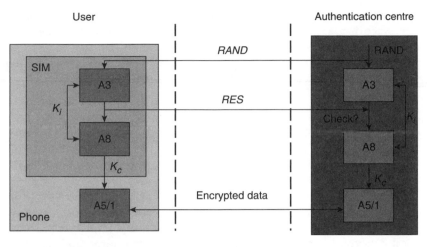

Figure 12.7. GSM authentication and encryption

3. Alice's SIM card uses K_i and *RAND* to compute a response *RES* using algorithm A3:

$$RES = A3_{K_i}(RAND).$$

The response *RES* is sent back to Bob.

4. Bob, who maintains a database of all the user keys, selects the appropriate key K_i for Alice and then computes the expected response in the same way. If the result matches the received *RES* then Alice is authenticated.

5. Alice and Bob both use K_i and *RAND* to compute an encryption key K_c using algorithm A8:

$$K_c = A8_{K_i}(RAND).$$

This simple protocol relies on the belief that only the mobile user and the mobile operator authentication centre can possibly know the key K_i that has been installed on the user's SIM card.

GSM ENCRYPTION

While authentication is a service that is 'private' to a mobile user and their mobile operator, encryption must be provided using a mechanism that is common to all mobile operators, in order to facilitate cross-network calls. Thus the encryption algorithm A5/1 is fixed by the GSM standard (in fact GSM offers three different versions of A5, but A5/1 is the most commonly deployed). As indicated in Figure 12.7, it is implemented on the mobile phone itself, not the SIM card, since the phone has more computation power than the SIM.

The A5/1 algorithm is a stream cipher with a 64-bit key. It was designed to be implemented very efficiently in the hardware of a mobile phone. In GSM, A5/1 is used to encrypt all radio path communication (both signalling information and the message data) using the key K_c. Potentially, this key may be freshly generated each time a user makes a mobile call.

Encryption is also used to protect the transfer of temporary identification numbers, which are used instead of the IMSI to provide user anonymity.

FACILITATING GSM ROAMING

While we previously argued that authentication is a 'private' service between a user and their mobile operator, there is one situation where this is not strictly true. This happens when a mobile user is traveling outside the area serviced by their mobile operator, for example, overseas (this is referred to as *roaming*).

Although different mobile operators are in some sense part of a wider 'closed' GSM network, they are still individual businesses with their own private user relationships. It would thus be unacceptable for one operator to share its security critical data (particularly key K_i) with another for the purpose of facilitating roaming. On the other hand, it is equally unacceptable from a practical perspective for every authentication request from a roaming user to be referred back to the user's mobile operator, since this might result in extensive delays.

GSM has a clever solution to this problem, through the use of *authentication triplets*. When a roaming mobile user Alice first connects with Charlie, a local mobile operator with whom she has no direct business relationship, the following procedure is followed:

1. Charlie contacts Bob (Alice's mobile operator) and requests a batch of GSM authentication triplets.
2. Bob generates a fresh batch of randomly generated challenge numbers $RAND(1)$, $RAND(2)$, ..., $RAND(n)$ and computes the matching values for RES and K_c using Alice's key K_i. These form the batch of triplets:

$$TRIP(1) = (RAND(1), RES(1), K_c(1))$$

$$TRIP(2) = (RAND(2), RES(2), K_c(2))$$

$$\vdots$$

$$TRIP(n) = (RAND(n), RES(n), K_c(n)),$$

where $RES(j) = A3_{K_i}(RAND(j))$ and $K_c(j) = A8_{K_i}(RAND(j))$. Bob sends this batch of triplets to Charlie.
3. Charlie sends the challenge $RAND(1)$ to Alice.
4. Alice computes the response $RES(1)$ using $RAND(1)$ and key K_i and sends $RES(1)$ to Charlie.
5. Charlie checks that the received $RES(1)$ matches the value in the first triplet that he received from Bob. If it does then Charlie authenticates Alice. Note that Charlie has done this without needing to know the key K_i. Alice and Charlie can now safely assume that they share the encryption key $K_c(1)$.

6. The next time Alice contacts Charlie to request a new authentication, Charlie uses the second triplet received from Bob and sends the challenge *RAND*(2). Thus although Bob has to be involved in the first authentication attempt, there is no need to contact Bob again until the current batch of triplets have all been used up.

SECURITY OF GSM ALGORITHMS

Despite the justification that we made for the use of proprietary algorithms in GSM, the general concerns about the use of proprietary algorithms that we outlined in Section 1.5.3 have come to the fore since the initial development of GSM.

A popularly implemented early instantiation of the algorithms A3 and A8 was a proprietary algorithm called COMP128. The details of this algorithm were leaked in 1997 and weaknesses in COMP128 were subsequently found. New versions of this algorithm have since been introduced.

The initial design of A5/1 was also secret but the algorithm was subsequently reverse-engineered and some powerful attacks against it have now been demonstrated. We will see shortly that a different approach has been taken over UMTS algorithm selection.

Nonetheless, GSM has proved to be a successful security standard. GSM effectively solved the problem of cloning mobiles to gain unauthorised access to mobile telecommunications networks. GSM addressed the problem of eavesdropping on the radio path. It is interesting to note that GSM was also one of the first applications to demonstrate the advantages of basing security of consumer devices on smart cards.

12.3.4 UMTS

The main reason for developing a new standard for mobile telecommunications was not so much GSM security concerns, but rather to provide additional features and functionality, such as the ability to access internet services. However, the opportunity was taken during the development of UMTS to build on the successful aspects of GSM security, and further strengthen it where appropriate. The main cryptographic improvements over GSM are as follows:

Mutual entity authentication. GSM offers entity authentication only of the mobile user. Since the development of GSM, so-called *false base station attacks* have become much more feasible due to reductions in the costs of suitable equipment. In one example of such an attack, a mobile user connects to the false base station, which immediately suggests to the user that encryption is turned off. By additionally requiring the user to authenticate to the mobile base station, such attacks are prevented.

Prevention of triplet reuse. A GSM triplet can, in theory, be reused many times for the particular mobile that it was generated for. In UMTS this is prevented

441

by upgrading authentication triplets to *quintets*, which additionally include a sequence number that prevents successful replay and a MAC key.

Use of publicly known algorithms. UMTS adopts cryptographic algorithms based on well-established and well-studied techniques. While it does not quite use 'off-the-shelf' algorithms, due to the desire to tailor algorithms to the underlying hardware, the algorithms deployed are very closely based on standard algorithms and the modifications have been publicly evaluated.

Longer key lengths. Following the relaxation of export restrictions that were in place at the time of GSM development, the key lengths of the underlying cryptographic algorithms were increased to 128 bits.

Integrity of signalling data. UMTS provides additional integrity protection to the critical signalling data. This is provided using a MAC, whose key is established during the UMTS authentication (AKE) protocol.

UMTS SECURITY PROTOCOLS

We will omit the details of the UMTS security protocols since they are, in essence, just slightly more complex versions of the original GSM protocols. Entity authentication of the mobile user is conducted via a similar challenge–response mechanism to GSM, at the end of which encryption and MAC keys are established.

Entity authentication of the base station is added to UMTS through the use of a MAC. The freshness mechanism used as part of this authentication is a sequence number (see Section 8.2.2), which is maintained by the mobile user and the base station. This is preferable to also using a challenge–response protocol in the opposite direction since, as we discussed in Section 8.2.3, this would introduce one extra message exchange, as well as require the mobile user to randomly generate a challenge number. It would also be very inconvenient when roaming, since the local mobile operator would have to contact a user's home mobile operator during each authentication attempt.

Roaming works on exactly the same principle as for GSM, except that the additional fields of the authentication quintet provide protection against replays.

UMTS CRYPTOGRAPHIC ALGORITHMS

Just as for GSM, mobile operators are free to use their own cryptographic algorithms as part of the UMTS AKE protocol. However, UMTS recommends the use of a set of algorithms called MILENAGE, which is based on AES and implements all the functionality required for UMTS authentication.

Once again the encryption algorithm must be fixed across all mobile operators. The selected UMTS algorithm is KASUMI, which is a 128-bit block cipher based on a well-studied design known as MISTY. Since what we really want is a stream cipher, KASUMI is deployed in a mode of operation that deploys a block cipher as a stream cipher keystream generator (similar to some of those discussed in Section 4.6). UMTS also specifies 'backup' stream ciphers in the (unexpected) event that a serious vulnerability is found in KASUMI.

442

There are currently no known practical attacks against these cryptographic algorithms.

12.3.5 GSM and UMTS key management

Key management in GSM and UMTS is fairly straightforward.

KEY MANAGEMENT SYSTEM

GSM and UMTS have an entirely symmetric key management system, facilitated by the fact that a mobile operator is completely in control of all keying material relating to their users. We can think of the underlying key management system as a very simple key hierarchy (see Section 10.4.1) with the user keys K_i acting as individual user 'master keys' and the encryption keys K_c acting as data (session) keys.

KEY GENERATION

The user keys K_i are randomly generated, normally by the SIM manufacturer (on behalf of the mobile operator) using a technique of their choice. The encryption keys K_c are derived from the user keys K_i, using the mobile operator's chosen cryptographic algorithm.

KEY ESTABLISHMENT

The establishment of user key K_i is under the control of the SIM manufacturer (on behalf of the mobile operator) who installs K_i on the user's SIM card before it is issued to the user. The significant key management advantage that is being exploited here is that a mobile service has no utility until a customer obtains a physical object from the mobile operator (in this case a SIM card), hence key establishment can be tied to this process. The keys K_c are established during the AKE protocol used for entity authentication. It is clearly very important that the SIM manufacturer transfers all the keys K_i to the mobile operator using highly secure means, perhaps in the form of an encrypted database.

KEY STORAGE

The critical user keys K_i are stored in the hardware of the user's SIM card, which offers a reasonable degree of tamper-resistance. Only the encryption key K_c, and in UMTS a MAC key derived from K_i, leave the SIM card. These are session keys that are discarded after use.

KEY USAGE

Both GSM and UMTS enforce a degree of key separation by making sure that the long-term user key K_i is only ever indirectly 'exposed' to an attacker through its use to compute the short responses to the mobile operator's challenges. The key K_c that is used for bulk data encryption, and is thus most 'exposed' to an attacker, is a derived key that is not used more than once. In UMTS, separate keys for encryption and MACs are derived from K_i. The use of a SIM also makes key change relatively straightforward.

12.3.6 GSM and UMTS security issues

GSM broke new ground for the mass use of cryptography. It provided, and to an extent still provides, good security for a rapidly expanding mobile phone network. GSM was, by and large, well designed and the basic security architecture of GSM is preserved in UMTS, which tightens up on the security offered by GSM.

It is worth remembering, however, that GSM and UMTS are deliberately not designed to provide end-to-end security. The design goal of being 'as secure as the PSTN' means that, just like a conventional telephone call, a mobile telephone call may still be intercepted after it has been switched into the conventional PSTN infrastructure.

12.3.7 GSM and UMTS design issues

The main design issues emerging from our study of GSM and UMTS are the following:

Use of symmetric cryptography. The closed nature of the application environment lends itself to adoption of a fully symmetric solution. The properties of stream ciphers are highly suited to mobile telecommunications.

Adaptation to evolving constraints. GSM was designed under several constraints, including cryptographic export restrictions and the apparent lack of a need for mobile operator authentication. As the environment determining these constraints evolved, the redesigned security mechanisms of UMTS took these into account.

Shift from proprietary to publicly known algorithms. Mobile telecommunications provide a plausible environment for the adoption of proprietary cryptographic algorithms. However, subsequent weaknesses in some of the original GSM algorithms may well have influenced the use of publicly known algorithms in UMTS.

Flexibility, but only when appropriate. Just as we saw for WLAN security in Section 12.2, GSM and UMTS only prescribe particular cryptographic algorithms when this is essential, leaving a degree of flexibility to mobile operators. That said, in UMTS mobile operators are strongly encouraged to follow central recommendations.

12.4 Cryptography for secure payment card transactions

Financial sector organisations are the most established commercial users of cryptography. They oversee global networks that use cryptographic services to provide security for financial transactions. We will demonstrate some of the ways in which cryptography is used in the financial sector by considering some of the services offered by international payment card organisations.

12.4.1 Background to payment card services

A *payment card organisation* (PCO), such as Visa and MasterCard, essentially operates as a 'club' of member banks who cooperate in order to facilitate transactions. Figure 12.8 indicates the key players in this cooperative organisation.

Issuing banks issue payment cards to customers. *Acquiring banks* have relationships with merchants of goods. PCOs run networks that connects these banks and facilitate payments from issuing bank customers to acquiring bank merchants. The two main uses of a payment card network are to:

1. authorise payments;
2. arrange clearing and settlement of payments.

PCOs oversee the use of both credit and debit cards. The main difference between the two is the process by which the issuing bank decides to bill the customer. From a cryptographic perspective we will not distinguish between these two types of payment card.

In this section we will look at a number of different uses of cryptography with respect to payment cards. We begin by looking at the cryptographic security relating to magnetic stripe payment cards. We then consider the upgraded security

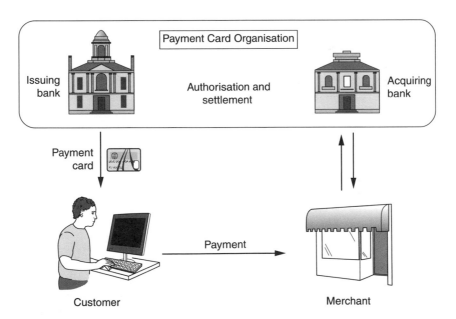

Figure 12.8. Payment card organisation infrastructure

offered by so-called *chip-and-PIN* cards, more correctly referred to as *Europay MasterCard Visa* (EMV) cards, named after the three major global payment card schemes operating in Europe who worked together to establish a common interoperable standard for payment card security. We then discuss the use of payment cards in online transactions. Finally we consider the use of payment cards as tokens for authenticating to other services.

12.4.2 Magnetic stripe cards

Most payment cards have magnetic stripes. Even payment cards with chips often retain the magnetic stripe and may resort to using it when they are deployed in environments that do not support EMV. The following description of cryptography used by magnetic stripe cards is based on the practices of Visa and MasterCard.

PIN PROTECTION

Our first example of cryptography being used by payment cards concerns online authentication of a user who inserts their magnetic stripe payment card into an ATM. Before releasing any funds, the ATM needs to know whether the user is genuine and whether they are entitled to make the requested withdrawal.

The process begins when the user is asked to enter their PIN into the ATM. The ATM clearly cannot verify this PIN on its own, so it needs to refer the PIN to the user's issuing bank. Since PINs are sensitive, this information should be encrypted. It is impractical for every ATM to share an encryption key with every issuing bank, so a process of key translation (see Section 10.4.1) is used:

1. The ATM encrypts the PIN and the authentication request message using a key shared by the ATM and the acquiring bank responsible for that ATM (each ATM should have a unique key of this type).
2. The acquiring bank decrypts the ciphertext and then re-encrypts it under a key known as the *acquirer working key*, which is a key shared by the acquiring bank and the PCO.
3. The PCO decrypts the ciphertext and re-encrypts it using an *issuer working key*, which is a key that the PCO shares with the issuing bank.
4. The issuing bank decrypts the ciphertext and makes the necessary checks of the PIN and the authentication request message. The response is then relayed back to the ATM.

Symmetric cryptography is used for this application mainly for legacy reasons, since this type of application predates the invention of public-key cryptography. However, symmetric cryptography is also feasible to use in this situation because the underlying infrastructure is 'closed' and thus symmetric keys can be managed. The symmetric algorithm employed is 2TDES (see Section 4.4.4). Again this is a legacy choice, since the original specifications used single DES.

Note that it would be dangerous simply to encrypt the PIN directly during this process, since the limited number of PINs will result in a limited number of possible ciphertexts representing encrypted PINs. If the same key were to be used to encrypt several PINs then an attacker could conduct a dictionary attack that matched a ciphertext representing an unknown PIN against a 'dictionary' of ciphertexts corresponding to known PINs. This threat is prevented by two important mechanisms:

Use of a PIN block. The PIN is never encrypted directly. Instead a *PIN block* is formed, one example of which consists of a 64-bit string containing the PIN being XORed to a 64-bit string containing the *Personal Account Number* (PAN) corresponding to the card. This means that two cards with the same PIN will not be encrypted to the same ciphertext under the same encryption key.

Session key encryption. Further security is provided by ensuring that ATMs use session keys, which are generated for a single PIN encryption event and then destroyed.

CARD VERIFICATION VALUES

One major problem with magnetic stripe cards is that they are relatively easy to clone. Early payment cards only included routine information such as the PAN and expiry date on the magnetic stripe. Since this information is easily obtained by a potential attacker (most of it is even displayed on the card itself, or can be obtained from receipts), it was very easy for an attacker to forge such a card.

The problem was alleviated by the inclusion of a cryptographic value known as the *Card Verification Value* (CVV) on the magnetic stripe (we adopt Visa terminology here, while MasterCard uses the term *Card Validation Code* for the same concept). The CVV consists of three digits that are extracted from a hex ciphertext, which is computed by encrypting the routine card information using a key known only to the issuer. The CVV is not displayed on the card and can only be created and verified by the card issuer.

Of course the CVV can be obtained by an attacker who has read off all the information contained on the magnetic stripe, for example, a rogue merchant. Payment cards thus include a second CVV value, CVV2, which is a cryptographic value computed in a similar (but slightly different) way to the CVV. The CVV2 is displayed on the reverse of the payment card, but is not included in the magnetic stripe. The CVV2 is primarily used as a simple check of the physical presence of a card, particularly in transactions made over the telephone or online (see Section 12.4.4).

PIN VERIFICATION VALUE

In order to improve availability, PCOs also provide a service which allows PINs to be verified when the card issuer is unable to process PIN verification requests. This is conducted using a *PIN Verification Value* (PVV), which is computed in a similar way to the CVVs, except that the PIN itself forms part of the plaintext that is encrypted in order to generate the PVV. The issuing bank needs to share the key that it uses to compute this PVV with the PCO.

The PVV is four digits long, so that its security is 'equivalent' to that of the PIN itself. Like the CVV, the PVV is normally stored on the magnetic stripe but not displayed on the card. During a PIN verification request, the PCO recomputes the PVV using the PIN that has been offered by the customer and checks whether this value matches the PVV on the magnetic stripe. If it does then the PIN verification is accepted.

Although CVVs and PVVs are short values, and hence theoretically could be exhaustively searched for by an attacker, PCOs use procedural controls to stop any apparent attack of this type. A typical control rejects the card after a maximum of three or four attempts. In this way a relatively weak cryptographic mechanism is strengthened by an appropriate management control.

PAYMENT CARD AUTHORISATION

When a payment card is inserted into a terminal, the main goal of the terminal is normally to determine the validity of the card and decide whether the transaction that is being requested is likely to go through. Prior to magnetic stripe cards, this process required a merchant to make a telephone call to the issuer. The ability for a terminal to extract data from the magnetic stripe and automatically contact the issuer in order to authorise a transaction certainly makes this process easier. However, it is important to note that with magnetic stripe cards this process still requires direct (online) communication with the card issuer. This requirement has restricted the adoption of payment cards of this type in countries with poor communication infrastructures.

12.4.3 EMV cards

EMV cards were introduced for two main reasons. The first reason was in order to improve the security of payment card transactions. The other reason was to lower telecommunication costs by introducing a secure means of authorising a transaction offline, hence reducing the number of times that a merchant might have to contact a card issuer.

The introduction of EMV cards has greatly increased the use of cryptography to protect payment card services since the chip on the card is capable of storing cryptographic keys. As we will see in Sections 12.4.4 and 12.4.5, they have also increased the diversity of secure services for which a card can be used.

PIN VERIFICATION

PIN verification becomes much more straightforward for EMV than for magnetic stripe cards, since the PIN can be stored on the chip itself. This allows a terminal to easily verify the PIN without having to contact the card issuer, or use a service based on a PVV.

OFFLINE DATA AUTHENTICATION

In order to authorise an EMV card transaction, a terminal must first decide whether to do an offline check, or whether to conduct a stronger online check that involves communicating with the card issuer. The decision as to which check to conduct depends on the transaction amount and the number of transactions conducted since the last online check.

Offline data authentication does not involve the card issuer. In its most basic form, it provides a means of gaining assurance that the information stored on an EMV card has not been changed since the payment card was created by the card issuer. In other words, it provides data origin authentication of the fundamental card data. The stronger mechanisms also provide entity authentication of the card. Offline data authentication of a payment card can be conducted directly by a terminal that the card has been inserted into.

It is impractical to provide this offline service using symmetric cryptography, since each terminal would need to share a symmetric key with every possible issuer. The use of key translation, as discussed in Section 12.4.2 for magnetic stripe PIN verification, requires the issuer to be online. Thus public-key cryptography, in the form of a digital signature scheme, is used to provide offline data authentication. For space efficiency reasons, EMV cards use a type of RSA digital signature scheme with message recovery (see Section 7.3.5) to provide this assurance.

EMV provides three offline data authentication mechanisms:

Static Data Authentication (SDA) is the simplest technique. All that is checked is the digital signature on the card data that is stored on the card. Verification of this digital signature requires access to the issuer's verification key. Clearly it is not reasonable to expect every terminal to have direct access to every issuer's verification key. Thus EMV employs a simple certificate hierarchy (see Section 11.3.3). In this case the card stores a public-key certificate containing the verification key of the issuer. This certificate is signed by the PCO, and the PCO's verification key is installed in every terminal supporting EMV.

Dynamic Data Authentication (DDA) goes one step further and provides this assurance in a dynamic way that differs for each transaction, hence providing another layer of security against card counterfeiting. During DDA, a challenge–response protocol is run that provides entity authentication of the card. In this case each card has its own RSA key pair and includes a public-key certificate for the card's verification key, signed by the issuer, as well as the issuer's public-key certificate, signed by the PCO. We thus have a three-level public-key certificate chain. The card computes a digital signature on the card data as well as some information unique to the current authentication session. The terminal uses the certificates offered by the card to verify this digital signature.

Combined Data Authentication (CDA) is similar to DDA, except that the card also signs the transaction data, thus providing assurance that the card and terminal have the same view of the transaction. This protects against man-in-the-middle attacks that seek to modify the transaction data communicated between card and terminal. In contrast, DDA can take place before the transaction details have been established.

ONLINE AUTHENTICATION

Online authentication is the stronger check, which requires communication with the card issuer. As with DDA, the objective of online card authentication is for a terminal to gain entity authentication assurance of a payment card that is involved in a transaction. This is provided by means of a simple challenge–response protocol, based on a symmetric key that is shared by the card issuer and the payment card, which stores it on the chip.

The only complication is that the terminal does not share this key, hence the issuer must be contacted online in order to verify the response. More specifically:

1. The terminal generates transaction data (which includes the payment card details) and a randomly generated challenge, which it then sends to the card.
2. The card computes a MAC on this data with the key that it shares with the issuer. This MAC is called the *authorisation request cryptogram*, and is passed on to the issuer.
3. The issuer computes its own version of the authorisation request cryptogram and compares it with the value received from the card. The issuer is also able to conduct a check that there are sufficient funds in the account to proceed with the transaction.

There are also situations where a payment card may require entity authentication of its issuer (for example, if it is being instructed to perform some internal management procedures, such as resetting counters). This can be built into the card authentication procedure as follows:

1. The card issuer treats the authorisation request cryptogram as a randomly generated challenge and computes a MAC on it using the key that it shares with the card. This response is sent to the card.
2. The card uses the key it shares with the card issuer to check this response. If it matches then it successfully authenticates the card issuer.

TRANSACTION CERTIFICATES

At the end of each transaction a *transaction certificate* (TC) is generated. This is a MAC computed on the details and outcome of the transaction and is passed back to the card issuer. The TC is computed using the key shared by the card and the card issuer. The TC is normally only required as evidence in the event of a subsequent dispute about certain aspects of the transaction.

SECURITY OF MANAGEMENT FUNCTIONS

A number of important management functions concerning security features of the payment card can be remotely managed by sending instructions to the card.

These include PIN changes, PIN unblocking instructions and changes to card data items (such as credit limits). These instructions are sent by the card issuer to the card (via a terminal). They are authorised by computing and verifying a MAC on the instruction, which is generated using a symmetric key that is shared by the card issuer and the card. Since this is a very different use of symmetric cryptography, in line with the principle of key separation (see Section 10.6.1) this key is different from the one used in online authentication.

12.4.4 Using EMV cards online

The previous security features of EMV cards all relate to applications where a card comes into contact with a terminal owned by a merchant. In this sense the card is physically 'present' and security features of the card can be directly employed.

However, an increasing number of transactions are conducted when the card is remote from the merchant, most commonly when a customer makes an online transaction. These are referred to as *card-not-present* (CNP) transactions. The potential for fraud in such transactions is high, since the most common information used to authenticate CNP transactions is simple card data (PAN, expiry date, CCV2), which is relatively easily acquired by a determined attacker. From the card holder perspective, the counter to this fraud threat has been the ability to challenge fraudulent transactions. However, this brings significant costs to the merchants, as well as being an inconvenience to the PCOs and cardholders when new cards have to be reissued to customers who have been fraud victims.

Secure Electronic Transactions (SET) was a standard that proposed a heavy architecture and set of procedures for securing CNP transactions. It relied on an overarching public-key management system and required all merchants to acquire special supporting equipment. Its complexity prevented it from being successful and so Visa and Mastercard developed a more lightweight approach known as *3DSecure*. The two main goals of 3DSecure are:

1. The card issuer is able to authenticate its payment card holders during a CNP transaction.
2. A merchant gains assurance that it will not later be financially punished because of a fraudulent transaction.

3DSecure is much more flexible than SET because it allows a card issuer to decide by what means it will authenticate its card holders during a CNP transaction. The overall benefits to all parties are that the increased transaction security allows the PCOs to charge merchants less money for using their services.

At its heart, 3DSecure relies on the following process:

1. A merchant that is 3DSecure-enabled puts in a request for authorisation of the card.

2. The card issuer contacts the card holder and requests authentication information. While EMV-CAP (see Section 12.4.5) provides a natural way to enable this, a common instantiation is for the card issuer and card holder to have pre-agreed a password, which the card holder must enter into a form presented to them in an embedded frame on their browser.

3. If authentication is successful, the card issuer computes a MAC on the critical transaction data, using a symmetric key known only to them. This MAC is known as a *Cardholder Authentication Verification Value* (CAVV) and acts as sort of 'signature', vouching for the authentication of the card holder and the transaction data. The CAVV will be used to resolve any subsequent disputes about the transaction.

3DSecure appears to be a popular technique and is widely adopted.

12.4.5 Using EMV cards for authentication

The increase in uptake of remote banking services, both online and over the telephone, presents banks with the challenge of coming up with strong entity authentication mechanisms in order to reduce the risk of fraud. A wide range of entity authentication mechanisms are used for access to remote banking services, including dynamic password schemes, as discussed in Section 8.5. Such solutions require bank customers to possess a device with cryptographic capability.

Since EMV cards have cryptographic capability, and EMV-supporting bank customers have such a card by default, it is natural to consider using the EMV card as part of an entity authentication mechanism. This is precisely the thinking behind the *Chip Authentication Program* (CAP), which specifies a range of entity authentication options (EMV-CAP explicitly refers to MasterCard technology, while Visa have a similar scheme known as *Dynamic Passcode Authentication*). These are supported by a *CAP reader*, which is a handheld device with a display and keypad. This is much the same as the token that we described in our example dynamic password scheme in Section 8.5.2, except that the CAP reader also has a slot into which an EMV card can be inserted. The customer authenticates directly to the EMV card via the CAP reader by means of a PIN. The CAP reader can then support several different entity authentication mechanisms:

Identify. This option displays a number on the CAP reader that is computed from a symmetric key on the EMV card and an EMV customer transaction counter, which is also stored and updated on the card. This mechanism is a type of sequence-number-based dynamic password scheme. The cryptographic computation essentially involves computing a CBC-MAC (see Section 6.3.3) on the input.

Response. This option works in almost the same way as our example dynamic password scheme in Section 8.5.2. In this case the bank provides the customer with a randomly generated challenge. The customer types the challenge into the CAP reader, which requests the EMV card to compute a response using the symmetric key on the EMV card (again, based on CBC-MAC). Finally, the customer provides the bank with the displayed response.

Sign. This is stronger version of the *response* mechanism, which involves the CBC-MAC being computed on basic transaction data (amount and recipient account) as well as the challenge value. This can be used to provide a type of 'digital signature' on the transaction. This is an example of the 'asymmetric trust relationship' use of MACs to provide non-repudiation that we discussed in Section 7.2.2.

The use of CAP has been gaining in popularity amongst European banks, where its provision of relatively strong two-factor authentication based on EMV cards does appear to have reduced certain types of fraud, such as those based on phishing attacks.

12.4.6 Payment card key management

We now briefly review some of the main key management issues relating to the cryptography employed by payment cards.

KEY MANAGEMENT SYSTEM

While the cryptography used by magnetic stripe cards is entirely symmetric, EMV uses a hybrid of symmetric and public-key cryptography. While PCOs allow issuing and acquiring banks to manage the keys of their own customers, the PCOs provide overarching key management services that link up these banks and facilitate secure transactions.

The model depicted in Figure 12.8 that underlies payment card transactions is essentially the same as the connected certification model that we presented in Figure 11.4. We argued in Section 11.3.2 that this model is suitable for public-key certificate management across a large distributed organisation. It is thus a good model to adopt given the distributed nature of a PCO's network of banks.

KEY GENERATION

A PCO generates its own master public-key pair. PCOs maintain master RSA key pairs of different lengths in order to cope with potential improvements in factorisation techniques.

Individual banks are responsible for the generation of all keys that are placed on their own cards. Banks are also responsible for generating their own RSA key pairs, which they submit to the PCOs for certification. The symmetric keys are all 2TDES keys. The keys stored on a customer's card are typically derived from the user's PAN and a master derivation key. The keys stored on the card are never used directly (in contrast to our slightly oversimplified description). Instead, session keys are derived from these long-term keys and a transaction counter, which is also maintained on the card and is communicated to relying parties during a transaction.

KEY ESTABLISHMENT

The advantage of a closed system of this type is that the keys stored on a card can be pre-installed during the manufacturing (or personalisation) process. This is slightly more complex for RSA key pairs, since they cannot be mass generated as efficiently as symmetric keys. The session keys used in individual transactions are established on the fly during the transaction, as just discussed.

A PCO's verification key is installed into terminals during their manufacture. PCOs also oversee an important symmetric key hierarchy. At the top level are *zone control master keys*, which are manually established using component form (see Section 10.3.3). These are used to establish the acquirer working keys and issuer working keys.

KEY STORAGE

All the long-term secret or private keys used in EMV payment card systems are protected in tamper-resistant hardware, either in the form of an issuer's hardware security module or the chip on the payment card.

KEY USAGE

In general, key separation is enforced in EMV. The two main security functions that involve encryption using keys stored on a card are conducted using separate symmetric keys.

12.4.7 Payment card security issues

A PCO's overall security goal is to keep fraud using its cards down to a manageable level. PCOs such as Visa and MasterCard thus maintain a risk management division whose function is to assess whether the current security controls are good enough. The evolution from magnetic stripes to EMV cards also reflects an adaptation to cope with new perceived threats.

3DSecure is a further response to the growing problems of online fraud. Of course, 3DSecure is only as secure as the authentication mechanism deployed by the issuing bank to authenticate its customers. Nonetheless, it seems to offer a reasonable compromise between security and usability that has helped to reduce the amount of CNP fraud.

12.4.8 Payment card cryptographic design issues

The main cryptographic design issues concerning payment card cryptographic security mechanisms are:

Use of well-respected cryptographic algorithms. Payment cards use 2TDES and RSA, which are well-established algorithms.

Targeted use of public-key cryptography. Payment cards uses public-key cryptography precisely when it delivers substantial benefits, namely in simplified key management for the support of offline data authentication.

Balance of control and flexibility. PCOs strictly control the part of the key management infrastructure that they need to, but otherwise devolve control to participating banks. This provides scalable key management and allows banks to develop their own relationships with their customers.

Efficient use of related data. Payment cards use data in a number of imaginative ways. For example, PANs are used to derive keys, and items of transaction data are used as challenges in authentication protocols. This is both efficient and clever.

12.5 Cryptography for video broadcasting

The next application that we will examine is fundamentally different from the previous ones. This is the use of cryptography to protect digital video content that is being broadcast, sometimes referred to as *pay-TV*. What is most fascinating about this application is that the security service requirements are fairly straightforward but the key management is very sophisticated. This is because the environment poses some unusual operational restrictions that require special key management techniques.

12.5.1 Video broadcasting background

Commercial television broadcasters have traditionally financed the provision of their services either through government subsidy or advertising revenue. This is primarily because most analogue broadcast content can be received by anyone with access to a suitable device, such as a television set. This makes alternative business models, such as those based on annual subscription, hard to enforce. For example, enforcement of the annual television license in the UK involves locating devices and attempting to retrospectively collect revenue.

An alternative option is to 'encrypt' analogue content using special techniques that are developed for particular broadcast technologies. This process is often referred to as *scrambling*. This requires a consumer of content to acquire dedicated hardware in order to use decryption to recover the content. This requirement thus presents an opportunity for revenue collection.

Digital video broadcast networks process digital content, thus making it possible to use the full range of modern cryptographic mechanisms to protect content. This, in turn, enables a wide variety of different business models. Most of these require consumers to obtain specific hardware (or occasionally software) in order to recover content. Common models include *full subscription services*

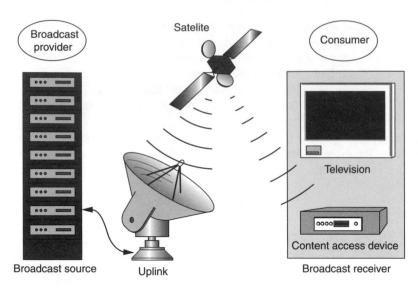

Figure 12.9. Digital video broadcast network

that allow consumers to access all broadcast content for a specific period of time, *package subscription services* that allow consumers to access 'bundles' of predefined broadcast content, and *pay-per-view services* that allow the purchase of specific broadcast content (for example, a live broadcast of a sports event). The compression of digital video broadcasts also allows more content to be broadcast than that of analogue over a similar bandwidth. It thus creates the opportunity for a much more diverse provision environment.

Figure 12.9 shows a simple example of a possible infrastructure for a digital video broadcast network. The *broadcast source* transmits the broadcast content, and is under the control of the *broadcast provider*. The broadcast content is transmitted to the *consumer* of the content, who requires access to a suitable *broadcast receiver* in order to receive the signal. In the example in Figure 12.9, the communication channel is over the air via a satellite link, hence the broadcast receiver takes the form of a satellite dish. However, a digital video broadcast could just as well be transmitted by other media, such as a fibre optic cable, in which case the broadcast receiver is any hardware device capable of receiving the content. As well as receiving the data transmitted by the broadcast source, the consumer requires a *content access device*, which has the capability of decrypting to recover the broadcast content. While this can be implemented in software, most content access devices are hardware devices that contain a smart card. The critical data that is required to control access to the broadcast content, such as cryptographic keys, will normally be stored on the smart card, thus allowing the potential for a content access device to be used to obtain content from different broadcast providers. In such cases we will choose to regard the 'content access device' as the hardware *and* the smart card, unless otherwise specified. Note that this generic network infrastructure is independent of the business model being used to sell the broadcast content.

In the subsequent discussion we will consider a generic broadcast video application, rather than a specific provider's system. We will assume, however, that the broadcast provider is using the *Common Scrambling Algorithm* (CSA), which is a standard proprietary encryption algorithm around which many providers base their security (see Section 12.5.3).

12.5.2 Video broadcasting security requirements

In order to appreciate the security requirements for digital video broadcasting, it is first necessary to appreciate two important constraints on the broadcast network environment:

One-way channel. The broadcast communication channel only operates in one direction: from broadcast source to broadcast receiver. There is no means by which a consumer can send information back to the broadcast source on this communication channel.

Uncontrolled access. Just as for analogue broadcasts, digital video broadcast content can be received by anyone with the right broadcast receiver technology (a satellite dish in our example in Figure 12.9).

The security requirement for digital video broadcast is thus, simply:

Confidentiality of the broadcast content. In order to control the revenue stream the broadcast provider must make the broadcast content essentially 'worthless' to anyone who has not purchased the necessary content access device. In other words, confidentiality is required on the broadcast channel, with only authorised consumers having access to the necessary decryption keys. It is important to note that this requirement for confidentiality does not arise due to the sensitivity of the broadcast content. On the contrary, the broadcast provider *wants* people to view this content, so long as they have paid to do so. This requirement is sometimes referred to as *conditional access*.

It is worth briefly considering why this is the only security service requirement.

Entity authentication. Most of our previous applications required some level of entity authentication, which would be one way of controlling which consumers get access to broadcast video content. However, this requires the consumer to be able to communicate with the broadcast source, which in this case is not possible. Entity authentication of the broadcast source is possible, but unnecessary, since the threat of an attacker posing as a broadcast source and sending false video broadcasts is not particularly relevant to most commercial broadcast environments.

Data integrity. There is no doubt that data integrity is important, since a video broadcast channel is potentially prone to errors in the transmission channel. However, the threat against data integrity is more likely to be accidental errors rather than deliberate ones introduced by a malicious attacker. Hence the solutions lie in the area of error-correcting codes (see Section 1.4.4) and not cryptographic mechanisms.

There are several other operational constraints that influence the design of the key management for digital video broadcasting. We will discuss these in Section 12.5.4.

12.5.3 Cryptography used in video broadcasting

Since confidentiality is required, we need to determine which encryption algorithm to use. The cryptographic design decisions behind this are almost identical to those for GSM encryption (see Section 12.3.3), namely:

A fully symmetric cryptographic architecture. Video broadcast networks are closed systems.

Stream ciphers for data encryption. Video broadcasts involve streaming data in real time over potentially noisy communication channels.

Fixing the encryption algorithm. Agreeing on use of a fixed encryption algorithm allows this algorithm to be implemented in all broadcast receivers, aiding interoperability.

Proprietary encryption algorithm. Choosing to design a proprietary encryption algorithm was justifiable for the same reasons as for GSM. In this case the expertise lay with members of the *Digital Video Group* (DVB), which is a consortium of broadcasters, manufacturers, network operators, software developers, and regulatory bodies with interests in digital video broadcasting. As for GSM, one of the influences behind the design was to make decryption as efficient as possible, since content access devices are less powerful than broadcast sources.

The proprietary encryption algorithm that was designed was CSA. While CSA was standardised by ETSI (see Section 12.3), it was only available for scrutiny under a non-disclosure agreement. However, in 2002, the CSA was implemented in a software application and subsequently reverse-engineered.

The CSA is essentially a double stream cipher encryption. The first encryption is based on a proprietary block cipher deployed in CBC mode, which means that it operates as a stream cipher (see Section 4.6.3). The second layer of encryption uses a dedicated stream cipher to encrypt the ciphertext produced during the first encryption (this is a slight simplification). The key length is 64 (only 48 of the bits are actually used for encryption) and the same encryption key is used for both encryption processes. It is not clear why this 'double encryption' layered design was adopted, but the natural reason would be as a form of insurance against one of the layers of encryption being broken.

12.5.4 Key management for video broadcasting

The primary key management task for digital video broadcasting is simple to state: the keys required to recover broadcast content should be available only to those consumers who are authorised to view the broadcast content. However, there are several complications that combine to make this a challenging task:

The number of potential consumers. A digital video broadcast network is likely to have a large number of consumers (in some cases this could be several million), hence the key management system design must be sufficiently scalable that it works in practice.

Dynamic groups of authorised consumers. The groups of consumers who are authorised to view digital broadcast content is extremely dynamic. Pay-per-view services provide the extreme example of this, where the group of authorised consumers is likely to be different for every content broadcast.

Constant service provision. In many applications a broadcast source will be constantly streaming digital video content that needs to be protected. There are no break periods in which key management operations could be conducted. Most key management must therefore be conducted on the fly.

Precision of synchronisation. As we know from Section 4.2.4, stream ciphers require the keys at each end of the communication channel to be synchronised. In digital video broadcasting this synchronisation has to happen between the broadcast source and *all* (and as we have just pointed out, this could be 'millions of') authorised consumers. This synchronisation must be close to being perfect, otherwise some consumers may incur a temporary loss of service.

Instant access. Consumers normally want instant access to broadcast content and will not tolerate delays imposed by key management tasks. A good example of the extreme nature of this problem arises in the case of subscription services, where consumers often choose to select a series of different broadcast channels, each for a very short period of time, in order to make a selection (often referred to as 'channel surfing'). Since these different channels need to be encrypted using different encryption keys, the content access device needs to have instant access to all the relevant decryption keys.

We will now look at how digital video broadcasting systems typically address these challenges.

VIDEO BROADCAST KEY MANAGEMENT SYSTEM DESIGN

As we indicated in Section 12.5.2, all video broadcast content must be encrypted during transmission. In Section 12.5.3 we identified that this must be using a symmetric key, which we will refer to as the *content encryption key* (CEK).

Since the broadcast source only transmits one version of an item of broadcast content, the content encryption key used to encrypt a specific item of content must be the same for all consumers. Since consumers have different access rights to digital content, the CEK for two different items of broadcast content must be different.

The challenge is thus to make sure that only consumers who are authorised to access content can obtain the appropriate CEK. In order to facilitate this, the operational constraints that we outlined impose the following key management design decisions:

Encrypted CEK is transmitted in the broadcast signal. The most important reason for this is the need for instant access. The CEK is transmitted along with the content itself and is made 'instantly available' by being continuously repeated, perhaps every 100 milliseconds or so. Clearly the CEK cannot be transmitted in the clear, otherwise anyone receiving the broadcast signal could obtain it and hence recover the content. Thus the CEK is transmitted in encrypted form. We will refer to the key used to encrypt the CEK as the *key encrypting key* (KEK).

CEK is frequently changed. Once someone has access to the CEK, they can use it to recover all broadcast content that is encrypted using it. Thus it is important to frequently change the CEK, for the reasons discussed in Section 10.6.2. In most video broadcast systems the CEK typically changes every 30 seconds, but this can happen as often as every five seconds.

CEK is transmitted in advance. In order to aid synchronisation and instant access, the CEK is issued in advance of the transmission of any content broadcast using it. Clearly this cannot be too far in advance because of the dynamic nature of the authorised consumer base. The compromise is to constantly transmit two (encrypted) CEKs, which consist of:

1. the current CEK that is being used to encrypt the current broadcast content;
2. the 'next' CEK that will be used to encrypt the next broadcast content.

Hence the content access device has time to recover the next CEK and have it instantly available as soon as the CEK is changed.

Use of symmetric key hierarchies. We have already seen that video broadcast schemes use KEKs to encrypt the CEKs. This of course just 'transfers' the access problem to making sure that only authorised consumers have access to the required KEKs. In order to manage this problem in a scalable way, video broadcast systems use symmetric key hierarchies (see Section 10.4.1), the details of which we will discuss shortly.

VIDEO BROADCAST KEY ESTABLISHMENT

We now discuss how a video broadcast scheme establishes the KEKs that are necessary for authorised consumers to obtain the CEKs that they are entitled to.

As previously mentioned, video broadcast schemes use symmetric key hierarchies. At the 'top' of each these hierarchies are keys that are shared only by the broadcast provider and a particular consumer, which we refer to as *consumer keys* (CKs). In a simple system, with relatively few consumers, these CKs could be used to encrypt the KEKs. However, there are two reasons why this is not very practical:

1. Most video broadcast systems have so many consumers that sending an encrypted KEK in this way would require too much bandwidth, since a unique ciphertext would have to be sent for each consumer.
2. Each KEK itself must be frequently changed, for similar reasons to the CEKs. This might happen, say, on a daily basis. Thus the bandwidth problems are further exacerbated by the need to frequently update the KEKs.

The compromise is to deploy *zone keys* (ZKs), which are keys shared by groups of consumers. Zone keys have longer lifetimes than KEKs, but shorter lifetimes than CKs. A relevant ZK is initially sent to a consumer encrypted using their CK. The consumer then uses the ZK to recover KEKs, which are used to recover CEKs. When a ZK needs to be changed, the new ZK does need to be sent to every consumer who requires it, but this event occurs much less frequently than for KEKs (which in turn occurs much less frequently than for CEKs).

The consumer keys, which sit at the top of these key hierarchies, are stored on the smart cards of the content access devices. They are thus established prior to the issuing of the smart cards to the consumers. A simple example set of key hierarchies is shown in Figure 12.10. In this example there are are five consumers, divided into two zones. In practice, multiple layers of zone keys can be deployed in order to enhance scalability.

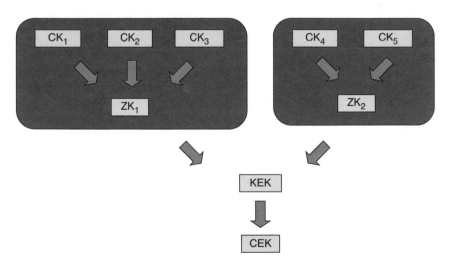

Figure 12.10. Digital video broadcast scheme key hierarchy

461

Video broadcast schemes provide a good example of the benefits of using a symmetric key hierarchy in order to provide scalable key management. It is worth noting that, unlike the encryption of the content, there are no standards mandating the encryption algorithms used to distribute keys in the hierarchy. Thus different content providers are free to choose their own methods for doing this.

VIDEO BROADCAST ACCESS CONTROL

Encryption of the broadcast content prevents anyone who does not have a content access device with a smart card containing a consumer key from recovering broadcast content. However, it should be apparent that a consumer who does have a valid CK will be able to recover content. This poses a potential problem when a consumer's contract with a broadcast provider ends since, in theory, the consumer will still be able to access broadcast content until the next update of the relevant ZK.

In practice, this problem is addressed by the enforcement of access control in the content access device (see Section 1.4.6). Each consumer is issued in advance with their *content access rights*, which identifies which content the consumer has permission to access. These rights are distributed to a consumer in a special management message, encrypted using the consumer's CK. These content access rights can be updated at any stage using a similar process. Before a content access device attempts to recover any content, it first checks the consumer's content access rights to find out whether the consumer is entitled to access the content. If they are then the content is recovered, otherwise the content access device refuses to proceed.

Thus video broadcast schemes have a two-tiered approach to protecting content. At one level there is access control, enforced by the content access device. The other level is cryptographic control, enforced by using the symmetric key hierarchy. A 'normal' consumer should be prevented by the hardware controls from determining their CK and thus cannot alter the content access rights that they have been issued with. However, even a consumer who is able to do this will ultimately be 'shut out' of their ability to access content through the key establishment controls that we previously described.

VIDEO BROADCAST KEY STORAGE

In hardware-based content access devices all the relevant keys, including the important consumer key, are stored on the smart card. However, there remains one potential point of vulnerability. Since content access devices are designed to be interoperable between different broadcast providers, the interface between the smart card and the rest of the content access device is standardised and hence well understood. This potentially allows an attacker to attempt to obtain a CK when it is transferred between the smart card and the rest of the content access device. For this reason, a shared symmetric key between the smart card and the rest of the content access device is often established, in order to secure this interface.

12.5.5 Video broadcast security issues

Digital video broadcast schemes appear to have the capability of providing strong protection for broadcast content. This is extremely important for the broadcast providers, since they rely on encryption to protect their source of revenue. The protection of the content ultimately relies on the security of CSA, which despite some concerns remains fairly well regarded. Although the key length is short by modern standards, the keys are frequently changed. The security of these keys also relies on the encryption algorithms and key management techniques deployed by a specific broadcast provider to protect all the keys in the key hierarchy.

12.5.6 Video broadcast design issues

Video broadcast networks have provided us with a very interesting application of cryptography, with the following design issues:

Use of symmetric cryptography. The closed nature of a video broadcast scheme facilitates the use of a fully symmetric cryptosystem.

Use of a symmetric key hierarchy. Video broadcast schemes provide a good example of the benefits of deploying a key hierarchy to support symmetric key management.

The influence of operational constraints. While the security requirements for video broadcast networks are fairly straightforward, the operational constraints require some innovative key management controls. Of particular interest are the techniques used in order to provide instant and synchronised access to broadcast content across a potentially large consumer base.

Partially standardised infrastructure. Video broadcast schemes follow some common standards, for example, for content encryption, while leaving other aspects such as higher-level key establishment open to custom design by individual broadcast providers. While this provides the opportunity for a diverse market of interoperable schemes, it also presents a potential source of vulnerability in specific systems.

Note that the security of video broadcast networks is just one example of a larger set of applications relating to the wider problem of *digital rights management*, which concerns technologies for limiting the access of users to digital content.

12.6 Cryptography for identity cards

The applications that we have looked at so far have all had fairly specific goals, and hence well-defined specific security requirements. Our next use of cryptography is quite different in this regard. National (citizen) identity cards are normally intended to be general purpose 'tokens' that can be used by a range of applications that require information relating to the identity of a citizen. They are thus tools that can be deployed in applications, rather than being applications in their own right. Since identity cards can be deployed with many different functionalities (and indeed many such schemes do not deploy cryptography at all), we will focus our discussion on one specific scheme, the Belgian *eID* card scheme, which was one of the first such schemes to provide cryptographic capability on each identity card. This is an example of cryptography being made widely available for use by other applications, rather than cryptography being deployed to provide specific support to a particular application.

12.6.1 eID background

Within a specific context, such as a workplace, most people accept cards that contain and/or display data relating to the identity of the holder. However, the attitude towards *national* identity card schemes is surprisingly diverse and, to an extent, cultural. In some countries, such as the UK, there is a great deal of hostility to such schemes. This is largely due to concerns over privacy issues, costs of deployment, data management and doubts about the utility of such a scheme. In many other countries, such as Belgium, national identity card schemes have been rolled out and are integrated into daily life.

The main application of national identity cards is to present independently issued evidence of the identity of the card holder. Such cards typically display a photograph of the card holder and some personal details, which may include a handwritten signature. However, the progress in smart card technology and the development of cryptographic applications has presented the opportunity for national identity cards to provide additional functionality and thus, perhaps, become more useful.

Figure 12.11. eID card

The eID card scheme was motivated by the establishment of the 1999 European Directive on Electronic Signatures, which created a framework that enabled electronic signatures (see Section 7.1.2) to become legally binding. The first eID cards were issued to Belgian citizens in 2003 and from 2005 all newly issued identity cards were eID cards.

The eID card has four core functions:

Visual identification. This allows the card holder to be visually identified by displaying a photograph on the card alongside a handwritten signature and basic information such as date of birth (see Figure 12.11). This functionality is also provided by previous Belgian identity cards.

Digital data presentation. This allows the data on the eID card to be presented in electronic form to a verifying party. The card data has a specific format and includes:

- a digital photograph of the card holder;
- an *identity file* which consists of:
  - personal data such as name, national identity number, date of birth, and special status (for example, whether the card holder has a disability);
  - a hash of the digital photograph of the card holder;
  - card-specific data such as chip number, card number and validity period;
- an *address file* which consists of the card holder's registered address.

Applications of digital data presentation include access control to facilities such as libraries, hotel rooms and sports halls.

Digital card holder authentication. This allows a card holder to use the eID card to 'prove' their identity in real time to a verifying party. In other words, it facilitates entity authentication of the card holder. The many listed applications of digital card holder authentication include remote access to various internet services, including official document requests (for example, birth certificates), access to an online tax declaration application, and access to patient record information.

Digital signature creation. This allows the card holder to use the eID card to digitally sign some data. Applications of digital signature creation include signing of electronic contracts and social security declarations. Digital signatures created using an eID card are legally recognised.

12.6.2 eID security requirements

The three digital functions of the eID card motivate the following three security requirements:

Data origin authentication of the card data. In order to provide digital data presentation, assurance that the card data has not been changed since the card was issued must be provided.

Ability to provide a data origin authentication service. In order to support digital card holder authentication, it is necessary for an eID card to be used as part of an entity authentication service. The eID card's role in this is to provide a data origin authentication service, which can then be used to support an entity authentication protocol between the card holder and a verifying party.

Ability to provide a non-repudiation service. In order to support digital signature creation, an eID card must be able to provide non-repudiation.

12.6.3 Cryptography used in eID cards

The cryptography in the eID card is relatively straightforward. The following design issues are important in determining the eID card's cryptographic capability:

Use of public-key cryptography. The open nature of the potential application space for eID cards dictates that public-key cryptography must be supported. It is impractical for an eID card to contain pre-loaded symmetric keys that will be 'meaningful' to all unknown future applications.

A digital signature scheme suffices. All three of the security requirements for eID cards can be met by using a digital signature scheme. The first requirement does not even require the digital signature scheme to be implemented on the eID card, however, the second and third requirements do need this. Note that the eID card is not required to have the capability to encrypt or decrypt data.

Use of a publicly known digital signature scheme. In order to encourage use of the eID card and aid interoperability, it is imperative that the digital signature scheme that is deployed is widely respected and supported.

The eID card scheme addresses these design issues by using RSA digital signatures with appendix (see Section 7.3.4). The initial eID cards used 1024-bit RSA, however, there are plans to support 2048-bit RSA in future cards. A number of hash functions are currently supported, including MD5 and SHA-1.

The eID card scheme thus presents an interesting case study of the use of public-key cryptography. We will now briefly look at how the three core digital functions are provided using an eID card and then take a look at how the public-key management is supported.

12.6.4 Provision of the eID card core functions

The eID card scheme is governed by an entity called the *National Register* (NR). The NR can be considered as a trusted third party that facilitates the scheme. As we will see in Section 12.6.5, the NR is responsible for issuing eID cards and hence also takes 'ownership' of the personal data contained on them.

Each eID card contains two signature key pairs and one additional signature key:

Authentication key pair. This key pair is used to support digital card holder authentication.

Non-repudiation key pair. This key pair is used to support digital signature creation.

Card signature key. This signature key can be used to authenticate the card, rather than the card holder. Only the NR knows the verification key that corresponds to a particular eID card. This signature key is only used for administrative operations between the card and the NR.

Note that the eID card enforces the principle of key separation (see Section 10.6.1) by having separate signature key pairs for the two different security services. As well as being an example of good key management practice, there are legal reasons for this separation since the non-repudiation verification key requires a higher level of certificate in order to facilitate legal recognition of digital signatures verified using it (see Section 12.6.5).

We now consider how the first two key pairs are used to support the three core digital eID card functions.

DIGITAL DATA PRESENTATION

This involves a verifying party reading the card data and then gaining assurance that the data on the card is correct. To gain this assurance, the verifying party needs to verify two digital signatures that are created by the NR and stored on the eID card:

Signed identity file. This is a digital signature generated by the NR on the identity file.

Signed identity and address file. This is a digital signature generated by the NR on a concatenation of the signed identity file and the address file. In other words, this takes the form:

$$sig_{NR}(sig_{NR}(\text{identity file}) \parallel \text{address file}).$$

A verifying party can then verify the card data by first using the verification key of the NR to verify the signed identity file. If this check is fine then they can proceed to verify the signed identity and address file.

The reason that the NR does not simply sign all the card data is that address changes are much more frequent than changes to the content of the identity file. Thus the NR can update an address on the card without having to reissue a new eID card. Hence a major administrative operation is saved at the expense of a slightly more complex verification process of the card data.

DIGITAL CARD HOLDER AUTHENTICATION

Each eID card holder can activate the signature keys on the eID card through the use of a PIN. The card holder also requires access to an *eID card reader*, which

467

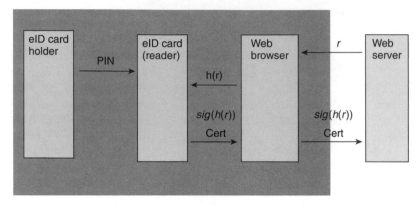

Figure 12.12. eID card holder authentication

may include a PIN pad. This provides an interface between the eID card and the card holder's computer. A typical card holder authentication process is illustrated in Figure 12.12. In this example, a visited web server is requesting authentication of the card holder:

1. The web server randomly generates a challenge r. This is sent to the card holder's browser, which displays a request to login.
2. The card holder enters their PIN into the eID card reader which, if correct, authorises the eID card to proceed with the authentication.
3. The card holder's browser computes a hash $h(r)$ of the challenge r, using a suitable hash function (see Section 6.2) and sends this to the eID card via the card reader.
4. The eID card digitally signs $h(r)$ using the authentication signature key and sends this to the web server via the card holder's browser, along with the card holder's authentication verification key certificate.
5. The web server verifies the received certificate and, if this is successful, verifies the signature and checks that it corresponds to the challenge r. If everything is in order, the card holder is successfully authenticated.

This process is a straightforward application of challenge–response to provide entity authentication (see Section 8.5). Note that the overall security of the authentication process relies on the security of the card holder's PIN. An attacker with access to both the eID card and the PIN can falsely authenticate to the web server.

DIGITAL SIGNATURE CREATION

The digital signature creation process is as described in Section 7.3.4, except that the card holder enters their PIN before the digital signature is created. The digital signature is generated using the non-repudiation signature key.

The non-repudiation verification key certificate is sent to the verifier along with the digital signature. The verifier should then perform all the standard verification checks, which may include checking the appropriate CRLs (see Section 12.6.5), before verifying the digital signature using the procedure outlined in Section 7.3.4.

12.6.5 eID key management

The eID card scheme provides an interesting example of a key management system supporting public-key cryptography. We will look at how the eID card scheme key management is supported, with a particular focus on the two phases in the certificate lifecycle identified in Section 11.2 as being particularly challenging, namely certificate issuing and certificate revocation.

eID CERTIFICATES

The eID card scheme key management is based on the closed certification model that we described in Section 11.3.2. It uses a certification hierarchy, as described in Section 11.3.3, in order to provide a scalable approach to certificate issuing. This certification hierarchy is indicated in Figure 12.13. The main CAs involved are:

Belgium Root CA. This CA is the root CA that oversees all the eID scheme certification. It possesses a 2048-bit RSA verification key certificate that is both self-signed and signed by a commercial CA.

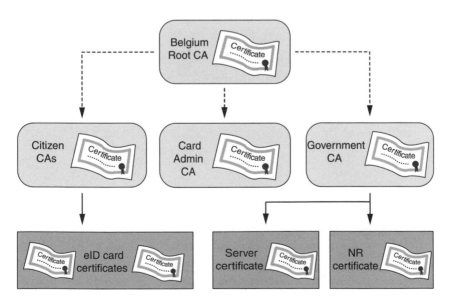

Figure 12.13. eID certification hierarchy

Citizen CAs. These CAs issue certificates to card holders and are responsible for signing the eID card authentication and non-repudiation verification key certificates. Citizen CAs have a 2048-bit RSA verification key signed by the Belgium Root CA.

Card Admin CA. This CA issues certificates to organisations carrying out administrative operation of the eID card scheme, such as those managing address changes and key pair generation. The Card Admin CA has a 2048-bit RSA verification key signed by the Belgium Root CA.

Government CA. This CA issues certificates to government organisations and web servers, including the NR. The Government CA has a 2048-bit RSA verification key signed by the Belgium Root CA.

Each eID card stores five certificates:

1. the Belgium Root CA certificate;
2. the Citizen CA certificate for the Citizen CA that issued the eID card's certificates;
3. the eID card authentication verification key certificate;
4. the eID card non-repudiation verification key certificate;
5. the NR certificate.

All eID card scheme certificates are X.509 Version 3 certificates (see Section 11.1.2). The card holder non-repudiation verification key certificate must, in addition, be a *qualified certificate*, which means that it satisfies further conditions, including that the precise identity of the certificate holder has been established. A certificate is required under European law to be qualified if any digital signatures produced using the corresponding signature key are to be legally binding.

eID CARD ISSUING PROCESS

The process of issuing an eID card is quite complex and involves several different organisations. It serves as a good illustration of the intricacies of generating public-key certificates, which we discussed in general terms in Section 11.2.2. The process is indicated in Figure 12.14 and consists of the following steps:

1. Either after requesting, or being invited to apply for, an eID card, the eID applicant attends a local government office. This office essentially acts as the RA (see Section 11.2.2). The applicant presents a photograph to the RA, which then verifies the personal details of the applicant and formally signs an *eID card request*.
2. The eID card request is sent from the local government office to the *card personaliser* (CP), and the NR is notified. The CP checks the eID card request. For simplicity we will assume the existence of a single CP, who is responsible for creating the physical aspects of the card and for inputting the relevant data onto the chip on the card.
3. The CP creates a new eID card and generates the required key pairs on the card itself. The CP then sends a request for certificates to the relevant Citizen CA via the NR, who issues a certificate serial number for each certificate.

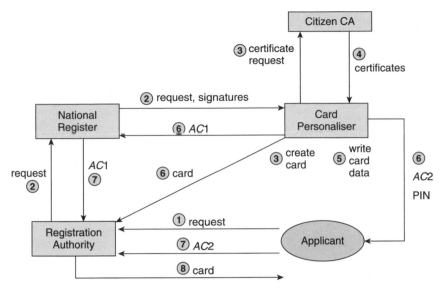

Figure 12.14. eID card issuing process

4. The Citizen CA generates certificates and sends them to the CP, who stores them on the card. The CA then immediately suspends these certificates.
5. The CP writes all the remaining card data onto the card and then deactivates the card.
6. The CP sends:

- the first part of an activation code AC1 to the NR;
- the second part of the activation code AC2 and a PIN to the applicant;
- the inactive eID card to the RA.

7. The applicant revisits the RA and presents AC2. This is then combined with AC1, which the RA requests from the database of the NR.
8. The CA activates the suspended card certificates and the active eID card is issued to the applicant.

eID CERTIFICATE REVOCATION

In Section 11.2.3 we discussed the challenges of public-key certificate revocation. As well as the reasons identified in Section 10.6.2 for revoking a public-key certificate, there are two special situations in which an eID card certificate has the status of being revoked:

1. the eID card non-repudiation verification key certificate is revoked for juveniles under the age of 18;
2. the eID card authentication verification key certificate is revoked for children under the age of 6.

The main technique used to manage certificate revocation in the eID card scheme is CRLs (see Section 11.2.3). A significant problem of the eID card scheme is that the potential size of CRLs is considerable. The eID card scheme Citizen CAs issue new *base CRLs* every three hours. During the period between updates of the base CRL, much smaller *delta CRLs* are issued, which identify changes to the last base CRL. In this way anyone who wishes to maintain their own local copy of the complete CRLs for the eID card scheme does not have to regularly download the full database. All CRLs are digitally signed by the issuing Citizen CA using 2048-bit RSA.

In general, applications using the eID card scheme are free to decide how to manage the certificate revocation information. Options include trusting the revocation status management to a third-party provider who operates an OCSP querying service (see Section 11.2.3), which itself will rely on the information provided in the Citizen CA CRLs.

eID SIGNATURE VALIDITY

Given the importance of some of the applications of eID cards, particularly with respect to digital signature creation, it is worth briefly commenting on the potential validity of digital signatures during two specific periods of time:

Digital signatures created after an incident but before revocation. As discussed in Section 11.2.3, a potential problem arises if a relying party verifies an eID card signature in the period between occurrence of a security incident (of a type that invalidates the eID card non-repudiation verification key certificate) and the revocation of that certificate. If the time of the incident can be precisely verified then, technically speaking, a digital signature created during this period is unlikely to be valid. Applications need to be aware of this potential problem and have procedures for coping with it. The Citizen CAs assist this process by frequently issuing base and delta CRLs.

Validity of digital signatures after expiry or revocation of the eID card (non-repudiation verification key certificate). So long as a digital signature is verified before expiry or revocation of the eID card (or its non-repudiation verification key certificate) then it should still be regarded as valid (and, indeed, may be legally binding) after the expiry or revocation date. One method for making this more explicit is for the signer who signs some data to obtain a digital signature from a trusted third party that attests to the validity of that signature at a specific point in time. Namely, the signer Alice presents her digital signature $sig_A(\text{data})$ to the TTP, who verifies this signature at time t and then generates the digital signature:

$$sig_{TTP}(sig_A(\text{data}) \| t).$$

The TTP thus acts as an archiving service. After the expiry or revocation of her eID card, Alice can still present the archived signature as evidence of its validity. Note that any future relying party does not need to verify Alice's original signature, but does have to trust the TTP. This process assumes that:

- The TTP's verification key has a longer lifetime than Alice's. On expiry of the TTP's verification key, Alice can always ask the TTP to resign the archived signature with its new signature key.
- No flaws are subsequently found in any of the processes or algorithms used to generate or validate Alice's digital signature.

12.6.6 Security issues

The eID card scheme represents a relatively straightforward use of cryptography. Its primary function is to issue citizens with smart cards that have digital signature capability. These applications can then engage with this cryptographic functionality in order to meet their own security requirements. The main 'security issues' are thus likely to arise from the specific ways in which these applications interact with eID cards. Since the eID card scheme supports digital signatures, it is also important to be aware of the many security issues that we discussed regarding the use of digital signatures in Section 7.4.

The main security issues for the eID cards themselves arise from the key management. Card issuing is a fairly complex and controlled process, since the implications of eID cards being either fraudulently issued, or issued with incorrect data, are potentially very serious. Certificate revocation is managed in a scalable way and it is up to individual applications to make sure that they obtain the latest revocation data in order to verify data signed using an eID card.

12.6.7 Design issues

The main design issues concerning the eID card scheme are as follows:

Use of public-key cryptography. While eID cards are issued within a closed environment, they are intended for use in open environments. Thus the use of public-key cryptography is appropriate.

Use of publicly known algorithms. To increase confidence and support interoperability, the eID card scheme uses the well-respected RSA digital signature scheme.

Use of certification hierarchies. The eID card scheme's national reach lends itself very naturally to a certification hierarchy, with central CAs supporting regional registration authorities.

Specific data handling. The eID card design demonstrates that in real applications different data items may require different management. This is reflected in the way that card data is digitally signed, which recognises that address data normally changes much more frequently than other types of personal data.

Flexibility. The eID card scheme is primarily an enabler for cryptographic applications. It therefore leaves specific applications a degree of flexibility on how they manage security of applications interacting with eID cards. In particular, applications must manage their own certificate revocation processing.

12.7 Cryptography for home users

Most of the previous applications use cryptography in a fairly transparent manner, in the sense that the end user may not even be aware of the underlying cryptography when they interact with the application. In this section we briefly consider some situations where an end user may take the active decision to use cryptography to protect some data. We focus our attention on a 'home user', by which we rather loosely mean a user who is not particularly computer literate and not part of a wider organisation with centralised security controls. Since there are so many tools and products providing cryptographic support to home users, we restrict ourselves to general remarks rather than specific analysis. The two applications that we will focus on are file encryption and email security.

12.7.1 File protection

Typically, there are two main reasons for a home user wanting to use cryptography to protect a file:

Additional storage protection. Most computer systems, including desktops, laptops, PDAs and smart phones, have basic security controls that provide some protection against unauthorised parties from accessing the files that are stored on them. Most home users rely on basic user access control mechanisms for this protection. The commonest such control is to provide entity authentication to the computer itself through the use of a password-based mechanism. However, such controls do not normally provide strong protection, since it is relatively easy to overcome them. In addition, different types of portable media exist for storing files, such as DVDs, memory cards and USB tokens, many of which have no default file storage protection mechanisms.

File transfer security. A user may wish to transfer a file from one computer system to another. While the end computer systems may be protected, the communication channel is potentially insecure.

In both of these cases, the primary security service that is required is confidentiality, since the main concern is unauthorised parties accessing the contents of the file.

474

FULL DISK ENCRYPTION

One option for a home user who is concerned about the security of files stored on their desktop or laptop is to deploy *full disk encryption*, which encrypts every bit of data contained on the computer system. Full disk encryption mechanisms are available both in hardware and software, with hardware mechanisms typically offering greater security and performance. Software mechanisms are easier to centrally manage, so are often preferred in corporate environments.

Full disk encryption is particularly attractive for laptops, which are at risk of becoming lost or stolen. The 'classical' physical attack on a stolen computer is for an attacker to remove the disk and reinstall it on a computer for which the attacker has administrator access.

There are two constraints which motivate the type of encryption deployed in full disk encryption mechanisms:

Performance. Encryption and decryption operations need to take place as fast as possible, ideally without any apparent delay. Thus most full disk encryption mechanisms encrypt each disk sector, which typically consist of around 512 bytes, independently.

Avoidance of storage overhead. In order to use disk space efficiently, the encryption operation should not result in significantly more data being stored than would otherwise have been stored without full disk encryption.

The performance requirement means that usually only symmetric encryption mechanisms are used. If we were to deploy a stream cipher for this purpose then we would need to store a unique value for each disk sector in order to make sure that the keystream used for each independent encryption was different (see Section 4.2.2), which results in an unacceptable storage overhead. Thus block ciphers are normally used.

Since sectors are encrypted independently and each sector is fairly small, ECB mode is unsuitable for the reasons that we discussed in Section 4.6.1. The other modes that we discussed in Section 4.6 all require additional sector-specific information, such as an IV in CBC mode and a counter in CTR mode, in order to guarantee that two identical sectors are not encrypted by the same key to the same ciphertext. The only other option is to make this sector-specific information predictable in some way, however, there are attacks known against some of our previously discussed modes if this is the case. As a result, several modes of operation of a block cipher, such as XTS mode, have been designed specifically for applications such as disk encryption. These tend to use predictable information such as the disk sector number and the position of a block of data within the sector to vary the encryption process each time it is applied.

One example of a full disk encryption mechanism is *BitLocker*, which is a feature provided by some versions of Microsoft operating systems. BitLocker provides its security through both hardware and software mechanisms by employing some of the functionality of the *Trusted Platform Module* (TPM) chip that is installed in some computer systems. BitLocker encryption is based on a modified version of AES in CBC mode.

Many full disk encryption mechanisms require the user to provide the disk decryption key either by entering a password or providing a security token. However, this control does require user interaction during the booting of the machine, which may be undesirable or inconvenient from a performance perspective. BitLocker allows such interaction, but also provides a more transparent service using the TPM that does not require it. The main additional requirement that this imposes is the need for a degree of data origin authentication of the encrypted data.

With respect to key management, generation and establishment of the necessary keys is relatively straightforward because this can be done locally. Of greater concern is storage of the key used to encrypt/decrypt the disk. Options for this include encrypting it using a key encrypting key that is derived on the fly from a passphrase (see Section 10.5.1) or storing it on a smart card. The main concern with a full disk encryption mechanism is the implications of the loss of the key used to protect the disk. It would thus be wise to make sure that the deployed mechanism provides a means of backing up important keys and that the backup mechanism itself is secure. One option is to store important keys on physically secured portable media.

VIRTUAL DISK ENCRYPTION

An alternative to encrypting an entire disk is to use *virtual disk encryption* mechanisms, which can be used to encrypt chunks of data, usually referred to as *containers*. Virtual disk encryption can be deployed on devices such as USB tokens, as well as on desktops and laptops. In most solutions the user is required to authenticate to the device, usually by means of a password, in order to access the encrypted files within the container. There are several advantages of virtual disk encryption over full disk encryption:

- Virtual disk encryption can be used to encrypt selected data on a disk, rather than the full disk.
- An encrypted container is normally portable, in the sense that it can be copied onto media such as a DVD. Thus virtual disk encryption can provide security for data transfer, as well as storage, in cases where the data can be physically transferred using portable media.

Just as for full disk encryption, care needs to be taken to make sure that the mechanisms and processes used to support user (entity) authentication to the device and key management are adequately addressed.

FILE ENCRYPTION

The greatest granularity of control over data encryption is to deploy file encryption, which encrypts individual files (or folders). One of the other main advantages of file encryption is that it can protect a file on a running computer system that an attacker has gained access to. Contrast this situation with, for example, a full disk encryption mechanism running on a computer that the user has authenticated to and then (foolishly) walked off and left unattended. Unlike full and virtual disk encryption, however, file (and folder) encryption do not normally prevent an attacker from learning data associated with the file, such as file size, file type and the folder name in which the file resides.

Some operating systems provide in-built file encryption, such as the *Encrypting File System* (EFS) deployed in many Microsoft operating systems. EFS uses hybrid encryption to protect a file by first encrypting it with a unique symmetric key, which is then itself encrypted using the user's public key. The user's private key is then required in order to decrypt. One issue with in-built file encryption of this type is that the protection is not always maintained when the encrypted file is transferred to another storage medium. However, there are many third-party software applications providing general file encryption capability, some of which support transfer of encrypted data.

File encryption is also appropriate for a user who only occasionally needs to encrypt a file, usually for transfer purposes. An example of encryption software for casual encryption of this type is *GNU Privacy Guard* (GPG). This uses hybrid encryption to encrypt files, as well as supporting digital signatures. A range of patent-free symmetric and public-key algorithms are supported. Users generate their own key pairs locally, using a passphrase to generate, and later activate, a key encrypting key that is used to protect the decryption key. Public-key management is lightweight and left at the user's discretion. Users could, for example, exchange public keys directly with known contacts or use a web of trust (see Section 11.4.1).

Finally, some application software supports encryption for specific data formats. For example, Adobe software allows users to encrypt pdf files. Adobe originally used RC4 but now also supports AES. The key is activated using a password, which can be sent to the recipient of an encrypted file in order to allow them to decrypt and view it.

12.7.2 Email security

Email has become a common communication mechanism for many people. Indeed, many of us use email almost every day. Thus users should at least consider the issue of email security. We will shortly discuss whether home users really need to secure their email or not.

EMAIL SECURITY REQUIREMENTS

There are two potential concerns about the security of email:

Confidentiality. By default, email messages are unprotected during their transfer from the email sender's device to the email receiver's device. During that transfer the email message resides on several email servers and internet routers, as well as passing through various potentially unprotected networks. There are many points at which, at least in theory, the contents of an email message could be viewed by someone other than the intended recipient. In addition, users sometimes mistakenly send email to the wrong recipient, for example, by replying to all the recipients of an email rather than just the original sender. Thus there is certainly a case that could be made for requiring confidentiality of some types of email message.

Data origin authentication. Email messages are structured using a simple protocol that facilitates their transfer. This protocol includes fields for specifying the sender, recipient and subject, as well as the message itself. An informed attacker can fairly easily generate forged emails. In addition, at most of the points at which an attacker can read a genuine email (see confidentiality concerns), the attacker could intercept and make changes to the email message before forwarding it on to the recipient. This also makes a case for requiring data origin authentication of email messages. Indeed, for some email messages we might even want to go further and require non-repudiation, but data origin authentication probably suffices for most traffic.

In certain corporate or government environments the above concerns are sufficiently important that email applications are deployed that provide these security services, sometimes applying protection by default to all email messages. We will shortly discuss the typical use of cryptography in these solutions, but first consider the appropriateness of secure email to a home user.

SHOULD HOME USERS SECURE THEIR EMAIL?

As we have just seen, in theory, email messages are insecure. It is thus unwise for anyone to send highly confidential information in the body of a normal email message. Confidential information is probably better protected by conveying it using an alternative communication channel, if available, perhaps by telephone.

However, home users need to be realistic about the threats facing their email. An informal risk assessment should be undertaken about the likelihood that someone does want to interfere with a home user's email. This should consider the environment within which the home user is operating (the other parties who may have access to the user's email, the general security practices of the home user, the local network, etc.), the wider infrastructure (for example, the reputation of the user's ISP) and the nature of the information that the user exchanges using email.

In most cases a home user is likely to conclude that securing email is unnecessary. However, it is certainly wise to carefully consider the possible implications of someone accessing information in a specific email message. Certain types of data should almost never be sent in an email. For example, credit card numbers in unprotected emails can be detected by automatic scanning of network traffic.

The main problem facing a home user who decides that they do want to protect the email that they send is the potential inconvenience to recipients. As we will see, securing email involves the use of cryptography, which then requires recipients to have the capability of processing a secure email message. This is why secure email applications generally work better in large organisations, which can provide the capability for securing internal email communication on all the email clients of employees.

One option for a home user who wishes to occasionally protect an email message is to send the sensitive data in a protected attachment. File encryption, as discussed in Section 12.7.1, is probably the easiest way to do this. However, if email requires security on a wider basis then it may be more convenient to use a dedicated email security application, which we now discuss.

EMAIL SECURITY APPLICATIONS

There are two well-known standards for protection of email, each of which are implemented by a wide range of email security applications. Both *Open Pretty Good Privacy* (OpenPGP) and *Secure/Multipurpose Internet Mail Extensions* (S/MIME) broadly work in the same way, although precise implementations may have minor differences. They both provide confidentiality and data origin authentication (non-repudiation) through support for encryption and digital signatures. They are either supported by default in certain email clients or can be installed through plug-ins.

There are three ways in which email messages can be protected using these applications:

Confidentiality only. This is provided by hybrid encryption (see Section 5.5.2). The symmetric encryption key is either generated using a deterministic generator (see Section 8.1.4) or a software-based non-deterministic generator (see Section 8.1.3). The body of the email message is then encrypted using this symmetric key, and the symmetric key is encrypted using the public key of the recipient.

Data origin authentication only. This is provided by a digital signature scheme with appendix (see Section 7.3.4). The email message is first hashed and then signed using the signature key of the sender. The receiver will need to obtain the corresponding verification key in order to verify the resulting digital signature.

Confidentiality and data origin authentication. This is typically provided by following the MAC-then-encrypt construction (see Section 6.3.6). In other words, a symmetric encryption key is generated and the email message is digitally signed, as described above. The email message and the resulting signature are then both encrypted using the symmetric encryption key. Finally the symmetric encryption key is itself encrypted using the public encryption key of the recipient.

The main differences between OpenPGP and S/MIME are with respect to:

Cryptographic algorithms supported. OpenPGP implementations support a range of cryptographic algorithms. On the other hand, S/MIME is more restrictive and specifies the use of AES or Triple DES for symmetric encryption and RSA for digital signatures and public-key encryption (the original S/MIME proposal came from RSA Data Security Inc.).

Public-key management. Again, OpenPGP is more flexible and can be supported by almost any form of public-key management system. The default public key management model for OpenPGP is to use a web of trust (see Section 11.4.1), although more formal public-key management can also be supported. On the other hand, S/MIME is based on the use of X.509 Version 3 certificates (see Section 11.1.2) supported by a structured public-key management system relying on Certificate Authorities.

AN ALTERNATIVE APPROACH TO EMAIL SECURITY

Since the approaches to email security that we have just discussed all rely on the use of public-key cryptography, the problem of assurance of purpose of public keys needs to be addressed by whichever public-key management system is used to support an email security application.

In Section 11.4.2 we explained the potential benefits of identity-based public-key cryptography in addressing the problem of providing assurance of purpose of public keys. The IDPKC concept requires unique identifiers that can be associated with users of the system. In email security applications such a potential unique identifier exists in the form of the email address of the recipient. Thus, using IDPKC, an email sender is potentially able to send an encrypted email to *any* recipient simply by encrypting the email using the recipient's email address.

The advantages offered by this concept have resulted in the commercial development of email security applications based on IDPKC. As we discussed in Section 11.4.2, one of the potential drawbacks with IDPKC is the need for an online centrally-trusted key centre (TKC). Thus IDPKC is most suited to large organisations where such a TKC can easily be provided, rather than home users. However, a home user could well receive encrypted email from such an organisation without needing any formal relationship with the sender. In this case:

1. The sender (from the organisation supporting IDPKC) sends an encrypted email to the recipient (the home user), using the recipient's email address as the encryption key.
2. The recipient receives an email message informing them that they have received an encrypted email message and inviting them to visit a secure website in order to view the contents.
3. The recipient clicks on the provided web link and is directed via an SSL-protected channel to the organisation's TKC web server. This generates the necessary private decryption key and recovers the email, which is then displayed to the recipient.

The obvious concern with this approach is that the IDPKC approach requires the recipient of the email to trust the sending organisation enough to visit the website and request decryption of the protected email. From the organisation's perspective, however, there is no need to rely on third-party public-key certificates.

The organisation is also able, through the TKC, to check the contents of secure email sent from their employees, which is sometimes a requirement (for example, for checking for malware or other undesirable content).

12.8 Summary

In this chapter we examined a number of cryptographic applications. Each of these applications varied in terms of the cryptographic services that it required and the constraints within which it operated. For each of these applications we identified the cryptographic requirements, detailed the cryptography deployed and discussed the appropriate key management. We examined these applications in a fairly consistent manner, with the intention that this same methodology could be used to analyse the cryptographic design of other applications that we have not covered in this chapter.

Hopefully this examination of some important applications of cryptography has provided a good illustration of the fundamental principles that were outlined in the earlier chapters. Of particular importance are the following general issues that should have been made clear during our analysis:

- Applications tend to aim for 'sufficient' security rather than 'best' security. The use of cryptography often represents both a computational and/or usability overhead, hence it should not be needlessly deployed in order to provide security services that are not required.
- As we have seen throughout our discussions, security and efficiency often have to be traded off against one another. Getting the right balance is not always easy. The development of several of the applications that we have examined show that designers are often forced to readjust this balance over time. Naturally enough, the tendency is (to err) towards efficiency in early versions of cryptographic applications.
- Application constraints play an important role in cryptographic design. They often dictate both the cryptography deployed and the ways in which keys are managed.
- The use of proprietary cryptographic algorithms comes with a degree of risk. While many applications initially adopted proprietary cryptographic algorithms for legitimate reasons, in a number of high-profile cases the underlying primitives were reverse-engineered and found to contain flaws. In most cases these early versions have been replaced by systems using publicly known algorithms.
- Despite the wide variety of cryptographic algorithms that have been designed and made publicly available, only a very select few are deployed in real applications.
- Symmetric cryptography remains the preferred choice for most applications. Public-key cryptography is selectively deployed only when the key

481

management requirements of symmetric cryptography cannot be easily supported, which tends to be the case for applications in open environments. Even then, its use tends to be restricted to the essential operations.

- Key management is absolutely critical to the security of a cryptographic application. Key management is relatively straightforward in some applications, but much more complex in others. Indeed, key management issues can often dictate what kind of cryptography is used in an application.

12.9 Further reading

The applications that we discussed in this chapter were just examples. While some other books on cryptography include information on applications, in most cases details about the cryptography used in a particular application are more readily obtained from resources directly concerning the application itself. A notable exception is the wide range of security applications discussed in Anderson [23], which includes chapters on banking security, telecommunications security and digital rights management.

There is a vast amount of further information available concerning SSL (TLS). One of the most comprehensive sources of information is Rescorla [161]. There are numerous IETF standards covering aspects of TLS, with RFC 5246 [57] being the most fundamental one. Several more general network security books include good coverage of SSL, including Garfinkel and Spafford [88] and Stallings [183], the latter of which is also a good source of information about SSH and IPsec. Advice on implementation of TLS is included in NIST 800-52 [136].

The saga behind the cryptography used in WLAN standards is well documented. An excellent overview of WLAN security, which includes details of all the crypto-graphic issues, is Edney and Artaugh [67]. The main WLAN security standard is IEEE 802.11 [15], which has numerous more recent amendments. WLAN security is also covered in a number of other dedicated books, including the practical perspectives provided by Cache and Liu [44]. Some more general books such as Stallings [183] include chapters on WLAN security. WPA2 entity authentication can be done using EAP, which is defined in RFC 3748 [20].

A comprehensive discussion of UMTS security is Niemi and Nyberg [130]. A very accessible introduction to GSM security is Pagliusi [150]. Both GSM and UMTS are covered by Chandra [46]. The official EMV standards for card payments are all available online from EMVCo [71]. A good overview of EMV is included as a chapter in Mayes and Markantonakis [120], where there are also chapters on mobile telecommunications security and the security of video broadcasting. A more detailed coverage of technical issues concerning the more general area of digital rights management is Zeng, Hu and Lin [208]. An overview of security of the eID card scheme can be found in De Cock et al. [48].

A number of good resources exist relating to cryptography for home users. NIST 800-111 provides advice on encryption of storage devices, including some useful background information. Cryptographic secure file storage is also discussed in Cobb [47]. A good tool for disk encryption is TrueCrypt [192], on whose website a great deal of interesting information can be found about the underlying cryptographic mechanisms used. Email security is covered by informative chapters in Stallings [183], Garfinkel and Spafford [88] and Cobb [47]. NIST also dedicate special publication NIST 800-45 [138] to this subject.

12.10 Activities

1. Consider two different 'worlds' with respect to cryptographic applications:

   World 1: the early 1970s;
   World 2: today.

   The cryptographic applications discussed in this chapter belong to the second of these 'worlds' (indeed, many were unimaginable in the first of these 'worlds'). At a fairly high and generic level, compare these two 'worlds' by considering the following issues for each of them. In each of the two worlds:

   (a) Who is using cryptography and for what applications?
   (b) What type of cryptography is deployed?
   (c) What security services are implemented?
   (d) What technology is used to conduct cryptographic operations?
   (e) How secure is a typical 'communication channel'?
   (f) How secure are the 'end points' (the sender and receiver's local environ-
       ments)?
   (g) How reliable are the cryptographic mechanisms that are used?
   (h) How straightforward is key management?
   (i) Are there any security issues relating to cryptography in the first 'world' that
       do not apply to the second 'world'?
   (j) Are there any security issues relating to cryptography in the second 'world'
       that do not apply to the first 'world'?
   (k) Summarise the discussion by commenting on whether the role and
       effectiveness of cryptography has changed between these two 'worlds'.

2. Many cryptographic applications support a range of different cryptographic algorithms.

   (a) Which of the applications discussed in this chapter support a range of
       cryptographic algorithms, rather than recommending a fixed encryption
       algorithm?
   (b) Discuss the pros and cons of supporting a range of cryptographic algorithms
       in an application.
   (c) Why might a relatively 'weak' cryptographic algorithm be included amongst
       a set of supported cryptographic algorithms?
   (d) What security issues might arise from including a relatively 'weak' crypto-
       graphic algorithm in a set of supported cryptographic algorithms?

3. The security provided by SSL to secure a web session depends, partially, on the handling of the underlying public-key certificates.

   (a) Explain how an SSL client can determine whether a server that they are communicating with has supplied them with a valid public-key certificate during the SSL Handshake Protocol.
   (b) A university department decides to self-sign a public-key certificate for its own web server. What might go wrong when a prospective student tries to establish an SSL-protected connection with the departmental web server?
   (c) A local government office decides to use a third-party payment provider to process payments for electronic services offered through the government website. What might go wrong when a local resident tries to make a secure payment from the government website using SSL?
   (d) Comment on the extent to which you think that the way in which current web browsers manage certificate problems that arise during SSL sessions is effective.

4. SSL is generally regarded as a well-designed protocol.

   (a) Explain why the use of SSL does not necessarily prevent phishing attacks.
   (b) To what extent do you regard this as a design failure of SSL itself, or the wider system in which it is deployed?

5. SSL provides a secure channel at the Transport Layer of the Internet Protocol Suite. On the other hand, SSH provides a secure channel at the Application Layer and IPsec provides a secure channel at the Internet Layer. By reading up about SSH and IPsec, compare SSL with SSH and IPsec from the perspective of:

   (a) Security services provided;
   (b) Cryptographic primitives and algorithms supported;
   (c) Examples of real-world use of the protocols;
   (d) Key management requirements.

6. Consider the following statement: *The design of WEP is not fundamentally flawed, but rather represents a misjudged efficiency–security tradeoff.* By considering the flaws in WEP, to what extent do you support this statement?

7. CCM mode is adopted by a number of wireless network applications, including WPA2. Find a description of CCM mode and explain, with the aid of diagrams, how CCM mode encryption/authentication and decryption/verification work.

8. GSM and UMTS both provide a degree of security to users of mobile phone technology.

   (a) Explain the role of the SIM card in GSM/UMTS security.
   (b) What potential threats to mobile phone users do the security mechanisms in GSM and UMTS *not* provide any protection against?
   (c) Why do GSM and UMTS not employ public-key cryptography?

9. Mobile phones are becoming more general computing platforms, with more and more functionality and support for applications. What implications do you think this has for the future functionality, security and management of cryptography on mobile phones?

10. EMV is largely based on a symmetric key infrastructure.

    (a) Explain precisely where, and why, EMV uses public-key cryptography.
    (b) Identify which operations within EMV essentially provide non-repudiation, and justify the cryptographic mechanisms used by EMV to provide this service.
    (c) Why does EMV not currently deploy AES?

11. EMV cards are supported online by 3DSecure, which replaces a previous architecture known as *Secure Electronic Transactions* (SET).

    (a) Briefly explain the main cryptographic design features of SET and explain why it did not become well established.
    (b) Identify the main features of 3DSecure that have led to its successful adoption on a large scale.

12. Find an example of an application supporting EMV-CAP.

    (a) Provide some details on how EMV-CAP is used to support the overall security requirements of that application.
    (b) What advantages are there of using EMV-CAP for your application as opposed to other authentication technologies?

13. Broadcast networks have some very specific properties. Explain how the nature of a broadcast channel provides particular challenges to the design of a cryptographic architecture to support a broadcast application.

14. Recall the various issues that we discussed in Chapter 7 concerning the use of digital signatures in practical applications. Which of these issues do you regard as being the most significant when using a Belgian eID card to provide a non-repudiation service?

15. The Belgian eID card issuing process is complex and involves several different organisations.

    (a) Identify the different organisations involved and explain what role they each play in the process.
    (b) Why are these various roles provided by *different* organisations?

16. Belgium is not the only country to issue identity cards that have cryptographic capability to its citizens. Find another example of a national identity card scheme based on smart cards and attempt to find out:

    (a) what functionality the card is intended to have;
    (b) what security services it requires;
    (c) what cryptography it deploys;

(d) how the necessary keys are managed;

(e) how the card protects the data contained on it.

17. Full disk encryption is an option for users who are concerned that their computer disk might be accessed or stolen.

   (a) Explain at least three different ways in which an attacker could overcome basic login password protection on a laptop in order to access the files on the machine.

   (b) Why, in general, do you think data origin authentication is not a requirement for file encryption systems?

   (c) Describe one of the modes of operation that has been proposed for full disk encryption and explain what properties it has that are particularly suitable for this type of application.

18. File encryption is supported by many operating systems and third-party software applications.

   (a) Explain why most file encryption mechanisms use hybrid encryption.

   (b) Select an example of a file encryption mechanism using hybrid encryption and explain:

      i. how a user accesses an encrypted file;

      ii. which encryption algorithms are supported;

      iii. where the user's private key is stored;

      iv. what mechanisms exist to support a user who has lost their private key (or forgotten how to activate it).

19. Discuss the relative advantages and disadvantages of using full disk encryption, virtual disk encryption and file encryption from:

   (a) a security perspective;

   (b) a usability perspective;

   (c) a management perspective.

20. Amongst the most important data managed by home users is personal data relating to information such as contact information, usernames and passwords. A number of commercial and open source products exist to assist users manage and secure this type of personal data. Choose an example of a technology that claims to protect personal data on a portable device. Write a short report commenting on the security mechanisms (including cryptographic mechanisms) deployed and the extent to which personal data is protected in the event that the portable device is stolen.

21. We discussed email security from the perspective of a home user securing email through the use of a standard email client.

   (a) Compare the security of email accessed through an OpenPGP-compliant email client with that of email accessed via an SSL-protected channel to a webmail application.

(b) Some organisations choose to use an OpenPGP-compliant gateway server to conduct cryptographic operations on behalf of users. A recipient who is not a member of the organisation is required to visit the gateway server to retrieve encrypted email. Compare the key management issues of this approach with the use of IDPKC to secure email.

22. Consider a transport ticketing application for a large city that allows travelers to pay for their journeys using smart cards that contain pre-loaded monetary value. Travelers activate payment by presenting their smart cards to payment gateways at the start and end of their journey. Following the approach of the other cryptographic applications discussed in this chapter, for this ticketing application:

    (a) What are the main security requirements?
    (b) What are the application constraints that influence the design of suitable security mechanisms?
    (c) Which cryptographic primitives are suitable for deployment in this application?
    (d) Which cryptographic algorithms and key lengths do you suggest are supported?
    (e) How should key management be conducted?

23. Following the approach of other cryptographic applications discussed in this chapter (as outlined above), discuss the cryptographic design and key management of the different versions of Bluetooth, which allows short-range wireless communication between two Bluethooth-enabled devices.

13 Closing Remarks

We have now completed our introduction to everyday cryptography. We have seen that cryptography is essentially a toolkit of mathematical techniques for implementing the core security services that are required to protect information. We have learnt many important lessons about cryptography along the way. In particular:

Cryptography is much more than encryption. The term 'cryptography' derives from the Greek for 'hidden writing', which inappropriately implies that cryptography is primarily about providing confidentiality. Although confidentiality is important, the cryptographic toolkit consists of far more than just tools for encryption. Cryptographic primitives can be employed to provide a host of different security services. As well as confidentiality mechanisms, we have studied mechanisms for providing data integrity, data origin authentication, entity authentication and non-repudiation. While cryptographers have designed many even more specialised tools, the majority of applications of cryptography can be built from the mechanisms that we discussed in this book.

Cryptography is an everyday technology. Cryptography has become a technology that most of us use almost every day of our lives. We have examined several of these applications in this book. However, the majority of users do not realise that they are using cryptography on a daily basis. Cryptography may literally mean 'hidden writing', but it is really the *use* of cryptography that is hidden in most applications. In many cases we have no alternative to cryptography for providing most of these security services, so it is reasonable to expect that this everyday use of cryptography will continue for the foreseeable future.

Cryptography is a process. Cryptography does nothing on its own. While it is a crucial underlying component of any information security architecture, cryptography is nothing more than that. Achieving the security services that cryptographic mechanisms are designed to provide requires cryptography to be treated as a process. The correct cryptographic mechanisms need to be selected, combined and used in an appropriate manner. Cryptography needs to be carefully incorporated into other technologies. Cryptographic keys undergo a complete lifecycle, which must be overseen by sound key management. If any

488

stage of this process is deficient then it is likely that the desired security services are not provided, despite the use of cryptography.

Cryptography is not only for mathematicians. It is certainly true that most cryptographic mechanisms rely on mathematical ideas. However, we hope that we have made the case that understanding what cryptography does, and how it can be used, does not require extensive mathematical knowledge.

Cryptography must be handled with care. Bruce Schneier later expressed some regret that some people treated his book *Applied Cryptography* [168] as a complete source of cryptographic knowledge. His mistake was that by popularising and explaining cryptographic principles, he gave some readers too much confidence that they now knew everything. We hope that we have provided enough caveats to make it clear that this book should not be treated in such a way. This book is a starting point for a cryptographic adventure, not a comprehensive guide. We have concentrated on principles at the expense of detail. In cryptography, unlike certain other subjects, detail is often absolutely crucial. Cryptography is not a subject for 'do-it-yourself' amateurs, even well-informed ones. The best advice is to always listen to the experts, consult the standards, and pursue a policy of safely following the knowledgeable crowd. Those who stray from this advice by attempting to exhibit cryptographic flare and creativity are rarely rewarded. Cryptographic standards are normally painstakingly prepared and scrutinised. It is generally wise to follow them.

Our explanation of the cryptographic toolkit and key management has focussed on fundamental principles and illustrative applications, rather than the latest trends. In doing so, we hope that the careful reader should now be in a position not just to understand the everyday use of cryptography, but also to interpret future developments in cryptographic technology and applications. We hope the case has been made that cryptography is clever, useful, important and fun, which is a charmingly rare combination.

Mathematics Appendix

In this appendix we look at the basic mathematical concepts that underlie some of the material in the book. We stress that study of this appendix is *not required* in order to read this book. The explanation of these ideas assumes little or no prior knowledge.

The topics covered in this appendix are:

- Decimal, binary and hex;
- XOR;
- Modular arithmetic;
- Primes, coprimes and greatest common divisors;
- Modular inverses;
- Why RSA works;
- Primitive elements;
- Why ElGamal works.

A.1 Decimal, binary and hex

Everyone is familiar with *decimal numbers*. These are the numbers that we use every day and are the numbers that we normally write and perform calculations with. Representing numbers in decimal is just one possible way of writing a number. There are many other ways of writing a number (for example, Roman numbers and Chinese characters). This section introduces two other ways of writing numbers: *binary* and *hex*. Binary and hex are particularly useful in digital communication. In fact, at the most fundamental level, binary numbers are the basis of all computing.

In this section we make extensive use of the notation for exponentiation, as discussed in Section 1.6.1. For example, if we write 10^7 (10 to the power 7) then we mean 10 multiplied by itself seven times:

$$10^7 = 10 \times 10 \times 10 \times 10 \times 10 \times 10 \times 10.$$

Note that it is standard mathematical convention to say that any number raised to the power 0 is 1. Thus, for example, $10^0 = 1$.

A.1.1 Decimal

Before explaining binary or hex, it is first necessary to understand some of the principles behind the more familiar decimal numbers.

WRITING A NUMBER IN DECIMAL

Consider the number 359. What do each of 3, 5 and 9 actually represent? Observe that.

$$359 = 300 + 50 + 9$$
$$= (3 \times 100) + (5 \times 10) + (9 \times 1)$$
$$= (3 \times 10^2) + (5 \times 10^1) + (9 \times 10^0).$$

All we have done in these last three lines is to rewrite the number 359 in a form that shows how it can be represented as a sum of multiples of powers of ten. This is why our most familiar numbers are often referred to as *decimal* numbers: the digits that we use to write them indicate the multiples of powers of ten that are added together to make up the number. Observe two things:

1. The digits of a decimal number can take any of the values from 0 up to 9.
2. Every digit in a decimal number will be multiplied by some power of 10. The powers of 10 start with 0 (the furthest digit to the right) and then increase from right to left.

Decimal numbers are sometimes also referred to as *base 10* numbers. This is because the representation of the number in digits is 'based' on the powers of 10, as we have just seen. We normally do not bother indicating that a number is written in base 10, since this tends to be assumed by default. However, because we will be changing numbers from one base into another, we will often need to indicate the base being used. To indicate that the number 359 is a decimal number we will thus sometimes write it as 359_{10}.

LEADING ZEROS

As a last remark about decimal (indeed, any number base), any number of 0's can be put in front of a decimal number without changing its value. These are called *leading zeros*. For example,

$$00013 = 013 = 13.$$

This is consistent with our previous way of expressing decimal numbers since:

$$00013 = (0 \times 10^4) + (0 \times 10^3) + (0 \times 10^2) + (1 \times 10^1) + (3 \times 10^0)$$
$$= 0 + 0 + 0 + (1 \times 10^1) + (3 \times 10^0)$$
$$= (1 \times 10^1) + (3 \times 10^0) = 13.$$

491

Of course, when writing numbers in decimal we do not normally use any leading zeros.

A.1.2 Binary

We now look at binary numbers.

WRITING A NUMBER IN BINARY

Binary numbers are numbers written in base 2. Binary numbers follow very similar rules to decimal numbers. In fact the only real change is that the role of the number 10 in writing a decimal number is replaced by the number 2. Thus the new rules are:

1. The digits of a binary number can take the value 0 or 1.
2. Every digit in a binary number will be multiplied by some power of 2. The powers of 2 start with 0 (the furthest digit to the right) and then increase from right to left.

Consider the binary number 1101_2 (note that we have used the subscript 2 just to make it clear that we mean the number 1101 in binary and not the decimal number one thousand one hundred and one, which we would have written 1101_{10}). Using the above rules (and comparing them with the explanation of decimal numbers), we see that each binary number is a sum of multiples of powers of 2:

$$1101_2 = (1 \times 2^3) + (1 \times 2^2) + (0 \times 2^1) + (1 \times 2^0).$$

Similarly, the number 110010_2 is the sum of multiples of powers of 2 expressed by:

$$110010_2 = (1 \times 2^5) + (1 \times 2^4) + (0 \times 2^3) + (0 \times 2^2) + (1 \times 2^1) + (0 \times 2^0).$$

Every binary number has a decimal equivalent, and every decimal number has a binary equivalent. We now explain how to convert from one to the other.

CONVERTING BINARY TO DECIMAL

Converting from binary to decimal is easy. Simply express the binary number as its sum of multiples of powers of 2, and then add them up. So, what is 1101_2 in decimal? We know that:

$$1101_2 = (1 \times 2^3) + (1 \times 2^2) + (0 \times 2^1) + (1 \times 2^0)$$

$$= (1 \times 8) + (1 \times 4) + (0 \times 2) + (1 \times 1)$$

$$= 8 + 4 + 0 + 1$$

$$= 13.$$

So what we are saying is that the number 1101 in binary is the same as the number 13 in decimal, in other words $1101_2 = 13_{10}$.

CONVERTING DECIMAL TO BINARY

Converting a decimal number into binary is essentially just the reverse of the process for converting binary into decimal. Recall that a binary number such as 1101_2 specifies a sum of multiples of powers of 2. These multiples can only take the values 0 or 1, so a binary number really specifies a sum of *some of* the powers of 2. More precisely:

- if the multiple is 0 then the corresponding power of 2 is not included in the sum;
- If the multiple is 1 then the corresponding power of 2 is included in the sum.

In fact any number can be *uniquely* expressed as a sum of powers of 2. So the question of how to convert a given decimal number into binary is equivalent to asking precisely which of the powers of 2 add up to that decimal number.

For a small number such as 14 we can easily determine this by trial and error. It does not take very long to work out that the powers of 2 that add up to 14 are 8, 4 and 2. Thus, by reversing the binary to decimal process, we see that:

$$14_{10} = 8 + 4 + 2$$
$$= (1 \times 8) + (1 \times 4) + (1 \times 2) + (0 \times 1)$$
$$= (1 \times 2^3) + (1 \times 2^2) + (1 \times 2^1) + (0 \times 2^0)$$
$$= 1110_2.$$

In general, and in particular to convert large decimal numbers into binary, we need some kind of algorithm (system) for working out the binary equivalent of a decimal number. For simplicity, we will illustrate this process using a small number, namely 25_{10}.

1. *Find the highest power of 2 that is smaller than 25.* Clearly it is not possible for a power of 2 that is larger than 25 to be part of the sum of powers of 2 that adds up to 25, so we find the largest power of 2 less than 25. This is 16. Thus 25_{10} can be expressed as a sum of powers of 2 that are all less than or equal to 16. In other words:

$$25_{10} = (? \times 16) + (? \times 8) + (? \times 4) + (? \times 2) + (? \times 1).$$

2. *Determine whether each of the ? symbols is 0 or 1.* Consider the ? coefficient next to 16. All of the remaining powers of 2 (8, 4, 2 and 1) only add up to 15. Thus we must have 16 in our sum of powers of 2 that add up to 25, otherwise we could only sum to 15. Hence the coefficient of 16 must be 1. So:

$$25_{10} = (1 \times 16) + (? \times 8) + (? \times 4) + (? \times 2) + (? \times 1).$$

Now the remaining four powers of 2 must add to $25 - 16 = 9$. Consider the ? coefficient next to 8. All of the remaining powers of 2 (4, 2 and 1) only add up to 7. Thus we must have 8 in our sum of powers of 2 that add up to 25, otherwise we could only sum to $16 + 7 = 23$. Hence the coefficient of 8 must be 1. Thus:

$$25_{10} = (1 \times 16) + (1 \times 8) + (? \times 4) + (? \times 2) + (? \times 1).$$

Now the remaining three powers of 2 must add to $25 - 16 - 8 = 1$. Consider the ? coefficient next to 4. If 4 was included in our sum of powers of 2 then our sum of powers of 2 would be greater than 25, since $16 + 8 + 4 = 28$. Hence the coefficient of 4 must be 0. Thus:

$$25_{10} = (1 \times 16) + (1 \times 8) + (0 \times 4) + (? \times 2) + (? \times 1).$$

Now the remaining two powers of 2 must add to $25 - 16 - 8 = 1$. Consider the ? coefficient next to 2. If 2 was included in our sum of powers of 2 then our sum of powers of 2 would be greater than 25, since $16 + 8 + 2 = 26$. Hence the coefficient of 2 must be 0. Thus:

$$25_{10} = (1 \times 16) + (1 \times 8) + (0 \times 4) + (0 \times 2) + (? \times 1).$$

Now the remaining power of 2 must add to $25 - 16 - 8 = 1$. Consider the ? coefficient next to 1. Clearly in order to complete our sum the coefficient of 1 must be 1. So:

$$25_{10} = (1 \times 16) + (1 \times 8) + (0 \times 4) + (0 \times 2) + (1 \times 1).$$

Thus we have determined all the coefficients and so:

$$25_{10} = 11001_2.$$

This is a simple algorithm, although a bit awkward to perform by hand. It should be clear, however, that this conversion algorithm is very easily performed on a computer.

THE 3.3 TRICK

We tend to have an intuitive feel for decimal numbers because we use them every day without thought or question. In cryptography we often represent keys in binary. For example, an AES key can be 128 bits long, which means that it consists of 128 binary bits. This means that there are 2^{128} possible keys in the keyspace, but what does this mean in terms of our more familiar decimal numbers? Fortunately, there is a quick and easy way to get a fairly rough, but good, approximation to this relationship. It is known as the *3.3 trick*:

- To change a power of 2 into a power of 10, divide the power of 2 by 3.3.
- To change a power of 10 into a power of 2, multiply the power of 10 by 3.3.

Thus, knowing that there are are 2^{128} possible AES keys, we need to divide 128 by 3.3. The answer is close to 39, so 2^{128} is approximately 10^{39}.

Similarly, if we want to know how many bits long a symmetric key should be in order to guarantee a keyspace of at least one million, we need to determine what power of 2 is approximately equal to 10^6. We thus need to multiply 6 by 3.3, which is almost 20, so 10^6 is approximately 2^{20}. Thus around 20 bits will suffice.

Of course this is not really a *trick* at all. Note that $2^3 = 8$ and $2^4 = 16$. We can in fact write any number between 8 and 16 as a power of 2, where the 'power' will be a number between 3 and 4 (the details are easily found from any wider introduction to exponentiation). The number 3.3 arises because $2^{3.3}$ is a close approximation to 10.

A.1.3 XOR

Now that we are familiar with binary numbers, it is worth mentioning a very important way of combining two binary numbers, which is commonly used in cryptography. This is the function *exclusive or*, better known as XOR, and usually denoted by the symbol $\oplus$.

When used to combine single binary digits, XOR takes two bits as input, and results in a third bit. The result is calculated according to the following rules:

$$0 \oplus 0 = 0$$

$$0 \oplus 1 = 1$$

$$1 \oplus 0 = 1$$

$$1 \oplus 1 = 0.$$

In other words, the result of the XOR of two bits is 1 if the two inputs are different, and the result is 0 if the two inputs are the same.

When the XOR function is applied to binary numbers that are more than one bit long, the XOR of the two binary numbers is the result of the XOR of each individual bit. For example:

$$11010 \oplus 10011 = 01001 = 1001.$$

This follows because:

$$1 \oplus 1 = 0, \quad 1 \oplus 0 = 1, \quad 0 \oplus 0 = 0, \quad 1 \oplus 1 = 0, \quad 0 \oplus 1 = 1.$$

We can also XOR two binary numbers of different lengths by first padding the smaller of the two numbers with leading zeros until it is the same length as the larger number. The two numbers can then be XORed in the normal way. For example, to compute $11010 \oplus 101$ we first pad out 101 to 00101 and then compute:

$$11010 \oplus 00101 = 11111.$$

A.1.4 Hex

The other base that we need is *hexadecimal*, better known as *hex*, which is base 16. The main reason that we need hex is that it provides a compact way of representing binary numbers. This is particularly helpful for cryptographic keys, which are often very long when represented in binary.

WRITING A NUMBER IN HEX

For hex numbers, we use the base number 16 instead of 10 in decimal (and 2 in binary). Thus:

1. The digits of a hex number can, in theory, take any of the values between 0 and 15.
2. Every digit in a hex number will be multiplied by some power of 16. The powers of 16 start with 0 (the furthest digit to the right) and then increase from right to left.

The first requirement causes a slight problem, since it will be hard to determine whether 12 means the digit 1 followed by the digit 2, or whether we mean the hex 'digit' 12. Thus we replace the hex digits 10, 11, 12, 13, 14 and 15 by A, B, C, D, E and F, respectively. So, in practice, the digits of a hex number take any of the values between 0 and 9, and between A and F.

CONVERTING HEX TO DECIMAL

Converting from hex to decimal follows the same principles as binary to decimal, except that now we are using multiples and powers of 16. Consider the hex number $B5F_{16}$. It follows that:

$$B5F_{16} = (B \times 16^2) + (5 \times 16^1) + (F \times 16^0)$$
$$= (11 \times 16^2) + (5 \times 16^1) + (15 \times 16^0)$$
$$= (11 \times 256) + (5 \times 16) + (15 \times 1)$$
$$= 2816 + 80 + 15$$
$$= 2911_{10}.$$

Thus $B5F$ in hex is 2911 in decimal.

CONVERTING BETWEEN BINARY AND HEX

A useful feature of hex is that there is a very simple way of converting between binary and hex (which does not work for converting either of them to, or from, decimal). This uses Table A.1, which displays the binary equivalents of the 16 hex digits.

Converting from hex to binary simply involves replacing each hex digit with its binary equivalent from Table A.1. For example, to convert $B5F_{16}$ into binary we first make the substitutions:

$$B_{16} = 1011_2, \quad 5_{16} = 0101_2, \quad F_{16} = 1111_2$$

from Table A.1 to get:

$$B5F_{16} = 101101011111_2.$$

496

Table A.1: Decimal and binary equivalents of hex digits

Decimal	Binary	Hex
0	0000	0
1	0001	1
2	0010	2
3	0011	3
4	0100	4
5	0101	5
6	0110	6
7	0111	7
8	1000	8
9	1001	9
10	1010	*A*
11	1011	*B*
12	1100	*C*
13	1101	*D*
14	1110	*E*
15	1111	*F*

Converting from binary to hex is just substituting the other way. For example, to convert 11000111_2 into hex we make the substitutions:

$$1100_2 = C_{16}, \quad 0111_2 = 7_{16}$$

from Table A.1, to get:

$$11000111_2 = C7_{16}.$$

In the case where the binary number cannot be neatly divided into groups of four bits, we add leading zeros until it can. Thus to convert 1110011111_2 into hex we first add two leading zeros:

$$1110011111_2 = 001110011111_2.$$

We now make the substitutions:

$$0011_2 = 3_{16}, \quad 1001_2 = 9_{16}, \quad 1111_2 = F_{16}$$

from Table A.1 to get:

$$1110011111_2 = 39F_{16}.$$

A.1.5 ASCII

Although computers process binary numbers, the majority of data that we exchange does not consist of binary numbers themselves, but rather consists of alphanumeric symbols, punctuation and other keyboard characters. Thus there needs to be a standard convention for converting these items into binary, before they can be processed by digital devices.

The *American Standard Code for Information Interchange* (ASCII) is the convention that most computers use to conduct this conversion. ASCII specifies an 8-bit binary number for each keyboard character. These are numbered 000 up to 127 in decimal (hence, strictly, only 7 binary digits are needed). Each of these can thus also be represented as two hex digits. Some sources give ASCII values between 128 and 255 but these have not been agreed as a standard and are strictly ASCII extensions.

As an example, the 'greater than' symbol > appears in position 62 of the full ASCII table. To find out the ASCII binary representation we just convert 62_{10} into binary and then pad out to 8 bits using leading zeros, if necessary. In other words:

$$62_{10} = 111110_2 = 00111110_2 = 3E_{16}.$$

A.2 Modular arithmetic

This section introduces modular arithmetic. Modular arithmetic is used in many different cryptographic primitives, particularly public-key algorithms such as RSA.

A.2.1 Motivation

Modular arithmetic is a familiar idea, dressed in mathematical terminology. This is best illustrated by several examples from everyday use.

DAYS OF THE WEEK

When we work out what day of the week something will happen on, we often (unconsciously) make mental calculations such as 'two days after Tuesday is

Thursday'. We could write this in a pseudo-mathematical way as follows:

$$\text{Tuesday} + 2 = \text{Thursday}.$$

When such a calculation takes us beyond the end of a particular week then we will make statements such as 'three days after Friday is Monday'. Although this is actually Monday of the *following* week, this does not cause us any problem since we are treating all Mondays as 'the same' for this purpose. So:

$$\text{Friday} + 3 = \text{Monday}.$$

Similarly we can make statements such as:

$$\text{Thursday} - 2 = \text{Tuesday},$$

and

$$\text{Friday} + 7 = \text{Friday}.$$

We can restate this simple idea by now replacing the days of the week, starting with Monday, by the numbers 0 to 6 (so Monday is 0, Tuesday is 1, and Sunday is 6). It is now possible to write all our previous pseudo-mathematical equations as mathematical equations. In other words:

$$1 + 2 = 3$$
$$4 + 3 = 0$$
$$3 - 2 = 1$$
$$4 + 7 = 4.$$

Computing the days of the week in this manner is an example of *modulo* 7 (often abbreviated to *mod* 7) *arithmetic*. It is just like normal arithmetic except that we 'wrap back around' when we reach the number 7 by treating 7 as beginning again at 0.

MONTHS OF THE YEAR

Another example of modular arithmetic is when we calculate the months of the year. When we try to work out what month of the year something will happen in, we often make calculations such as 'three months after January is April'. We can write this as:

$$\text{January} + 3 = \text{April}.$$

Similarly, 'four months after October is February' is:

$$\text{October} + 4 = \text{February}.$$

499

By replacing January to December with the numbers 0 to 11, we can write these calculations as:

$$0 + 3 = 3$$

$$9 + 4 = 1$$

This is modulo 12 arithmetic. There are many other examples of this type of 'unconscious' use of modular arithmetic. For example, the 24-hour clock provides an example of modulo 24 arithmetic.

A.2.2 Modular numbers

We can perform modular arithmetic using any positive integer as the modulus, where by *positive integer* we mean a whole number that is bigger than 0 (in other words a number such as 2, 18, 754, etc.). When working modulo n (mod n), where n is some positive integer which we call the *modulus*, the only numbers that we deal with are:

$$0, 1, 2, 3, \ldots, n - 1.$$

Thus, instead of having numbers that go on forever, when working modulo n we only have n different numbers to work with. For example, mod 6 arithmetic only uses the numbers 0, 1, 2, 3, 4 and 5, and mod 359 arithmetic only uses the numbers 0, 1, 2, 3, \ldots, 355, 356, 357, 358. Using modular arithmetic we will later see that we can add, subtract and multiply numbers. So long as the answer is less than the modulus, these operations are just the same as if there was no modulus being used. For example, when working modulo 358, $57 + 101 = 158$. However, we need to consider what happens when the answer takes us beyond the modulus value.

ADDING MULTIPLES OF THE MODULUS

First, let us consider what happens if we add two numbers modulo n and end up with n itself. For example, when working modulo 7, what happens when we compute $3 + 4$? We know that $3 + 4 = 7$, but in modulo 7 arithmetic there is no number 7.

Recall the example based on days of the week. When working modulo 7 we see that asking 'what is $3 + 4$?' in modulo 7 arithmetic is equivalent to asking 'what day comes four days after Thursday?'. The answer is Monday, which is day 0, so:

$$3 + 4 = 0 \bmod 7.$$

The 'mod 7' at the end of the line indicates that we are performing the calculation modulo 7. Unless it is clear from the context, it is important to include this indicator, since the answer to 'what is $3 + 4$?' depends very much on what modulus we are working with.

The important lesson is that when working modulo n, adding n to a number will not change it. Again, thinking of the days of the week example, seven days after Tuesday it is Tuesday again:

$$2 + 7 = 2 \bmod 7.$$

In fact, 14 days after Tuesday it is Tuesday again:

$$2 + 14 = 2 \bmod 7.$$

Also, seven days before Tuesday is also Tuesday:

$$2 - 7 = 2 \bmod 7.$$

Thus, in modulo n arithmetic, the number n behaves just like 0 does for the numbers that we normally use. This is an important principle of modular arithmetic.

ONE NUMBER MODULO ANOTHER

Consider two numbers a and n, where a and n are both positive integers. Although a is a positive integer, suppose that we want to know what value a would take if we considered it as a number modulo n. This question is often phrased as 'what is the value of a modulo n'?

It is important to recognise that there will be an answer to this question. This is because any number can be expressed uniquely modulo any other number. Since we have just seen that in modulo n arithmetic all multiples of n are 0, we can see that the answer to our question is that a will take the value that is the *remainder* when we divide a by n.

To see a simple example, let $a = 6$ and $n = 5$. We know that 5 is the same as 0 in modulo 5 arithmetic. Since 6 is just one more than 5, it follows that 6 will be the same as 1 in modulo 5 arithmetic. This is just another way of saying that when we divide 6 by 5 we get a remainder of 1. Thus 6 is equal to 1 when 6 is considered as a number modulo 5. In other words,

$$6 = 1 \bmod 5.$$

Similarly, let $a = 5417$ and $n = 7$. We can divide 5417 by 7 using traditional arithmetic to discover that:

$$5417 = (773 \times 7) + 6.$$

Since we know that $7 = 0$ when we are working modulo 7, it follows that (773×7) will also be 0. Thus 5417 is equal to 6 when we work modulo 7, which we write:

$$5417 = 6 \bmod 7.$$

Returning to our analogy, if we ask 'what day of the week is it 5417 days after Wednesday?' we now know that in 5417 days it will be 6 days after Wednesday, so it will be Tuesday!

We will also need the following idea later. Suppose that we know that a positive integer a takes the value r modulo n. In other words, we know that when we divide a by n we get the remainder r. This tells us is that it is possible to write a as:

$$a = (k \times n) + r,$$

for some number k. We do not necessarily know what k is, but there must be a k for which this is true. Returning to our previous example, knowing that 5417 takes the value 6 modulo 7 allows us to claim that:

$$5417 = (k \times 7) + 6,$$

for *some* number k (in fact it is easy to work out, in this case, that $k = 773$).

TERMINOLOGY AND NOTATION

We have kept our terminology as simple as possible. However, other texts may explain modular arithmetic in a slightly different language. For example, the process of calculating one number modulo another is sometimes called modular *reduction*. Thus we might say that 5417 *reduces to* 6 modulo 7. Also, just to make sure that it is recognised that a modular reduction has taken place, often the symbol $\equiv$ is used instead of $=$. Thus we would write $5417 \equiv 6 \bmod 7$ rather than $5417 = 6 \bmod 7$. This idea is often expressed by stating that 5417 *is congruent to* 6 modulo 7.

Note that while 5417 is congruent to 6 mod 7, it is also congruent to 13 mod 7, and 20 mod 7. In fact it is congruent to any multiple of 7 with 6 added. However, when asked 'what number is congruent to 5417 mod 7?', there will only be one answer that lies between 0 and 6. This is the default answer, and usually the most useful one.

NEGATIVE MODULAR NUMBERS

We can also work with negative numbers in modular arithmetic. These behave almost the same way. To start with, we can regard any negative multiple of the modulus n as being equal to 0 modulo n. In other words, -7 and -14 are both equal to 0 modulo 7. More generally, any negative integer can be uniquely expressed as a number modulo n. For example, suppose that we wish to compute $-17 \bmod 10$. We divide -17 by 10 and take the remainder. When we do this we need to have a positive remainder because our answer modulo 10 must be one of the numbers between 0 and 9. Thus we see that:

$$-17 = (-2 \times 10) + 3.$$

In other words:

$$-17 = 3 \bmod 10.$$

A.2.3 Modular arithmetic operations

We now consider how to compute basic arithmetic operations modulo n.

ADDITION, SUBTRACTION AND MULTIPLICATION

The good news is that the basic arithmetic operations of addition, subtraction and multiplication behave just as we would expect them to. In other words, we can add numbers, subtract them, or multiply them, just as we would 'normal' numbers. We just need to remember to reduce the answer modulo n. Thus, for example:

$$3 + 3 = \quad 6 = 1 \bmod 5$$

$$5 + 4 = \quad 9 = 2 \bmod 7$$

$$3 - 5 = -2 = 7 \bmod 9$$

$$4 \times 5 = \quad 20 = 2 \bmod 18$$

$$3 \times 3 \times 3 = \quad 27 = 3 \bmod 4$$

$$0 \times 6 = \qquad 0 \bmod 7.$$

Importantly, division is intentionally left out of this list because it does not work in quite the same way as it does for normal numbers. There is a way to deal with division, but we discuss this later.

MODULAR REDUCTION: BEFORE OR AFTER?

One issue worth clarifying when doing a calculation such as $15 + 20 \bmod 6$ is whether we should reduce 15 and 20 modulo 6 before, or after, they have been added together. Fortunately, it does not matter, since will still get the same answer. This is best seen by example:

1. *Add then reduce*: We first compute $15 + 20 = 35$ and then note that $35 = 5 \bmod 6$. So $15 + 20 = 5 \bmod 6$.
2. *Reduce then add*: We first compute $15 = 3 \bmod 6$, and then $20 = 2 \bmod 6$. Now we add the answers, in other words $15 + 20 = 3 + 2 = 5 \bmod 6$.

A.3 The mathematics of RSA

This section contains the remaining mathematical tools that we need in order to understand the RSA cryptosystem.

A.3.1 Primes and coprimes

Before we learn how to 'divide' in modular arithmetic, we need to explore the concept of division in a bit more detail.

PRIMES

A *divisor* of a number is any number that divides into it 'neatly' with no remainder left over. For example, 3 is a divisor of 6, 5 is a divisor of 145, and 17 is a divisor of 187. Note also that 46 is a divisor of 46, and 1 is a divisor of 10023. Indeed, every number has at least two divisors, namely the number itself and 1. Most numbers have more divisors than that.

A *prime* is a number that has no divisors other than itself and 1. For example, 17 is prime because 17 and 1 are the only numbers that divide into 17. Also 2 is a prime, so is 3, and 5, and 7. On the other hand 18 is not prime because 2, 3, 6 and 9 are also divisors of 18. Primes have many special mathematical properties, which is why they form the basis for so many different cryptographic algorithms.

GREATEST COMMON DIVISORS

The *greatest common divisor* (usually abbreviated to gcd) of two numbers is the largest whole number that divides neatly into both numbers without leaving a remainder. In other words, the gcd of a and b is the largest number that is a divisor of both a and b.

For example, the gcd of 14 and 21 is 7, since 7 is the largest divisor of both 14 and 21. We normally write this as:

$$\gcd(14, 21) = 7.$$

Similarly, $\gcd(6, 8) = 2$, since 2 is the largest divisor of both 6 and 8.

Every pair of numbers has a greatest common divisor. Since 1 is a divisor of every number, it follows that there is always at least one common divisor. In some cases 1 is the greatest common divisor, but for many pairs of numbers there is a larger common divisor than 1.

COPRIMES

We say that two numbers are *coprime* if their greatest common divisor is 1. In other words, two numbers are coprime if the only divisor that they have in common is the number 1. Or, using our gcd notation, two numbers a and b are coprime if $\gcd(a, b) = 1$. For example, 42 and 55 are coprime. But 42 and 56 are not coprime, since 2 divides into 42 and 56 (as do many other numbers).

Primality and coprimality are different concepts. Primality is a measure applied to a single number on its own. Coprimality is a measure applied to two numbers to compare them with one another. However, it is true that two different primes are always coprime to one another.

A.3.2 Multiplicative inverses

Before considering division in modular arithmetic, we need to reconsider what division means in normal arithmetic.

DEFINITION OF MULTIPLICATIVE INVERSE

The *multiplicative inverse* of a chosen number is the number that we multiply the chosen number by to get 1. In other words:

$$3 \times \text{'the multiplicative inverse of 3'} = 1.$$

So what is the multiplicative inverse of 3 in our normal number system? The answer is one third, since:

$$3 \times \frac{1}{3} = 1.$$

In a similar way, the multiplicative inverse of 127 is $\frac{1}{127}$. The multiplicative inverse of a number is indicated by writing the number to the power -1. Thus, for example:

$$3^{-1} = \frac{1}{3}.$$

An important issue is that not every number has a multiplicative inverse. For example, in our normal number system, the number 0 does not have a multiplicative inverse, since there is no number that, when multiplied by 0, results in the answer 1.

DIVISION USING MULTIPLICATIVE INVERSES

Division by a number can thus be described as the process of multiplying a number by its multiplicative inverse. For example, dividing by 10 is just the same as multiplying by $\frac{1}{10}$, the multiplicative inverse of 10. In other words, division by 10 is the same as multiplying by 10^{-1}. Similarly, division by 127 is the same as multiplying by $127^{-1} = \frac{1}{127}$.

This might sound like we are just playing with words, but we are not. Considering division as multiplication by multiplicative inverses is very helpful when we return to the problem of how to divide in modular arithmetic.

MODULAR INVERSES

We now consider the multiplicative inverse of one number modulo another, sometimes referred to as a *modular inverse*. We will see that, in contrast to our normal number system:

- many numbers other than 0 do not have a multiplicative inverse modulo another number;
- there exist numbers other than 1 that are their own multiplicative inverse modulo another number.

We begin with an example. Let us try to find the multiplicative inverse of 2 modulo 7. In other words, we need to find a number that, when multiplied by 2, results in 1 mod 7. Recall that when working mod 7, the only numbers are 0, 1, 2, 3, 4, 5 and 6, so $\frac{1}{2}$ cannot be the answer.

It is not obvious what the answer is, or indeed if there is an answer at all. One rather crude way of finding a solution is to try out all of the numbers mod 7 until we find out if there is an answer:

$$2 \times 0 = 0 \bmod 7$$

$$2 \times 1 = 2 \bmod 7$$

$$2 \times 2 = 4 \bmod 7$$

$$2 \times 3 = 6 \bmod 7$$

$$2 \times 4 = 1 \bmod 7$$

$$2 \times 5 = 3 \bmod 7$$

$$2 \times 6 = 5 \bmod 7.$$

So the modular inverse of 2 is 4. In other words, $2^{-1} = 4 \bmod 7$. We can also search for the multiplicative inverse of 6 modulo 10:

$$6 \times 0 = 0 \bmod 10$$

$$6 \times 1 = 6 \bmod 10$$

$$6 \times 2 = 2 \bmod 10$$

$$6 \times 3 = 8 \bmod 10$$

$$6 \times 4 = 4 \bmod 10$$

$$6 \times 5 = 0 \bmod 10$$

$$6 \times 6 = 6 \bmod 10$$

$$6 \times 7 = 2 \bmod 10$$

$$6 \times 8 = 8 \bmod 10$$

$$6 \times 9 = 4 \bmod 10.$$

So, there is no multiple of 6 that is equal to 1 mod 10. Thus 6 does not have an inverse mod 10. In other words, the modular inverse $6^{-1} \bmod 10$ does not exist.

The previous examples raise the interesting question: when does a number have a multiplicative inverse modulo another number? This is essentially the question: when can we divide in modular arithmetic? It turns out that a number has an inverse modulo another number precisely when the two numbers are coprime. Thus, for example, $\gcd(2, 7) = 1$, which means that 2 and 7 are coprime, and thus $2^{-1} \bmod 7$ exists. Similarly, $\gcd(5, 17) = 1$, which means that 5 and 17 are coprime, and thus $5^{-1} \bmod 17$ exists. On the other hand, $\gcd(6, 10) = 2$, which means that 6 and 10 are not coprime, and thus $6^{-1} \bmod 10$ does not exist.

THE EXTENDED EUCLIDEAN ALGORITHM

We need to be able to find modular inverses in order to set up key pairs for the RSA cryptosystem. RSA works with modular numbers that are very large, so the idea of exhaustively trying out all the possible numbers less than our modulus is not going to be a practical method of finding modular inverses.

Fortunately there is a process, known as the *Extended Euclidean Algorithm*, which can be used to calculate modular inverses. The Extended Euclidean Algorithm is not complicated, but neither is it simple to explain in a few paragraphs. We thus refer the interested reader elsewhere and choose to accept that we can find modular inverses easily, whenever we need them, using the Extended Euclidean Algorithm.

A.3.3 RSA key pair setup

We now explain how all the simple ideas that we have just discussed come together in the RSA cryptosystem.

There are four basic steps involved in setting up an RSA public and private key pair. Although we covered this material in Section 5.2, we provide a reminder here using the mathematical terms that we have just explained:

1. *Generating the modulus.* Choose two primes p and q and let $n = p \times q$.
2. *Generating e.* Choose e to be a number smaller than $(p - 1) \times (q - 1)$ that is coprime to $(p - 1) \times (q - 1)$. The reason that we require this is because we want e to have a modular inverse.
3. *Forming the public key.* Let the public key be (n, e).
4. *Generating the private key.* The private key d is the unique modular inverse of e modulo $(p - 1) \times (q - 1)$. This number d can be calculated using the Extended Euclidean Algorithm by anyone who knows p and q.

An example of this process was given in Section 5.2.1.

A.3.4 Why RSA works

We now explain why RSA works. This section contains simple mathematical arguments based on information that we have just described. However, there is no need to concern yourself with the detailed discussion in this section unless you want to know exactly why RSA works. If you simply want to understand the main mathematical 'mechanics' behind RSA then this has already been done.

We know from Section 5.2.2 that RSA encryption consists of taking a plaintext P and computing $C = P^e \bmod n$, while decryption is given by $P = C^d \bmod n$. We now provide an explanation as to why these two operations 'reverse' one another.

507

We will assume that (n, e) is an RSA public key and that d is the corresponding private key. We will sometimes use the notation ab to mean $a \times b$, just as we did in Section 5.2. We will also use a mathematical result attributed to Fermat that states that for any number B that satisfies $\gcd(B, n) = 1$, it follows that:

$$B^{(p-1)(q-1)} = 1 \bmod n.$$

Now, expressing the RSA decryption formula mathematically, we have:

$$C^d = (P^e)^d = P^{ed} \bmod n.$$

Remember that because d is the modular inverse of e we have that $ed = 1 \bmod (p-1)(q-1)$. This means that there is some positive integer k for which it is true that:

$$ed = k(p-1)(q-1) + 1.$$

Thus, by replacing this in our above expression for the decryption function:

$$C^d = P^{ed} = P^{k(p-1)(q-1)+1} \bmod n.$$

Now all we do is rewrite this expression by rearranging the powers of P. There are no mathematical tricks here, we just follow the rules that describe how powers of a number behave. So:

$$C^d = P^{k(p-1)(q-1)+1} \bmod n$$

$$= P^{k(p-1)(q-1)} \times P \bmod n$$

$$= (P^{(p-1)(q-1)})^k \times P \bmod n.$$

The result due to Fermat that we quoted at the start can now be used. Writing P instead of B, we see that (so long as the greatest common divisor of P and n is 1) this result says:

$$P^{(p-1)(q-1)} = 1 \bmod n.$$

Thus we see that:

$$C^d = (1)^k \times P = P \bmod n,$$

which is what we hoped decryption would achieve.

The only case that we have not covered is when $\gcd(P, n)$ is not equal to 1. Note that this is an extremely rare case and only happens in the highly unlikely event that either $P = up$, for some $u < q$, or $P = vq$, for some $v < p$. If $P = up$ then $P = 0 \bmod p$ and so $P^{ed} = 0 \bmod p$. In other words, $P^{ed} = P = 0 \bmod p$. Since P is a multiple of p, in this case it cannot be a multiple of q as well, and so the greatest common divisor of P and q is 1. Thus we can apply Fermat's result and the above RSA argument to see that $P^{ed} = P \bmod q$. We have now shown that $P^{ed} = P \bmod p$ and $P^{ed} = P \bmod q$. It follows by a simple number theory result that $P^{ed} = P \bmod n$. If $P = vq$ then we apply a similar argument to show the same result.

A.4 The mathematics of ElGamal

The version of the ElGamal cryptosystem that we described in Section 5.3 also relies on modular arithmetic. We only need to explain one further concept in order to understand the basic mathematics behind ElGamal.

A.4.1 ElGamal public keys

Recall from Section 5.3.1 that each ElGamal public key involves three numbers. The first is a prime p, while the second number g has the special property that it is a *primitive* element. We now explain the significance of this.

PRIMITIVE ELEMENTS

Let p be a prime. A number g between 1 and $p - 1$ is said to be *primitive* (or is a *primitive element*) modulo p if the numbers:

$$g, g^2, g^3, g^4, g^5, g^6, \ldots, g^{p-1} \bmod p,$$

are all different. If this is the case then, since there are $p - 1$ of them, they must consist of 1, 2, 3, $\ldots$, $p - 1$ in some order.

Table A.2 indicates the powers of 11 modulo 23. The first and third rows indicate the powers that 11 is being raised to, while the rows below show the result of computing 11 raised to that power, modulo 23. For example, $11^2 = 121 = 6 \bmod 23$, so 6 appears below 11^2 in Table A.2.

We can see from inspecting Table A.2 that 11 is a primitive element modulo 23. Note, however, that not every number between 1 and $p - 1$ is primitive modulo p. Table A.3 indicates the powers of 2 modulo 23. In this case, not all the numbers 1, 2, 3, $\ldots$, 22 appear amongst the second and fourth rows of Table A.3 (in fact only half of them do) and so 2 is not a primitive element modulo 23.

IMPORTANCE OF PRIMITIVE ELEMENTS TO ElGamal

The ElGamal public-key component g must be a primitive element modulo p. The main reason that this restriction is made is in order to make sure that when we

Table A.2: Powers of 11 modulo 23

11^1	11^2	11^3	11^4	11^5	11^6	11^7	11^8	11^9	11^{10}	11^{11}
11	6	20	13	5	9	7	8	19	2	22
11^{12}	11^{13}	11^{14}	11^{15}	11^{16}	11^{17}	11^{18}	11^{19}	11^{20}	11^{21}	11^{22}
12	17	3	10	18	14	16	15	4	21	1

Table A.3: Powers of 2 modulo 23

2^1	2^2	2^3	2^4	2^5	2^6	2^7	2^8	2^9	2^{10}	2^{11}
2	4	8	16	9	18	13	3	6	12	1

2^{12}	2^{13}	2^{14}	2^{15}	2^{16}	2^{17}	2^{18}	2^{19}	2^{20}	2^{21}	2^{22}
2	4	8	16	9	18	13	3	6	12	1

raise g to different powers, which we do when computing the third component y of an ElGamal public key as well as during the encryption process itself, the result can be *any* number modulo p. If g is not primitive then the security of ElGamal is greatly reduced.

For example, if the non-primitive element $g = 2$ is used as part of an ElGamal public key alongside $p = 23$ then we can see from Table A.3 that g^k can only take half of the possible values. An attacker who tries to decrypt a ciphertext by exhaustively searching for the value k that was used when forming $C_1 = g^k$ will have a much easier job than if we had used a primitive element for g, since there are two different values of k that will work, halving the effort required.

A.4.2 Why ElGamal works

Recall that an ElGamal public key is of the form (p, g, y), where x is the corresponding private key and $y = g^x$. In Section 5.3.2 we also learnt that ElGamal encryption consists of randomly generating a value k and then computing $C_1 = g^k$ and $C_2 = Py^k$, where P is the plaintext. We then observed that decryption consists of dividing C_2 by the answer to $(C_1)^x \bmod p$. We now explain why this works.

Suppose that Bob receives the ciphertext (C_1, C_2). Bob begins by using his private key x to transform C_1 into something more useful. He thus computes:

$$(C_1)^x = (g^k)^x = (g^x)^k = y^k \bmod p.$$

This follows because it does not matter in which order the two exponentiations are computed. Thus raising g to the power k and then to the power x is the same as raising g to the power x and then to the power k.

Bob now divides this value into C_2. Of course we now know that such 'division' is done by multiplying by the modular inverse. Thus Bob needs to find the modular inverse of y^k modulo p, which we denote by $(y^k)^{-1}$. Bob can find this using the

Extended Euclidean Algorithm. Then Bob computes:

$$C_2 \times (y^k)^{-1} = (Py^k) \times (y^k)^{-1} \bmod p$$
$$= P \times (y^k \times (y^k)^{-1}) \bmod p$$
$$= P \times 1 = P \bmod p,$$

which is what we require.

A.5 Further reading

Several of the recommended existing cryptography books, such as Menezes, van Oorschot and Vanstone [123], Mel and Baker [122] and Stinson [185], also include explanations of some the basic mathematics that we have discussed, although these vary in the level of detail and degree of assumed knowledge. For further details of basic number theory there are a number of good options, of which Tattersall [190] is one of the more accessible.

Bibliography

[1] ISO/IEC 10116. Information technology – Security techniques – Modes of operation for an n-bit block cipher algorithm. International Organisation for Standardisation.

[2] ISO/IEC 10118. Information technology – Security techniques – Hash functions. International Organisation for Standardisation.

[3] ISO 11568. Information technology – Banking – Key management (retail). International Organisation for Standardisation.

[4] ISO/IEC 11770. Information technology – Security techniques – Key management. International Organisation for Standardisation.

[5] ISO 13491. Information technology – Banking – Secure cryptographic devices (retail). International Organisation for Standardisation.

[6] ISO/IEC 13888. Information technology – Security techniques – Non-repudiation. International Organisation for Standardisation.

[7] ISO/IEC 14888. Information technology – Security techniques – Digital signatures with appendix. International Organisation for Standardisation.

[8] ISO 15782. Information technology – Banking – Certificate management. International Organisation for Standardisation.

[9] ISO/IEC 15945. Information technology – Security techniques – Specification of TTP services to support the application of digital signatures. International Organisation for Standardisation.

[10] ISO/IEC 15946. Information technology – Security techniques – Cryptographic techniques based on elliptic curves. International Organisation for Standardisation.

[11] ISO/IEC 18031. Information technology – Security techniques – Random bit generation. International Organisation for Standardisation.

[12] ISO/IEC 18033. Information technology – Security techniques – Encryption algorithms. International Organisation for Standardisation.

[13] ISO/IEC 19772. Information technology – Security techniques – Authenticated encryption. International Organisation for Standardisation.

[14] ISO 21188. Public key infrastructure for financial services – Practices and policy framework. International Organisation for Standardisation.

[15] IEEE 802.11. Wireless LAN Medium Access Control (MAC) and Physical Layer (PHY) Specifications. IEEE Standards Association.

[16] ISO/IEC 9594. Information technology – Open Systems Interconnection – The Directory. International Organisation for Standardisation.

[17] ISO/IEC 9796. Information technology – Security techniques – Digital signature schemes giving message recovery. International Organisation for Standardisation.

[18] ISO/IEC 9797. Information technology – Security techniques – Message Authentication Codes (MACs). International Organisation for Standardisation.

[19] ISO/IEC 9798. Information technology – Security techniques – Entity authentication. International Organisation for Standardisation.

[20] B. Aboba, L. Blunk, J. Vollbrecht, J. Carlson, and H. Levkowetz. RFC 3748, Extensible Authentication Protocol (EAP). Internet Engineering Task Force, 2004.

[21] C. Adams and S. Lloyd. *Understanding Public-Key Infrastructure*, 2nd Edition. Addison-Wesley, 2003.

[22] R. Anderson. Why cryptosystems fail. *Communications of the ACM*, **37**(11):32–40, 1994.

[23] R. Anderson. *Security Engineering: A Guide to Building Dependable Distributed Systems*, 2nd Edition. Wiley, 2008.

[24] R. Anderson, E. Biham, and L. Knudsen. Serpent: A proposal for the Advanced Encryption Standard. Technical report, http://www.cl.cam.ac.uk/rja14/.

[25] ANSI. X9 TR-31:2005, Interoperable secure key exchange key block specification for symmetric algorithms. American National Standards Institute.

[26] ANSI. X9.24, Retail financial services symmetric key management. American National Standards Institute.

[27] J. Attridge. An overview of hardware security modules. SANS Institute InfoSec Reading Room, 2002.

[28] P. S. L. M. Barreto and V. Rijmen. The Whirlpool hashing function. Technical report, http://www.crypto.ruhr-uni-bochum.de/en_sclounge.html, 2003.

[29] H. Beker and F. Piper. *Cipher Systems: The Protection of Communications*. Northwood, 1982.

[30] M. Bellare, P. Rogaway, and D. Wagner. The EAX mode of operation. In *Fast Software Encryption*, volume 3017 of *Lecture Notes in Computer Science*, pages 389–407. Springer, 2004.

[31] C. H. Bennett and G. Brassard. Quantum cryptography: Public key distribution and coin tossing. In *Proceedings of the IEEE International Conference on Computers, Systems, and Signal Processing*, pages 175–179. IEEE, 1984.

[32] R. L. Benson. The Venona story. Technical report, Center for Cryptologic History, National Security Agency, 2001.

[33] N. Biggs. *Codes: An Introduction to Information Communication and Cryptography*. Springer, 2008.

[34] M. Bishop. *Computer Security: Art and Science*. Addison Wesley, 2002.

[35] M. Blaze. Safecracking for the computer scientist. Technical report, University of Pennsylvania, http://www.crypto.com/papers/safelocks.pdf, 2004.

[36] M. Blaze, W. Diffie, R. L. Rivest, B. Schneier, T. Shimomura, E. Thompson, and M. Wiener. Minimal key lengths for symmetric ciphers to provide adequate commercial security. Technical report, http://people.csail.mit.edu/rivest/bsa-final-report.pdf, 1996.

[37] Bluetooth Special Interest Group. Simple pairing white paper v10r00. Bluetooth Special Interest Group, 2006.

[38] M. Bond. Attacks on cryptoprocessor transaction sets. In *Proceedings of CHES 2001*, volume 2162 of *Lecture Notes in Computer Science*, pages 220–234. Springer, 2001.

[39] D. Boneh. Twenty years of attacks on the RSA cryptosystem. *Notices of the American Mathematical Society*, **46**:203–213, 1999.

[40] C. Boyd and A. Mathuria. *Protocols for Authentication and Key Establishment*. Springer, 2003.

[41] D. Brown. *The Da Vinci Code*. Corgi, 2004.

[42] D. Brown. *Digital Fortress*. Corgi, 2004.

[43] J. Buchmann. *Introduction to Cryptography*. Springer-Verlag, 2004.

[44] J. Cache and V. Liu. *Hacking Exposed Wireless: Wireless Security Secrets and Solutions*. McGraw-Hill Osborne, 2007.

[45] Certicom. ECC tutorial. http://www.certicom.com.

[46] P. Chandra. *Bulletproof Wireless Security: GSM, UMTS, 802.11, and Ad Hoc Security*. Newnes, 2005.

[47] C. Cobb. *Cryptography for Dummies*. Hungry Minds, 2004.

[48] D. De Cock, B. Van Alsenoy, B. Preneel, and J. Dumortier. The Belgian eID approach. In W. Fumy and M. Paeschke, editors, *Handbook of eID Security – Concepts, Practical Experiences, Technologies*. Publicis Publishing, 2011.

[49] D. Cooper, S. Santesson, S. Farrell, S. Boeyen, R. Housley, and W. Polk. RFC 5280, Internet X.509 Public Key Infrastructure Certificate and Certificate Revocation List (CRL) Profile. Internet Engineering Task Force, 2008.

[50] COPACOBANA. A codebreaker for DES and other ciphers. http://www.copacobana.org/.

[51] Common Criteria. The Common Criteria Portal. http://www.commoncriteriaportal.org/.

[52] CrypTool. Open source e-learning application. http://www.cryptool.org.

[53] M. Curtin and J. Dolske. A brute force search of DES keyspace. Technical report, Usenix, 1998.

[54] J. Daemen and V. Rijmen. *The Design of Rijndael: AES – the Advanced Encryption Standard*. Springer-Verlag, 2002.

[55] A. W. Dent and C. J. Mitchell. *User's Guide to Cryptography and Standards*. Artech House, 2004.

[56] G. Dhillon. *Principles of Information Systems Security: Texts and Cases*. Wiley, 2006.

[57] T. Dierks and E. Rescorla. RFC 5246, The Transport Layer Security (TLS) Protocol Version 1.2. Internet Engineering Task Force, 2008.

[58] W. Diffie. The first ten years of public-key cryptography. *Proceedings of the IEEE*, **76**(5):560–577, 1988.

[59] W. Diffie and M. Hellman. New directions in cryptography. *IEEE Trans. Information Theory*, **IT-22**:644–654, 1976.

[60] W. Diffie and M. Hellman. Exhaustive cryptanalysis of the NBS Data Encryption Standard. *IEEE Computer*, **10**(6):74–84, 1977.

[61] W. Diffie, P.C. van Oorschot, and M.J. Wiener. Authentication and authenticated key exchanges. *Designs, Codes and Cryptography*, **2**:107–125, 1992.

[62] H. Dobbertin, A. Bosselaers, and B. Preneel. RIPEMD-160, a strengthened version of RIPEMD. In *Fast Software Encryption*, volume 1039 of *Lecture Notes in Computer Science*, pages 71–82. Springer-Verlag, 1996.

[63] D. Eastlake, J. Schiller, and S. Crocker. RFC 4086, Randomness Requirements for Security. Internet Engineering Task Force, 2005.

[64] ECRYPT. The Side Channel Cryptanalysis Lounge. European network of excellence in cryptology II. http://www.crypto.ruhr-uni-bochum.de/en_sclounge.html.

[65] C. Mitchell (Ed.). *Trusted Computing*. IET, 2005.

[66] N. Smart (Ed.). ECRYPT II Yearly report on algorithms and keysizes (2010–2011). European network of excellence in cryptology II, 2011. http://www.ecrypt.eu.org/.

[67] J. Edney and W. A. Arbaugh. *Real 802.11 Security: WI-Fi Protected Access and 802.11i*. Addison Wesley, 2003.

[68] T. ElGamal. A public-key cryptosystem and a signature scheme based on discrete logarithms. *IEEE Trans. Information Theory*, **IT-31**:469–472, 1985.

[69] J. H. Ellis. The history of non-secret encryption. *Cryptologia*, **23**(3):267–273, 1999.

[70] C. Ellison and B. Schneier. Ten risks of PKI: What you're not being told about public key infrastructure. *Computer Security Journal*, **16**(1):1–7, 2000.

[71] EMVCo. EMV Integrated Circuit Card Specifications for Payment Systems. EMVCo. http://www.emvco.com.

[72] J. -J. Quisquater, L. C. Guillou, and T. A. Berson. How to explain zero-knowledge protocols to your children. In *Advances in Cryptology – CRYPTO '89*, volume 435 of *Lecture Notes in Computer Science*, pages 628–631. Springer-Verlag, 1990.

[73] S. Farrell and R. Housley. RFC 3281, An Internet Attribute Certificate Profile for Authorization. Internet Engineering Task Force, 2002.

[74] N. Ferguson and B. Schneier. *Practical Cryptography*. Wiley, 2003.

[75] N. Ferguson, B. Schneier, and T. Kohno. *Cryptography Engineering: Design Principles and Practical Applications*. Wiley, 2010.

[76] FIPS. Automated Password Generator (APG). Federal Information Processing Standard FIPS 181, 1993.

[77] FIPS. Data Encryption Standard (DES). Federal Information Processing Standard FIPS 46-3, 1999.

[78] FIPS. Advanced Encryption Standard (AES). Federal Information Processing Standard FIPS 197, 2001.

[79] FIPS. Security Requirements for Cryptographic Modules. Federal Information Processing Standard FIPS 140-2, 2001.

[80] FIPS. Secure Hash Standard. Federal Information Processing Standard FIPS 180-2, 2002.

[81] FIPS. The Keyed-Hash Message Authentication Code (HMAC). Federal Information Processing Standard FIPS 198, 2002.

[82] FIPS. Digital Signature Standard (DSS). Federal Information Processing Standard FIPS 186-3, 2009.

[83] W. Ford and M. S. Baum. *Secure Electronic Commerce: Building the Infrastructure for Digital Signatures and Encryption*, 2nd Edition. Prentice Hall, 2000.

[84] Electronic Frontier Foundation. *Cracking DES*. O'Reilly, 1998.

[85] J. Fridrich. *Steganography in Digital Media: Principles, Algorithms, and Applications*. Cambridge University Press, 2010.

[86] S. Friedl. An illustrative guide to cryptographic hashes. Unixwiz.net Tech Tips, 2005. http://unixwiz.net/techtips/iguide-crypto-hashes.html.

[87] M. Gardner. *Codes, Ciphers and Secret Writing (Test Your Code Breaking Skills)*. Dover, 2003.

[88] S. Garfinkel and G. Spafford. *Web Security, Privacy and Commerce*. O'Reilly, 2001.

[89] D. Giry. Bluekrypt: Cryptographic key length recommendation. http://www.keylength.com.

[90] O. Goldreich. *Foundations of Cryptography: Vol 1*. Cambridge University Press, 2001.

[91] O. Goldreich. *Foundations of Cryptography: Vol 2*. Cambridge University Press, 2004.

[92] D. Gollmann. *Computer Security*, 2nd Edition. Wiley, 2007.

[93] P. Gregory and M. A. Simon. *Biometrics For Dummies*. Wiley, 2008.

[94] M. Haahr. Random.org. http://www.random.org/.

[95] H. Handschuh and B. Preneel. Minding your MAC algorithms. *Information Security Bulletin*, **9**(6):213–220, 2004.

[96] D. Hankerson, A. J. Menezes, and S. Vanstone. *Guide to Elliptic Curve Cryptography*. Springer, 2004.

[97] D. Harel. *Computers Ltd, What they really can't do*. Oxford University Press, 2000.

[98] R. Harris. *Enigma*. Arrow, 2009.

[99] A. Hodges. *Alan Turing: The Enigma*. Vintage, 1992.

[100] J. Pipher, J. Hoffstein, and J. H. Silverman. *An Introduction to Mathematical Cryptography*. Springer, 2008.

[101] A. K. Jain, P. Flynn, and A. A. Ross (Eds.). *Handbook of Biometrics*. Springer, 2007.

[102] D. Johnson, A. Menezes, and S. Vanstone. The Elliptic Curve Digital Signature Algorithm (ECDSA). Certicom, 2001.

[103] M. Joye and G. Neven (Eds.). *Identity-based Cryptography*. IOS Press, 2008.

[104] D. Kahn. *The Codebreakers: The Comprehensive History of Secret Communication from Ancient Times to the Internet*. Simon & Schuster, 1997.

[105] J. Katz and Y. Lindell. *Introduction to Modern Cryptography*. CRC Press, 2007.

[106] C. Kaufman. RFC 4306, Internet Key Exchange (IKEv2) Protocol. Internet Engineering Task Force, 2005.

[107] K. Kenan. *Cryptography in the Database: The Last Line of Defense*. Addison-Wesley, 2005.

[108] A. Kerckhoffs. La cryptographie militaire. *Journal des sciences militaires*, **IX**:161–191, 1883.

[109] N. Koblitz. *A Course in Number Theory and Cryptography*. Springer-Verlag, 2001.

[110] B.-J. Koops. Crypto Law Survey. http://rechten.uvt.nl/koops/cryptolaw/.

[111] KPMG. Digital certificates, authentication, and trust on the Internet. KPMG Risk and Advisory Services, 2002.

[112] KPMG. Key management and policy framework. KPMG Risk and Advisory Services, 2002.

[113] H. Krawczyk, M. Bellare, and R. Canetti. RFC 2104, HMAC: Keyed-Hashing for Message Authentication. Internet Engineering Task Force, 1997.

[114] RSA Laboratories. One-Time Password Specifications (OTPS). http://www.rsa.com/rsalabs/.

[115] RSA Laboratories. Public-key Cryptography Standards (PKCS). http://www.rsa.com/rsalabs/.

[116] X. Lai and J. L. Massey. A proposal for a new block encryption standard. In *Advances in cryptology – EUROCRYPT '90: Workshop on the theory and application of cryptographic techniques*, volume 473 of *Lecture Notes in Computer Science*, pages 389–404. Springer-Verlag, 1991.

[117] S. Levy. *Crypto: How the Code Rebels Beat the Government: Saving Privacy in the Digital Age*. Penguin, 2002.

[118] S. Levy. *Crypto: Secrecy and Privacy in the New Cold War*. Penguin, 2002.

[119] W. Mao. *Modern Cryptography*. Prentice Hall, 2004.

[120] K. Mayes and K. Markantonakis (Eds.). *Smart Cards, Tokens, Security and Applications*. Springer, 2008.

[121] G. McGraw. *Software Security: Building Security In*. Addison-Wesley, 2006.

[122] H. X. Mel and D. Baker. *Cryptography Decrypted*. Addison-Wesley, 2001.

[123] A. Menezes, P. van Oorschot, and S. Vanstone. *Handbook of Applied Cryptography*. CRC Press, 1997.

[124] D. L. Mills. RFC 1305, Network Time Protocol (Version 3). Internet Engineering Task Force, 1992.

[125] R. A. Mollin. *An Introduction to Cryptography*. Chapman & Hall/CRC Press, 2001.

[126] T. Moses. Quantum computing and cryptography: Their impact on cryptographic practice. Entrust, Inc., 2009.

[127] M. Myers, C. Adams, D. Solo, and D. Kemp. RFC 2511, Internet X.509 Certificate Request Message Format. Internet Engineering Task Force, 1999.

[128] M. Myers, R. Ankney, A. Malpani, S. Galperin, and C. Adams. RFC 2560, X.509 Internet Public Key Infrastructure Online Certificate Status Protocol – OCSP. Internet Engineering Task Force, 1999.

[129] C. Neuman, T. Yu, S. Hartman, and K. Raeburn. RFC 4120, The Kerberos Network Authentication Service (v5). Internet Engineering Task Force, 2005.

[130] V. Niemi and K. Nyberg. *UMTS Security*. Wiley-Blackwell, 2003.

[131] NIST. Computer Security Resource Center. National Institute of Standards and Technology. http://csrc.nist.gov/.

[132] NIST. Cryptographic Hash Project. National Institute of Standards and Technology, Computer Security Resource Center. http://csrc.nist.gov/groups/ST/hash/index.html.

[133] NIST. Introduction to public key technology and the Federal PKI infrastructure. National Institute of Standards and Technology Special Publication 800-32, 2001.

[134] NIST. Recommendations for block cipher modes of operation. National Institute of Standards and Technology Special Publication 800-38A, 2001.

[135] NIST. Recommendations for block cipher modes of operation: The CCM mode for authentication and confidentiality. National Institute of Standards and Technology Special Publication 800-38C, 2004.

[136] NIST. Guidelines for the selection and use of Transport Layer Security implementations. National Institute of Standards and Technology Special Publication 800-52, 2005.

[137] NIST. Guidelines for media sanitization. National Institute of Standards and Technology Special Publication 800-88, 2006.

[138] NIST. Guidelines on electronic mail security. National Institute of Standards and Technology Special Publication 800-45, 2007.

[139] NIST. Recommendations for key management. National Institute of Standards and Technology Special Publication 800-57, 2007.

[140] NIST. Recommendations for the Triple Data Encryption Algorithm (TDEA) block cipher. National Institute of Standards and Technology Special Publication 800-67, 2008.

[141] NIST. Recommendation for key derivation using pseudorandom functions (revised). National Institute of Standards and Technology Special Publication 800-108, 2009.

[142] NIST. A framework for designing cryptographic key management systems. Draft National Institute of Standards and Technology Special Publication 800-130, 2010.

[143] NIST. Recommendation for password-based key derivation, Part 1: storage applications. National Institute of Standards and Technology Special Publication 800-132, 2010.

[144] NIST. Recommendations for block cipher modes of operation: The XTS-AES mode for confidentiality on storage devices. National Institute of Standards and Technology Special Publication 800-38E, 2010.

517

[145] NIST. A statistical test suite for random and pseudorandom number generators for cryptographic applications. National Institute of Standards and Technology Special Publication 800-22, Revision 1a, 2010.

[146] D. O'Mahony, M. Peirce, and H. Tewari. *Electronic Payment Systems for E-commerce*, 2nd Edition. Artech House, 2001.

[147] IEEE P1363.1. Draft Standard for Public-Key Cryptographic Techniques Based on Hard Problems over Lattices. IEEE Standards Activities Department.

[148] IEEE P1363.3. Draft Standard for Identity-based Public-key Cryptography Using Pairings. IEEE Standards Activities Department.

[149] C. Paar and J. Pelzl. *Understanding Cryptography: A Textbook for Students and Practitioners*. Springer, 2009.

[150] P. Pagliusi. A contemporary foreword on GSM security. In *Proceedings of the International Conference on Infrastructure Security*, volume 2437 of *Lecture Notes in Computer Science*, pages 129–144. Springer, 2002.

[151] European Parliament. Directive 1999/93/EC of the European Parliament and of the Council on a community framework for electronic signatures, 1999.

[152] K. G. Paterson, F. Piper, and R. Schack. Quantum cryptography: A practical information security perspective. *Quantum Communication and Security, Proceedings NATO Advanced Research Workshop*, pages 175–180, 2007.

[153] K. G. Paterson and G. Price. A comparison between traditional public key infrastructures and identity-based cryptography. *Information Security Technical Report*, 8(3):57–72, 2003.

[154] K. G. Paterson and A. K. L. Yau. Lost in translation: Theory and practice in cryptography. *IEEE Security and Privacy*, 4(3):69–72, 2006.

[155] M. Paterson. *Voices of The Codebreakers: Personal Accounts of the Secret Heroes of World War II*. David & Charles, 2007.

[156] R. A. Perlner and D. A. Cooper. Quantum resistant public key cryptography: A survey. In *IDtrust '09: Proceedings of the 8th Symposium on Identity and Trust on the Internet*, volume 373, pages 85–93. ACM, 2009.

[157] F. Piper and S. Murphy. *Cryptography: A Very Short Introduction*. Oxford University Press, 2002.

[158] G. Price. PKI challenges: An industry analysis. In *Proceedings of the 4th International Workshop for Applied PKI (IWAP 2005)*, pages 3–16. IOS Press, 2005.

[159] S. Purser. *A Practical Guide to Managing Information Security*. Artech House, 2004.

[160] E. Rescorla. RFC 2631, Diffie–Hellman Key Agreement Method. Internet Engineering Task Force, 1999.

[161] E. Rescorla. *SSL and TLS: Building and Designing Secure Systems*. Addison Wesley, 2000.

[162] D. Rijmenants. Cipher machines and cryptology. http://users.telenet.be/d.rijmenants/.

[163] R. L. Rivest, A. Shamir, and L. Adleman. A method for obtaining digital signatures and public-key cryptosystems. *Communications of the ACM*, 21:120–126, 1978.

[164] M. Robshaw and O. Billet (Eds.). *New Stream Cipher Designs: The eSTREAM Finalists*, volume 4986 of *Lecture Notes in Computer Science*. Springer, 2008.

[165] P. Rogaway, M. Bellare, and J. Black. OCB: A block-cipher mode of operation for efficient authenticated encryption. *ACM Transactions on Information and System Security (TISSEC)*, 6:365–403, 2003.

[166] B. Schneier. Cryptanalysis of SHA-1. *Crypto-gram Newsletter* February 18th, 2005. http://www.schneier.com/blog/archives/2005/02/cryptanalysis_o.html.

[167] B. Schneier. Why digital signatures are not signatures. *Crypto-gram Newsletter* February 15th, 2000. http://www.schneier.com/crypto-gram-0011.html#1.

[168] B. Schneier. *Applied Cryptography*, 2nd Edition. Wiley, 1996.

[169] B. Schneier. Security pitfalls in cryptography, 1998. http://www.schneier.com/essay-028.html.

[170] B. Schneier. *Secrets and Lies: Digital Security in a Networked World*. Wiley, 2004.

[171] B. Schneier, D. Whiting, D. Wagner, C. Hall, N. Ferguson, and J. Kelsey. *Twofish Encryption Algorithm : A 128-Bit Block Cipher*. Wiley, 1999.

[172] SECG. Standards for Efficient Cryptography Group. http://www.secg.org.

[173] C. Shannon. A mathematical theory of communication. *Bell System Technical Journal*, **27**:379–423 and 623–656, 1948.

[174] C. Shannon. Communication theory of secrecy systems. *Bell System Technical Journal*, **28**:656–715, 1949.

[175] S. Singh. Crypto corner. http://www.simonsingh.net/Crypto_Corner.html.

[176] S. Singh. *The Code Book: The Secret History of Codes and Code-breaking*. Fourth Estate, 2002.

[177] S. Singh. *The Cracking Code Book*. HarperCollins, 2009.

[178] N. P. Smart. *Cryptography: An Introduction*. McGraw-Hill, 2002.

[179] M. Smith. *Station X: The Code Breakers of Bletchley Park*. Pan, 2004.

[180] R. J. Spillman. *Classical and Contemporary Cryptology*. Prentice-Hall, 2004.

[181] T. St Denis. *Cryptography for Developers*. Syngress Media, 2006.

[182] W. Stallings. *Cryptography and Network Security*, 5th Edition. Pearson, 2010.

[183] W. Stallings. *Network Security Essentials: Applications and Standards*, 4th Edition. Pearson, 2010.

[184] N. Stephenson. *Cryptonomicon*. Arrow, 2000.

[185] D. R. Stinson. *Cryptography: Theory and Practice*, 3rd Edition. Chapman & Hall/CRC Press, 2006.

[186] G. Stix. Best kept secrets. *Scientific American*, **292**:78–83, 2005.

[187] C. Stoll. *The Cuckoo's Egg: Tracking a Spy Through the Maze of Computer Espionage*. Pocket Books, 2005.

[188] X. Suo, Y. Zhu, and G. Scott Owen. Graphical passwords: A survey. In *Proceedings of Annual Computer Security Applications Conference*, pages 463–472, 2005.

[189] J. Talbot and D. Welsh. *Complexity and Cryptography: An Introduction*. Cambridge University Press, 2006.

[190] J. J. Tattersall. *Elementary Number Theory in Nine Chapters*, 2nd Edition. Cambridge University Press, 2005.

[191] W. Trappe and L. C. Washington. *Introduction to Cryptography: With Coding Theory*, 2nd Edition. Pearson, 2005.

[192] TrueCrypt. Free open-source on-the-fly encryption. http://www.truecrypt.org/.

[193] UKPA. Standard 70: Card Acceptor to Acquirer Interface Standards. UK Payments Administration, 2010.

[194] S. Vaudenay. *A Classical Introduction to Cryptography: Applications for Communications Security*. Springer, 2005.

[195] R. Walton. Cryptography and trust. *Information Security Technical Report*, **11**(2):68–71, 2006.

[196] L. C. Washington. *Elliptic Curves: Theory and Cryptography*, 2nd Edition. CRC Press, 2008.

[197] P. Wayner. *Disappearing Cryptography: Information Hiding: Steganography and Watermarking*. 3rd Edition. Morgan Kaufmann, 2008.

[198] D. Welsh. *Codes and Crypography*. Clarendon Press, 1988.

[199] M. J. Wiener. Efficient DES key search. Technical report, School of Computer Science, Carleton University, 1994.

[200] Wikipedia. Digital signatures and law. http://en.wikipedia.org/wiki/Digital_signatures_and_law.

[201] Wikipedia. One-time password. http://en.wikipedia.org/wiki/One-time_password.

[202] Wikipedia. Padding (cryptography). http://en.wikipedia.org/wiki/Padding_(cryptography).

[203] Wikipedia. RC4. http://en.wikipedia.org/wiki/RC4.

[204] Wikipedia. Web of trust. http://en.wikipedia.org/wiki/Web_of_trust.

[205] J. Yan, A. Blackwell, R. Anderson, and A. Grant. Password memorability and security: Empirical results. *IEEE Security and Privacy*, September/October:25–31, 2004.

[206] A. L. Young and M. Yung. *Malicious Cryptography: Exposing Cryptovirology*. Wiley, 2004.

[207] E. Zabala. Rijndael inspector. http://www.formaestudio.com/rijndaelinspector/.

[208] W. Zeng, H. Yu, and C.-Y. Lin (Eds.). *Multimedia Security Technologies for Digital Rights Management*. Academic Press, 2006.

Index